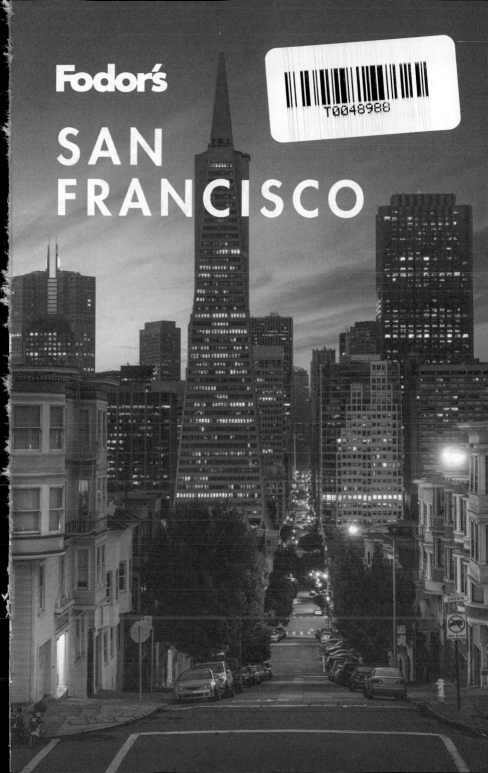

Fodor's

SAN FRANCISCO

T0048988

Welcome to San Francisco

With its myriad hills and spectacular bay, San Francisco beguiles with natural beauty, vibrant neighborhoods, and contagious energy. From the hipster Mission District to the sassy Castro, from bustling Union Square to enduring Chinatown, this dynamic town thrives on variety. The city makes it wonderfully easy to tap into the good life, too: between San Francisco's vibrant arts scene, tempting boutiques, parks perfect for jogging or biking, and all those stellar locavore restaurants and cocktail bars, it's the ultimate destination for relaxed self-indulgence. As you plan your upcoming travels, please confirm that places are still open and let us know when we need to make updates by writing to us at editors@fodors.com.

TOP REASONS TO GO

★ **Foodie heaven:** Top restaurants, hip ethnic favorites, farmers' markets, food trucks.

★ **Distinctive neighborhoods:** Buzzing, walkable streets invite discovery.

★ **Golden Gate Bridge:** Electric orange and towering, this glorious span inspires awe.

★ **Waterfront activities:** Whether you hike, bike, or stroll it, the bay is magnetic.

★ **Accessible art:** From famous street murals to top-notch museums, art is everywhere.

Contents

Fodor's Features

MAPS

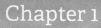

Chapter 1

EXPERIENCE SAN FRANCISCO

25 ULTIMATE EXPERIENCES

San Francisco offers terrific experiences that should be on every traveler's list. Here are Fodor's top picks for a memorable trip.

1 Ride a Cable Car

Clatter and jiggle up mansion-topped Nob Hill, then hold on for the hair-raising descent toward Fisherman's Wharf, with sun glittering off the bay and Alcatraz in the distance. *(Ch. 4–8)*

2 Wander through Chinatown

Have delicious dim sum, watch the nimble hands at Golden Gate Fortune Cookie Factory, then take in the hundreds of red lanterns at Tin How Temple. *(Ch. 6)*

3 Frolic in Golden Gate Park

San Francisco's green beating heart, a three-mile-long park, stretches from the Haight to the Pacific Ocean, and offers museums, gardens, and two windmills. *(Ch. 10–11)*

4 See a Classic Film at the Castro Theatre

One of America's last great independent theaters, this grand 1922 playhouse is a hodgepodge of art deco, Spanish, and Asian influences and features a pipe organ that entertains preshow. *(Ch. 12)*

5 Picnic in the Presidio

Larger than Golden Gate Park, the Presidio is home to public art, an extensive network of hiking trails, a historic fort, two cemeteries, and the beautiful new Presidio Tunnel Tops park. *(Ch. 9)*

6 Browse City Lights Bookstore

A San Francisco landmark, this independent shop and publisher was a Beat-era hangout for writers and remains a vital part of the city's literary scene. Browse three levels of books. *(Ch. 6)*

7 Visit Mission Dolores and Dolores Park

Mission Dolores's 18th-century chapel, with its painted wooden ceiling, is the oldest standing building in the city. Just down the road, Dolores Park is a favorite with the locals. *(Ch. 13)*

8 Gaze upon the Palace of Fine Arts

Perched on a lagoon near the Marina's yacht harbor, this beautiful terra-cotta domed structure was built in 1915 for an expo and has been a popular photo op ever since. *(Ch. 9)*

9 Take in the Views at Coit Tower

It's all about the city and bay views here. The tower sits at the top of Telegraph Hill's Filbert Steps, a steep stairway through glorious gardens. *(Ch. 6)*

10 Find a Ghost at Alcatraz

Walk the cellblock of America's most infamous federal pen as you hear about desperate escape attempts and notorious crooks like Al "Scarface" Capone and George "Machine Gun Kelly." *(Ch. 5)*

11 Eat at the Ferry Building

Discover cafés, restaurants, a farmers' market, and merchants peddling everything from wine and olive oil to oysters and mushrooms. Plaza tables offer great people-watching. *(Ch. 5)*

12 See Your Favorite Band at the Fillmore

This is the club that all the big names want to play. Catch a show and view the amazing collection of rock posters upstairs, then get free apples and posters on the way out. *(Ch. 8)*

13 Feel the Wind on Twin Peaks

Windswept and desolate, Twin Peaks yields sweeping vistas of San Francisco and neighboring counties. You can get a real feel for the city's layout here. *(Ch. 12)*

14 Dive into Urban Ruins at the Sutro Baths

Explore the ruins and staircases of what was once the largest indoor saltwater swimming pool in the world, to a soundtrack of pounding Pacific waves. *(Ch. 10)*

15 Tipple at the Tonga Room & Hurricane Bar

Since the 1940s this kitschy tiki bar has served up signature mai tais with a backdrop of fake palm trees, a lagoon (bands play pop standards on a floating barge), and faux monsoons. *(Ch. 7)*

16 Walk across a Rainbow in the Castro

Take your selfies at the rainbow crosswalks at 18th and Castro, check out the Rainbow Honor Walk honoring brave pioneers, and visit the GLBT Historical Society Museum. *(Ch. 12)*

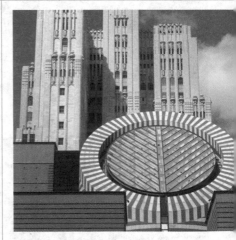

17 Seek Out the Mission's Murals

Street art is at its most concentrated in the Mission, where small alleys and other spots have become magnets for artists creating murals, many with themes of social justice and Latino heritage. *(Ch. 13)*

18 Explore SFMOMA

With about 170,000 square feet of galleries, SFMOMA is one of the largest museums in America devoted to modern and contemporary art. It's easy to spend a day here. *(Ch. 3)*

19 Amble across the Golden Gate Bridge

Walking the 1.7 miles to Marin County—steel shaking beneath your feet, and the water 200 feet below—is much more than a superlative photo op (though it's that, too). *(Ch. 9)*

20 Explore Historic North Beach

Signs of the area's Italian heritage linger on in establishments like century-old foccacia purveyors Liguria Bakery and trattorias along Columbus Avenue. *(Ch. 6)*

21 Admire the Redwoods of Muir Woods

Walking among some of the last old-growth redwoods on the planet, trees hundreds of feet tall and a millennium or more old, is a magical experience. *(Ch. 14)*

22 Stand in Line at Tartine

Experience loaves of tangy country bread and morning buns dusted with brown sugar, cinnamon, and orange zest at this cult Mission District bakery. *(Ch. 13)*

23 Climb the Vallejo Steps

Though very steep, the walk up to Ina Coolbrith Park and beyond is possibly the most pleasurable thing to do on Russian Hill, thanks to glorious city views. *(Ch. 7)*

24 Watch the Giants at Oracle Park

San Francisco's Major League Baseball team calls SoMa's Oracle Park home. *(Ch. 3)*

25 Explore Point Reyes

The 71,000-acre Point Reyes National Seashores has hiking trails, secluded beaches, and a scenic lighthouse. *(Ch. 14)*

WHAT'S WHERE

1 SoMa, Mission Bay, and Dogpatch. Anchored by SFMOMA and Yerba Buena Gardens, SoMa (like adjacent Mission Bay and Dogpatch) is a once-industrial neighborhood in transition, with luxury condos, stylish restaurants, and cool dance clubs, but some parts are still gritty.

2 Union Square, Civic Center, and the Tenderloin. Hotels and upscale stores are plentiful around bustling Union Square. Monumental city government buildings and performing arts venues dominate Civic Center, but it's also a chronic magnet for unhoused people, as is the Tenderloin.

3 The Waterfront. This area includes Fisherman's Wharf, the Embarcadero, and the Financial District and offers access to boats to Alcatraz. If you wander the touristy shops and attractions of Fisherman's Wharf, Pier 39, and Ghirardelli Square, the only locals you'll meet will be the ones with visitors in tow. The city's northeastern waterfront Embarcadero area is anchored at the foot of Market Street by the Ferry Building and its

San Francisco Bay

Pier 39

Bay St.

The Embarcadero

NORTH BEACH

TELEGRAPH HILL

Ferry Building

Jackson Square

THE EMBARCADERO

4 **CHINATOWN**

FINANCIAL DISTRICT

Powell St.

Grant Ave.

Market St.

1st St.

San Francisco-Oakland Bay Bridge

UNION SQUARE

2nd St.

3rd St.

2

Yerba Buena Gardens

SF MoMA

SOMA

1

4th St.

5th St.

Mission St.

6th St.

Folsom St.

Harrison St.

Bryant St.

Brannan St.

Townsend St.

King St.

7th St.

Berry St.

8th St.

9th St.

10th St.

MISSION BAY

DOGPATCH

0   1 mi

0   1 km

marketplace, filled with culinary delights. The promenade that starts in back has great views of the bay. In the Financial District, Jackson Square is a pleasant diversion for history buffs and has some of the city's ritziest shops.

4 **Chinatown and North Beach.** Remnants of Old San Francisco show forth in the city's traditionally Chinese and Italian neighborhoods.

5 **Nob Hill and Russian Hill.** Topped by staid, elegant mansions and luxury hotels that ooze reserve and breeding, Nob Hill is old-money San Francisco. Russian Hill's steep streets hold a vibrant, classy neighborhood that's very au courant. Locals flock to Polk and Hyde Streets, the main commercial avenues, for excellent neighborhood eateries and pleasant window shopping at charming, often family-owned shops.

6 **Pacific Heights and Japantown.** The Pacific Heights neighborhood boasts some of San Francisco's most opulent real estate and grand Victorians—but in most cases you'll have to be content with an exterior view. A tight-knit Japanese American population supports

WHAT'S WHERE

Japantown, of interest to visitors mostly for the shopping and dining opportunities.

7 The Marina and the Presidio. With fancy wine shops, trendy boutiques, fashionable cafés and restaurants, and pricey waterfront houses, the Marina is home to many young urban professionals. The exquisite 1915 Palace of Fine Arts is here, too. Locals go to the Presidio, the huge, wooded shoreline park west of the Marina, for an amble through enchanting forests or on the sand in the shadow of the Golden Gate Bridge.

8 The Western Shoreline. A natural gem underappreciated by locals and visitors alike, the city's windswept Pacific shore stretches for miles.

9 Golden Gate Park. Covering more than 1,000 acres of greenery, with sports fields, two windmills, museums, gardens, a playground, and small lakes, Golden Gate Park is San Francisco's backyard.

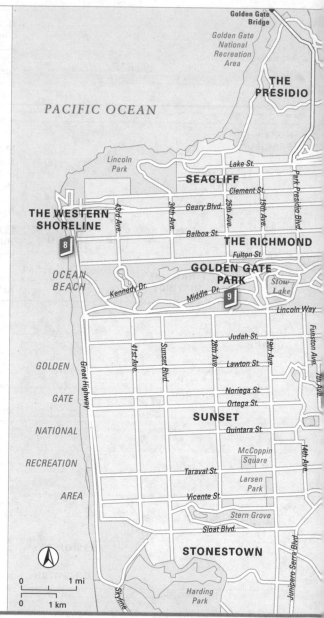

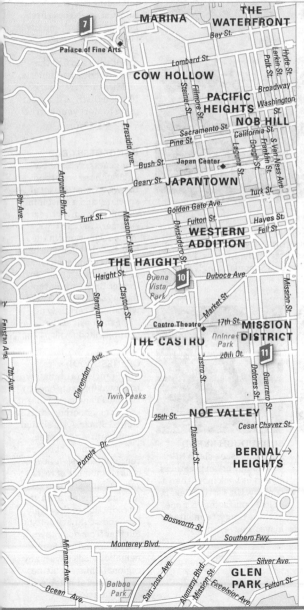

10 **The Haight, the Castro, Hayes Valley, and Noe Valley.** If you're looking for '60s souvenirs, the Haight has them, along with some of the city's loveliest Victorian houses (and most aggressive panhandling). Hip locals come for the secondhand shops, cheap brunch, and low-key bars and cafés. The Castro is proudly rainbow-flag-waving, in-your-face fab, and it's a friendly neighborhood that welcomes visitors of all stripes. Catch a film at the vintage Castro Theatre. South of the Castro, Noe Valley is a cute, pricey neighborhood favored by young families. The main strip, 24th Street, is lined with coffee shops, eateries, and boutiques.

11 **Mission District, Bernal Heights, and Potrero Hill.** When the sun sets, people descend on the Mission from all over the Bay Area for destination restaurants, excellent value-price global eateries, and a hip bar scene. Colorful murals are a major draw during the day. Neighborhoods to explore near the Mission include Bernal Heights and Potrero Hill.

What to Eat and Drink in San Francisco

MICHELIN-STARRED CUISINE
Northern California's culinary intensity and creativity have earned five restaurants three Michelin stars. The Bay Area's three-star Atelier Crenn and Sonoma's SingleThread are especially hot now.

LOCAL WINE
Drink deep: San Francisco sits smack-dab in wine paradise surrounded by Napa and Sonoma, the Sierra Foothills, the Santa Cruz Mountains, and the Central Coast. Chardonnay is a major varietal in most regions. Pinot Noir is the main varietal for coastal areas while Cabernet Sauvignon rules Napa Valley.

SOURDOUGH BREAD
San Francisco's claim to sourdough-bread greatness stretches back more than a century. Hit Tartine Bakery or its Manufactory for one of these tangy, fermented loaves. Leave room for pastries!

MISSION BURRITO
Named for San Francisco's Mission District, this burrito has three identifiers: the size (gigantic), the variety of ingredients (including rice, considered unusual when these first became popular), and the tightly packed weight. Every local has an opinion about where to find the "best" burrito. La Taqueria, on Mission Street in the Mission District, is a great place to start your burrito research crawl.

DUNGENESS CRAB
Dungeness crab, with a habitat in the waters off the West Coast, is a local specialty and a must if in season (November to early summer). You can try it at many restaurants in the Bay Area, but you'd be hard pressed to find somewhere more revered than Swan Oyster Depot, a great spot for any seafood fix. There will almost certainly be a line for a seat at the counter, but do wait.

CHINESE FOOD
San Francisco's Chinatown is known for being one of the oldest and most vibrant ethnic neighborhoods in the United States. As in similar communities across the U.S., the number of regions represented is significant, as is the number of restaurants. China Live and Z&Y (Sichuan cuisine) are a great introduction to the neighborhood's culinary delights. Further from downtown, the Richmond and Sunset neighborhoods have many regional Chinese cuisines represented at notable restaurants.

Dungeness crab

CIOPPINO

San Francisco's diverse history and incredible confluence of cultures makes for unique dishes like cioppino, which is essentially the Bay Area's own version of bouillabaisse. The dish is credited to Italian immigrants who began fishing California's generous waters. With a broth made from tomatoes and red wine, this seafood-filled soup is worth seeking out. Try the version at Scoma's by Fisherman's Wharf.

STEAM BEER

San Francisco has more than a dozen breweries which specialize in a variety of beer styles. But, let's not get too carried away with any beer trends since America's first craft brewery resides on Potrero Hill. Anchor Brewing's smooth, always pleasant Steam Beer is one of the world's iconic beers and it just manages to always taste slightly better here in its own home city.

A CITY OF COCKTAILS

From award-winning, inventive bars like True Laurel and Pacific Cocktail Haven, to classic cocktails known worldwide like Irish coffee and mai tais, San Francisco has a deep history with cocktails. The city's beloved bars often have a unique ambience and design to go with their drinks.

LOCAL COFFEE

Local chains like Blue Bottle Coffee (now more global), Four Barrel, and Réveille have cult followings. Be sure to support independently owned coffee shops as you wander: there's no shortage of talent or expertly roasted beans.

10 Best Photo Ops in San Francisco

THE PAINTED LADIES

Familiar to fans of the TV show *Full House*, the so-called Painted Ladies or Seven Sisters are a row of seven color-ful and beautifully maintained Queen Anne–style houses just off Alamo Square Park. Take photos at midday for clear city views.

THE PALACE OF FINE ARTS

This stirringly lovely terra-cotta–color domed structure on a lagoon near the Marina's yacht harbor has an otherworldly quality about it. Built in 1915 for an exposition, the palace is a San Francisco architect's version of a Roman ruin, and it's been eliciting gasps ever since. It's a popular wedding spot, which is good if you like happy couples in your photos.

TWIN PEAKS

These two adjacent peaks near Noe Valley are at the near geographic center of San Francisco, with an elevation of 925 feet. Especially pretty (and popular, but chilly) at sunrise and sunset, the peaks provide sweeping 180-degree views of the Bay Area, with a great perspective on downtown San Francisco, the Bay Bridge, and the tips of the Golden Gate Bridge.

LANDS END COASTAL TRAIL

This four-mile trail winds and twists along the rugged cliffs of San Francisco Bay, offering stunning views of the Golden Gate Bridge and surprisingly woodsy forest. At the 1.3-mile mark, turn left at the wooden staircase to explore Mile Rock Beach and the Lands End Labyrinth. On a clear day, you can see the Golden Gate Bridge in the distance.

THE PRESIDIO
As the gateway to the Golden Gate Bridge, San Francisco's 1,500-acre Presidio offers incredible views of the bridge and the sprawling landscape that surrounds it. Enjoy spectacular bridge photo opportunities from Crissy Field or the Presidio Tunnel Tops. The Presidio also abuts Baker Beach, a stretch of sand with an alternative perspective.

MUIR WOODS NATIONAL MONUMENT
Naturalist John Muir wrote, "Most people are on the world, not in it—have no conscious sympathy or relationship to anything about them..." It's hard not to feel connected as you walk the shaded paths of Muir Woods amid the towering majesty of the redwood groves.

UNION SQUARE
This lively spot is the place to capture the cable cars as they rumble by. The towering Dewey Monument pillar, topped triumphantly by Nike, the Greek goddess of victory, is a beautiful sculpture. Relax on the steps and photograph what many call the heart of the city.

TREASURE ISLAND
Tiny, man-made Treasure Island is generally off the tourist track, so your photos won't be crowded with selfie-takers. Sitting right in the middle of San Francisco Bay, it offers gorgeous views of the San Francisco skyline, especially at night when everything is lit up.

HAWK HILL
At a high point on the south-facing Marin Headlands, Hawk Hill lies opposite the city with vistas of the Pacific and of the Golden Gate Bridge as it enters San Francisco. True to its name, it's also a great spot for nature-watching. Hawk Hill is the site of the autumnal raptor migration and also serves as a habitat for the Mission Blue Butterfly.

BERNAL HEIGHTS
This somewhat stumpy-looking mound rises unenthusiastically above the houses of the surrounding neighborhood. But, pictures taken *from* Bernal Heights Hill offer 360-degree panoramic views. Take a sunset stroll here for stunning San Francisco shots.

Under the Radar

KABUKI SPRINGS & SPA
Enter the peaceful lobby and prepare to be transported at the Japanese-style communal baths at this Japantown spa popular with locals of all ages. The extensive spa menu includes facials, salt scrubs, and mud and seaweed wraps. Enjoy banging the gong if fellow bathers are ruining your zen with chitchat.

SALESFORCE PARK
Perhaps because it's a park above a major public transit center and dwarfed by the soaring Salesforce Tower, this gorgeous green oasis in the heart of the SoMa-Downtown area is an absolute breath of fresh air for families and business people alike. Somehow it manages to never feel crowded, which is very needed because it's often extremely congested below on street level.

16TH AVENUE STEPS
At the base of this glorious stairway mosaic in the Inner Sunset, you can take in the beautiful artwork, from an underwater theme to dragonflies and butterflies and even a starry night skyscape. At the top, you get beautiful city views.

MT. DAVIDSON
In the shadow of Twin Peaks, but actually taller, this "mountain" the next hill over is topped with a eucalyptus-filled park. Finding the road up is tricky (entrance at Dalewood and Myra Ways), but once there you'll have amazing views—while tourists look for parking on Twin Peaks.

POLLY ANN AND MITCHELL'S
San Francisco is filled with hip ice cream shops, but two of the older shops stand out for their unusual offerings. Polly Ann Ice Cream has ice cream flavors like Thai tea, lychee, and black sesame. Mitchell's offers tropical flavors, including *langka* (jackfruit) and *ube* (purple yam).

THE WARMING HUT
Walking over the Golden Gate Bridge can be a blustery experience at any time, but head down to sea level and you'll find a port in a storm. The Warming Hut offers warm drinks and gifts, and it's the perfect spot to stock up on picnic supplies to enjoy while exploring the waterfront.

16th Avenue Steps

CHURCH OF 8 WHEELS

You haven't lived until you've roller-skated in church, specifically at the former Sacred Heart Church in the Western Addition, now a bona fide roller disco for holy and not-so-holy rollers. Friday and Saturday nights are for adults only, with plenty of old-school funk to get your groove on.

RISE OVER RUN

As beautiful as the views can be, there's one theme every visitor leaves SF's rooftop bars thinking about: it's cold! The city's infamous wind and fog are not good partners for rooftop drinking. However, this gorgeous rooftop bar atop The LINE SF hotel (Tenderloin) has a nifty solarium that keeps you warm and dry while offering an excellent view. In good weather, you can also sit outside. Regardless of the weather, it's home to the best food and drink of any rooftop spot in the city.

CRANE COVE PARK

This beautiful park at the border of Mission Bay and Dogpatch is a great example of neglected industrial waterfront turned into a charming green space—complete with a beach (though swimming is not recommended). The views of Chase Center, the Bay Bridge, and the East Bay are worth a visit on their own.

What to Watch and Read

THE MALTESE FALCON
There was a time when the city's most notorious antiheroes weren't billionaires in T-shirts but rather chain-smoking, hard-boiled detectives. In *The Maltese Falcon*, detective Sam Spade crisscrosses an atmospheric 1930s San Francisco to locate a jeweled statue. The novel, written by Dashiell Hammett, is a legendary piece of noir fiction, and the 1941 film, which starred an in-his-prime Humphrey Bogart and was nominated for three Oscars, is a must-watch.

THE JOY LUCK CLUB
San Francisco's Chinatown is one of the largest and most famous immigrant enclaves in the United States. Amy Tan's 1989 novel and the 1993 film based on it provide a glimpse into the lives of four women who emigrated from China and their relationships with their American-born daughters.

THE ROCK
Set on Alcatraz, San Francisco's infamous island prison, *The Rock* (1996) sets Nicholas Cage and Sean Connery against a rogue unit of special-forces Marines who threaten to launch rockets filled with nerve gas into the city unless they're paid a ransom of $100 million.

THE MAYOR OF CASTRO STREET
Randy Shilts's 1982 biography of gay civil rights icon Harvey Milk is perhaps the most well-regarded and authoritative reckoning of his life to date. Milk was a bombastic, emblematic figure whose advocacy and assassination permanently shaped the political landscape of San Francisco and the entire United States.

INFINITE CITY: A SAN FRANCISCO ATLAS
In this 2010 book, Rebecca Solnit offers her own narrative of the city as well as those of collaborating artists, writers, and mapmakers. The end result is a fascinating visual representation of San Francisco's diverse geographical and cultural layers.

MRS. DOUBTFIRE
Longtime Bay Area resident Robin Williams had a stunning, iconic career, but for many *Mrs. Doubtfire* (1993) is his quintessential film role. Williams plays a freshly divorced dad who dresses up as an older British nanny to care for his children. The beautiful, Victorian-style "Mrs. Doubtfire House," at 2640 Steiner Street in Pacific Heights, is a popular attraction even though it can be viewed only from the street.

TALES OF THE CITY
Few books offer such a longitudinal view of a place; Armistead Maupin's stories started running in serial format in the *San Francisco Chronicle* in 1978 (and later in the *San Francisco Observer*) before they were compiled into novels. As a result the books are grounded in the events of the day, so the AIDS epidemic is represented and gay characters play an important and influential role.

GUN, WITH OCCASIONAL MUSIC
Set in San Francisco and Oakland, Jonathan Lethem's 1994 novel, a compelling, not-quite-dystopian vision of the near-yet-distant future, highlights what San Francisco might become with just a little (okay, a lot of) rampant genetic experimentation.

VERTIGO
One of Alfred Hitchcock's career-defining films, *Vertigo* (1958) was filmed on location in San Francisco and the surrounding Bay Area. The movie offers a smorgasbord of quintessential sights, bringing both presence and authenticity to a captivating story of love, mystery, and murder.

MR. PENUMBRA'S 24-HOUR BOOKSTORE

Robin Sloan's 2012 novel about a quirky used-book store in San Francisco does double duty. It's a story of mystery, love, code-breaking, secret societies, and adopted and inherited culture, but it's also a narrative about the potential dangers of rapid technological advancement, tribalism, and other issues currently impacting San Francisco.

THE ROOM

The Room (2003) is widely considered to be one of the worst films ever produced, and for good reason. It's a disjointed mess with atrocious acting, a nonsensical plot, and a script that defies belief. However, thanks to its sheer ridiculousness (and raucous midnight screenings at arthouse theaters), both *The Room* and its creator, director, and principal actor Tommy Wiseau have become cult film legends. *The Disaster Artist,* the 2017 dramatic mockumentary detailing its inception and production, is also incredibly fun to watch.

SILICON CITY: SAN FRANCISCO IN THE LONG SHADOW OF THE VALLEY

Written by a documentary filmmaker, *Silicon City* (2018) interviews a broad swath of San Franciscans, including both older bohemians who are concerned about the changes to their longtime home and technocratic millennials pushing a future tied to rapid growth. Cary McClelland's book delves into San Francisco's cultural shifts through the eyes of both new and longtime residents and examines how people of differing backgrounds, and philosophies, live side by side.

CHEZ PANISSE CAFÉ COOKBOOK

Located in Berkeley, Chez Panisse taught lessons to cooks, chefs, and diners that now seem so obvious—cook with fresh ingredients, eat local meat and produce, and treat your guests like friends. The *Chez Panisse Café Cookbook* (1999) by Alice Waters captures this unstuffy ethos and is as much about relationships and culinary philosophy as it is about recipes. If you can't make it to the restaurant itself, this book will help get you there in flavor and in spirit.

ZODIAC

During the late '60s, the city and its surrounding areas were terrorized by a person known only as the "Zodiac Killer." Seven people were killed, and the assailant—who to this day remains unknown—sent taunts, cryptic codes, and ciphers to local newspapers, causing both curiosity and panic. Robert Graysmith's book (1986) and the David Fincher film adaptation (2007) each chronicle the efforts to catch the Zodiac Killer and are well-received thrillers.

THE LAST BLACK MAN IN SAN FRANCISCO

With its ever-increasing socioeconomic gap and perpetually high cost of living, longtime San Francisco residents have been squeezed out of the city for several decades. Perhaps no demographic in San Francisco has left the city in higher numbers than its Black population. This powerful 2019 film shows a younger generation trying to save their family home in the city and facing the difficult reality of modern day San Francisco—a city with so much natural beauty but one that is growing increasingly impossible for many people to live in. San Francisco native Danny Glover is one of the film's supporting actors.

San Francisco with Kids

ON THE MOVE

Adventure Cat sailing. Them: playing on the trampoline at the bow of this 55-foot catamaran. You: enjoying a drink and the bay sunset on the stern deck.

Cable cars. This one's a no-brainer. But don't miss the **Cable Car Terminus** at Powell and Market Streets, where conductors push the iconic cars on giant turntables, and the **Cable Car Museum,** where you can see how cable cars work.

F-line trolleys. Thomas the Tank Engine fan in tow? Hop on one of the F-line's neat historic streetcars.

■TIP➔ Bonus: this line connects other kid-friendly sights, like Fisherman's Wharf, Pier 39, and the San Francisco Railway Museum.

SNEAK IN SOME CULTURE

Mission District murals. Kids can appreciate the colorful murals in the Mission's alleys and on buildings, especially if you follow it up with a meal at one of the area's excellent eateries.

Walt Disney Family Museum. Older children may appreciate the videos and displays about the life and times of the man behind Mickey Mouse, including a detailed model of Disneyland.

Stern Grove Festival. Enjoying a delicious picnic in a eucalyptus grove, your kids might not even complain that they're listening to—gasp—classical music (or Latin jazz or opera).

THE GREAT OUTDOORS

Aquatic Park beach. Does your brood include a wannabe Michael Phelps? Then head to this popular beach, one of the few places around the city where it's safe to swim. However, it's best to stick close to shore here given how cold the water is and how sometimes swimmers encounter unpredictable seals.

Golden Gate Promenade. If your kids can handle a 4.3-mile loop, this one's a beauty—winding from Marina Green, through Crissy Field, to Fort Point under the Golden Gate Bridge.

Muir Woods National Monument. If these redwood trees look tall to you, imagine seeing them from two or four feet lower.

Stow Lake. When feeding bread to the ducks gets old, rent a rowboat or pedal boat at this Golden Gate Park favorite.

JUST PLAIN FUN

Dim sum. A rolling buffet from which kids point and pick—likely an instant hit during a break on a Chinatown stroll.

Fisherman's Wharf, Hyde Street Pier, Ghirardelli Square, and Pier 39. The phrase "tourist trap" may come to mind, but in this area you can clamber around old ships, snack on chocolate, and laugh at the sea lions.

Oracle Park. Emerald grass, a hot dog in your hand, baseball ... and suddenly, you're 10 again, too.

San Francisco Zoo. Between Grizzly Gulch, Lemur Forest, and Koala Crossing, you can make a day of it.

Yerba Buena Gardens. Head here for ice-skating, bowling, a carousel, a playground, and the Children's Creativity Museum, a hands-on arts-and-technology center.

LEARN A THING OR TWO

California Academy of Sciences. Penguins, free-flying tropical butterflies, giant snakes—what's not to like? Then ride the SkyStar Ferris wheel right outside the academy complex afterwards.

Exploratorium. A hands-on children's creativity and science museum on the waterfront.

Top Walking Tours

All About Chinatown. On a delightful two-hour, behind-the-scenes look at the neighborhood, owner Linda Lee and her guides explore historic buildings and new murals, stroll through a food market, and stop at a Buddhist temple. At herbal markets, you'll learn the therapeutic benefits of ginseng, geckos, and more. A dim sum lunch is an added option. ⊠ *660 California St., Chinatown* ☎ *415/982–8839* ⊕ *allaboutchinatown.com* ⊠ *From $55, $85 with lunch.*

Don Herron's Dashiell Hammett Tour. Brush up on your noir slang and join trench-coated guide Herron for a walk by the mystery writer's haunts and the locations from some of Hammett's novels. At three hours for $20, it's one of the best deals going. But make sure to contact Herron in advance as tours are almost entirely by appointment for private groups only now. ⊠ *Civic Center* ⊕ *www.donherron.com* ⊠ *$20.*

Foot! Fun Walking Tours. You'll likely find yourself breathless with laughter, not just gasping after a steep hill. The tour leaders are all entertainers and history buffs; they've got offerings like the Nob Hill tour "Hobnobbing with Gobs of Snobs."⊠ *San Francisco* ☎ *415/793–5378* ⊕ *www.foottours.com* ⊠ *From $30 for adults.*

Local Tastes of the City Tours. If you want to snack your way through a neighborhood as you walk it, consider hanging with cookbook author Tom Medin or one of his local guides. You'll learn why certain things just taste better in San Francisco—like coffee and anything baked with sourdough. You'll also gorge yourself into oblivion: the North Beach tour, for instance, might include multiple stops for coffee and baked goods. ⊠ *San Francisco* ☎ *415/665 0480* ⊕ *www.sffoodtour.com* ⊠ *From $69.*

Precita Eyes Mural Walks. For an insider's look at the Mission District's vibrant murals, contact this place for the latest information on tours. The nonprofit organization has nurtured this local art form since 1977. Walks are on weekends, but you can arrange private tours at other times. Muralists lead the tours. ⊠ *Mission District* ☎ *415/285–2287* ⊕ *www. precitaeyes.org* ⊠ *From $20.*

San Francisco City Guides. An outstanding free service supported by the San Francisco Public Library since 1978, these walking tours have themes that range from individual neighborhoods to local history (the gold rush, the 1906 quake, ghost walks) to architecture. Although the tours are free and the knowledgeable guides are volunteers, it's appropriate to make a donation for these nonprofit programs. ⊠ *San Francisco* ☎ *415/375–0468* ⊕ *www.sfcityguides.org* ⊠ *Free; $20 donation suggested.*

Wok Wiz Chinatown Tour. The late cookbook author and Chinatown booster Shirley Fong-Torres founded Wok Wiz, and her team continues to lead these walks. Conversation topics include folklore and, of course, food. The tour called "I Can't Believe I Ate My Way Through Chinatown!" includes breakfast and lunch. ⊠ *Chinatown* ☎ *650/355–9657* ⊕ *www.wokwiz.com* ⊠ *From $35.*

Free and Almost Free

San Francisco offers loads of free diversions. Here are our picks for the best free things to do, in alphabetical order by category. Also check out ⊕ *sf.funcheap. com* for a calendar of random, offbeat, and often free one-offs.

FREE MUSEUMS AND GALLERIES
- Fort Point National Historic Site
- Octagon House
- San Francisco Cable Car Museum
- San Francisco Railway Museum
- Wells Fargo History Museum

FREE MUSEUM TIMES
The first week of every month brings a bonanza of free museum options. Be aware that free times draw crowds.

- Asian Art Museum, first Sunday of every month
- de Young Museum, first Tuesday of every month
- GLBT Historical Society Museum, first Wednesday of every month
- Legion of Honor, first Tuesday of every month
- Yerba Buena Center for the Arts (galleries), always free

FREE CONCERTS
- The Golden Gate Park Band plays free public concerts on multiple days a week, April through November, on the Music Concourse in the namesake park.
- The San Francisco Conservatory of Music offers frequent free recitals year-round at its Civic Center home.
- Stern Grove Festival concerts are held in the Sunset on Sunday afternoon from June through August, ranging from opera to jazz to pop music. Admission is free but advance tickets are required.

- Yerba Buena Gardens Festival hosts concerts and performances from May through October, including world music, dance, and even puppet shows.

FREE TOURS
- The free San Francisco City Guides walking tours (note: a $20 donation is suggested) are easily one of the best deals going. Knowledgeable, enthusiastic guides lead walks that focus on a particular neighborhood, theme, or historical period.
- City Hall offers free docent-led tours of its grandiose HQ on Fridays.

MORE GREAT EXPERIENCES FOR $7 OR LESS
- See baseball at Oracle Park, for free! Go to the Portwalk, beyond the right-field wall, for a standing-room (slightly obstructed) view through the open fence. Twenty-four people are allowed, and you must leave after three innings.
- Do your own walking tour of the Mission District's fantastic outdoor murals, then grab a bite at a taqueria.
- Walk across the Golden Gate Bridge—an obvious but breathtaking choice.
- Choose a perfect treat at the Ferry Building's fabulous marketplace and stroll the waterfront promenade.
- Tour the grounds around the Palace of Fine Arts, circling its lagoon. Next, walk through the Presidio to the Letterman Digital Arts Center campus to see the Yoda fountain and life-size figure of Darth Vader inside the building beyond.
- Take the kids to Koret Children's Quarter in Golden Gate Park and go for a ride ($2 for adults and $1 for children ages 6–12) on a vintage carousel.
- Hike up to the top of Telegraph Hill for sweeping city and bay views.

SAN FRANCISCO'S CABLE CARS

The moment it dawns on you that you severely underestimated the steepness of the San Francisco hills will likely be the same moment you look down and realize those tracks aren't just for show—or just for tourists.

Van Ness Ave., California
59
& Market Streets

Sure, locals rarely use the cable cars for commuting these days. (That's partially due to the $8 fare—hear that, Muni?) So you'll likely be packed in with plenty of fellow sightseers. You may even be approaching cable-car fatigue after seeing its image on so many souvenirs. But if you fear the magic is gone, simply climb on board, and those jaded thoughts will dissolve. Grab the pole and gawk at the view as the car clanks down an insanely steep grade toward the bay. Listen to the humming cable, the clang of the bell, and the occasional quip from the gripman. It's an experience you shouldn't pass up, whether on your first trip or your fiftieth.

HOW CABLE CARS WORK

The mechanics are pretty simple: cable cars grab a moving subterranean cable with a "grip" to go. To stop, they release the grip and apply one or more types of brakes. Four cables, totaling 9 miles, power the city's three lines. If the gripman doesn't adjust the grip just right when going up a steep hill, the cable will start to slip and the car will have to back down the hill and try again. This is an extremely rare occurrence—imagine the ribbing the gripman gets back at the cable car barn!

Gripman: Stands in front and operates the grip, brakes, and bell. Favorite joke, especially at the peak of a steep hill: "This is my first day on the job, folks . . ."

Conductor: Moves around the car, deals with tickets, alerts the grip about what's coming up, and operates the rear wheel brakes.

❶ Cable: Steel wrapped around flexible sisal core; 2 inches thick; runs at a constant 9½ mph.

❷ Bells: Used for crew communication; alerts other drivers and pedestrians.

❸ Grip: Vice-like lever extends through the center slot in the track to grab or release cable.

❹ Grip Lever: Left-hand lever; operates grip.

❺ Car: Entire car weighs 8 tons.

❻ Wheel Brake: Steel brake pads on each wheel.

❼ Wheel Brake Lever: Foot pedal; operates wheel brakes.

❽ Rear Wheel Brake Lever: Applied for extra traction on hills.

❾ Track Brake: 2-foot-long sections of Monterey pine push down against the track to help stop the car.

❿ Track Brake Lever: Middle lever; operates track brakes.

⓫ Emergency Brake: 18-inch steel wedge, jams into street slot to bring car to an immediate stop.

⓬ Emergency Brake Lever: Right-hand lever, red; operates emergency brake.

ROUTES

Cars run at least every 15 minutes, from around 6 am to about 1 am.

Powell–Hyde line: Most scenic, with classic Bay views. Begins at Powell and Market streets, then crosses Nob Hill and Russian Hill before a white-knuckle descent down Hyde Street, ending near the Hyde Street Pier.

Powell–Mason line: Also begins at Powell and Market streets, but winds through North Beach to Bay and Taylor streets, a few blocks from Fisherman's Wharf.

California line: Runs from the foot of Market Street, at Drumm Street, up Nob Hill and back. Great views (and aromas and sounds) of Chinatown on the way up. Sit in back to catch glimpses of the bay. ■TIP→ **Take the California line if it's just the cable-car experience you're after— the lines are shorter, and the grips and conductors say it's friendlier and has a slower pace.**

RULES OF THE RIDE

Tickets. There are ticket booths at all three turnarounds. You must purchase your ticket in advance.

■TIP→ **If you're planning to use public transit a few times, or if you'd like to ride back and forth on the cable car without worrying about the price, consider a one-day (or multiday) Muni Visitor Passport. You can get passports online, at the Powell Street turnaround, the TIX booth on Union Square, or the Fisherman's Wharf cable-car ticket booth at Beach and Hyde streets. Also consider Muni Mobile or a Clipper Card; see sfmta.com. Cash purchases require exact change.**

All Aboard. You can board on either side of the cable car. It's legal to stand on the running boards and hang on to the pole, but keep your ears open for the gripman's warnings. ■TIP→ **Grab a seat on the outside bench for the best views.**

Most people wait (and wait) in line at one of the cable car turnarounds, but you can also hop on along the route. Board wherever you see a white sign showing a figure climbing aboard a brown cable car; wave to the approaching driver, and wait until the car stops.

Riding on the running boards can be part of the thrill.

CABLE CAR HISTORY

HALLIDIE FREES THE HORSES

In the 1850s and '60s, San Francisco's streetcars were drawn by horses. Legend has it that the horrible sight of a car dragging a team of horses downhill to their deaths roused Andrew Smith Hallidie to action. The English immigrant had invented the "Hallidie Ropeway," essentially a cable car for mined ore, and he was convinced that his invention could also move people. In 1873, Hallidie and his intrepid crew prepared to test the first cable car high on Russian Hill. The anxious engineer peered down into the foggy darkness, failed to see the bottom of the hill, and promptly turned the controls over to Hallidie. Needless to say, the thing worked . . . but rides were free for the first two days because people were afraid to get on.

SEE IT FOR YOURSELF

The Cable Car Museum (✉ 1201 Mason St, ⊕ cablecarmusem.org) is one of the city's best free offerings and an absolute must for kids. (You can even ride a cable car there, since all three lines stop between Russian Hill and Nob Hill.) The museum, which is inside the city's last cable-car barn, takes the top off the system to let you see how it all works. Eternally humming and squealing, the massive powerhouse cable wheels steal the show. You can also climb aboard a vintage car and take the grip, let the kids ring a cable-car bell (briefly, please!), and check out vintage gear dating from 1873.

■ TIP➜ The gift shop sells cable car paraphernalia, including an authentic gripman's bell (it'll sound like Powell Street in your house every day). For significantly less, you can pick up a key chain made from a piece of worn-out cable. Books, T-shirts, hats, and models are also on sale.

CHAMPION OF THE CABLE CAR BELL

Each fall (though the month can vary widely : check ⊕ sfmta.com for update) the city's best and brightest come together to crown a bell-ringing champion at Union Square. The crowd cheers gripmen and conductors as they stomp, shake, and riff with the rope. But it's not a popularity contest; the ringers are judged by former bell-ringing champions and others who take each ping and gong very seriously.

Chapter 2

TRAVEL SMART

Updated by
Trevor Felch

★ **STATE CAPITAL**
Sacramento

⚕ **POPULATION**
815,201 (San Francisco city)

💬 **LANGUAGE**
English

$ **CURRENCY**
U.S. dollar

☎ **AREA CODE**
415

⚠ **EMERGENCIES**
911

🚗 **DRIVING**
On the right

⚡ **ELECTRICITY**
120–220 v/60 cycles;
plugs have two or three
rectangular prongs

🕐 **TIME**
Pacific Time; three hours
behind New York

🌐 **WEB RESOURCES**
www.sftravel.com
www.visitcalifornia.com
www.sfgate.com
www.sfchronicle.com

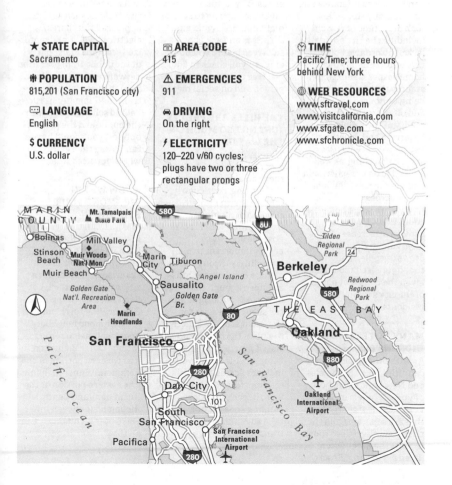

Know Before You Go

PACK FOR SAN FRANCISCO, NOT CALIFORNIA
California has drawn in many a traveler with endless sunny days, but the average high in the Bay Area is only 63.8°F and nights tend to drop into the low 50s. So, while the city is beautiful, it doesn't exactly have beach weather. Even summer is marked by foggy, windy conditions.

SF HAS A HIGH RATE OF STREET HOMELESSNESS
San Francisco is famous for a great many things, but for a multitude of reasons, including the city's acute lack of affordable housing, this unfortunately includes homelessness. The circumstances that lead to people being unhoused are varied and often tragic, and the reality of the problem can be jarring and upsetting: expect to see tent cities and panhandling, as well as used drug paraphernalia and human waste in public places across the city. San Francisco's latest homeless count in 2022 actually showed a decrease of 3.5% from 2019 to a population of 7,754 people, though that figure isn't too reliable given the transient nature of the city's unhoused residents.

MANY HOTELS CHARGE HIDDEN FEES
As with other major American cities, like Los Angeles and New York, the majority of upscale hotels in San Francisco now charge fees that are separate from the published advertised room rate for the hotel. Often listed as "Urban," "Resort," "Amenity," and/or "Facility" fees, these tack-on rates are usually around $25 per night but can run to $45 per night or more. Avoid any surprises and ask about such fees before you book or when you check in (and feel free to contest them in person and on social media).

THE HILLS ARE PRETTY, JUST NOT SO MUCH ON THE WAY UP
The city's hills offer spectacular views, but they can also be physically challenging, particularly for those with limited stamina or mobility. Exploring on foot is both possible and rewarding, but it's important to plan accordingly if you're not up for a climb. Some hills are steep enough that they have steps built right into the sidewalk (easier for some, but still not exactly a walk in the park!), and the city is committed to being ADA-friendly, which includes accessible public transportation. If you're up to it, pack practical walking shoes; if not, take advantage of public transportation.

YOU CAN RELY ON PUBLIC TRANSIT
While public transportation is a feature of nearly every major city, few places have the sheer variety offered by San Francisco. The Bay Area Rapid Transit (BART) system is a mix of both heavy rail and subway and serves San Francisco, Oakland, and a variety of suburban areas. At the same time, San Francisco has hybrid Muni buses, Muni Metro Light Rail, cable cars, historic streetcars, electric trolleys, and a range of privately run options, such as taxis, app-based rideshares, electric bicycles, and motorized scooters. Many parts of the public transportation network are quite well run, though buses fall prey to traffic and sometimes run behind schedule. Between the public and the private options, you should have a fairly easy time getting to where you need to go.

KNOW WHICH RICHMOND YOU'RE RENTING IN
The Richmond District, also known as "the Richmond," is a neighborhood in the northwest corner of San Francisco; Richmond is a city 20 miles northeast of San Francisco in the East Bay. Drilling further down: the Richmond neighborhood's sub-neighborhoods include Outer Richmond (the western portion of the Richmond), Inner Richmond (the eastern portion of the Richmond), and Central Richmond (between Inner and Outer Richmonds). Got all that?

THERE ARE MORE THAN 1,000 MURALS

Along with L.A. and Chicago, San Francisco is one of the top three cities for murals in the United States, and walls and alleys all over town are adorned with vivid colors and poignant messages. The Mission District alone boasts almost 500. Some highlights are the Chris Ware mural at 826 Valencia Street, the multitude of murals in Balmy Alley and Clarion Alley, and the Hidden Garden Steps.

THE PIERS ARE TOURIST TRAPS, BUT THAT'S OKAY

San Francisco's northern waterfront public piers are absolutely, 100% a set of loud and crowded tourist traps. But there's a reason these piers are such a famous magnet for visitors—they're kind of awesome! The straight, weatherworn expanse of Fisherman's Wharf is iconic, and Pier 39's basking sea lions and multitude of vendors make it a lively and popular destination. Even if you don't think of yourself as the kind of person that these sights would appeal to, give them a shot. Wander along the Embarcadero, stop for some crab legs and oysters along the way, and enjoy one of the most leisurely parts of the city.

SIDE TRIPS ARE A MUST

San Francisco is a vibrant and engaging place, but you'll be doing yourself a disservice if you only stick to the major tourist neighborhoods. The city of Oakland has been transformed in recent years,

with pockets of Piedmont Avenue and other streets lined with hip restaurants, bars, and shops. Berkeley is home not just to a famous university but also to a variety of museums, cafés, and legendary restaurants. And don't forget the beautiful scenery along the coast from Bodega Bay to Half Moon Bay and all the incredible wine to be had in nearby Sonoma and Napa.

PRIVATE PARKS ARE PUBLIC

It's a little-known fact that cities often require privately owned buildings to provide public spaces. In San Francisco those are known as POPOS (Privately Owned Public Open Spaces), and they're all over the city just waiting for you to come sit, feel like a local, and enjoy some fresh air in a pleasant setting. These spaces are legally required to be labeled with visible signage indicating both how they can be accessed and what their hours of operation are. In the off chance those signs are hard to find (or simply aren't there), the San Francisco Planning Department provides a searchable, interactive map (⊕ sfplanninggis. org/popos) that lets you see which sites have amenities, such as bathrooms, food, tables, and seating.

IT'S NOT CHEAP

San Francisco is not only one of the most expensive cities in the entire world in which to live, it's also an expensive one to visit. Between the high prices of flights, hotels, and meals, if you're budget-conscious you'll need to plan a bit to

maximize your resources. CityPASS (⊕ www.citypass. com) bundles together public transit passes and museum tickets for both ease and savings, and the customizable Go City pass (⊕ gocity.com/en-us) lets you build your own itinerary from scratch while still economizing. The city's public transportation network also sells unlimited-ride day passes.

YOUR DOG IS VERY WELCOME

If you're a dog lover or like to travel with your dog, San Francisco is a good option for you. There are hundreds of acres in and around the city where your pup can romp off-leash, and every neighborhood has one or two parks with sizable dog-run areas. People are out and about everywhere with their dogs, socializing with other people with dogs. There are dog-friendly bars; dog-friendly beaches, like Baker Beach, Ocean Beach, and Lands End Beach; dog-friendly cabor dog friendly gyms, pet-friendly apartment rentals and hotels; dog-friendly wineries in Napa; and lots of dog-friendly walking tours. In April, the annual DogFest is a huge celebration of all things canine in Duboce Park.

Getting Here and Around

Air

Nonstop flights from New York to San Francisco take about 5½ hours, and with the three-hour time change, it's possible to leave JFK by 8 am and be in San Francisco by 10:30 am. Nonstop times are approximately 1½ hours from Los Angeles, 3 hours from Dallas, 4½ hours from Chicago, 5½ hours from Atlanta, 11 hours from London, and 13½ hours from Sydney.

AIRPORTS

The major gateway to San Francisco is San Francisco International Airport (SFO), 15 miles south of the city off U.S. 101.

Oakland International Airport (OAK) is across the bay, not much farther away from downtown San Francisco (via I–80 East and I–880 South), but traffic on the Bay Bridge lengthens travel times considerably.

San Jose International Airport (SJC) is about 40 miles south of San Francisco; travel time varies with traffic, but plan on between an hour and 1½ hours.

Depending on the price difference, you might consider flying into Oakland or San Jose. Oakland's an easy-to-use alternative because there's public transportation between the airport and downtown San Francisco. Getting to San Francisco from San Jose, though, can be time-consuming via public transportation or costly via rideshare or taxi. Heavy fog is infamous for causing chronic delays into and out of San Francisco.

GROUND TRANSPORTATION FROM SAN FRANCISCO INTERNATIONAL AIRPORT

Transportation signage at the airport is color-coded by type and is quite clear. A taxi ride to downtown costs around $60; rideshare companies like Lyft and Uber are a popular option and start around $25 for a shared ride into the city. However, prices can vary greatly depending on the time of day and overall demand. SuperShuttle is a good choice for groups looking to be driven via a van.

For travelers to or from the East Bay, East Bay Shuttle is a choice for nonstop service to any major airport in the Bay Area. MSN Door to Door operates van service to Marin County, Sonoma County, and Napa County starting at $83 for the first passenger, and a few bucks more for each additional person. Marin Airporter buses cost $25 (cash only, unless reserved ahead online) and require no reservations but stop only at designated stations in Marin; buses run every hour, from 5 am to midnight.

You can take BART directly to downtown San Francisco; the trip takes about 30 minutes and costs $10. There are both booths with attendants and vending machines for ticket purchases. Travelers must have a Clipper Card to board or a first-time purchase for BART will include one (paper tickets are not sold). Trains leave from the international terminal every 15 or 20 minutes.

Another inexpensive way to get to San Francisco (though not as convenient as BART) is via two SamTrans buses: No. 292 (1 hour, 18 minutes), No. 398 (40 to 60 minutes) and the 397 OWL (55 minutes). Fares are $2.25. Board the SamTrans buses on the lower level.

To drive to downtown San Francisco, take U.S. 101 North to the Civic Center/9th Street, 7th Street, or 4th Street/Downtown exits. For the Embarcadero or Fisherman's Wharf, take I–280 North (the exit is to the right, just north of the airport, off U.S. 101) and get off at the 4th Street/King Street exit. King Street becomes the Embarcadero a few blocks east of the exit. The Embarcadero winds around the waterfront to Fisherman's Wharf.

FROM OAKLAND INTERNATIONAL AIRPORT

A taxi to downtown San Francisco costs around $80; rideshare companies like Lyft and Uber offer rides for around $50. SuperShuttle operates vans to San Francisco and Oakland. MSN Door to Door serves Marin County for $83 or more for the first passenger, and a few bucks more for each additional person.

The best way to get to San Francisco via public transit is to take BART, which is free upon boarding but requires ticket purchase at the Coliseum/Oakland International Airport BART station (BART fares vary depending on where you're going; the ride to downtown San Francisco from here costs $10.20).

By car, take Airport Drive east to I–880 North to I–80 West over the Bay Bridge. This will likely take at least an hour.

FROM SAN JOSE INTERNATIONAL AIRPORT

A taxi to downtown San Jose costs about $20 to $25; a trip to San Francisco runs about $150 to $165. Lyft and Uber rides to downtown San Jose start around $12; a trip to San Francisco starts around $55.

To drive to downtown San Jose, take Airport Boulevard east to Route 87 South. To get to San Francisco, take Route 87 North to U.S. 101 North or I–880 South to I–280 North. The trip takes roughly an hour to 1 hour, 30 minutes.

At $10.50 for a one-way ticket, Caltrain provides the most affordable option for traveling between San Francisco and San Jose's airport. However, the nearby Santa Clara Station isn't attached to San Jose International Airport. And the Caltrain station in San Francisco at 4th and King Streets isn't in a conveniently central location. It's on the eastern side of the South of Market (SoMa) neighborhood and not easily accessible by other public transit. You'll need to take a taxi or walk from the nearest bus line. From San Francisco, it takes 90 minutes to reach the Santa Clara Caltrain station, from which you'll need to catch the VTA Bus No. 60 or order a rideshare for the roughly 10 minute drive to and from San Jose International Airport.

Boat

Several ferry lines run out of San Francisco. Blue & Gold Fleet operates a number of tours, plus service to Sausalito ($14.25 one-way). Tickets are sold at Pier 39; boats depart from Pier 41. Alcatraz Cruises operates the ferries to Alcatraz Island ($42) from Pier 33. Boats leave 14 times a day (more in summer), and the journey itself takes 30 minutes. Allow at least 2½ hours for a round-trip jaunt. Golden Gate Ferry operates daily to and from Sausalito and Larkspur ($14 and $13.50 one-way), leaving from Pier 1, behind the Ferry Building. The San Francisco Bay Ferry operates daily between Alameda's Main Street Terminal, Oakland's Jack London Square, and San Francisco's Ferry Building ($4.50 one-way). Purchase tickets online via the Clipper Card website or app or at terminal vending machines (tickets for the ferry to Oakland/Alameda can also be purchased on board).

Bus

Greyhound serves San Francisco with buses from many major U.S. cities. The Greyhound depot is located at the Salesforce Transit Center in SoMa. Tickets can be purchased online; seating is first-come, first-served. Cash, checks, and credit cards are accepted.

Getting Here and Around

🚋 Cable Car

Don't miss the sensation of moving up and down some of San Francisco's steepest hills in a clattering cable car. Jump aboard as it pauses at a designated stop, and wedge yourself into any available space. Then just hold on.

The fare (for one direction) is $8. Buy tickets in advance at the kiosks at the cable-car turnarounds at Hyde and Beach Streets and at Powell and Market Streets. Or consider MuniMobile or a Clipper Card; see ⊕ sfmta.com. Cash purchases require exact change.

The Powell–Mason and Powell–Hyde lines begin at Powell and Market Streets near Union Square and terminate at Fisherman's Wharf; lines for these routes can be long, especially in summer. The California Street line runs east and west from Market and California Streets to Van Ness Avenue. It's a shorter and less thrilling ride, but there's often no wait.

🚗 Car

Driving in San Francisco can be a challenge because of the one-way streets, snarly traffic, and steep hills.

Be sure to leave plenty of room between your car and other vehicles when on a steep slope. This is especially important when you've braked at a stop sign on a steep incline. Whether with a stick shift or an automatic transmission, every car rolls backward for a moment once the brake is released. When it's time to pull forward, keep your foot on the brake while tapping lightly on the accelerator. Once the gears are engaged, let up on the brake and head uphill.

■ TIP→ Remember to curb your wheels when parking on hills—turn wheels away from the curb when facing uphill, toward the curb when facing downhill. You can get a ticket if you don't do this.

Market Street runs southwest from the Ferry Building, then becomes Portola Drive as it rounds Twin Peaks (which lie just south of the giant radio-antennae structure Sutro Tower). It can be difficult to drive across Market. The major east–west streets north of Market are Geary Boulevard (it's called Geary Street east of Van Ness Avenue), which runs to the ocean; Fulton Street, which begins at the back of the Opera House and continues along the north side of Golden Gate Park to Ocean Beach; Oak Street, which runs east from Golden Gate Park toward downtown, then flows into northbound Franklin Street; and Fell Street, the left two lanes of which cut through Golden Gate Park and empty into Lincoln Way, which continues to the ocean.

Among the major north–south streets are Divisadero, which heading south becomes Castro Street at Waller Street and continues just past Cesar Chavez Street; Van Ness Avenue, which heading south becomes South Van Ness Avenue after it crosses Market Street; and Park Presidio Boulevard, which heading south from the Richmond District becomes Crossover Drive within Golden Gate Park and empties into 19th Avenue.

GASOLINE

Gas stations are hard to find; look for them on major thoroughfares, such as Market Street, Geary Boulevard, Mission Street, or California Street.

PARKING

San Francisco is a terrible city for parking. In the Financial District and Civic Center neighborhoods, parking is forbidden on most streets between 3 or 4 pm and 6 or 7 pm. Check street signs carefully to confirm because illegally parked cars are towed immediately. Downtown parking lots are often full, and most are expensive. The city-owned Sutter-Stockton, Ellis-O'Farrell, and 5th-and-Mission garages have the most reasonable rates in the downtown area. Large hotels often have parking available, but many charge in excess of $40 a day.

Whether you are parking in a garage or on the street, never leave any items of value in your car. Vehicle break-ins are a frequent and unfortunate reality, and they can happen anywhere at any hour (even in safe neighborhoods).

ROAD CONDITIONS

Although rush hours are 6–10 am and 3–7 pm, you can hit gridlock on any day at any time, especially over the Bay Bridge and leaving or entering the city from the south. Sunday-afternoon traffic can be heavy as well.

The most comprehensive traffic updates are available through the city's 511 service, which can be accessed online (⊕ www.511.org), where real-time data shows you the traffic on your route, or by calling ☎ 511. On the radio, tune in to an all-news radio station, such as KQED 88.5 FM or KCBS 740 AM/106.9 FM.

Be wary of nonindicated lane changes.

San Francisco is the only major American city uncut by freeways. To get from the Bay Bridge to the Golden Gate Bridge, you'll have to take surface streets, specifically Van Ness Avenue, which doubles as U.S. 101 through the city. It can be frustrating, so allow extra time.

RULES OF THE ROAD

The speed limit on city streets is 25 mph unless otherwise posted. A right turn on a red light after stopping is legal unless posted otherwise, as is a left on red at the intersection of two one-way streets.

Take the 511 👁

Several transportation organizations—the Metropolitan Transportation Commission, the California Highway Patrol, the California Department of Transportation, and more—pool their data into a free, one-stop telephone (☎ 511) and Web (⊕ www.511.org) resource for the Bay Area. The service provides the latest info on traffic conditions, routes, and fares for all public transit and also has info about bicycle and other transportation.

Ⓜ Metro/Public Transport

BART

BART (Bay Area Rapid Transit) trains, which run until midnight, travel under the bay via tunnel to connect San Francisco with Oakland, Berkeley, and other cities and towns beyond. Within San Francisco, stations are mostly downtown and in the Mission.

Trains travel frequently from early morning until evening on weekdays. After 8 pm weekdays and on weekends, there's often a 20-minute wait between trains on the same line. Trains also travel south from San Francisco as far as Millbrae. BART trains connect downtown San Francisco to San Francisco International Airport; the ride costs $10.

Intracity San Francisco fares are $2.15; intercity fares are $3.60 to $14.35. BART bases its ticket prices on miles traveled and doesn't offer price breaks by zone. The easy-to-read maps posted in BART stations list fares based on destination, radiating out from the current station.

Getting Here and Around

During rush hours, trains within the city are crowded—even standing room can be hard to come by. Cars at the far front and back of the train are less likely to be filled to capacity. Smoking, eating, and drinking are prohibited on trains and in stations.

Like with any major city subway system, be alert on BART trains. The system is largely safe, but it's always best to avoid being distracted or alone while on platforms and trains.

BUS OPERATORS

Outside the city, AC Transit serves the East Bay, and Golden Gate Transit serves Marin County and a few cities in southern Sonoma County.

MUNI

The San Francisco Municipal Railway, or Muni, operates light-rail vehicles, the historic F-line streetcars along Fisherman's Wharf and Market Street, buses, and the world-famous cable cars. Light-rail travels along Market Street to the Mission District and Noe Valley (J line), Ingleside (K line), and the Sunset District (L, M, and N lines) while also passing through the West Portal, Glen Park, and Castro neighborhoods. The N line continues around the Embarcadero to the Caltrain station at 4th and King Streets; the T-line light-rail runs from the Chinatown to Union Square, SoMa, the 4th and King Caltrain station, and south past Mission Bay and Hunters Point to Sunnydale Avenue and Bayshore Boulevard. Muni provides 24-hour service on select lines to all areas of the city.

On buses and streetcars, the fare is $3 ($2.50 with a Clipper Card). Exact change is required, and dollar bills are accepted in the fare boxes. For all Muni vehicles

other than cable cars, transfers are issued free upon request at the time the fare is paid that allow for 120 minutes of travel. Cable cars cost $8 and include no transfers (⇨ see Cable-Car Travel).

One-day ($13), three-day ($31), and seven-day ($41) Visitor Passports valid on the entire Muni system can be purchased at several outlets, including the cable-car ticket booth at Powell and Market Streets and the visitor information center downstairs in Hallidie Plaza. A monthly ticket is available for $81, which can be used on all Muni lines (including cable cars) and on BART within city limits. The San Francisco CityPass ($76), a discount ticket booklet to several major city attractions, also covers all Muni travel for seven consecutive days.

■ TIP→ Save money by purchasing your Passports on MuniMobile, the mobile ticketing app of the San Francisco Metropolitan Transportation Authority (SFMTA).

VTA

The Valley Transit Authority (VTA) provides light rail and bus service to the Santa Clara Valley. Fares range from $2.50 for a single ride (with two hours of free transfers) to $7.50 for a day pass. The VTA's routes are particularly useful at evening rush hour when U.S. 101 and I–280 have considerable traffic, and for getting to Levi's Stadium.

🚕 Taxi

Taxi service is notoriously bad in San Francisco, and finding a cab can be frustrating. Popular nightlife locales, such as the Mission, SoMa, North Beach, and the Castro, are the easiest places to hail a cab off the street; hotel taxi stands are also an option. If you're going to the airport, make a reservation or book a shuttle instead. Taxis in San Francisco charge $4.15 for the first 0.2 mile, 65¢ for each additional 0.2 mile, and 65¢ per minute in stalled traffic; a $5.50 surcharge is added for trips from the airport. There's no charge for additional passengers or for luggage. For trips farther than 15 miles outside city limits, multiply the metered rate by 1.5; tolls and tip are extra.

That said, San Francisco's poor taxi service was a direct factor in the creation of ridesharing services, such as Uber and Lyft, which are easy to use and prominent throughout the city. If you're willing to share a car with strangers, a trip within the city can run as low as $4; rates go up for private rides and during peak-demand times. These services are especially economical when going to or from the airport, where a shared ride starts at about $25—half the cost of a cab.

Many San Franciscans use rideshare apps for going *to* SFO, but often use taxis for trips *from* the airport because they are much easier to find than arranging rideshare cars after landing.

🚆 Train

Amtrak trains travel to the Bay Area from some cities in California as well as the greater United States. The Coast Starlight passes through the Bay Area on the way from Los Angeles to Seattle, but contrary to its name, the train runs mostly inland through the Central Valley while in Northern California; the most scenic stretch is in Southern California.

Amtrak also has several routes between San Jose, Oakland, and Sacramento. The California Zephyr travels from Chicago to the Bay Area, with spectacular vistas as it crosses the Sierra Nevada. San Francisco doesn't have an Amtrak train station but does have an Amtrak bus stop at the Ferry Building, from which shuttle buses transport passengers to trains in Emeryville. Shuttle buses also connect the Emeryville train station with BART and other points in downtown San Francisco. You can buy a California Rail Pass, which gives you 7 days of travel in a 21-day period, for $159.

Caltrain connects San Francisco to Palo Alto, San Jose, Santa Clara, and many smaller cities en route. Trains leave from the main depot at 4th and Townsend Streets, and a rail-side stop at 22nd and Pennsylvania Streets. One-way fares are $3.75 to $15, depending on the number of zones through which you travel; tickets are valid for four hours after purchase time. A ticket is $8.25 from San Francisco to Palo Alto, at least $10.50 to San Jose. You can also buy a day pass ($7.50–$30) for unlimited travel in a 24-hour period. It's worth waiting for an express train for trips over an hour. On weekdays, trains depart three or four times per hour during the morning and evening, but only once or twice per hour during non-commute hours. Weekend trains run once per hour, with two bullet trains per day, one in late morning and one in early evening. The system shuts down after midnight. There are no onboard ticket sales. You must buy tickets before boarding the train or risk paying up to $230 for fare evasion.

Essentials

🏃 Activities

Bikers and hikers traverse the majestic Golden Gate Bridge, bound for the Marin Headlands or the winding trails of the Presidio. Runners, strollers, and cyclists head for Golden Gate Park's wooded paths, and water lovers satisfy their addictions by kayaking, sailing, and kite-surfing in the bay and along the rugged Pacific coast. Swimmers usually stick to sheltered parts of the bay or swimming pools.

Prefer to watch from the sidelines? The Giants (baseball) play in San Francisco, as do the Golden State Warriors (basketball; at the Chase Center in Mission Bay); the A's (baseball) play in Oakland; and the 49ers (football) are based in Santa Clara. But the city has plenty of other periodic sporting events to spectate, including that roving costume party, the Bay to Breakers race in May. For events listings and local perspectives on Bay Area sports, pick up a copy of the *San Francisco Chronicle* (⊕ *www.sfchronicle.com*) or go online to visit *SFGate* (⊕ *www.sfgate. com*).

BASEBALL
Oakland Athletics
BASEBALL & SOFTBALL | **FAMILY** | Baseball's Oakland Athletics, also called the Oakland A's, has a loyal following among locals in the East Bay and enjoys a fierce rivalry with the San Francisco Giants across the bay. The team hopes to move from its Oakland Coliseum stadium to a proposed new waterfront ballpark at Jack London Square, but that project has repeatedly stalled and fans are discouraged that it might not happen. Major League Baseball is also allowing the team to consider relocating to another city; stay tuned. ⊠ *Oakland Coliseum, 7000 Coliseum Way, Oakland* ☎ *877/638–4900* ⊕ *mlb.com/athletics.*

★ San Francisco Giants
BASEBALL & SOFTBALL | **FAMILY** | Three World Series titles (2010, 2012, and 2014) and the retro-modern design of Oracle Park lead to sellout home games, so make plans in advance. ⊠ *Oracle Park, 24 Willie Mays Plaza, SoMa* ☎ *415/972–2000* ⊕ *www.mlb.com/giants.*

BIKING
San Francisco is known for its treacherously steep hills, so it may be surprising to see so many cyclists. This is actually a great city for biking—there are ample bike lanes, it's not hard to find level ground with great scenery (especially along the water), and if you're willing to tackle a challenging uphill climb, you're often rewarded with a fabulous view—and a quick trip back down. Along with the roads within Golden Gate Park itself, "the Wiggle" is a mostly flat, frequently used route that connects the park with Market Street.

If you're driving on downtown and SoMa streets, make sure to be extra careful given the number of stop signs, streetlights, and frequently frustrated drivers because of traffic.

FOOTBALL
San Francisco 49ers
FOOTBALL | State-of-the-art Levi's Stadium, 45 miles south of San Francisco, has more than 13,000 square feet of HD video boards. Home games usually sell out far in advance. Ticketmaster (⊕ *www.ticketmaster.com*) and StubHub (⊕ *www.stubhub.com*) are sources for single-game tickets. ⊠ *Levi's Stadium, 4900 Marie P. DeBartolo Way, Santa Clara* ✛ *From San Francisco, take U.S. 101 S to Lawrence Expressway and follow signs* ☎ *800/745–3000 Ticketmaster, 415/464–9377 Santa Clara stadium* ⊕ *www.49ers. com.*

RUNNING

San Francisco is spectacular for running. There are more than seven miles of paved trails in and around **Golden Gate Park**; circling Stow Lake and then crossing the bridge and running up the path to the top of Strawberry Hill is a total of 2½ miles. An enormously popular route is the two-mile raised bike path that runs from Lincoln Way along the ocean, at the southern border of Golden Gate Park, to Sloat Boulevard, which is the northern border of the San Francisco Zoo. (Stick to the park's interior when it's windy, as ocean gusts can kick up sand.) From Sloat Boulevard, you can pick up the **Lake Merced** bike path, which loops around the lake and the golf course, to extend your run another five miles.

The paved path along the **Marina** provides a 1½-mile (round-trip) run along a flat, well-maintained surface and has glorious bay views. Start where Laguna Street meets Marina Boulevard, then run west along the Marina Green toward the Golden Gate and St. Francis Yacht Clubs, near the docks at the northern end of Marina Boulevard. On weekends, beware: you'll have to wind through the crowds—but those views are worth it. You can extend your Marina run by jogging the paths through the restored wetlands of Crissy Field, just past the yacht harbor, then up the hill to the Golden Gate Bridge.

The *San Francisco Bike Map & Walking Guide*, available at booksellers or through the San Francisco Bicycle Coalition (⊕ *sfbike.org/resources/maps-routes*), which indicates hill grades on city streets by color, is a great resource. Online, check the San Francisco Road Runners Club site (⊕ *www.sfrrc.org*) for some recommended routes and links to several local races.

🍴 Dining

San Francisco is one of America's top food cities. Some of the biggest landmarks are restaurants, and, for some visitors, chefs are just as big a draw as Alcatraz. In fact, on a Saturday, the Ferry Building—a temple to local eating—may attract more visitors than the Golden Gate Bridge.

Chefs are drawn to the superb ingredients plucked from the soil and the sea. Chances are that the Meyer lemons, fava beans, or strawberries on your plate that are preserved, pureed, or pickled were harvested within the last 48 hours, if not this morning. The briny abalone, crab, oysters, squid, and tuna that are poached, seared, smoked, or carpaccio'ed are caught just offshore. You will also get to taste unusual varieties, like lollipop kale, agretti greens, and yuzu citrus.

Today the most interesting kitchens are using these ingredients in regional cuisines, like Korean, Japanese, Italian, or South American. So get ready to dig into kung pao pastrami, porcini doughnuts with raclette béchamel, and yucca gnocchi. That fig-on-a-plate reputation is so cliché.

But the playground isn't just in haute cuisine kitchens. Culinary hot spots are just as likely to be a burger, pizza, or barbecue joint—with a few classically trained chefs dedicating their lives to making a better margherita pizza. And you can just as easily find superb *banh mi*, ramen noodles, and juicy *al pastor* tacos in the kitchens of Little Saigon, Japantown, or the Mission District.

The impact of the COVID-19 pandemic on the restaurant scene in the Bay Area, as in many other parts of the globe, has been widespread and severe. Many

Essentials

restaurants and bars now have shorter hours or more condensed menus. Call the restaurant or check their website for the latest information. One upside is that temporary parklets and pedestrian-friendly slow streets have become permanent fixtures, lending an air of alfresco European leisure to the streets of San Francisco.

RESERVATIONS

Snagging reservations at restaurants with a lot of buzz has gotten notoriously difficult, with 5:30 or 9:30 often the pick. These choices aren't terrible, if you plan on it. For a reservation at peak dining hours, though, our best advice is to call or look online as far in advance as possible (usually 30 months to the calendar day)—try eating there earlier in the week if the Friday and Saturday tables are full. You can also try calling a restaurant in the early afternoon the day of, when they're making their reservation confirmation calls and may have a last-minute opening. If you're calling a few days ahead of time, ask if you can be put on a waiting list. Also, ask whether there's a bar or counter you can dine at—these are usually offered first-come, first-served. Some places set aside tables for walk-in business (and not for advance reservations), in which case you can just show up and make the most of the wait. As a last resort, some popular San Francisco restaurants are also open for lunch.

HOURS

Unless otherwise noted, the restaurants listed are open daily for lunch and dinner. Prime time for dinner is around 7:30 or 8 pm, and although there are places for night owls to fuel up, most restaurants stop serving around 10 pm. Restaurants, along with bars and clubs, may serve alcohol between the hours of 6 am and 2 am.

WHAT TO WEAR

In general, San Franciscans are neat but casual dressers; only at the top-notch dining rooms do you see a more formal style. But the way you dress may influence how you're treated—and where you're seated. Generally speaking, jeans will suffice at most table-service restaurants in the $ to $$$ range. No restaurants in the city require a jacket and tie for men anymore, though you certainly will see some at the most refined establishments. Note that shorts, sweatpants, and sports jerseys are rarely appropriate. When in doubt, call the restaurant and ask.

CHILDREN

As in many other cities, small kids generally aren't seen in the fanciest restaurants. For families with young children, we recommend many family-friendly places with great food. Restaurants that are particularly good for families are marked as such.

PARKING

Most high-end restaurants offer valet parking—worth considering in crowded neighborhoods, such as North Beach, Russian Hill, Union Square, and the Mission. There's often a nominal charge and a time restriction on validated parking.

Remember, parking in San Francisco is often a dicey proposition given the high number of thefts. It's always recommended to use rideshare, taxi, or public transit for traveling to restaurants.

PRICES

If you're watching your budget, be sure to ask the price of daily specials. The charge for these dishes can sometimes be out of line with the menu. If you eat early or late, you may be able to take advantage of a prix-fixe deal not offered at peak hours. Many upscale restaurants offer lunch deals with special menus at bargain prices. Bar seating or casual portions of higher-end restaurants often have a slightly less expensive "bar bites" menu. Also, keep in mind that several of the city's best bars also serve excellent food, which is usually less expensive than their restaurant peers.

Credit cards are widely accepted, but a few restaurants (particularly smaller ones) accept only cash. Also, keep in mind that a restaurant listed as $$$ may actually have a good deal or two, such as an early prix-fixe dinner or a great bar scene and good, reasonably priced bar food to go with it.

⇨ *Prices in the reviews are the average cost of a main course at dinner or, if dinner is not served, at lunch.*

What It Costs in U.S. Dollars

$	$$	$$$	$$$$
AT DINNER			
under $20	$20–$30	$31–$40	over $40

TIPPING AND TAXES

In most restaurants, tip the waiter 18%–20%. (To figure out a 20% tip quickly, just move the decimal spot one place to the left of your pretax bill and double that.) Bills for parties of five or more sometimes include the tip (you can always add more). A few restaurants in the Bay Area are experimenting with a gratuity-included policy for all parties. There are only a handful of such places, and the movement is led by some of the best chefs. Tip at least $1 per drink at the bar; $2 or $3 if it's a labor-intensive cocktail. Also be aware that some restaurants, now required to fund the city's new universal-health-care ordinance, are passing these costs along to their customers indirectly instead of raising menu prices—usually in the form of a 3%–4%

surcharge or a $1–$3.50-per-head charge. (San Francisco sales tax is currently at 8.63%.) Diners in San Francisco generally do not include these health care figures/fees/taxes when calculating gratuity—tip is almost always solely based on the base pretax total.

🛜 Internet

The city of San Francisco offers free Wi-Fi service in selected parks and areas in and around the city. All public libraries also provide Internet access, and most hotels have a computer stationed in the lobby with free (if shared) high-speed access for guests. Some hotels charge a small fee to provide a high-speed connection in the room; others offer it free of charge. In addition, many cafés throughout San Francisco, Marin County, and the East Bay offer complimentary Wi-Fi, but a few continue to charge a fee.

🛏 Lodging

San Francisco accommodations are diverse, ranging from cozy bed-and-breakfasts and kitschy motels to chic boutique hotels, grande dames, and sleek high-rises. Though the tech boom has skyrocketed the prices of even some of the most dependable low-cost options, some Fodor's faves still offer fine accommodations without prices that rival the city's steep hills. In fact, the number of reasonably priced accommodations is impressive.

When contemplating a stay in San Francisco, consider timing. Many business-oriented hotels offer weekend deals (such properties are busiest from Monday through Thursday), with the opposite often true at lodgings geared more to leisure travelers. When there's

Essentials

a big convention in town, even the humblest accommodations can double in price or more.

For travelers looking for a more intimate experience with local hosts, vacation rental properties booked through Airbnb or VRBO may be the way to go. Prices are often cheaper, especially if shared among a group of guests who plan to do some of the cooking themselves.

Once you settle into your perfect room, remember this advice: when in doubt, ask the concierge. This holds true for almost any request, whether you have special needs or burning desires—if anyone can get you tickets to that sold-out show or a table at the hottest restaurant, it's the concierge.

RESERVATIONS

Reservations are always advised, especially during the peak seasons—from August through November, during Fleet Week (October) and Salesforce Dreamforce Convention (September), and weekends in December. Celebrations like Chinese New Year (late January or early February), Mother's Day and Bay to Breakers (mid-May), and Gay Pride (June) also require reservations.

FACILITIES

When pricing accommodations, always ask what facilities are included and what entails an additional charge. One big unexpected extra might be parking fees, which are off the charts in San Francisco; another is the per-night "resort" or "amenity" fee that may be added to rates at more expensive hotels. A seemingly expensive hotel that provides free parking and a hearty breakfast, for instance, can end up costing you less than one that charges for parking and breakfast. All the hotels listed have private baths, central heating, and private phones unless otherwise noted. Many

places don't have air-conditioning, but you probably won't need it. Even in September and October, when the city sees its warmest days, the temperature rarely climbs above 70°F.

Nearly all hotels have Wi-Fi available, and though many offer the service for free, some charge for quicker connections, multiple devices, or both. Larger hotels often have high-speed checkout capability. Pools are a rarity, but most large properties have gyms or health clubs, and sometimes full-scale spas; hotels without facilities usually have arrangements for guests at nearby gyms, sometimes for a fee. At the end of each review, we state whether any meals (and in San Francisco, this means breakfast) are included in the room rate. Mirroring a trend elsewhere in the country, some hotels no longer provide room service, so if that's an amenity you require, be sure to inquire.

PARKING

Several properties on Lombard Street and in the Civic Center area have free parking (but not always in a covered garage), and occasionally hotel package deals include parking. Hotels in the Union Square and Nob Hill areas charge $30 to $70 per day for garage parking; many hotels charge extra fees for SUVs. Some bed-and-breakfasts have limited free parking available, but many don't, requiring you to park on the street. Depending on the neighborhood, this can be easy or quite difficult, so ask for realistic parking information when you call. Some hotels offer a choice of valet parking with unlimited in-out privileges or self-parking. The cost is generally less for the latter, in part because no tip is involved. Given the expense of parking, and the ease of getting around San Francisco on public transportation, you may well want to leave the car at home or wait to rent one

Where Should I Stay?

	NEIGHBORHOOD VIBE	PROS	CONS
SoMa	Square one for the business set, with luxury high-rises, old classics, and a few bargains.	Near the museums, Oracle Park, Yerba Buena Gardens, and the convention center. Many fine eateries.	Construction brings noise and traffic. Be cautious walking around at any time of day.
Union Square	A hub for visitors, with a wide range of options.	Excellent shopping. Home to the theater district. Great public transit access.	Often crowded and noisy. Take caution in the area, especially at night.
Fisherman's Wharf	Mostly chain hotels in a touristy area.	Near attractions like Ghirardelli Square and Pier 39. Cable-car lines and bay-cruise piers are nearby. Easy access to walking/ jogging/biking on the waterfront.	City ordinances limit wharf hotels to four stories, so good views are out. Very touristy.
Financial District	A mini Midtown Manhattan, largely catering to business travelers.	Excellent city and bay views. Easy access to restaurants and nightlife.	Some streets are iffy at night. Pricey hotels. Many businesses close at night and on weekends.
Nob Hill	Home of San Francisco's high society, and some of the best-known luxury hotels.	Many hotels boast gorgeous views and notable restaurants. Easy access to Union Square and Chinatown.	Hotels here will test your wallet, while the area's steep hills may try your endurance.
Pacific Heights	A quiet, residential neighborhood with a few tony accommodations.	Away from the street life and noise of downtown. Local feel. Lots of free parking.	Getting downtown from these neighborhoods can be challenging via public transportation.

Essentials

until you're ready to leave town. Keep in mind that tourists are unfortunately often targeted by thieves who look for rental cars and expect to find luggage left in them. Be vigilant—never leave your belongings in your rental car.

PRICES

San Francisco hotel prices rank among the highest in the country. Weekend rates for double rooms in high season (typically summer for leisure travelers) average about $250 a night citywide except during large conventions, such as the one hosted by Salesforce, when even the humblest downtown lodgings command $500 or more. At other times, even in high season, decent lower-cost accommodations are relatively plentiful. Most hotels price rooms dynamically, with rates for dates a few days forward or months down the line fluctuating from hour to hour depending on availability—if you have your heart set on a particular property and its prices are high for your desired dates, it's wise to check back often either online or by phone.

You'll sometimes, but not always, find a hotel's best rates on its website. If looking for a same-day room, check out apps, such as HotelTonight, or access the last-minute pages of Expedia and other travel sites for the best deals. Whenever you're making a reservation, inquire about special rates and packages.

⇨ Prices are the lowest cost of a standard double room in high season.

What It Costs in U.S. Dollars

$	$$	$$$	$$$$
HOTELS			
under $200	$200–$350	$351–$500	over $500

Nightlife

After hours, the city's business folk and workers give way to costume-clad party-goers, hippies and hipsters, downtown divas, frat boys, and those who prefer something a little more clothing-optional. Downtown and the Financial District remain pretty serious even after dark, and Nob Hill is staid, though you can't beat views from penthouse lounges, the most famous being the Top of the Mark (in the InterContinental Mark Hopkins). Nearby North Beach is an even better starting point for an evening out.

Always lively, North Beach's options include family-friendly dining spots, historic bars from the city's bohemian past (among them Jack Kerouac's old haunts), and even comedy clubs where stars like Robin Williams and Jay Leno cut their teeth. In SoMa there are plenty of places to catch a drink before a Giants game and brewpubs to celebrate in afterward. SoMa also hosts some of the hottest dance clubs, along with some saucy gay bars. While Union Square can be a bit trendy, even the swanky establishments have loosened things up in recent years.

Heading west to Hayes Valley, a more sophisticated crowd dabbles in the burgeoning "culinary cocktail movement." Up-and-coming singles gravitate north of here to Cow Hollow and the Marina. Polk Gulch was the city's gay mecca before the Castro and still hosts some wild bars, but things get downright outlandish in the Castro District. Hipsters populate the Mission and Haight Districts by night. Keep in mind, though, that some of the best times San Francisco has to offer are off the beaten path. And a good party can still be found in even the sleepiest of neighborhoods, such as Bernal Heights and Outer Richmond.

Sports bars and hotel bars tend to be open on Sunday, but others may be closed. A few establishments—especially wine bars and bars attached to restaurants—also close on Monday.

🧳 Packing

Walking shoes. A pair of comfortable walking shoes is your must-pack item. This is a walking town, with notoriously steep and uneven streets, and if you fail to pack for it, your feet will pay. If you are planning an outdoorsy day or side trip from the city, you will need a pair of hiking boots or shoes with good treads.

A good raincoat. San Francisco is in California, but it doesn't adhere to your idea of California weather. It does stay mild year-round, but this is a peninsula surrounded by water on three sides, so you will want to plan for foggy mornings.

Sweaters. San Francisco weather can be a bit unpredictable. One minute you could be comfortable, and the next, shivering with the cold. Having a sweatshirt or sweater with you at all times will alleviate this.

Scarf. Lightweight and easy layers offset those sudden chills. In spring or from September to November, you can bring a lightweight one, but you will want warmer options for the rest of the year.

Backpack. A lightweight daypack is handy for toting those layers, along with sunscreen, a hat (the sun *does* often come out), and a change of shoes if you are planning a variety of activities, say, hiking, sightseeing, and then drinks.

Wine-bottle protectors. If your visit to San Francisco allows time to visit Napa and Sonoma's amazing vineyards, you may want to bring a few bottles home with you. Protect those precious souvenirs (and everything in your suitcase) with bubble-wrap wine-bottle protectors.

🌐 Passport

All visitors to the United States require a passport that is valid for six months beyond your expected period of stay.

🎭 Performing Arts

The heart of the mainstream theater district lies on or near Geary Street, mostly west of Union Square, though touring Broadway shows land a little farther afield at big houses like the Orpheum and the Golden Gate. But theater can be found all over town. For a bit of culture shock, slip out to eclectic districts, maybe the Mission or the Castro, where smaller theater companies reside and short-run and one-night-only performances happen on a regular basis.

The city's opera house and symphony hall present the musical classics, and venues like the Fillmore and the Warfield host major rock and jazz talents, but the city's extensive festival circuit broadens the possibilities considerably. Stern Grove presents a popular, free summer music festival; Noise Pop is the premier alt-rock showcase; and Hardly Strictly Bluegrass is a beloved celebration of bluegrass, country, and roots music, attracting hundreds of thousands of attendees from all over every year. Outside Lands in Golden Gate Park is the region's leading music festival with marquee global headliners each summer from the alt-rock, pop, and hip-hop genres.

Essentials

➕ Safety

Contrary to what the headlines might say, San Francisco is generally a safe place for travelers who observe all normal urban precautions. Use common sense and, unless you know exactly where you're going, steer clear of certain neighborhoods late at night, especially if you're walking alone. Even during the daytime in safe neighborhoods, make sure to be aware of your surroundings. Don't walk around with flashy jewelry or immersed in conversation on your phone AirPods and unable to hear what's around you. However, be extra alert in the following areas, or avoid them:

The Tenderloin. This neighborhood west of Union Square and above Civic Center can be seedy, with drug dealers, homeless people, hustlers, and X-rated joints. It's roughly bordered by Taylor, Polk, Geary, and Market Streets. It is strongly recommended to not walk here at any time of day. To visit the neighborhood, take a taxi or rideshare to your particular destination.

Western Addition. Past incidents of gang activity have made this neighborhood somewhat sketchy. Don't stray too far off Fillmore Street in this general area.

Civic Center. After a show here, walk west to Gough Street; avoid Market Street between 6th and 10th Streets. If walking to the Civic Center BART, make sure to be in a group.

Some areas in Golden Gate Park. These include the area near the Haight Street entrance, where teens often smoke and deal drugs, and around the pedestrian tunnels on the far west end of the park.

Like many large cities, San Francisco has many homeless people. Although most are no threat, some are more aggressive and can persist in their pleas for cash until it feels like harassment. If you feel uncomfortable, don't reach for your wallet.

According to the *San Francisco Chronicle*'s SFNext Index, San Francisco property crime figures are generally high compared to its peers, while violent crime numbers are generally low compared to several large American cities. However, in large part because of the region's steep real estate prices, drug and mental health epidemics, and the COVID-19 pandemic, San Francisco has seen a noticeable uptick in assaults and thefts (targeting businesses, cars, or pedestrians) in neighborhoods that were previously considered generally safe. Tourist areas are unfortunately a popular target for these crimes. Always be aware of your surroundings and trust your instincts. If something doesn't feel comfortable, then it isn't safe.

💼 Shopping

Each neighborhood has its own distinctive finds, whether it's 1960s housewares, cheeky stationery, or vintage Levi's. If shopping in San Francisco has a downside, it's that real bargains can be few and far between. Sure, neighborhoods like the Lower Haight and the Mission have thrift shops and other inexpensive stores, but you won't find many discount outlets in the city, where rents are sky-high and space is at a premium.

Serious shoppers head straight to Union Square, San Francisco's main shopping area and the site of most of its department stores, including Macy's, Neiman Marcus, and Saks Fifth Avenue. Nearby are such platinum-card international boutiques as Yves Saint Laurent, Cartier, Emporio Armani, Gucci, Hermès, and Louis Vuitton.

Seasonal sales, usually in late January and late July into August, are good opportunities for finding deep discounts on clothing. The *San Francisco Chronicle* and *San Francisco Examiner* advertise sales. Sample sales are usually held by individual manufacturers, so check your favorite company's website before visiting.

Tipping

Tipping Guidelines for San Francisco

Bartender	About 15%, starting at $1 a drink at casual places
Bellhop	$1–$5 per bag, depending on the level of the hotel
Hotel concierge	$5 or more, if he or she performs a service for you
Hotel doorman, room service, or valet	$3–$4
Hotel maid	$5 a day (either daily or at the end of your stay, in cash)
Taxi driver	15%–20%, but round up the fare to the next dollar amount
Tour guide	10% of the cost of the tour
Waiter	18%–20%, with 20% being the norm at high-end restaurants

Visa

Except for citizens of Canada and Bermuda, most visitors to the United States must have a visa. If you are from one of the 38 designated members of the Visa Waiver Program, then you only require an ESTA (Electronic System for Travel Authorization) as long as you are staying for 90 days or less. However, some changes were made in the Visa Waiver Program in 2015, and nationals of Visa-Waiver nations who have traveled to Iran, Iraq, Libya, North Korea, Somalia, Sudan, Syria, or Yemen no longer qualify for ESTA. Also, if you have been denied a visa to visit the United States, your application for the ESTA program most likely will be denied.

When to Go

You can visit San Francisco comfortably any time of year, though summer is high season for leisure travelers, including families with children. Thanks to its proximity to the Pacific Ocean, the city has fairly consistent weather throughout the year. Possibly the best months are September and October, when the summerlike weather (warmer than August) at that time brings outdoor concerts and festivals (however, this can also be fire season in Northern California). Springtime ranges greatly from cold and wet to very hot in May and June but is generally dry and pleasant. The climate here always feels Mediterranean and moderate—with a foggy, sometimes chilly bite. The temperature rarely drops below 40°F, and anything warmer than 80°F is considered a heat wave. Be prepared for rain in winter, especially December and January. Winds off the ocean can add to the chill factor. That old joke about summer in San Francisco feeling like winter is true at heart, but once you move inland, it gets warmer. (And some locals swear that the thermostat has inched up in recent years.)

A Waterfront Walk: The Ferry Building to Fisherman's Wharf

One of the great pleasures of San Francisco is a stroll along the bay, with its briny scent, the cry of the gulls, and boats bobbing on the waves. The flat, two-mile walk along the Embarcadero from the Ferry Building offers a chance to take in some of the city's blockbuster sights, along with spectacular bay vistas.

THE FERRY BUILDING: FOODIE MECCA

Standing sentry at the foot of Market Street, the **Ferry Building** offers organic, seasonal delights from such local treasures as Mariposa Baking Company, Fatted Calf charcuterie, and Humphry Slocombe Ice Cream. Take your picnic to a bench out back and take in the bay and the Bay Bridge.

EMBARCADERO: NEW LIFE FOR OLD PIERS

Heading north on the Embarcadero (the piers go up in number), watch for a mélange of historical info on black-and-white pillars, engraved in the sidewalk, and on plaques. These line **Pier 1**, where the giant paddle wheeler *San Francisco Belle* docks. **Pier 7** juts out far into the bay; an evening stroll here is lovely (if chilly) under the street lamps.

Just two blocks beyond at Pier 15 is the city's excellent hands-on science museum, the **Exploratorium**.

NORTH BEACH DETOUR: TELEGRAPH HILL

For a brief visit inland to get prime lookouts from above the Embarcadero, consider heading west on Filbert or Greenwich and ascending one of the steep staircases clinging to **Telegraph Hill** for spectacular views and a peek into the lush stairway gardens along the way up to **Coit Tower**. Then return down the stairs to continue along the Embarcadero.

A Waterfront Walk: The Ferry Building to Fisherman's Wharf

WHERE TO START:
In front of the Ferry Building.

TIME/LENGTH:
30–60 minutes at a moderate pace, without stops. With a picnic and park breaks, this walk could be a three-hour affair. The total distance is two miles.

WHERE TO STOP:
At the cable-car turnaround or resting your feet at the Buena Vista.

BEST TIME TO GO:
Sunny days are best for strolling the waterfront. Start off at the Ferry Building in the morning, ideally on a Saturday, when farmers' market stalls fill the plaza. The street-theater scene from Pier 39 to Fisherman's Wharf is liveliest on weekends, too.

WORST TIME TO GO:
Rain puts a huge damper on this walk, which is all about being outside. Weekends are bustling, but they can mean large crowds at the big-ticket attractions—Alcatraz and Fisherman's Wharf.

GETTING AROUND:
If you're driving, park at the north end—it's much cheaper—and do the walk backward from north to south. Pedicabs will offer rides along the way, and the light-rail F-line is always available for the weary.

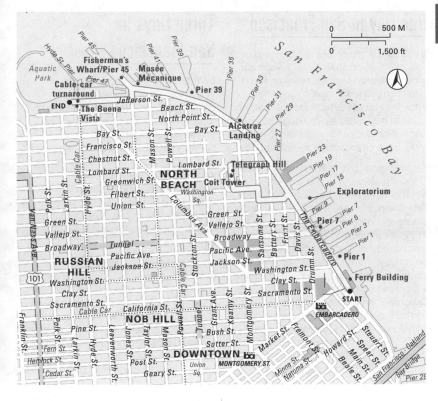

EMBARCADERO NORTH END: TOURIST SAN FRANCISCO

Continuing north up the Embarcadero, **Alcatraz Landing** (Pier 33) is a good spot to pick up souvenirs even if you're not taking the highly recommended tour. **Pier 39** is just around the corner, with its cornucopia of souvenir vendors; thankfully, sea lion–watching is still free.

A few blocks farther north is **Fisherman's Wharf**, at Pier 45. Bypass the wax museum and make a beeline for the fabulous vintage arcade **Musée Mécanique** (at the foot of Taylor Street). For crab- and bunny-shape sourdough loaves, stop by Boudin Bakery, just down Taylor on Jefferson.

LAST STOP: HISTORIC VESSELS AT THE HYDE STREET PIER

Follow the towering masts to the foot of Hyde Street and the collection of exquisitely restored ships there. Afterward, head up Hyde to the **cable-car turnaround**, where you can grab an Irish coffee at the **Buena Vista**, which opened in 1916. The coffee-whiskey cocktail should provide enough of a jolt to help with your walk back to the Ferry Building if it's a round-trip journey.

Great Itineraries

One Day in San Francisco

If you have a day or less in San Francisco, your sightseeing strategy is very simple: either pick one major museum or one attraction you really want to see and work the rest of your day around that, *or* avoid all major attractions altogether, and just walk and take the cable car to get a feel for the city's diverse neighborhoods.

For the former, we'd recommend the San Francisco Museum of Modern Art (or SFMOMA, as it's known) and the **Golden Gate Bridge**. For the latter, start in **Union Square**, but don't be too early: the focus of this neighborhood is shopping, and most doors don't open until 10 am (11 am on Sunday). At the cable-car turnaround at Powell and Market Streets, hop aboard either line and ride over Nob Hill and into **Chinatown**. Browse the produce stalls and markets, peruse herb shops, and explore alleyways. Have your camera ready as you pass from Chinatown into **North Beach**, the old Italian quarter: Broadway looking down Columbus and Grant is one of the most interesting cultural intersections of the city. Walk Columbus Avenue—stopping for espresso, of course—then head toward Coit Tower up Filbert Street, which becomes the Filbert Steps, one of the city's many stairways. Keep your eyes—and ears—open for the famous wild parrots of **Telegraph Hill**. Take in the views at the top and Coit Tower's WPA-era murals of California's history, then head back into North Beach for dinner or cocktails.

Three Days in San Francisco

DAY 1

With more time, you have a chance to see the sights, eat all the amazing food, and really get to know the city. The **Mission District** is the first stop, for breakfast and coffee: perhaps a cappuccino at Four Barrel Coffee and croissants at Tartine. With some pastries in hand and fortified by caffeine, head to nearby **Dolores Park**. The park's southwest corner offers your first of many steep climbs. It also presents a panoramic view of the city skyline.

It's a short walk to Castro Street, the heart of the city's gay population and culture. Allow time to browse the shops and snap some photos of the ornate marquee and giant rainbow flag at the classic movie palace **Castro Theatre** at Castro and Market. From here, it's a steep climb, but short trek mileage-wise, to the city's "it" corridor, Divisadero and its chic cafés and vintage shops. At Hayes Street, hang a right and ahead is **Alamo Square Park**, with the backdrop of the beautifully painted Painted Ladies Victorian homes, made famous by the TV show *Full House*. This is *the* view of San Francisco.

It's all downhill from here … at least until the late afternoon. Stroll down the hill along Hayes Street and check out the sleek boutiques of Hayes Valley. Lunch just a few blocks away at Zuni Café, a fine-dining staple that defines California cuisine.

Back on your feet, continue down Market Street, San Francisco's "Champs-Élysée," which sadly is also one of its more struggling corridors, as is evident in the street life. There are many important sights to see here, including the Twitter headquarters and its must-photograph "@Twitter" sign at Market and 10th Streets. Walk one block off Market Street to admire magnificent **City Hall** and its grand rotunda. Catch a ride here to the beautiful Chinatown Gate entrance to **Chinatown** at Grant and Bush Streets. Continue along Grant Street to Columbus Avenue and explore North America's oldest Chinatown. Hang a left at Columbus; after it crosses Broadway, Chinatown evolves into the city's Italian neighborhood, North Beach. The Italian influence continues to dwindle but can be found in cozy espresso cafés, like Mario's Bohemian Cigar Store Cafe overlooking Washington Square Park. After a much-needed espresso jolt, get ready for another steep climb up **Telegraph Hill**, home of a community of parrots and Coit Tower, with its mesmerizing views at the top.

Back down the hill, immediately head to Columbus Avenue and have a coffee or a drink. Wrap up the day with dinner at Mister Jiu's, the city's game-changing contemporary Chinese restaurant by chef Brandon Jew. Everything is stellar and has an intriguing spin, but be sure to start with the shrimp chips and sea urchin cheong fun.

DAY 2

Start in Union Square and admire the grand outdoor plaza that could fit in any European capital. It's surrounded by the city's luxury department stores, and the 97-foot Victory Monument column commemorating Commodore George Dewey's defeat of the Spanish fleet at Manila in 1898 resides in the center. Give your legs a rest this morning and take the Powell-Hyde cable car that weaves up and down Nob Hill and Russian Hill from its loading spot by Union Square. After the requisite selfies as you dangle from the outdoor poles, get off the cable car at Lombard Street. This flower-adorned, curvy street is best viewed in the morning before there are more tourists than blossoms. When you're ready, walk a block or two away and request a car to head to Pier 33, where the **Alcatraz** boats depart. Generally, 2½ to 3 hours is a good amount of time for the boat ride and tour of "The Rock," a federal prison until the '60s.

■TIP➔ **Avoid disappointment and secure Alcatraz tickets in advance online.**

Back on the mainland, walk along the **Embarcadero**, a former elevated freeway turned palm tree–lined thoroughfare along the bay that is the de facto official venue for San Francisco joggers and stroller walking. For lunch, head to the **Ferry Building**, which is indeed the public transit ferry terminal, in addition to being a spectacular food hall filled with all sorts of vendors and artisans showcasing why the Bay Area is one of the greatest places to eat in the world. Save room for desserts such as chocolates by Recchiuti. As a bonus, if it's Tuesday, Thursday, or Saturday, the city's most extensive farmers' market gathers outside the building (note that it wraps up by 2 pm).

Spend the late afternoon in the sprawling **San Francisco Museum of Modern Art (SFMOMA)**, a magnificent museum of modern art that is a 460,000-square-foot behemoth, with more than 1,000 works from its large collection on display. You won't make it through all the galleries, so start with highlights, like the third-floor sculpture garden with a living wall and signature works by the likes of Wayne Thiebaud and Andy Warhol, plus Alexander Calder's mobiles.

Great Itineraries

Finally, take a short car ride up steep Nob Hill to the city's premier grande dame hotel, The Fairmont. Quite the contrast to the hotel's stately elegance, its beloved watering hole, Tonga Room & Hurricane Bar, is as kitsch as it gets with its lagoon and ultra-tiki atmosphere. The mai tais aren't so bad, either.

DAY 3
After you've explored the city's urban and residential sides, this final day is all about nature. If it's a weekend, get a head start on the brunch crowds by racing out toward the Pacific. Enjoy San Francisco's "unofficial official meal" at Outerlands, a surfer-cool, reclaimed wood–paneled restaurant that is often cited as the city's best brunch. If it's a weekday, consider breakfast sandwiches from Devil's Teeth Baking Company or a seafood lunch from Hook Fish Co. Walk a few blocks to Ocean Beach and enjoy the sea salt–kissed air.

If there were more time today to do it, the walk all the way to the **Golden Gate Bridge** is one of the most stunning in the country, but it would take several hours. Take a car to Baker Beach, just to the western edge of the bridge. The views from here of the bridge are magnificent, even dreamy. Afterward, climb up the steep Battery to Bluffs Trail, hang a left on Lincoln Boulevard, follow the trail along the road for another gorgeous Golden Gate overlook, and follow the trail to the Golden Gate Bridge's parking lot. The views from the bridge are beautiful, but the experience can take a lot of time and is frightening if you are even vaguely afraid of heights. Today, bypass the popular walk across the bridge and follow the steps down to Fort Point at its base. The walk from here to Crissy Field, an expansive grassy area that used to be a military airfield, is one of the more spectacular in the whole Bay Area. There are two bridges in view, the skyline, and lots of fresh air. Yes, welcome to California. End your walk at the Palace of Fine Arts, an elegant, colossal monument built in 1915 for the Panama–Pacific International Exposition world's fair.

For one final neighborhood, dinner, and drink, use the "Mrs. Doubtfire home" as the starting address, at 2640 Steiner Street. This is the heart of Pacific Heights, the city's deep-pockets district, with splendid mansions and views on each block. Walk down nearby Fillmore Street and admire the price tags and high-end boutiques. Then, for your final dinner, head to the wildly inventive State Bird Provisions, to enjoy a feast of globe-spanning contemporary creations served dim sum–style.

■TIP➜ **Make reservations at State Bird Provisions at least a month in advance.**

If You Have More Time

With more time, you can begin to explore the Bay Area. Cross the bay to **Oakland** or **Berkeley** and check out Oakland's restaurants and breweries or spend an afternoon scouting the university in Berkeley. Alternatively, you can head north from the city to majestic **Muir Woods National Monument**; if you've never seen the redwoods—the tallest living things on earth—this is a must. World-famous Napa Valley or lower-key Sonoma County each merit an overnight stay. Silicon Valley, Stanford University, the Peninsula coastline, and wine tasting in the Santa Cruz Mountains all merit day trips or overnight stays as well.

Contacts

✈ Air

**CONTACTS Oakland
International Airport.** (*OAK*).
✉ *1 Airport Dr., Oakland*
☎ *510/563–3300* ⊕ *www.
oaklandairport.com.* **San
Francisco International Airport.** (*SFO*). ✉ *McDonnell
and Links Rds., San Fran-
cisco* ☎ *800/435–9736,
650/821–8211* ⊕ *www.
flysfo.com.* **San Jose
International Airport.** (*SJC*).
✉ *1701 Airport Blvd., San
Jose* ☎ *408/392–3600*
⊕ *www.flysanjose.com.*

⚓ Boat

**CONTACTS Alameda/
Oakland Ferry.** ☎ *877/643–
3779* ⊕ *sanfrancisco-
bayferry.com.* **Alcatraz
Cruises.** ☎ *415/981–7625*
⊕ *www.alcatrazcruises.
com.* **Blue & Gold Fleet.**
☎ *415/705 0200* ⊕ *www.
blueandgoldfleet.com.*
Ferry Building Marketplace.
✉ *1 Ferry Bldg., at foot
of Market St. on Embar-
cadero, San Francisco*
☎ *415/983–8030* ⊕ *www.
ferrybuildingmarketplace.
com.* **Golden Gate Ferry.**
☎ *415/455–2000* ⊕ *www.
goldengate.org/ferry.*

🚌 Bus

CONTACTS Greyhound.
✉ *Salesforce Transit
Center, 425 Mission St.,
SoMa* ☎ *415/495–1569*
⊕ *www.greyhound.com.*

Ⓜ Public
Transport

**BART Bay Area Rapid Tran-
sit.** (*BART*). ☎ *510/465–
2278* ⊕ *www.bart.gov.*

**MUNI San Francisco
Municipal Transportation
Agency.** (*Muni*). ☎ *311,
415/701–2311* ⊕ *www.
sfmta.com.*

🚕 Taxi

CONTACTS Flywheel Taxi.
☎ *855/359–2420* ⊕ *fly-
wheeltaxi.com.* **Luxor Cab.**
☎ *415/202 4141* ⊕ *www.
luxorcab.com.* **Yellow Cab.**
☎ *415/333–3333* ⊕ *yellow-
cabsf.com.*

🚆 Train

CONTACTS Amtrak.
☎ *800/872–7245* ⊕ *www.
amtrak.com.* **Caltrain.**
☎ *800/660–4287* ⊕ *www.
caltrain.com.* **San Francisco
Caltrain station.** ✉ *700 4th
St., near Townsend St.,
SoMa* ☎ *800/660–4287*
⊕ *www.caltrain.com/
stations.*

📍 Visitor
Information

**SAN FRANCISCO San
Francisco Visitor Information
Center.** ✉ *Moscone Center,
749 Howard St., between
3rd and 4th Sts., SoMa*
☎ *415/391–2000* ⊕ *www.
sftravel.com.*

**METRO AREA Marin
Convention & Visitors
Bureau.** ✉ *1 Mitch-
ell Blvd., Suite B, at
Redwood Hwy., San
Rafael* ☎ *415/925–2060,
866/925–2060* ⊕ *www.
visitmarin.org.* **Visit
Berkeley Information Center.**
✉ *2030 Addison St.,
Suite 102, Berkeley* ✛ *1
block north of Downtown
Berkeley BART station*
☎ *510/549–7040* ⊕ *www.
visitberkeley.com.*

STATE Visit California.
✉ *555 Capitol Mall,
Suite 1100, Sacramen-
to* ☎ *877/225–4367,
916/444–4429* ⊕ *www.
visitcalifornia.com.*
California Welcome Center.
✉ *Pier 39, Beach St. and
the Embarcadero, Bldg. B,
2nd level, San Francisco*
☎ *415/716–1423* ⊕ *www.
visitcalifornia.com.*

Chapter 3

SOMA, MISSION BAY, AND DOGPATCH

3

Updated by
Trevor Felch

⊙ Sights   🍴 Restaurants   🛏 Hotels   🛍 Shopping   🍸 Nightlife

★★★☆☆   ★★★☆☆   ★★★★☆   ★★★☆☆   ★★★★☆

NEIGHBORHOOD SNAPSHOT

TOP EXPERIENCES

■ **San Francisco Museum of Modern Art (SFMOMA):** Explore the vast trove of modern masterpieces at this sprawling museum, one of the largest in the country dedicated to modern art.

■ **Oracle Park:** Cheer on the Giants and savor the beautiful views (and garlic fries) at the gorgeous waterfront ballpark.

■ **Club-hopping in SoMa:** Shake it with the cool, friendly crowd that fills SoMa's dance clubs until the wee hours, and all weekend long at the EndUp.

■ **Yerba Buena Gardens:** Gather picnic provisions and choose a spot on the grass in downtown's oasis.

■ **Dining in Dogpatch:** One of the hippest neighborhoods in town is home to outstanding restaurants and chic galleries.

GETTING HERE

For most SoMa visitors who stick close to the area around Yerba Buena Gardens and the Moscone Center, getting here is a matter of walking roughly 10 minutes from Union Square, less from Market Street transit.

The "Central Subway" unveiled in 2022 connects Chinatown and Union Square directly to Moscone Center, the Caltrain station, Mission Bay, and Dogpatch via the T-line light rail.

After dark, a cab or rideshare is recommended anywhere in SoMa. Regardless of the time of day, do not walk in the area bordered by 10th Street, 5th Street, Market Street and Howard Street.

PLANNING YOUR TIME

■ You could spend all day museum-hopping in SoMa. Allow at least two hours for gigantic SFMOMA. An hour each should do it for the Museum of the African Diaspora, the Contemporary Jewish Museum, and the Yerba Buena Center for the Arts, a little less than that for the smaller museums.

■ SoMa after dark is another adventure entirely. More interested in merlot or megaclubs than Matisse? Start here around 8 pm for dinner, then move on to a bar or dance spot.

■ Mission Bay is great for leisurely walking, while Dogpatch is best enjoyed with a meal or three. The two neighborhoods can fill up an entire day, especially when paired with an event at Chase Center.

SoMa (short for "south of Market") is one of San Francisco's most sprawling neighborhood, covering a largely industrial part of the city below Market Street between the Mission District, the Financial District, and the Embarcadero.

It's home to many tech company offices, nightclubs and notable restaurants. It's also home to several major sights for visitors, including Oracle Park, the Moscone Center and the magnificent SFMOMA.

Mission Bay resides just on the other side of Mission Creek from SoMa. The two are connected by a pair of drawbridges, one of which the Muni T-line crosses. Mission Bay is the city's "newest" neighborhood where construction continues at a rapid pace. It's a relaxed, park-filled, walkable area that often feels like a quiet suburb in a big city. The neighborhood includes the NBA's Golden State Warriors and many UCSF hospitals. Dogpatch is a formerly industrial, now mostly chic neighborhood adjacent to Mission Bay. Compared to SoMa, Dogpatch is tiny, yet has several exciting restaurants, cafés, and boutiques. It's also the rare San Francisco neighborhood that remains visual arts–centric with several studios and galleries scattered throughout.

SoMa

SoMa is less a neighborhood than a sprawling area of wide, traffic-heavy boulevards lined with office skyscrapers and ultrachic condo high-rises. The COVID-19 pandemic hit this area particularly hard, as many of the neighborhood's office workers and residents departed with the increase in working from home for tech companies. Still, it's a noteworthy area for locals and tourists who are drawn to the cultural offerings and concentration of eateries and bars, including a number of destination restaurants. In terms of sightseeing, gigantic and impressive SFMOMA tops the list, followed by the specialty museums of the Yerba Buena arts district.

SoMa was once known as "South of the Slot" (read: the Wrong Side of the Tracks) in reference to the cable-car slot that ran up Market Street. Ever since gold-rush miners set up their tents here in 1848, SoMa has played a major role in housing immigrants to the city.

The 2010s influx of techies (and their money) changed the neighborhood once again: the skid row of 6th Street, between Market and Mission Streets, now coexists with trendy bars and cafés that cater to Twitter's headquarters. Once a scary section of SoMa, the neighborhood is trying hard to rebrand itself as the hip Mid-Market area. However, it is still on the rough side and extreme caution is essential in the area

⊙ Sights

@Twitter Sign
NOTABLE BUILDING | Those who want to take a picture of the @Twitter sign at Twitter's headquarters—or, yes, tweet from Twitter—can see the sign

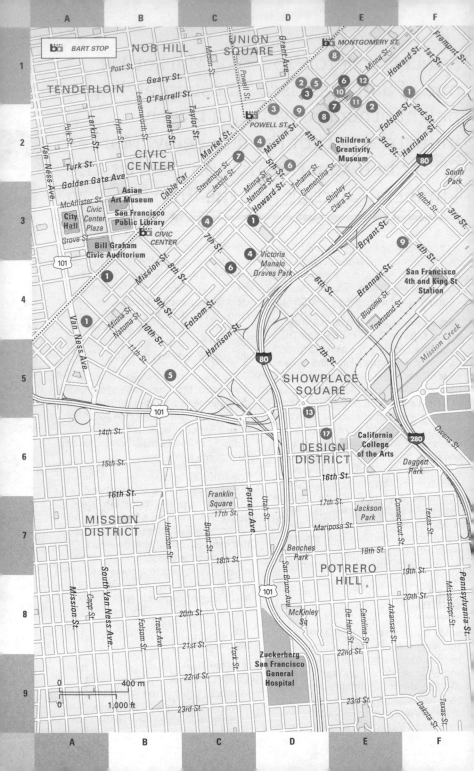

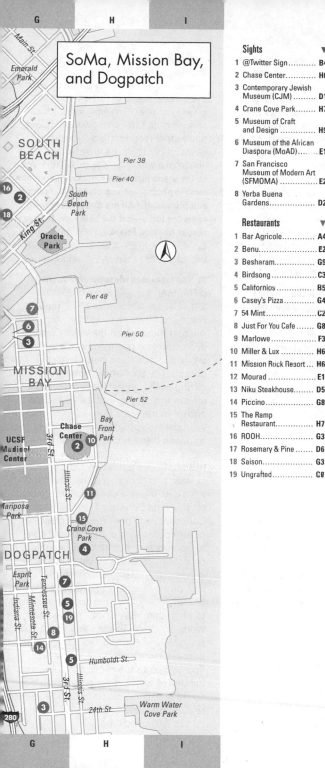

SoMa, Mission Bay, and Dogpatch

Sights ▼

1 @Twitter Sign............ B4
2 Chase Center............ H6
3 Contemporary Jewish Museum (CJM) D1
4 Crane Cove Park........ H7
5 Museum of Craft and Design H9
6 Museum of the African Diaspora (MoAD)........ E1
7 San Francisco Museum of Modern Art (SFMOMA) E2
8 Yerba Buena Gardens.................. D2

Restaurants ▼

1 Bar Agricole.............. A4
2 Benu...................... E2
3 Besharam................ G9
4 Birdsong C3
5 Californios B5
6 Casey's Pizza G4
7 54 Mint C2
8 Just For You Cafe G8
9 Marlowe F3
10 Miller & Lux H6
11 Mission Rock Resort ... H6
12 Mourad E1
13 Niku Steakhouse........ D5
14 Piccino G8
15 The Ramp Restaurant............... H7
16 ROOH...................... G3
17 Rosemary & Pine D6
18 Saison.................... G3
19 Ungrafted............... C9

Quick Bites ▼

1 Bini's Kitchen............ D3
2 Birdbox................... G3
3 Cafe Réveille G4
4 Deli Board C3
5 Neighbor Bakehouse... G8
6 Sightglass Coffee........ C4
7 Wooly Pig................ G8

Hotels ▼

1 The Clancy, Autograph Collection................. F1
2 Four Seasons Hotel San Francisco........... D1
3 Hotel Zelos San Francisco........... D2
4 Hotel Zetta San Francisco........... D2
5 Hyatt Regency San Francisco Downtown SOMA D1
6 InterContinental San Francisco........... D2
7 LUMA Hotel San Francisco........... G4
8 Palace Hotel San Francisco............ E1
9 San Francisco Marriott Marquis D2
10 The St. Regis San Francisco............ E1
11 W San Francisco E1

prominently displayed outside the gorgeous art-deco building that houses the company's main offices at Market and 10th Streets (though there are far fewer employees working in office now thanks to a certain new company owner). You can tweet inside while shopping in the building's ground-floor market or picking up lunch from the vendors around the market's small café/bar area. To truly appreciate this micro-neighborhood, enjoy a local beer across Market Street at The Beer Hall or catch some music with craft cocktails at Mr. Tipple's—both are prime happy-hour spots for the Mid-Market crowd. ⊠ *1355 Market St., SoMa* ☏ *415/767–5130* ⊕ *visitthemarket.com.*

Contemporary Jewish Museum (CJM)

OTHER MUSEUM | Architect Daniel Libeskind designed the postmodern CJM, whose impossible-to-ignore diagonal blue cube juts out of a painstakingly restored power substation. A physical manifestation of the Hebrew toast *l'chaim* (to life), the cube may have obscure philosophical origins, but Libeskind created a unique, light-filled space that merits a stroll through the lobby even if the current exhibits (the museum is non-collecting and does not have permanent holdings) don't entice you into the galleries. Exhibits, usually two or three at a time, vary, from a look at the history of famous puppeteer Frank Oz (*Star Wars* and the Muppets) to an immersive series about the 19th-century Jewish immigrant and photographer Shimmel Zohar. ■TIP➔ **San Francisco's best Jewish deli, Wise Sons, operates a counter in the museum. Try their smoked salmon bagel sandwich or a slice of chocolate babka.** ⊠ *736 Mission St., SoMa* ☏ *415/655–7800* ⊕ *www.thecjm.org* ⊠ *$16* ⊗ *Closed Mon.–Wed.*

Museum of the African Diaspora (MoAD)

OTHER MUSEUM | Dedicated to the influence that people of African descent have had in places all over the world, MoAD focuses on temporary exhibits in its four galleries over three floors. With floor-to-ceiling windows onto Mission Street, the museum fits perfectly into the cultural scene of Yerba Buena and is well worth a 30-minute foray. Most striking is its front window centerpiece: a three-story mosaic, made from thousands of photographs, that forms the image of a young girl's face. ■TIP➔ **Walk up the stairs inside the museum to view the mosaic photographs up close—Malcolm X and Muhammad Ali are there, along with everyday folks—but the best view is from across Mission Street.** ⊠ *685 Mission St., SoMa* ☏ *415/358–7200* ⊕ *www.moadsf.org* ⊠ *$12* ⊗ *Closed Mon. and Tues.*

★ San Francisco Museum of Modern Art (SFMOMA)

ART·MUSEUM | Opened in 1935, the San Francisco Museum of Modern Art was the first museum on the West Coast dedicated to modern and contemporary art, and after a three-year expansion designed by Snøhetta, it emerged in 2016 as one of the largest modern art museums in the country and the revitalized anchor of the Yerba Buena arts district. With gallery space over seven floors, the museum displays only a portion of its more than 33,000-work collection and has numerous temporary exhibits. Allow at least two hours here; you could spend a full day. The museum's holdings include art from the Doris and Donald Fisher Collection, one of the world's greatest private collections of modern and contemporary art. Highlights include deep collections of works by German abstract expressionist Gerhard Richter and American painter Ellsworth Kelly and an Agnes Martin gallery. The third floor is dedicated to photography. Also look for seminal works by Diego Rivera, Alexander Calder, Matisse, and Picasso. Don't miss the third-floor sculpture terrace. The first floor is free to the public and contains a handful of works. Save time by reserving timed tickets online. ⊠ *151 3rd St., SoMa* ☏ *415/357–4000* ⊕ *www.sfmoma.org* ⊠ *$25* ⊗ *Closed Wed.*

Above the Yerba Buena Gardens, SFMOMA's striped "eye" can be spotted.

Yerba Buena Gardens

GARDEN | FAMILY | These two blocks encompass the Yerba Buena Center for the Arts, the Metreon, and Moscone Convention Center, but the gardens themselves are the everyday draw. Office workers and convention-goers escape to the green swath of the East Garden, the focal point of which is the memorial to Martin Luther King Jr. Powerful streams of water surge over large, jagged stone columns, mirroring the enduring force of King's words, which are carved on the stone walls and on glass blocks behind the waterfall. Moscone North is behind the memorial, and an overhead walkway leads to Moscone South and its rooftop attractions.

■ TIP→ The gardens are liveliest during the week and during the Yerba Buena Gardens Festival, from May through October (www.ybgfestival.org), with free performances.

Atop the Moscone Center perch a few lures for kids. The historic Looff carousel (🎟 *$5 for 2 rides; $3 with museum admission*) twirls daily 10–5. The carousel is attached to the Children's Creativity Museum (🌐 *creativity.org*), an interactive arts-and-technology center (🎟 *$15*) geared to children ages 3–12. Outside in the children's garden, kids adore the slides, including a 25-foot tube slide, at the play circle. Also part of the complex are an ice-skating rink and a bowling alley. ✉ *Bordered by 3rd, 4th, Mission, and Folsom Sts., SoMa* ☎ *415/651–3684* 🌐 *yerbabuenagardens.com* 🎟 *Free.*

🍴 Restaurants

Bar Agricole

$$ | MODERN AMERICAN | This sharply designed spot is just as notable for its food menu as its renowned mixed drinks. Owner Thad Vogler is the city's leading voice on single-origin spirits, so any visit should include a few sips of Bar Agricole's own spirits. **Known for:** impeccable spirit-forward cocktails; exciting vegetable-centric dishes; sourdough with tinned fish or duck liver. [$] *Average main: $25* ✉ *1540 Mission St., SoMa*

☎ *415/341–0101* 🌐 *baragricole.com*
⏲ *Closed Sun. and Mon. No lunch.*

★ Benu
$$$$ | **MODERN AMERICAN** | Chef Corey Lee's three-Michelin-star fine dining mecca is a must-stop for those who hop from city to city collecting memorable meals. Lee, formerly of French Laundry, meticulously ties together cooking techniques and ingredients commonly seen in different cuisines of Asia—such as *xiaolongbao* (soup dumplings) and kimchi—with a deft gastronomic touch. **Known for:** high-end dining; phenomenal wine pairings; stellar service. [$] *Average main: $375* ✉ *22 Hawthorne St., SoMa* ☎ *415/685–4860* 🌐 *www.benusf.com* ⏲ *Closed Sun. and Mon. No lunch.*

★ Birdsong
$$$$ | **MODERN AMERICAN** | Despite its gritty location a block from Market Street's roughest section (take a cab or rideshare directly to the restaurant), this sweeping, elaborate tasting-menu restaurant with a refined forest-wilderness theme is a destination for discerning fine-dining lovers from all over the country. Chef and co-owner Christopher Bleidorn spread his wings here at his first solo project after working in the kitchen at some of San Francisco's top kitchens (Atelier Crenn, Saison, Benu), and each of the 11 or so dishes he and his team creates is a masterpiece in presentation and taste. **Known for:** incredible aged meat dishes; beautiful open-kitchen setting; creek-raised trout prepared three ways. [$] *Average main: $295* ✉ *1085 Mission St., SoMa* ☎ *415/369–9161* 🌐 *www.birdsongsf.com* ⏲ *Closed Sun. and Mon. No lunch.*

★ Californios
$$$$ | **MODERN MEXICAN** | This Californian-Mexican tasting-menu concept by chef Val M. Cantu continues to be one of the hottest tickets in the entire Bay Area. Cantu and his team's creations, along with Charlotte Randolph's acclaimed wine program, remain as special as ever (the restaurant had a great run in smaller Mission District digs before moving to SoMa), crafting what is possibly the country's leading Mexican-influenced fine dining experience. **Known for:** house-made tortillas used in brilliant ways; wonderful patio; grilled banana with cold-smoked caviar. [$] *Average main: $307* ✉ *355 11th St., SoMa* ☎ *415/757–0994* 🌐 *www.californiossf.com* ⏲ *Closed Sun. and Mon. No lunch.*

54 Mint
$$$ | **ITALIAN** | Overlooking the always interesting Mint Plaza, a European-style plaza that surrounds the former U.S. Mint, this brick-walled, cozy-modern restaurant is one of San Francisco's best Roman trattorias, with both rustic traditional cooking and gentle spins on classic recipes. The exceptional cocktails by Jacopo Rosito are worth a trip on their own, and diners can wrap up dinner properly with an amaro and an espresso—this place truly feels and tastes like Rome. **Known for:** bottarga, sea urchin, and burrata bruschetta; homemade pastas; classic and creative Negroni renditions. [$] *Average main: $31* ✉ *16 Mint Plaza, SoMa* ✥ *Plaza can be accessed from 5th St. or Mission St.* ☎ *415/543–5100* 🌐 *54mint.com.*

Marlowe
$$$ | **AMERICAN** | Hearty American bistro fare and hip design draw crowds to this neighborhood favorite that's ambitious enough to be a citywide draw. The menu boasts one of the city's best burgers, and the dining room gleams with white penny-tile floors and marble countertops. **Known for:** refined takes on comfort food like roast chicken and deviled eggs; strong drinks; festive atmosphere. [$] *Average main: $36* ✉ *500 Brannan St., SoMa* ☎ *415/777–1413* 🌐 *marlowesf.com* ⏲ *Closed Mon. No lunch Tues. and Wed.*

Mourad
$$$$ | **MOROCCAN** | With Mourad's stunning, grand design, it's easy to get distracted from the intricate cocktails and excellent cooking served here on the

ground level of the magnificent 1920s art-deco PacBell building. However, chef-owner Mourad Lahlou is the great voice for his native Morocco's cuisine in the Bay Area, and this restaurant is his showcase, where dish after dish is as splendid as the bathrooms' tile work and the chandeliers above the dining room. **Known for:** glass-enclosed wine cellar "bridge" above the bar and dining room; family-style chicken and short rib dinners; duck basteeya (a sweet-savory pastry). $ *Average main: $48* ⌂ *140 New Montgomery St., Suite 1, SoMa* ☎ *415/660–2500* ⊕ *www.mouradsf.com* ⊗ *Closed Sun. and Mon. No lunch.*

Niku Steakhouse

$$$$ | **STEAKHOUSE** | The idea of a chic, contemporary steak house didn't really exist in San Francisco before this runaway favorite opened by the Design District's traffic circle. It's one of two high-end restaurants for the popular Omakase Group (the other being nearby luxury sushi bar Omakase), and perfectly balances a menu of creative small plates and flame-kissed mains. **Known for:** Wagyu fat brownie dessert; expense account meat-heavy dinners; superb wine and cocktails. $ *Average main: $105* ⌂ *61 Division St., SoMa* ☎ *415/829–7817* ⊕ *nikusteakhouse.com* ⊗ *No lunch.*

★ ROOH

$$$ | **MODERN INDIAN** | Traditional Indian dishes get a captivating, innovative spin at this hot spot near Oracle Park. Look for tandoori octopus and chili garlic escargots, complemented by equally inventive cocktails and a splashy, colorful space. **Known for:** SF's best butter chicken; green pea, goat cheese, and truffle kulcha bread; best dining choice before a Giants game. $ *Average main: $32* ⌂ *333 Brannan St., SoMa* ☎ *415/525–4174* ⊕ *www.roohsf.com* ⊗ *No lunch.*

Rosemary & Pine

$$$$ | **MODERN ITALIAN** | The Design District is filled with chic, breezy showrooms and galleries that evoke the California "good life" vibe, like this excellent restaurant from chef Dustin Falcon and the Omakase Group. The menu is a seamless blend of Italian and Californian influences, where vadouvan spaghetti with duck sugo might precede king salmon and a citrus sabayon. **Known for:** crispy burrata fra diavolo; terrific cocktails; excellent pastas. $ *Average main: $46* ⌂ *1725 Alameda St., SoMa* ☎ *415/757–0594* ⊕ *rosemaryandpinesf.com.*

Saison

$$$$ | **MODERN AMERICAN** | This two-Michelin-starred restaurant is one of the city's greatest dining destinations. The culinary team teases the deepest flavors from premium ingredients in a tasting-menu that may highlight fire-grilled duck followed by a broth of its grilled bones, or the signature, showstopping sea urchin on grilled bread. **Known for:** elegant decor; world-class wine list; polished start-to-finish experience. $ *Average main: $298* ⌂ *178 Townsend St., SoMa* ☎ *415/828–7990* ⊕ *www.saisonsf.com* ⊗ *Closed Sun. and Mon.*

☕ Coffee and Quick Bites

Bini's Kitchen

$ | **NEPALESE** | Chef-owner Bini Pradhan's Nepalese restaurant introduced many city diners to the wonderful dishes of her home country. Pradhan started in San Francisco with the wonderful La Cocina kitchen incubator program (a nonprofit that helps women, immigrants, and people of color) and years later is the region's leading voice for Himalayan cooking. **Known for:** Nepali roti bread; Gurkha chicken curry; momo dumplings. $ *Average main: $15* ⌂ *1001 Howard St., SoMa* ☎ *415/361–6911* ⊕ *biniskitchen.com* ⊗ *No dinner.*

Birdbox

$$ | **AMERICAN** | The search for San Francisco's greatest fried chicken ends at this casual counter-service restaurant. It started as a COVID-19 pandemic concept

at fine dining sibling Birdsong and became so popular that it received its own brick-and-mortar space. **Known for:** best cornbread in town; sour cream and onion–seasoned fried chicken; Claude the Claw sandwich. [$] *Average main: $20* ✉ *680A 2nd St., SoMa* 🌐 *birdboxsf.com* ⏲ *Closed Mon. and Tues.*

Deli Board

$$ | **SANDWICHES** | Everyone has their opinion about the greatest sandwiches in this city filled with amazing bread; but more often than not, locals will name this quirky, humorous lunch specialist. Here, sandwiches are truly an art and usually are taller than can be eaten in one bite. **Known for:** Mick roast beef sandwich on sesame seed French roll; festive, friendly atmosphere; Leroy Brown turkey-pastrami-salami sandwich. [$] *Average main: $21* ✉ *1058 Folsom St., SoMa* ☎ *415/552–7687* 🌐 *deliboardsf.com* ⏲ *Closed Mon. No dinner.*

★ **Sightglass Coffee**

$ | **CAFÉ** | The stunning interior design of Sightglass's three San Francisco cafés demands several photographs on each visit, but quickly all eyes settle on the pitch-perfect shots of espresso and cups of robust coffee from beans roasted at their airy, bi-level SoMa café and roastery. This is the heart of their operation and a must-visit for any coffee lover. **Known for:** photogenic space and drinks; vanilla cold brew; good selection of pastries. [$] *Average main: $6* ✉ *270 7th St., SoMa* ☎ *415/861–1313* 🌐 *sightglasscoffee.com.*

Hotels

The Clancy, Autograph Collection

$$ | **HOTEL** | This 18-floor Marriott-affiliated hotel is arguably the best of the few mid-range hotels in SoMa. **Pros:** spacious rooms; great location for walking between Moscone Center and the Embarcadero; very good in-house coffee shop. **Cons:** hard to arrive/leave at rush hour; a little too flashy; bland bathrooms. [$] *Rooms from: $275* ✉ *299 2nd St., SoMa* ☎ *415/947–0700* 🌐 *marriott.com* 🔑 *410 rooms* 🍴 *No Meals.*

★ **Four Seasons Hotel San Francisco**

$$$$ | **HOTEL** | Occupying 12 floors of a skyscraper, the Four Seasons delivers subdued elegance in rooms with contemporary artwork, fine linens, floor-to-ceiling windows that overlook Yerba Buena Gardens or downtown, and bathrooms with soaking tubs. **Pros:** located in the heart of everything; one of the city's best hotel bars and restaurants; top-level service. **Cons:** can be difficult to find; house car doesn't transport guests nearby after 9 pm; entrances are iffy to walk to from outside. [$] *Rooms from: $570* ✉ *757 Market St., SoMa* ☎ *415/633–3000* 🌐 *www.fourseasons.com/sanfrancisco* 🔑 *277 rooms* 🍴 *No Meals.*

Hotel Zelos San Francisco

$ | **HOTEL** | A high-style haven on the top five floors of the green-tiled Pacific Building, the Zelos offers a luxurious oasis above the busiest part of town, with spacious rooms decked out with modern art pieces, eye-catching textured carpeting, and sleek furniture echoing a 1930s sensibility. **Pros:** snappy design; convenient to public transit; home to one of the city's premier cocktail bars. **Cons:** allergenic down comforters; can be too much of a scene; chaotic street entrance. [$] *Rooms from: $167* ✉ *12 4th St., SoMa* ☎ *415/348–1111* 🌐 *zhotelssf.com* 🔑 *202 rooms* 🍴 *No Meals.*

Hotel Zetta San Francisco

$ | **HOTEL** | With a playful lobby lounge, London-style brasserie The Cavalier, and slick-yet-homey tech-friendly rooms, this trendy spot behind a stately 1913 neoclassical facade is a leader on the SoMa hotel scene. **Pros:** tech amenities and arty design; in-room spa services; noteworthy fitness center. **Cons:** lots of hubbub and traffic; need to leave the building for breakfast; frenetic aesthetic. [$] *Rooms from: $196* ✉ *55 5th St., SoMa*

☎ *415/543–8555* 🌐 *zhotelssf.com* 🛏 *116 rooms* 🍴 *No Meals.*

Hyatt Regency San Francisco Downtown SOMA
$$ | **HOTEL** | Soaring 36 stories, this Hyatt anchors one of the most prominent areas in the city, between Market Street, Moscone Center, and SFMOMA. **Pros:** good fitness center with Pelotons; stellar La Societé bistro in-house; feels exciting again after years of being stale. **Cons:** bland room design; bustling lobby; hardwood floors in room. [$] *Rooms from: $273* ✉ *50 3rd St., SoMa* ☎ *415/974–6400* 🌐 *hyatt.com* 🛏 *686 rooms* 🍴 *No Meals.*

InterContinental San Francisco
$$ | **HOTEL** | The arctic-blue glass exterior and Zen-like lobby may mimic an airport concourse, but it's merely a prelude to generally expansive, nicely thought-out guest rooms supplied with all the ultra-modern tech conveniences sophisticated travelers expect. **Pros:** excellent restaurant and above-average hotel bar; less pricey than its peers; state-of-the-art air filtration system. **Cons:** decor lacks character; borders a rough area; lacks special amenities. [$] *Rooms from: $237* ✉ *888 Howard St., SoMa* ☎ *415/616–6500* 🌐 *www.icsanfrancisco.com* 🛏 *556 rooms* 🍴 *No Meals.*

★ **Palace Hotel San Francisco**
$$$ | **HOTEL** | Open since 1875 and rebuilt after the 1906 earthquake, this legendary hotel continues to be one of the city's elite places to stay, with a prominent location at the border of SoMa and downtown plus a delightful mix of modern amenities (an indoor lap pool beneath a glass-domed ceiling) and deluxe architectural details of a bygone era. **Pros:** oozes history and Gilded Age grandeur; well-trained staff; excellent fitness center. **Cons:** entrance is frequently understaffed; small bathrooms; street noise (ask for an upper-floor room). [$] *Rooms from: $360* ✉ *2 New Montgomery St., SoMa* ☎ *415/512–1111* 🌐 *marriott.com* 🛏 *556 rooms* 🍴 *No Meals.*

San Francisco Marriott Marquis
$$ | **HOTEL** | The distinctive design of the 39-story Marriott has been compared to a parking meter and a jukebox, but the guest rooms, decorated in tasteful neutrals, satisfy the business set with ergonomic chairs, wide desks, and a host of technological amenities. **Pros:** spectacular views from upper-floor rooms; walking distance to many attractions; in-house FedEx Office. **Cons:** the snazzy design is outside, not in the guest rooms; curtains don't fully block out light; hectic lobby and entrance area. [$] *Rooms from: $256* ✉ *780 Mission St., SoMa* ☎ *415/896–1600* 🌐 *www.marriott.com* 🛏 *1,500 rooms* 🍴 *No Meals.*

★ **The St. Regis San Francisco**
$$$$ | **HOTEL** | Across from Yerba Buena Gardens and SFMOMA, the luxurious and modern St. Regis is favored by celebrities and others drawn to guest rooms and suites decorated with gold rush–inspired colors of silver, iron, and copper; leather-paneled headboards; 3D graphic art pieces by Christo Saba; and lots of natural light from windows offering city views. **Pros:** outstanding service; wonderful pool and spa; large rooms and bathrooms. **Cons:** expensive rates; no coffee machines; hectic lobby and entrance area. [$] *Rooms from: $585* ✉ *125 3rd St., SoMa* ☎ *415/284–4000* 🌐 *marriott.com* 🛏 *260 rooms* 🍴 *No Meals.*

W San Francisco
$$ | **HOTEL** | **FAMILY** | Chic, urbane, and nicely laid out, the W's colorful guest rooms (and unique Spectacular Studio indoor-outdoor suites with a heated patio) come with an abstract "gold rush" theme (both the 1800s one and the current tech wave) and include such comforts as upholstered window seats, pillow-top mattresses, Nespresso machines, and sleek baths with MOMO amenities by Davines. **Pros:** nicely designed fitness center; guest rooms

feel refreshingly not like a chain; exciting cocktails at the Living Room bar. **Cons:** annoying motion sensor bathroom lights; feels like a convention center at peak times; not great in-room noise insulation. [$] *Rooms from: $208* ✉ *181 3rd St., SoMa* ☎ *415/777–5300* 🌐 *marriott.com* 🛏 *411 rooms* 🍴 *No Meals.*

🍸 Nightlife

BARS

The House of Shields

BARS | History and great cocktails collide at one of the city's most legendary bars. There are rumors that President Warren G. Harding met his final fate here, but other accounts say that happened across the street at the Palace Hotel. Today, it's a favorite watering hole for the Financial District happy hour set, then a quieter, casual date spot later on. The cocktails are prepared with the same care and quality as at its flashier, newer peers. ✉ *39 New Montgomery St., SoMa* ☎ *415/769–8109* 🌐 *thehouseofshields.com.*

Kaiyo Rooftop

BARS | Slowly but surely San Francisco is developing a reputation for great rooftop restaurant-bars high above the city. Among the best is on the 12th floor of the Hyatt Place near Oracle Park, where the setting looks like a tropical rain forest in the middle of urban sprawl, and the food and drink focuses on Nikkei cuisine (Japanese-Peruvian) like at its sibling in Cow Hollow. Reservations are recommended, and make sure to bundle up. ✉ *701 3rd St., SoMa* ☎ *415/800–8141* 🌐 *kaiyosf.com* 🕒 *Closed Mon.*

Kona's Street Market

BARS | The sibling to Union Square bar stalwart P.C.H. is just as compelling for locals and travelers alike looking for some of the city's greatest cocktails. With colorful lighting and wall decor made of comic book and karate film prints, the space is a feast for the eyes. But it's really all about the outstanding cocktails inspired by street markets on different continents. ✉ *32 3rd St., SoMa* ☎ *415/432–7006* 🌐 *konastreetmarket.com* 🕒 *Closed Sun. and Mon.*

MoMo's

BARS | This stylish restaurant and trendy bar has an outdoor patio perfect for sunny days with pizzas, burgers, and beers. But, this fan favorite is really all about its proximity to Oracle Park—it's the ballpark area's unofficial gathering place before and after games. ✉ *760 2nd St., at King St., SoMa* ☎ *415/227–8660* 🌐 *www.sfmomos.com* 🕒 *Closed Sun.*

★ The Pied Piper

BARS | The Palace Hotel's clubby, wood-paneled watering hole takes its name from the 1909 Maxfield Parrish mural *The Pied Piper of Hamelin,* which covers most of the wall behind the bar. The Pied Piper lures an upscale clientele for two-olive martinis, Manhattans, and other trad libations. ✉ *The Palace Hotel, 2 New Montgomery St., SoMa* ☎ *415/546–5089* 🌐 *www.piedpipersf.com.*

The View Lounge

COCKTAIL LOUNGES | Art-deco-influenced floor-to-ceiling windows frame superb views on the 39th floor of the San Francisco Marriott Marquis. You won't feel out of place here just getting a drink or two rather than dinner, but the small bites are usually delicious. It can get crowded at happy hour on weekdays and all night on weekends. ✉ *780 Mission St., SoMa* ☎ *415/442–6003* 🌐 *marriott.com.*

BREWPUBS AND BEER GARDENS

Black Hammer Brewing Company

BREWPUBS | The city's best brewery within actual walking distance of downtown resides on a warehouse stretch of SoMa that is better known for Bay Bridge on-ramp traffic than food and drink. The cozy, colorful tasting room is always friendly and full of great fresh beers on tap. It's hard to pick from the extensive list of brews, but there's a wide variety of styles and usually a few funky choices and gluten-removed options included. ✉ *544 Bryant St., SoMa* ☎ *628/222–4664* ⊕ *blackhammerbrewing.com.*

CABARET
AsiaSF

CABARET | Saucy, sexy, and fun, this is one of the best places in town for dinner with a show. The entertainment, as well as the gracious food service, is provided by some of the city's most gorgeous transgender women, who strut in impossibly high heels on top of the catwalk bar, vamping to tunes like "Cabaret" and "Big Spender." The creative Asian-influenced cuisine is surprisingly good. Make reservations, and go on a weekday to avoid the bachelorette parties. ✉ *201 9th St., SoMa* ☎ *415/255–2742* ⊕ *asiasf.com.*

DANCE CLUBS
DNA Lounge

DANCE CLUBS | The music changes nightly at the venerable DNA Lounge, with Monday Night burlesque and comedy shows, themed weekend dance parties, and a wide range of music styles each evening. Multiple dance floors and bars across two levels mean that the festivities are rarely uncomfortably crowded and always huge amounts of fun. ✉ *375 11th St., SoMa* ☎ *415/626–1409* ⊕ *www. dnalounge.com* ⊗ *Closed Tues. and Wed.*

The EndUp

DANCE CLUBS | With an all-night (and most of the morning) dance party starting at 10 pm on Saturday, the EndUp is SF's most popular after-hours place, with possibly the best sound system in the city. Weekends often see day parties that make it so 3 am and 3 pm seem to blur together. It can be a bit of a meat market, but this San Francisco institution doesn't adhere to any particular scene, with DJs playing a variety of music styles. ■TIP→ **Said sound system is cranked. Even the cool kids wear earplugs.** ✉ *401 6th St., SoMa* ⊕ *theendupsf.com.*

LGBTQ+ NIGHTLIFE
Lone Star Saloon

BARS | This watering hole is popular with bikers, bears, and the men who love them. The inside bar has an old tavern feel, with a pool table and a long wooden bar you half expect the bartender to sling a beer down. Weekend "Beer Busts" unfold on the great outdoor patio bar. The action can get steamy during events like Gay Pride or the Folsom Street Fair. ✉ *1354 Harrison St., SoMa* ☎ *415/863–9999* ⊕ *www.lonestarsf.com.*

SF Eagle

BARS | This spacious indoor-outdoor leather bar is a holdover from the days before SoMa's gentrification. The Sunday afternoon "Beer Busts" remain a high point of the leather set's week, Mondays are for karaoke, and there are DJs and live music generally Thursday and Friday. This remains a welcoming place for people from all walks of life. ✉ *398 12th St., SoMa* ⊕ *sf-eagle.com.*

🎭 Performing Arts

DANCE
Alonzo King LINES Ballet

BALLET | Since 1982 this company has been staging the fluid and gorgeous ballets of choreographer and founder Alonzo King, sometimes in collaboration with top-notch global musicians and visual artists. Ballets incorporate both classical and modern techniques, with experimental set design, costumes, and music. The San Francisco seasons are in spring and fall with performances at the Yerba Buena Center for the Arts. ✉ *700 Howard St., SoMa* ☎ *415/863–3040* ⊕ *linesballet. org* 🎟 *Tickets from $40.*

PERFORMING ARTS CENTERS
Yerba Buena Center for the Arts

ARTS CENTERS | Across the street from SFMOMA and abutting a lovely urban garden, this performing arts complex schedules interdisciplinary art exhibitions, touring and local dance troupes, music, film programs, and contemporary theater events. You can depend on the quality of the productions at Yerba Buena. Dance groups that perform here include the Smuin Ballet (⊕ *smuinballet.org*), ODC/Dance (⊕ *odc.dance*), and Alonzo King's LINES Ballet (⊕ *linesballet.org*). Lamplighters (⊕ *lamplighters.org*), an alternative opera that specializes in Gilbert & Sullivan, also sometimes performs here. ✉ *701 Mission St., SoMa* ☎ *415/978–2787* ⊕ *ybca.org*.

🛍 Shopping

ART GALLERIES
Crown Point Press
ART GALLERIES | What started as a print workshop in 1962 now includes studios as well as a large, airy gallery displaying etchings, intaglios, engravings, and aquatints by local and internationally renowned artists. ✉ *20 Hawthorne St., SoMa* ☎ *415/974–6273* ⊕ *crownpoint.com* ☯ *Closed Sun.*

Hackett Mill
ART GALLERIES | This gallery prides itself on its friendly staffers, who will educate you about the art (or leave you alone if you prefer). Artists include Conrad Marca-Relli, Esteban Vincente, Kenzo Okada, and Robert De Niro Sr. Specialties are American modern, postwar abstract expressionist, and Bay Area figurative art. ✉ *300 Beale St., SoMa* ☎ *415/362–3377* ⊕ *www.hackettmill.com*.

Varnish Fine Art
ART GALLERIES | Jen Rogers and Kerri Stephens's gallery specializes in thought-provoking works such as those by San Francisco–based artist Brian Goggin, known for his public art piece *Defenestration*. Ransom & Mitchell, two other noteworthy locals the gallery represents, blend photography and set design to create a truly surreal visual experience. ✉ *16 Jessie St., Suite C120, SoMa* ☎ *415/433–4400* ⊕ *www.varnishfineart.com* ☞ *Open by appointment only.*

BOOKS
Alexander Book Company
BOOKS | The three floors here are stocked with literature, poetry, and children's books, with a focus on hard-to-find works by people of color. ✉ *50 2nd St., SoMa* ☎ *415/495–2992* ⊕ *www.alexanderbook.com* ☯ *Closed weekends.*

★ Chronicle Books
BOOKS | A local beacon of publishing produces inventively designed fiction, cookbooks, art books, and other titles, as well as postcards, planners, and address books—all of which you can purchase at its home near Oracle Park. ✉ *680 2nd St., SoMa* ☎ *415/537–4200* ⊕ *www.chroniclebooks.com* ☯ *Closed weekends.*

FOOD AND DRINK
DECANTsf
WINE/SPIRITS | Wine geeks love the retail choices and the exciting offerings poured at this hybrid wine store–bar. This is the place to ask questions about quieter regions and rarely seen grapes—the co-owners are gifted sommeliers and love to share their passion with guests. The shop puts together some of the greatest cheese, charcuterie, and tinned fish boards in town. ✉ *1168 Folsom St., SoMa* ☎ *415/913–7256* ⊕ *decantsf.com* ☯ *Closed Mon.*

K&L Wine Merchants
WINE/SPIRITS | This wine shop has an ardent cult following around town. The friendly staffers promise to sell only what they taste themselves, and weekly events (Thursday through Saturday) open the tastings to customers. The best-seller list for varietals and regions for both the under- and over-$30 categories appeals to the wine lover in everyone. ✉ *855 Harrison St., SoMa* ☎ *415/896–1734* ⊕ *www.klwines.com*.

JEWELRY AND COLLECTIBLES
★ SFMOMA Museum Store
MUSEUM SHOP | This is an excellent stop for unique souvenirs, including a large selection of watches and jewelry, as well

For San Francisco Giants games at Oracle Park, there isn't a bad seat in the house.

as artists' monographs and artful house-wares. Posters, calendars, and children's art sets round out the merchandise. ✉ *151 3rd St., SoMa* ☎ *415/357–4035* ⊕ *museumstore.sfmoma.org.*

MUSIC

Guitar Solo

MUSIC | This shop stocks high-quality acoustic guitars, CDs, and thousands of titles of sheet music—and has its own record label to boot. The custom guitars, ukuleles, and mandolins make this a true musician's choice. ✉ *230 Townsend St., SoMa* ☎ *415/896–1922* ⊕ *www. gspguitar.com.*

 Activities

BASEBALL

★ San Francisco Giants

BASEBALL & SOFTBALL | **FAMILY** | Three World Series titles (2010, 2012, and 2014) and the retro-modern design of Oracle Park lead to sellout home games, so make plans in advance. ✉ *Oracle Park, 24 Willie*

Mays Plaza, SoMa ☎ *415/972–2000* ⊕ *www.mlb.com/giants.*

KAYAKING

★ City Kayak

KAYAKING | **FAMILY** | There are few better ways to see the San Francisco skyline than kayaking on the bay. This popular kayak and stand up paddleboard outfitter offers rentals, classes, and guided tours. Long-haul kayakers often head past the Bay Bridge and turn around near the Ferry Building for quite the spectacular workout. However, the most popular route goes to McCovey Cove behind the Oracle Park's rightfield wall (remember all those Barry Bounds home runs in the water?) and continues under two draw bridges to the houseboats on Mission Creek. ✉ *Pier 40, SoMa* ☎ *888/966–0953* ⊕ *citykayak.com* ✉ *From $36.*

Oracle Park: Where Giants Tread

The size of Oracle Park hits you immediately—the field, McCovey Cove, and the Lefty O'Doul drawbridge all look like miniature models. At just under 13 acres, the San Francisco Giants' ballpark is one of the country's smallest. After Boston's Fenway Park, Oracle Park has the shortest distance to the wall; from home plate it's just 309 feet to the tall right-field wall. But there's something endearing about its petite stature—not to mention its location, with yacht masts poking up over the outfield and the blue bay sparkling beyond.

In 2000 the Giants played their first game at Oracle Park (then called Pacific Bell Park and later SBC Park and AT&T Park). All told, $357 million was spent on the facility, and it shows in the retro redbrick exterior, the quaint clock tower, handsome bronze statues, and above-average food. There isn't a bad seat in the house, and the park has an unusual level of intimacy and access. Concourses circle the field on one level, and in some ticketed areas you can stand inches from players as they exit the locker rooms. At street level, non-ticket-holders can get up close outside a gate in right field. The giant Coke bottle and mitt you see beyond the outfield are part of the Coca-Cola Fan Lot playground. Don't miss the edible garden, the model cable car, and the specialty Crazy Crab sandwich, all located in the centerfield area. Park tours are led daily at 10:30 and 12:30 and cost $25.

The Famous "Splash Hit"

Locals show up in motorboats and inflatable rafts, ready to scoop up home-run balls that clear the right-field wall and land in McCovey Cove. Hitting one into the water isn't easy: the ball has to clear a 25-foot wall, the elevated walkway, and the promenade outside. Barry Bonds had the first "splash hit" on May 1, 2000.

Getting There

Parking is very limited and pricey ($35 and up), plus traffic can be gridlock before games. Take public transportation. Muni lines N and T (to CalTrain/Mission Bay and Sunnydale, respectively) stop in front of the park, and Muni bus lines 30 and 45 stop a block away. Or arrive in style—take the ferry from Jack London Square in Oakland (⊕ www.sanfranciscobay-ferry.com).

Mission Bay

San Francisco is a small city, but it can't really build much more. There is one major exception: Mission Bay. The name is confusing because the area isn't attached to the Mission District (it's bordered by Mission Creek). The most famous "locals" in the neighborhood are the NBA's Golden State Warriors, who play at the dazzling Chase Center. In this area between Oracle Park and Dogpatch, it's impossible to miss the construction and the tall, shiny new glass condo buildings (skyscrapers by San Francisco housing standards) that feel more like L.A. or Miami. But it's also easy to see the energy of a new neighborhood, a rarity in quirky and old San Francisco.

Possibly more than any other neighborhood in the city, you'll see kids playing in parks and dogs enjoying the sunshine here. It's a very family-friendly and pedestrian-friendly area. Families from all over

The Chase Center is home to the Golden State Warriors NBA team, major concerts and events, and a slew of dining options.

the Bay Area enjoy spending weekend days playing miniature golf at Stagecoach Greens and enjoying lunch or dinner from the food trucks in the Spark Social multipurpose park complex.

Sights

★ Chase Center

SPORTS VENUE | In 2019 the NBA's Golden State Warriors moved from Oakland to this spectacular arena, which opened with a concert by Metallica with the San Francisco Symphony and continues to be a major stop for entertainers like Trevor Noah, Carrie Underwood, and Andrea Bocelli. Don't miss a walk around the beautiful bayfront grounds; a highlight is Olafur Eliasson's stunning *Seeing Spheres* installation.

The area around Chase Center is called Thrive City; its focal point is the beautiful plaza on the Third Street side of Chase Center, where fans gather to celebrate Warriors wins. There is a popular bleacher-like seating amphitheater facing the plaza that includes a statue of the late former mayor Ed Lee, who helped bring the Warriors to San Francisco. The other main highlight of Thrive City is dining. A few popular San Francisco establishments have branches here, including Gott's Roadside, Dumpling Time, Harmonic Brewing, and a pair of wine bars from Mission Bay Wine & Cheese and Dogpatch's Ungrafted. ✉ *1 Warriors Way, Mission Bay, Mission Bay* ☎ *415/479–4667* 🌐 *chasecenter.com.*

Restaurants

Casey's Pizza

$$ | **PIZZA** | **FAMILY** | Casey Crynes' East Coast–style pies are larger and have slightly thicker and sturdier crusts compared to the typical Neapolitan ones. New York expats love that these slices can actually be folded. **Known for:** bacon kale pizza; strong local beer and wine selection; a favorite pre–game stop. [$] *Average main: $29* ✉ *1170 4th St., Mission Bay* ☎ *415/814–2482* 🌐 *caseyspizzas.com* 🕒 *Closed Mon. No lunch.*

Miller & Lux

$$$$ | STEAKHOUSE | A splashy contemporary steak house attached to a basketball arena? It sounds like a bizarre combination, but it truly works at chef Tyler Florence's restaurant on the side of the Chase Center. **Known for:** steak with green peppercorn Bordelaise sauce; perfectly balanced Manhattans and martinis; posh, sharp design headlined by curved leather booths. $ *Average main: $45* ✉ *700 Terry A. Francois Blvd., Mission Bay* ☎ *415/872–6699* ⊕ *millerandluxrestaurant.com* ⊗ *No lunch.*

Mission Rock Resort

$$ | SEAFOOD | Fresh seafood and waterfront views are some of the many reasons to swing by this fun restaurant in the shadow of the Chase Center. Local fish is emphasized, whether as a fried petrale sole sandwich or black cod in an elaborate dinner entrée with warm fregola and mushroom pilaf. **Known for:** oysters in a variety of preparations; Dungeness crab and bay shrimp roll; margaritas. $ *Average main: $25* ✉ *817 Terry A Francois Blvd., Mission Bay* ☎ *415/701–7625* ⊕ *missionrockresort.com* ⊗ *Closed Mon.*

🍵 Coffee and Quick Bites

Cafe Réveille

$ | CAFÉ | FAMILY | San Francisco has plenty of great food options and coffee destinations, but rarely do the two merge together as well as they do at this Mission Bay roastery, which excels at sandwiches on fresh focaccia, virtuous lunch bowls, and coffee in myriad forms. With tall ceilings, ample windows, and a pleasant parklet, the café almost has a Parisian indoor-outdoor feel. **Known for:** top-tier breakfast sandwich and burrito; excellent cappuccino; maybe the city's best açai bowl. $ *Average main: $15* ✉ *610 Long Bridge St., Mission Bay* ⊕ *www.cafereveille.com* ⊗ *No dinner.*

🛏 Hotels

LUMA Hotel San Francisco

$$ | HOTEL | Located just over a block away from Oracle Park, the second-ever location of this emerging boutique hotel brand is the first-ever hotel in rapidly growing Mission Bay. **Pros:** great technology additions; beautiful art; very good coffee and pastries in Twyne Coffee Bar. **Cons:** near major construction; entrance can be a scene because of rooftop bar; no nightlife in the area except on 17th floor. $ *Rooms from: $283* ✉ *100 Channel St., Mission Bay* ☎ *888/589–9988 reservations, 415/266–9999* ⊕ *lumahotelsf. com* ⇗ *299 rooms* ⦿| *No Meals.*

🍸 Nightlife

Cavaña

BARS | The almost 360-degree views of San Francisco and the bay are dazzling at this hip rooftop bar on the LUMA Hotel. Fire pits, hand warmers, and strategic wind barriers make this one of the warmer outdoor SF drinking destinations. But the real stars are the intricate cocktails inspired by Central and South American cultures and ingredients. ✉ *LUMA Hotel San Francisco, 100 Channel St., Mission Bay* ☎ *415/757–1470* ⊕ *cavanasf.com.*

Dogpatch

East of the Mission District and Potrero Hill and a short T–Third Muni light-rail ride from SoMa, the increasingly hip Dogpatch neighborhood has been on the rise since the tech boom of the 2010s started. Red-hot galleries have hit a critical mass, decamping from aging Union Square and even New York to fill the Minnesota Street Project, a giant warehouse of art space; and the Museum of Craft and Design is another neighborhood anchor. Artisans, designers, and craftspeople eager to protect the area's historical industrial legacy have all moved here in recent years, providing a solid customer base for shops, boutique restaurants, and artisanal food producers (but no bank!). If you're staying in a vacation home and planning to cook, make sure to visit Olivier Butchery, considered by many as the city's top butcher shop.

Sights

Crane Cove Park

CITY PARK | FAMILY | A former industrial part of the bay waterfront was beautifully redesigned into a city park with two lawn areas; plenty of space for dogs, joggers, and picnickers; splendid East Bay and Bay Bridge views; and, yes, a small beach. However, it's not recommended to actually swim in the area—it's best to kayak or just dip your toes in the water. This is an urban renewal triumph enjoyed by all ages. ✉ *Crane Cove Park, at 18th St. and Illinois St., Dogpatch* 🌐 *sanfranciscoparksalliance.org.*

Museum of Craft and Design

ART MUSEUM | Right at home in this once-industrial neighborhood now bursting with creative energy, this small, four-room space—definitely a quick view—mounts temporary art and design exhibitions. The focus might be sculpture, metalwork, furniture, or jewelry, though it might also be industrial design, architecture, the connection of scent and objects, or very on-trend subjects like data and computer encoding. The beautifully curated shop is perfect for unique souvenirs and imagination-spurring items for the home office. ✉ *2569 3rd St., Dogpatch* ☎ *415/773–0303* 🌐 *sfmcd.org* 🎫 *$10* 🕒 *Closed Mon. and Tues.*

Restaurants

Besharam

$$ | MODERN INDIAN | Every night is a party with excellent cocktails and vegetarian dishes from chef-owner Heena Patel's home state of Gujarat, on the western coast of India. A graduate of the La Cocina kitchen incubator, Patel has created a menu of snacks and entrées split between four different cities within Gujarat. **Known for:** maska paneer with homemade cheese; pani puri snacks; dahi wada fritters with chilled yogurt. [$] *Average main: $25* ✉ *1275 Minnesota St., Dogpatch* ☎ *415/580–7662* 🌐 *besharamrestaurant.com* 🕒 *Closed Mon. and Tues. No lunch.*

Just For You Cafe

$ | AMERICAN | Whether you're looking for a New Orleans-, Mexican-, or California-inspired breakfast or lunch, this beloved café is the place for you. The signature pillowy beignets deserve all the considerable hype and people drive an hour just to try them. **Known for:** beignet sampler with three flavors; outstanding brioche French toast; breakfast burritos. [$] *Average main: $18* ✉ *732 22nd St., Dogpatch* ☎ *415/647–3033* 🌐 *justforyoucafe.com* 🕒 *No dinner.*

★ Piccino

$$ | MODERN ITALIAN | Look for the sunny yellow building, and you've reached the pinnacle of Californian-Italian dining in San Francisco. With one of the greatest parklets in the city, and a serene dining room surrounded by large windows and an open kitchen, this restaurant is a huge reason why Dogpatch became an "it" neighborhood. **Known for:** beef and pork polpette (meatballs); pastas; excellent thin-crust pizzas. [$] *Average main: $28* ✉ *1001 Minnesota St., Dogpatch* ☎ *415/824–4224* 🌐 *piccino.com* 🕒 *Closed Mon. and Tues.*

The Ramp Restaurant

$$ | AMERICAN | This waterfront, outdoor gathering place brings diners from all over town for sunny day brunches and a beachy-bohemian Key West vibe. This is San Francisco's definitive destination for leisurely daytime eating and drinking—always slinging beers, burgers, and fish tacos to guests fighting hangovers or just relaxing before an afternoon of work. **Known for:** famous Bloody Mary;

clam chowder in a bread bowl; gorgeous views. $ *Average main: $21* ✉ *855 Terry A Francois Blvd., Dogpatch* ☎ *415/621–2876* ⊕ *rampsf.com* ⊗ *Closed Mon.*

★ Ungrafted

$$ | MODERN AMERICAN | Wife-and-husband team Rebecca Fineman and Chris Gaither are both Master Sommeliers, and, on cue, the wine program at this destination-worthy seasonal-driven restaurant, wine bar, and wine shop is absolutely fantastic. Gaither supervises the floor and his friendly, fun way of explaining wine even makes rookies get excited about obscure grapes and unknown vineyard regions. **Known for:** exquisite Champagne selection; pork belly carbonara with Korean rice cakes; za'atar pull-apart bread. $ *Average main: $30* ✉ *2419 3rd St., Dogpatch* ☎ *415/814–2129* ⊕ *ungraftedsf.com* ⊗ *Closed Sun. and Mon.*

☕ Coffee and Quick Bites

Neighbor Bakehouse

$ | BAKERY | Baker extraordinaire Greg Mindel's croissants, pastries, and other treats draw big crowds every morning. It's walk-up only, so plan on enjoying your tarts, bostocks, sourdough loaves, and coffee (drip only; no espresso drinks) elsewhere. **Known for:** long lines; pistachio berry twice-baked croissant; ham and cheese croissant. $ *Average main: $6* ✉ *2343 3rd St., Dogpatch* ⊕ *neighborsf.com* ⊗ *Closed Mon. and Tues.*

Wooly Pig

$ | SANDWICHES | This standout sandwich shop wonderfully balances a menu of signature Vietnamese banh mi and other sandwiches given a unique spin with ingredients from different Asian cultures.

At dinner time, there's a comforting ginger chicken *jook* (porridge), Japanese curry, and more. **Known for:** breakfast sandwich on an English muffin; curry-spiced fried chicken sandwich; cubano sandwich with char siu (Chinese barbecue) ham. $ *Average main: $16* ✉ *2295 3rd St., Dogpatch* ☎ *415/592–8015* ⊕ *woolypigsf.com* ⊗ *No dinner weekends.*

▼ Nightlife

BARS

The Sea Star

BARS | Few San Francisco bars can match the drink quality paired with the friendly atmosphere here. Cocktails are creative and well-made; the craft beer roster is strong; there's a pool table; and dogs often watch sports at the bar with their human owners. Then there's the main decor talking piece: an octopus chandelier below the Gilded Age–evoking chandelier. ✉ *2289 3rd St., Dogpatch* ☎ *415/552–5330* ⊕ *theseastarsf.com.*

Third Rail

BARS | High-quality, not-fussy cocktails are showcased at this friendly, low-key bar. The botanical-heavy Mt. Tam gin cocktail is a longtime favorite, but there's no going wrong on the menu split between shaken and stirred drinks. Food is almost exclusively unique kinds of jerky—a perfect snack with a drink or two. ✉ *628 20th St., Dogpatch* ⊕ *thirdrailbarsf.com* ⊗ *Closed Mon.*

Chapter 4

UNION SQUARE, CIVIC CENTER, AND THE TENDERLOIN

4

Updated by
Denise Leto

⊙ Sights	🍴 Restaurants	🛏 Hotels	🛍 Shopping	🍸 Nightlife
★★☆☆☆	★★★☆☆	★★★★★	★★★★★	★☆☆☆☆

NEIGHBORHOOD SNAPSHOT

TOP EXPERIENCES

■ **Retail therapy:** Prime your credit cards and dive right in, from department stores like Bloomingdale's to the boutiques of Maiden Lane.

■ **Union Square:** Grab a seat and soak up the grandeur—and the sun—in the heart of the city's signature plaza.

■ **Asian Art Museum:** Stand face-to-face with a massive gold Buddha at one of the world's most expansive collections of Asian art.

■ **San Francisco Opera, Ballet, and Symphony:** Enjoy San Francisco's world-class performing arts companies in the shadow of spectacular City Hall.

■ **Little Saigon:** Take your pick of excellent Vietnamese restaurants along Larkin Street in the Tenderloin, but take a cab—the neighborhood is vibrant but sketchy, especially at night.

PLANNING YOUR TIME

■ Set aside at least an hour to scope out the stores and sights around Union Square—or most of the day if you're a shopper—but don't bother arriving before 10 am, when the first shops open.

■ Plan on spending at least two hours at the Asian Art Museum and no more than a half hour at City Hall. Except for these two mainstays, you'll have little reason to visit the Civic Center area unless you have tickets to the opera, symphony, or other cultural event.

GETTING HERE

In Union Square, cars equal hassle traffic is slow and parking is pricey. Take advantage of the confluence of public transit at Powell and Market Streets: buses, Muni light-rail vehicles, and BART (Powell Street Station for both), cable cars, and F-line streetcars run here.

Parking is easier in Civic Center and the Tenderloin, but in both neighborhoods, most visitors will be more comfortable with a ride service, especially after dark.

FUN FACT

■ Fans of Dashiell Hammett's noir masterpiece *The Maltese Falcon* can experience the author's San Francisco in Union Square. The Flood Building, home of the San Francisco offices of Pinkerton's National Detective Agency (and Hammett's workplace in the 1920s), contains a replica of the falcon. Another can be found around the corner at John's Grill, opened in 1908, where Hammett—as well as Sam Spade—dined.

The Union Square area bustles with big-city bravado. In Union Square—a plaza but also the neighborhood around it—the crowds zigzag among international brands, trailing glossy shopping bags.

Just east is one of the city's poorest districts, the Tenderloin, where rough life on the streets brushes up against a new wave of investment. Here you'll find excellent Vietnamese food, a fancy new design hotel, a brand-new IKEA, and startlingly public drug use and street crime.

Another hop east is Civic Center, where wonderful museums and gold-domed City Hall share space with the city's unhoused.

Union Square

The city's finest department stores put on their best faces in Union Square, along with such exclusive emporiums as Tiffany & Co., Chanel, Gucci, and Bulgari, and such big-name retailers as Nike and Apple. Visitors lay their heads at several dozen hotels within a three-block walk of the square, and the downtown theater district is nearby. Union Square is shopping-centric; non-shoppers will find fewer enticements here.

◉ Sights

Lotta's Fountain
FOUNTAIN | Saucy gold rush–era actress, singer, and dancer Lotta Crabtree so excited the city's miners that they were known to shower her with gold nuggets and silver dollars after her performances. This peculiar, rather clunky gold-colored fountain adorned with regal lions was her way of saying thanks to her fans.

Given to the city in 1875, the fountain became a meeting place for survivors after the 1906 earthquake; each April 18, the anniversary of the quake, San Franciscans gather here. An image of redheaded Lotta herself, in a very pink, rather risqué dress, appears in one of the Anton Refregier murals in Rincon Center. ⊠ *Traffic triangle at intersection of 3rd, Market, Kearny, and Geary Sts., Union Sq.*

Maiden Lane
STREET | Known as Morton Street in the raffish Barbary Coast era, this former red-light district reported at least one murder a week during the late 19th century, though things cooled down after the 1906 fire. These days Maiden Lane is a chic, designer-boutique-lined pedestrian mall. Wrought-iron gates close the street to traffic most days between 11 and 6, when the lane becomes an alfresco hot spot dotted with umbrella-shaded tables. It's also popular with photographers and Instagrammers for its quaint-chic aesthetic. At 140 Maiden Lane is the only Frank Lloyd Wright building in San Francisco, fronted by a large brick archway. The curving ramp and skylights of the interior, which houses exclusive Italian menswear boutique Isaia, are said to have been his model for the Guggenheim Museum in New York. ⊠ *Between Stockton and Kearny Sts., Union Sq.*

Union Square
PLAZA/SQUARE | The marquee destination for big-name shopping in the city and within walking distance of many hotels,

Union Square's Backstory 👁

The heart of San Francisco's downtown since 1850, Union Square takes its name from the violent pro-Union demonstrations staged here before the Civil War. At center stage, Robert Ingersoll Aitken's Dewey Monument commemorates Commodore George Dewey's victory over the Spanish fleet at Manila in 1898. The 97-foot Corinthian column, topped by a bronze figure symbolizing naval conquest, was dedicated by Theodore Roosevelt in 1903; it withstood the 1906 earthquake. After the earthquake, the square was dubbed "Little St. Francis" because of the temporary shelter erected for residents of the St. Francis hotel. Actor John Barrymore (grandfather of actress Drew Barrymore and a notorious carouser) was among the guests pressed into volunteering to stack bricks in the square. His uncle, thespian John Drew, remarked, "It took an act of God to get John out of bed and the United States Army to get him to work."

Union Square is home base for many visitors. Four globular contemporary lamp sculptures by the artist R. M. Fischer preside over the landscaped, 2½-acre park anchored by the monument to Admiral George Dewey. The area also has a café with outdoor seating, an open-air stage, and the city's favorite holiday season ice-skating rink. The square hosts a kaleidoscope of characters: office workers sunning and brown-bagging, street musicians, shoppers taking a rest, kids chasing pigeons, and a fair number of homeless people. The constant clang of cable cars traveling up and down Powell Street helps maintain a festive mood. ⊠ *Bordered by Powell, Stockton, Post, and Geary Sts., Union Sq.*

The Westin St. Francis San Francisco on Union Square

HOTEL | Built in 1904 and barely established as the most sumptuous hotel in town before it was ravaged by fire following the 1906 earthquake, this grande-dame hotel designed by Walter Danforth Bliss and William Baker Faville reopened in 1907 with the addition of a luxurious Italian Renaissance–style residence designed to attract loyal clients from among the world's rich and powerful. The hotel's checkered past includes the ill-fated 1921 bash in the suite of the silent-film superstar Fatty Arbuckle, at which a woman became ill, leading to her death. Arbuckle endured three sensational trials for rape and murder before being acquitted, by which time his career was kaput. In 1975, Sara Jane Moore, standing among a crowd outside the hotel, attempted to shoot then-President Gerald Ford. Of course, the grand lobby contains no plaques commemorating these events. ■ TIP→ **Some visitors make the St. Francis a stop whenever they're in town, soaking up the lobby ambience or enjoying a cocktail at the Clock Bar or holiday tea at the Oak Room Restaurant.** ⊠ *335 Powell St., at Geary St., Union Sq.* ☎ *415/397–7000* ⊕ *westinstfrancis.com.*

🍴 Restaurants

It's hard to find authentic San Francisco dining here, as locals dislike battling the crowds. But if you know where to look, you can find good places tucked away in narrow side alleys and hotel lobbies.

Bouche

$$$$ | **MODERN FRENCH** | They don't hand out awards for the the smallest restaurant in San Francisco, but this charmer right on top of the Stockton Tunnel

A monument to Admiral George Dewey stands tall in Union Square, a spacious plaza surrounded by hotels and big-name shops.

outside Union Square would definitely be a contender. It's a perfect example of a French bistro given a California spin—the best of both worlds seamlessly cooked together in a value prix-fixe menu. **Known for:** charming ambience and food; counter seating in front of kitchen; fougasse bread. [$] *Average main: $55* ✉ *603 Bush St., Union Sq.* ☎ *415/956–0396* 🌐 *www.bouchesf.com* 🕒 *Closed Mon. No lunch.*

★ Kin Khao

$$$ | THAI | Casual eaters of Americanized Thai food probably won't recognize much at this modern, Michelin-star restaurant, but travelers to Thailand will likely see a few familiar items on the short, focused menu. Ingredients are sourced—more accurately, tracked down with dedication—from regional purveyors to create a range of powerful, unique dishes ranging from a mushroom curry mousse with crispy rice cakes to spicy charred squid. **Known for:** fish sauce chicken wings; sharp cocktails and wine program; odd location in the back of a hotel. [$] *Average main: $38* ✉ *Parc 55 Hotel, 55 Cyril Magnin St., Union Sq.* ☎ *415/362–7456* 🌐 *www.kinkhao.com* 🕒 *Closed Mon. and Tues. No lunch.*

★ Liholiho Yacht Club

$$$$ | MODERN AMERICAN | Inspired but not defined by the chef's native Hawaii, Ravi Kapur's lively restaurant is known for big-hearted, high-spirited cooking. It offers contemporary riffs on staples like poke and Spam, as well as squid served with crispy tripe and manila clams in coconut curry. **Known for:** beef tongue on poppy-seed steamed buns; giant mains that serve two to four people; beautifully composed cocktails. [$] *Average main: $42* ✉ *871 Sutter St., Union Sq.* ☎ *415/440–5446* 🌐 *lycsf.com* 🕒 *Closed Sun. No lunch.*

Mensho Tokyo SF

$ | JAPANESE | Look for the lines on busy Geary Street where Union Square blurs into the edges of the Tenderloin, and you'll find what eager ramen fans consider the city's best bowl. This was the first U.S. outpost of a prominent Tokyo-based ramen shop, and the quality and

Union Square, Civic Center, and the Tenderloin

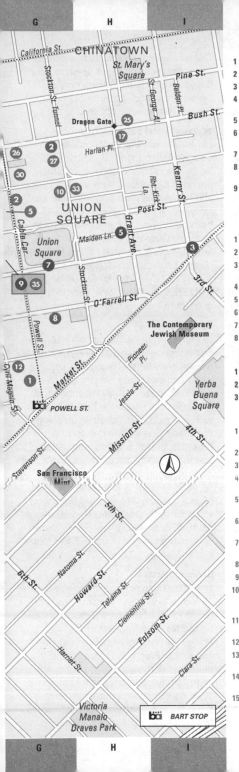

Sights ▼

1 Asian Art Museum........**C8**
2 City Hall.................**B8**
3 Lotta's Fountain..........**I3**
4 Louise M. Davies
   Symphony Hall..........**A9**
5 Maiden Lane............**H3**
6 San Francisco
   Public Library..........**C8**
7 Union Square...........**G3**
8 War Memorial
   Opera House............**A9**
9 The Westin St. Francis
   San Francisco on
   Union Square............**G4**

Restaurants ▼

1 Bodega SF...............**F5**
2 Bouche..................**G2**
3 Brenda's French
   Soul Food...............**B6**
4 Kin Khao................**F5**
5 Lers Ros................**B5**
6 Liholiho Yacht Club.....**D3**
7 Mensho Tokyo SF.......**D4**
8 ONE65...................**G4**

Quick Bites ▼

1 Arsicault................**D7**
2 Beanstalk Cafe..........**F2**
3 Saigon Sandwich........**C6**

Hotels ▼

1 Axiom Hotel
   San Francisco...........**G5**
2 Beacon Grand...........**G3**
3 Beresford Arms.........**D4**
4 The Cartwright Hotel
   Union Square.............**F2**
5 Chancellor Hotel on
   Union Square...........**G3**
6 The Clift Royal
   Sonesta Hotel...........**E4**
7 Cornell Hotel
   de France................**F2**
8 The Donatello...........**F3**
9 Golden Gate Hotel.......**F2**
10 Grand Hyatt
   San Francisco
   Union Square...........**G3**
11 Hilton San Francisco
   Union Square...........**F5**
12 Hotel Abri...............**G5**
13 Hotel Adagio,
   Autograph Collection....**E4**
14 Hotel Emblem
   San Francisco...........**F2**
15 Hotel G
   San Francisco...........**F4**
16 Hotel Nikko
   San Francisco...........**F4**
17 Hotel Triton..............**H2**
18 Hotel Zeppelin...........**F3**
19 The Inn at
   Union Square............**F3**
20 JW Marriott
   San Francisco
   Union Square............**F3**
21 Kensington Park
   Hotel....................**F3**
22 King George Hotel.......**F4**
23 The LINE SF.............**F6**
24 The Marker
   San Francisco...........**E4**
25 Orchard
   Garden Hotel...........**H2**
26 Orchard Hotel..........**G2**
27 Palihotel
   San Francisco...........**G2**
28 Parc 55
   San Francisco...........**F5**
29 Phoenix Hotel..........**B6**
30 San Francisco Marriott
   Union Square...........**G2**
31 San Francisco
   Proper Hotel............**E7**
32 Staypineapple
   San Francisco...........**E4**
33 Taj Campton Place
   San Francisco...........**H3**
34 Warwick
   San Francisco...........**E4**
35 The Westin St. Francis
   San Francisco on
   Union Square............**G4**

consistency of its noodles and broths continue to be spectacular. **Known for:** "tori paitan" chicken ramen; excellent vegan ramen; open late. [$] *Average main: $18* ✉ *672 Geary St., Union Sq.* ☎ *415/800–8345* 🌐 *mensho.tokyo* ⏲ *No lunch.*

ONE65

$$$$ | FRENCH | It's hard to describe this ode to France's many culinary specialties without a map diagram, as this is a full six-story, four-concept venue just a block from Union Square. The shimmering gem of the house is upstairs, the exquisite fine-dining tasting menu space O' by Claude Le Tohic; the other floors are taken up by a modern cocktail bar (Elements), a more casual bistro and grill (closed for remodeling at time of writing), and a ground-floor bakery and patisserie. **Known for:** cocktails high above the street at moody, urbane Elements lounge; patisserie's macarons; stellar house-baked breads. [$] *Average main: $195* ✉ *165 O'Farrell St., Union Sq.* ☎ *415/814–8888* 🌐 *www.one65sf.com.*

☕ Coffee and Quick Bites

Beanstalk Cafe

$ | SANDWICHES | Robin's-egg-blue banquettes and metal chairs in different colors add to the cheer at this sunny spot. Drop in for hearty local coffee and excellent breakfast and lunch sandwiches, including those on the popular cragel, a combination of a croissant and a bagel. **Known for:** pleasant, airy space; quality coffee drinks; cragel (croissant and bagel) sandwiches. [$] *Average main: $13* ✉ *724 Bush St., Union Sq.* ⏲ *No dinner.*

🛏 Hotels

Scores of hotels—populated by first-time visitors, corporate travelers, and savvy globetrotters—surround Union Square, which is a central shopping district. Easy access to public transportation, attractions, the Financial District, and Moscone Center convention activity has influenced major hotel chains to set up shop here, but you'll also find boutique hotels, several inns, and, a few blocks off Union Square, some value options.

★ Axiom Hotel San Francisco

$$ | HOTEL | Green, pet-friendly, and equipped with high-speed fiber-optic Wi-Fi, the tech-oriented Axiom nimbly provides a boutique experience business and leisure travelers applaud. **Pros:** fun, hip vibe; nicely designed rooms and bathrooms; on-site café open morning to night. **Cons:** the smallest rooms are notably tiny; somewhat congested area; nearby panhandlers. [$] *Rooms from: $229* ✉ *28 Cyril Magnin St., Union Sq.* ☎ *415/392–9466* 🌐 *www.axiomhotel.com* 🛏 *152 rooms* 🍴 *No Meals.*

Beacon Grand

$$ | HOTEL | This 1928 landmark—renovated and reopened in 2022—welcomes guests in its ornate, high-ceilinged lobby and classically elegant rooms that come equipped with 21st-century tech amenities but evoke the hotel's heyday with gorgeously restored wood plank floors and plush white comforters. **Pros:** thoughtful, beautiful renovation of historic property; excellent Union Square location; good 24-hour gym. **Cons:** limited services for business travelers; classic rooms can feel cramped; disappointing value for hefty destination fee. [$] *Rooms from: $275* ✉ *450 Powell St., Union Sq.* 🌐 *www.beacongrand.com* 🛏 *416 rooms* 🍴 *No Meals.*

Beresford Arms

$ | HOTEL | FAMILY | Fancy moldings and 10-foot-tall windows grace the red-carpeted lobby of this brick Victorian listed on the National Register of Historic Places that has rooms of varying size and setup. **Pros:** good value for the neighborhood; suites with kitchenettes and Murphy beds; excellent bathrooms. **Cons:** no a/c; older architecture and design; can be noisy at night. [$] *Rooms from: $169* ✉ *701 Post St., Union Sq.*

☎ 415/673–2600 ⊕ www.beresford.com ⇨ 95 rooms ⏹ Free Breakfast.

The Cartwright Hotel Union Square

$$ | HOTEL | A relatively inexpensive option (look for online specials), this 1913 Edwardian is part of the Best Western chain's Premier Collection, and it retains a period feel, especially in the tile-floor lobby with a fireplace and adjoining wood-paneled bar. **Pros:** comfortable pillow-top beds; free Wi-Fi; staff that cares. **Cons:** few amenities; small bathrooms; uninspired decor. Ⓢ *Rooms from: $270* ⊠ *524 Sutter St., Union Sq.* ☎ *415/421–2865, 800/780–7234* ⊕ *www.bestwestern.com* ⇨ *114 rooms* ⏹ *No Meals.*

Chancellor Hotel on Union Square

$ | HOTEL | Built to accommodate visitors to the 1915 Panama-Pacific International Exposition, this favorite of budget travelers has cable car views from its modest lobby. **Pros:** free Wi-Fi; good value for Union Square; friendly staff. **Cons:** small bathrooms; no breakfast available; no a/c (ceiling fans). Ⓢ *Rooms from: $150* ⊠ *433 Powell St., Union Sq.* ☎ *415/362–2004, 800/428–4748* ⊕ *www.chancellorhotel.com* ⇨ *137 rooms* ⏹ *No Meals.*

The Clift Royal Sonesta Hotel

$$ | HOTEL | Built for the 1915 Panama-Pacific International Exposition world's fair, this longtime favorite bridges the gap between hip modern and timeless classic style. **Pros:** discreet and helpful staff; one of the city's top hotel bars; close to public transportation, shopping, and theaters. **Cons:** street noise (book on upper floors to avoid); nearby neighborhood can be rough; simple room designs. Ⓢ *Rooms from: $239* ⊠ *495 Geary St., Union Sq.* ☎ *415/775–4700* ⊕ *www.sonesta.com/ sanfrancisco* ⇨ *372 rooms* ⏹ *No Meals.*

★ Cornell Hotel de France

$ | HOTEL | In their six-story structure dating back to 1910, hosts Claude and Micheline Lambert have created a bit of Paris a few blocks from Union Square, with rooms individually decorated with pastel colors, a stenciled ceiling, and prints of works by Picasso, Chagall, Klimt, and other European artists. **Pros:** excellent room quality and design; updated bathrooms; special packages and discounts. **Cons:** several blocks from the center of things; surrounding area mildly dodgy after dark; small lobby. Ⓢ *Rooms from: $165* ⊠ *715 Bush St., Union Sq.* ☎ *415/421–3154* ⊕ *www.cornellhotel.com* ⇨ *50 rooms* ⏹ *Free Breakfast.*

The Donatello

$$ | HOTEL | A Tuscan-theme Wyndham owners' club and boutique hotel may hardly be a traditional San Francisco arrangement, but it's the setup for one of the prime Union Square places to stay for luxury without grande-dame prices or pomp and circumstance. **Pros:** giant-size rooms by SF standards; on-site Zingari Ristorante; feels more like a home than a hotel. **Cons:** located away from the main areas of Nob Hill and Union Square; shared spaces with residents; not particularly stylish. Ⓢ *Rooms from: $250* ⊠ *501 Post St., Union Sq.* ☎ *415/441–7100* ⊕ *www.clubdonatello.org* ⇨ *45 rooms* ⏹ *No Meals.*

★ Golden Gate Hotel

$$ | B&B/INN | FAMILY | Travelers looking for charming accommodations around Union Square will enjoy this four-story Edwardian building with bay windows, an original birdcage elevator, hallways lined with historical photographs, and rooms decorated with antiques, wicker pieces, and Laura Ashley bedding and curtains. **Pros:** friendly staff; spotless rooms; good location for walkers. **Cons:** some rooms share a bath; resident cat; some small rooms. Ⓢ *Rooms from: $234* ⊠ *775 Bush St., Union Sq.* ☎ *415/392–3702, 800/835–1118* ⊕ *www.goldengatehotel.com* ⇨ *23 rooms* ⏹ *Free Breakfast.*

Grand Hyatt San Francisco Union Square
$$ | **HOTEL** | **FAMILY** | Location is the main draw at this hotel, where rooms done in warm autumnal tones, with textured custom furniture, original artwork, and teak beds, are showing their age but still offer high-tech features: windows can be blacked out from your bed, and you can stream from your mobile or other device to a swiveling flat-screen. **Pros:** stellar views from upper floors; on-site restaurant and lounge cover breakfast and afternoon snacks; weekend deals. **Cons:** small bathrooms; some rooms and area showing age; self-parking is in one of the city's busiest garages. [$] *Rooms from: $250* ✉ *345 Stockton St., Union Sq.* ☎ *415/398–1234* 🌐 *www.hyatt.com* 🛏 *668 rooms* 🍴 *No Meals.*

Hilton San Francisco Union Square
$$ | **HOTEL** | This is the largest hotel in California—sometimes the lobby feels like downtown at rush hour—and many rooms in the silvery tower enjoy views that rank among San Francisco's finest. **Pros:** great views from Cityscape Lounge; outdoor pool; $25 daily destination charge can be applied in restaurant/bar credit. **Cons:** dodgy area; Wi-Fi is only free if you're a Hilton member; some rooms show wear. [$] *Rooms from: $250* ✉ *333 O'Farrell St., Union Sq.* ☎ *415/771–1400* 🌐 *www.hiltonsanfranciscohotel.com* 🛏 *1,919 rooms* 🍴 *No Meals.*

Hotel Abri
$ | **HOTEL** | Near Union Square shops, theaters, and restaurants, this appealing hotel has small but tastefully appointed rooms with smart TVs, device docking stations, comfortable bedding, and fancy bath products. **Pros:** online specials offer great values; excellent work-from-room setup; great location for walking and public transit. **Cons:** no on-site gym or restaurant; area can be dicey; on-street parking very difficult. [$] *Rooms from: $175* ✉ *127 Ellis St., Union Sq.* ☎ *866/823–4669, 415/392–8800* 🌐 *hotelabrisf.com* 🛏 *91 rooms* 🍴 *No Meals.*

Monument to San Francisco

In front of the Grand Hyatt hotel at 345 Stockton Street gurgles an intricate bronze fountain depicting whimsical bas-relief scenes of San Francisco. It's one of many local public works by San Francisco sculptor Ruth Asawa. Look closely at this one and you can find an amorous couple behind one of the Victorian bay windows.

Hotel Adagio, Autograph Collection
$$ | **HOTEL** | The Spanish-colonial facade of this 16-story theater-row hotel complements its chic interior, with good-size rooms that have beautiful sea-blue carpets and plenty of tech amenities. **Pros:** Marriott-run property with boutique-hotel charm; central location for sightseeing; good drinks and scene at lobby bar, the Mortimer. **Cons:** street noise; area can be dicey at night; adjacent to a popular outdoor bar. [$] *Rooms from: $246* ✉ *550 Geary St., Union Sq.* ☎ *415/775–5000* 🌐 *www.hoteladagiosf.com* 🛏 *171 rooms* 🍴 *No Meals.*

Hotel Emblem San Francisco
$ | **HOTEL** | Inspiration is everywhere at this intimate hotel, with a prominent literary theme that celebrates San Francisco's Beat poets, from its lobby wall of books and poetry-laced carpet to in-room libraries and typewriters. **Pros:** fun, creative vibe; solid eating and drinking options; amenities available by request include diffusers, a humidifier, and bath bombs. **Cons:** some guests might feel the hotel is trying too hard to be hip; no on-site fitness option; some small rooms. [$] *Rooms from: $159* ✉ *562 Sutter St., Union Sq.* ☎ *415/433–4434* 🌐 *www.viceroyhotelsandresorts.com/en/emblem* 🛏 *96 rooms* 🍴 *No Meals.*

Hotel G San Francisco

$ | HOTEL | Both homey and innovative, the Hotel G has tiled lobby floors, large windows, and high ceilings (giving even the smallish standard rooms an airy feel) that pay homage to the building's century-plus history, while smart TVs, Bluetooth radios, Nespresso machines, and Wi-Fi keep it firmly in the present. **Pros:** fun design; central location; gym facility accessible around the clock. **Cons:** street noise; wooden or concrete flooring can be loud; small bathrooms and small windows. $ *Rooms from: $195* ✉ *386 Geary St., Union Sq.* ☎ *415/986–2000* ⊕ *www.hotelgsanfrancisco.com* ⇦ *149 rooms* ⚫ *No Meals.*

Hotel Nikko San Francisco

$$ | HOTEL | FAMILY | Known for impeccable service and satin-smooth style, this youngish grande dame takes its visual cues from traditional kimonos and Japanese calligraphy, with rooms that soothe upscale business and leisure travelers with muted colors offset by judicious splashes of stronger hues. **Pros:** dog-friendly, including a pet terrace; large indoor rooftop pool; Feinstein's at the Nikko, classy, intimate cabaret venue. **Cons:** formal vibe; daily $39 fee for fitness center and pool use; so-so neighborhood. $ *Rooms from: $200* ✉ *222 Mason St., Union Sq.* ☎ *415/394–1111, 800/248–3308* ⊕ *www.hotelnikkosf.com* ⇦ *532 rooms* ⚫ *No Meals.*

Hotel Triton

$ | HOTEL | With a strong location at the convergence of Chinatown, the Financial District, and Union Square, this boutique anchor attracts a design-conscious crowd and is highlighted by its intricately decorated lobby featuring marble floors, a wood-beam ceiling, and art from around the world. **Pros:** arty environs; exceptionally pet-friendly; beautiful Café de la Presse next door offers discount for guests. **Cons:** small rooms and baths; cramped hallways; dated room decor. $ *Rooms from: $195* ✉ *342 Grant Ave.,*

Union Sq. ☎ *415/394–0500* ⊕ *www.hoteltriton.com* ⇦ *140 rooms* ⚫ *No Meals.*

★ Hotel Zeppelin

$ | HOTEL | A frothy homage to 1950s Beat writers, 1960s hippies and rockers, and other local agents of change, the hip Hotel Zeppelin appeals to a youngish crowd with high-tech amenities and an inviting, sometimes boisterous, game room with a pool table, quick-shot basketball wall, and other entertainments. **Pros:** plucky design; fun-loving vibe; responsive concierge reachable by text for advice or requests. **Cons:** smallish rooms; frenetic pace; informal service. $ *Rooms from: $194* ✉ *545 Post St., Union Sq.* ☎ *415/563–0303, 888/539–7510* ⊕ *www.zhotelssf.com/zeppelin* ⇦ *196 rooms* ⚫ *No Meals.*

The Inn at Union Square

$$$ | B&B/INN | Built in 1922 and smartly updated, this six-story inn is strictly 21st century, with amenities that include high-quality bath products, soft robes, free high-speed Wi-Fi (included in the daily $20 amenity fee), and in-room service tablets. **Pros:** nicely laid-out rooms; morning tea and coffee; dreamy Beautyrest Victoria Park Plush beds. **Cons:** some rooms can be noisy; interiors feel stuffy; cramped hallways. $ *Rooms from: $365* ✉ *440 Post St., Union Sq.* ☎ *415/397–3510* ⊕ *www.unionsquare.com* ⇦ *30 rooms* ⚫ *No Meals.*

JW Marriott San Francisco Union Square

$$ | HOTEL | Bullet elevators whisk guests skyward from the grand, third-floor marble lobby with a Matisse-inspired bronze sculpture to contemporary guest rooms that are outfitted with business-oriented clientele in mind and situated around a dramatic, 19-story atrium. **Pros:** large rooms; luxurious bathrooms; spectacular public spaces. **Cons:** lacks character; service is polite but not particularly warm; expensive parking. $ *Rooms from: $265* ✉ *515 Mason St., Union*

Sq. ☎ *415/771–8600* 🌐 *www.jwmarriottunionsquare.com* 🛏 *344 rooms* 🍴 *No Meals.*

Kensington Park Hotel

$$ | **HOTEL** | Built in the 1920s in a Moorish and Gothic style, this former Elks Club retains its period feel and features, with rich marble and dark-wood accents, crystal chandeliers, vaulted ceilings, and antique furnishings in the lobby and vintage touches in the comfortable guest rooms. **Pros:** friendly, personal service; no amenity fees; period feel. **Cons:** some rooms have street noise; rooms average 220 square feet; small bathrooms. [$] *Rooms from: $245* ✉ *450 Post St., Union Sq.* ☎ *415/788–6400, 800/553–1900* 🌐 *www.kensingtonparkhotel.com* 🛏 *93 rooms* 🍴 *No Meals.*

King George Hotel

$$ | **HOTEL** | With its compact yet thoughtfully designed rooms and its Mason Social Club—a lively, Union Jack–theme bar/living room/game room—the King George has upped its game to match its service and hospitality, points of pride since the hotel's 1914 opening. **Pros:** colorful rooms; good rates available online; marble bathrooms. **Cons:** low ceilings in hallways; location on the edge of the Tenderloin; baths and some closets are minuscule. [$] *Rooms from: $325* ✉ *334 Mason St., Union Sq.* ☎ *415/781–5050* 🌐 *www.kinggeorge.com* 🛏 *153 rooms* 🍴 *No Meals.*

The Marker San Francisco

$$ | **HOTEL** | Behind a cheery 1910 Beaux-Arts facade and with smartly designed public spaces, the Marker delivers a comfortable experience amid the theater district hubbub, plus one of the area's better restaurant/bars with the Italian-themed Tratto. **Pros:** desk and lots of outlets for working from the room; colorful, nicely appointed rooms; BeeKind bath products are luxurious and sustainable. **Cons:** close to sketchy Tenderloin neighborhood; some discount-rate rooms are very small; windowless fitness center is very basic. [$] *Rooms from: $212* ✉ *501 Geary St., Union Sq.* ☎ *415/292–0100, 800/237-2508* 🌐 *www.themarkersf.com* 🛏 *208 rooms* 🍴 *No Meals.*

★ **Orchard Garden Hotel**

$$ | **HOTEL** | Feel virtuous and eco-friendly while enjoying a junior terrace room with private outdoor space and views of downtown at this service-oriented and environmentally friendly boutique hotel close to the Financial District and Chinatown that was the city's first LEED-certified hotel. **Pros:** free Wi-Fi and no resort fees; rooftop deck with sweeping city views; noise-reducing walls and windows. **Cons:** no on-site fitness center; lacks character of older establishments; minimalist aesthetic. [$] *Rooms from: $265* ✉ *466 Bush St., Union Sq.* ☎ *877/525–7749* 🌐 *www.theorchardgardenhotel.com* 🛏 *86 rooms* 🍴 *No Meals.*

Orchard Hotel

$$ | **HOTEL** | Unlike many of the area's other boutique hotels, which occupy century-old buildings, the Orchard was built in 2000—though the marble lobby, with dramatic architectural embellishments like arched openings, vaulted ceilings, and stone floors, evokes another era. **Pros:** cutting-edge technology; sizable rooms; green pedigree. **Cons:** can be pricey (but look for deals on hotel website); uphill from Union Square; area outside hotel is safe but grungy. [$] *Rooms from: $289* ✉ *665 Bush St., Union Sq.* ☎ *877/525–7750* 🌐 *www.theorchardhotel.com* 🛏 *104 rooms* 🍴 *No Meals.*

Palihotel San Francisco

$$ | **HOTEL** | Situated at the foot of the Stockton Tunnel, this beautiful property is now under the careful, hip eye of the Palisociety boutique hotel group, but its strong suits continue to be food and drink, a prime location, and a modern-meets-vintage aesthetic. **Pros:** superb cocktail bar; historic property; artsy decor. **Cons:** smallish rooms; city noise; sketchy characters in the block by tunnel entrance. [$] *Rooms from: $265* ✉ *417*

Stockton St., Union Sq. ☎ *415/400–0500* 🌐 *www.palisociety.com/hotels/san-francisco* 🛏 *82 rooms* 🍴 *No Meals.*

Parc 55 San Francisco

$$ | **HOTEL** | One of the largest hotels in town, the Parc 55 (a Hilton hotel) brims with activity, but its size is by no means overwhelming, thanks to features like the acclaimed Kin Khao restaurant and spacious but dated standard rooms with flat-screen TVs, handsome desks, and ergonomic chairs. **Pros:** close to public transportation, shops, and restaurants; some rooms have stellar views; good-size rooms. **Cons:** dated rooms; immediate area can be seedy at night; expensive breakfast. [$] *Rooms from: $285* ✉ *55 Cyril Magnin St., near 5th and Market Sts., Union Sq.* ☎ *415/392–8000* 🌐 *www.parc55hotel.com* 🛏 *1,024 rooms* 🍴 *No Meals.*

San Francisco Marriott Union Square

$$ | **HOTEL** | **FAMILY** | Business travelers appreciate the 30-floor Marriott's easily accessible plugs, movable desks, ergonomic chairs, and laptop connectors to flat-screen TVs—and its prime location near shopping, restaurants, nightspots, and public transportation. **Pros:** convenient location; in-room pull-out sofas and roll-away bed options; food and drink credit and cable car tickets offset the daily $25 "destination fee". **Cons:** noisy street; lacking in atmosphere; bland fitness center. [$] *Rooms from: $235* ✉ *480 Sutter St., Union Sq.* ☎ *415/398–8900, 866/912–0973* 🌐 *www.marriott.com* 🛏 *400 rooms* 🍴 *No Meals.*

★ **Staypineapple San Francisco**

$$ | **HOTEL** | Three blocks west of Union Square and loaded with high- and low-tech amenities, this Pineapple Hospitality boutique property delivers value in a stylish package, starting with the lobby's paintings and sculptures and the giant black-and-white art above the adjacent bar. **Pros:** cheery and stylish decor; loaded with amenities and extras like loaner bikes and afternoon pineapple cupcakes; fun vibe. **Cons:** many rooms are small; $30 per day amenity fee; iffy neighborhood after dark. [$] *Rooms from: $245* ✉ *580 Geary St., Union Sq.* ☎ *415/441–2700, 866/866–7977* 🌐 *www.staypineapple.com* 🛏 *93 rooms* 🍴 *No Meals.*

Taj Campton Place San Francisco

$$$ | **HOTEL** | Beauty and highly attentive service remain the hallmarks of this top-tier hotel, whose rooms are elegantly decorated in a contemporary Italian style, with sandy earth tones and handsome pearwood paneling and cabinetry. **Pros:** discreet, attentive service; Michelin-starred French-influenced Cal-Indian restaurant; rooftop fitness center. **Cons:** some questionable characters and busy sidewalk right outside hotel; smallest rooms 250 square feet; $30 obligatory resort fee. [$] *Rooms from: $360* ✉ *340 Stockton St., Union Sq.* ☎ *415/781–5555* 🌐 *www.tajcamptonplace.com* 🛏 *110 rooms* 🍴 *No Meals.*

Warwick San Francisco

$$ | **HOTEL** | The handsome, if small, rooms at this 1913 theater district hotel evoke an aristocratic feel with geometric wallpaper, black-and-white framed historic photos curated by the San Francisco Public Library, and ornate wooden furnishings. **Pros:** artsy rooms with timeless feel, gorgeous cocktail bar and paella restaurant; good online rates. **Cons:** thin walls and small rooms; not much for $31 daily amenity fee; some guests complain of unaddressed maintenance issues. [$] *Rooms from: $225* ✉ *490 Geary St., Union Sq.* ☎ *415/928–7900* 🌐 *www.warwickhotels.com/san-francisco* 🛏 *74 rooms* 🍴 *No Meals.*

The Westin St. Francis San Francisco on Union Square

$$ | **HOTEL** | The survivor of two major earthquakes, some headline-grabbing scandals, and even an attempted presidential assassination, this richly appointed and superbly located grande dame dating to 1904 is comprised of the landmark building, renovated in 2018, and

a modern 32-story tower whose glass elevators reveal Union Square views from the upper floors. **Pros:** prime Union Square location; correctly named Heavenly Bed; Chateau Montelena wine-tasting room and the excellent Clock Bar. **Cons:** rooms in original building can be small; public spaces lack the panache of days gone by; no dinner at on-site Oak Room Restaurant. $ *Rooms from: $279* ✉ *335 Powell St., Union Sq.* ☎ *415/397–7000, 888/627–8546* 🌐 *www.marriott.com* 🛏 *1,195 rooms* 🍴 *No Meals.*

Nightlife

Known more for the surrounding theater district, the square has its share of nightlife. You'll find places pouring interesting cocktails, a good mix of locals and tourists, and nods to nightspots and eras past.

BARS

Iron Horse Cocktails

COCKTAIL LOUNGES | Tucked away on lovely Maiden Lane, this warm and welcoming two-level space offers respite from the bustle of Union Square. Talented bartenders make good use of fresh fruit in reasonably priced seasonal cocktails, while muted jazz, dim lighting, and oil paintings in gilded frames create an intimate vibe. Upstairs tables overlooking the lane are particularly cozy. ✉ *25 Maiden La., Union Sq.* 🌐 *www.ironhorsesf.com.*

Le Colonial

COCKTAIL LOUNGES | Down an easy-to-miss alley off Taylor Street is what appears to be a two-story plantation house in the center of the city. Without being kitschy, the top-floor bar successfully evokes French-colonial Vietnam, thanks to creaky wooden floors, wicker Victorian sofas, and a patio with potted palms. It's open Friday and Saturday only, when live music accompanies tasty French-Vietnamese food and tropical cocktails. ✉ *20 Cosmo Pl., off Taylor St., between Post and Sutter Sts., Union Sq.* ☎ *415/931–3600* 🌐 *www.lecolonialsf.com.*

Pacific Cocktail Haven

COCKTAIL LOUNGES | Retro tiki kitsch meets tropical sophistication at award-winning PCH, a lively favorite for evening cocktails. As the name suggests, Asia Pacific flavors—shiso, ume, li hing mui, pandan—abound on the booklike cocktail menu, and the talented bartenders make reliable recommendations. Fun theme nights and whimsical mugs are common. ✉ *550 Sutter St., Union Sq.* 🌐 *www.pacificcocktailsf.com.*

Redwood Room

COCKTAIL LOUNGES | Opened in 1933, this lounge at the Clift Hotel is a San Francisco icon. The art-deco bar itself and the wood-paneled room are constructed from a single old redwood tree, giving a distinct only-in-California sense of place. Cocktails are a mix of high-quality classics and slightly creative newcomers. ✉ *The Clift Royal Sonesta Hotel, 495 Geary St., Union Sq.* ☎ *415/929–2372 table reservations* 🌐 *redwoodroomsf.com.*

Performing Arts

THEATER

American Conservatory Theater

THEATER | One of the nation's leading regional theater companies presents about eight plays a year, from classics to contemporary works, often in repertory. The season runs from early fall to late spring. In December ACT stages a beloved version of Charles Dickens's *A Christmas Carol.* ✉ *415 Geary St., Union Sq.* ☎ *415/749–2228* 🌐 *www.act-sf.org.*

Curran Theater

THEATER | Some of the biggest touring shows come to this local gem, which has hosted classical music, dance, and stage performances since its 1922 opening. Productions are of the long-running Broadway musical variety, such as *Stomp* and *The Book of Mormon.* ✉ *445 Geary St., Union Sq.* ☎ *415/358–1220* 🌐 *sfcurran.com.*

🛍 Shopping

Serious shoppers head straight to Union Square, San Francisco's main shopping area and the site of department stores including Macy's, Neiman Marcus, and Saks Fifth Avenue. Nearby are such platinum-card international boutiques as Yves Saint Laurent, Cartier, Giorgio Armani, Gucci, Hermès, and Louis Vuitton. The Westfield San Francisco Centre, anchored by Bloomingdale's and Nordstrom, is notable for its gorgeous atriums and top-notch dining options.

■TIP➜ Most retailers in the square don't open until 10 am or later, so there isn't much advantage to getting an early start unless you're grabbing breakfast nearby. If you're on the prowl for art, be aware that many galleries are closed on Sunday and Monday.

ART GALLERIES
Hang Art
ART GALLERIES | A spirit of fun imbues this inviting space that showcases local emerging artists. Prices range from a few hundred dollars to several thousand, making it an ideal place for novice collectors to get their feet wet. ⊠ 567 Sutter St., 2nd fl., near Mason St., Union Sq. ☎ 415/434–4264 ⊕ hangart.com.

CLOTHING
Cable Car Clothiers
MEN'S CLOTHING | This classic British menswear store, open since 1939, is so fully stocked that a whole room is dedicated to hats, pants are cataloged like papers in file cabinets, and entire displays showcase badger-bristle shaving brushes. The cable-car logo gear, from silk ties to pewter banks, makes for dashing souvenirs. ⊠ 110 Sutter St., Suite 108, Union Sq. ☎ 415/397–4740 ⊕ cable-carclothiers.com.

Levi's
MIXED CLOTHING | A San Francisco icon, founded in 1853, Levi's offers every style, size, color, and cut of 501s for men and women at its massive flagship store. You can even get a custom fitting if you book ahead of time. ⊠ 815 Market St., Union Sq. ☎ 415/501–0100 ⊕ www.levi.com.

ELECTRONICS
Apple Store Union Square
ELECTRONICS | Apple's flagship San Francisco store is a two-level, open-air tech temple to Macs, iPads, iPhones, and Apple Watches. Inside, it's more about getting your iPhone fixed at the Genius Grove, but outside everyone is using those phones to take pictures of the modern structure. ⊠ 300 Post St., Union Sq. ☎ 415/486–4800 ⊕ www.apple.com.

HOUSEWARES AND GIFTS
Samuel Scheuer
HOUSEWARES | A San Francisco staple since the 1930s, this decadent shop draws designers and other fans for its luxurious bed and bath items and linens. The pretty tablecloths, runners, napkins, fragrant candles, and luxurious bath accessories are popular gifts. ⊠ 340 Sutter St., between Grant Ave. and Stockton St., Union Sq. ☎ 415/392–2813 ⊕ www.scheuerlinens.com ⊙ Closed Sun.

Williams Sonoma
HOUSEWARES | Behind a historical facade lies the massive mothership of the Sonoma-founded kitchen-store empire. La Cornue custom stoves beckon you in, and two grand staircases draw you up to the world of dinnerware, linens, and chefs' tools. Antique tart tins, eggbeaters, and pastry cutters from the personal collection of founder Chuck Williams line the walls. ⊠ 340 Post St., Union Sq. ☎ 415/362–9450 ⊕ www.williams-sonoma.com.

JEWELRY
Shreve & Co.
JEWELRY & WATCHES | Along with gems in dazzling settings, San Francisco's oldest retail store—it's been in business since 1852—carries luxury watches by Jaeger-LeCoultre and others. On Saturdays well-heeled couples scope out hefty diamond engagement rings. ⊠ 150 Post

St., Union Sq. ☎ *415/421–2600* ⊕ *shreve. com* ⊗ *Closed Sun.*

TEXTILES
★ Britex Fabrics
FABRICS | Walls of Italian wool in deep, rich colors, yards of faille-striped silk, and neat stacks of fresh cotton prints await your creative touch. A San Francisco institution for more than 70 years, the two-story Britex also sells an endless variety of buttons as well as thread and trim. If sewing is your thing, this will be a visit to paradise. ⊠ *117 Post St., Union Sq.* ☎ *415/392–2910* ⊕ *www.britexfabrics.com* ⊗ *Closed weekends.*

Civic Center

San Francisco's eye-catching, gold-domed City Hall presides over this patchy neighborhood bordered roughly by Franklin, McAllister, Hyde, and Grove Streets. The optimistic "City Beautiful" movement of the early 20th century produced the Beaux Arts–style complex for which the district is named, including City Hall, the War Memorial Opera House, and the old public library, now the home of the Asian Art Museum. The wonderful Main Library on Larkin Street between Fulton and Grove Streets is a modern variation on Civic Center's architectural theme.

The Civic Center area may have been set up on City Beautiful principles, but illusion soon gives way to reality. The buildings are grand, but many of the city's most destitute residents eke out an existence on the neighborhood's streets and plazas. Tickets to shows, concerts, operas, or ballet at one of the grand performance halls are the main reason many venture here, and major city events like the Pride parade and Giants' victory celebrations draw big crowds.

⊙ Sights

★ Asian Art Museum
ART MUSEUM | You don't have to be a connoisseur of Asian art to appreciate this newly expanded museum, whose monumental exterior conceals a light, open, and welcoming space. The fraction of the museum's collection on display (about 2,500 pieces out of 18,000-plus total) is laid out thematically and by region, making it easy to follow historical developments.

Begin on the third floor, where highlights of Buddhist art in Southeast Asia and early China include a large, jewel-encrusted, exquisitely painted 19th-century Burmese Buddha and clothed rod puppets from Java. On the second floor you can find later Chinese works, as well as exquisite pieces from Korea and Japan. The ground floor is devoted to temporary exhibits and the museum's wonderful gift shop. During spring and summer, visit on Thursday evenings for extended programs and sip drinks while a DJ spins tunes. ⊠ *200 Larkin St., Civic Center* ☎ *415/581–3500* ⊕ *asianart.org* 🎫 *$20, free 1st Sun. of month; $10 Thurs. 5–8* ⊗ *Closed Tues. and Wed.*

★ City Hall
GOVERNMENT BUILDING | This imposing 1915 structure with its massive gold-leaf dome—higher than the U.S. Capitol's—is as close to a palace as you'll find in San Francisco: the classic granite-and-marble behemoth was modeled after St. Peter's Basilica in Rome. Architect Arthur Brown Jr., who was also behind Coit Tower and the War Memorial Opera House, designed an interior with grand columns and a sweeping central staircase. The 1899 structure it replaced had taken 27 years to erect, but it collapsed in about 27 seconds during the 1906 earthquake.

City Hall was seismically retrofitted in the late 1990s, but the sense of history remains palpable, and you can learn about it on a free tour. Some noteworthy

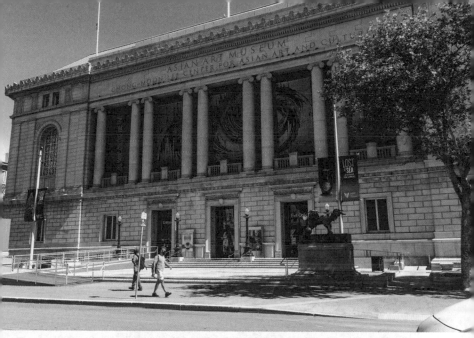

The Asian Art Museum displays art and artifacts from throughout the continent, some as much as 6,000 years old.

events that have taken place here include the hosing of civil-rights and freedom-of-speech protesters (1960); the assassinations of Mayor George Moscone and Harvey Milk (1978); the torching of the lobby by angry members of the gay community in response to the light sentence given to their killer (1979); and the first domestic partnership registrations of gay couples (1991). In 2004, Mayor Gavin Newsom took a stand against then-current state and federal law by issuing marriage licenses to same-sex partners.

Across Polk Street from City Hall is Civic Center Plaza, with an outdoor café, flower beds, and a playground. This sprawling space is generally clean but somewhat grim, as many homeless people hang out here. ⊠ *1 Dr. Carlton B. Goodlett Pl., Civic Center* ☎ *415/554–4000, 415/554–6139 tour reservations* ⊕ *sfgov.org/cityhall/city-hall-tours* ⊠ *Free* ⊙ *Closed weekends.*

★ Louise M. Davies Symphony Hall
PERFORMANCE VENUE | Fascinating and futuristic, this 2,739-seat hall is the home of the San Francisco Symphony.

The glass wraparound lobby and pop-out balcony are visible from outside, as is the Henry Moore bronze sculpture on the sidewalk. The hall's 59 adjustable Plexiglas acoustical disks cascade from the ceiling like hanging windshields. Concerts range from typical symphonic fare to more unusual performances, such as singer Al Green and film screenings with a live orchestra performing the score. ⊠ *201 Van Ness Ave., Civic Center* ☎ *415/552–8338* ⊕ *www.sfsymphony. org.*

San Francisco Public Library
LIBRARY | Topped with a swirl like an art-deco nautilus, the library's seven-level glass atrium fills the building with light. Local researchers take advantage of centers dedicated to gay and lesbian, African American, Chinese, and Filipino history. The sixth-floor San Francisco History Center has fun exhibits of city ephemera, including a treat for fans of noir fiction: novelist Dashiell Hammett's typewriter. ⊠ *100 Larkin St., Civic Center* ☎ *415/557–4400* ⊕ *sfpl.org.*

War Memorial Opera House

PERFORMANCE VENUE | After San Francisco's original opera houses were destroyed in the 1906 quake, architect Arthur Brown Jr. was commissioned to design this stunning Renaissance-style building. Named in tribute to the city's soldiers lost in World War I, it was inaugurated in 1932 with a performance of *Tosca*. It has since played host to two major historic events: the drafting of the United Nations charter in 1945 and the ceremony six years later in which the United States restored sovereignty to Japan. Modeled after its European counterparts, the building has a vaulted and coffered ceiling, marble foyer, two balconies, and a huge silver art-deco chandelier that resembles a sunburst. The San Francisco Opera performs here from September into December and in summer; the opera house hosts the San Francisco Ballet from December through May. ✉ *301 Van Ness Ave., Civic Center* ☎ *415/621–6600* 🌐 *sfwarmemorial.org.*

Coffee and Quick Bites

★ Arsicault

$ | **BAKERY** | This white, high-ceilinged space offers what some claim are the best croissants—not only outside France, but in the world. You simply can't go wrong with anything on the menu. **Known for:** exquisite croissants; enthusiastic following; specials run out quickly. [$] *Average main: $6* ✉ *87 McAllister St., Civic Center* ☎ *415/926–5155* 🌐 *arsicault-bakery.com.*

Nightlife

Lawyers, politicians, and others in the government biz populate this neighborhood by day, and at night the scene tends to remain buttoned-up.

MUSIC CLUBS

Warfield

LIVE MUSIC | A former movie palace is now one of the city's largest rock venues, with folding chairs or standing space (depending on the event) downstairs and theater seating upstairs. The historic venue has booked everyone from Prince and the Grateful Dead to the Killers. ✉ *982 Market St., Civic Center* ☎ *415/345–0900* 🌐 *www.thewarfieldtheatre.com.*

Performing Arts

DANCE

★ San Francisco Ballet

BALLET | For ballet lovers, the nation's oldest professional company is reason alone to visit San Francisco. The primary season runs from January through May with a repertoire including full-length ballets such as *Don Quixote* and *Sleeping Beauty*; the December presentation of *The Nutcracker* is truly spectacular. The company also performs bold new dances from star choreographers such as William Forsythe and Mark Morris, alongside modern classics by George Balanchine and Jerome Robbins. ✉ *War Memorial Opera House, 301 Van Ness Ave., Civic Center* ☎ *415/865–2000* 🌐 *www.sfballet.org.*

MUSIC

★ San Francisco Opera

OPERA | Founded in 1923, this internationally recognized organization has occupied the War Memorial Opera House since the building's completion in 1932. From September–December and June–July, the company presents a wide range of operas, from *Carmen* to an operatic version of *It's a Wonderful Life*. The opera often takes on ambitious world premieres as well as unconventional, edgy projects designed to attract younger audiences. Translations are projected above the stage during most non-English productions. ✉ *War Memorial Opera House, 301 Van Ness Ave., Civic Center* ☎ *415/864–3330 tickets* 🌐 *sfopera.com.*

★ San Francisco Symphony

MUSIC | One of America's top orchestras performs from September through May, with additional summer performances

The critically acclaimed San Francisco Ballet performs a blend of traditional and modern works.

of light classical music and show tunes. The symphony is known for its daring programming of 20th-century American works, often performed with soloists of the caliber of André Watts, Gil Shaham, and Renée Fleming. ✉ *Louise M. Davies Symphony Hall, 201 Van Ness Ave., Civic Center* ☎ *415/864–6000* ⊕ *www.sfsymphony.org.*

SPOKEN WORD AND READINGS
★ City Arts & Lectures
READINGS/LECTURES | Each year this program includes more than 20 fascinating conversations with writers, composers, actors, politicians, scientists, and others. Past speakers have included Diane Keaton, Ken Burns, and Patti Smith. ✉ *Sydney Goldstein Theater, 275 Hayes St., Civic Center* ☎ *415/392–4400* ⊕ *www.cityarts.net.*

THEATRE
New Conservatory Theatre Center
THEATER | This three-stage complex focuses on contemporary LGBTQ+-themed works and newer small-production musicals, as well educational plays and classes for young people. ✉ *25 Van Ness Ave., Civic Center* ☎ *415/861–8972* ⊕ *www.nctcsf.org.*

🛍 Shopping

FARMERS' MARKETS
Heart of the City Farmers' Market
MARKET | After you experience the Ferry Building's fancy Saturday celebrity-chef extravaganza, head to the city's workaday market (Wednesday and Sunday). Vendors at the city's only farmer-operated farmers' market sell heaps of fresh produce, along with baked goods, jams, potted herbs, and plenty of delicious snacks and on-the-go lunches from local artisans. ✉ *United Nations Plaza, along Market St., Civic Center* ☎ *415/558–9455* ⊕ *hotcfarmersmarket.org.*

Built as a bordello in 1907, the Great American Music Hall now pulls in top-tier performers.

Tenderloin

Stretching west of Union Square and north of Civic Center, the Tenderloin is the poster child for the city's challenges: low-income families huddle in tiny apartments; single-room-occupancy hotels offer shelter a step up from living on the street; drug dealing and prostitution are common; and very few green spaces break up the monotony of high-rises. So why would anyone go out of their way to come here? Well, exceptional Vietnamese food, for one thing, but these days more than just the great pho is luring people. Trendy watering holes and coffee shops are springing up, with a handful of intrepid hipsters moving in after them. The Tenderloin may be on its way to becoming the next Mission, but for now it remains a gritty slice of San Francisco.

■ **TIP→ Some parts of the Tenderloin are more dangerous than others, and a single street can change from block to block. Little Saigon's Larkin Street corridor is relatively safe during the day, as are most streets north of Ellis (an area that realtors insist on calling the TenderNob for its proximity to Nob Hill). Avoid walking the last two blocks of Turk Street and Golden Gate Avenue before they meet Market Street, along with Hyde Street and Leavenworth Street between Ellis Street and Turk Street. Don't walk alone or look at your phone when walking here.**

🍴 Restaurants

A land of dive bars, panhandlers, and some of the best pho and banh mi in the city, this seedy district encompasses Little Saigon. Locals come here for great cheap eats, including not just Vietnamese but naans and masalas.

Bodega SF

$$$ | **VIETNAMESE** | Chef Matthew Ho cut his teeth at his family's excellent, barebones Bodega Bistro, an anchor of the Little Saigon restaurant scene for years. This new incarnation elevates traditional Vietnamese recipes with a modern twist

and the freshest ingredients. **Known for:** well-paired cocktails; hopping late-night dining scene; complex and delightful beef carpaccio. [$] *Average main: $32* ✉ *138 Mason St., Tenderloin* 🌐 *bodegarestaurants.com* 🕒 *Closed Tues.*

Brenda's French Soul Food
$ | **CREOLE** | The good times roll at the city's definitive choice for New Orleans cooking. Brunch is the preferred meal here, but it's just as good to come for a weekday lunch of gumbo or a fried chicken dinner when the scene is a little more subdued. **Known for:** delicious beignets; broiled oysters; lots of charm and fun. [$] *Average main: $19* ✉ *652 Polk St., Tenderloin* ☎ *415/345–8100* 🌐 *frenchsoulfood.com* 🕒 *Closed Tues. and Wed.*

Lers Ros
$ | **THAI** | Try something beyond the same old pad thai at this authentic Thai standby. Thai herb sausage and papaya salad with salted egg are good appetizers to share, while the pork belly with crispy rind and basil leaves and duck *larb* (meat salad) come packed with flavor and heat. **Known for:** exciting, rarely seen dishes; extensive menu; post-drinking hangout. [$] *Average main: $19* ✉ *730 Larkin St., Tenderloin* ☎ *415/931–6917* 🌐 *lersros.com.*

Coffee and Quick Bites

Saigon Sandwich
$ | **VIETNAMESE** | Stop by this hole in the wall for some of the best—and cheapest!—takeout banh mi in the city. Favorites include *thit* (roast pork) and *ga* (roast chicken). **Known for:** generous portions; really low prices; bare-bones storefront. [$] *Average main: $5* ✉ *560 Larkin St., between Eddy and Turk Sts., Tenderloin* ☎ *415/474–5698* 🌐 *www.facebook.com/saigonsandwich* 🕒 *No dinner.*

Little Saigon 🍴

The best Vietnamese food in the city can be found along Larkin Street between Turk and O'Farrell Streets, where Vietnamese Americans own most of the businesses. Marketing types call this corridor Little Saigon; locals associate it with the Tenderloin. You can find cheap, often fantastic food here, particularly pho (beef- or chicken-broth noodle soup). Check out Turtle Tower (✉ *645 Larkin St.*) for pho, Hai Ky Mi Gia (✉ *707 Ellis St.*) for braised duck-leg noodles, and Sing Sing (✉ *309 Hyde St.*) or Saigon Sandwich (✉ *560 Larkin St.*) for banh mi.

Hotels

The Tenderloin contains some hip boutique hotels. Many transients live here, and the streets can feel seedy even during the day.

The LINE SF
$$ | **HOTEL** | This art-driven hotel draws creatives and tech workers with its effortlessly chic design, central location, and rooftop bar. **Pros:** inspired design featuring local art; central location; 24-hour fitness center with Peloton bikes. **Cons:** valet parking only; gritty neighborhood; unusually high amenity fee. [$] *Rooms from: $307* ✉ *33 Turk St., Tenderloin* ☎ *415/475–0000* 🌐 *www.thelinehotel.com/san francisco* 🛏 *236 rooms* 🍽 *No Meals.*

Phoenix Hotel
$ | **HOTEL** | A magnet for the music- and film-industry crowd, the Phoenix is retro and low-key, with colorful furniture and original pieces by local artists, as well as modern amenities like free Wi-Fi. **Pros:** mellow staffers set the cool tone; heated outdoor pool but no resort fee; free parking. **Cons:** seedy location; no

elevators; frequent party vibe. $ *Rooms from: $185* ✉ *601 Eddy St., Tenderloin* ☎ *415/776–1380* ⊕ *www.phoenixsf.com* ⤶ *44 rooms* ⦿ *No Meals.*

★ San Francisco Proper Hotel

$$$ | **HOTEL** | Inside the magnificent, flatiron-shape Beaux Arts–style building is one of the city's most spectacular places to stay, a sharp, upscale, ultra-hip boutique hotel; in contrast, outside is one of the roughest intersections for street life in San Francisco. **Pros:** gorgeous lobby; excellent restaurant and cocktails; tech elements like wireless speakers and smart TV. **Cons:** high price for difficult location; too cool for many tastes; $36 daily fee for amenities. $ *Rooms from: $375* ✉ *1100 Market St., Tenderloin* ⤖ *Entrance at 45 McAllister St.* ☎ *415/737–7777, 888/730–4299* reservations ⊕ *properhotel.com/san-francisco* ⤶ *131 rooms* ⦿ *No Meals.*

🍸 Nightlife

The Loin is known for its grittiness, but it's also centrally located and could be the perfect place to start (or end) your night on the town.

BARS

★ Bourbon & Branch

COCKTAIL LOUNGES | Although this spot reeks of Prohibition-era speakeasy cool, it's not exclusive (though it's highly recommended to book a reservation). The place has sex appeal, with tin ceilings, bordello-red silk wallpaper, intimate booths, and low lighting; loud conversations and cell phones are not allowed. The menu of spirit-forward cocktails and quality bourbon and whiskey is substantial. A speakeasy within the speakeasy called Wilson & Wilson is more exclusive but just as funky. ✉ *501 Jones St., Tenderloin* ☎ *415/346–1735* ⊕ *www.bourbonandbranch.com.*

Charmaine's

COCKTAIL LOUNGES | Euro-chic yet comfortable, this rooftop lounge serves up jaw-dropping skyline views along with sophisticated small bites and expert cocktails—it's not hard to reach the $65 per person minimum spend. The indoor space is cozy and intimate, and the outdoor tables with personal fire pits are popular, so reservations are a good idea. ✉ *San Francisco Proper Hotel, 1100 Market St., entrance at 45 McAllister St., Tenderloin* ☎ *628/895–2039* ⊕ *www.properhotel.com/san-francisco/restaurants-bars/charmaines.*

MUSIC CLUBS

Great American Music Hall

LIVE MUSIC | You'll find top-drawer entertainment at this eclectic venue. Acts range from the best in blues, folk, and jazz to up-and-coming alternative artists. The colorful marble-pillared club, built in 1907 as a bordello, accommodates dancing at some shows. Pub grub is available most nights. ✉ *859 O'Farrell St., Tenderloin* ☎ *415/885–0750* ⊕ *gamh.com.*

🎭 Performing Arts

THEATER

Golden Gate Theatre

THEATER | Stylishly refurbished, this movie theater is now primarily a musical house. Touring productions of Broadway shows and revivals are its mainstays. ✉ *1 Taylor St., Tenderloin* ☎ *888/746–1799* ⊕ *www.broadwaysf.com.*

★ Orpheum Theatre

THEATER | The biggest touring shows perform at this gorgeously restored 2,200-seat venue. The theater, opened in 1926, is as much an attraction as the shows. It was modeled after a 12th-century French cathedral and is considered one of the most beautiful theaters in the world; the interior walls have ornate stonework, and the gilded plaster ceiling is perforated with tiny lights. ✉ *1192 Market St., Tenderloin* ☎ *888/746–1799* ⊕ *www.broadwaysf.com.*

Chapter 5

THE WATERFRONT

Updated by
Trevor Felch

Sights	Restaurants	Hotels	Shopping	Nightlife
★★★☆☆	★★★☆☆	★★☆☆☆	★★☆☆☆	★★☆☆☆

NEIGHBORHOOD SNAPSHOT

TOP EXPERIENCES

■ **Ferry Building:** Join locals eyeing produce and foods prepared by some of the city's best chefs at San Francisco's premier Saturday farmers' market.

■ **Hyde Street Pier:** Sing sea chanteys and raise the sails aboard the 19th-century square-rigged ship *Balclutha,* then hit the Buena Vista for an Irish coffee.

■ **Alcatraz:** Go from a scenic bay tour to "the hole"—solitary confinement in absolute darkness—while inmates and guards tell you stories about what life was really like on the Rock.

■ **F-line:** Grab a polished wooden seat aboard one of the city's vintage streetcars and clatter down the tracks toward the Ferry Building's spire.

■ **Exploratorium:** Play with the ultimate marble run or explore yourself in the Science of Sharing exhibit at this spectacular hands-on science museum.

GETTING HERE

The Powell–Hyde and Powell–Mason cable-car lines both end near Fisherman's Wharf. The walk from downtown through North Beach to the northern waterfront is lovely, and if you stick to Columbus Avenue, the incline is relatively gentle. F-line trolleys run all the way down Market to the Embarcadero, then north to the wharf.

PAUSE HERE

Situated between the Ferry Building and Bay Bridge, *Cupid's Span* is a stunning 60-foot-tall sculpture designed by husband-and-wife team Claes Oldenburg and Coosje van Bruggen. Supposedly, Cupid left his bow and arrow in the ground here—like so many people leave their hearts in San Francisco (per Tony Bennett's song). Pause here and soak up the grandeur of the Bay Bridge, the Embarcadero, and the skyline surrounding you. There are some nearby benches and tables to sit at. Then look at the nearby water because you'll almost certainly see a seal or two popping up in this spot.

PLANNING YOUR TIME

■ If you're planning to go to Alcatraz, be sure to buy your tickets in advance, as tours frequently sell out. Alcatraz ferries leave from Pier 33—so there isn't a single good reason to suffer Pier 39's tacky, overpriced attractions. If you're a sailor at heart, though, definitely spend an hour with the historic ships of the Hyde Street Pier.

FERRIES

■ The bay is a huge part of San Francisco's charm, and getting out on the water gives you an attractive and unique (though windy) perspective on the city.

■ A ride on a commuter ferry is cheaper than a cruise, and just as lovely.

■ The **Blue & Gold Fleet** (⊕ blueandgoldfleet.com) offers scenic bay cruises around Alcatraz and under the Golden Gate Bridge.

■ The **Red and White Fleet** (⊕ redandwhite.com) offers cruises to the Golden Gate Bridge and the Bay Bridge—and beautiful sunset trips—all of which deliver splendid views of San Francisco.

San Francisco's waterfront neighborhoods have fabulous views and utterly different personalities.

Kitschy, overpriced Fisherman's Wharf struggles to maintain the last shreds of its existence as a working wharf, while Pier 39 is a full-fledged consumer circus. The Ferry Building draws well-heeled locals with its culinary pleasures, firmly connecting the Embarcadero and downtown. Between the Ferry Building and Pier 39, a former maritime no-man's-land, are the Exploratorium, a $90-million cruise-ship terminal, Alcatraz Landing, fashionable waterfront restaurants, and restored, pedestrian-friendly piers.

Fisherman's Wharf

The crack of fresh Dungeness crab, the aroma of sourdough warm from the oven, the cry of the gulls—in some ways you can experience Fisherman's Wharf today as it has been for more than 100 years. Italians began fishing these waters in the 19th century as immigrants to booming Barbary Coast San Francisco. A handful of family businesses established generations ago continue to this day, like the Alioto-Lazio Fish Company, selling crab fresh off the boat here since the 1940s.

As the local fishing industry has contracted and environmental awareness has changed fishing regulations, Fisherman's Wharf has morphed. Fewer families make a living off the sea here, fewer fishing boats go out, and more of the wharf survives on tourist dollars. You'll see more schlock here than in any other neighborhood in town: overpriced food alongside discount electronics stores, bargain-luggage outlets, and cheap T-shirts and souvenirs.

It's enough to send locals running for the hills, but there are things here worth experiencing. Explore maritime history aboard the fabulous ships of the Hyde Street Pier, amuse yourself early-20th-century style with the mechanical diversions at Musée Mécanique, and grab a bowl of chowder or some Dungeness crab from one of the stands along Jefferson Street to get a taste (and distinct shellfish aroma) of what made Fisherman's Wharf what it is in the first place. If you come early, you can avoid the crowds and get a sense of the Wharf's functional side: it's not entirely an amusement-park replica.

◉ Sights

Aquatic Park
BEACH | This urban beach, surrounded by Fort Mason, Ghirardelli Square, and Fisherman's Wharf, is a quarter-mile-long strip of sand. The gentle waters near shore are shallow, safe for kids to swim or wade, and fairly clean. Locals come out for quick dips in the frigid water. Members of the Dolphin Club and the South End Rowing Club come every morning for a swim, and a large and raucous crowd braves the cold on New Year's Day. **Amenities:** food and drink; showers; toilets. **Best for:** sunset; walking. ⊠ *San Francisco Maritime National Historical Park, 499 Jefferson St., at Hyde St., Fisherman's Wharf* ⊕ *www.nps.gov/safr.*

Cartoon Art Museum
OTHER MUSEUM | **FAMILY** | Snoopy, Wonder Woman, Batman, and other colorful cartoon icons greet you at the Cartoon Art Museum, established with an endowment from the late cartoonist-icon

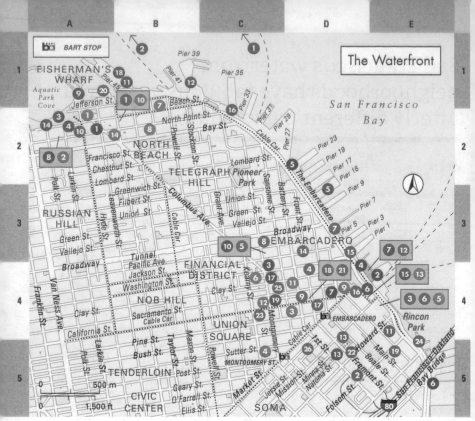

The Waterfront

Sights ▼

1 Alcatraz C1
2 Angel Island
   State Park B1
3 Aquatic Park A2
4 Cartoon Art Museum ... A2
5 Exploratorium D3
6 F-line D4
7 Ferry Building E3
8 Ghirardelli Square A2
9 Hyde Street Pier A1
10 Jackson Square
   Historic District C3
11 Musée Mécanique B1
12 Pier 39 .... B1
13 Salesforce Park D5
14 San Francisco National
   Maritime Museum A2
15 San Francisco
   Railway Museum E4
16 SS *Jeremiah O'Brien* C2
17 Transamerica
   Pyramid C4
18 USS *Pampanito* B1

19 Wells Fargo
   History Museum C4

Restaurants ▼

1 Abacá B2
2 Akikos D5
3 Angler E4
4 Bar Sprezzatura D4
5 BIX C3
6 Boulevard E4
7 Coqueta D3
8 Cotogna C3
9 Estiatorio Ornos D4
10 Gary Danko A2
11 GOZU E4
12 Hog Island
   Oyster Company E3
13 International Smoke
   San Francisco D4
14 Kokkari Estiatorio D3
15 La Mar Cebicheria
   Peruana D3
16 One Market D4
17 Pabu Izakaya D4

18 Perbacco D4
19 Prospect E5
20 Scoma's A1
21 Tadich Grill D4
22 Town Hall D5
23 The Vault Garden C4
24 Waterbar E5
25 Wayfare Tavern C4
26 Yank Sing D5

Quick Bites ▼

1 Cafe de Casa A2
2 Grande Crêperie E4
3 Maison Nico C4
4 Peaches Patties D4
5 Pier 23 Cafe D2
6 Red's Java House E5
7 Terminus Cafe
   and Bar D4

Hotels ▼

1 Argonaut Hotel A2
2 Fairmont Heritage
   Place A2
3 Four Seasons Hotel
   San Francisco at
   Embarcadero D4
4 Galleria Park Hotel C5
5 Harbor Court Hotel E4
6 Hilton San Francisco
   Financial District C4
7 Hotel Zephyr B1
8 Hotel Zoe
   Fisherman's Wharf B2
9 Hyatt Regency
   San Francisco D4
10 Kimpton Alton Hotel B2
11 Le Méridien
   San Francisco D4
12 Omni San Francisco
   Hotel C4
13 1 Hotel
   San Francisco E4
14 San Francisco Marriott
   Fisherman's Wharf A2

Charles M. Schulz. The museum's strength is its changing exhibits, which have highlighted subjects such as emerging artists, the evolution of animation, and artwork that highlights the landmarks of San Francisco. Serious fans of cartoons—especially those on the quirky underground side—will likely enjoy the exhibits; those with a casual interest may be bored. The store here carries cool titles to add to your collection. ⊠ *781 Beach St., Fisherman's Wharf* ☎ *415/227–8666* ⊕ *www.cartoonart.org* ⊠ *$10.*

Ghirardelli Square

STORE/MALL | FAMILY | Most of the redbrick buildings in this complex were once part of the Ghirardelli factory, which the prominent chocolate company purchased in 1893. Tourists visit to pick up the famous chocolate and indulge in ice cream sundaes at this dessert paradise, though you can purchase the chocolates all over town and save yourself a trip to what is essentially a glamorized mall food court (Ghirardelli's factory is now in the East Bay). But it's still a must-visit destination for chocolate lovers. Placards throughout the square describe the factory's history, and the giant Ghirardelli sign above the square, erected in 1923, remains one of the city's visual icons.

Once you're tired of chocolate, there are a few notable restaurants within the square. Palette Tea House serves some of the city's most artistic dim sum, Square Pie Guys has the Bay Area's gold standard for Detroit-style square pizza, Barrio offers enjoyable tacos and margaritas, and there's a great beer garden setting at the San Francisco Brewing Co. ⊠ *900 N. Point St., Fisherman's Wharf* ☎ *415/775–5500* ⊕ *www.ghirardellisq.com.*

Hyde Street Pier

HISTORY MUSEUM | FAMILY | If you want to get to the heart of the Wharf, there's no better place to do it than at this pier. Don't pass up the centerpiece collection of historic vessels, part of the San Francisco Maritime National Historical Park,

almost all of which can be boarded. The *Balclutha*, an 1886 full-rigged three-masted sailing vessel that's more than 250 feet long, sailed around Cape Horn 17 times. Kids especially love the *Eureka*, a side-wheel passenger and car ferry, for her onboard collection of vintage cars. The *Hercules* is a steam-powered tugboat, and the *C. A. Thayer* is a beautifully restored three-masted schooner.

Across the street from the pier and a museum in itself is the maritime park's Visitor Center (⊠ *499 Jefferson St.* ☎ *415/447–5000*), whose fun, large-scale exhibits make it an engaging stop. See a huge First Order Fresnel lighthouse lens from the Farallon Islands and a shipwrecked boat. Then stroll through time in the exhibit "The Waterfront," where you can touch the timber from a gold rush–era ship recovered from below the Financial District, peek into 19th-century storefronts, and see the sails of an Italian fishing vessel. ⊠ *Hyde and Jefferson Sts., Fisherman's Wharf* ☎ *415/447–5000* ⊕ *www.nps.gov/safr* ⊠ *Ships $15 (ticket good for 7 days).*

Musée Mécanique

OTHER MUSEUM | FAMILY | Once a staple at Playland at the Beach, San Francisco's early 20th-century amusement park, the antique mechanical contrivances at this time-warp arcade—including peep shows and nickelodeons—make it one of the most worthwhile attractions at the Wharf. Some favorites are the giant and rather creepy "Laffing Sal"; an arm-wrestling machine; the world's only steam-powered motorcycle; and mechanical fortune-telling figures that speak from their curtained boxes. Note the depictions of race that betray the prejudices of the time: stoned Chinese figures in the "Opium-Den" and clown-faced African Americans eating watermelon in the "Mechanical Farm." ■**TIP→ Admission is free, but you'll need quarters to bring the machines to life.** ⊠ *Pier 45, Shed A,*

Pier 39's shops and amusements lure millions of tourists each year.

Fisherman's Wharf ☎ 415/346–2000 ⊕ *museemecaniquesf.com* ✉ *Free.*

Pier 39

STORE/MALL | FAMILY | The city's most popular waterfront attraction draws millions of visitors each year, who come to browse through its shops and concessions hawking every conceivable form of souvenir. The pier can be quite crowded, and the numerous street performers may leave you feeling more harassed than entertained. Arriving early in the morning ensures you a front-row view of the sea lions that bask here, but be aware that most stores don't open until 9:30 or 10 (later in winter).

Follow the sound of barking to the northwest side of the pier to view the sea lions flopping about the floating docks. During the summer, orange-clad naturalists offer fascinating facts about the playful pinnipeds—for example, that most of the animals here are males.

At the Aquarium of the Bay (⊕ *aquariumofthebay.org*), moving walkways

transport you through a space surrounded on three sides by water filled with indigenous San Francisco Bay marine life, from the orange Garibaldi (the state marine fish) to sharks. ✉ *Beach St., at Embarcadero, Fisherman's Wharf* ☎ *415/705–5500* ⊕ *www.pier39.com.*

San Francisco National Maritime Museum

HISTORY MUSEUM | FAMILY | You'll feel as if you're out to sea when you step inside this sturdy, ship-shape (literally), Streamline-Moderne structure, dubbed the Bathhouse Building and built in 1939 as part of the New Deal's Works Progress Administration. The first floor of the museum, part of the San Francisco Maritime National Historical Park, has stunningly restored undersea dreamscape murals and some of the museum's intricate ship models. The first-floor balcony overlooks the beach and has lovely WPA-era tile designs. ■**TIP→ If you've got young kids in tow, the museum makes a great quick, free stop. Then pick up ice cream at Ghirardelli Square across the street and enjoy it on the beach or next door**

in Victorian Park, where you can watch the cable cars turn around. ✉ *Aquatic Park, foot of Polk St., Fisherman's Wharf* ☎ *415/447–5000* 🌐 *www.nps.gov/safr* ⏲ *Closed Mon. and Tues.*

SS *Jeremiah O'Brien*

NAUTICAL SIGHT | A participant in the D-Day landing in Normandy during World War II, this Liberty Ship freighter is one of two such vessels still in working order. On board you can peek at the crew's living quarters and the officers' mess hall. The large display of the Normandy invasion, one of many exhibits on board, was a gift from France. To keep the 1943 ship in sailing shape, the steam engine—which appears in the film *Titanic*—is operated dockside a few times a year on special "steaming weekends." Most recently, the ship escaped damage from a major 2020 fire at its home dock, Pier 45. Visitors can explore the ship at the dock or enjoy one of the bay cruises that happen on select days throughout the year. ✉ *Pier 45, Fisherman's Wharf* ☎ *415/544–0100* 🌐 *www.ssjeremiahobrien.org* 🎟 *$20.*

USS *Pampanito*

NAUTICAL SIGHT | Get an intriguing, if mildly claustrophobic, glimpse into life on a submarine during World War II on this small, 80-person sub, which sank six Japanese warships and damaged four others. ■ **TIP→ There's not much in the way of interpretive signs, so use the free audio tour to learn about what you're seeing.** ✉ *Pier 45, Fisherman's Wharf* ☎ *415/775–1943* 🌐 *maritime.org/uss-pampanito* 🎟 *From $25.*

🍴 Restaurants

To the north of the Ferry Building lies Fisherman's Wharf, a jumbled mix of seafood dining rooms, sidewalk vendors, and trinket shops that visitors religiously trudge through and San Franciscans invariably dismiss as a tourist trap. But even locals may come for a cracked crab.

★ Abacá

$$ | FILIPINO | Defeating the cliché that restaurants in hotels can't be citywide draws, chef Francis Ang's longtime Pinoy Heritage pop-up is thriving at its permanent home within the Kimpton Alton Hotel. Ang's exciting contemporary Filipino cooking has gained rave reviews from national publications and well-deserved awards. **Known for:** innovative desserts and terrific weekend morning pastries; any pancit noodle dish; cocktails that are as exciting as the food. [$] *Average main: $26* ✉ *Kimpton Alton Hotel, 2700 Jones St., Fisherman's Wharf* ☎ *486–0788* 🌐 *restaurantabaca.com* ⏲ *No dinner Sun. No lunch weekdays.*

Gary Danko

$$$$ | MODERN AMERICAN | This classic for prix-fixe dining has earned legions of fans—and a Michelin star—for its refined and creative seasonal California cooking, displayed in dishes like glazed oysters with Ossetra caviar and juniper-crusted venison. The banquette-lined rooms, with stunning floral arrangements, are as memorable as the food and impeccable service. **Known for:** tableside cheese cart; soufflé for dessert; reservations are hard to get. [$] *Average main: $122* ✉ *800 N. Point St., Fisherman's Wharf* ☎ *415/749–2060* 🌐 *garydanko.com* ⏲ *Closed Tues. and Wed. No lunch.*

Scoma's

$$$$ | SEAFOOD | Ask locals where to eat at Fisherman's Wharf and you'll usually get a blank look, but the answer is this San Francisco classic that is undoubtedly the leader among its peers (or piers?). The Pier 47 spot was a coffee shop when brothers Al and Jay Scoma bought it in 1965 (the homey coffeehouse vibe still lingers around the retro-meets-contemporary space), and the restaurant continues to be a great stop for excellent fresh fish and seafood preparations. **Known for:** excellent crab Louis; one of the city's best cioppinos; surprisingly great cocktails and wine. [$] *Average* *main: $46* ✉ *1965 Al Scoma Way, Pier 47, Fisherman's Wharf* ☎ *415/771–4383* ⊕ *scomas.com.*

☕ Coffee and Quick Bites

Cafe de Casa
$ | **BRAZILIAN** | Start the morning on the outskirts of Fisherman's Wharf with an açaí bowl and strong coffee, or enjoy puffy chicken-and-cheese-filled coxinha pastries as a lunchtime snack at this cheery stop by a quiet, grassy square. It's a breath of fresh air for visitors who are tired of crab and clam chowder. **Known for:** fresh juices; pão de queijo cheese roll; Brazilian-style hot dog snack. $ *Average main: $14* ✉ *2701 Leavenworth St., Fisherman's Wharf* ☎ *345–1055* ⊕ *cafedecasa.com* ☯ *Closed Sun. No dinner.*

🛏 Hotels

The hub of San Francisco's kitschy tourist trade, Fisherman's Wharf draws families to its chain hotels and smaller properties. Accommodations are generally playful, and many have swimming pools. The downside is that some lodgings lie far from other tourist attractions.

★ Argonaut Hotel
$$ | **HOTEL** | **FAMILY** | The nautically themed Argonaut's spacious guest rooms have exposed-brick walls, wood-beam ceilings, and best of all, windows that open to the sea air and the sounds of the waterfront; many rooms enjoy Alcatraz and Golden Gate Bridge views. **Pros:** above average seafood restaurant; near Hyde Street cable car; toys for the kids. **Cons:** nautical theme isn't for everyone; cramped public areas; far from crosstown attractions. $ *Rooms from: $289* ✉ *495 Jefferson St., at Hyde St., Fisherman's Wharf* ☎ *415/563–0800, 800/790–1415 reservations* ⊕ *www.argonauthotel.com* ⌇ *252 rooms* ⦿ *No Meals.*

Fairmont Heritage Place
$$$$ | **HOTEL** | **FAMILY** | Located in the former Ghirardelli chocolate factory, these one- to three-bedroom residences deliver elevated comfort and style, with fully equipped gourmet kitchens, brick walls, plush bedding, in-room laundry facilities, fireplaces, and modern furniture in chocolate and lavender hues. **Pros:** bay and Alcatraz views from most rooms; magnificent outdoor terrace with fire pits; pre-arrival grocery shopping can be provided. **Cons:** limited food and beverage service; steep prices; loud street noise. $ *Rooms from: $815* ✉ *900 N. Point St., Suite D100, Fisherman's Wharf* ☎ *415/268–9900* ⊕ *www.fairmont.com/ghirardelli* ⌇ *53 suites* ⦿ *No Meals.*

Hotel Zephyr
$$ | **HOTEL** | **FAMILY** | Directly facing Alcatraz with unobstructed bay and island vistas, this Fisherman's Wharf hotel pays tribute to San Francisco's shipyard past and features an impressive outdoor adult playground with fire pits, giant interactive games, and a periscope. **Pros:** creative decor; water views from many rooms; fun atmosphere. **Cons:** very touristy area; scruffy exterior architecture; funky vibe is not for everyone. $ *Rooms from: $223* ✉ *250 Beach St., Fisherman's Wharf* ☎ *415/617–6565* ⊕ *www.hotelzephyrsf.com* ⌇ *361 rooms* ⦿ *No Meals.*

Hotel Zoe Fisherman's Wharf
$ | **HOTEL** | A little removed from the heart of the wharf area craziness, this smart-looking boutique hotel with guest-room interiors inspired by luxury Mediterranean yachts aims for subtle contemporary elegance in the form of lightly stained woods and soft-brown and cream fabrics and walls. **Pros:** cozy feeling; nice desks and sitting areas in rooms; open-air courtyard with fire pits. **Cons:** congested touristy area; smaller rooms can feel too tight; no on-site fitness center. $ *Rooms from: $190* ✉ *425 N. Point St., at Mason St., Fisherman's Wharf* ☎ *415/561–1100,*

Did You Know?

San Francisco is only seven miles long by seven miles wide—which makes it really easy to see a lot in just one day.

800/648–4626 🌐 *www.hotelzoesf.com* 🛏 *221 rooms* 🍴 *No Meals.*

Kimpton Alton Hotel
$$ | **HOTEL** | **FAMILY** | A breath of fresh air in touristy Fisherman's Wharf, the popular and approachable boutique hotel chain is hands down the leading hotel option for travelers on the waterfront between the Presidio and the downtown area. **Pros:** nicely sized rooms in all tiers; outstanding in-house restaurant; a chain that doesn't feel like a chain. **Cons:** remote location; limited natural light; small bathroom sinks. [$] *Rooms from: $209* ✉ *2700 Jones St., Fisherman's Wharf* ☎ *771–9000, 833/642–9132 reservations* 🌐 *altonhotelsf.com* 🛏 *248 rooms* 🍴 *No Meals.*

San Francisco Marriott Fisherman's Wharf
$ | **HOTEL** | **FAMILY** | Reliable and slightly refined, this chain property is a good choice for families and business travelers wanting to be on the fringes of Fisherman's Wharf, highlighted by a lobby that plays on the aquatic theme and smartly designed rooms with tech amenities. **Pros:** excellent work-from-room setup; comfortable bedding; charming by Marriott standards. **Cons:** bland fitness center; on a busy street; nearby hotels have better views. [$] *Rooms from: $199* ✉ *1250 Columbus Ave., Fisherman's Wharf* ☎ *415/775–7555* 🌐 *www.marriott.com* 🛏 *285 rooms* 🍴 *No Meals.*

Nightlife

BARS

★ The Buena Vista
CAFÉS | At the end of the Hyde Street cable-car line, the Buena Vista packs 'em in for its famous Irish coffee—which, according to owners, was the first served stateside (in 1952). The place oozes nostalgia with its white-jacketed bartenders and timeless atmosphere, drawing devoted locals as well as out-of-towners relaxing after a day of sightseeing. It's narrow and can get crowded, but this spot is a sip of history and provides a fine alternative to the overpriced tourist joints nearby. ✉ *2765 Hyde St., at Beach St., Fisherman's Wharf* ☎ *415/474–5044* 🌐 *www.thebuenavista.com.*

No Uphill Battle

Don't want to get stuck slogging up 20-degree inclines? Then buy the foldout *San Francisco Bike Map & Walking Guide* ($4), which indicates street grades by color and delineates bike routes that avoid major hills and heavy traffic. Find it in bicycle shops and some bookstores or at the San Francisco Bicycle Coalition's website (🌐 *sfbike.org*).

Activities

BICYCLING

A completely flat, sea-level route, the Embarcadero hugs the eastern and northern bay and gives a clear view of open waters, the Bay Bridge, and sleek high-rises. The route from Pier 40 to Aquatic Park takes about 30 minutes to ride, and there are designated bike lanes the entire way. As you ride west, you'll pass the Bay Bridge, the Ferry Building, Coit Tower (look inland near Pier 19), and historic ships at the Hyde Street Pier. At Aquatic Park there's a nice view of the Golden Gate Bridge. If you're not tired yet, continue along the Marina and through the Presidio's Crissy Field. You may want to time your ride so you end up at the Ferry Building, where you can reward yourself with some great food. **■ TIP→ Be alert—cars move quickly here, and streetcars and tourist traffic can cause congestion. Near Fisherman's Wharf you can bike on the promenade, but watch out for pedestrians.**

Bay City Bike

BIKING | With three locations in Fisherman's Wharf, Bay City Bike isn't hard to find. The shop has an impressive fleet of rental bikes—in many sizes and types—and friendly staff to help you map your biking adventure. They also offer guided tours to the Golden Gate Bridge or Golden Gate Park. ⊠ *2661 Taylor St., at Beach St., Fisherman's Wharf* ☎ *415/346–2453* ⊕ *baycitybike.com* ⊠ *From $36 per day.*

Blazing Saddles

BIKING | This outfitter with multiple locations around San Francisco also offers guided tours—most of which involve biking the Golden Gate Bridge—as well as self-guided options with their app. Go slowly on the bridge and watch for pedestrians. ⊠ *2715 Hyde St., near Beach St., Fisherman's Wharf* ☎ *415/202–8888* ⊕ *www.blazingsaddles. com* ⊠ *From $29 per day for rentals.*

BOATING AND SAILING

San Francisco Bay has year-round sailing, but tricky currents and strong winds make the bay hazardous for inexperienced navigators. However, on group sails you can enjoy the bay while leaving the work to the experts.

Adventure Cat Sailing Charters

BOATING | Near Fisherman's Wharf, Adventure Cat takes passengers aboard one of two 55-foot-long catamarans. The kids can sit and soak up the water spray on the trampoline-like net between the two hulls while adults sip drinks on the wind-protected sundeck. Bay cruises, sunset sails, and city lights evening trips are options. Soda, wine, and beer are sold at an on-board bar. ⊠ *Pier 39, Dock J, Fisherman's Wharf* ☎ *415/777–1630, 800/498–4228* ⊕ *www.adventurecat.com* ⊠ *From $60 for a 90-minute bay cruise.*

WHALE-WATCHING

Between January and April, hundreds of gray whales migrate along the coast; the rest of the year humpback and blue whales feed offshore at the Farallon

Islands. The best place to watch them from shore is Point Reyes in Point Reyes National Seashore, in Marin County (⇨ *see Chapter 14*).

For a better view, head out on a whale-watching trip. Seas around San Francisco can be rough, making motion-sickness tablets a must. Dress warmly, wear sunscreen, and pack rain gear and sunglasses; binoculars come in handy, too. Tour companies don't provide meals or snacks, so bring your own lunch and water. Make reservations at least a week ahead.

San Francisco Whale Tours

WILDLIFE-WATCHING | Once it's springtime, it's also humpback whale season. From April to October, this wildlife-focused operator leaves Pier 39 on its "Kitty Kat" catamaran and heads past the Golden Gate Bridge to the Pacific in pursuit of those humpbacks, along with seals and sometimes also gray whales. Guests are allowed to bring food, wine, and beer, but keep in mind that it is a very bumpy trip. ⊠ *Pier 39, Fisherman's Wharf* ☎ *415/706–7364* ⊕ *sanfranciscowhaletours.com.*

Embarcadero

Stretching from below the Bay Bridge to Fisherman's Wharf, San Francisco's flat, accessible waterfront invites you to get up close and personal with the bay, the picturesque and constant backdrop to this stunning city. For decades the Embarcadero was obscured by a raised freeway and known best for the giant buildings on its piers that further cut off the city from the water. With the freeway gone and a few piers restored for public access, the Embarcadero has been given a new lease on life. Millions of visitors may come through the northern waterfront every year, lured by Fisherman's Wharf and Pier 39, but locals tend to stop short of these, opting instead for the gastronomic pleasures of the Ferry

Escape from Alcatraz

Federal-prison officials liked to claim that it was impossible to escape Alcatraz, and for the most part, that assertion was true. For seasoned swimmers, though, the trip has never posed a problem—in fact, it's been downright popular.

In the 1930s, in an attempt to dissuade the feds from converting Alcatraz into a prison, a handful of schoolgirls made the swim to the city. At age 60, fitness guru and native son Jack LaLanne did it (for the second time) while shackled and towing a 1,000-pound rowboat. Every year thousands take the chilly plunge during the annual Escape from Alcatraz Triathlon and Sharkfest Swim events. Heck, a dog made the crossing in 2005 and finished well ahead of most of the (human) pack. And since 2006, seven-year-old Braxton Bilbrey remains the youngest "escapee" on record. Incidentally, those reports of shark-infested waters are true, but the sharks are almost never dangerous species.

Building or the jogging route offered by the palm-tree-lined sidewalks. Between the wharf and South Beach Park, though, you'll find tourists and San Franciscans alike soaking up the sun, walking out over the water on a long pier to see the sailboats, savoring the excellent restaurants and old-time watering holes, and watching the street performers that crowd Embarcadero Plaza on a sunny day—these are the simple joys that make you happy you're in San Francisco, whether for a few days or a lifetime.

◉ Sights

★ Alcatraz

JAIL/PRISON | **FAMILY** | Thousands of visitors come every day to walk in the footsteps of Alcatraz's notorious criminals. The stories of life and death on "the Rock" may sometimes be exaggerated, but it's almost impossible to resist the chance to wander the cell block that tamed the country's toughest gangsters and saw daring escape attempts of tremendous desperation. Fewer than 2,000 inmates ever did time on the Rock, including Al "Scarface" Capone, Robert "The Birdman" Stroud, and George "Machine Gun Kelly."

Some tips for escaping to Alcatraz: (1) Buy your ticket in advance. Visit the website for Alcatraz Cruises to scout out available departure times for the ferry. (2) Dress smart. Bring a jacket to ward off the chill from the boat ride and wear comfortable shoes. (3) Go for the evening tour. The evening tour has programs not offered during the day, the bridge-to-bridge view of the city twinkles at night, and your "prison experience" will be amplified as darkness falls. (4) Be mindful of scheduled and limited-capacity talks.

The boat ride to the island is brief (15 minutes) but affords beautiful views of the city, Marin County, and the East Bay. The audio tour, highly recommended, includes observations by guards and prisoners about life in one of America's most notorious penal colonies. Plan your schedule to allow at least three hours for the visit and boat rides combined. ✉ Pier 33, Embarcadero ☎ 415/981–7625 ⊕ www.nps.gov/alca 🚢 From $42.

Continued on page 123

ALCATRAZ

"They made that place purely for punishment, where men would rot. It was designed to systematically destroy human beings ... Cold, gray, and lonely, it had a weird way of haunting you—there were those dungeons that you heard about, but there was also the city ... only a mile and a quarter away, so close you could almost touch it. Sometimes the wind would blow a certain way and you could smell the Italian cooking in North Beach and hear the laughter of people, of women and kids. That made it worse than hell."

—Jim Quillen, former Alcatraz inmate

Gripping the rail as the ferryboat pitches gently in the chilly breeze, you watch formidable Alcatraz rising ahead. Imagine making this trip shackled at the ankle and waist, the looming fortress on the craggy island ahead, waiting to swallow you whole. Thousands of visitors come every day to walk in the footsteps of Alcatraz's notorious criminals. The stories of life and death on "the Rock" may sometimes be exaggerated, but it's almost impossible to resist the chance to wander the cellblock that tamed the country's toughest gangsters and saw daring escape attempts of tremendous desperation.

LIFE ON THE ROCK

The federal penitentiary's first warden, James A. Johnston, was largely responsible for Alcatraz's (mostly false) hell-on-earth reputation. A tough but relatively humane disciplinarian, Johnston strictly limited the information flow to and from the prison when it opened in 1934. Prisoners' letters were censored, newspapers and radios were forbidden, and no visits were allowed during a convict's first three months in the slammer. Understandably, imaginations ran wild on the mainland.

A LIFE OF PRIVILEGE

Monotony was an understatement on Alcatraz; the same precise schedule was kept daily. The rulebook stated, "You are entitled to food, clothing, shelter, and medical attention. Anything else you get is a privilege." These privileges, from the right to work to the ability to receive mail, were earned by following the prison's rules. A relatively minor infraction meant losing privileges. A serious breach, like fighting, brought severe punishments like time in the Hole (a.k.a. the Strip Cell, since the prisoner had to strip) or the Oriental (an absolutely dark, silent cell with a hole in the ground for a toilet).

THE SPAGHETTI RIOT

Johnston knew that poor food was one of the major causes of prison riots, so he insisted that Alcatraz serve the best chow in the prison system. But the next warden at Alcatraz slacked off, and in 1950, one spaghetti meal too many sent the inmates over the edge. Guards deployed tear gas to subdue the rioters.

A PRISONER'S DAY

6:30 am: Wake-up call. Prisoners get up, get dressed, and clean cells.

6:50 am: Prisoners stand at cell doors to be counted.

7:00 am: Prisoners march single-file to mess hall for breakfast.

7:20 am: Prisoners head to work or industries detail; count.

9:30 am: 8-minute break; count.

11:30 am: Count; prisoners march to mess hall for lunch.

12:00 pm: Prisoners march to cells; count; break in cells.

12:20 pm: Prisoners leave cells, march single-file back to work; count.

2:30 pm: 8-minute break; count.

4:15 pm: Prisoners stop work, two counts.

4:25 pm: Prisoners march into mess hall and are counted; dinner.

4:45 pm: Prisoners return to cells and are locked in.

5:00 pm: Prisoners stand at their doors to be counted.

8:00 pm: Count.

9:30 pm: Count; lights out.

12:01 am–5 am: Three counts.

INFAMOUS INMATES

Fewer than 2,000 inmates ever did time on the Rock; though they weren't necessarily the worst criminals, they were definitely the worst prisoners. Most were escape artists, and others, like Al Capone, had corrupted the prison system from the inside with bribes.

Name Al "Scarface" Capone

On the Rock 1934–1939

In for Tax evasion

Claim to fame Notorious Chicago gangster and bootlegger who arranged the 1929 St. Valentine's Day Massacre.

Hard fact Capone was among the first transfers to the Rock and arrived smiling and joking. He soon realized the party was over. Capone endured a few stints in the Hole and Warden Johnston's early enforced-silence policy; he was also stabbed by a fellow inmate. The gangster eventually caved, saying "it looks like Alcatraz has got me licked," thus cementing the prison's reputation.

Name Robert "The Birdman" Stroud

On the Rock 1942–1959

In for Murder, including the fatal stabbing of a prison guard

Claim to fame Subject of the acclaimed but largely fictitious 1962 film *Birdman of Alcatraz.*

Hard fact Stroud was actually known as the "Bird Doctor of Leavenworth." While incarcerated in Leavenworth prison through the 1920s and '30s, he became an expert on birds, tending an aviary and writing two books. The stench and mess in his cell discouraged the guards from searching it—and finding Stroud's homemade still. His years on the Rock were birdless.

Name George "Machine Gun" Kelly

On the Rock 1934–1951

In for Kidnapping

Claim to fame Became an expert with a machine gun at the urging of his wife, Kathryn. Kathryn also encouraged his string of bank robberies and the kidnapping for ransom of oilman Charles Urschel. While stashed in Leavenworth on a life sentence, Kelly boasted that he would escape and then free Kathryn. That got him a one-way ticket to Alcatraz.

Hard fact Was an altar boy on Alcatraz and was generally considered a model prisoner.

NO ESCAPE

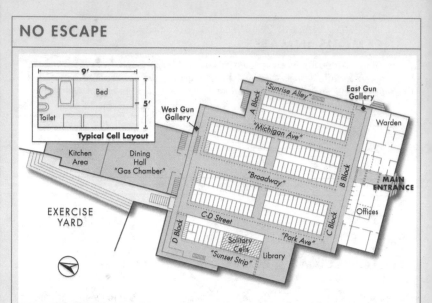

Alcatraz was a maximum-security federal penitentiary with one guard for every three prisoners. The biggest deterrent to escape, though, was the 1.4 miles of icy bay waters separating the Rock from the city. Only a few prisoners made it off the island, and only one is known to have survived. And that story about the shark-infested waters? There are sharks in the bay, but they're not the man-eating kind.

Bloodiest Attempt: In 1946, six prisoners hatched a plan to surprise a guard, seize weapons, and escape through the recreation yard. They succeeded up to a point, arming themselves and locking several guards into cells, but things got ugly when the group couldn't find the key that opened the door to the prison yard. Desperate, they opened fire on the trapped guards. Warden Johnston called in the Marines, who shelled the cell house for two days in the so-called Battle of Alcatraz. Three ringleaders were killed in the fighting; two were executed for murder; and one, who was just 19 years old, got 99 years slapped on to his sentence.

Craftiest Attempt: Over six months, three convicts stole bits and pieces from the kitchen and machine shop to make drills and digging pieces. They used these basic tools to widen a vent into the utility corridor. They also gathered bits of cardboard, toilet paper, and hair from the prison's barbershop to make crude models of their own heads. Then, like teenagers sneaking out, they put the decoy heads in their cots and walked away—up the pipes in the utility corridor to the roof, then down a drainpipe to the ground. They set sail in a raft made from prison raincoats, and are officially presumed dead.

Most Anticlimactic: In 1962, one prisoner spent an entire year loosening the bars in a window. Then he slipped through and managed to swim all the way to Fort Point, near the Golden Gate Bridge. He promptly fell asleep there and was found an hour later by some teenagers.

6 TIPS FOR ESCAPING TO ALCATRAZ

"Broadway," once the cell blocks' busiest corridor.

1. Buy your ticket in advance. Visit the website for Alcatraz Cruises (☎ 415/981–7625 ⊕ cityexperiences.com) to scout out available departure times for the ferry. Prepay by credit card—the ticket price covers the boat ride and the audio tour—and print your ticket at home. Bring it to Pier 33 up to an hour before sailing and experience just a touch of schadenfreude as you overhear attendants tell scores of too-late passengers that your tour is sold out.

2. Dress smart. Bring that pullover you packed to ward off the chill from the boat ride and Alcatraz Island. Also: sneakers. Some Alcatraz guides are fanatical about making excellent time.

3. Go for the evening tour. You'll get even more out of the experience if you do it at night. The evening tour has programs not offered during the day, the bridge-to-bridge view of the city twinkles at night, and your "prison experience" will be amplified as darkness mournfully falls while you shuffle around the cell block.

4. Unplug and go against the flow. If you miss a cue on the excellent audio tour and find yourself out of synch, don't sweat it—use it as an opportunity to switch off the tape. No one will stop you if you walk back through a cell block on your own, taking the time to listen to the haunting sound of your own footsteps on the concrete floor.

5. Be mindful of scheduled and limited-capacity talks. Some programs only happen once a day; the schedule is posted in the cell house and at the dock on the island. Certain talks have limited capacity seating, so keep an eye out for a cell house staffer handing out passes shortly before the start time.

6. Talk to the staff. One of the island's greatest resources is its staff, who practically bubble over with information. Pick their brains, and draw them out about what they know.

PRACTICALITIES

Visitors at the Alcatraz dock waiting to depart "Uncle Sam's Devil's Island."

GETTING THERE

All cruises are operated by Alcatraz Cruises, the park's authorized concessionaire. Check ⊕ *cityexperiences.com* for all tour options and reservations. Please book in advance. Locals aren't kidding when they mention how often visitors are disappointed.

TIMING

The boat ride to Alcatraz is only about 15 minutes long, but you should allow about three hours for your entire visit. The delightful F-line vintage streetcars are the most direct public transit to the dock; on weekdays the 10-Townsend bus will get you within a few blocks of Pier 33.

FOOD

There is no food service on the boats or on the island. Food cannot be brought past the dock on the island, so don't even think about an Alcatraz picnic. Bottled water is okay, though. The café

STORM TROOPER ALERT!

When he was filming *Star Wars*, George Lucas recorded the sound of Alcatraz's cell doors slamming shut and used the sound bite in the movie whenever Darth Vader's star cruiser closed its doors.

at Alcatraz Landing is closed. Plan your meals for before or after the trip.

KIDS ON THE ROCK

Parents should be aware that the audio tour, while engaging and worthwhile, includes some startlingly realistic sound effects. (Some children might not get a kick out of the gunshots from the Battle of Alcatraz—or the guards' screams, for that matter.) If you stay just one minute ahead in the program, you can always fast forward through the violent moments on your little one's audio tour.

Angel Island State Park

STATE/PROVINCIAL PARK | For an outdoorsy adventure and some fascinating though sometimes disturbing history, consider a day at this island northwest of Alcatraz, the bay's largest natural island. Used by the Coast Miwok as a favored camp, explored by Spaniards in 1775, and declared a U.S. military reserve 75 years later, the island was used as a screening ground for Asian, mostly Chinese, immigrants—who were often held for months, even years, before being granted entry—from 1910 until 1940. You can visit the restored Immigration Station, from the dock where detainees landed to the barracks where you can see the poems in Chinese script they etched onto the walls.

In 1963 the government designated Angel Island a state park. Today people come for picnics, hikes (such as one to the top of Mt. Livermore and a scenic five-mile path that winds around the island's perimeter), and tram tours that explain the park's history. Golden Gate Ferry is the only Angel Island ferry service with departures from San Francisco; boats leave from the Ferry Building. ⊠ Angel Island State Park, 1 Ferry Bldg., Embarcadero ☎ 415/435–5390 park information, 415/455–2000 ferry information ⊕ www.parks.ca.gov ⛴ $28 round-trip for ferry and admission.

★ Exploratorium

SCIENCE MUSEUM | FAMILY | Walking into this fascinating museum of "science, art, and human perception" is like visiting a mad-scientist's laboratory, but one in which most of the exhibits are supersize and you can play with everything. Signature experiential exhibits include the Tinkering Studio and a glass Bay Observatory building, where the exhibits help visitors better understand what they see outside. Get an Alice-in-Wonderland feeling in the Distorted Room, where you seem to shrink and grow as you walk across the slanted, checkered floor. In the Shadow Box, a powerful flash freezes an image of your shadow on the wall; jumping is a favorite pose. More than 650 other exhibits focus on sea and insect life, computers, electricity, patterns and light, language, the weather, and more. Don't miss a walk around the outside of the museum afterward for superb views and a lesson about the bay's sediment and water motion in the Bay Windows presentation. ⊠ Pier 15, Embarcadero ☎ 415/528–4444 general information ⊕ www.exploratorium.edu ⛴ $40 ⊗ Closed Mon.

★ Ferry Building

MARKET | The jewel of the Embarcadero, erected in 1896 and now home to an outstanding food marketplace, is topped by a 230-foot clock tower modeled after the campanile of the cathedral in Seville, Spain. On the morning of April 18, 1906, the tower's four clock faces stopped at 5:17—the moment the great earthquake struck—and stayed still for 12 months.

Today San Franciscans flock to the street-level marketplace, stocking up on supplies from local favorites such as Acme Bread, Blue Bottle Coffee, El Porteño (empanadas), the gluten-free Mariposa Baking Company, and Humphry Slocombe (ice cream). For sit-down dining, there's the Hog Island Oyster Company and the seasonal Californian duo of Bouli Bar and Boulette's Larder. On the plaza side, the outdoor tables at Gott's Roadside and Fort Point Ferry Building offer great people-watching and excellent casual bites and sips. On Saturday morning the plazas outside the building buzz with an upscale farmers' market. Extending south from the piers north of the building to the Bay Bridge, the waterfront promenade out front is a favorite among joggers and picnickers, with a view of sailboats plying the bay. True to its name, the Ferry Building still serves actual ferries: from its eastern flank they sail to Sausalito, Larkspur, Tiburon, Angel Island, and the East Bay. ⊠ Embarcadero,

1 Ferry Bldg., at foot of Market St., Embarcadero ☎ *415/983–8000* 🌐 *www.ferrybuildingmarketplace.com.*

F-line

TRANSPORTATION | The city's system of vintage electric trolleys, the F-line, gives the cable cars a run for their money as a beloved mode of transportation. The beautifully restored streetcars—some dating from the 19th century—run from the Castro District down Market Street to the Embarcadero, then north to Fisherman's Wharf. Each car is unique, restored to the colors of its city of origin, from New Orleans and Philadelphia to Melbourne and Milan. ■**TIP→ Pay with a Clipper card or purchase tickets on board; exact change is required.** ✉ *Embarcadero* 🌐 *www.streetcar.org* 🎟 *$3.*

San Francisco Railway Museum

OTHER MUSEUM | FAMILY | A labor of love from the same vintage-transit enthusiasts responsible for the F-line's revival, this one-room museum and store celebrates the city's streetcars and cable cars with photographs, models, and artifacts. The permanent exhibit includes the replicated end of a streetcar with a working cab—complete with controls and a bell—for kids to explore; the cool, antique Wiley birdcage traffic signal; and models and display cases to view. Right on the F-line track, just across from the Ferry Building, this is a great quick stop. ✉ *77 Steuart St., Embarcadero* ☎ *415/974–1948* 🌐 *www.streetcar.org/museum* 🎟 *Free* 🕓 *Closed Sun. and Mon.*

🍴 Restaurants

Locals and visitors alike flock here for gorgeous bay views, a world-class waterfront esplanade, and a Ferry Building that's much better known for its food than its boat rides. Some of the best bakers and cooks in the city have started here or have their satellites here.

Angler

$$$ | SEAFOOD | Immaculately fresh seafood and a wood-burning hearth are the centerpieces of this bustling yet luxurious sibling to Saison. The menu descriptions might be brief, but it's really all about the ingredients and impeccable technique—whether it's a grilled hand-dived scallop or the signature thinly sliced potato with Sonoma cheeses—fulfilling their full potential on the plate with a few smart embellishments. **Known for:** taxidermy-filled back room with Bay Bridge views; tuna tartare with tomato jelly; Instagram-favorite radicchio salad. [$] *Average main: $39* ✉ *132 The Embarcadero, Embarcadero* ☎ *415/872–9442* 🌐 *anglerrestaurants.com/san-francisco* 🕓 *No lunch Sun. and Mon.*

★ Boulevard

$$$$ | MODERN AMERICAN | Celebrated local chef Nancy Oakes' high-profile, high-priced eatery in the historic 1889 Audiffred Building has been attracting well-dressed locals and flush out-of-towners since 1993. A striking belle époque interior (originally designed by Pat Kuleto and later touched up by Ken Fulk, both star local architects) is the setting for sophisticated American food with a French accent and a distinct local California produce twist. ■**TIP→ The main dining room has a three-course set menu with several options in each course, while most of that menu is available à la carte in the bar area. Known for:** any pork chop preparation; polished service; lively bar area. [$] *Average main: $115* ✉ *1 Mission St., Embarcadero* ☎ *415/543–6084* 🌐 *www.boulevardrestaurant.com* 🕓 *Closed Sun. and Mon. No lunch.*

Coqueta

$$$ | SPANISH | With its Bay Bridge views and stellar Spanish tapas, celebrity chef Michael Chiarello's San Francisco restaurant is a big hit that's equal parts rustic and chic, a lively destination for both small bites and larger meals. Toothpicked *pintxos* (small snacks) like quail egg with sausage are a tasty way to start, but the real draws are the inventive cocktails, luscious paella, and dazzling selection of cured meats. **Known for:** smoked salmon montadito (a small sandwich); sangria from a porrón (a pitcher that people also drink from); churros with chocolate. $ *Average main: $36* ⊠ *Pier 5, on the Embarcadero, near Broadway, Embarcadero* ☎ *415/704–8866* ⊕ *coquetasf.com.*

★ **GOZU**

$$$$ | CONTEMPORARY | Chef-owner Marc Zimmerman's first personal restaurant project is the city's most compelling beef-centric dining experience. Elaborate small dishes, several of which incorporate prestigious Wagyu beef elements (blood, fat, or obscure parts, for example), make up a captivating tasting menu served to diners, most of whom are seated at a U-shaped counter that overlooks a centerpiece robata grill. **Known for:** a steak restaurant that isn't a typical steak house; Japanese whisky list; ultra high-end yet relaxed dining. $ *Average main: $225* ⊠ *201 Spear St., Embarcadero* ☎ *415/523–9745* ⊕ *www.gozusf.com* ⊗ *Closed Sun. and Mon. No lunch.*

Hog Island Oyster Company

$$ | SEAFOOD | A thriving oyster farm north of San Francisco in Tomales Bay serves up its harvest at this raw bar and restaurant in the Ferry Building, where devotees come for impeccably fresh oysters and clams on the half shell. Other mollusk-centered options include first-rate clam chowder, grilled oysters, and steamed mussels and clams; the kitchen also makes one of the city's best grilled cheese sandwiches. **Known for:** crowds slurping dozens of oysters; local produce salads; superior Bloody Mary. $ *Average main: $23* ⊠ *1 Ferry Bldg., Embarcadero at Market St., Embarcadero* ☎ *415/391–7117* ⊕ *hogislandoysters.com.*

La Mar Cebicheria Peruana

$$$$ | PERUVIAN | Right on the water's edge, this casually chic outpost, global mega-chef Gastón Acurio's first outside Peru, imports the signature flavors of his home country's cuisine to San Francisco. Fresh seafood is a big draw here, including a long list of ceviches and the can't-miss *causas* (whipped potatoes topped with a choice of fish, shellfish, or vegetable salads). **Known for:** pisco cocktails; beautiful back patio; empanadas and tiradito (a dish with raw fish). $ *Average main: $46* ⊠ *Pier 1½, between Washington and Jackson Sts., Embarcadero* ☎ *415/397–8880* ⊕ *lamarsf.com.*

One Market

$$$ | MODERN AMERICAN | A three-decade-old favorite for business lunches and special dinners, this white-tablecloth spot caters to suits brokering deals and well-dressed romantic dates, who carve their way through upscale dishes accented by local produce and often intricate sauces. Its menu skews seasonal and meaty, and its largish bar, which offers its own food menu of New York deli–style dishes and numerous cocktails, is popular for Financial District/pre-commute happy hour. **Known for:** tasty fried chicken; Tonya Pitts's standout wine program; butterscotch pudding. $ *Average main: $36* ⊠ *1 Market St., Embarcadero* ☎ *415/777–5577* ⊕ *onemarket.com* ⊗ *Closed Sun. and Mon. No lunch Sat.*

Prospect

$$$$ | MODERN AMERICAN | This contemporary-minded younger sibling of Boulevard, one of the city's most beloved dining institutions, deserves to be known for its own virtues. The food menu rotates frequently based on the seasons and is a nice mix of elevated snacks like outrageously good chicken-fried oysters and more refined small plates, entrées, and pastas. **Known for:** sleek dining room and bar; prime rib eye roast; terrific fries and house-baked Hokkaido milk bread. $ *Average main: $41* ⊠ *300 Spear St., Embarcadero* ☎ *415/247–7770* ⊕ *prospectsf.com* ⊗ *Closed weekends. No lunch.*

Waterbar

$$$$ | **SEAFOOD** | Come for seafood with a view: sky-high aquariums dominate the dining room, and the bay is just beyond, but the biggest attraction is the food. Every fin and shell of the sea, from the oak-roasted striped bass to the black cod from the Mendocino Coast, is sustainably sourced. **Known for:** cured fish and iced shellfish starters; always feels like a celebration; delightful Pat Kuleto–designed interior. [$] *Average main: $42 ✉ 399 The Embarcadero, between Folsom and Harrison Sts., Embarcadero ☎ 415/284–9922 🌐 www.waterbarsf.com.*

☕ Coffee and Quick Bites

Grande Crêperie

$ | **FRENCH** | **FAMILY** | The team behind French baking sensation Le Marais serves some of the greatest savory buckwheat galettes and sweet crêpes in the Bay Area at a kiosk on the water side of the Ferry Building. It's the perfect stop for breakfast, lunch, or a dessert snack. **Known for:** exquisite pastries; chocolate crêpe with local fruits; mushroom and cheddar galette. [$] *Average main: $15 ✉ Ferry Bldg., Suite 46, Embarcadero 🌐 grandecreperie.com 🕒 No dinner.*

Peaches Patties

$ | **JAMAICAN** | San Francisco has very few Caribbean restaurants, but luckily locals and tourists can try some excellent Jamaican cuisine from Shani Jones' catering company-turned-permanent kiosk on the Embarcadero sidewalk side of the Ferry Building. Homemade patties (savory pastries filled with meats or vegetables) are the namesake signature dish, complemented by the island's iconic jerk chicken and frequently a hearty stew or two. **Known for:** sorrel (a hibiscus beverage) or ginger beer to drink; curry chicken patties; lunchtime deal of a patty, plantains, and side of vegetables. [$] *Average main: $17 ✉ Ferry Bldg., Suite 50, Embarcadero ☎ 562–7589 🌐 peachespatties.com 🕒 No dinner.*

Pier 23 Cafe

$$ | **AMERICAN** | Beer arrives at your table in buckets at this waterfront café-saloon, which has ample seating at plastic tables on a wooden deck. Although you'd expect to sit elbow to elbow with fishers, you're more likely to share the space with twenty- and thirtysomethings drawn by the cocktails and casual seafood and sandwiches from the kitchen, and of course the prime vantage point for gazing across the bay. **Known for:** clam chowder; live music; Key West–like vibe on the bay. [$] *Average main: $24 ✉ Pier 23, The Embarcadero, Embarcadero ☎ 415/362–5125 🌐 www.pier23cafe.com 🕒 Closed Mon. and Tues. No dinner.*

Red's Java House

$ | **AMERICAN** | For a real cup of joe without any sense of pretension, join the savvy dock workers, carpenters, and young suits at decades-old Red's Java House, where the coffee typically follows a cheeseburger and a beer and the gorgeous view of the East Bay is priceless. **Known for:** hearty breakfast dishes; no lettuce or tomato on the burgers; throwback mid-century atmosphere. [$] *Average main: $10 ✉ Pier 30, Embarcadero ✥ Between Embarcadero and Bryant St. 🌐 www.redsjavahouse.com 🕒 No dinner.*

🛏 Hotels

The boutique hotels along the Embarcadero are convenient, though at a cost. Rooms tend to be on the smallish side (this is the high-rent district), yet stylish. On the upside, views of the bay are dramatic, and easy access to the Ferry Building makes foodies rejoice.

Harbor Court Hotel

$$ | **HOTEL** | This Spanish Colonial Revival–style hotel has nice touches that enliven the guest quarters, including 42-inch high-definition TVs, quirky mathematical wall clocks, ultra-comfortable beds with Frette linens, and the convenience of being attached to the Ozumo sushi

restaurant. **Pros:** convenient and quiet location; friendly, professional staffers; Bay Bridge and Ferry Building views from some rooms. **Cons:** small bathrooms; some rooms lack views; continental breakfast is uninspired for the steep price. $ *Rooms from: $227* ✉ *165 Steuart St., Embarcadero* ☎ *415/882–1300, 888/538–8552* ⊕ *www.harborcourt-hotel.com* ⇄ *131 rooms* ⦿*| No Meals.*

Hyatt Regency San Francisco

$$ | **HOTEL** | This perfectly located property near the Ferry Building has a dramatic 17-story atrium lobby that starred in several 1970s flicks, most notably the disaster epic *The Towering Inferno.* **Pros:** sharp contemporary design; near restaurants and shopping; even the smallest rooms are a decent size. **Cons:** unremarkable dining choices; chaotic street entrance; nondescript amenities. $ *Rooms from: $295* ✉ *5 Embarcadero Center, Embarcadero* ☎ *415/788–1234* ⊕ *hyatt.com* ⇄ *821 rooms* ⦿*| No Meals.*

1 Hotel San Francisco

$$$ | **HOTEL** | The sustainability and green-everything boutique hotel concept planted its flag in San Francisco in 2022 after a substantial renovation of the Hotel Vitale, a longtime Embarcadero stalwart. **Pros:** one of the city's best spas; beautiful, spacious rooms; excellent restaurant with sidewalk patio. **Cons:** Embarcadero-facing rooms get lots of traffic noise; subpar fitness center; wellness-environment theme can feel contrived. $ *Rooms from: $398* ✉ *8 Mission St., Embarcadero* ☎ *278–3700, 833/602–7111* ⊕ *1hotels.com/san-francisco* ⇄ *200 rooms.*

🅨 Nightlife

The waterfront's eastern section tends to get quiet once the dinner hour winds down, which isn't a surprise given that it's an area consisting mainly of apartments and upscale restaurants. Most evening visitors go to bars elsewhere and focus on romantic strolls and

photographs of the Bay Bridge lights while on the Embarcadero.

BARS
Hi Dive

BARS | For a city with so much waterfront mileage, it's shocking how few waterfront bars San Francisco has. This very welcoming, somewhat retro, kind of divey bar almost directly underneath the Bay Bridge is the perfect place for a local IPA or a margarita on the patio on a sunny day. ✉ *Pier 28, Embarcadero* ☎ *977–0170* ⊕ *hidivesf.com.*

🅐 Shopping

Four sprawling buildings of shops, restaurants, offices, and a popular independent movie theater—plus the Hyatt Regency hotel—make up the Embarcadero Center. Most stores are branches of upscale national chains, such as Sephora and Banana Republic.

FARMERS' MARKETS
★ Ferry Plaza Farmers' Market

MARKET | The partylike Saturday edition of the city's most upscale and expensive farmers' market places baked goods, gourmet cheeses, smoked fish, and fancy pots of jam alongside organic basil, specialty mushrooms, heirloom tomatoes, and juicy-ripe locally grown fruit. Smaller markets also take place on Tuesday and Thursday year-round, rain or shine—and the many passionate San Francisco home cooks who frequent them will come even in a rainstorm. ✉ *Ferry Plaza, at Market St., Embarcadero* ☎ *415/291–3276* ⊕ *www.ferrybuildingmarketplace.com.*

FOOD AND DRINK
Recchiuti Confections

CHOCOLATE | Michael and Jacky Recchiuti began making otherworldly chocolates in San Francisco in 1997, using traditional European techniques. Now considered among the best confectioners in the world, they stock their store here with their full chocolate line, including several unique items like dark chocolate truffles made with Napa Valley sparkling wine and a box of burnt caramel truffles decorated with images of San Francisco's iconic places. ⊠ *Ferry Building Marketplace, 1 Ferry Bldg., Suite 30, Embarcadero at foot of Market St., Embarcadero* ☎ *415/834–9494* ⊕ *www.recchiuti.com.*

TOYS

Exploratorium

TOYS | FAMILY | The educational gadgets sold here are so clever and engaging that kids won't know they're learning while playing. Space- and dinosaur-related games are popular, as are science videos and optical illusion gifts. ⊠ *Pier 15, at The Embarcadero and Green St., Embarcadero* ☎ *415/528–4390* ⊕ *www.exploratorium.edu* ⊗ *Closed Mon.*

 ## Activities

BOATING AND SAILING

Rendezvous Charters

SAILING | This sailing school is sometimes a trip operator that offers individually ticketed trips on large sailing yachts, including sunset sails and Sunday brunch cruises. Ticketed trips tend to close from mid-October through March (although they continue to do private chartered sails throughout the year), so call in advance to confirm availability. ⊠ *Pier 40, Suite 4, South Beach Harbor, Embarcadero* ☎ *415/543–7333* ⊕ *www.rendezvouscharters.com* ⊠ *Sailings from $60.*

Financial District

During the latter half of the 19th century, when San Francisco was a brawling, extravagant gold-rush town, today's Financial District (FiDi, for short) was underwater. Yerba Buena Cove reached all the way up to Montgomery Street, and what's now Jackson Square was the heart of the Barbary Coast, bordering some of the roughest wharves in the world. These days, Jackson Square is a genteel and upscale neighborhood wedged between North Beach and the Financial District, but buried below Montgomery Street lie remnants of those wild days: more than 100 ships abandoned by frantic crews and passengers caught up in gold fever rest under the foundations of buildings here.

The Financial District of the 21st century is a decidedly less exciting affair: it's all office towers with mazes of cubicles now. When the sun sets, this quarter empties out fast. The few sights here will appeal mainly to gold-rush history enthusiasts; others can spend time elsewhere.

⊙ Sights

Jackson Square Historic District

HISTORIC DISTRICT | This was the heart of the Barbary Coast of the Gay '90s—the 1890s, that is. Although most of the red-light district was destroyed in the fire that followed the 1906 earthquake, the remaining old redbrick buildings, many of them now occupied by advertising agencies, law offices, and antiques firms, retain hints of the romance and rowdiness of San Francisco's early days.

With its gentrified gold rush–era buildings, the 700 block of Montgomery Street just barely evokes the Barbary Coast days, but this was a colorful block in the 19th century and on into the 20th. Writers Mark Twain and Bret Harte were among the contributors to the spunky *The Golden Era* newspaper, which occupied No. 732 (now part of the building at No. 744).

Restored 19th-century brick buildings line Hotaling Place, which connects Washington and Jackson Streets; it's named for the A. P. Hotaling Company whiskey distillery, the largest liquor repository on the West Coast in its day. The exceptional Gold Rush City walking tour offered by City Guides (☎ *415/557–4266*) brings this area's history to life. ⊠ *Bordered by Columbus Ave., Broadway, and Washington and Sansome Sts., Financial District.*

★ Salesforce Park

CITY PARK | FAMILY | Ask a hundred San Franciscans about Salesforce Park and the city's tallest building, the 1,070-foot Salesforce Tower, and you'll get a hundred different opinions. The tower opened in 2018 and is now the second-tallest building west of the Mississippi. This splashy, impossible-to-miss, rocket-shape glass high-rise dominates the city's skyline and has become the symbol of the city's tech-money elite. It is photogenic, but some feel it dominates photos of the city too often. Building visits are limited to employees and people coming for business purposes.

The true highlight of the Salesforce mini-neighborhood is Salesforce Park, a sprawling urban park with 13 ecosystems atop the four-block-long Salesforce Transit Center. It's a downtown green gem, a true civic accomplishment. This is a favorite destination for families, walkers, and workers trying to get fresh air on their lunch break. A beer garden from Barebottle Brewing Co. in Bernal Heights has swiftly become the happy hour destination of choice for downtown office workers. For a weekday coffee break, there's a branch of local favorite Andytown Coffee Roasters on the seventh floor of the spectacular 181 Fremont skyscraper; it's attached to the park via skybridge. The park can be reached via elevators, escalators, or a thrilling gondola ride from the base of the Salesforce Tower at Fremont and Mission Streets. ⊠ *425 Mission St., Financial District* ✛ *Roughly between Beale and 2nd Sts., and Mission and Howard Sts.* ☎ *415/597–5000* ⊕ *salesforcetransit-center.com.*

Transamerica Pyramid

NOTABLE BUILDING | It's neither owned by Transamerica nor is it a pyramid, but this 48-floor, 853-foot-tall obelisk *is* the most photographed of the city's high-rises. Excoriated in the design stages as "the world's largest architectural folly," the

Whiskey Rhyme 👁

The Italianate Hotaling building at 451 Jackson Street survived the disastrous 1906 quake and fire—a miracle considering the thousands of barrels of inflammable liquid inside. A plaque on the side of the structure repeats a famous query: "If, as they say, god spanked the town for being over frisky, why did he burn the churches down and save Hotaling's whiskey?"

icon was quickly hailed as a masterpiece when it opened in 1972. Today it's probably the city's most recognized structure after the Golden Gate Bridge, and it's the second-tallest in the city after the Salesforce Tower. You can't go up the pyramid, but the best views and photo-ops are of the building itself anyway. Note that the building is undergoing a substantial construction renovation, so there will be fencing around its perimeter likely for all of 2023 and possibly into 2024. ■ **TIP→ A fragrant redwood grove along the east side of the building, with benches and a cheerful fountain of leaping frogs, is a placid downtown oasis in which to unwind.** ⊠ *600 Montgomery St., Financial District* ⊕ *transamericapyramid.com.*

Wells Fargo History Museum

HISTORY MUSEUM | At this fun two-story museum, you can get a taste of the early years of the gold rush when San Francisco had no formal banks and miners often entrusted their gold dust to saloon keepers. In 1852, Wells Fargo opened its first bank in the city on this block, and the company soon established banking offices in mother-lode camps throughout California. One popular exhibit is a simulated ride in a replica of an early stagecoach. The museum also displays samples of nuggets and gold dust from mines, an old telegraph machine on which you can practice sending codes, and tools the '49ers used to coax gold from the ground. ✉ *420 Montgomery St., Financial District* ☎ *415/396–2619* 🌐 *www.wellsfargohistory.com* 🎫 *Free* 🕒 *Closed weekends.*

🍴 Restaurants

The center of commerce, with some very good restaurants (housed in old Barbary Coast buildings), the FiDi caters to the business elite with prices to match. Engineers and software developers looking for a fast lunch head to modest Indian, Mexican, and Chinese places, as well as sandwich shops.

Akikos
$$$$ | **SUSHI** | The title of "best omakase" has many worthwhile contenders in the city, but many would name this newcomer as the most captivating sushi-centric tasting menu. It's undoubtedly a splurge and can feel a little Vegas-flashy, yet the raw and gently torched fish nigiri preparations are nothing short of remarkable. **Known for:** superb sake and cocktail selection; shokupan (milk bread) topped with tuna and caviar; pricey but worth it. [$] *Average main: $250* ✉ *430 Folsom St., Financial District* ☎ *415/397–3218* 🌐 *akikosrestaurant.com* 🕒 *Closed Sun. and Mon. No lunch Sat.*

Bar Sprezzatura
$$$ | **VENETIAN** | Guests can almost smell the Adriatic salt water–kissed air while digging into *cicchetti* (similar to open-faced crostini bites with various toppings) and other clever Venetian-inspired dishes at this gorgeous restaurant next to the Embarcadero Center. As delightful as the food is, the glamorous design and intricate cocktails are just as noteworthy. **Known for:** pizza al taglio with whipped artichoke; epic Cicchetti Martini presentation with snacks and olive brine; fish crudo. [$] *Average main: $31* ✉ *1 Maritime Plaza, 300 Clay St., Suite 100, Financial District* ☎ *628/466–0230* 🌐 *barsprezzatura.com* 🕒 *Closed weekends.*

BIX
$$$ | **MODERN AMERICAN** | With its Jazz Age vibe, live music, discreet alley location behind the Transamerica Pyramid, and spectacular bar and bi-level dining room, BIX would be worth a visit for the impressive setting alone. However, it's also one of the city's finest restaurants for special occasions that don't require a tasting menu; continental and upscale American fare get fresh modern takes, often with a few haute elements. **Known for:** classic cocktails; potato pillows with caviar; career servers who remember your name after one visit. [$] *Average main: $38* ✉ *56 Gold St., Financial District* ☎ *415/433–6300* 🌐 *bixrestaurant.com* 🕒 *No lunch.*

Cotogna
$$$ | **ITALIAN** | The draw at this urban trattoria is chef Michael Tusk's flavorful, rustic, seasonally driven Italian cooking, headlined by pastas, beautifully grilled or spit-roasted meats, and homemade gelato. The look inside and outside is comfortably chic, with wood tables, quality stemware, and fantastic Italian wines by the bottle and glass. **Known for:** raviolo with brown butter and egg in center; tough to get reservations; peak seasonal produce in antipasti. [$] *Average main: $38* ✉ *490 Pacific Ave., Financial District* ☎ *415/775–8508* 🌐 *www.cotognasf.com* 🕒 *Closed Sun. and Mon.*

Estiatorio Ornos
$$$$ | **MEDITERRANEAN** | One of Downtown San Francisco's most storied restaurant spaces is now on a permanent Mediterranean vacation. After a longtime tenure as Aqua (where Michael Mina's legendary career began) and later as Mina's flagship namesake restaurant, the prominent California Street dining room's latest concept looks towards Greece and Mina's Egyptian heritage. **Known for:** terrific Greek wine selection; tableside baklava cart; must-order grilled octopus.

Average main: $45 ✉ *252 California St., Financial District* ☎ *415/417–3969* ⊕ *michaelmina.net* ⊘ *Closed Sun. No lunch.*

International Smoke San Francisco

$$$ | **CONTEMPORARY** | Ayesha Curry teamed up with the city's most prolific chef/entrepreneur, Michael Mina, on this hip spot inside the glitzy Millennium Tower. Don't call it a barbecue restaurant—it's more of an open flame, smoke-driven style of cooking inspired by various global cuisines. **Known for:** gourmands and mega sports fans eating together; prix-fixe "Fuego" menu; bacon-washed bourbon old-fashioned. *Average main: $32* ✉ *301 Mission St., Financial District* ☎ *415/660–2656* ⊕ *internationalsmoke. com.*

Kokkari Estiatorio

$$$$ | **GREEK** | Satisfy your craving for outstanding Greek taverna food—albeit at luxe steak house prices—from a dizzying selection of mezes such as stuffed grape leaves to main courses that showcase Athenian standards like moussaka, lemon-oregano chicken, and grilled lamb chops. There's a lively after-work scene in this chic farmhouse setting with wood-beamed ceilings, a roaring wood oven, and candlelight. **Known for:** grilled octopus; whole fish entrées; semolina custard wrapped in phyllo. *Average main: $45* ✉ *200 Jackson St., Financial District* ☎ *415/981–0983* ⊕ *kokkari.com* ⊘ *No lunch weekends.*

Pabu Izakaya

$$$$ | **JAPANESE** | This energetic Japanese dining venue (part of Michael Mina's high-powered group) is a sleek, wonderful place that hosts both date nights and business deals at its tables and cocktail bar. The substantial menu can be overwhelming, so it's best to just graze around the sushi rolls, robata grill items, and a few small and large plates like homemade pork gyoza and miso yaki black cod. **Known for:** stellar sake and cocktail program; "happy spoon" oyster

with salmon roe and sea urchin; chef's nigiri and sashimi selections. *Average main: $42* ✉ *101 California St., Financial District* ☎ *535–0184* ⊕ *michaelmina.net* ⊘ *Closed Sun. No lunch.*

Perbacco

$$$ | **NORTHERN ITALIAN** | From the idyllic hazelnut budino to the pappardelle with short rib ragù, this longtime power dining favorite's menu is a delectable paean to northern Italy. With a long marble bar and open kitchen, this brick-lined, ultra polished space oozes big-city charm, attracting business types and Italian food aficionados alike to the FiDi well after evening rush hour ends. **Known for:** agnolotti del plin (a type of pasta filled with meat); crisp and friendly service; vitello tonnato (cold veal with a tuna-flavored sauce) appetizer. *Average main: $37* ✉ *230 California St., Financial District* ☎ *415/955–0663* ⊕ *www.perbaccosf.com* ⊘ *Closed Sun. and Mon. No lunch Sat.*

Tadich Grill

$$$ | **SEAFOOD** | Locations and owners have changed more than once since this old-timer started as a coffee stand in 1849, but the crowds keep coming. Snag one of the private booths (complete with a bell to summon the brusque, white coated waiters) and sample seafood—always the name of the game here—such as the Dungeness crab cocktail or local sanddabs (a type of flounder). **Known for:** delicious cioppino; one- (or three-) martini lunches; hangtown fry (a type of omelet from gold-rush days). *Average main: $39* ✉ *240 California St., Financial District* ☎ *415/391–1849* ⊕ *tadichgrillsf.com* ⊘ *Closed Sun. No lunch Sat.*

Town Hall

$$$ | **AMERICAN** | American fare with Southern flair is the headline at this power broker's pit stop where barbecue gulf shrimp, juicy fried chicken, and butterscotch-chocolate pot de crème highlight a menu with enough variety (and large enough portions) to satisfy nearly

everyone. The converted-warehouse space, with dark-wood floors, exposed brick walls, and contemporary art, comfortably blends old with new. **Known for:** must-order buttermilk biscuits; signature veal meatballs; mix of classic New Orleans and creative cocktails. ⓢ *Average main: $32* ⊠ *342 Howard St., Financial District* ☎ *415/908–3900* ⊕ *townhallsf. com* ⊙ *Closed Sun. and Mon. No lunch.*

The Vault Garden

$$$$ | **MODERN AMERICAN** | Most of the early pandemic pop-ups and pivots in San Francisco slowly faded away back to their previous selves in 2021 and 2022. However, this "Garden" concept (really a tented patio on part of the spacious plaza of one of SF's tallest skyscrapers) is a permanent fixture featuring excellent seasonal California cuisine and a few elevated comfort classics that help lift this destination into the upper tier of SF dining options. **Known for:** Parker House rolls; photogenic food and atmosphere; excellent cocktails. ⓢ *Average main: $45* ⊠ *555 California St., Financial District* ☎ *415/508–4675* ⊕ *thevault555.com* ⊙ *Closed Sun.–Mon.*

Wayfare Tavern

$$$ | **AMERICAN** | This energetic and upscale American tavern owned by TV chef and personality Tyler Florence is rich with upscale turn-of-the-20th-century Americana, including brick walls, comfortable booths, and a billiards room. It also tips its hat to tradition—and comfort—on the menu with deviled eggs, fresh seafood, and several signature dishes that are considered the best of their categories in the city (the burger with Marin Brie, for one), plus noteworthy cocktails that complete the full experience. **Known for:** buttermilk-brined fried chicken with herbs; giant warm popovers start each meal; house-made doughnuts. ⓢ *Average main: $34* ⊠ *558 Sacramento St., Financial District* ☎ *415/722–9060* ⊕ *www.wayfaretavern.com.*

Yank Sing

$ | **CHINESE** | This bustling, lunch-only restaurant serves some of San Francisco's best dim sum to office workers on weekdays and boisterous families on weekends, and the take-out counter makes a satisfying meal on the run. The several dozen varieties prepared daily include the classic and the creative; steamed pork buns, shrimp dumplings, scallop skewers, and basil seafood dumplings are among the many delights. **Known for:** Peking duck on weekends; Shanghai soup dumplings; energetic vibe. ⓢ *Average main: $16* ⊠ *49 Stevenson St., Financial District* ☎ *415/541–4949* ⊕ *yanksing. com* ⊙ *No dinner.*

☕ Coffee and Quick Bites

★ Maison Nico

$ | **FRENCH** | Some of San Francisco's most exquisite French pastries are baked daily at this serene, cheery shop. On the savory side, most choices tend to be some form of pâté-filled pastry and are presented with all the artistry of haute cuisine; sweets are split between croissant-type items and proper dessert treats. **Known for:** Parisian feel; flaky brioche feuilleetée filled with almond paste; duck pithivier (similar to a meat pie). ⓢ *Average main: $14* ⊠ *710 Montgomery St., Jackson Square* ☎ *415/359–1000* ⊕ *maisonnico.com* ⊙ *Closed Mon. and Tues.*

Terminus Cafe and Bar

$ | **AMERICAN** | With coffee, sandwiches, and salads by day, and superb drinks at night, this spot right by the California St. cable car terminus is a charming place to visit. Its atmosphere is refreshingly low-key for FiDi—the rare downtown establishment that feels like a true neighborhood gathering place. **Known for:** relaxed atmosphere; excellent kale salad; not flashy yet unique cocktails. ⓢ *Average main: $12* ⊠ *16 California St., Financial District* ☎ *415/960–8405* ⊕ *terminussf.com.*

Hotels

The large hotels here lure business travelers with some of the city's finest luxury accommodations—with hefty price tags to boot. With public transportation, Union Square, the Ferry Building, Chinatown, and North Beach a short walk away, leisure travelers find this area a good base as well.

Four Seasons Hotel San Francisco at Embarcadero
$$$ | **HOTEL** | Each luxurious room at the city's second Four Seasons has spectacular city and bay views; the hotel occupies the top 11 floors in two wings connected by a glass skybridge atop one of San Francisco's tallest and most recognizable buildings. **Pros:** great fitness center; spacious rooms; sleek design. **Cons:** in a business area that's quiet nights and weekends; clunky website; no swimming pool. [$] *Rooms from: $446* ✉ *222 Sansome St., Financial District* ☎ *415/276–9888* 🌐 *www.fourseasons.com/embarcadero* 🛏 *155 rooms* 🍴 *No Meals.*

Galleria Park Hotel
$ | **HOTEL** | At the edge of the FiDi and Union Square areas, this boutique hotel manages to be both hip and welcoming, with modern touches on historical bones and smallish guest rooms with all the technological amenities modern travelers require. **Pros:** park terrace with walking track; complimentary wine at daily Sipping Hour; in-house Blue Bottle Coffee. **Cons:** relatively small deluxe rooms; city noise; no restaurant. [$] *Rooms from: $179* ✉ *191 Sutter St., Financial District* ☎ *415/781–3060* 🌐 *www.galleriapark.com* 🛏 *177 rooms* 🍴 *No Meals.*

Hilton San Francisco Financial District
$ | **HOTEL** | **FAMILY** | Business travelers patronize this hoppin' Hilton for its airy guest rooms and large work desks, but even in high season the weekend rates drop significantly, luring leisure travelers. **Pros:** technology lounge; good-size rooms with bay or city views; great location at intersection of FiDi, Chinatown, and North Beach. **Cons:** feels corporate; no valet parking and self parking is pricey; 11 am checkout time. [$] *Rooms from: $179* ✉ *750 Kearny St., Financial District* ☎ *415/433–6600* 🌐 *www.hilton.com* 🛏 *543 rooms* 🍴 *No Meals.*

Le Méridien San Francisco
$$ | **HOTEL** | The stylishly contemporary Le Méridien scores well on both form and function, with compelling artwork throughout the lobby and guest rooms outfitted with polished granite sinks, wall-size San Francisco maps, and floor-to-ceiling windows. **Pros:** spacious rooms; interesting artwork; accommodating staff. **Cons:** area grows sleepy after dark; no on-site parking option; low, funky bed style. [$] *Rooms from: $208* ✉ *333 Battery St., Financial District* ☎ *415/296–2900* 🌐 *marriott.com* 🛏 *360 rooms* 🍴 *No Meals.*

Omni San Francisco Hotel
$$ | **HOTEL** | In a 1926 Florentine Renaissance–style structure that once housed banks and other financial enterprises, the Omni draws travelers seeking historical flavor and a downtown location. **Pros:** comfortable rooms with historical flavor; great on-site bar; "get fit" kits for working out in-room, plus well-equipped fitness center. **Cons:** deluxe and premier rooms could use more natural light; traditional look; in-house food offerings are pedestrian. [$] *Rooms from: $209* ✉ *500 California St., Financial District* ☎ *415/677–9494* 🌐 *www.omnisanfrancisco.com* 🛏 *362 rooms* 🍴 *No Meals.*

Nightlife

Not surprisingly, the nightlife scene here revolves around people recovering from extended workdays or still trying to seal the deal. Wiggle in among the shop talkers and enjoy a stiff martini.

BARS
Pagan Idol

BARS | Giving the Tonga Room a run for its money as the most kitschy tiki bar in town, Pagan Idol features a secret back room complete with erupting volcano, giant tikis, and a starry night sky. The folks from Bourbon & Branch are behind this faux pirate ship, so even if the cocktails are served in goofy tiki glasses with paper umbrellas, rest assured they're on the money. ⊠ *375 Bush St., Financial District* ☎ *415/985–6375* ⊕ *www.paganidol. com* ⊗ *Closed Sun. and Mon.*

Rickhouse

BARS | An after-work FiDi crowd fills this brick-walled and dimly lit, speakeasy-ish drinking spot, revered for its extensive whiskey menu and curated list of seasonal cocktails. ⊠ *246 Kearny St., Financial District* ☎ *415/398–2827* ⊕ *www.rickhousebar.com* ⊗ *Closed Sun. and Mon.*

The Treasury

BARS | With a striking, almost elegant interior, this is a prime happy hour spot in the afternoon, then a citywide cocktail destination afterward. You can't go wrong with any of the cocktails, but the bar has a particular affinity for sherry. ⊠ *200 Bush St., Suite 101, Financial District* ☎ *415/578–0530* ⊕ *www.thetreasurysf. com* ⊗ *Closed weekends.*

COMEDY
Punch Line

COMEDY CLUBS | A launch pad for the likes of Robin Williams and Ellen DeGeneres, this medium-sized club books some of the nation's top comedy talents. ⊠ *444 Battery St., Financial District* ☎ *415/397–7573* ⊕ *www.punchlinecomedyclub.com.*

🎫 Performing Arts

THEATER
42nd Street Moon

THEATER | This group produces delightful "semi-staged" concert performances of rare chestnuts from Broadway's golden age, such as *Fiorello!* and *Anything Goes.* ⊠ *Gateway Theatre, 215 Jackson St., Financial District* ☎ *415/255–8207* ⊕ *42ndstmoon.org.*

Chapter 6

CHINATOWN AND NORTH BEACH

Updated by
Denise Leto

⊙ Sights	🍴 Restaurants	🛏 Hotels	🛍 Shopping	🍸 Nightlife
★★★☆☆	★★★★★	★☆☆☆☆	★★★★☆	★★★★☆

NEIGHBORHOOD SNAPSHOT

TOP EXPERIENCES

■ **Tin How Temple:** Climb the narrow stairway to this space in Chinatown with hundreds of red lanterns, then step onto the tiny balcony and take in the alley scene below.

■ **Ross Alley:** Breathe in the scented air as you watch the nimble hands of workers at Chinatown's Golden Gate Fortune Cookie Factory on this narrow one-block, shop-lined alley first built in the gold rush days of 1849.

■ **Chinatown walk and dine:** Stroll down Grant Avenue and Stockton Street, Chinatown's main thoroughfares, and enjoy steamed pork buns and red-bean sesame balls from the decades-old shops.

■ **Espresso:** Or cappuccino, americano, mocha— however you take your caffeine, this is the neighborhood for it. Grabbing a coffee constitutes sightseeing here, so find a worthy spot and get to work.

■ **Colorful watering holes:** The high concentration of bars with character, like Specs' and Vesuvio, makes North Beach perfect for a pub crawl.

■ **Browsing books at City Lights:** Illuminate your mind at this Beat-era landmark. Its ample selection, author events, and keen staff make it as cool as ever.

VIEWFINDER

North Beach offers no shortage of beautiful vantage points. It's well worth the trip up Telegraph Hill to Coit Tower, where sweeping city and bay views abound. Just as lovely—and less crowded—are the views on the way up (or down), along the Filbert or Vallejo Steps, which are themselves borderline magical. A much less well-known vista can be had from the top floor of the North Beach Parking Garage (⌧ *735 Vallejo St.*). Not only does the parking structure have views of the Bay Bridge and Coit Tower, it gets bonus points for fortunes (à la fortune cookies) spray-painted in every parking stall.

GETTING HERE

■ It's an easy walk to Chinatown from Union Square, both Powell lines of the cable-car system pass through, and getting there on the new Central Subway requires just one stop from Powell. Avoid driving— parking is a hassle.

■ The Powell–Mason cable- car line can drop you by Washington Square Park, in the heart of North Beach. The 30–Stockton and 15–3rd Street buses run from Mar- ket Street. North Beach is a snap to explore on foot.

■ It's an easy stroll between Chinatown and North Beach.

PLANNING YOUR TIME

■ Allow at least two hours to tour compact China- town. Come on a weekday before lunchtime to avoid the crowds. You won't need more than 20 minutes at any of the sights, but take your time exploring the shops and alleys and having a few bites along the way.

■ There's no bad time of day to visit North Beach. The cafés buzz from morn- ing to night, the shops along the main drags stay open until at least 6 pm, and late- night revelers are out past 2 am. Sunday is quieter, since some shops close. Plan to linger for a few hours.

A few blocks uphill from Union Square is the abrupt beginning of dense and insular Chinatown—the oldest such community in the country. When the street signs have Chinese characters, produce stalls take up most of the sidewalk, and whole roast ducks hang in deli windows, you'll know you've arrived.

The neighborhood fills the 17 blocks and 41 alleys bordered roughly by Bush, Kearny, and Powell Streets and Broadway. A number of neighborhood businesses closed or struggled during the COVID-19 pandemic, and, as in other parts of San Francisco and in cities around America, the community is seeing an unfortunate rise in anti–Asian American incidents. The city is trying hard to support this landmark neighborhood and keep its largely elderly population safe.

At its northern end, Chinatown overlaps with North Beach, described by San Francisco novelist Herbert Gold as "the longest-running, most glorious, American bohemian operetta outside Greenwich Village." Indeed, to anyone who has spent some time in its eccentric old bars and cafés, North Beach evokes everything from the Barbary Coast days to the no-less-rowdy Beatnik era.

Italian delis appear frozen in time, rife with homages to writers Jack Kerouac and Allen Ginsberg, and the area is dotted with adult-entertainment meccas nodding to North Beach's bawdy history, the modern equivalent of its once-wild sin city legacy. Although the outdoor café tables seem like a contrived scene of European alfresco dining, the real heart and soul of this part of the city remains inside the iconic enclaves, away from the throngs of tourists.

Chinatown

Chinatown is very much both a residential *and* a tourist neighborhood, with some overly tourist-focused souvenir shops. Yet it is still an incredibly unique, welcoming place that residents love to share. Each day sees a joyful mix of curious visitors eating pork buns and gazing at the architecture, while longtime locals walk by after to shop for the night's dinner. Join the flow along Grant Avenue and its side streets: good-luck banners of crimson and gold hang beside dragon-entwined lampposts and pagoda roofs, and honking cars chime in with shoppers bargaining in Cantonese or Mandarin.

◉ Sights

Chinatown Gate
NOTABLE BUILDING | At the official entrance to Chinatown, stone lions flank the base of the pagoda-topped gate; the lions, dragons, and fish up top symbolize wealth, prosperity, and other

Chinatown Gate is an inviting entrance to the second-largest Chinatown outside of Asia.

good things. The four Chinese characters immediately beneath the pagoda represent the philosophy of Sun Yat-sen, the leader who unified China in the early 20th century. Sun Yat-sen, who lived in exile in San Francisco for a few years, promoted the notion of friendship and peace among all nations based on equality, justice, and goodwill. The vertical characters under the left pagoda read "peace" and "trust," the ones under the right pagoda "respect" and "love." The whole shebang telegraphs the internationally understood message of "photo op." Immediately beyond the gate, dive into souvenir shopping on Grant Avenue, Chinatown's tourist strip. ⊠ Grant Ave. at Bush St., Chinatown.

Chinese Culture Center
COLLEGE | Chiefly a place for the community to gather for calligraphy and tai chi workshops, the center operates a gallery with interesting temporary exhibits by Chinese and Chinese American artists. Excellent political, historical, and food-focused walking tours of Chinatown depart from the gallery. ⊠ Hilton San Francisco Financial District, 750 Kearny St., 3rd fl., Chinatown ☎ 415/986–1822 ⊕ www.cccsf.us ✉ Center and gallery free (donations suggested), tour $45 ☉ Closed Sun.

Golden Gate Fortune Cookie Factory
FACTORY | FAMILY | Follow your nose down Ross Alley to this tiny but fragrant cookie factory. Two workers sit at circular motorized griddles and wait for dollops of batter to drop onto a tiny metal plate, which rotates into an oven. A few moments later, out comes a cookie that's pliable and ready for folding. It's easy to peek in for a moment, and hard to leave without getting a few free samples and then buying a bagful of fortune cookies for snacks and wisdom later. ⊠ 56 Ross Alley, between Washington and Jackson Sts., west of Grant Ave., Chinatown ☎ 415/781–3956 ⊕ www.goldengatefortunecookies.com ✉ Free.

Kong Chow Temple
TEMPLE | This ornate temple to the god of honesty and trust sets a somber, spiritual tone right away with a sign warning

visitors not to touch anything. Chinese stores and restaurants often display his image because he's thought to bring good luck in business. Chinese immigrants established the temple in 1851; its congregation moved to this building in 1977. Take the elevator up to the fourth floor, where incense fills the air. You can show respect by placing a dollar or two in the donation box and by leaving your phone stowed. Amid the statuary, flowers, and richly colored altars (red wards off evil spirits and signifies virility, green symbolizes longevity, and gold connotes majesty), a couple of plaques announce that "Mrs. Harry S. Truman came to this temple in June 1948 for a prediction on the outcome of the election … this fortune came true." ■TIP➡ **The temple's balcony has a good view of Chinatown.** ✉ *855 Stockton St., 4th fl., Chinatown* ☎ *415/788–1339* 💲 *Free.*

Old St. Mary's Cathedral + Chinese Mission
RELIGIOUS BUILDING | Dedicated in 1854, this church served as the city's Catholic cathedral until 1891. The verse below the massive clock face beseeched naughty Barbary Coast boys: "Son, observe the time and fly from evil." Across the street from the church in St. Mary's Square, a Beniamino Bufano statue of Sun Yat-sen towers over the site of the Chinese leader's favorite reading spot during his years in San Francisco. On Tuesdays at 12:30 pm, the church hosts free chamber music concerts (⊕ *noontimeconcerts. org*). ■TIP➡ **A surprisingly peaceful spot, St. Mary's Square also has a couple of small, well-kept playgrounds, perfect for a break from the hustle and bustle of Chinatown.** ✉ *660 California St., at Grant Ave., Chinatown* ⊕ *www.oldsaintmarys.org.*

Portsmouth Square
PLAZA/SQUARE | Chinatown's living room buzzes with activity: the square, with its pagoda-shape structures, is a favorite spot for morning tai chi, and by noon dozens of men huddle around Chinese chess tables, engaged in competition. Kids scamper about the square's two grungy playgrounds. Back in the late 19th century this land was near the waterfront. The square is named for the USS *Portsmouth*, the ship helmed by Captain John Montgomery, who in 1846 raised the American flag here and claimed the then-Mexican land for the United States. A couple of years later, Sam Brannan kicked off the gold rush at the square when he waved his loot and proclaimed, "Gold from the American River!" Robert Louis Stevenson, the author of *Treasure Island,* often dropped by, chatting up the sailors who hung out here. Some of the information he gleaned about life at sea found its way into his fiction. A bronze galleon sculpture, a tribute to Stevenson, anchors the square's northwest corner. A plaque marks the site of California's first public school, built in 1847. ✉ *Bordered by Walter Lum Pl. and Kearny, Washington, and Clay Sts., Chinatown* ⊕ *sfrecpark.org.*

★ Tin How Temple
TEMPLE | In 1852, Day Ju, one of the first three Chinese to arrive in San Francisco, dedicated this temple to the Queen of the Heavens and the Goddess of the Seven Seas, and the temple looks largely the same today as it did more than a century ago. Duck into the inconspicuous doorway, climb three flights of stairs, and be surrounded by the aroma of incense in this tiny, altar-filled room. In the entryway, elderly ladies can often be seen preparing "money" to be burned as offerings to various Buddhist gods or as funds for ancestors to use in the afterlife. Hundreds of red-and-gold lanterns cover the ceiling; the larger the lamp, the larger its donor's contribution to the temple. Gifts of oranges, dim sum, and money left by the faithful, who kneel while reciting prayers, rest on altars to different gods. Tin How presides over the middle back of the temple, flanked by one red and one green lesser god. Taking photographs is not allowed. ✉ *125 Waverly Pl., between Clay and Washington Sts., Chinatown* 💲 *Free, donations accepted.*

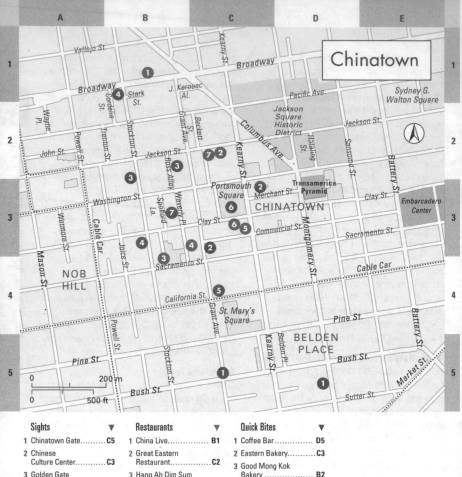

Chinatown

Sights ▼
1 Chinatown Gate.......... **C5**
2 Chinese Culture Center............ **C3**
3 Golden Gate Fortune Cookie Factory................... **B2**
4 Kong Chow Temple..... **B3**
5 Old St Mary's Cathedral + Chinese Mission......... **C4**
6 Portsmouth Square................... **C3**
7 Tin How Temple......... **B3**

Restaurants ▼
1 China Live............... **B1**
2 Great Eastern Restaurant............... **C2**
3 Hang Ah Dim Sum Tea Room............... **B4**
4 Mister Jiu's............... **C3**
5 R & G Lounge............. **C3**
6 Sam Wo Restaurant............... **C3**
7 Z & Y Restaurant......... **C2**

Quick Bites ▼
1 Coffee Bar............... **D5**
2 Eastern Bakery........... **C3**
3 Good Mong Kok Bakery................... **B2**
4 Hing Lung Co. **B1**

🍽 Restaurants

Step beneath the gateway on Grant Avenue and meander the alleyways, into the restaurants and bakeries along Jackson, Clay, and Washington Streets. A food market, along Stockton, is a riot of unusual fruits, vegetables, and other delicacies. Restaurants feature the cuisine of (mostly) China's Guangdong Province, that is, the Cantonese style, but you'll also find restaurants focused on Sichuan, Hunanese, and Shanghai cuisine. The area has several bakeries and takeout dim sum specialists.

China Live

$$ | CHINESE | It's been compared to a Chinatown version of Eataly, but George Chen's ultra-ambitious market, restaurant, bar, and fine-dining-experience project is its own unique place. The main ground-floor Market Restaurant excels at a wide variety of specialties from dumplings to duck, served in a refined, industrial-style dining room surrounded by different cooking areas; upstairs, the intimate Eight Tables is one of San Francisco's most elaborate special-occasion tasting-menu experiences. **Known for:** sheng jian bao pork dumplings; "nine essential flavors of Chinese cuisine" dish at Eight Tables; outstanding tea selection. Ⓢ *Average main: $26* ✉ *644 Broadway, Chinatown* ☎ *415/788–8188* ⊕ *chinalivesf. com* ⊙ *No lunch.*

Great Eastern Restaurant

$$ | CHINESE | FAMILY | Dine here for fresh, simply prepared Cantonese cuisine, especially the seafood—from tanks that occupy a corner of the main dining room—as well as kid favorites, such as stir-fried noodles, cashew chicken, and fried rice. Dim sum starts at 10 am, but there aren't any carts—you order off a paper sheet, and the dumplings come out of the kitchen piping hot. **Known for:** shrimp dumplings; ornate pagoda-roof exterior; then-president Barack Obama ate takeout from here. Ⓢ *Average main:*

Look Up! 👁

When wandering around Chinatown, don't forget to look up! Above the chintziest souvenir shop might loom an ornate balcony or a curly pagoda roof. The best examples are on the 900 block of Grant Avenue (at Washington Street) and at Waverly Place.

$25 ✉ *649 Jackson St., Chinatown* ☎ *415/986–2500* ⊕ *www.greateasternsf. com* ⊙ *Closed Tues.*

Hang Ah Dim Sum Tea House

$ | CHINESE | Enjoying the barbecue pork buns and curry chicken at this Chinatown icon dating to 1920 is a bite into both culinary history and San Francisco's past. Located on an alley, it's one of the smaller, more homey, and less frenetic sit-down dim sum choices in the city, with a small dining room simply decorated with pieces of Chinese art and a few Bruce Lee movie posters. **Known for:** the country's first dim sum house; soup dumplings; red-bean bun desserts decorated like cute animals. Ⓢ *Average main: $15* ✉ *1 Pagoda Pl., between Sacramento and Clay Sts., Chinatown* ☎ *415/982–5686* ⊕ *hangahdimsumsf.com.*

Mister Jiu's

$$$$ | CHINESE | Brandon Jew's ambitious, graceful restaurant offers the chef's delicious contemporary, farm-to-table interpretation of Chinese cuisine that sometimes tweaks classic dishes with a California spin (hot-and-sour soup with nasturtiums) or enhances fresh produce with unique Chinese flavors (local asparagus with smoked tofu). The elegant dining room—accented with plants and a chrysanthemum chandelier—provides beautiful views of Chinatown, while the menu breathes new life into it. **Known for:** sea urchin cheong fun (rice noodle rolls); standout cocktails; large-format roast duck with pancakes. $ *Average main: $49* ✉ *28 Waverly Pl., Chinatown* ☎ *415/857–9688* ⊕ *misterjius.com* ☾ *Closed Sun. and Mon. No lunch.*

R&G Lounge

$$ | **CHINESE** | **FAMILY** | Salt-and-pepper Dungeness crab is a delicious draw at this bright, three-level Cantonese eatery that always has a packed crowd for its crustacean specialties—crab portions can easily be split for three—and dim sum. A menu with photographs will help you sort through other Hong Kong specialties, including Peking duck and shrimp-stuffed bean curd. **Known for:** three treasures with shrimp and black bean sauce; stir-fry "special beef"; high-energy crowd of all ages. $ *Average main: $24* ✉ *631 Kearny St., Chinatown* ☎ *415/982–7877* ⊕ *www. rnglounge.com.*

Sam Wo Restaurant

$ | **CHINESE** | Few restaurants in San Francisco can match the history of this city treasure that has been around since 1908. You'll want to try as much as possible from the menu, which is a unique mix of Cantonese dishes, a few items from other regions of China, a couple Southeast Asia–inspired noodles, and more familiar Chinese American fare. **Known for:** iconic sign; jook (rice porridge); barbecue pork noodle roll. $ *Average main: $13* ✉ *713 Clay St., Chinatown* ☎ *415/989–8898* ⊕ *samworestaurant. com* ☾ *Closed Tues.*

Z & Y Restaurant

$$ | **SICHUAN** | San Francisco's signature Sichuan restaurant is a wonderful place to sample the often spicy, mouth-numbing (that's the "mala" heat, then the cooling effect of the peppers and chilies) cuisine of that northern China region. It's a long menu, so ask for advice from the servers. **Known for:** house spicy fresh fish; "couple's delight" beef-three-ways appetizer; energetic dining room. $ *Average main: $25* ✉ *655 Jackson St.,*

Chinatown ☎ *415/981–8988* ⊕ *zandyrestaurant.com* ☾ *Closed Tues.*

☕ Coffee and Quick Bites

Coffee Bar

$ | **CAFÉ** | For seriously good local roast in Chinatown, head to this tiny storefront at the entrance to St. Mary's Square. **Known for:** high-quality joe in out-of-the-way spot; unique seasonal coffee drinks; Havana Latte, with sweetened condensed milk. $ *Average main: $5* ✉ *433 Kearny St., Chinatown* ⊕ *www.original-coffeebarsf.com* ☾ *Closed weekends.*

Eastern Bakery

$ | **BAKERY** | Claiming to be Chinatown's oldest bakery, this packed space is a must-stop, with the goods to back up its rep. Try the moon cakes and egg custard tarts. **Known for:** Chinatown's oldest bakery, opened in 1924; moon cakes and flaky dan tat (egg tarts); addictive coffee crunch cake topped with toffee pieces. $ *Average main: $6* ✉ *720 Grant St., Chinatown* ⊕ *www.easternbakery.com* ▭ *No credit cards.*

Good Mong Kok Bakery

$ | **CHINESE** | At this line-around-the-corner, no-English-spoken bakery, the delicious dim sum is strictly to-go, so picnic at Woh Hei Yuen Park on Powell Street or Portsmouth Square. **Known for:** taciturn service; low prices and good value; large portions of authentic and yummy dim sum. $ *Average main: $7* ✉ *1039 Stockton St., Chinatown* ⊕ *www. goodmongkok.com.*

Hing Lung Co.

$ | **CHINESE** | It's impossible to miss this Stockton Street Cantonese barbecue butchery icon—just look for the air-drying ducks and pigs hanging from above and the sign in the window that reads "Go duck yourself," the name by which many locals know this to-go favorite. Roast duck, crispy roast pork, and succulent honey barbecue pork are the marquee

Continued on page 147

CHINATOWN

Chinatown's streets flood the senses. Incense and cigarette smoke mingle with the scents of briny fish and sweet vanilla. Rooflines flare outward, pagoda-style. Loud Cantonese bargaining and honking car horns rise above the sharp clack of mah-jongg tiles and the eternally humming cables beneath the street.

Most Chinatown visitors march down Grant Avenue, buy a few trinkets, take a few photos of paper lanterns and dragon-draped lamp posts, and call it a day. Do yourself a favor and dig deeper. This is one of the largest Chinese communities outside Asia, and there is far more to it than buying a back-scratcher near Chinatown Gate. To get a real feel for the neighborhood, wander off the main drag. Step into a temple or an herb shop and wander down a flag-draped alley.

Whatever you do, don't leave without eating something. Noodle houses, bakeries, tea houses, and dim sum shops seem to occupy every other storefront. There's a feast for your eyes as well: in the market windows on Stockton and Grant, you'll see hanging whole roast ducks, fish, and shellfish swimming in tanks, and strips of shiny, pink-glazed Chinese-style barbecued pork.

CHINATOWN'S EARLY HISTORY

The Street of Gamblers (Ross Alley), 1898 (top). The first Chinese telephone operator in Chinatown (bottom).

Sam Brannan's 1848 cry of "Gold!" didn't take long to reach across the world to China. Struggling with famine, drought, and political upheaval at home, thousands of Chinese jumped at the chance to try their luck in California. Most came from the Pearl River Delta region, in the Guangdong province, and spoke Cantonese dialects. From the start, Chinese businesses circled around Portsmouth Square, which was conveniently central. Bachelor rooming houses sprang up, since the vast majority of new arrivals were men. By 1853, the area was called Chinatown.

COLD WELCOME

The Chinese faced discrimination from the get-go. Harrassment became outright hostility as first the gold rush, then the work on the Transcontinental Railroad petered out. Special taxes were imposed to shoulder aside competing "coolie labor." Laws forbidding the Chinese from moving outside Chinatown kept the residents packed in like sardines, with nowhere to go but up and down—thus the many basement establishments in the neighborhood. State and federal laws passed in the 1870s deterred Chinese women from immigrating, deeming them prostitutes. In the late 1870s, looting and arson attacks on Chinatown businesses soared.

The coup de grace, though, was the Chinese Exclusion Act, passed by the U.S. Congress in 1882, which slammed the doors to America for "Asiatics." This was

Chinatown's Grant Avenue.

Women and children flooded into the neighborhood after the Great Quake.

the country's first significant restriction on immigration. The law also prevented the existing Chinese residents, including American-born children, from becoming naturalized citizens. With a society of mostly men (forbidden, of course, from marrying white women), many San Franciscans hoped that a Chinatown neighborhood would not have a strong presence in the city.

OUT OF THE ASHES
When the devastating 1906 earthquake and fire hit, city fathers thought they'd seize the opportunity to kick the Chinese out of Chinatown and get their hands on that desirable piece of downtown real estate. Then Chinatown businessman Look Tin Eli had a brainstorm of Disneyesque proportions.

He proposed that Chinatown be rebuilt, but in a tourist-friendly, stylized, "Oriental" way. Anglo-American architects would design new buildings with pagoda roofs and dragon-covered columns. Chinatown would attract more tourists—the curious had been visiting on the sly for decades—and add more tax money

to the city's coffers. Ka-ching: the sales pitch worked.

PAPER SONS
For the Chinese, the 1906 earthquake turned the virtual "no entry" sign into a flashing neon "welcome!" All the city's immigration records went up in smoke, and the Chinese quickly began to apply for passports as U.S. citizens, claiming their old ones were lost in the fire. Not only did thousands of Chinese become legal overnight, but so did their sons in China, or "sons," if they weren't really related. Whole families in Chinatown had passports in names that weren't their own; these "paper sons" were not only a windfall but also an uncomfortable neighborhood conspiracy. The city caught on eventually and set up an immigration center on Angel Island in 1910. Immigrants spent weeks or months being inspected and interrogated while their papers were checked. Roughly 250,000 people made it through. With this influx, including women and children, Chinatown finally became a more complete community.

A GREAT WALK THROUGH CHINATOWN

■ Start at the Chinatown Gate and walk ahead on Grant Avenue, entering the souvenir gauntlet. (You'll also pass Old St. Mary's Cathedral.)

■ Make a right on Clay Street for a great view of the Transamerica Pyramid ahead. The *Ross Alley 1889* mural to your right depicts a Chinatown alley (a stop on this walk) after the Chinese Exclusion Act. Next, turn left and walk to spacious Portsmouth Square.

■ Head up Washington Street to the Old Chinese Telephone Exchange building, now the East West Bank. Across Grant, look left for Waverly Place. Here Free Republic of China (Taiwanese) flags flap over some of the neighborhood's most striking buildings, including Tin How Temple.

■ At the Sacramento Street end of Waverly Place stands the First Chinese Baptist Church of 1908. Across the way, Mister Jiu's restaurant bridges the gap between the neighborhood's history and modern seasonal California dining. Make a U-turn at Sacramento Street and visit the Tin How Temple (No. 125) on your return toward Washington Street.

■ Head back to Washington Street and check out the many herb shops.

■ Follow the scent of vanilla down Ross Alley to the Golden Gate Fortune Cookie Factory, where many fortunes and crunchy, crescent-shape cookies have been produced since 1962.

■ Turn left on Jackson Street; ahead is the real Chinatown's main artery, Stockton Street, where most residents do their grocery shopping. Both sides of Stockton Street in this stretch north to Broadway alternate between herbal stores, bustling markets, butcher and fish shops, and on-the-go dim sum stops like Good Mong Kok Bakery and Wing Sing Dim Sum. Look toward the back of stores for Buddhist altars with offerings of oranges and grapefruit. From here you can loop one block east back to Grant.

items on the concise menu, and must-try signature tastes of Chinatown history. **Known for:** char siu (barbecue pork) with deliciously thick char; perfectly roasted duck; runs out of favorites later in the day. $ *Average main: $14* ✉ *1261 Stockton St., Chinatown* ☎ *415/397–5521* ☾ *Closed Mon. and Tues.*

Nightlife

BARS

Cold Drinks Bar

COCKTAIL LOUNGES | China Live's stylish upstairs, vintage Shanghai–inspired bar focuses on scotch and intricate cocktails with no shortage of creativity. The renowned AvroKO firm's sharp-as-a-tuxedo design, with dramatic lighting and a black-and-gold motif, is as glamorous a setting for drinking as any in this city. ✉ *644 Broadway, 2nd fl., Chinatown* ☎ *415/788–8188* ⊕ *chinalivesf.com.*

Moongate Lounge

COCKTAIL LOUNGES | The upstairs, slightly more casual and hip bar/lounge companion to Mister Jiu's is a destination in its own right. Lunar themes are everywhere, from the drinks' names and colors to the mystical lighting and design accents in a suave space that previously was a banquet room. Smaller bites have the same seasonal and technique-driven Chinese-Californian bent as the more upscale food downstairs. ✉ *28 Waverly Pl., 2nd fl., Chinatown* ☎ *415/857–9688* ⊕ *www.moongatelounge.com.*

🎭 Performing Arts

Noontime Concerts at Old St. Mary's Cathedral

MUSIC | The Gothic Revival church, completed in 1872 and rebuilt after the 1906 earthquake, hosts a notable free chamber-music series on Tuesday at 12:30. ✉ *660 California St., Chinatown* ☎ *415/777–3211* ⊕ *www.noontimeconcerts.org.*

🛍 Shopping

ART GALLERY

Jessica Silverman Gallery

ART GALLERIES | One of the city's leading galleries devoted to emerging contemporary artists resides along Chinatown's main thoroughfare. Jessica Silverman has been instrumental in launching the careers of several artists and constantly puts together interesting exhibitions. ✉ *621 Grant Ave., Chinatown* ☎ *415/255–9508* ⊕ *jessicasilvermangallery.com.*

CLOTHING

Kim + Ono

SOUVENIRS | Hand-painted robes, kimonos, formal dresses, and jackets are sold at this second generation family-owned spot. Chic Asia-inspired gifts and smaller items make great souvenirs. ✉ *729 Grant Ave., Chinatown* ☎ *415/989–8588* ⊕ *kimandono.com.*

FOOD AND DRINK

★ Vital Tea Leaf

OTHER FOOD & DRINK | Tea enthusiasts will feel at peace in this bright, spacious haven for sipping. You'll find more than 400 different varieties of tea here, and the staff is extremely knowledgeable on the health benefits of each and every one. ✉ *1044 Grant Ave., between Jackson St. and Pacific Ave., Chinatown* ☎ *415/981–2388* ⊕ *vitaltealeaf.net.*

HOUSEWARES

The Wok Shop

HOUSEWARES | The store carries woks, of course, but also anything else you could need for Chinese cooking and eating—bamboo steamers, ginger graters, wicked-looking cleavers—plus artistic chopstick holders and accessories for Japanese cooking, including sushi paraphernalia and tempura racks. ✉ *718 Grant Ave., at Sacramento St., Chinatown* ☎ *415/989–3797* ⊕ *www.wokshop.com.*

A North Beach Walk

To hit the highlights of the neighborhood, start off with a browse at Beat landmark **City Lights Bookstore**. For cool boutique shopping, head north up **Grant Avenue**. Otherwise, it's time to get down to the serious business of people-watching. Make a left onto **Columbus Avenue** when you leave the bookstore and walk the strip until you find a respectable coffee café or pastry display howling your name.

Sugar-loaded, continue down Columbus to **Washington Square**, where you can walk or take the 39 bus up **Telegraph Hill** to Coit Tower's views. Be sure to take in the gorgeous gardens along the **Filbert Steps** on the way down. Finally, reward yourself by returning to **Columbus Avenue** for a drink at one of the atmosphere-steeped watering holes like **Vesuvio** or **Specs'**.

TOYS AND GADGETS
Chinatown Kite Shop
TOYS | This family-run shop has been selling bright, fun-shaped kites—dragons, butterflies, sharks—since the 1960s. There's a lot more than kites, too, with feng shui items, art tiles, and even iPhone cases that can go home as local souvenirs. ✉ *717 Grant Ave., near Sacramento St., Chinatown* ☎ *415/989–5182*.

North Beach

North Beach truly was a beach at the time of the gold rush—the bay extended into the hollow between Telegraph and Russian Hills. Among the first immigrants to Yerba Buena during the early 1840s were young men from the northern provinces of Italy. The Genoese started the fishing industry in the newly renamed boomtown of San Francisco, as well as a much-needed produce business. Later, Sicilians emerged as leaders of the fishing fleets and eventually as proprietors of the seafood restaurants lining Fisherman's Wharf. Meanwhile, their Genoese cousins established banking and manufacturing empires.

This was once an almost exclusively Italian American neighborhood, but today the area's premium rental market has

driven away many of these residents to other neighborhoods. The neighborhood lies alongside a still-robust Chinese community that is now being joined by transplanted yuppie populations. Still, walk down narrow Romolo Place (off Broadway east of Columbus) or Genoa Place (off Union west of Kearny) or Medau Place (off Filbert west of Grant) and you can catch a hint of the Italian roots of this neighborhood. Locals may think the city's finest Italian restaurants are elsewhere, but North Beach has some gems and is, after all, the place that puts folks in mind of Italian food, with addresses worth seeking out despite some kitschy traps. The street foods of choice are bags of focaccia or massive subs from Liguria Bakery, Molinari's, or Freddie's, eaten warm or cold. Random aromas fill the air: coffee beans, cured salami, Italian dolce, and—depending on the corner you've turned—pungent garlic.

⊙ Sights

Beat Museum
HISTORY MUSEUM | "Museum" might be a stretch for this tiny storefront that's half bookstore, half memorabilia collection. You can see the 1949 Hudson from the movie version of *On the Road* and the shirt Neal Cassady wore while driving Ken Kesey's Merry Prankster bus,

City Lights bookstore is a literary icon with three floors of books and zines.

"Further." There are also manuscripts, letters, and early editions by Jack Kerouac, Allen Ginsberg, and Lawrence Ferlinghetti. But the true treasure here is the passionate and well-informed staff, which often includes the museum's founder, Jerry Cimino: your short visit may turn into an hours-long trip through the Beat era. ■ TIP➔ **Excellent walking tours go beyond the museum to take in favorite Beat watering holes and hangouts in North Beach.** ✉ *540 Broadway, North Beach* ☎ *800/537–6822, 415/399–9626* ⊕ *www.kerouac.com* ✉ *$8* ☺ *Closed Tues. and Wed.*

★ City Lights Bookstore

STORE/MALL | The exterior of this famous bookstore is iconic in itself, from the replica of a revolutionary mural destroyed in Chiapas, Mexico, by military forces to the art banners hanging above the windows. Designated a landmark by the city, the hangout of Beat-era writers and independent publishers remains a vital part of San Francisco's literary scene. Browse the three levels of poetry, philosophy, politics, fiction, history, and local zines, to the beat of creaking wood floors.

Back in the day, writers like Allen Ginsberg and Jack Kerouac would read here (and even receive mail in the basement). The late poet Lawrence Ferlinghetti, who cofounded City Lights in 1953, cemented its place in history by publishing Ginsberg's *Howl and Other Poems* in 1956. The small volume was ignored in the mainstream—until Ferlinghetti and the bookstore manager were arrested for obscenity and corruption of youth. In the landmark First Amendment trial that followed, the judge exonerated both men. *Howl* went on to become a classic.

Stroll Kerouac Alley, branching off Columbus Avenue next to City Lights, to read the quotes from Ferlinghetti, Maya Angelou, Confucius, John Steinbeck, and the street's namesake embedded in the pavement. ✉ *261 Columbus Ave., North Beach* ☎ *415/362–8193* ⊕ *citylights.com.*

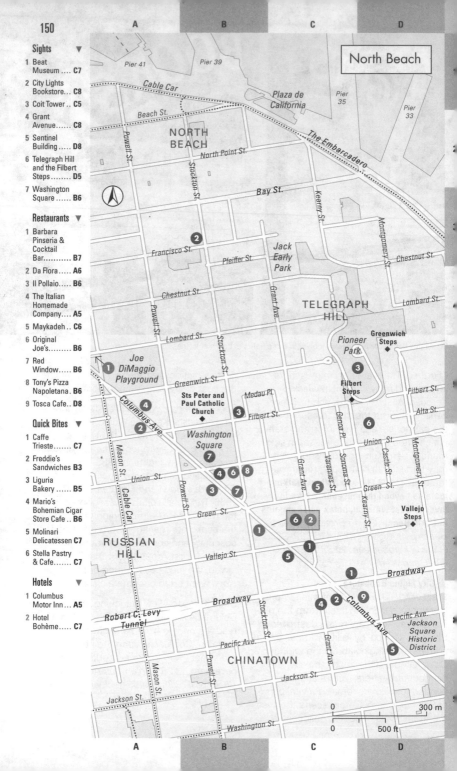

Sights ▼

1 Beat Museum **C7**
2 City Lights Bookstore... **C8**
3 Coit Tower .. **C5**
4 Grant Avenue...... **C8**
5 Sentinel Building **D8**
6 Telegraph Hill and the Filbert Steps **D5**
7 Washington Square **B6**

Restaurants ▼

1 Barbara Pinseria & Cocktail Bar........... **B7**
2 Da Flora **A6**
3 Il Pollaio..... **B6**
4 The Italian Homemade Company.... **A5**
5 Maykadeh .. **C6**
6 Original Joe's......... **B6**
7 Red Window..... **B6**
8 Tony's Pizza Napoletana. **B6**
9 Tosca Cafe.. **D8**

Quick Bites ▼

1 Caffe Trieste....... **C7**
2 Freddie's Sandwiches **B3**
3 Liguria Bakery **B5**
4 Mario's Bohemian Cigar Store Cafe .. **B6**
5 Molinari Delicatessen **C7**
6 Stella Pastry & Cafe....... **C7**

Hotels ▼

1 Columbus Motor Inn ... **A5**
2 Hotel Bohème..... **C7**

North Beach

Pier 41
Pier 39
Plaza de California
Pier 35
Pier 33

Cable Car
Beach St.
NORTH BEACH
North Point St.
The Embarcadero
Powell St.
Stockton St.
Bay St.
Kearny St.
Montgomery St.
Francisco St.
Pfeiffer St.
Jack Early Park
Chestnut St.
Chestnut St.
Grant Ave.
Lombard St.
TELEGRAPH HILL
Powell St.
Lombard St.
Stockton St.
Pioneer Park
Greenwich Steps
Joe DiMaggio Playground
Greenwich St.
Sts Peter and Paul Catholic Church
Medau Pl.
Filbert Steps
Filbert St.
Alta St.
Columbus Ave.
Mason St.
Washington Square
Filbert St.
Genoa Pl.
Union St.
Castle St.
Montgomery St.
Cable Car
Union St.
Powell St.
Varennes St.
Sonoma St.
Green St.
Green St.
Grant Ave.
Kearny St.
Vallejo Steps
RUSSIAN HILL
Vallejo St.
Broadway
Robert C. Levy Tunnel
Broadway
Stockton St.
Columbus Ave.
Pacific Ave.
Jackson Square Historic District
Pacific Ave.
Grant Ave.
CHINATOWN
Mason St.
Powell St.
Jackson St.
Jackson St.
Jackson St.
Washington St.

0 300 m
0 500 ft

Topped by Coit Tower, Telegraph Hill has spectacular bay and city views.

Coit Tower

VIEWPOINT | Among San Francisco's most distinctive skyline sights, this 210-foot tower is often considered a tribute to firefighters because of the donor's special attachment to the local fire company. As the story goes, a young gold rush–era girl, Lillie Hitchcock Coit (known as Miss Lil), was a fervent admirer of her local fire company—so much so that she once deserted a wedding party and chased down the street after her favorite engine, Knickerbocker No. 5, while clad in her bridesmaid finery. When Lillie died in 1929, she left the city $125,000 to "expend in an appropriate manner … to the beauty of San Francisco."

You can ride the elevator to the top of the tower to enjoy the 360-degree view of the Bay Bridge and the Golden Gate Bridge; due north is Alcatraz Island. Most visitors saunter past the 27 fabulous Depression-era murals inside the tower that depict California's economic and political life, but take the time to appreciate the first New Deal art project, supported by taxpayer money. It's also possible to walk up and down to the tower (if you're in shape): a highlight is the descent toward the Embarcadero via the Filbert Steps, a series of stairways that are a shaded green oasis in the middle of the city. ⋈ *Telegraph Hill Blvd., at Greenwich St. or Lombard St., North Beach* ☎ *415/362–0808* ⊕ *sfrecpark.org* 🖭 *Free; elevator to top $10.*

Grant Avenue

STREET | Originally called Calle de la Fundación, Grant Avenue is the oldest street in the city, but it's got plenty of young blood. Dusty bars such as The Saloon mix with independent boutiques, odd curio shops, and curated gourmet shops. While the street runs from Union Square through Chinatown, North Beach, and beyond, the fun stuff in this neighborhood is jammed into the four blocks from Columbus Avenue north to Filbert Street. ⋈ *North Beach.*

The Birds

While on Telegraph Hill, you might be startled by a chorus of piercing squawks and a rushing sound of wings. No, you're not about to have a Hitchcock bird-attack moment. These small, vivid green parrots with cherry-red heads number in the hundreds; they're descendants of former pets that escaped or were released by their owners. (The birds dislike cages, and they bite if bothered—must've been some disillusioned owners along the way.)

The parrots like to roost high in the aging cypress trees on the hill, chattering and fluttering, sometimes taking wing en masse. They're not popular with some residents, but they did find a champion in local bohemian Mark Bittner, a former street musician. Bittner began chronicling their habits, publishing a book and battling the homeowners who wanted to cut down the cypresses. A 2003 documentary, *The Wild Parrots of Telegraph Hill*, made the issue a cause célèbre. In 2007, City Hall, which recognizes a golden goose when it sees one, stepped in and brokered a solution to keep the celebrity birds in town. The city would cover the homeowners' insurance worries and plant new trees for the next generation of wild parrots.

Sentinel Building

NOTABLE BUILDING | A striking triangular shape and a gorgeous green patina make this 1907 flatiron building unmissable, and the Financial District's skyscrapers make a great backdrop for it. In the 1970s filmmaker Francis Ford Coppola bought the building to use for his production company. The ground floor houses Coppola's swanky wine bar, Café Zoetrope. ⊠ *916 Kearny St., at Columbus Ave., North Beach.*

★ Telegraph Hill and the Filbert Steps

NEIGHBORHOOD | Residents here have some of the city's best views, as well as the most difficult ascents to their aeries. The hill rises from the east end of Lombard Street to a height of 284 feet and is capped by Coit Tower. If you brave the slope, though, you'll be rewarded with a "secret treasure" San Francisco moment. Filbert Street starts up the hill, then becomes the Filbert Steps when the going gets too steep. You can cut between the Filbert Steps and another flight, the Greenwich Steps, on up to the hilltop. As you climb, you pass some of the city's oldest houses and are surrounded by beautiful, flowering private gardens. In some places the trees grow over the stairs, so it feels like you're walking through a green tunnel; elsewhere, you'll have wide-open views of the bay. The cypress trees that grow on the hill are a favorite roost of local avian celebrities, the wild parrots of Telegraph Hill; you'll hear the cries of the cherry-headed conures if they're nearby. The name comes from the hill's status as the first Morse code signal station back in 1853. ⊠ *Bordered by Lombard, Filbert, Kearny, and Sansome Sts., North Beach.*

Washington Square

PLAZA/SQUARE | Once the daytime social heart of San Francisco's Italian district, this grassy patch has changed character numerous times over the years. The Beats hung out here in the 1950s, hippies camped out in the 1960s and early '70s, and nowadays you're more likely to see picnickers and residents doing community dance, yoga, or tai chi. You might also see homeless people hanging out on the benches and young locals sunbathing or running their dogs. Lillie Hitchcock Coit, in yet another show of affection for

San Francisco's firefighters, donated the statue of two firemen with a rescued child. Camera-toting visitors focus on the Romanesque splendor of Saints Peter and Paul Church (Filbert Street side of the square), a 1924 building with Disneyesque stone-white towers that are local landmarks. Mass reflects the neighborhood; it's given in English, Italian, and Chinese. ✉ *Bordered by Columbus Ave. and Stockton, Filbert, and Union Sts., North Beach* 🌐 *sfrecpark.org.*

🍴 Restaurants

One of the city's oldest neighborhoods, North Beach continues to speak Italian, albeit in fewer households than it did when Joe DiMaggio was hitting home runs at the local playground.

Columbus Avenue, North Beach's primary commercial artery, and nearby side streets boast dozens of moderately priced Italian restaurants and coffee bars that San Franciscans flock to for a dose of strong community feeling. But beware, there are a few tourist traps that are after the college crowd, who come here for cheap drinks and then want to fill up on cheap food.

Barbara Pinseria & Cocktail Bar

$$ | ITALIAN | Calabrian-born SF resident Francesco Covucci is determined to continue the Italian legacy of North Beach with trendy, casual, quality-driven regional Italian eateries (he also owns Il Casaro Pizzeria at 348 Columbus Avenue). Here you can slam Roman-style *pinsa*, which is a modern style of ciabatta-shape pizza made of a multigrain flour mix and gourmet toppings like burrata and pesto or pear, walnut, and Gorgonzola. **Known for:** Roman pasta specialties; casual industrial-chic decor; craft cocktails and wines from Italy and California. [$] *Average main: $22* ✉ *431 Columbus Ave., North Beach* ☎ *415/445–3009* 🌐 *www.sfbarbara.com.*

Da Flora

$$ | ITALIAN | Wife-and-husband duo chef Jen McMahon and Oakland native Darren Lacy (front of house) strive to create the neighborhood's most thoughtful Italian dining experience. Handwritten menus and linen napkins set the tone for ingredient-driven, high-quality regional Italian–inspired cuisine. **Known for:** house-baked focaccia and fresh pastas; red walls and cozy, romantic decor; decadent Italian desserts. [$] *Average main: $27* ✉ *701 Columbus Ave., North Beach* ☎ *415/981–4664* 🌐 *daflora.com* 🕓 *Closed Sun.–Tues. No lunch.*

Il Pollaio

$ | CAFÉ | One of North Beach's last blue-collar eateries has immense character, as if a *rosticceria* (a type of casual roast meat eat-in or take-away) was plopped here from a small quarter of Rome. This is a simple spot to get classic, hearty meals like half a roasted chicken and sides. **Known for:** an icon for a chicken or rib-eye dinner since 1984; simple, cafeteria-style tables and chairs; BYOB option, though there's wine and beer. [$] *Average main: $19* ✉ *555 Columbus Ave., North Beach* ☎ *415/362–7727* 🌐 *www.ilpollaiosf.com* 🕓 *Closed Sun.*

The Italian Homemade Company

$ | ITALIAN | FAMILY | In Italy, the bastion of fresh pasta is Emilia-Romagna, and a trio of entrepreneurs hailing from the region give respect to its claim to carb fame in a mini-empire of fast-casual pasta eateries, with the one in North Beach as its flagship. Come for treats like slabs of lasagna that fool you into thinking you're calorie-loading in Bologna, as well as stuffed ravioli and gnocchi. **Known for:** varieties of piadina (Italian flatbreads with meats, cheeses, and vegetables); mix-and-match pastas and sauces; great quality for the price. [$] *Average main: $13* ✉ *716 Columbus Ave., North Beach* ☎ *415/712–8874* 🌐 *italianhomemade.com.*

★ **Maykadeh**

$$ | MIDDLE EASTERN | Persian dining is mostly done in homes, with fine dining a modern concept, but Maykadeh hits the mark with authenticity in Persian cooking as well as saucy, elevated, French-influenced twists. Those in the know come for succulent lamb specialties with saffron rice, served in a dining room with an old-school, white-shirt-and-tie vibe. **Known for:** loyal following of Iranians, Iranian Americans, and Persian food enthusiasts; eggplant dip appetizer; kebabs and marinated meats good for sharing. $ *Average main: $26* ✉ *470 Green St., North Beach* ☎ *415/362–8286* ⊕ *maykadehrestaurant.com.*

Original Joe's

$$$ | ITALIAN | After a fire destroyed the old-school Italian American restaurant's Tenderloin building in 2007, it moved to North Beach; the "new" place has its charms, but it's quite a different restaurant, with far more sophisticated decor that includes some mid-century design elements. Original Joe's took over the former location of Fior D'Italia and carried on that space's legacy as a destination for fine dining, now marrying a higher-end experience with classic Italian American fare like eggplant parmigiana, saucy meatballs, and fettuccine dishes. **Known for:** classic Cal-Ital food; housemade ravioli; excellent bar. $ *Average main: $32* ✉ *601 Union St., North Beach* ☎ *415/775–4877* ⊕ *originaljoessf.com* ⊘ *No lunch Mon.–Thurs.*

Red Window

$$ | TAPAS | This colorful Spanish-style tapas/pintxos bar deserves a spot especially if you need a quick bite with an appetite-stimulating vermouth-based aperitif before heading off to dinner. The food is delicious, with delightful ambience, and it's a not-to-miss for anyone who could use a night off from Italian. **Known for:** excellent low-ABV cocktails made tableside; patatas bravas piled into thin slices and then fried; fun, welcoming atmosphere. $ *Average main: $20* ✉ *500 Columbus Ave., North Beach* ☎ *415/757–0600* ⊕ *www.theredwindow.com* ⊘ *No lunch weekdays.*

Tony's Pizza Napoletana

$$ | PIZZA | FAMILY | Repeatedly crowned the World Champion Pizza Maker at the World Pizza Cup in Naples, Tony Gemignani is a carb-friendly legend in the city for his flavorful dough and myriad versions. The multiple gas, electric, and wood-burning ovens in his casual, modern pizzeria turn out many different styles of pies—the famed Neapolitan-style Margherita, but also Sicilian, Roman, and Detroit styles—with salads, antipasti, homemade pastas, and calzone rounding out the menu. **Known for:** Cal-Italia pie with aged balsamic drizzle; NYC pizza parlor vibes; slice stand next door if you can't wait. $ *Average main: $29* ✉ *1570 Stockton St., North Beach* ☎ *415/835–9888* ⊕ *tonyspizzanapoletana.com.*

Tosca Cafe

$$$ | ITALIAN | The leather booths and chairs are in high demand at this dark and clubby boho classic from 1919, where well-heeled locals and visitors delight in food that skews to the Cal-Italian genre, meaning local catches and seasonal produce as well as Italian flair in dishes such as halibut crudo and meatballs swimming in red sauce. This is also a great place to park on a stool at the bar, linger over a craft cocktail, and soak up the old–San Francisco vibe. **Known for:** Italian cocktails; raw bar and caviar menu; Tuscan fried chicken. $ *Average main: $34* ✉ *242 Columbus Ave., North Beach* ☎ *415/986–9651* ⊕ *toscacafesf.com* ⊘ *Closed Sun. and Mon. No lunch.*

☕ Coffee and Quick Bites

Caffe Trieste

$ | CAFÉ | Caffe Trieste gives a glimmer of North Beach soul, along with generous slices of cake and possibly the best cappuccino in town that isn't trying to be part of a hipster latte-art competition. Open since 1956 and claiming to be the West Coast's first espresso coffeehouse, this fixture draws a diverse crowd, from young artists writing to the tune of their espresso buzz to old-timers reading the paper as they sip their drip cup. **Known for:** Saturday afternoon music; neighborhood vibe; retail annex next door. $ *Average main: $5* ⊠ *601 Vallejo St., at Grant Ave., North Beach* ☎ *415/392–6739* ⊕ *coffee.caffetrieste.com.*

Freddie's Sandwiches

$ | ITALIAN | For a take-out sando shop for those in the North Beach know, Freddie's is where you need to go. The calling cards of this off-the-tourist-track time capsule, owned by Ed Sweileh, are the combo layered with mortadella, pressed ham, cheese, and salami galore, and the protein trio turkey, ham, and bacon club. **Known for:** corner store vibe; plenty of sandwich choices; excellent value for the price. $ *Average main: $12* ⊠ *300 Francisco St., North Beach* ☎ *415/433–2882* ⊕ *orderfreddiessandwiches.com* ⊙ *Closed Sun. No dinner.*

Liguria Bakery

$ | BAKERY | The Soracco family has been baking Liguria's focaccia genovese for more than a century, and their fresh-baked Italian flatbreads (such as plain, rosemary, and tomato slathered with green onions) are the city's best. Bring cash and arrive before noon: when the focaccia is gone, the bakery closes. **Known for:** selling out daily; a San Francisco time capsule; the best focaccia in town. $ *Average main: $8* ⊠ *1700 Stockton St., North Beach* ⊙ *Closed Sun. and Mon.*

Mario's Bohemian Cigar Store Cafe

$ | ITALIAN | This intimate, triangular spot with a beautiful antique oak bar serves great hot focaccia sandwiches, sourcing from Liguria Bakery. Try the toasted combo (ham, salami, cheese), the breaded eggplant, or the meatball drenched in marinara. **Known for:** great Washington Square views; old-school San Francisco vibe; loaded focaccia sandwiches. $ *Average main: $13* ⊠ *566 Columbus Ave., North Beach* ⊕ *marios-bohemian-cigar-store-cafe.square.site.*

★ Molinari Delicatessen

$ | SANDWICHES | The whip-quick, no-nonsense, food-smart staff behind the counter at this take-out delicatessen have been serving up the most delicious, and quite possibly the biggest, sandwiches in town since 1896. Grab a number, revel in the time warp that Sinatra in the background provides, marvel at the Italian-style cured meats, and let the artists build you an unforgettable combo; then head to Washington Square Park for a picnic. **Known for:** Italian combo sandwich; family business has old-time Italian vibe; traditional Italian products. $ *Average main: $14* ⊠ *373 Columbus Ave., at Vallejo St., North Beach* ☎ *415/421–2337* ⊕ *www.themolinarideli.com* ⊙ *Closed Sun. No dinner.*

Stella Pastry & Cafe

$ | BAKERY | For a quarter so rich in Italian history, North Beach sadly lacks authentic Italian *dolce* (sweet) offerings; indeed, this lone sweets bakery is it. Stella has been around since 1942 and has since changed hands from the original owners but still sticks to offering an array of Italian-American-style biscotti, tiramisu, and cannoli with creamy, cloyingly sweet predilections. **Known for:** Sacripantina cake, heavy with zabiglione; coffee and cappucino; American-style cannoli. $ *Average main: $4* ⊠ *446 Columbus Ave., North Beach* ☎ *415/986–2914.*

 Hotels

Columbus Motor Inn

$$ | HOTEL | FAMILY | Close to Chinatown and Fisherman's Wharf, this affordable lodging with basic rooms decked out with oversize pillows, earth-toned bedding, and large flat-screen TVs is a great pick if you brought your family and have

a car to park. **Pros:** free parking; affordable rooms deep-cleaned regularly; lively location. **Cons:** lacks amenities; decor is not stylish; street-facing accommodations can be noisy. [$] *Rooms from: $210* ✉ *1075 Columbus Ave., North Beach* ☎ *415/885–1492* 🌐 *www.columbusmotorinn.com* 🛏 *45 rooms* 🍴 *No Meals.*

Hotel Bohème

$$ | HOTEL | Located in the heart of North Beach, this small hotel takes you back in time with cast-iron beds, large mirrored armoires, and memorabilia recalling the Beat generation—whose leading light, Allen Ginsberg, often stayed here (legend has it that in his later years he could be seen sitting in a window, typing away). **Pros:** convenient to North Beach shops and pastry spots; homey rooms; helpful staff. **Cons:** street parking is scarce; no a/c; small rooms. [$] *Rooms from: $225* ✉ *444 Columbus Ave., North Beach* ☎ *415/433–9111* 🌐 *hotelboheme.com* 🛏 *15 rooms* 🍴 *No Meals.*

🍸 Nightlife

BARS

Bodega

WINE BARS | For a glass (or a bottle) of natural wine served with delicious, fresh small plates from burrata and radish salads to flavorful sweet potato tacos, head to this popular neighborhood wine bar. The rotating selection of artisanal wines from small producers, mainly in France, Italy, and California, pairs well with the eclectic, casual atmosphere. The weekend breakfast burritos are legendary. ✉ *700 Columbus St., North Beach* ☎ *415/634–7002* 🌐 *www.bodegasf.com.*

15 Romolo

BARS | Easy to miss on an alley and overshadowed by neighboring adult-entertainment venues that are parallel along the Columbus strip, this craft cocktail den with a Basque theme serves up tipples of sherry, a few thoughtful wine picks, and creative cocktails. Pair your drink with tasty, Spanish-driven bistro snacks, such as pressed tuna baguette sandos, house-made pickles, *pintxos* (Basque tapas with bread), and *croquetas* (a fried snack). With a non-Internet jukebox and a photo booth, this place oozes vintage hipster vibes but with old-world sensibilities. ✉ *15 Romolo Pl., off Broadway east of Columbus Ave., North Beach* ☎ *415/398–1359* 🌐 *www.15romolo.com.*

Specs' Twelve Adler Museum Cafe

BARS | If you're into bohemian dive bars, you can groove on this hidden hangout for artists, poets, and heavy-drinking old-timers. Specs' bar is a women-owned and-run institution and a beloved fixture. It's one of the few remaining old-fashioned watering holes in North Beach that still smack of the Beat years and the 1960s. Though it's just off a busy street, Specs' is strangely immune to the hustle and bustle outside. ✉ *12 William Saroyan Pl., off Columbus Ave., between Pacific Ave. and Broadway, North Beach* ☎ *415/421–4112* 🌐 *www.specsbarsf.com.*

Tony Nik's

BARS | For a dive bar with old San Francisco soul, go no further for a nightcap involving an old-fashioned, martini, or Negroni after a night of pizza crushing. ✉ *1534 Stockton St., North Beach* ☎ *415/693–0990* 🌐 *tonyniks.com/history.php.*

O Pioneers!

The corner of Broadway and Columbus Avenue witnessed a historic breakthrough. Here stood the Condor Club, where in 1964 Carol Doda became the country's first dancer to break the topless barrier. A bronze plaque honors the milestone.

★ Vesuvio

BARS | If you're hitting only one bar in North Beach, it should be this one. The low-ceilinged second floor of this raucous boho saloon hangout, little altered since its 1960s heyday (when Jack Kerouac frequented the place), is a fine vantage point for watching the colorful Broadway and Columbus Avenue intersection. Another part of Vesuvio's appeal is its diverse clientele, from older neighborhood regulars and young couples to bacchanalian posses. ✉ *255 Columbus Ave., at Broadway, North Beach* ☎ *415/362–3370* ⊕ *www.vesuvio.com.*

COMEDY

Cobb's Comedy Club

COMEDY CLUBS | Well-known stand-up comics have appeared here, though there's more emphasis on up-and-comers. You might also see local sketch comedy and comic singer-songwriters. No one under 18 is admitted, and there is a minimum drink purchase in addition to the entrance fee. ✉ *915 Columbus Ave., North Beach* ☎ *415/928–4320* ⊕ *www.cobbscomedy.com.*

MUSIC CLUBS

Bimbo's 365 Club

LIVE MUSIC | The plush main room and adjacent lounge of this club retain a retro vibe perfect for the "Cocktail Nation" programming that keeps the crowds entertained. For a taste of the original San Francisco nightclub scene, you can't beat it. Indie low-fi and pop bands such as Mustache Harbor and Tainted Love have played here. ✉ *1025 Columbus Ave., at Chestnut St., North Beach* ☎ *415/474–0365* ⊕ *bimbos365club.com.*

The Saloon

LIVE MUSIC | Hard-drinkin' in-the-know locals favor this raucous spot, renowned for great blues. Built in the 1860s, the onetime bordello is purported to be the oldest bar in the city. This is not the place to order anything mixed besides maybe a gin and tonic. Get a bottle or can of beer, enjoy the scene, and chat with anyone next to you. Just keep quiet when the music is jamming. ✉ *1232 Grant Ave., near Columbus Ave., North Beach* ☎ *415/989–7666* ⊕ *sfblues.weebly.com.*

🛍 Shopping

CLOTHING

AB Fits

MIXED CLOTHING | The affable staff can help guys and gals sort through the jeans selection, one of the hippest in the city, from hyperlocal to international brands. On-staff experts pride themselves on being able to match the pants to the person. Occasional release parties are hosted; sign up for the mailing list to get a taste of local fashion and art life combined. ✉ *1519 Grant Ave., between Filbert and Union Sts., North Beach* ☎ *415/982–5726* ⊕ *www.abfits.com.*

Knitz and Leather

MIXED CLOTHING | Local artisans Julia Relinghaus and Katharina Ernst have been producing one-of-a-kind and custom products for more than 30 years. Ernst's bold knitted sweaters and accessories will help you stand out from the crowd, and Relinghaus's exquisite, high-quality leather jackets for men and women are the kind of investment you make for fine leather. ✉ *1453 Grant Ave., North Beach* ☎ *415/391–3480.*

SFOG North Beach

MIXED CLOTHING | The artists at this screen-printing boutique offer homespun souvenirs in the form of colorful graphic T-shirts and hoodies paying homage to the city. Favorites include tees saluting North Beach and various signature San Francisco street signs. You can often see the giant screen printer behind the counter in action. ✉ *1314 Grant Ave., North Beach* ⊕ *sfognorthbeach.com.*

FOOD AND DRINK
Graffeo Coffee Roasting Company
OTHER FOOD & DRINK | This emporium and working roastery, open since 1935, is one of the best-loved coffee stores in a city devoted to high-quality roasted java. The shop sells craft roast whole-bean bags only. It's worth the jaunt if only for the aromas. ⊠ *735 Columbus Ave., at Filbert St., North Beach* ☎ *415/986–2420* ⊕ *www.graffeo.com.*

Sotto Casa
FOOD | A specialty Italian grocer for lovers of Slow Food, this shop is owned by Abruzzo-born Lorenzo Scarpone, who founded SF's Slow Food chapter; he also moonlights as a wine importer. Stop by for dried pastas from ancient villages like Gragnano; imported Italian specialty cheeses; aged balsamic vinegar from Modena; holiday cookies and specialties; and canned goods, such as San Marzano tomatoes. Also on offer are Roman roasted coffee and bottles of extra-virgin olive oil from Scarpone's family's production in Abruzzo. ⊠ *1351 Grant Ave., North Beach* ☎ *415/475–7774* ⊕ *www.sotto-casa.com.*

Victoria Pastry Company
FOOD | In business since the early 1900s and a throwback to the North Beach of old, this bakery has display cases full of Italian pastries (although most hard-core Italian food experts would disapprove of them), traditional holiday cookies, and buttercream-based cakes. ⊠ *700 Filbert St., between Columbus Ave. and Powell St., North Beach* ☎ *415/781–2015.*

★ XOX Truffles
CANDY | The decadent confection comes in countless flavors here, from the traditional (cocoa-powder-coated Amaretto) to the unusual (flavored with rum-coconut liqueur and coated with coconut flakes). There's something for everyone, even vegans. Bonus: all espresso drinks come with a complimentary truffle. ⊠ *754 Columbus Ave., between Greenwich and Filbert Sts., North Beach* ☎ *415/421–4814* ⊕ *xoxtruffles.com.*

HOUSEWARES
Biordi Art Imports
CERAMICS | A North Beach landmark, this store sells ceramics of the quality found in the artisan clusters of Italy. The excellent selection of hand-painted Italian pottery, imported mainly from Tuscany, Umbria, and Sicily, has been shipped worldwide by this proud, family-run business since it was opened by Italian immigrants in 1946. Their specialty is Umbrian Deruta ceramics and some Palio di Siena Contrade pieces, and they work directly with generational artisans. ⊠ *412 Columbus Ave., at Vallejo St., North Beach* ☎ *415/392–8096* ⊕ *biordi.com.*

MUSIC MEMORABILIA
San Francisco Rock Posters & Collectibles
ANTIQUES & COLLECTIBLES | The huge selection of rock-and-roll memorabilia, including posters, handbills, and original art, makes this spot a groovy cave for the nostalgic vintage '60s. Also available are posters from more recent shows, many at the legendary Fillmore Auditorium. ⊠ *1851 Powell St., between Filbert and Greenwich Sts., North Beach* ☎ *415/956–6749* ⊕ *rockposters.com.*

PAPER AND STATIONERY
Lola of North Beach
SOUVENIRS | For an alternative to Hallmark with a SF vibe, try this intimate shop offering gadgets, knickknacks, and tongue-in-cheek novelties, plus cards, stationery, and postcards. Many products make great souvenirs, from Golden Gate Bridge onesies for babies to city-skyline socks for adults. Local artists are well represented. ⊠ *454 Columbus Ave., North Beach* ☎ *415/678–5327* ⊕ *www.lolaofnorthbeach.com.*

Chapter 7

NOB HILL AND RUSSIAN HILL

7

Updated by
Denise Leto

👁 Sights	🍴 Restaurants	🛏 Hotels	🛍 Shopping	🍸 Nightlife
★★★☆☆	★★★☆☆	★★★★☆	★★☆☆☆	★★☆☆☆

NEIGHBORHOOD SNAPSHOT

TOP EXPERIENCES

■ **Macondray Lane:** Duck into this secret, lush garden lane and walk its narrow, uneven cobblestones.

■ **Vallejo Steps:** Make the steep climb up to lovely Ina Coolbrith Park, then continue up along the glorious garden path of the Vallejo Steps to a spectacular view at the top.

■ **San Francisco Art Institute:** Contemplate a Diego Rivera mural and stop at the café for organic coffee and a priceless view of the city and the bay. It may be the best—and cheapest—way to spend an hour in the neighborhood.

■ **Cable Car Museum:** Ride a cable car all the way back to the barn, hanging on tight as it *clack-clack-clacks* its way up Nob Hill, and then go behind the scenes at the museum.

■ **Playing "Bullitt" on the steep streets:** For the ride of your life, take a drive up and down the city's steepest streets on Russian Hill. A trip over the precipice of Filbert or Jones will make you feel as if you're falling off the edge of the world.

GETTING HERE

The thing about Russian and Nob Hills is that they're both especially steep hills. If you're not up for the hike, a cable car is certainly the most exciting way to reach the top. Take the California line for Nob Hill and the Powell–Hyde line for Russian Hill. Buses serve the area as well, such as the 1–California bus for Nob Hill, but the routes run only east–west. The cable cars tackle the steeper north–south streets. Driving yourself is a hassle, since parking is a challenge on these crowded, precipitous streets.

PLANNING YOUR TIME

■ Since walking Nob Hill is (almost) all about gazing at exteriors, touring the neighborhood during daylight hours is a must. The sights here don't require a lot of visiting time—say a half hour each at the Cable Car Museum and Grace Cathedral—but allow time for the walk itself. An afternoon visit is ideal for Russian Hill, so you can browse the shops. You could cover both neighborhoods in three or four hours. Finish up with a sunset cocktail at a swanky hotel lounge or the retro-tiki Tonga Room.

VIEWFINDER

■ Tucked along the side of Russian Hill, terraced Ina Coolbrith Park is a pocket-size spot worth seeking out for its sweeping city and bay views and secret–San Francisco vibe. Best way to get here is via cable car—take the Powell–Mason line to Mason and Vallejo streets, then walk half a block to the Vallejo Steps at the base of the park.

Nob Hill exudes history and good breeding: topped with some of the city's most elegant hotels, gloriously Gothic Grace Cathedral, and private blue-blood social clubs, it's the pinnacle of privilege. One hill over, Russian Hill is another old-family bastion with jaw-dropping views.

Nob Hill

Nob Hill was officially dubbed during the 1870s when the "Big Four"—Charles Crocker, Leland Stanford, Mark Hopkins, and Collis P. Huntington, who were involved in the construction of the transcontinental railroad—built their hilltop estates. The lingo is thick from this era: those on the hilltop were referred to as "nabobs" (originally meaning a provincial governor from India) and "swells," and the hill itself was called Snob Hill, a term that survives to this day. By 1882 so many estates had sprung up on Nob Hill that Robert Louis Stevenson called it "the hill of palaces." The 1906 earthquake and fire, though, destroyed all the palatial mansions except for portions of the James Flood brownstone. History buffs may choose to linger here, but for most visitors, a casual glimpse from a cable car will be enough.

⇨ *For more details on the Cable Car Museum, see the Cable Cars feature in Chapter 1, Experience San Francisco.*

◉ Sights

Cable Car Museum
OTHER MUSEUM | FAMILY | One of the city's best free offerings, this museum is an absolute must for kids and compelling

for adults too. You can even ride a cable car here—all three lines stop between Russian Hill and Nob Hill. The facility, which is inside the city's last remaining cable-car barn, takes the top off the system to show you how it all works. Eternally humming and squealing, the massive powerhouse cable wheels steal the show. You can also climb aboard a vintage car and take the grip, let the kids ring a cable-car bell, and check out vintage gear dating from 1873. ⊠ *1201 Mason St., Nob Hill* ☎ *415/474–1887* ⊕ *www.cablecarmuseum.org* 🎫 *Free* 🕐 *Closed Mon.*

Collis P. Huntington Park
CITY PARK | The elegant park west of the Pacific Union Club and east of Grace Cathedral occupies the site of a mansion owned by railroad baron Collis P. Huntington. He died in 1900, the mansion was destroyed in the 1906 fire, and in 1915 his widow—by then married to Huntington's nephew—donated the land to the city. The Huntingtons' neighbors, the Crockers, once owned the *Fountain of the Tortoises,* based on the original in Rome's Piazza Mattei. ■**TIP**➜ **The benches around the fountain offer a welcome break after climbing Nob Hill.** ⊠ *Taylor and California Sts., Nob Hill* ⊕ *sfrecpark.org.*

Sights ▼

1	Cable Car Museum	G5
2	Collis P. Huntington Park	G6
3	The Fairmont Hotel	H6
4	Grace Cathedral	G6
5	Ina Coolbrith Park	G3
6	The Mark Hopkins Hotel	H7
7	Lombard Street	D1
8	Macondray Lane	F2
9	Nob Hill Masonic Center	G7
10	Pacific-Union Club	H6
11	Vallejo Steps	F3

Restaurants ▼

1	Acquerello	C7
2	Del Popolo	H8
3	Harris' Restaurant	B5
4	Helmand Palace	B3
5	House of Prime Rib	C6
6	Nisei	C3
7	Seven Hills	D3
8	Sons & Daughters	I7
9	Swan Oyster Depot	C7

Quick Bites ▼

1	Bob's Donuts	C6
2	The Boys' Deli	C4
3	The Coffee Movement	H5
4	Hot Sauce and Panko	E5
5	Le Beau Market	E6
6	Maison Danel	D9
7	Swensen's Ice Cream	D3

Hotels ▼

1	Fairmont San Francisco	H6
2	InterContinental Mark Hopkins	H7
3	Petite Auberge	H8
4	The Ritz-Carlton, San Francisco	I6
5	Stanford Court San Francisco	H6
6	White Swan Inn	H8

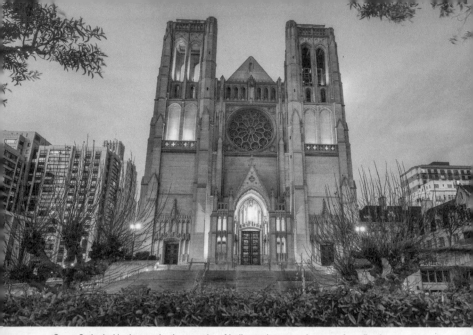

Grace Cathedral in the evening is a wonder of Italianate beauty and a space for reflection.

Fairmont San Francisco

HOTEL | The hotel's dazzling opening was delayed a year by the 1906 quake, but since then, the marble palace has hosted presidents, royalty, movie stars, and local nabobs. Things have changed since its early days, however: on the eve of World War I, you could get a room for as low as $2 per night, meals included. Nowadays, prices go as high as $18,000, which buys a night in the eight-room, contemporary art–filled penthouse suite.

Swing through the opulent lobby on your way to tea (served on weekends from 1:30 to 3:30) at the Laurel Court restaurant; peek through the foyer's floor-to-ceiling windows for a glimpse of the hotel's garden and beehives, where the honey served with tea is produced. Don't miss an evening cocktail in the kitschy Tonga Room, complete with tiki huts and a floating bandstand. Snap a picture with the eight-foot-tall bronze Tony Bennett statue outside the lobby. This site was selected as the statue's home to commemorate the singer's 90th birthday because his first performance of "I Left My Heart in San Francisco" was in the hotel's Venetian Room. ⊠ *950 Mason St., Nob Hill* ☎ *415/772–5000* ⊕ *www. fairmont-san-francisco.com.*

★ Grace Cathedral

CHURCH | Not many churches can boast an altarpiece by Keith Haring and two labyrinths, but this one, the country's third-largest Episcopal cathedral, does. The soaring Gothic-style structure took 14 (often interrupted) years to build, beginning in 1927 and eventually wrapping up in 1964. The gilded bronze doors at the east entrance were taken from casts of Lorenzo Ghiberti's incredible *Gates of Paradise*, designed for the Baptistery in Florence, Italy. A sculpture of St. Francis by Beniamino Bufano greets you as you enter.

The 34-foot-wide limestone labyrinth is a replica of the 13th-century stone maze on the floor of Chartres Cathedral. All are encouraged to walk the ⅛-mile-long labyrinth, a ritual based on the tradition of meditative walking. There's also a granite

Walking the Hills

Start a tour of Nob Hill and Russian Hill with a cable-car ride up to **California** and **Powell Streets** on Nob Hill (all lines go here). Walking two blocks west, you can pass all the Big Four mansions-cum-hotels on the hill. Peek at the Keith Haring triptych in impressive **Grace Cathedral** and stroll around manicured **Huntington Park.** While on top of the hill, walk over to the southeast corner of Clay and Jones Streets, home to the art-deco Clay-Jones Apartments building (the highest point on Nob Hill). Next, enjoy the view of the Bay Bridge and the Transamerica Pyramid from the intersection, then head down to the **Cable Car Museum** to see the machinery in action. Next, make your way to Russian Hill—a cable car is a fine way to reach the peak—to visit some of the city's loveliest hidden lanes and stairways. At **Mason** and **Vallejo Streets**, head up the **Vallejo Steps**, passing contemplative, terraced **Ina Coolbrith Park** and private gardens. Take in the sweeping city and bay view from the top of the hill, then head right on **Jones Street** and duck under the trellis to shady **Macondray Lane.** For another alleyway photo-op, head a block west to Leavenworth and briefly backtrack south to see **Waldo Alley,** where clever locals dressed up its sign pole with red and white stripes as an ode to the namesake "Where's Waldo" puzzle-book character. From here it's a five-block hike to crooked **Lombard Street.** If you've still got some steam, go another block to see **Diego Rivera's mural** and the surprise panoramic view from the **San Francisco Art Institute.**

outdoor labyrinth on the church's northeast side. The AIDS Interfaith Chapel, to the right as you enter Grace, contains a bronze triptych by the late artist Keith Haring (a gift from Yoko Ono) and panels from the AIDS Memorial Quilt. The church offers self- and docent-led tours. ■TIP→ **Especially dramatic times to view the cathedral are during Tuesday-evening yoga (6:15 pm), Thursday-night evensong (5:15 pm), and special holiday programs.** ⊠ *1100 California St., Nob Hill* ☎ *415/749–6300* ⊕ *www.gracecathedral. org* 🎫 *Entrance and self-guided tours $12, docent-led tours $20.*

The Mark Hopkins Hotel

HOTEL | Built on the ashes of railroad tycoon Mark Hopkins's grand estate, this 19-story hotel built in 1926 displays a combination of French château and Spanish Renaissance architecture, with noteworthy terra-cotta detailing. Over the decades it has hosted statesmen, royalty, and Hollywood celebrities. The 11-room penthouse was turned into a glass-wall cocktail lounge in 1939: the Top of the Mark is remembered fondly by thousands of World War II veterans who jammed the lounge before leaving for overseas duty. Wives and sweethearts watching the ships depart gave the room's northwest nook its name—Weepers' Corner. ■TIP→ **With its 360-degree views, the lounge is a wonderful spot for a grand brunch or a nighttime drink.** ⊠ *999 California St., Nob Hill* ☎ *415/392–3434* ⊕ *www.sfmarkhopkins.com.*

Nob Hill Masonic Center

NOTABLE BUILDING | Erected by Freemasons in 1957, the hall is familiar to locals mostly as a concert and lecture venue, where such notables as Van Morrison and Trevor Noah have appeared. But you don't need a ticket to check out the outdoor war memorial or artist Emile Norman's impressive lobby mosaic. Mainly in rich greens and yellows, it depicts the Masons' role in California history. ✉ *1111 California St., Nob Hill* ☎ *415/776–7457* ⊕ *www.facebook.com/sfmasonic.*

Pacific-Union Club

NOTABLE BUILDING | The former home of silver baron James Clair Flood cost a whopping $1.5 million in 1886, when even a stylish Victorian like the Haas-Lilienthal House cost less than $20,000. All that cash did buy some structural stability—the Flood residence (to be precise, its shell) was the only Nob Hill mansion to survive the 1906 earthquake and fire. The Pacific-Union Club, a bastion of the wealthy and powerful, purchased the house in 1907 and commissioned Willis Polk to redesign it; the architect added the semicircular wings and third floor. The ornate fence design dates from the mansion's construction. It is now a members-only private social club. ✉ *1000 California St., Nob Hill.*

🍴 Restaurants

Unfortunately, Nob Hill's food isn't as unparalleled as its scenic outlooks. Real estate is too expensive for chefs to roll the dice on a new venture, but you'll find hotel dining rooms and established institutions.

Del Popolo

$$ | **PIZZA** | **FAMILY** | The puffy, perfectly charred Neapolitan pizzas from this Lower Nob Hill neighborhood bistro-pizzeria are the stuff of legend. Del Popolo gained a cult following after beginning as a state-of-the-art pizza truck outfitted with a wood-fired oven, and the crowds continue to gather nightly for the stellar pies—though being a restaurant means that it also has a convivial, cozy dining room, friendly servers, and great wines. **Known for:** margherita pizza; stunning firewood-filled arch backdrop behind the wood-fired oven; delightful salads and antipasti. Ⓢ *Average main: $22* ✉ *855 Bush St., Nob Hill* ☎ *415/589–7940*

⊕ *www.delpopolosf.com* ⊘ *Closed Sun. and Mon. No lunch.*

★ Sons & Daughters

$$$$ | **AMERICAN** | The constantly evolving tasting menu that chef-owner Teague Moriarty serves at his standout, Michelin-star restaurant serves as a primer for how to do highly seasonal cuisine right. Though the preparations are intricate and often luxurious, there is a pretension-free, contemporary elegance that makes this one of the most relaxed (and fun) fine-dining experiences in the city. **Known for:** cozy but chic dining room anchored by an ornate fireplace; excellent house-made bread; attentive service. Ⓢ *Average main: $225* ✉ *708 Bush St., Nob Hill* ☎ *415/994–7933* ⊕ *www. sonsanddaughterssf.com* ⊘ *Closed Mon. and Tues. No lunch.*

☕ Coffee and Quick Bites

The Coffee Movement

$ | **CAFÉ** | Nob Hill's design and architecture tend to be resolutely old-school, except with this impossibly hip coffee shop. Coffee and espresso drinks are excellent, plus there's a tasting flight of the day's offerings for the most avid coffee nerd. **Known for:** perfect cappucinos; popular with the Instagram set; friendly baristas. Ⓢ *Average main: $5* ✉ *1030 Washington St., Nob Hill* ☎ *415/237–3375* ⊕ *thecoffeemovement.com.*

Le Beau Market

$ | **SANDWICHES** | **FAMILY** | Neighborhood residents love the dauntless Le Beau, one of the few remaining family-run grocery stores in the city. It's fun to browse around, and their sandwiches are a highlight. **Known for:** turkey butta sandwich; barbecue chicken sandwich; charming staff and vibe. Ⓢ *Average main: $13* ✉ *1263 Leavenworth St., Nob Hill* ☎ *415/885–3030* ⊕ *www.lebeaumarket. com.*

Hotels

The steep Nob Hill is alive with hostelries proffering treatment fit for (and provided to) kings, queens, and politicians. Stay here, and at the end of a long day of sightseeing, a cable car can whisk you practically to your hotel's doorstep. The dining scene can be a schlep from your hotel, but the allure of sleeping atop San Francisco can erase that inconvenience.

Fairmont San Francisco

$$ | **HOTEL** | Dominating the top of Nob Hill like a European palace, the Fairmont indulges guests in luxury: rooms in the main building, adorned in sapphire blues with platinum and pewter accents, have high ceilings, decadent beds, and marble bathrooms, while rooms in the newer Tower, many with fine views, have a neutral color palette with bright-silver notes. **Pros:** huge bathrooms; stunning lobby; great location. **Cons:** some older rooms are small; challenging hills for those on foot; $35 per night amenity fee. [$] *Rooms from: $301* ✉ *950 Mason St., Nob Hill* ☎ *415/772–5000, 866/550–4491* 🌐 *www.fairmont.com/san-francisco* 🛏 *606 rooms* 🍴 *No Meals.*

InterContinental Mark Hopkins

$$ | **HOTEL** | The circular redbrick drive of this towering 1926 architectural landmark leads to an opulent, mirrored, marble-floor lobby that's the gateway to luxurious rooms aglow with gold, cream, and yellow tones. **Pros:** spectacular views from upper floors; steeped in history; last-minute deals often possible online. **Cons:** old-style decor; small bathrooms in some rooms and suites; steep climb from Union Square. [$] *Rooms from: $239* ✉ *999 California St., Nob Hill* ☎ *415/392–3434* 🌐 *www.sfmarkhopkins.com* 🛏 *380 rooms* 🍴 *No Meals.*

Petite Auberge

$ | **B&B/INN** | The French provincial room decor of Petite Auberge—bright flowered wallpaper and an armoire that compensates for a lack of closet space—pleases Francophiles seeking Old World charm. **Pros:** classic character without feeling old; cute outdoor courtyard; personalized service. **Cons:** street noise in front rooms; lowest-price rooms can be too tight of a squeeze; limited amenities. [$] *Rooms from: $189* ✉ *863 Bush St., Nob Hill* ☎ *415/928–6000* 🌐 *www.petiteauberge-sf.com* 🛏 *26 rooms* 🍴 *Free Breakfast.*

Close-Up on the Brocklebank

The grand Brocklebank Apartments, on the northeast corner of Sacramento and Mason Streets across from the Fairmont San Francisco, might look eerily familiar. In 1958 the complex was showcased in Alfred Hitchcock's *Vertigo* (Jimmy Stewart starts trailing Kim Novak here), and in the 1990s it popped up in the television miniseries based on Armistead Maupin's *Tales of the City.*

★ The Ritz-Carlton, San Francisco

$$$ | **HOTEL** | A tribute to beauty and attentive, professional service, the Ritz-Carlton emphasizes luxury and elegance, which are evident in the Ionic columns that grace the neoclassical facade and the crystal chandeliers that illuminate marble floors and walls in the lobby. **Pros:** terrific service; beautiful furnishings; lobby wine-tasting lounge. **Cons:** nothing is a bargain; hilly location; no pool. [$] *Rooms from: $450* ✉ *600 Stockton St., Nob Hill* ☎ *415/296–7465, 800/542–8680* 🌐 *www.ritzcarlton.com/sanfrancisco* 🛏 *336 rooms* 🍴 *No Meals.*

Stanford Court San Francisco

$$ | **HOTEL** | Railroad baron Leland Stanford's mansion once stood at the top-tier location where the Stanford Court is today, and the warm tones and handsome leather chairs are reminiscent of a

grander time. **Pros:** attention to techno-logical detail; classic yet modern style; off-season packages. **Cons:** $36 nightly amenity fee; cheaper rooms are small and lack design interest; exterior rooms get outside noise. $ *Rooms from: $274* ✉ *905 California St., Nob Hill* ☎ *415/989–3500* ⊕ *www.stanfordcourt.com* ⇥ *393 rooms* ⦿ *No Meals.*

White Swan Inn
$$ | B&B/INN | A cozy library with a crackling fireplace and comfortable chairs and sofas is the heart of this inviting Eng-lish-style bed-and-breakfast, a sister prop-erty to the French-style Petite Auberge next door. **Pros:** cozy antidote to nearby chain hotels; nice lounge and patio area; unique touches like board games and its own city treasure hunt. **Cons:** thin walls make for noisy rooms; nearby streets can feel gritty at night; some rooms need an update. $ *Rooms from: $209* ✉ *845 Bush St., Nob Hill* ☎ *415/775–1755* ⊕ *www.whiteswaninnsf.com* ⇥ *26 rooms* ⦿ *Free Breakfast.*

Nightlife

BARS
Stookey's Club Moderne
COCKTAIL LOUNGES | With swing jazz on the soundtrack, bartenders in white jackets, and an immaculately detailed art-deco interior, it's always a trip back to the Bing Crosby–Ella Fitzgerald era at this charm-ing Lower Nob Hill cocktail bar. ✉ *895 Bush St., Nob Hill* ☎ *415/771–9695* ⊕ *www.stookeysclubmoderne.com.*

Tonga Room and Hurricane Bar
THEMED ENTERTAINMENT | Since the 1940s, the Tonga Room has supplied the city with high Polynesian kitsch. Fake palm trees, grass huts, a lagoon (three-piece combos play pop standards on a floating barge), and faux monsoons—courtesy of sprinkler-system rain and simulated thun-der and lightning—grow more surreal as you quaff mai tais and other fruit-flavored cocktails. ✉ *Fairmont San Francisco, 950 Mason St., Nob Hill* ☎ *415/772–5144* ⊕ *www.fairmont-san-francisco.com.*

Top of the Mark
COCKTAIL LOUNGES | A famous magazine photograph immortalized the bar atop the Mark Hopkins as a hot spot for World War II servicemen on leave or about to ship out. The view remains sensational. Enter-tainment on many evenings ranges from solo piano to six-piece jazz ensembles (sometimes with a cover charge). Drinks and small bites can vary in quality, but you're really here to drink in the view and history. ✉ *InterContinental Mark Hopkins, 999 California St., Nob Hill* ☎ *415/392–3434* ⊕ *www.topofthemark.com.*

Shopping

ART GALLERIES
Bond Latin Gallery
ART GALLERIES | Some of the vibrant works on show in this cozy Latin American art gallery come from such artists as Diego Rivera, Frida Kahlo, and Francisco Toledo. ✉ *792 Sutter St., Nob Hill* ☎ *415/362–1480* ⊕ *www.bondlatin.com.*

CLOTHING
Cris Consignment
WOMEN'S CLOTHING | This upscale designer consignment shop is full of nearly new items for a lot less than new prices. Chloé and Chanel are a couple of the many high-end labels to grace the racks. Not only is this shop brimming with one-of-a-kind tops, dresses, and coats, but it smells like a spring garden, and they include a sprig of fresh flowers with every purchase. ✉ *1813 Polk St., Nob Hill* ☎ *415/474–1191* ⊕ *shopcrisconsignment. com* ⊙ *Closed Mon. and Tues.*

Russian Hill

A tony residential neighborhood of spiffy pieds-à-terre, Victorian flats, Edwardian cottages, and boxlike condos, Russian Hill has some of the city's loveliest stairway walks, sweetest hidden garden-ways, and steepest streets—not to mention wonderful bay views. Several stories explain the origin of Russian Hill's name. One legend has it that Russian farmers raised vegetables here for Farallon Islands seal hunters; another attributes the name to a Russian sailor of prodigious drinking habits who drowned in a well on the hill. A plaque at the top of the Vallejo Steps gives credence to the version that says sailors of the Russian-American Company were buried here in the 1840s. Be sure to visit the sign for yourself—its location offers perhaps the finest vantage point on the hill.

◉ Sights

★ Ina Coolbrith Park

CITY PARK | If you make it all the way up here, you may have the place all to yourself, or at least feel like you do. The park's terraces are carved from a hill so steep that it's difficult to see if anyone else is there or not. Locals love this park because it feels like a secret—one of the city's magical hidden gardens, with a meditative setting and spectacular views of the bay peeking out from among the trees. A poet, Oakland librarian, and niece of Mormon prophet Joseph Smith, Ina Coolbrith introduced Jack London and Isadora Duncan to the world of books. For years she entertained literary greats in her Macondray Lane home near the park. In 1915 she was named poet laureate of California. ⊠ *Vallejo St. between Mason and Taylor Sts., Russian Hill* ⊕ *www.sfparksalliance.org.*

★ Lombard Street

STREET | The block-long "Crookedest Street in the World" makes eight switchbacks down the east face of Russian Hill between Hyde and Leavenworth Streets. Join the line of cars waiting to drive down the steep hill, or avoid the whole mess and walk down the steps on either side of Lombard. You take in super views of North Beach and Coit Tower either

way—though if you're the one behind the wheel, you'd better keep your eye on the road lest you become yet another of the many folks who ram the garden barriers. ■TIP➔ **Can't stand the traffic? Thrill seekers of a different stripe may want to head two blocks south of Lombard to Filbert Street. At a gradient of 31.5%, the hair-raising descent between Hyde and Leavenworth Streets is one of the city's steepest. Go slowly!** ⊠ *Lombard St. between Hyde and Leavenworth Sts., Russian Hill.*

★ Macondray Lane

STREET | San Francisco has no shortage of impressive, grand homes, but Macondray Lane is the quintessential hidden garden. Enter under a lovely wooden trellis and proceed down a quiet, cobbled pedestrian lane lined with Edwardian cottages and flowering plants and trees. A flight of steep wooden stairs at the end of the lane leads to Taylor Street—on the way down you can't miss the bay views. If you've read any of Armistead Maupin's Tales of the City books, you may find the lane vaguely familiar; it's the thinly disguised setting for parts of the series. ⊠ *Between Jones and Taylor Sts., and Union and Green Sts., Russian Hill.*

★ Vallejo Steps

VIEWPOINT | Several Russian Hill buildings survived the 1906 earthquake and fire and remain standing. Patriotic firefighters saved what's become known as the Flag House (⊠ *1652–56 Taylor St.*) when they spotted the American flag on the property. The owner, a flag collector, fearing the house would burn, wanted it to go down with "all flags flying." At the southwest corner of Ina Coolbrith Park, it is one of a number of California shingle–style homes in this neighborhood, several of which the architect Willis Polk designed.

Polk drew up the plans for the nearby Polk-Williams House (⊠ *Taylor and Vallejo Sts.*) and lived in one of its finer sections, and he was responsible for 1034–1036 Vallejo, across the street. He also laid out the Vallejo Steps themselves, which climb the steep ridge across Taylor Street from the Flag House. The precipitous walk up to Ina Coolbrith Park and beyond is possibly the most pleasurable thing to do while on Russian Hill. **■TIP→ If the walk up the steps will be too taxing, park at the top by heading east on Vallejo from Jones and enjoy the scene from there.** ✉ *Taylor and Vallejo Sts., steps lead up toward Jones St., Russian Hill.*

🍴 Restaurants

Harris' Restaurant

$$$$ | STEAKHOUSE | Red-meat connoisseurs will appreciate this old-school restaurant, home to some of the best dry-aged steaks in town, including Kobe-style Wagyu rib eye. Enjoy a generous martini or Manhattan and you'll feel transported back in time at one of the city's few lavish, wood-paneled classic steak houses. **Known for:** classic atmosphere; extensive wine list; live jazz. [$] *Average main: $70* ✉ *2100 Van Ness Ave., Russian Hill* ☎ *415/673–1888* 🌐 *www.harrisrestaurant.com* 🕓 *Closed Mon. No lunch.*

Helmand Palace

$$ | AFGHAN | This handsomely outfitted spot will introduce you to the aromas and tastes of traditional Afghan cooking, with sauces and spices reminiscent of Indian cuisine and an emphasis on lamb. Highlights include *aushak* (leek-filled ravioli served with yogurt and ground beef) and *kadoo* (a sweet-savory dish of sugared pumpkin in a beef sauce). **Known for:** basmati rice pudding; neighborhood gem; generous portions. [$] *Average main: $23* ✉ *2424 Van Ness Ave., Russian Hill* ☎ *415/345–0072* 🌐 *www.helmandsf.com* 🕓 *No lunch.*

Nisei

$$$$ | JAPANESE FUSION | As the American child of a Japanese immigrant—the definition of *nisei*—Chef David Yoshimura wants us to know that there's more to Japanese cuisine than ramen and sushi. At his new, low-key and elegant black-walled restaurant—already awarded its first Michelin star—Yoshimura puts his own creative spin on *washoku*, traditional seasonal Japanese cooking, to deliver what he calls "Japanese soul food." **Known for:** excellent cocktails at Bar Iris; innovative flavor combinations; inventive Japanese food with a strong flavor profile. [$] *Average main: $223* ✉ *2316 Polk St., Russian Hill* 🌐 *www.restaurantnisei.com* 🕓 *Closed Mon. and Tues. No lunch.*

Seven Hills

$$$ | MODERN ITALIAN | This longtime Nob Hill favorite recently moved into a new, far more spacious home in Russian Hill. The setting might be livelier and grander, but the consistently excellent contemporary-upscale Italian cuisine and superb wine list remain as great as ever. **Known for:** excellent pastas; well-curated wine list; burrata and house-made charcuterie. [$] *Average main: $35* ✉ *1896 Hyde St., Russian Hill* ☎ *415/775–1550* 🌐 *www.sevenhillssf.com* 🕓 *No lunch.*

☕ Coffee and Quick Bites

The Boy's Deli

$ | SANDWICHES | Tucked into the back of a tiny produce market is a counter serving up some of the biggest, juiciest, best sandwiches in town for lunch—strictly to go. Try the turkey-bacon-pesto Sanfranpsycho sandwich. **Known for:** generous portions; in-the-know spot; long lines at lunchtime. [$] *Average main: $14* ✉ *Polk & Green Produce Market, 2222 Polk St., Russian Hill* ☎ *415/776–3099* 🌐 *theboysdeli.com* 🕓 *No dinner.*

Hot Sauce and Panko

$ | KOREAN FUSION | This quaint, family-run Korean fried chicken–focused establishment serves quite possibly the leading wings in the city. Cover the crispy, tender wings with your choice of more than a dozen sauces, from tangy lime-fish to fiery habanero-mango, and take them to go. **Known for:** more than a dozen sauce options (they're for sale, too); waffles for DIY fried chicken sandwiches; closes at 7 pm (5 pm Sundays). $ *Average main: $10 ⊠ 1468 Hyde St., Russian Hill* ☏ *415/359–1908* ⊕ *hotsauceandpanko. com* ☺ *Closed Mon. and Tues.*

Swensen's Ice Cream

$ | ICE CREAM | FAMILY | The original Swensen's has been a neighborhood favorite since 1948. **Known for:** house-made ice cream; fun throwback; deeply rooted San Francisco history. $ *Average main: $8 ⊠ 1999 Hyde St., Russian Hill* ⊕ *www.swensensicecream.com.*

🍸 Nightlife

Union Larder

WINE BARS | This cheery, modern industrial–designed spot is truly wonderful and refreshingly casual. The excellent list of wines by the glass is always impressive. Nicely composed small plates, cheese, and house-made charcuterie are worthy companions to all the Chardonnay and Zinfandel. ⊠ *1945 Hyde St., Russian Hill* ☏ *415/323–4845* ⊕ *unionlarder.com* ☺ *Closed Sun.–Mon.*

Polk Gulch

Polk Gulch, the microhood surrounding north-south Polk Street, hugs the western edges of Nob Hill and Russian Hill but is nothing like either. It's actually two microhoods: Upper Polk Gulch, fairly classy in its northern section, runs from about Union Street south to California Street; Lower Polk Gulch, the rougher southern part, continues down from California to Geary or so.

Polk Gulch was the city's gay neighborhood into the 1970s, hosting San Francisco's first Pride parade in 1972 and several festive Halloween extravaganzas. The area became known for transgender bars and gay prostitution but has "straightened" out—lost its edge, some would say. Today the friendly saloon the Cinch, the last remnant of gay Polk, and a few holdovers from that earlier time share space with newer mid-range restaurants, a passel of bars and nightclubs, and some browsable, funky stores, plus two great doughnut shops.

Downhill and down-market from its hilltop neighbors, Polk Gulch has seen some gentrification (especially north of California Street) from the tech-boom years, but the Upper Gulch still has a fraternity-house party vibe. The Lower Gulch feels closer in spirit to the edgy Tenderloin, which it borders. Come to see a lively, scrappy, down-to-earth slice of the city that's forever in transition.

🍴 Restaurants

★ Acquerello

$$$$ | ITALIAN | Chef and co-owner Suzette Gresham has elicited swoons over the years with high-end but soulful Italian cooking that is worth every penny. Her cuttlefish "tagliatelle" is a star of the menu, which features both classic and cutting-edge dishes. **Known for:** sensational prix-fixe dining; city's premier Italian cheese selection; extensive Italian wine list. $ *Average main: $165 ⊠ 1722 Sacramento St., Polk Gulch* ☏ *415/567–5432* ⊕ *www.acquerellosf.com* ☺ *Closed Sun. and Mon. No lunch.*

House of Prime Rib

$$$$ | STEAKHOUSE | Van Ness's temple to a British Sunday roast is one of San Francisco's most timeless dinner experiences. Waiters continuously wheel prime rib carving stations around a sprawling complex that feels like the vast dining hall of a Cotswolds manor, complete with fireplaces and chandeliers. **Known for:** worthy martinis; ambience of a London high-society club; leaving you too full for dessert. $ *Average main: $59 ⊠ 1906 Van Ness Ave., Polk Gulch* ☏ *415/885–4605, 415/885–4606* ⊕ *www.houseof-primerib.net* ☺ *No lunch.*

★ Swan Oyster Depot
$$ | **SEAFOOD** | Half fish market and half diner, this small, slim, family-run seafood operation, open since 1912, has no tables, just a narrow marble counter with about 18 stools. Some locals come in to buy perfectly fresh salmon, halibut, crabs, and other seafood to take home; everyone else hops onto one of the rickety stools to enjoy a dozen oysters, other shellfish, or a bowl of clam chowder—the only hot food served. **Known for:** memorable Dungeness crab Louie salad; fresh oysters and seafood; clam chowder. [$] *Average main: $29* ✉ *1517 Polk St., Polk Gulch* ☎ *415/673–1101* 🌐 *swanoysterdepot.us* 💳 *No credit cards* 🕘 *Closed Sun. No dinner.*

Coffee and Quick Bites

Bob's Donuts
$ | **BAKERY** | **FAMILY** | This legendary 24-hour doughnut shop has been a neighborhood anchor since the 1960s. The homemade doughnuts, whether an apple fritter or classic raised maple, are always excellent, at 10 am or 10 pm. **Known for:** cake crumb doughnut; Bob's Challenge for devoted doughnut lovers; timeless, low-key atmosphere. [$] *Average main: $3* ✉ *1621 Polk St., Polk Gulch* ☎ *415/776–3141* 🌐 *www.bobsdonutssf.com.*

Maison Danel
$ | **CAFÉ** | Paris's joie de vivre is everywhere at this teahouse-patisserie-bakery that looks like it should be in Saint-Germain-des-Prés. The sweets and baked goods are just as magnificent as the vintage Parisian atmosphere. **Known for:** afternoon tea and lunch/brunch; "Paris–San Francisco" version of the famous Paris-Brest dessert pastry; macarons. [$] *Average main: $16* ✉ *1030 Polk St., Polk Gulch* ☎ *415/685–5900* 🌐 *www.maisondanel.com* 🕘 *Closed Tues.–Wed.*

Nightlife

BARS

Amelie
WINE BARS | A slice of modern French life, this cozy and romantic wine bar is an ideal spot for oenophiles, with a list strong in French selections. Vintage-theater seating is available up front—perfect for mingling with strangers. The prices are reasonable, the pours handsome. Sit at the red-lacquer bar to learn about wine and pick up a French phrase or two. ✉ *1754 Polk St., Polk Gulch* ☎ *415/292–6916* 🌐 *www.sfamelie.com.*

Kozy Kar
BARS | Outrageous and full of sexual energy, this tiny space with an even tinier dance floor may be the heterosexual equivalent of San Francisco's gay-bar scene. It may all be on the racy side, but it's never creepy or uncomfortable. ✉ *1548 Polk St., Polk Gulch* ☎ *415/346–5699* 🌐 *www.kozykar.com.*

Macondray
COCKTAIL LOUNGES | Your best option for a refined craft cocktail on Polk Street, this cheery, plant-filled bar serves solid, never precious drinks, balancing the line between serious and fun. The food menu leans toward seafood like rock crab–stuffed eggs and a signature lobster roll. ✉ *2209 Polk St., Polk Gulch* ☎ *415/829–3464* 🌐 *www.macondraysf.com.*

LGBTQ+ NIGHTLIFE

The Cinch Saloon
BARS | This Wild West–motif neighborhood gay bar has pinball machines, pool tables, a smoking patio, and several theme nights and drag shows on the schedule. The Cinch is not the least bit trendy, which is part of the charm for regulars of this landmark 1970s bar. ✉ *1723 Polk St., Polk Gulch* ☎ *415/776–4162* 🌐 *www.facebook.com/thecinchsaloon.*

Chapter 8

PACIFIC HEIGHTS AND JAPANTOWN

8

Updated by
Denise Leto

⊙ Sights	⑪ Restaurants	🛏 Hotels	⊜ Shopping	ⓨ Nightlife
★★☆☆☆	★★★★☆	★★☆☆☆	★★★☆☆	★★☆☆☆

SAN FRANCISCO'S ARCHITECTURE

California Academy of Sciences

San Francisco's architecture scene underwent a dramatic growth spurt in the first two decades of the 21st century. Boldface international architects spearheaded major projects like Salesforce Tower (2018), the Chase Center (2019), and SFMOMA's dramatic expansion (2016). And with those additions came heated local debates.

The development flurry is thrown into sharp relief by the previous decades spent carefully preserving the city's historic buildings. Genteel Victorian homes are a San Francisco signature, and this residential legacy is fiercely protected.

Residents aren't shy about voicing opinions on the "starchitect" plans, either. As high-profile designs unfold and new condo neighborhoods break ground, criticism will surely escalate. One thing that gratifies everyone: the impressive advances made in eco-friendly building practices that are a recurring theme in the new, prominent building projects.

SAN FRANCISCO MUSEUM OF MODERN ART (SFMOMA)

Renowned Swiss architect Mario Botta's first shot at designing a museum resulted in the distinctive, sturdy geometrical forms that reflect his signature style. Here a black-and-white cylindrical tower anchors the brick structure. Botta called the huge, slanted skylight the "city's eye, like the Cyclops." A new wing, designed by Snøhetta, opened in 2016, adding more than 100,000 square feet of gallery and public space.

DE YOUNG MUSEUM OF FINE ART

Love it or hate it, the structure is a must-see destination in Golden Gate Park. After the original Egyptian-revival edifice was deemed seismically unsafe, the Pritzker-winning Swiss team Herzog & de Meuron won the commission to rebuild. Their design's copper facade and, in particular, the 144-foot observation tower—a twisted parallelogram grazing the treetops—drew fire from critics, who compared the design to a "rusty aircraft carrier." But the copper hue is mellowing with age, and the panoramic view from the ninth-floor observation deck is a hit.

CALIFORNIA ACADEMY OF SCIENCES

An eco-friendly, energy-efficient adventure in biodiversity, Renzo Piano's audacious design for this natural history museum comes equipped with a rain forest, a planetarium, skylights, and a retractable ceiling over the central courtyard. But it's the "living roof," covered in native plants, that generates the most comment.

MISSION BAY, RINCON HILL, AND TRANSBAY DISTRICT

San Francisco's cityscape is undergoing tremendous change, especially moving south from Market Street

San Francisco Victorian homes

along the waterfront. Glass-sheathed, condo-crammed high-rises are taking over what was a working-class area of warehouses and lofts, led by Oracle Park, the Giants' baseball ballpark. The ultramodern Transbay Terminal, with a rooftop park, opened in 2018, as did soaring Salesforce Tower, now San Francisco's tallest building. The blocky Mission Bay Conference Center on the University of California, San Francisco (UCSF) campus, by Mexican architect Ricardo Legorreta, has changed the landscape of nearby Mission Bay, as has the Warriors' waterfront home, the Chase Center basketball arena and entertainment complex.

PRESIDIO

The development of this parkland continues at a relatively slow pace. Its historic military-base buildings are being put to new uses—everything from a printing press to a spa. Additions include a digital arts center by George Lucas, a Walt Disney Museum, the beautifully renovated mid-century Presidio Theatre, and the hip Inn at the Presidio and Lodge at the Presidio boutique hotels.

de Young Museum of Fine Art

NEIGHBORHOOD SNAPSHOT

TOP EXPERIENCES

■ **Fillmore Street shopping:** Browse the superfine shops along Pacific Heights' main drag.

■ **Picnicking at Lafayette Park:** Gather supplies along Fillmore Street and climb to the top of this park. It's surrounded by spectacular homes and has a sweeping view of the city.

■ **Asian shops in the Japan Center:** Grab an adorable *taiyaki* (a fish-shape cone with soft-serve ice cream) at Uji Time or browse the wonderful Kinokuniya Bookstore and the tea implements at Asakichi.

■ **Spa serenity at Kabuki Springs:** Enter the peaceful lobby and prepare to be transported at the Japanese-style communal baths.

■ **Historical architecture:** Check out the grand vintage homes along the tree-lined streets of Pacific Heights.

PLANNING YOUR TIME

Give yourself an hour to wander Fillmore Street, more if you're planning to eat here or picnic in one of the parks. Checking out the stunning homes in Pacific Heights is best done by car, unless you have serious stamina; a half hour is enough. Shops and restaurants are the highlights of Japantown; lunchtime is ideal.

Allow at least an hour to wander around Alamo Square Park and the Divisadero corridor. The street has great restaurants, so plan to eat here.

GETTING HERE

■ Steep streets in Pacific Heights make for impressive views and rough walking; consider taking a car or taxi here. For Pacific Heights proper, take the 12–Folsom to its terminus at Van Ness and Pacific Avenues and walk west. For Fillmore Street, catch the 1–California or the 22–Fillmore bus. The 38 and 38R–Geary run right by Japantown, and the 24–Divisadero and 21–Hayes are the routes for the Alamo Square/Western Addition area.

FUN FACT

■ Some of the city's richest and most famous make their homes in Pacific Heights. Well-known residents include former Speaker of the House Nancy Pelosi (whose elderly husband was famously attacked here in 2022) and prolific romance novelist Danielle Steel.

Pacific Heights and Japantown are something of an odd couple: privileged, old-school San Francisco and the workaday commercial center of Japanese-American life in the city, stacked virtually on top of each other.

The extravagant mansions of Pacific Heights gradually give way to the more modest Victorians and unassuming housing tracts of Japantown. The most interesting spots here huddle in the Japan Center, the neighborhood's two-block centerpiece, and along Post Street. You can find plenty of authentic Japanese treats in the shops and restaurants.

Pacific Heights

Pacific Heights defines San Francisco's most expensive and dramatic real estate. Grand Victorians line the streets, mansions and town houses are priced in the two-digit millions, and there are magnificent views from almost any point in the neighborhood. Old money and new, personalities in the limelight and those who prefer absolute media anonymity live here; few outsiders see anything other than English Tudor imports, baroque bastions, and the pleasing facades of Queen Anne charmers. Nancy Pelosi and Dianne Feinstein, Larry Ellison, and Gordon Getty all own impressive homes here, but not even pockets as deep as those can buy a large garden—space is simply at too much of a premium. Luckily, two of the city's most spectacular parks are located here. The boutiques and restaurants along Fillmore Street, which range from glam to funky, are a draw for the whole city.

◉ Sights

★ Alta Plaza Park
CITY PARK | FAMILY | Golden Gate Park's longtime superintendent, John McLaren, designed this 12-acre park in the early 1900s, modeling its steep south-facing terracing on that of the Grand Casino in Monte Carlo. At any time of day, you're guaranteed to find San Francisco's exercise warriors running up the park's south steps. From the top of those steps, you can see Marin to the north, downtown to the east, Twin Peaks to the south, and Golden Gate Park to the west. ■ TIP→ Kids love the many play structures at the large, enclosed playground at the top; dogs love the off leash area in the park's southeast corner. ⊠ Bordered by Clay, Steiner, Jackson, and Scott Sts., Pacific Heights ⊕ www.altaplazapark.com.

Atherton House
HISTORIC HOME | The somewhat quirky design of this Victorian-era house incorporates Queen Anne, Stick-Eastlake, and other architectural elements. Many claim the house—now apartments—is haunted by the ghosts of its 19th-century residents, who (supposedly) regularly whisper, glow, and generally cause a mild fuss. It's not open to the public. ⊠ 1990 California St., Pacific Heights.

Broadway Estates
HISTORIC HOME | Broadway uptown, unlike its garish North Beach stretch, has plenty of prestigious addresses. The three-story

A Pacific Heights Walk

Start at **Broadway and Webster Streets**, where four notable estates stand within a block of one another. Two are on the north side of Broadway west of the intersection, one is on the same side to the east, and the last is half a block south on Webster. Head south down Webster and hang a right onto Clay to **Alta Plaza Park**, or skip the park and turn left on Jackson to the **Whittier Mansion**, at Jackson and Laguna Streets. Head south down Laguna and cross Washington Street to **Lafayette Park**. Walk on Washington along the edge of the park, past the formal French **Spreckels Mansion** at the corner of Octavia Street, and

continue east two more blocks to Franklin Street. Turn left (north); halfway down the block stands the handsome **Haas-Lilienthal House**. Head back south on Franklin Street, stopping to view a grand Georgian-style residence (⊠ *1735 Franklin St.*) and the Queen Anne–style Coleman House with a gorgeous purple stained-glass window on the home's north side (⊠ *1701 Franklin St.*). At California Street, turn right (west) to see two **Italianate Victorians** and the **Atherton House**. Continue west to Laguna Street and turn left (south); past Pine Street sits a sedate block of **Laguna Street Victorians**.

palace at 2222 Broadway, which has an intricately filigreed doorway, was built by Comstock silver-mine heir James Clair Flood and later donated to a religious order. The Convent of the Sacred Heart purchased the Grant House at 2220 Broadway. These two buildings, along with a Flood property at 2120 Broadway, are used as private school buildings today. A gold-mine heir, William Bowers Bourn II, commissioned Willis Polk to build the nearby brick mansion at 2550 Webster Street. Two blocks away, movie fans will surely recognize the "Mrs. Doubtfire" apartment at Broadway and Steiner (⊠ *2640 Steiner St.*). It's the home where Robin Williams donned his disguise as a lovable British nanny in the beloved 1993 comedy. ⊠ *Pacific Heights.*

Haas-Lilienthal House

HISTORIC HOME | A small display of photographs on the bottom floor of this elaborate, gray 1886 Queen Anne house makes clear that despite its lofty stature and striking, round third-story tower, the 11,500-square-foot house was modest compared with some of the giants that fell victim to the 1906 earthquake and

fire. San Francisco Heritage, a foundation to preserve San Francisco's architectural history, operates the home, whose carefully kept rooms provide a glimpse into late-19th-century life through period furniture, authentic details (like the antique dishes in the kitchen built-in), and photos of the Haas family, who occupied the house for three generations until 1972.

■**TIP→ You can admire hundreds of gorgeous San Francisco Victorians from the outside, but this is the only one that's open to the public, and it's worth a visit.**

You can download free maps of two nearby walking tours highlighting the neighborhood's historic architecture on the house's website. ⊠ *2007 Franklin St., between Washington and Jackson Sts., Pacific Heights* ☎ *415/441–3000* ⊕ *www. haas-lilienthalhouse.org* ⤴ *Tours $10.*

Lafayette Park

CITY PARK | **FAMILY** | Clusters of trees dot this four-block-square oasis for sunbathers and dog-and-Frisbee teams. On the south side of the park, squat but elegant 2151 Sacramento Street, a private condominium, is the site of a home occupied

Did You Know?

These pastel Victorian homes in Pacific Heights are closer to the original hues sported back in the early 1900s. It wasn't until the 1960s that the bold, electric colors now seen around San Francisco gained popularity. Before that, the most typical house paint color was a standard gray.

Pacific Heights, Japantown, and Western Addition

Moscone Park

Presidio of San Francisco

COW HOLLOW

PACIFIC HEIGHTS

CPMC Pacific Heights

PRESIDIO HEIGHTS

Alta Plaza Park

UCSF Laurel Heights

ANZA VISTA

UCSF Med Ctr at Mt Zion

Color Fountain Park

University of San Francisco

Alamo Square Park

PANHANDLE

Golden Gate Park

Buena Vista Park

Duboce Park

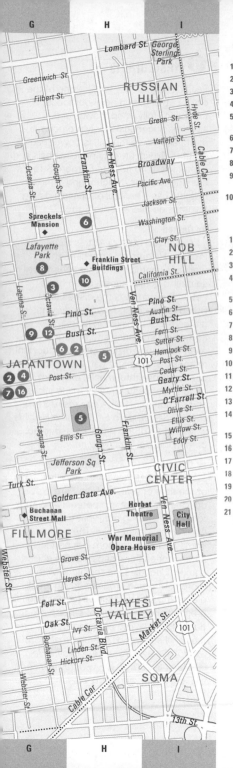

Sights ▼

1 Alamo Square Park...... **F8**
2 Alta Plaza Park........... **E4**
3 Atherton House **G4**
4 Broadway Estates **F3**
5 Cathedral of Saint Mary
of the Assumption **H5**
6 Haas-Lilienthal House.. **H3**
7 Japan Center............ **G5**
8 Lafayette Park........... **G4**
9 Laguna Street
Victorians................ **G4**
10 Two Italianate
Victorians................ **H4**

Restaurants ▼

1 As Quoted **B5**
2 Automat.................. **D7**
3 Che Fico.................. **E7**
4 Daeho Kalbijjim
& Beef Soup............. **G5**
5 4505 Burgers & BBQ ... **E8**
6 Hina Yakitori.............. **E7**
7 Ju-Ni **D7**
8 Marufuku Ramen **F5**
9 Merchant Roots.......... **F6**
10 Nopa **E8**
11 Nopalito.................. **E8**
12 Octavia................... **G4**
13 The Progress............. **F6**
14 Roam Artisan
Burgers **F4**
15 Routier **D4**
16 Sasa..................... **G5**
17 Sociale................... **A5**
18 Sorrel.................... **C4**
19 SPQR.................... **F5**
20 Spruce **A4**
21 State Bird
Provisions **F6**

Quick Bites ▼

1 b Patisserie.............. **D4**
2 Crown & Crumpet
Tea Salon **G5**
3 Jane on Fillmore **F4**
4 The Mill **E7**

Hotels ▼

1 Hotel Drisco **D3**
2 Hotel Majestic **H5**
3 Kimpton Hotel Enso...... **F5**
4 Laurel Inn **C4**
5 Mansion on Sutter...... **H5**
6 Queen Anne Hotel **G5**

by Sir Arthur Conan Doyle in the late 19th century. Coats of arms blaze in the front stained-glass windows. Across from the park's eastern edge is another eye-catching historic home: the Queen Anne (and distinctly yellow) C. A. Belden House at 2004 Gough Street.

The park's northern border is anchored by the stately Spreckels Mansion, built originally for sugar heir Adolph B. Spreckels and his wife, Alma. It is now the 55-room home of celebrated romance novelist Danielle Steel. Giant, immaculately trimmed hedges hide most of the mansion from public view—and have been quite the topic of debate among locals for many years. The park itself is a lovely neighborhood space where Pacific Heights residents laze in the sun or exercise their pedigreed canines while gazing at downtown's skyline or the Bay and Marin County hills in the distance to the north. ✉ *Bordered by Laguna, Gough, Sacramento, and Washington Sts., Pacific Heights* 🌐 *sfrecpark.org.*

Laguna Street Victorians

HISTORIC HOME | On the west side of the 1800 block of Laguna Street, these oft-photographed private houses cost between $2,000 and $2,600 when they were built in the 1870s. Nowadays, you'd need to add three zeros to those prices; an entire house might sell for upward of $5 million. No bright colors here, though—most of the paint jobs are in soft beiges or pastels. ✉ *Between Bush and Pine Sts., Pacific Heights.*

Two Italianate Victorians

HISTORIC HOME | Two Italianate Victorians stand out on the 1800 block of California Street. The beauty at 1834, the Wormser-Coleman House, was built in the 1870s. Coleman bought the lot next door, giving this private property an unusually spacious yard for the city, even for this luxurious neighborhood. ✉ *1818 and 1834 California St., Pacific Heights.*

🍴 Restaurants

Pacific Heights may well be one of the city's better-known neighborhoods, thanks to Hollywood movies and jaw-dropping mansions. More down-to-earth, and down the hill, is Lower Pac Heights, which attracts professionals and postgrads, who flock to Fillmore Street's bustling eateries. Neighboring Presidio Heights has a handful of upscale dining favorites on Sacramento Street.

As Quoted

$ | **AMERICAN** | **FAMILY** | At this sleek Presidio Heights daytime café, the wellness-centric menu manages to be so delicious that guests often don't notice how virtuous the dishes are. Bread for the open-faced sandwiches is gluten-free and baked in-house; several items are vegetarian and/or vegan; and even the pappardelle is made of zucchini ribbons instead of wheat. **Known for:** post-yoga healthful meals; excellent gluten-free toasts; freshly made juices and smoothies. [$] *Average main: $18* ✉ *3613 Sacramento St., Presidio Heights* ☎ *415/914–0689* 🌐 *www.eatasquoted.com* 🕒 *Closed Sun. No dinner.*

★ Octavia

$$$ | **MODERN AMERICAN** | Regardless of the time of year, Melissa Perello's upscale restaurant is a perennial favorite for diners seeking out what California cuisine really tastes like. The warm, immaculate dining room is a perfect setting for edgier dishes like the chilled squid-ink noodles starter, along with more comforting produce-driven small plates and entrées. **Known for:** exciting preparations with peak-of-season produce; spicy deviled egg starter; truly professional service. [$] *Average main: $35* ✉ *1701 Octavia St., Lower Pacific Heights* ☎ *415/408–7507* 🌐 *www.octavia-sf.com* 🕒 *Closed Sun. and Mon. No lunch.*

Roam Artisan Burgers

$ | **BURGER** | **FAMILY** | All the burgers at this laid-back spot, part of a popular Bay Area mini-chain, are responsibly sourced, and the beef is 100% grass-fed. Choose a patty (beef, bison, vegetarian, elk, or turkey), then select a preset "style" or invent your own from the many creative toppings. **Known for:** notable vegetarian burger; popular with families; the "fry-fecta" trio of fry styles for a side. [$] *Average main: $16* ✉ *1923 Fillmore St., Pacific Heights* ☎ *415/800–7801* 🌐 *www.roamburgers.com.*

Sociale

$$$ | **NORTHERN ITALIAN** | The COVID-19 pandemic's outdoor dining requirement led San Franciscans to discover the city's premier patios—like the one at this Presidio Heights stalwart. Whether you're dining on that patio or in the elegant dining room, Italian and seasonal Californian cooking mingle together on the menu. **Known for:** fantastic pastas; chocolate oblivion cake; Barolo and Barbaresco wine choices. [$] *Average main: $31* ✉ *3665 Sacramento St., Presidio Heights* ☎ *415/921–3200* 🌐 *sfsociale.com* ⏲ *Closed Sun. and Mon. No lunch Tues. and Wed.*

★ **Sorrel**

$$$$ | **MODERN AMERICAN** | After a long run as one of San Francisco's most important dining pop-ups, Alex Hong's refined seasonal Californian cooking can be found in one of San Francisco's most dramatic dining settings, with a skylight and floral arrangements that epitomize California "good life" architecture. That vibe is reflected in dishes like a springtime dry-aged duck with green garlic and kumquat, where Hong beautifully blends contemporary techniques and local ingredients. **Known for:** exemplary pastas; beautifully composed tasting menu; upscale dinner party vibe. [$] *Average main: $46* ✉ *3228 Sacramento St., Presidio Heights* ☎ *415/525–3765* 🌐 *www.sorrelrestaurant.com* ⏲ *Closed Mon. and Tues. No lunch.*

★ **SPQR**

$$$$ | **ITALIAN** | This modern Italian favorite continues to be a special destination for chef Matthew Accarrino's inventive seasonal cooking. The five-course tasting menu includes tempting antipasti, superlative pastas like mustard capellini with guinea hen ragù, and a few hearty secondi; save space for the fantastic desserts. **Known for:** chicken liver mousse antipasti; vintages from less-known Italian wine regions; fried chicken on Sundays. [$] *Average main: $96* ✉ *1911 Fillmore St., Pacific Heights* ☎ *415/771–7779* 🌐 *www.spqrsf.com* ⏲ *Closed Mon.–Wed. No lunch Thurs. and Fri.*

Spruce

$$$$ | **MODERN AMERICAN** | This elegant restaurant caters to an older crowd who sink happily into its oversized faux-ostrich leather chairs. The tasting menu is equally refined, with ingredients often sourced from the restaurant's farm south of the city and charcuterie made in-house; celeriac velouté with brandied-chestnut mousseline and salmon with horseradish soubise reflect the contemporary Californian menu's elegant French leanings. **Known for:** beloved burger on an English-muffin bun; giant chocolate chip cookies; expensive Napa Valley and French wines. [$] *Average main: $98* ✉ *3640 Sacramento St., Pacific Heights* ☎ *415/931–5100* 🌐 *www.sprucesf.com.*

☕ Coffee and Quick Bites

b Patisserie

$ | **BAKERY** | Your search for the perfect *kouign-amann* (a traditional glazed, butter-enriched Breton pastry made of croissant dough) ends in this buzzy café from baking wizard Belinda Leong. **Known for:** chocolate banana almond croissant; impeccable kouign-amann; dedication to seasonal offerings. [$] *Average main: $7* ✉ *2821 California St, Pacific Heights* ☎ *415/440–1700* 🌐 *bpatisserie.com* ⏲ *Closed Mon. and Tues. No dinner.*

Jane on Fillmore

$ | CAFÉ | Stop into this bright spot for their famous avocado mash, homemade baked goods and cookies, and coffee from beans roasted in-house. Look for other Janes around the city, including on Larkin Street in the Tenderloin, on Grant Avenue in Chinatown, and Jane the Bakery on Geary Street in Japantown. **Known for:** cute space and hipster vibe; excellent house-made breads; addictive cheddar chive biscuits. $ Average main: $10 ⊠ 2123 Fillmore St., Pacific Heights ⊕ www.itsjane.com ⊗ No dinner.

🛏 Hotels

★ Hotel Drisco

$$$$ | HOTEL | You can pretend you're a denizen of one of San Francisco's wealthiest neighborhoods at this understated, elegant Edwardian hotel built in 1903. **Pros:** gorgeous rooms and public spaces; great service and amenities; quiet residential neighborhood. **Cons:** not a close walk to restaurants or major sights; steep prices; no complimentary chauffeur service in the afternoon or evening. $ Rooms from: $520 ⊠ 2901 Pacific Ave., Pacific Heights ☎ 415/346–2880, 800/634–7277 ⊕ hoteldrisco.com ⇦ 48 rooms ⦿ Free Breakfast.

Hotel Majestic

$$ | HOTEL | Opened in 1902, the five-story Majestic is the city's oldest continually operating hotel; its elegant lobby is a graceful haven of antique chandeliers, plush Victorian chairs, antiquarian French books, and Edwardian architecture. **Pros:** nicely upgraded classic hotel; spacious rooms; good value. **Cons:** bus ride or over-10-minute walk to activities and restaurants; old style; website works erratically. $ Rooms from: $258 ⊠ 1500 Sutter St., Pacific Heights ☎ 415/441–1100, 800/869–8966 ⊕ www.thehotelmajestic. com ⇦ 58 rooms ⦿ No Meals.

Laurel Inn

$$ | HOTEL | FAMILY | The blue-and-tan facade of this boutique Hyatt property, punctuated on two sides by garage entrances, hints at its 1963 motor-inn origins, yet the spacious rooms feel modern. **Pros:** stylish, good-size rooms; family- and pet-friendly rooms; excellent bar. **Cons:** no on-site restaurant; cheapest rooms are very small; additional fee for gym or spa. $ Rooms from: $250 ⊠ 444 Presidio Ave., Pacific Heights ☎ 415/567–8467, 800/552–8735 ⊕ www.jdvhotels. com/hotels/california/san-francisco/the-laurel-inn ⇦ 49 rooms ⦿ No Meals.

Mansion on Sutter

$$$ | B&B/INN | San Francisco doesn't get much more old-school elegant than this Lower Pac Heights Victorian mansion transformed into a luxurious, intimate lodging with spacious, individually decorated rooms. **Pros:** luxury everywhere; the rare pet-friendly Victorian hotel; exceptionally comfortable beds. **Cons:** small gym; inconvenient location; subpar breakfast and fitness center. $ Rooms from: $360 ⊠ 1409 Sutter St., Lower Pacific Heights ☎ 415/213–2746 ⊕ www. mansiononsutter.com ⇦ 12 rooms ⦿ Free Breakfast.

Queen Anne Hotel

$$ | B&B/INN | Built in the 1890s as a girls' finishing school, this Victorian mansion is a taste of old San Francisco, with a large parlor and guest rooms that have classic touches, such as painted cherub murals and, in some, wood-burning fireplaces. **Pros:** lots of design character; library/salon will invite you to linger; old-time vibe. **Cons:** substantial walk to tourist areas; no restaurant or gym; some stuffy, airless rooms. $ Rooms from: $205 ⊠ 1590 Sutter St., Pacific Heights ☎ 415/441–2828 ⊕ www.queenanne. com ⇦ 48 rooms ⦿ Free Breakfast.

Nightlife

The Snug

COCKTAIL LOUNGES | A welcoming yet refined drinking destination, this Lower Pac Heights bar is exactly what the well-heeled and fun-loving neighborhood needed. It's the rare bar that emphasizes clever cocktails, in-high-demand local craft beer, and smartly selected wine in equal parts. Elevated takes on bar bites like yellowtail poke and sesame naan with shiitake mushroom hummus are created by a chef formerly at some of the country's gastronomic heavyweights (Benu, Alinea). As a reflection of its firm belief in living wages, in lieu of tips the Snug adds a 20% "fair-wage surcharge" to every bill. ⊠ *2301 Fillmore St., Lower Pacific Heights* ⊕ *www.thesnugsf.com.*

🛍 Shopping

With grocery and hardware stores sitting alongside local clothing ateliers and international designer outposts, Pacific Heights mixes small-town America with big-city glitz. After you've splurged on a cashmere sweater or a hand-blown glass vase, snag a seat at b Patisserie for coffee or a bite: it's the perfect way to pass an afternoon watching the parade of old money, new money, dogs, and strollers.

BOOKS

Browser Books

BOOKS | FAMILY | Opened in 1976, one of the city's most beloved independent bookstores resides quietly among the chic fashion boutiques lining Fillmore Street. All ages will find ample choices, from contemporary fiction to children's books to a large selection of Buddhist Dharma literature. The store is owned by Inner Richmond favorite Green Apple Books. ⊠ *2195 Fillmore St., Lower Pacific Heights* ☎ *415/567–8027* ⊕ *www. greenapplebooks.com.*

CLOTHING

Dottie Doolittle

CHILDREN'S CLOTHING | FAMILY | Mothers shop here for charming silk dresses and other special-occasion outfits for their little ones. Less pricey togs for infants (boys to size 12 and girls to size 16) are also for sale. There are lots of fun toys, from stuffed animals to mini picnic sets, worth glancing at as well. ⊠ *3680 Sacramento St., Pacific Heights* ☎ *415/563–3244* ⊕ *www.dottiedoolittle. com* ⊙ *Closed Sun.*

★ Margaret O'Leary

WOMEN'S CLOTHING | If you can only buy one piece of clothing in San Francisco, make it a hand-loomed cashmere sweater by this Irish-born local legend. The perfect antidote to the city's wind and fog, the sweaters are so beloved by San Franciscans that some of them never wear anything else. Pick up an airplane wrap for your trip home. ⊠ *2400 Fillmore St., Pacific Heights* ☎ *415/771–9982* ⊕ *www.margaretoleary.com.*

FOOD AND DRINK

D&M Wines and Liquors

WINE/SPIRITS | This family-owned business appears to be just another neighborhood liquor store, but it's actually a rare and wonderful specialist. In a city obsessed with wine, these spirits devotees distinguish themselves by focusing on rare, small-production Armagnac and Calvados brandy, and Champagne. Look up from the bottles to admire the stained-glass lampshades, too. ⊠ *2200 Fillmore St., Pacific Heights* ☎ *415/346–1325* ⊕ *dandm.com* ⊙ *Closed Sun. and Mon.*

★ Verve Wine

WINE/SPIRITS | Wine nerds will fall in love with this trendy, upscale destination from Master Sommelier Dustin Wilson. Many wine drinkers will also recognize him from the 2012 documentary *Somm* (and its sequels). High-quality, smaller producers from prominent and lesser-known regions share wall space in this exceptionally organized boutique. ⊠ *2358*

Fillmore St., Lower Pacific Heights
☎ 415/896–4935 ⊕ vervewine.com.

HOUSEWARES AND GIFTS
Nest
SOUVENIRS | A cross between a Parisian antiques show and a Jamaican flea market, this store can get even the most monochrome excited about color. Turn up the volume on your SF souvenirs with vintage artist journals, rare Oaxacan jewelry, hard-to-find Herb Caen books, and classic Paris and Barcelona map scarves. ⊠ 2300 Fillmore St., Pacific Heights ☎ 415/292–6199 ⊕ nestsf.com.

Sue Fisher King Company
HOUSEWARES | When Martha Stewart or the buyers at Williams Sonoma need inspiration, they come to see how Sue has set her sprawling table or dressed her stately bed. Her specialty is opulent linens for every room. And when Pacific Heights residents are looking for an impeccable hostess or bridal gift, they come by for a hand-embroidered velvet pillow or a piece of Amanda Moffat pottery. ⊠ 3067 Sacramento St., Pacific Heights ☎ 415/922–7276 ⊕ www.sue-fisherking.com ☉ Closed Sun.

JEWELRY AND COLLECTIBLES
Goldberry Jewelers
JEWELRY & WATCHES | Margie Rogerson opened this store to showcase her platinum-only designs. While she carries a large selection of engagement rings, her specialty is colored stones: rubies, sapphires, and emeralds. Their colors really sparkle against the background of this all-white and Lucite space. It's open by appointment only. ⊠ 3516 Sacramento St., Pacific Heights ☎ 415/734–7305 ⊕ goldberry.com.

Japantown

Though still the spiritual center of San Francisco's Japanese-American community, Japantown feels somewhat adrift. The Japan Center mall, for instance, comes across as rather sterile, and whereas Chinatown is densely populated and still largely Chinese, Japantown struggles to retain its unique character.

Also called Nihonmachi, Japantown is centered on the southern slope of Pacific Heights, north of Geary Boulevard, between Fillmore and Laguna Streets. The Japanese community in San Francisco started around 1860; after the 1906 earthquake and fire, many of these newcomers settled in the Western Addition. By the 1930s, they had opened shops, markets, meeting halls, and restaurants, and also established Shinto and Buddhist temples. But during World War II the area was virtually gutted when many of its residents, including second- and third-generation Americans, were forced into so-called relocation camps. During the 1960s and 1970s, redevelopment further eroded the neighborhood, and most Japanese Americans now live elsewhere in the city.

Still, when several key properties in the neighborhood were sold in the aughts, a group rallied to "save Japantown," and some new blood finally infused the area with energy: Robert Redford's Sundance corporation revived the Kabuki Theatre (now owned by AMC); local, hip hotel group Joie de Vivre (now JdV by Hyatt) took over the Hotel Kabuki; and the J-Pop center, New People, brought Japanese pop culture and a long-missing youthful vibe. Beginning in 2024, the city plans to revamp the currently dreary Peace Plaza, with a focus on making this important space more inviting.

■ TIP→ Japantown is a relatively safe area, but the Western Addition, south of Geary Boulevard, can be dangerous even during the daytime. Also avoid going too far west of Fillmore Street on either side of Geary.

👁 Sights

Japan Center

STORE/MALL | FAMILY | Cool and curious trinkets, noodle houses and sushi joints, a destination bookstore, and a peek at Japanese culture high and low await at this five-acre complex designed in 1968 by noted American architect Minoru Yamasaki. The Japan Center includes the shop- and restaurant-filled Kintetsu Mall and Kinokuniya Building; the excellent Kabuki Springs & Spa; the Hotel Kabuki; and the AMC Kabuki reserved-seating cinema/restaurant complex. ✉ *Bordered by Geary Blvd. and Fillmore, Post, and Laguna Sts., Japantown* 🌐 *www.sfjapantown.org/japan-center-malls.*

🍴 Restaurants

The epicenter of Japantown is the Japan Center mall, with several restaurants dishing out ramen, sushi, and *donburi* (rice bowls). There's also a glut of karaoke bars, sushi shops, and ramen restaurants along Buchanan Street's pedestrian way, between Post and Sutter Streets.

Daeho Kalbijjim & Beef Soup

$$$$ | KOREAN | This ever-popular specialist in *kalbijjim*, a Korean braised beef short rib soup, is set in an industrial-feeling space, with serene images of mountains on the walls. Each soup is large enough to feed a small family and comes with a choice of toppings, like rice cakes or oozing cheese (melted tableside, it's an Instagram sensation). **Known for:** Korean short rib soup; influencer hot spot; lively, fun atmosphere. [$] *Average main: $46* ✉ *1620 Post St., Japantown* ☎ *415/563–1388* 🌐 *daehokalbijjim.com.*

Marufuku Ramen

$ | RAMEN | Hakata-style *tonkotsu* (pork) and extra-intense chicken *paitan* ramen are the specialties of this modern-looking Japan Center restaurant that serves what many consider the city's finest bowl of ramen. As a result, long lines can be daunting, but tables move pretty quickly inside the bustling yet relaxed space decorated with wood design elements and dangling Edison bulbs. **Known for:** superb ramen; gyoza and pork buns; lively, contemporary vibe. [$] *Average main: $18* ✉ *Kinokuniya Bldg., 1581 Webster St., Suite 235, Japantown* ☎ *415/872–9786* 🌐 *www.marufukuramen.com.*

Sasa

$$ | SUSHI | Japantown has a host of sushi options at all price points, but this longtime staple on the second floor of the Japan Center stands out for its excellent rolls, nigiri, and sashimi. The omakase menu, with eight pieces of sushi and nigiri, is a fraction of the cost of its downtown peers, but close to equal in quality and diner satisfaction. **Known for:** "mystery box" mini chirashi bowl; uni spoon with quail egg and ikura (cured salmon roe); an oasis in a busy mall. [$] *Average main: $30* ✉ *Japan Center East Mall, 22 Peace Plaza, Suite 530, Japantown* ☎ *628/600–6945* 🌐 *sasasf.com* 🕒 *No lunch Mon.*

☕ Coffee and Quick Bites

Crown & Crumpet Tea Salon

$ | BRITISH | FAMILY | In the lobby of the New People building, this mini tea shop looks like a little girl's fantasy, with pretty flowered and polka-dotted tablecloths, fancy settings, and nods to the British royal family. Most guests opt for high tea with scones, crumpets, and finger sandwiches, or you can stop in for a sandwich or salad. **Known for:** nursery tea and craft kits for kids; fun and frilly tea-shop decor; unconventional lobby setting. [$] *Average main: $18* ✉ *1746 Post St., Japantown* ☎ *415/771–4252* 🌐 *www.crownandcrumpet.com* 🕒 *Closed Tues. and Wed. No dinner.*

Hotels

Kimpton Hotel Enso

$$ | HOTEL | FAMILY | With minimalist design and a nod to Zen serenity, this updated and rebranded Kimpton property named for the Zen circle of togetherness welcomes guests into its elegant lobby, lighted by fixtures reminiscent of Japanese lanterns and decorated with plants and a table made of reclaimed Japanese whiskey barrels. **Pros:** children's scooters to loan; complimentary morning coffee and afternoon wine hour; indoor/outdoor fitness center. **Cons:** somewhat far from the action; guests must join hotel rewards club to get free Wi-Fi; minimalist room design. [$] *Rooms from: $275* ✉ *1800 Sutter St., Japantown* ☎ *800/994–6103 reservations, 415/921–4000 hotel* 🌐 *www.ensohotelsf.com* 🛏 *225 rooms* 🍴 *No Meals.*

Shopping

Unlike shops in the ethnic enclaves of Chinatown, North Beach, and the Mission, the five-acre Japan Center is under one roof. The three-block complex includes a reasonably priced public garage and three shop-filled buildings. Especially worthwhile are the West Mall and the Kinokuniya Building, where shops sell things like bonsai trees, tapes and records, jewelry, antique kimonos, *tansu* (Japanese chests), electronics, and colorful glazed dinnerware and teapots.

BOOKS

Kinokuniya Bookstore

BOOKS | FAMILY | The selection of English-language books about Japanese culture—everything from medieval history to origami instructions—is one of the finest in the country. Kinokuniya is also the city's biggest seller of Japanese-language books. Glossy Asian fashion magazines attract the young and trendy; the manga and anime books and magazines are wildly popular, too. ✉ *Kinokuniya Bldg., 1581 Webster St., Japantown* ☎ *415/567–7625* 🌐 *usa.kinokuniya.com.*

HOUSEWARES AND GIFTS

Soko Hardware

HOUSEWARES | This shop specializes in beautifully crafted Japanese tools for gardening and woodworking. In addition to the usual hardware-store items, you can find seeds for Japanese plants and books about topics such as making *shoji* (paper screens). There are also lots of Japanese teapots and cookware vessels to browse. It's a great destination for a unique souvenir and a fun experience to see a truly historic San Francisco business. ✉ *1698 Post St., Japantown* ☎ *415/931–5510* 🌐 *www.sokohardware.com* 🕒 *Closed Mon.*

SHOPPING CENTERS

Buchanan Mall

MALL | FAMILY | The shops lining this open-air mall next to the Peace Plaza (look for the giant pagoda) are geared more toward locals, but there are some fun Japanese-goods stores here, too. Start your exploration with exquisite Japanese homewares in a gallery-like space at SF76 (✉ *1758 Buchanan St.* 🌐 *www.sf-76.com*). Look for Hasami and Tomoro pottery and ceramics by local artists. It's easy to spend hours among the fabulous origami and craft papers at Paper Tree (✉ *1743 Buchanan St.* 🌐 *paper-tree.com*). After shop browsing, have a seat on the steps around local artist Ruth Asawa's twin origami-style fountains, which sit in the middle of the mall. Wrap up a visit with lunch at Hinodeya Ramen (✉ *1737 Buchanan St.* 🌐 *hinodeyaramen.com*), serving lighter *dashi* (clear-broth) ramen, a rarity in the city. ✉ *Buchanan St., between Post and Sutter Sts., Japantown.*

New People

MALL | The younger generation's counterpart to the Japan Center, this fresh shopping center combines a cinema, a tea parlor, and shops with a successful synergy. The downstairs New People

Cinema shows classic and cutting-edge Asian (largely Japanese) films. Upstairs you can peruse Japanese pop-culture items and anime-inspired fashion, like handmade, split-toe shoes at SOU • SOU and Lolita fashion at Baby, the Stars Shine Bright. ⊠ *1746 Post St., Japantown* ⊕ *www.newpeopleworld.com.*

🏃 Activities

SPAS
★ Kabuki Springs & Spa
SPAS | The serene spa is one Japantown destination that draws locals from all over town, from hipsters to grandmas, Japanese American or not. Balinese urns decorate the communal bath area of this house of tranquility. The extensive service menu includes facials, salt scrubs, and mud and seaweed wraps, in addition to massage. You can take your massage in a private room with a bath or in a curtained-off area. The communal baths ($45) contain hot and cold tubs, a large Japanese-style bath, a sauna, a steam room, and showers. The clothing-optional baths are open for men only on Thursday and Saturday; women bathe on Wednesday, Friday, and Sunday. Bathing suits are required on Tuesday, when the baths are coed. Men and women can reserve a private room daily. ⊠ *1750 Geary Blvd., Japantown* 🕾 *415/922–6000* ⊕ *kabukisprings.com* 🕙 *Closed Mon.*

Western Addition

The Western Addition is traditionally one of the city's most diverse neighborhoods. It struggles in some areas with poverty and gang violence, yet the same neighborhood includes the trendy, dining-rich Divisadero corridor and Alamo Square Park with its iconic Painted Ladies. The Lower Fillmore area in its post–World War II heyday was known as the Harlem of the West for its profusion of jazz night spots, where such legends as Billie

Holliday, Duke Ellington, and Charlie Parker would play. These days the neighborhood tries to maintain its historic African American cultural core and its link to that heritage with events like the beloved annual Fillmore Jazz Festival in June. More live music rings at The Fillmore, the auditorium made famous in the 1960s by Bill Graham and the iconic bands he booked there, and at the blues-centric Boom Boom Room.

👁 Sights

★ Alamo Square Park
CITY PARK | **FAMILY** | Whether you've seen them on postcards or on the old TV show *Full House,* the colorful "Painted Ladies" Victorian houses are some of San Francisco's world-renowned icons. The signature view of these beauties with the downtown skyline in the background is from the east side of this hilly park. Tourists love the photo opportunities, but locals also adore the park's tennis courts, dog runs, and ample picnic area—with great views, of course. After taking plenty of photos, swing by the park's northwest corner and admire the William Westerfeld House (⊠ *1198 Fulton St.*), a splendid five-story late-19th-century Victorian mansion. ■**TIP ⯈ If it's a sunny day, grab picnic provisions from Bi-Rite Market. Thursday through Sunday, the Lady Falcon Coffee Club truck is stationed in the park, offering a great caffeine pick-me-up.** ⊠ *Bordered by Steiner, Hayes, Scott, and Fulton Sts., Western Addition* ⊕ *sfrecpark.org.*

Cathedral of Saint Mary of the Assumption
CHURCH | This striking cathedral stands out with its sweeping contemporary design. Italian architects Pietro Belluschi and Pier Luigi Nervi intended to create a spectacular cathedral that reflects both the Catholic faith and modern technology. It was controversial when it opened in 1971, yet now is applauded for its grand, curving roof that rises to a height of 190 feet, with sections that form a

cross highlighted with intricate stained-glass work. The cathedral is open daily for visitors other than during Mass, and it usually has docents on duty in the late morning hours. Most locals know the cathedral as Our Lady of Maytag for its resemblance to a washing machine agitator. ✉ *1111 Gough St., Western Addition* 🌐 *smcsf.org.*

🍴 Restaurants

This area is a patchwork of culturally and economically diverse neighborhoods bordering the Lower Haight, the Fillmore District, and Japantown, and the neighborhood reflects that diversity with Italian, Japanese, and Indian restaurants housed in 1950s-era and Victorian buildings in the span of a couple of city blocks. Some of San Francisco's hottest tables, from morning to late night, can be found along the busy Fillmore and Divisadero commercial corridors.

Automat

$$ | MODERN AMERICAN | FAMILY | Marquee pop-up turned all-day restaurant, this worthwhile casual establishment is tucked away on a residential street far from the activity of Divisadero. Here family-friendly focus meets refined technique, featuring excellent sandwiches during the daytime, then the rare option of a prix fixe, counter-service dinner menu. **Known for:** kids' menu for kids of all ages; casual fine-dining menu and vibe; superb house-baked breads. [$] *Average main: $28* ✉ *1801 McAllister St., at Baker St., Western Addition* ☎ *415/296–6680* 🌐 *www.automatsf.com* 🕒 *Closed Mon. No dinner Sun.*

Che Fico

$$$ | MODERN ITALIAN | This consistently popular spot sets itself apart with homemade charcuterie, plus antipasti, pastas, and pizza that often take traditional standbys for a creative spin or a California slant from local produce. The clever, beautifully balanced cocktails and fun twists on homey desserts are must-orders. **Known for:** pineapple pizza; hard-to-get reservations; Roman Jewish specialties. [$] *Average main: $39* ✉ *838 Divisadero St., Western Addition* ☎ *415/416–6959* 🌐 *www.chefico.com* 🕒 *Closed Sun. and Mon. No lunch.*

4505 Burgers & BBQ

$$ | BARBECUE | FAMILY | The smoker works overtime from noon to night at this hipster-chic barbecue shack, churning out an array of succulent meats that can be had by the plate, the pound, or as a sandwich. Every plate comes with two sides, and you should certainly make the frankaroni one of them: possibly the work of the devil, this is macaroni-and-cheese with pieces of hot dog ... deep fried. **Known for:** partially outdoor seating in shipping containers; decadent sides; self-named and possibly correct "Best Damn Cheeseburger." [$] *Average main: $20* ✉ *705 Divisadero St., Western Addition* ☎ *415/231–6993* 🌐 *www.4505burgersandbbq.com.*

Hina Yakitori

$$$$ | JAPANESE | San Franciscans are spoiled with an incredible abundance of cuisines and restaurants specializing in niche dishes—but *yakitori* (Japanese grilled meat skewers) remained elusive until the Ju-Ni team and chef Tommy Cleary opened this upscale omakase destination near Alamo Square Park, focused on chicken yakitori. The *binchotan* (Japanese charcoal) grill adds the pivotal smoky touch to the skewers that hold all parts of the chicken and make up the heart of the tasting menu. **Known for:** intimate prix-fixe-only dining experience; modern arts meet Japanese serene design space; refined, tiny composed dishes. [$] *Average main: $165* ✉ *808 Divisadero St., Western Addition* ☎ *415/817–1944* 🌐 *www.hinasf.com* 🕒 *Closed Sun. and Mon. No lunch.*

Ju-Ni

$$$$ | SUSHI | With just a dozen counter seats—its name means "12" in

Japanese—this NoPa (North of the Panhandle) omakase sushi favorite is one of the Bay Area's most exquisite sushi experiences. Diners sit in pods of four at the sushi bar, with one sushi chef serving each quartet in the serene-meets-modern room. **Known for:** Wagyu and uni à la carte sushi; sake selection; high quality with high prices. $ *Average main: $225* ✉ *1335 Fulton St., Western Addition* ☎ *415/655–9924* ⊕ *www.junisf.com* ⊗ *Closed Sun. and Mon. No lunch.*

Merchant Roots

$$$$ | CONTEMPORARY | After starting as part grocer/part lunch café/part tasting menu, this tiny Fillmore spot is now fully devoted to the elaborate tasting menus of chef-owner Ryan Shelton. Themes and dishes change every few months (it could be "flowers" or "Alice in Wonderland"), but the one constant is Shelton's incredible imagination and ability to transform those themes into elaborate, technique-driven composed dishes. **Known for:** SF's best chocolate chip cookies; warm and welcoming ambience; excellent wine program. $ *Average main: $168* ✉ *1365 Fillmore St., Western Addition* ☎ *530/574–7365* ⊕ *www.merchantroots.com* ⊗ *Closed Mon., Tues., and every other Sun. No lunch.*

★ Nopa

$$$ | AMERICAN | This is the good-food granddaddy of the hot corridor of the same name. The Cali-rustic fare draws dependable crowds regardless of the night, with attractions including a beloved Moroccan vegetable tagine; crisp-skin rotisserie chicken; and a juicy hamburger with thick-cut fries. **Known for:** high-quality comfort food with smart twists; lively vibe; a constant and diverse crowd. $ *Average main: $32* ✉ *560 Divisadero St., Western Addition* ☎ *415/864–8643* ⊕ *nopasf.com* ⊗ *No lunch.*

Nopalito

$$ | MEXICAN | FAMILY | Those in the mood for a fresh take on both common and seldom-seen Mexican dishes will adore Nopa's nearby little sibling. All the tortillas are made from organic house-ground masa, and Mexico's peppers find their way into many of the spice-filled offerings. **Known for:** house-made tortillas; pork shoulder–filled pozole rojo; tequila or mezcal drinks. $ *Average main: $27* ✉ *306 Broderick St., Western Addition* ☎ *415/437–0303* ⊕ *www.nopalitosf.com* ⊗ *Closed Mon.*

The Progress

$$$$ | MODERN AMERICAN | The second, grander restaurant from the chef-owners of State Bird Provisions is hardly just a little sibling: it features its own type of exciting, seasonally driven cooking, with no shortage of global influences. The lofty, bustling setting within an early 20th-century theater is a stunner of a backdrop, and some regulars love to sit at the small, cheery bar at the front and enjoy their dinner like an audience watching a grand dining-room stage. **Known for:** large barbecue duck platter; superb cocktails; top-notch desserts. $ *Average main: $42* ✉ *1525 Fillmore St., Western Addition* ☎ *415/673–1294* ⊕ *thepro-gress-sf.com* ⊗ *No lunch.*

Routier

$$$ | BISTRO | This charming establishment from an all-star chef trio has quickly become a favorite for classic bistro cooking with plenty of unique elements. A vintage Parisian dining room and marble-topped bar set the stage for fresh takes on French cuisine with a Californian accent. **Known for:** potato pavé bites; standout cocktails; must-order baguette and desserts. $ *Average main: $31* ✉ *2801 California St., Lower Pacific Heights* ☎ *415/766–9997* ⊕ *routiersf.com* ⊗ *Closed Mon. and Tues. No lunch.*

★ State Bird Provisions

$$ | MODERN AMERICAN | It's hard to score a reservation for a normal dinner hour at Lower Fillmore's game-changing restaurant, but once you nab a golden ticket, you'll be rewarded with fascinating bites served from roving carts and an à la

carte printed menu. The food has an artsy bent to it, and the colorful dining room with pegboard walls adds to a vibe that's part high-school art room, part bohemian dinner party. **Known for:** buttermilk fried quail; cart service and à la carte dining; "World Peace" peanut milk dessert drink. $ *Average main: $29* ⊠ *1529 Fillmore St., Western Addition* ☎ *415/795–1272* ⊕ *www.statebirdsf.com* ⊗ *No lunch.*

☕ Coffee and Quick Bites

★ The Mill

$ | **BAKERY** | "Four-dollar toast" is a phrase used around San Francisco referring to gentrification—and it was inspired by this sun-drenched, Wi-Fi-less café. At this project between one of the city's leading bakers, Josey Baker, and the Mission's Four Barrel Coffee, toasts slathered with jam or spreads are the specialty during the day. **Known for:** stellar loaves of bread; precious, post-yoga vibe; one pizza topping served Monday nights. $ *Average main: $8* ⊠ *736 Divisadero St., Western Addition* ☎ *415/345–1953* ⊕ *www.the-millsf.com* ⊗ *No dinner Tues.–Sun.*

▽ Nightlife

BARS

Horsefeather

COCKTAIL LOUNGES | Creative, produce-driven cocktails and a chic, low-key vibe make this a locals' frequent top choice for a fun night out. The always interesting (but never too bizarre) cocktails range from a breezy California Cooler with celery juice to the rum-and-whiskey-based Breakfast Punch featuring clarified Cinnamon Toast Crunch–infused milk. Weekend brunch is excellent, as is the delightfully messy double cheeseburger. The kitchen stays open late nightly. ⊠ *528 Divisadero St., Western Addition* ☎ *415/817–1939* ⊕ *www.horsefeatherbar.com.*

MUSIC CLUBS

Boom Boom Room

LIVE MUSIC | One of San Francisco's liveliest music spots is this Fillmore blues favorite, opened in 1997 by the "King of the Boogie," John Lee Hooker. The club has a fun blend of blues, funk, and hip-hop shows most nights of the week. ⊠ *1601 Fillmore St., at Geary Blvd., Western Addition* ☎ *415/673–8000* ⊕ *boomboomroom.com.*

The Fillmore

LIVE MUSIC | With performances by everyone from the Counting Crows to Jimi Hendrix, this legendary auditorium dating back to 1912 has seen it all. It remains one of San Francisco's essential concert destinations for a variety of music styles. Check out the cool collection of rock posters upstairs before the show and enjoy complimentary apples after—a fun tradition for concertgoers. ⊠ *1805 Geary Blvd., Western Addition* ☎ *415/346–6000* ⊕ *www.thefillmore.com.*

🏃 Activities

SKATING

The Church of 8 Wheels

SKATING | Dance or roll along to disco-era tunes at this retro-themed skating rink inside an old church. It's all ages during the day, and adults-only after dark. ⊠ *554 Fillmore St., Western Addition* ☎ *415/752–1967* ⊕ *www.churchof-8wheels.com* ⊠ *$15, skate rental $5.*

Chapter 9

THE MARINA AND THE PRESIDIO

Updated by
Trevor Felch

👁 **Sights**
★★★★☆

🍽 **Restaurants**
★★★☆☆

🛏 **Hotels**
★★☆☆☆

💼 **Shopping**
★★★★☆

🍸 **Nightlife**
★★☆☆☆

THE GOLDEN GATE BRIDGE

Two orange-red towers reach into the sky, floating above the mist like ghost ships on foggy days. If there's one image that instantly conjures San Francisco, it's the majestic Golden Gate Bridge, one of the most recognizable sights in the world.

Spanning the Golden Gate—the mouth of the San Francisco Bay, after which the bridge was named—between San Francisco and pastoral Marin County, the bridge has won both popular and critical acclaim, including being named one of the seven wonders of the modern world. With its simple but powerful art-deco design, the 1.7-mile suspension span and its 750-foot towers were built to withstand winds of more than 100 mph. It's also not a bad place to be in an earthquake: designed to sway almost 28 feet, the Golden Gate Bridge (unlike the Bay Bridge) was undamaged by the 1989 Loma Prieta quake. If you're on the bridge when it's windy, stand still and you can feel it swaying a bit.

⊘ *Pedestrians: Mar.–Oct., daily 5 am–8 pm; Nov.–Feb., daily 5 am–6:30 pm; hours change with daylight saving time. Bicyclists: daily 24 hrs.*

A DAY OVER THE BAY

Crossing the Golden Gate Bridge under your own power is a sensation that's hard to describe. Especially as you approach midspan, hovering more than 200 feet above the water makes you feel as though you're outside of time—exhilarating, a little scary (not recommended for those who are afraid of tall heights), definitely chilly. (And be careful taking selfies—the wind can steal phones!). From the bridge's eastern-side walkway, the only side pedestrians are allowed on, you can take in the San Francisco skyline and the bay islands; look west for the wild hills of the Marin Headlands, the curving coast south to Lands End, and the Pacific Ocean. On sunny days, sailboats dot the water, and brave windsurfers test the often-treacherous tides beneath the bridge. A vista point on the Marin County side provides a spectacular city panorama. The views are fantastic however you cross—by foot, bicycle, or motorized vehicle—but driving or cycling will allow you to fully appreciate the bridge from multiple vantage points in and around the Presidio.

THE MAN WHO BUILT THE BRIDGE

In the early 1900s, San Francisco was behind the times. Sure, the city had the engineering marvel of the cable car and hundreds of streetcar lines, but as the largest U.S. city served mainly by ferries, this town needed a bridge. Enter Joseph Strauss, a structural engineer, dreamer, and poet who promised that not only could he build a bridge, but he could also do it on the cheap. Strauss was a force of nature. He worked tirelessly over the next 20-odd years, first as a bridge booster and then overseeing its design and construction. Though the final structure bore little resemblance to his original plan, Strauss guarded his legacy,

The iconic orange-red bridge is often enveloped by clouds of swirling fog known as "Karl."

refusing to recognize the seminal contributions of engineer Charles Ellis. In 2007, the Golden Gate Bridge District finally recognized Ellis's role, though Strauss, who died less than a year after the bridge's opening day in 1937, would be pleased with the inscription on his own statue, which stands sentry in the southern parking lot: "The Man Who Built the Bridge."

VISITING THE BRIDGE TODAY

Most visits start in the Visitor Plaza, where the Strauss statue, the Equator Coffee-Round House at the Golden Gate Bridge café, and the bridge's Welcome Center are located. At the outdoor exhibits, you can learn about the bridge's unique science and safety traits, and read about the personalities behind its design and construction, all while taking in the panoramic views. The surrounding Battery East Trail features several stunning viewpoints of the bridge and also connects the bridge with Crissy Field back down at sea level. City Guides (⊕ *sfcityguides.org*) offers free walking tours of the bridge every Thursday and Sunday at 11 am.

If you want to ride across the bridge and avoid the crowds, bike early or on a weekday.

NEIGHBORHOOD SNAPSHOT

TOP EXPERIENCES

- **Golden Gate Bridge:** Get a good look at the iconic span from the Presidio, then bundle up and walk over the water.

- **Shopping in Cow Hollow and the Marina:** Browse hip boutiques and people-watch at stylish cafés on Union Street, Cow Hollow's main drag.

- **Palace of Fine Arts:** Bring a picnic to this beautiful faux-Roman remnant of the 1915 Panama-Pacific International Exposition and travel back in time to the city's post-earthquake-and-fire coming-out party.

- **Crissy Field:** Join jogging, cycling, and kitesurfing locals along this restored strip of sand and marshland where the bay laps the shore, a stone's throw from the Golden Gate Bridge.

- **Presidio wanderings:** Lace up your walking shoes and follow one of the wooded trails; the city will feel a hundred miles away.

FUN FACT

- When the Golden Gate Bridge first opened, it actually wasn't open to automobiles—it was open to pedestrians only. Vehicular traffic started on May 28, 1937, one day after the official opening date.

GETTING HERE

For those without wheels, the free year-round shuttle PresidiGo, which runs two routes through the Presidio, is a dream. The PresidiGo's route to downtown runs every hour and the route within the Presidio runs each half hour. Pick up the shuttle at the transit center (located by the Visitor's Center at Lincoln Boulevard and Graham Street).

PLANNING YOUR TIME

Walking across the Golden Gate Bridge takes about an hour round-trip, but leave some time to take in the view on the other side. If you aren't in a hurry, plan to spend at least two to three hours in the Presidio, and be sure to allow 15 minutes to stroll around the stunning Palace of Fine Arts. In a pinch, make a 30- to 45-minute swing-through for the views. Shoppers can burn up an entire afternoon browsing the Marina's Chestnut Street and Cow Hollow's Union Street. Weekends are liveliest, while Mondays are quiet, since some shops close.

Yachts bob at their moorings, satisfied-looking folks jog along the Marina Green, and multimillion-dollar homes overlook the bay in the picturesque, if somewhat sterile, Marina neighborhood. Just west of this waterfront area is a more natural beauty: the Presidio. Once a military base, this beautiful, sprawling park is mostly green space, with hills, woods, and the marshlands of Crissy Field.

The Marina

Well-funded postcollegiates and the nouveaux riches flooded the Marina after the 1989 Loma Prieta earthquake sent many residents running for more solid ground, changing the tenor of this formerly low-key neighborhood. A young, fairly homogeneous, well-to-do crowd floods the Chestnut Street–area cafés and bars whether it's a weekday afternoon or weekend night. (Some things don't change—even before the quake, the Marina Safeway was a famed pickup place for straight singles, hence the nickname "Dateway.") Joggers and kite-flyers head to the Marina Green, the strip of lawn between the yacht club and the mansions of Marina Boulevard.

⊙ Sights

Fort Mason Center
ARTS CENTER | Originally a depot for the shipment of supplies to the Pacific during World War II, the fort was converted into a cultural center in 1977 and is now home to the vegetarian restaurant Greens and shops, galleries, and performance spaces.

The Museo Italo Americano (⊠ Bldg. C ☎ 415/673–2200 ⊕ museoitaloamericano.org ⊗ Closed Mon.) is a small gallery that hosts one exhibit at a time, worth a glance if you're already at Fort Mason.

From March through September, Friday evening at Fort Mason means Off the Grid (⊕ offthegridsf.com); the city's food-truck gathering happens at locations around town, and this is one of the oldest and most popular. ⊠ 2 Marina Blvd., Marina ☎ 415/345–7500 ⊕ fortmason.org.

★ Palace of Fine Arts
NOTABLE BUILDING | This stunning, rosy rococo palace on a lagoon seems to be from another world—it's the sole survivor of the many tinted-plaster structures (a temporary neoclassical city of sorts) built for the 1915 Panama-Pacific International Exposition, the world's fair that celebrated San Francisco's recovery from the 1906 earthquake and fire. The expo buildings originally extended about a

mile along the shore. Bernard Maybeck designed this faux-Roman classic beauty, which was reconstructed in concrete and reopened in 1967.

The pseudo-Latin language adorning the Palace's exterior urns continues to stump scholars. The massive columns (each topped with four "weeping maidens"), great rotunda, and swan-filled lagoon have been used in countless fashion lay-outs, films, and wedding photo shoots. Other than its use for major events and exhibitions inside the building, it's really an outdoor architecture attraction that's perfect for an hour of strolling and relaxing. After admiring the lagoon, look across the street to the house at 3460 Baker Street. If the statues out front look familiar, they should—they're original casts of the "garland ladies" you can see in the Palace's colonnade. ⊠ 3301 Lyon St., at Beach St., Marina ☎ 415/886–1296 ⊕ palaceoffinearts.com ⌷ Free.

Wave Organ

PUBLIC ART | FAMILY | Conceived by environmental artist Peter Richards and fashioned by master stonecutter George Gonzales, this unusual wave-activated acoustic sculpture at the entrance of a harbor gives off subtle harmonic sounds produced by seawater as it passes through 25 tubes. The sound is loudest at high tide. The granite and marble used for walkways, benches, and alcoves that are part of the piece were salvaged from a gold rush–era cemetery. ⊠ 83 Marina Green Dr., Marina ⌖ North of Marina Green at end of jetty by Yacht Rd.; park in lot north of Marina Blvd. at Lyon St. ⊕ www.exploratorium.edu/visit/wave-organ.

🍴 Restaurants

Chestnut Street is full of lively, hip res-taurants, almost all of which have popular sidewalk seating areas, leading to one of the more energetic street scenes in the city. For the most part, this isn't the area for creative high-end cooking. Many restaurants here are wine bars or Ital-ian-focused, along with a few outposts of San Francisco's favorite fast-casual mini-chains. A few side streets between Lombard Street and Chestnut Street are also full of restaurants, ranging from family-friendly Peruvian dining to swanky seasonal Californian eats.

A16

$$$ | ITALIAN | Named after a highway that runs through southern Italy, this bustling contemporary trattoria specializes in the food from that region, done very, very well. The menu is stocked with pizza, rustic pastas like maccaronara with ragù Napoletano (a meat sauce), and entrées like braised short rib with polenta. **Known for:** spicy arrabbiata pizza; one of the city's best Italian wine programs; dark chocolate budino tart. $ Average main: $38 ⊠ 2355 Chestnut St., Marina ☎ 415/771–2216 ⊕ www.a16pizza.com ⊘ No lunch Mon.–Thurs.

Causwells

$$ | AMERICAN | There are two personali-ties to Chestnut Street's sleek grown-up diner—the double-stack burger that draws burger hounds from dozens of miles away, and the rest of the honest, spruced-up comfort-food menu. It's a local institution that feels partially like a bistro and partially like a modern tavern, and a place where the buzz from the innovative cocktails and delicious eats never disappears. **Known for:** banana bread "grilled cheese"; excellent brunch; always feels like a party. $ Average main: $22 ⊠ 2346 Chestnut St., Marina ☎ 415/447–6081 ⊕ www.causwells.com ⊘ Closed Mon. No lunch Tues.–Thurs.

Greens

$$ | VEGETARIAN | Even as diet trends come and go, this vegetable-focused icon (opened in 1979) continues to be a steadfast favorite for carnivores and vegetarians alike. Despite the lack of meat, the hearty and creative dishes—such as griddle cakes with crimson

lentils and spiced cashew cream—really satisfy, and floor-to-ceiling windows give diners a sweeping view of the Marina and the Golden Gate Bridge. **Known for:** magnificent wood-heavy decor; delightful fresh spring rolls filled with locally made tofu; seasonal produce–driven pizzas. $ *Average main: $30* ✉ *Fort Mason Center, 2 Marina Blvd., Bldg. A, Marina* ☎ *415/771–6222* ⊕ *greensrestaurant.com* ⊗ *Closed Mon.*

Jaranita
$$ | **PERUVIAN** | This excellent, festive restaurant (part of celebrity chef Gastón Acurio's global group) presents a concise menu of Peru culinary staples like ceviche and flaky empanadas. You won't miss the obligatory pisco sour (Jaranita doesn't have a full liquor license), because the "Nikkei Sour" with citrus sake is just as special. **Known for:** beautifully decorated "Yunza" tree; pollo a la brasa (Peruvian roast chicken); leisurely mimosa-filled brunches. $ *Average main: $29* ✉ *3340 Steiner St., Marina* ☎ *655–9585* ⊕ *jaranitasf.com* ⊗ *Closed Mon. and Tues. No lunch Wed.–Fri.*

Maybeck's
$$$$ | **MODERN AMERICAN** | This California-cuisine-centric restaurant might be named after the architect of the nearby Palace of Fine Arts, but it's very much a hip place for contemporary cooking. The menu wildly varies in terms of inspiration, from charred avocado to truffle spaghetti, but each dish is compelling and consistently executed perfectly. **Known for:** beef Wellington on Wednesdays; fantastic desserts; pasta. $ *Average main: $42* ✉ *3213 Scott St., Marina* ☎ *400–8500* ⊕ *maybecks.com* ⊗ *Closed Sun. and Mon. No lunch.*

☕ Coffee and Quick Bites

Dynamo Donut & Coffee
$ | **BAKERY** | **FAMILY** | The tiny kiosk on the Marina's yacht harbor is the perfect spot to grab a pick-me-up before a stroll to the Palace of Fine Arts or along the beach. The doughnuts by a former Foreign Cinema pastry chef are universally terrific, from the vanilla bean standby to chocolate star anise, and there's locally roasted coffee for an extra pre-hike jolt. **Known for:** doughnut flavors specific to each month; maple bacon apple doughnut; vegan doughnut options. $ *Average main: $4* ✉ *110 Yacht Rd., Marina* ☎ *920–1978* ⊕ *dynamodonut.com* ⊗ *Closed Mon. and Tues.*

Lucca Delicatessen
$ | **SANDWICHES** | Hungry Marina residents gather daily to order excellent, often enormous sandwiches at this neighborhood legend. It's the signature takeaway spot for Marina Green and Crissy Field picnic-goers and has been around since the days of the Hoover Administration. **Known for:** prepared pastas; "#1 Italian Combo" sandwich with assorted cold cuts; friendly, efficient staff. $ *Average main: $15* ✉ *2120 Chestnut St., Marina* ☎ *415/921–7873* ⊕ *luccadeli.com.*

🛏 Hotels

Marina is where the beautiful (and rich) go to see and be seen. However, that luxury is limited to homes because it's a heavily residential area; hotel options are mainly just reasonably priced, usually nondescript motels and motor inns on Lombard Street, with enticements that might include kitchenettes or free parking. The proximity to boutiques, eateries, and happening bars, as well as Crissy Field and the Presidio, make this area a popular choice for value-conscious groups and families.

Marina Motel
$ | **HOTEL** | **FAMILY** | Bougainvillea, fuchsia, and other foliage—real and trompe l'oeil—add color and verve to this 1939 motor court operated by the granddaughters of the original owners, creating a magical mood when everything's in bloom and hummingbirds flit through the

quiet courtyard. **Pros:** variety of room sizes; full kitchens in some units; free parking is gold in this neighborhood. **Cons:** loud rooms facing Lombard Street; no a/c (usually not a problem here); rooms look a bit dated. $ *Rooms from: $171* ✉ *2576 Lombard St., Marina* ☎ *415/921–3430* ⊕ *www.marinamotel.com* ⇔ *39 rooms* ⦾ *No Meals.*

⨂ Nightlife

BARS

California Wine Merchant

WINE BARS | Part cluttered shop, part cozy bar, Chestnut Street's marquee wine destination is a longtime favorite for grabbing a glass or three. Featured wines come from some of the state's most highly regarded vintners of all sizes and celebrity standings. The neighborhood has many wine bars, but this is where the locals go when the focus is on the wine itself. ✉ *2113 Chestnut St., Marina* ☎ *415/567–0646* ⊕ *www.californiawinemerchant.com.*

The Interval

COCKTAIL LOUNGES | Even many locals don't realize that the Fort Mason Center is home to one of the city's most impressive and scene-free cocktail bars. As part of the Long Now Foundation, a nonprofit devoted to long-term thinking, the bar serves cocktails that reflect the group's approach, finding innovative ways to serve tried-and-true libations. The Navy Gimlet with clarified lime juice is a modern-day San Francisco classic. ✉ *Fort Mason Center, 2 Marina Blvd., Bldg. A, Marina* ☎ *415/561–6582* ⊕ *www.theinterval.org.*

COMEDY

BATS Improv

COMEDY CLUBS | In addition to teaching workshops on improvisation, this group based in a renovated warehouse stages performances such as "Guilty Pleasures: Improvised Soaps" and "Spontaneous Broadway." As is always the case for improv, the quality varies, but it's reliably fun. Tickets can be purchased in advance or at the door and have a suggested price range of $5 to $50 depending on what each patron feels comfortable paying. ✉ *Bayfront Theater, Fort Mason Center, 2 Marina Blvd., Bldg. B, 3rd fl., at Buchanan St., Marina* ☎ *415/474–6776* ⊕ *www.improv.org.*

⨂ Performing Arts

THEATER

Magic Theatre

THEATER | Once the late Sam Shepard's favorite showcase, pint-size Magic presents works by rising and established playwrights who create thought-provoking plays that explore the world's diversity. It has produced a number of world premieres. ✉ *Fort Mason Center, 2 Marina Blvd., Bldg. D, at Laguna St., Marina* ☎ *415/441–8822* ⊕ *www.magictheatre.org.*

⨂ Shopping

CLOTHING

Marine Layer

MIXED CLOTHING | It doesn't take much time in San Francisco to learn about the city's frequent fog and chilly wind, both of which are the cozy inspiration for this local label's distinctive soft-textured, stylish clothing for men and women of all ages. If you're at any restaurant or event in the city, there's a good chance that several residents are wearing a Marine Layer design. ✉ *2106 Chestnut St., Marina* ☎ *415/400–4136* ⊕ *www.marinelayer.com.*

Cow Hollow

Between old-money Pacific Heights and the well-heeled, post-collegiate Marina lies comfortably upscale Cow Hollow. The neighborhood's name harks back to the 19th-century dairy farms whose

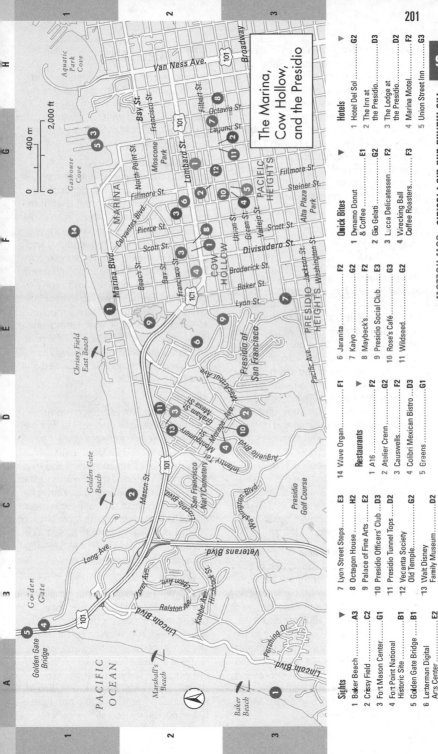

9

The Marina, Cow Hollow, and the Presidio

400 m
2,000 ft

Sights ▸
1 Baker Beach.............. **A3**
2 Crissy Field............... **C2**
3 Fort Mason Center....... **G1**
4 Fort Point National
   Historic Site............. **B1**
5 Golden Gate Bridge...... **B1**
6 Letterman Digital
   Arts Center.............. **E2**
7 Lyon Street Steps......... **E3**
8 Octagon House........... **H2**
9 Palace of Fine Arts...... **E2**
10 Presidio Officers' Club... **D3**
11 Presidio Tunnel Tops.... **D2**
12 Vecanta Society
    Old Temple.............. **G2**
13 Walt Disney
    Family Museum.......... **D2**
14 V/ave Organ.............. **F1**

Restaurants ▸
1 A16 .... **F2**
2 Atelier Crenn............. **G2**
3 Causwells................. **F2**
4 Colibri Mexican Bistro... **D3**
5 Greens **G1**
6 Jaranta.................... **F2**
7 Kaiyo..................... **G2**
8 Maybeck's................. **F2**
9 Presidio Social Club...... **E3**
10 Rose's Café.............. **G3**
11 Wildseed................. **F2**

Quick Bites ▸
1 Dynamo Donut
   & Coffee **E1**
2 Gio Gelati **G2**
3 Lucca Delicatessen....... **F2**
4 Wrecking Ball
   Coffee Roasters......... **F3**

Hotels ▸
1 Hotel Del Sol............. **G2**
2 The Inn at
   the Presidio............. **D3**
3 The Lodge at
   the Presidio............. **D2**
4 Marina Motel............. **F2**
5 Union Street Inn......... **G3**

owners eked out a living here despite the fact that there was more sand than grass. A patch of grass remains a scarce commodity in this mostly residential area, but Cow Hollow does have a lively commercial strip, centered around Union Street. To get a feel for this accessible bastion of affluence, stroll down Union. Browse the cosmetics and jewelry stores, snazzy clothing boutiques, and shops selling home decor for every taste (if not budget), then rest your feet at one of the many good restaurants or sidewalk cafés.

Sights

Octagon House

HISTORIC HOME | This eight-sided home sits across the street from its original site on Gough Street; it's one of two remaining octagonal houses in the city (the other is on Russian Hill), and the only one open to the public. White quoins accent each of the eight corners of the pretty blue-gray exterior, and a colonial-style garden completes the picture. The house is full of antique American furniture, decorative arts (paintings, silver, rugs), and documents from the 18th and 19th centuries. Note that the home is only open on the second Sunday and second and fourth Thursday of each month, and is closed all January. ✉ *2645 Gough St., near Union St., Cow Hollow* ☎ *415/441–7512* ⊕ *nscda-ca.org/octagon-house* ⌦ *Free, donations encouraged.*

Vedanta Society Old Temple

RELIGIOUS BUILDING | A light-green pastiche of colonial, Queen Anne, Moorish, and Hindu opulence, with turrets battling red-top onion domes and Victorian detailing everywhere, this 1905 structure is considered the first Hindu temple in the West. Vedanta, an underlying philosophy of Hinduism, maintains that all religions are paths to one goal. It's an interesting building to study from the street. ✉ *2963 Webster St., Cow Hollow* ☎ *415/922–2323* ⊕ *www.sfvedanta.org.*

🍴 Restaurants

Just up the hill from the Marina—and slightly quieter, with more young families—is Cow Hollow. Union Street is the main strip, dense with restaurants, cafés, and boutiques that mostly cater to the trendy A-list crowd.

★ Atelier Crenn

$$$ | MODERN FRENCH | Dinner at the spectacularly inventive flagship of San Francisco's most celebrated chef of the moment, Dominique Crenn, is an exploration of both Crenn's journey as a chef and California's distinct geography and history. Each course is usually eye-opening (and downright delicious) and many dishes feature produce from Crenn's own Bleu Belle Farm. **Known for:** extraordinary, whimsical pescatarian tasting menu; stellar desserts; hip-elegant atmosphere. Ⓢ *Average main: $365* ✉ *3127 Fillmore St., Cow Hollow* ☎ *415/440–0460* ⊕ *www.ateliercrenn.com* ⊙ *Closed Sun. and Mon. No lunch.*

Kaiyo

$$ | PERUVIAN | San Francisco has a handful of Peruvian restaurants, but this uber-hip Union Street spot is the first Nikkei (Japanese-Peruvian) restaurant. Skip the pedestrian appetizers and have fun sampling around the *tiraditos* (dishes with raw fish) and sushi rolls. **Known for:** creative pisco cocktails; shrimp tempura and yellowtail Lima roll; multiple kinds of "cebiche". Ⓢ *Average main: $24* ✉ *1838 Union St., Cow Hollow* ☎ *415/525–4804* ⊕ *kaiyosf.com* ⊙ *Closed Mon.*

Rose's Café

$$ | AMERICAN | FAMILY | Although it's open morning until night, this cozy café is most synonymous with brunch. Sleepy-headed locals turn up for delights like the smoked ham, fried egg, and Gruyère breakfast sandwich; evening favorites lean toward roast chicken, pastas, and seasonal-rustic fare. **Known for:** pizzas for morning and night; house-baked goods; grilled salmon cozy (a

Park Yourself in a Parklet 👁

Since 2010, San Francisco has been reclaiming parking spaces and turning them into parklets, tiny parks open to the public. These dot the city—more than five dozen and counting—from mobile, red-metal containers with built-in benches and plantings to Powell Street's eight-section high-design aluminum parklet. The Mission has the highest concentration, mostly along Valencia Street, but one of the most creative—an old Citroën van turned into seating and planters—is in front of the Rapha bike shop on Filbert near Fillmore in Cow Hollow.

With the outdoor dining rules in place at the start of the COVID-19 pandemic, the number of restaurant and bar parklets across the city soared, with unique alfresco dining setups created out of necessity in every neighborhood. They have been such a hit that many of these pandemic parklets will stay permanently.

unique pita-like sandwich). $ *Average main: $28 ⊠ 2298 Union St., Cow Hollow ☎ 415/775–2200 ⊕ rosescafesf.com.*

Wildseed

$$ | **VEGETARIAN** | This hip, bustling Union Street destination proves that plant-based cuisine can be exciting and delicious, along with being virtuous for the body (well, at least most dishes are) and better for the environment. The highly eclectic menu includes dishes from wild mushroom "zeppole" fritters to a spicy yellow Thai curry. **Known for:** mushroom-and-spinach patty Wildseed burger; terrific cocktails; weekend brunch-only dishes. $ *Average main: $22 ⊠ 2000 Union St., Cow Hollow ☎ 415/872–7350 ⊕ www.wildseedsf.com.*

☕ Coffee and Quick Bites

Gio Gelati

$ | **ICE CREAM** | **FAMILY** | San Francisco is filled with wonderful ice cream shops, but for the real-deal smooth, airy gelato, this Union Street gelato maker is the address to know. It's all about the ingredients here—pistachios from Sicily, local fruits in season, a sour cherry variety from a particular part of Italy—and the results are delightful whether it's a hot, sunny day or the fog feels as cool as the gelato. **Known for:** tiramisu flavor; Piemonte hazelnut flavor; espresso (in gelato or a proper espresso shot on its own). $ *Average main: $7 ⊠ 1998 Union St., Cow Hollow ☎ 415/867–1306 ⊕ giogelati. com.*

Wrecking Ball Coffee Roasters

$ | **CAFÉ** | The Instagram set knows this almost table-free Union Street roaster and café as the place with the pineapple wallpaper. Everyone enjoys some of the finest lattes and espresso shots around, usually to-go, but sometimes sipped on the low bench in front of that famous backdrop. **Known for:** coffee geeks nerding out; excellent espresso-based drinks; Instagram favorite. $ *Average main: $5 ⊠ 2271 Union St., Cow Hollow ☎ 638–9227 ⊕ www.wreckingballcoffee.com.*

🛏 Hotels

Upscale urbanites toting iPhones and gazillion-dollar strollers call Cow Hollow home. Visitors will appreciate the boutiques lining Union Street, the excellent eateries, and the small selection of B&Bs and motor inns (some are definitely more refurbished than others).

Hotel Del Sol

$ | **HOTEL** | **FAMILY** | This rejuvenated, beach-theme 1950s motor lodge with nicely appointed rooms and a fun, heated outdoor pool is all alone in a higher, hipper class of Cow Hollow/Marina boutique hotels. **Pros:** charming courtyard; great selection of suites; cheery design. **Cons:** no on-site fitness center; smallest rooms are truly tiny; self parking is pricey for the neighborhood. [$] *Rooms from: $129* ✉ *3100 Webster St., Cow Hollow* ☎ *415/921–5520* 🌐 *hoteldelsol.com* 🛏 *57 rooms* 🍴 *Free Breakfast.*

★ Union Street Inn

$$ | **B&B/INN** | Antiques, unique artwork, fine linens, and windows opening to a lovely courtyard or Union Street view make this charming Edwardian inn popular with honeymooners and those looking for a romantic getaway with an English countryside ambience. **Pros:** personal service; relaxing atmosphere; beautiful secret garden. **Cons:** parking garage is two blocks away; old-fashioned decor; no elevator. [$] *Rooms from: $297* ✉ *2229 Union St., Cow Hollow* ☎ *415/346–0424* 🌐 *unionstreetinn.com* 🛏 *6 rooms* 🍴 *Free Breakfast.*

Nightlife

In between the Marina and Pacific Heights, this small yet affluent neighborhood has a similar lively scene to the bordering Marina district, but generally is slightly pricier and slightly less raucous.

BARS

Balboa Cafe

BARS | Here you'll spy young (thirtysomething) and upwardly mobile former frat boys and sorority girls sipping on powerful espresso martinis and munching on tasty burgers served sandwich-style on a baguette—considered by some to be the best in town. Classic cocktails are proper and stiff, bartenders always have something witty to say, and the wine list is one of the neighborhood's best. ✉ *3199 Fillmore St., at Greenwich St., Cow Hollow* ☎ *415/921–3944* 🌐 *www.balboacafe.com.*

The Black Horse London Pub

BARS | Barely seven stools fit in San Francisco's smallest bar. There are just as many bottled beers (served from a bathtub!) as seats, and be sure to bring some cash since credit cards aren't accepted. It's as bare-bones as it gets, but there's sports on TV, a fun dice game, and most important, a neighborhood camaraderie that is increasingly hard to find. ✉ *1514 Union St., Cow Hollow* 🌐 *www.blackhorselondon.com.*

For the Record

COCKTAIL LOUNGES | While the Marina and Cow Hollow are filled with bars, this throwback record album–themed charmer is surprisingly the only (non-restaurant-affiliated) craft cocktail bar in the area. The sharply designed space has a clubby meets groovy feel with tufted leather banquettes and Summer of Love floral wallpaper. Cocktails are ambitious and exciting but, like the bar's atmosphere, completely free of pretension. ✉ *2120 Greenwich St., Cow Hollow* ☎ *415/855–4607* 🌐 *fortherecordsf.com* 🕒 *Closed Mon.*

Perry's

BARS | One of San Francisco's oldest singles bars still packs 'em in, but it's also a favorite restaurant for all ages. You can dine on great hamburgers (and a stellar Reuben) as well as more substantial fare to pair with local beers and simple cocktails, while gabbing about the 49ers with the well-scrubbed, khaki-clad, baseball-cap-wearing patrons. ✉ *1944 Union St., at Laguna St., Cow Hollow* ☎ *415/922–9022* 🌐 *www.perryssf.com.*

★ West Coast Wine & Cheese

WINE BARS | Whether you're in the mood for a Paso Robles Grenache Blanc or an Oregon Pinot Noir, you'll find it at this narrow, sleek locals' favorite. The kitchen isn't much more than a stovetop but does some pretty impressive work beyond cheese and charcuterie. Take advantage of the ability to order half pours and sample more wines. ✉ *2165 Union St., Cow Hollow* ☎ *415/376–9720* ⊕ *www.westcoastsf.com.*

🛍 Shopping

The former dairy pastures of yesteryear are a quaint yet sophisticated fashion and home-decor hot spot today. If you're tired of browsing the clothing and shoe stores, you can explore two of San Francisco's favorite longtime florist shops, The Bud Stop (✉ *2200 Union St.*) and Le Bouquet (✉ *2205 Union St.*). They're across the street from each other, creating the city's most flowery intersection.

CLOTHING
Current
WOMEN'S CLOTHING | Located a few blocks off of Union Street, this shop's name perfectly sums up how in vogue its selection of women's clothing is. The boutique keeps thing edgy and comfortable but never veers too far in either direction for stylish tops, pants, skirts, dresses, and even colorful cardigans. It is without question a San Francisco favorite for contemporary, fun, but functional designs. ✉ *3108 Fillmore St., Cow Hollow* ⊕ *shop-current.com.*

FOOD AND DRINK
The Caviar Company
FOOD |"The Caviar Sisters" Petra and Saskia Bergstein created this sustainability-minded brand that has developed a cult following among caviar connoisseurs and chefs in the Bay Area. Their chic above-street-level boutique on Union Street allows the public to pick out some of the finest caviar products in town—and feel good about it. ✉ *1954 Union St., Cow Hollow* ☎ *415/580–7986* ⊕ *thecaviarco.com* ☺ *Closed Sun.*

The Epicurean Trader
FOOD | Located around the city, this small group of markets presents a terrific selection of gourmet foods and high-quality artisanal food and drink products. Paninis, baguettes and espresso drinks are also available for hungry Union Street shoppers. However, it's best known for the extensive selections of craft spirits and cocktail ingredients, making this the shopping headquarters for San Francisco's home bartenders. ✉ *1909 Union St., Cow Hollow* ☎ *888/780–1628* ⊕ *theepicureantrader.com.*

PlumpJack Wines
WINE/SPIRITS | Cow Hollow's go-to wine boutique is much more than "the wine shop" co-founded by Governor Gavin Newsom in the early 1990s (when he was 26 years old). A nice selection of imported wines complements the well-priced, well-stocked collection of hard-to-find California wines, creating one of the city's strongest wine rosters. Noe Valley has a sibling store. ✉ *3201 Fillmore St., at Greenwich St., Cow Hollow* ☎ *415/346–9870* ⊕ *plumpjackwines.com.*

FURNITURE, HOUSEWARES, AND GIFTS
ATYS
OTHER ACCESSORIES | Gadgets and home accessories with a sleek modern design are imported from all over Europe and Japan and sold at this charming store in a courtyard off Union Street. Among the eye-catching items are a Mies cuckoo clock and a wine rack made of leather loops. ✉ *2149B Union St., between Fillmore and Webster Sts., Cow Hollow* ☎ *415/441–9220* ⊕ *atysdesign.com* ☺ *Closed Mon.*

Topdrawer
OTHER ACCESSORIES | This hip, creative store features an interesting mix of Japanese items like bento boxes, along with stylish, useful gear for the creative professional set like travel tumblers, journals, and various kinds of bags for

everything from hiking trails to working from a coffee shop. ⊠ *1840 Union St., between Octavia and Laguna Sts., Cow Hollow* ☎ *415/771–1108* ⊕ *topdrawershop.com.*

SHOES, HANDBAGS, AND LEATHER GOODS

Birdie's

SHOES | Comfortable, chic flats are the beloved signature item at the flagship store of this shoe designer, with varieties ranging from the most comfortable slippers ever to sandals that could walk down a runway. These flexible shoes can work for the office or a casual night out. The Union Street boutique shows that multidimensional approach as well, with its plush design that invites lingering long after shoes have been purchased. ⊠ *1934 Union St., Cow Hollow* ☎ *415/263–9668* ⊕ *birdies.com.*

Shaw Shoes

SHOES | Not much in Cow Hollow's retail scene has been around since the 1970s except this venerable luxury shoe store. Fine Italian leather shoes for men and women are the specialty, from sleek pumps to sharp flats, along with trendy, upscale sneakers and sandals. Designer sunglasses and handbags are also sold, so shoppers can look suave from head to toe. ⊠ *2001 Union St., Cow Hollow* ☎ *415/922–5676* ⊕ *shawshoes.net* ⊘ *Closed Sun.*

 ## Activities

SPAS

Redmint

SPAS | With a mix of traditional and modern practices like acupuncture and full-body LED therapy, plus unique herbal and antioxidant ingredients, this Union Street spa is a perfect stop for a mind and body wellness break or to pick up some unique hand creams or facial mists. The serene, immaculate complex seamlessly blends the indoors and outdoors and includes an herbal bar (think coffee shop,

but for herbal drinks) and a beautiful courtyard. ⊠ *1958 Union St., Cow Hollow* ☎ *415/888–8693* ⊕ *www.redmint.com.*

Spa Radiance

SPAS | Elegant but casual Spa Radiance specializes in facials and draws the occasional celebrity. Try the Super Duper Plus Facial, which adds LED light therapy to the treatment, or one of the relaxing massages or body treatments. ⊠ *3011 Fillmore St., between Union and Filbert Sts., Cow Hollow* ☎ *415/346–6281* ⊕ *www.sparadiance.com.*

Presidio

At the foot of the Golden Gate Bridge, one of city residents' favorite in-town getaways is the 1,400-plus-acre Presidio, which combines accessible nature-in-the-raw with a window on the past. For more than 200 years and under the flags of three nations—Spain, Mexico, and the United States—the Presidio served as an army post, but in 1995 the U.S. Army officially handed over the keys to the National Park Service. The keys came without sufficient federal funding, though, and it seemed the Presidio would be sold piecemeal to developers.

An innovative plan combining public and private monies and overseen by the Presidio Trust (the federal agency created to run the park) was hatched to help the Presidio become self-sufficient, which it did in 2013. The trust has found paying tenants, such as George Lucas's Industrial Light and Magic, the Walt Disney Family Museum, and a few thousand lucky San Franciscans who live in restored army housing. Now this spectacular corner of San Francisco—surrounded by sandy beaches and rocky shores, and with windswept hills of cypress dotted with historical buildings—is a thriving park for the far reaches of the city and technically a national park (it's part of the Golden Gate National Recreation Area).

The Presidio with Kids

If you're in town with children (and you have a car), the sprawling, bayside Presidio offers enough kid-friendly diversions for one very full day. Start off at Presidio Wall Playground, on the Presidio's southern edge, which has a disproportionate number of structures that spin. Swing by George Lucas's Letterman Digital Arts Center to check out the Yoda fountain; then head to the Immigrant Point Overlook on Washington Boulevard, with views of the bay and the ocean. Children love the pet cemetery, with its sweet, leaning headstones; it's near the stables, where you might glimpse some of the park police's equestrian members. Older kids might enjoy a stop at the Walt Disney Family Museum to see the model of Disneyland and a replica of the ambulance jeep Walt Disney drove during World War I.

After some museum time, the kids probably will need to run around outside. Luckily, the Presidio Tunnel Tops and its acres of meadows and playgrounds are right outside of the museum. Follow the paths of the Presidio Tunnel Tops to the last stop, Crissy Field, where kids can ride bikes, skate, or run along the beach and clamber over the rocks; the view of the Golden Gate Bridge from below is captivating. Two nature centers here have fun, hands-on exhibits for kids. Finally, stop by the Warming Hut, at the western end of Crissy Field, for sandwiches and hot chocolate. You can also do a version of this day using the PresidiGo Shuttle, but you'll need to adapt your route according to the shuttle stops.

It's also a small community on its own with a gym, a few restaurants, and a beautifully renovated 600-seat theater where Bob Hope once performed. The Presidio has superb views (be sure to visit Inspiration Point and the cemetery for the most striking ones) and some of the best hiking and biking areas in San Francisco (Lovers' Lane Trail is a favorite for hikers); even a drive through this lush area is a treat. Start your visit at the Presidio Visitor Center (⊠ 210 Lincoln Blvd. ☎ 415/561–4323 ⊕ presidio. gov ⊗ Daily 10–5), then enjoy a day of exploring.

Sights

★ Baker Beach

BEACH | FAMILY | West of the Golden Gate Bridge is a mile-long stretch of soft sand beneath steep cliffs, beloved for its spectacular views and laid-back vibe (read:

good chance you'll see naked people here on the northernmost end). Its isolated location makes it rarely crowded, but many San Franciscans know that there is no better place to take in the sunset than this beach. Kids love climbing around the old Battery Chamberlin. This is truly one of those places that inspires local pride. **Amenities:** parking (free); toilets. **Best for:** nudists; solitude; sunsets. ⊠ Baker Beach, Presidio ⊹ Accessed from Bowley St. off Lincoln Blvd. ⊕ www.parksconservancy.org ⊠ Free.

Crissy Field

NATURE SIGHT | FAMILY | One of the most popular places for San Franciscans to get fresh air is this stretch of restored marshland along the sand of the bay, part of the Golden Gate National Recreation Area. Kids on bikes, folks walking dogs, and joggers share the paved path along the shore, often winding up at the Warming Hut, a combination café and fun gift store at its end, for a hot chocolate in the shadow of the Golden Gate Bridge. Midway along the Golden Gate Promenade that winds along the shore is the Greater Farallones National Marine Sanctuary Visitor Center, where kids can get a close-up view of small sea creatures and learn about the rich ecosystem offshore. Alongside the main green of Crissy Field, several renovated airplane hangars and warehouses are now home to the likes of rock-climbing gyms, an air trampoline park, and a craft brewery (the latter is not open to the public). The Quartermaster Reach Marsh by Crissy Field was reclaimed as wetland ecosystem in 2020 and is an excellent area to see some of the local bird population. ⊠ *1199 E. Beach, Presidio ⊕ Area north of Mason St. between Baker St. and Marine Dr.* ⊕ *www.presidio.gov/places/crissy-field.*

Fort Point National Historic Site

MILITARY SIGHT | **FAMILY** | Dwarfed today by the Golden Gate Bridge, this brick fortress constructed between 1853 and 1861 was designed to protect San Francisco from a Civil War sea attack that never materialized. It was also used as a coastal-defense fortification post during World War II, when soldiers stood watch here. This National Historic Site is now a sprawling museum of military memorabilia. The building, which surrounds a lonely, windswept courtyard, has a gloomy air and is suitably atmospheric. It's usually chilly, too, so bring a jacket. The top floor affords a unique angle on the bay.

■ **TIP→ Take care when walking along the front side of the building, as it's slippery and the waves can have a dizzying effect.**

The popular, guided candlelight tours, available only in winter, book up in advance, so plan ahead. Twice a day on days that the site is open (Fridays and weekends), rangers provide short orientations to the site's history. And, a few days a year, the site holds a Living History Day complete with Civil War reenactments, including a look at the music

Don't Look Down! 👁

Armed only with helmets, safety harnesses, and painting equipment, a crew of 34 painters keeps the Golden Gate Bridge clad in International Orange. Contrary to a favorite bit of local lore, they don't actually sweep on an entire coat of paint from one end of the bridge to the other, but instead scrape, prime, and repaint small sections that have rusted from exposure to the elements.

and medicine of that 1800s era. ⊠ *201 Marine Dr., off Lincoln Blvd., Presidio* ☏ *415/561–4959* ⊕ *www.nps.gov/fopo* 🖾 *Free* ☾ *Closed Mon.–Thurs.*

★ Golden Gate Bridge

BRIDGE | Instantly recognizable as an icon of San Francisco, the two reddish-orange towers of the majestic Golden Gate Bridge rise 750 feet over the Golden Gate at the mouth of San Francisco Bay, linking the city and Marin County. Designed in simple but powerful art-deco style and opened in 1937, the 1.7-mile suspension span and the towers were built to handle winds of more than 100 mph. Crossing the bridge under your own power, by foot or bicycle, is exhilarating, a bit scary—and definitely chilly. From the bridge's eastern-side walkway, the panoramic views of the city skyline, Marin Headlands, and Pacific Ocean are magnificent. ⊠ *Lincoln Blvd., near Doyle Dr. and Fort Point, Presidio* ☏ *415/921–5858* ⊕ *www.goldengate.org* 🖾 *Free.*

Letterman Digital Arts Center

OTHER ATTRACTION | **FAMILY** | Bay Area filmmaker George Lucas's 23-acre Letterman Digital Arts Center, a digital studio campus along the eastern edge of the land, is exquisitely landscaped and largely open to the public. If you have kids in tow or are a *Star Wars* fan yourself, make the pilgrimage to the Yoda Fountain between two of the arts-center buildings, then take your picture with the life-size Darth Vader statue in the lobby, open to the public on weekdays. The center's public restaurant, Sessions, is a good stop for a craft beer and some satisfying eats that often include produce or beef from Lucas's Skywalker Ranch. ⊠ *1 Letterman Dr., Presidio* ⊕ *www.presidio.gov/places/letterman-digital-arts-center* ⊙ *Lobby closed weekends.*

Lyon Street Steps

VIEWPOINT | Get ready for a workout—and a spectacularly rewarding view at the top—when tackling the 332 steps at the eastern edge of the Presidio. There will likely be no shortage of exercise seekers bounding up the steps, but feel free to conquer the climb slowly. The trimmed hedge landscaping is worthy of its own visit, but the views of the Presidio forests and the bay are the reason these steps are a top attraction. The opulent mansions surrounding them are equally stunning. ⊠ *2545 Lyon St., between Green St. and Broadway, Presidio* ⊕ *www.nps.gov.*

Presidio Officers' Club

HISTORY MUSEUM | An excellent place to begin a historical tour of the Presidio, the Officers' Club offers a walk through time from the Presidio's earliest days as the first nonnative outpost in present-day San Francisco to more than a century as a U.S. Army post. Start with the excellent short film about life here from the time of the Ohlone people to the present, then peruse the displays of artifacts, including uniforms and weaponry. In the Mesa Room, you can literally see layers of history: parts of the original adobe wall from the 1790s, the brick fireplace in the 1880s commander's office, and the Mission revival–style fireplace in the 1930s billiard room. Note that the Officers' Club is only open on Saturdays.

Excavation of the Presidio continues: outside, a canopy covers the Presidio Archaeology Field Station, where you can sometimes see archaeologists at work. There is a docent on hand each Friday and Saturday from 11 am to 2 pm to answer questions about the dig. ⊠ *50 Moraga Ave., Presidio* ☎ *415/561–5300* ⊕ *www.presidio.gov/officers-club* ⊠ *Free* ⊙ *Closed Sun.–Fri.*

★ Presidio Tunnel Tops

CITY PARK | FAMILY | With how seamlessly the Presidio Tunnel Tops landscape flows from the Presidio's Main Parade Lawn downhill to Crissy Field, it's almost impossible to envision the two not being connected. Yet, that was always the case until this impressive 14-acre green space with 1.8 miles of winding walking paths was completed in 2022. It's a park that is both function (bringing together two important areas atop a highway tunnel) and form (beautifully designed by James Corner Field Operations, the same firm that designed New York City's acclaimed High Line elevated park).

The Presidio Tunnel Tops are a marquee destination for many reasons, but there's no escaping that the park is best known for its panoramic view of the Golden Gate Bridge. There's plenty more to do, from grabbing lunch from a visiting food truck or letting kids explore the impressive two-acre Outpost playground that tells the Presidio's extensive history and evokes its natural habitat. There are three lawn areas for picnicking, a Campfire Circle where ranger talks are given, and 200,000 plants to gaze at.

Altogether, it's a fun breath of fresh air—and it's hard to believe that you're literally on top of the busy 101 highway. After exploring the Presidio Tunnel Tops, make sure to head over to their lesser-known "above the highway" park sibling, Battery Bluff. This park doesn't have the activities or amenities that makes the Tunnel Tops such a draw, but it's worth a visit for the views and to see the four

Art in the Presidio

Fans of Andy Goldsworthy, the British artist famed for his work with natural elements, will have a field day in the Presidio: the park contains four of his creations, all using materials reclaimed from the Presidio. *Spire*, created in 2008, is a 100-foot-high sculpture made of 37 Monterey cypress trees that reaches toward the sky in a grove near the Arguello Gate. Near the intersection of Presidio Boulevard and West Pacific Avenue, Goldsworthy created *Wood Line* in 2011. Felled eucalyptus trees weave lines through a cypress grove in a work that the artist says "draws the place." In 2013, Goldsworthy moved inside for the installation *Tree Fall*, in the Presidio's Powder Magazine. He covered a tree trunk and the ceiling above it, a dome suspended above the historic structure's walls, with clay from the Presidio, which cracked into lovely patterns. In 2014, Goldsworthy created *Earth Wall* in a wall around the patio at the Presidio Officers' Club. He collected curved eucalyptus branches from the site, affixed them in a sphere on the side of the concrete wall, then added a rammed-earth layer to the entire wall, burying the wood while thickening the wall. When it had dried, he used a chisel to reveal the ball, essentially excavating it in a nod to the layers of history at the Presidio. The Presidio Trust's website includes a 3-mile-loop walk that connects all four works. Call The Presidio's Andy Goldsworthy information line at ☎ 415/561–2767 for the latest update on opening times to see *Tree Fall* and *Earth Wall*.

preserved historic gun batteries. ✉ *210 Lincoln Blvd., Presidio* ☎ *415/561–4323* ⊕ *presidiotunneltops.gov.*

Walt Disney Family Museum

HISTORY MUSEUM | FAMILY | This beautifully refurbished brick barracks is a tribute to the man behind Mickey Mouse, Disney Studios, and Disneyland. The smartly organized displays include hundreds of family photos, and well-chosen videos play throughout. Disney's legendary attention to detail is evident in the cels and footage of *Fantasia, Sleeping Beauty*, and other animation classics. Galleries tell the story of Disney's life from his youth in the Midwest to lesser-known bits of his professional history, like the films Walt Disney made for the U.S. military during World War II. The liveliest exhibit, and the largest gallery, documents the creation of Disneyland with a fun, detailed model of what Disney imagined the park would be. Teacups spin, the Matterhorn looms, and that world-famous castle leads the way to Fantasyland. You won't be the first to leave humming "It's a Small World." In the final gallery, a series of cartoons and quotes chronicle the world's reaction to Disney's sudden death. Worth checking for are periodic special exhibitions that take a deep dive into film themes or historical periods surrounding Disney's life. ✉ *Main Post, 104 Montgomery St., off Lincoln Blvd., Presidio* ☎ *415/345–6800* ⊕ *www.waltdisney.org* 🎫 *$25* ⊘ *Closed Mon.–Wed.*

🍴 Restaurants

Colibri Mexican Bistro

$$ | MEXICAN | After an 18-year run near Union Square, this city favorite moved across town in 2022 to a beautiful adobe dining room and firepit-adorned patio in the Presidio Officers' Club. Guacamole and margaritas are must-orders, but the menu jumps much further into regional

The Golden Gate Promenade provides stunning views—and gusting winds.

Mexican specialties as well. **Known for:** outstanding cinnamon-spiced chocolate cake; mole poblano with chicken; long list of tequila and mezcal cocktails. $ *Average main: $28* ⊠ *50 Moraga Ave., Presidio* ☎ *415/678–5170* ⊕ *colibrimexicanbistro.com.*

Presidio Social Club

$$ | AMERICAN | FAMILY | American comfort classics meet seasonal California cooking in this restaurant in an old barracks building at the eastern edge of the Presidio. The restaurant has a blend of the nostalgic past and the trendy present (deviled eggs with smoked salmon and furikake; grilled beef liver and onions; homemade cheesecake), as well as a lively bar and ample patio seating that allows diners to soak up the Presidio's outdoor beauty. **Known for:** East–West chicken soup; popular brunch; barrel-aged cocktails. $ *Average main: $29* ⊠ *563 Ruger St., Presidio* ☎ *415/885–1888* ⊕ *www.presidiosocialclub.com* ⊗ *Closed Mon. and Tues. No lunch Wed.*

🛏 Hotels

Long heralded as the place where upscale San Franciscans come to play, the Presidio has a few worthy lodgings, among them a fancy inn occupying former officers' quarters and a sleek lodge in a renovated barracks building. Though the area has just a couple restaurants and nightlife options are nonexistent, the Presidio's historic cachet, wealth of hiking trails, and gorgeous bay-view beaches entice tourists and locals alike, the latter escaping the hectic city for a restful staycation.

The Inn at the Presidio

$$ | B&B/INN | Built in 1903, this two-story, Georgian revival–style structure once served as officers' quarters but these days is a standout boutique hotel where the rooms and suites have a nice sense of modern refinement and historical touches varying by the room, such as wrought-iron beds, vintage black-and-white photos, and Pendleton blankets. **Pros:** beautifully designed rooms, some with gas fireplaces; peaceful vibe; evening wine-and-cheese reception by firepits. **Cons:** lack of noise-blocking because of old building; two-night minimum on weekends; challenging to get a taxi. [$] *Rooms from: $350* ✉ *42 Moraga Ave., Presidio* ☎ *415/800–7356* 🌐 *www.presidiolodging.com* 🛏 *26 rooms* 🍴 *Free Breakfast.*

★ The Lodge at the Presidio

$$ | **B&B/INN** | The three-story Lodge occupies former Army barracks, built in the 1890s, and is at the Main Post green's northwestern edge, allowing some rooms to have Golden Gate Bridge views; all rooms are far more upscale and chic than military accommodations, with large flat-screen TVs, well-appointed bathrooms, work stations, and dreamy, custom-made pillow-top mattresses. **Pros:** gorgeous, spacious rooms; charming staff; feels like a vacation from the city. **Cons:** traffic noise; isolated from restaurants and nightlife; similar prices to downtown's more lavish luxury hotels. [$] *Rooms from: $350* ✉ *105 Montgomery St., Presidio* ☎ *415/561–1234* 🌐 *www.presidiolodging.com* 🛏 *42 rooms* 🍴 *Free Breakfast.*

Activities

HIKING

Golden Gate Promenade

HIKING & WALKING | During this great walk you pass through Crissy Field, taking in marshlands, kite-flyers, beachfront, and windsurfers, with the Golden Gate Bridge as a backdrop. The 4.3-mile roundtrip trek (or bike ride) is flat and easy—it should take less than two hours round-trip. Make sure to pack layers, as the temperature and winds can dramatically change over the course of the walk. ✉ *Presidio* 🌐 *www.presidio.gov.*

Presidio Hiking Trails

HIKING & WALKING | Hiking and biking trails wind through nearly 1,500 acres of woods and hills in the Presidio, past old redbrick military buildings and jaw-dropping scenic overlooks with bay and ocean views. The Bay Trail along Crissy Field to Fort Point, the steep Batteries to Bluffs Trail, and the winding forest stroll of the Ecology Trail are some of the standout hiking routes. Visit the Presidio's website for hiking and biking maps. ✉ *Presidio Visitor Center, 210 Lincoln Blvd., near Montgomery St., Presidio* ☎ *415/561–4323* 🌐 *presidio.gov/trails.*

Chapter 10

THE WESTERN SHORELINE

Updated by
Denise Leto

⊙ Sights	🍴 Restaurants	🛏 Hotels	💼 Shopping	🍸 Nightlife
★★★☆☆	★★★☆☆	★☆☆☆☆	★★☆☆☆	★★☆☆☆

NEIGHBORHOOD SNAPSHOT

TOP EXPERIENCES

■ **Lands End:** Head down the gorgeous Coastal Trail; you'll quickly find yourself in a forest with unparalleled views of the Golden Gate Bridge.

■ **Richmond food crawl:** Grab brunch at the Clement Street Sunday farmers' market (between Arguello Boulevard and 4th Avenue) in the Inner Richmond, also packed with great Burmese and Chinese restaurants. Cross into the Outer Richmond's Little Russia for prepared Russian and Ukrainian foods, deli items, and groceries along Geary Boulevard, between 17th and 21st Avenues.

■ **Legion of Honor Museum:** Travel back to 18th-century Europe through the paintings, drawings, and porcelain on display here.

■ **Ocean Beach:** Wrap up warmly and stroll along the strand on a brisk, cloudy day; you'll feel like a gritty local. Then thaw out over a bowl of steaming pho in the Richmond.

■ **Sunset at the Beach Chalet:** Top off a day of exploring with a cocktail overlooking Ocean Beach.

PLANNING YOUR TIME

The premier sights of the Western Shoreline are outdoors—gorgeous hiking trails and sandy stretches of coastline. The area is prone to low-lying fog and often biting chill, so bundle up before you start off on the Coastal Trail, which passes by the Legion of Honor museum. Continue west to catch the sunset from the Beach Chalet. If you don't want to do the entire 3-mile hike, you can spend an hour touring the museum, catch the stunning views just below it, and head to the beach.

GETTING HERE

■ To reach the Western Shoreline from downtown by Muni light-rail, take the N–Judah to Ocean Beach or the L–Taraval to the zoo. From downtown by bus, take the 38–Geary, which runs all the way to 48th and Point Lobos Avenues, just east of the Cliff House. Along the Western Shoreline, the 18–46th Avenue runs between the Legion of Honor and the zoo (and beyond).

FUN FACT

■ Until the 20th century, the area that would become the Richmond, the Sunset, and Golden Gate Park was covered with sand dunes and known as the Outside Lands. Around the turn of the century, when the rise of automobiles led to a drastic decline in the number of cable cars and street cars running in the city, some resourceful residents bought the castoffs, brought them out west, and moved into them, creating the neighborhood Carville-by-the-Sea. Only one such known residence remains today, on the Great Highway in the Outer Sunset, with a second story made of two connected cable cars.

Few American cities provide a more intimate and dramatic view of the power and fury of the surf attacking the shore than San Francisco does along its wild Western Shoreline.

From Lincoln Park in the north, along Ocean Beach from the Richmond south to the Sunset, a different breed of San Franciscan chooses to live in this area: surfers who brave the heaviest fog to ride the waves; writers who seek solace and inspiration in this city outpost; and dog lovers committed to giving their pets a good workout each day.

The Richmond District

In the mid-19th century, the western section of town just north of Golden Gate Park was known as the Outer Lands, and it was covered in sand dunes and seen fit for cemeteries and little else. Today it's the Richmond, comprised of two distinct neighborhoods: the Inner Richmond, from Arguello Boulevard to about 20th Avenue, and the Outer Richmond, from 20th to the ocean. (More formally, this area of San Francisco is called the Richmond District. Just don't confuse it with Richmond, a city 20 miles away in the East Bay.) Clement Street, packed with dining options, from French to Burmese, and with numerous Chinese groceries, is the Inner Richmond's favorite commercial strip. The street makes for great strolling and even better eating. The Outer Richmond has its share of restaurants—most along Geary Boulevard, some along Clement—including the city's highest concentration of Russian eateries and bakeries. But this mostly residential neighborhood is about

the foggy hinterlands that stretch west to the coast: dramatic Lincoln Park with Golden Gate views, the (currently closed) Cliff House, and often-chilly, uncrowded Ocean Beach.

From Lands End in Lincoln Park, you have some of the best views of the Golden Gate—the name was given to the opening of San Francisco Bay long before the bridge was built—and the Marin Headlands. From the Cliff House south to the sprawling San Francisco Zoo, the Great Highway and Ocean Beach run along the western edge of the city (south of Golden Gate Park, you're in the Sunset). If you're here in winter or spring, keep your eyes peeled for migrating gray whales. The wind is often strong, summer fog can blanket the ocean beaches, and the water is cold and too dangerous for swimming. Don't forget your jacket!

⊙ Sights

★ Legion of Honor
ART MUSEUM | Built to commemorate soldiers from California who died in World War I and set atop cliffs overlooking the ocean, the Golden Gate Bridge, and the Marin Headlands, this beautiful Beaux Arts building in Lincoln Park displays an impressive collection of 4,000 years of ancient and European art. A pyramidal glass skylight in the entrance court illuminates the lower-level galleries, which exhibit prints and drawings, European porcelain, and ancient Assyrian, Greek, Roman, and Egyptian art. The 20-plus

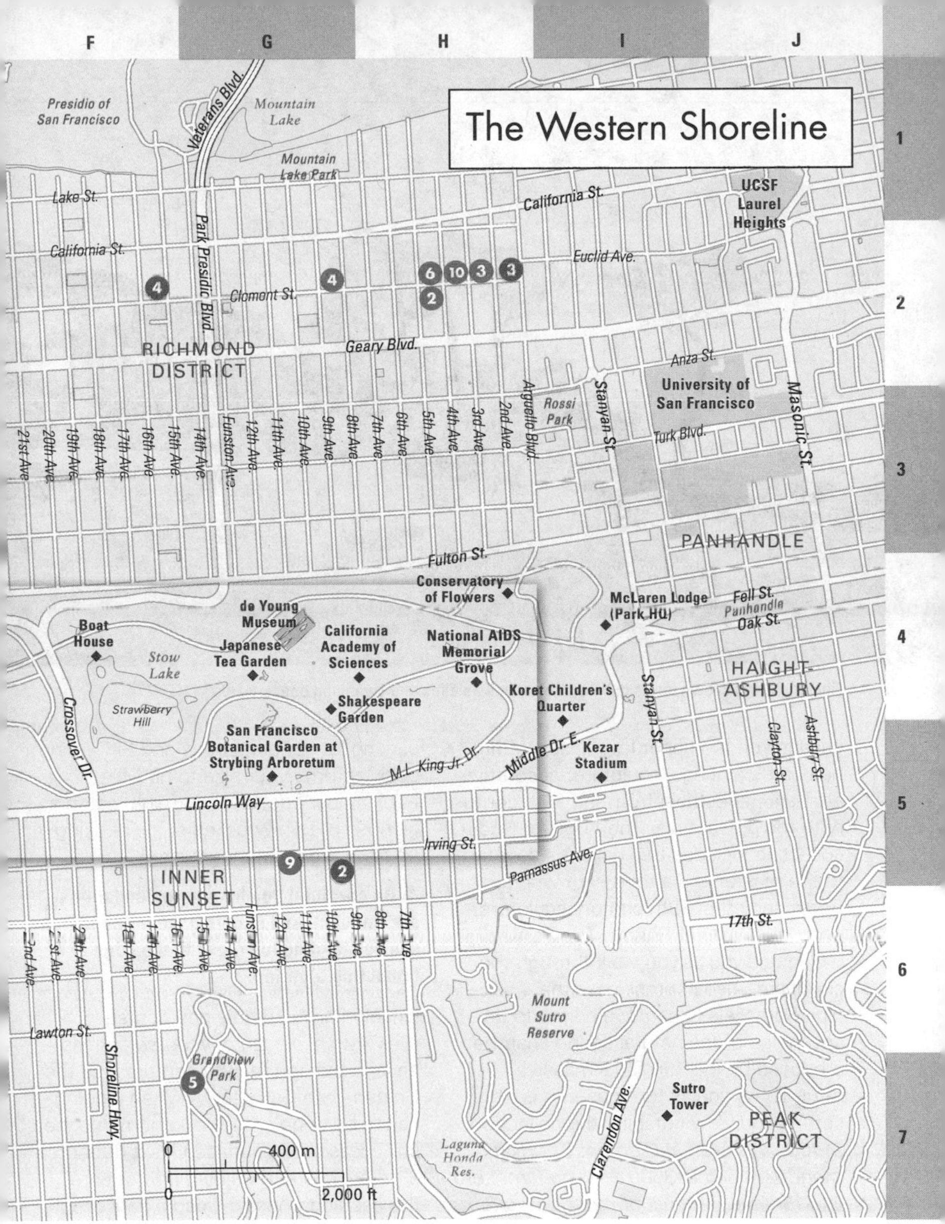
F
G
H
I
J
1
2
3
4
5
6
7
The Western Shoreline
Presidio of San Francisco
Mountain Lake
Mountain Lake Park
Veterans Blvd.
Lake St.
California St.
Park Presidio Blvd.
Clement St.
Euclid Ave.
UCSF Laurel Heights
RICHMOND DISTRICT
Geary Blvd.
Anza St.
University of San Francisco
Masonic St.
Turk Blvd.
Rossi Park
Arguello Blvd.
Stanyan St.
21st Ave.
20th Ave.
19th Ave.
18th Ave.
17th Ave.
16th Ave.
15th Ave.
14th Ave.
Funston Ave.
12th Ave.
11th Ave.
10th Ave.
9th Ave.
8th Ave.
7th Ave.
6th Ave.
5th Ave.
4th Ave.
3rd Ave.
2nd Ave.
PANHANDLE
Fulton St.
Conservatory of Flowers
McLaren Lodge (Park HQ)
Fell St.
Panhandle
Oak St.
de Young Museum
Boat House
Japanese Tea Garden
California Academy of Sciences
National AIDS Memorial Grove
Stow Lake
Strawberry Hill
Shakespeare Garden
Koret Children's Quarter
HAIGHT-ASHBURY
Crossover Dr.
San Francisco Botanical Garden at Strybing Arboretum
Middle Dr. E.
Kezar Stadium
M.L. King Jr. Dr.
Clayton St.
Ashbury St.
Lincoln Way
Irving St.
Parnassus Ave.
INNER SUNSET
17th St.
Mount Sutro Reserve
Lawton St.
Shoreline Hwy.
Grandview Park
Clarendon Ave.
Sutro Tower
PEAK DISTRICT
Laguna Honda Res.
0
400 m
0
2,000 ft

Quick Bites ▼

1 Andytown Coffee Roasters......... **C7**

2 Arizmendi Bakery....... **G5**

3 Arsicault................. **H2**

4 Breadbelly............... **F2**

5 Devil's Teeth Baking Company........ **B7**

Lincoln Park is known for its golf course as well as cliffs and sweeping ocean views.

galleries on the upper level display European art (paintings, sculpture, decorative arts, and tapestries) from the 14th century to the present day. The Auguste Rodin collection includes two galleries devoted to the master and a third with works by Rodin and other 19th-century sculptors. An original cast of Rodin's *The Thinker* welcomes you as you walk through the courtyard. Also impressive is the 4,526-pipe Spreckels Organ; live concerts take advantage of the natural sound chamber produced by the building's massive rotunda. As fine as the museum is, the setting and view outshine the collection. ⊠ *100 34th Ave., at Clement St., Richmond* ☎ *415/750–3600* ⊕ *www.famsf.org* ☞ *$15, free 1st Tues. of month; free Sat. for Bay Area residents* ⊘ *Closed Mon.*

★ Lincoln Park

CITY PARK | Lincoln Park is a wild, 275-acre park with windswept cliffs and panoramic views. The Coastal Trail, the park's most dramatic, leads out to Lands End; pick it up west of the Legion of Honor (at the end of El Camino del Mar) or from the parking lot at Point Lobos and El Camino del Mar. Time your hike to hit Mile Rock at low tide, and you might catch a glimpse of two wrecked ships peeking up from their watery graves.

⚠ **Be careful if you hike here; landslides are frequent, and people have fallen into the sea by standing too close to the edge of a crumbling bluff top.**

Lincoln Park's 18-hole golf course (⊕ *www.lincolnparkgolfcourse.com*) is on land that in the 19th century was the Golden Gate Cemetery. (When digging has to be done in the park, human bones still occasionally surface.) Next door on 33rd Avenue and California Street are the dazzling, mosaic Lincoln Park Steps, which rival the 16th Avenue Steps and the Hidden Garden Steps in the Sunset District. They provide a delightful backdrop for contemplation or an Instagram photo op. ⊠ *Entrance at 34th Ave. and Clement St., Richmond* ⊕ *sfrecpark.org.*

Ocean Beach

BEACH | Stretching 3 miles along the western side of the city from the Richmond to the Sunset, this sandy swath of the Pacific coast is good for flying kites, jogging, or walking the dog—but not for swimming. The water is so cold that surfers wear wet suits year-round, and riptides are strong—drownings are not infrequent. As for sunbathing, it's rarely warm enough here; think meditative walking instead of sun worshipping.

Paths on both sides of the Great Highway lead from Lincoln Way to Sloat Boulevard (near the zoo); the beachside path winds through landscaped sand dunes, and the paved path across the highway is good for biking and in-line skating (though you have to rent bikes elsewhere). The Beach Chalet restaurant and brewpub is across the Great Highway from Ocean Beach, about five blocks south of the Cliff House. **Amenities:** parking (no fee); showers; toilets. **Best for:** solitude; sunset; walking. ⊠ *San Francisco* ⊕ *Along Great Hwy. from Cliff House to Sloat Blvd. and beyond* ⊕ *www.parksconservancy.org.*

Sutro Baths

OTHER ATTRACTION | Along the oceanfront, to the north of the Cliff House, lie the ruins of the once-grand glass-roof Sutro Baths. Today visitors can explore this evocative historical site and listen to the pounding surf. Adolph Sutro, eccentric onetime San Francisco mayor, built the bath complex in 1896 so that everyday folks could enjoy the benefits of swimming. Six enormous baths—freshwater and seawater—and more than 500 dressing rooms plus several restaurants covered 3 acres and accommodated 25,000 bathers. Likened to Roman baths in a European glass palace, the baths were for decades a favorite destination of San Franciscans. The complex fell into disuse after World War II, was closed in 1952, and burned down (under questionable circumstances) during demolition in 1966. To get here, park in the main Lands End parking lot and walk down toward the ruins by the ocean. ⊠ *1004 Point Lobos Ave., Richmond* ☏ *415/426–5240* ⊕ *www.nps.gov/goga.*

Sutro Heights Park

CITY PARK | Crows and other large birds battle the heady breezes at this cliff-top park on what were once the grounds of the home of Adolph Sutro, an eccentric mining engineer and former San Francisco mayor. An extremely wealthy man, Sutro may have owned about 10% of San Francisco at one point, but he couldn't buy good taste: a few remnants of his gaudy, faux-classical statue collection still stand (including the lions at what was the main gate). Monterey cypresses and Canary Island palms dot the park, and photos on placards depict what things looked like before the house burned down in 1896.

All that remains of the main house is its foundation. Climb up for a sweeping view of the Pacific Ocean and the Cliff House below (which Sutro once owned), and try to imagine what the perspective might have been like from one of the upper floors. San Francisco City Guides (☏ *415/557–4266* ⊕ *www.sfcityguides. org*) runs a free Saturday tour of the park that starts at 2 pm; you must reserve ahead. ⊠ *Point Lobos and 48th Aves., Richmond* ⊕ *www.nps.gov/goga.*

🍴 Restaurants

The Richmond encompasses the land on the north side of Golden Gate Park, running to the ocean's edge. This is the land of authentic Asian food, particularly in the Inner Richmond, known as the new Chinatown, covering Clement Street from about 2nd to 13th Avenues. On the main thoroughfares of Clement, Balboa, and Geary Streets, you'll find bargain dim sum, Burmese salads, Korean barbecue, and noodle soups of all persuasions.

Burma Superstar

$$ | ASIAN | Locals make the trek to the "Avenues" for this perennially crowded spot's flavorful Burmese food, including its extraordinary signature tea leaf salad, a combo of spicy, salty, crunchy, and sour tastes that is mixed table-side. The modestly decorated, no-reservations restaurant is small and lines can be long during peak times, so leave your number and wait for the call. **Known for:** spicy curries; samusa soup; vegetarian options. $ *Average main: $20 ⊠ 309 Clement St., Richmond ☎ 415/387–2147 ⊕ www. burmasuperstar.com.*

Chapeau!

$$$ | FRENCH | A husband-and-wife team serves up classic French cooking and wines at this warm neighborhood bistro where you may run into romantic couples on date night or a small but convivial pre-wedding party. Favorites like bouillabaisse and filet mignon are beautifully served with loving attention. **Known for:** garlicky escargot; delicious cassoulet; loyal following. $ *Average main: $40 ⊠ 126 Clement St., Richmond ☎ 415/750–9787 ⊕ www.chapeausf.com ⊗ Closed Mon. and Tues. No lunch.*

Chili House

$$ | SICHUAN | This unassuming local establishment serves a fiery hot menu of Sichuan favorites as well as Peking duck and other northern Chinese dishes. Traditional Chinese lanterns, watercolors, and calligraphy decorate the walls, and diners are seated at square tables or larger round tables with revolving trays. **Known for:** fish in flaming chili oil; beef, tripe, and tendon in special chili sauce; cumin lamb. $ *Average main: $29 ⊠ 726 Clement St., Richmond ☎ 415/387–2658 ⊕ www. chilihousesf.com ⊗ Closed Tues.*

Mokuku

$$$ | JAPANESE | When the fog and wind roll into the Richmond, savvy locals dive straight into this all-you-can-eat joint serving Japanese shabu shabu and other hot pot options. Guests can pair an inventive soup base, like fire coconut crab or spicy miso, with the restaurant's signature, perfectly marbled Wagyu beef or Kurobuta pork for a satisfying meal. **Known for:** bar-top hot pot service; tatami mat dining room; karaoke night. $ *Average main: $35 ⊠ 332 Clement St., Richmond ☎ 415/702–6128 ⊕ www.mokukushabu. com ⊗ No lunch.*

Pizzetta 211

$ | PIZZA | FAMILY | This shoebox-size spot puts together thin-crust pies topped with the kinds of ingredients that are worth the constant wait. Almost half the menu changes on a biweekly basis, while dependable favorites include the tomato, basil, and mozzarella pizza; the Sardinian cheese, pine nut, and rosemary pie; and the San Marzano tomato sauce, wild arugula, and mascarpone pizza. **Known for:** creative topping combinations; good house-made desserts; short, changing menu. $ *Average main: $17 ⊠ 211 23rd Ave., Richmond ☎ 415/379–9880 ⊕ www.pizzetta211.com ⊗ Closed Tues.*

Tenglong

$ | CHINESE | FAMILY | Plenty of locals come to this tidy space known for remarkably friendly service and the dry chicken wings fried in garlic and roasted red peppers, as well as for thinly sliced Mongolian beef and dan dan noodles. Run by two former Hong Kong restaurant owners, it specializes in mostly southern Chinese fare, like Cantonese cuisine, and has a few Sichuan specialties, too. **Known for:** honey-walnut prawns; spicy seafood noodle soup; local hot spot. $ *Average main: $18 ⊠ 208 Clement St., Richmond ☎ 415/666–3515 ⊕ www.tenglongchinese.com ⊗ Closed Tues.*

☕ Coffee and Quick Bites

★ Arsicault

$ | BAKERY | The search for the best, flakiest croissant in San Francisco ends at this tiny French bakery off Clement Street. Other popular items include an assortment of scones, cookies, and *kouign-amann* (a Breton pastry); coffee and tea complete your treat. **Known for:** unassuming, take-out-only storefront; long lines; best croissants in the city. $ *Average main: $5* ⊠ *397 Arguello Blvd., Richmond* ⊕ *arsicault-bakery.com.*

Breadbelly

$ | **BAKERY** | Creative, Asian-inspired takes on homey pastries made with elevated ingredients such as bee pollen and maldon sea salt (with prices to match) draw enthusiastic crowds to this small storefront. The Kaya Toast—bright green coconut-pandan jam on the café's signature milk bread—is a must try. **Known for:** interesting ingredients in every item; long lines; bright green, Instagrammable Kaya Toast. $ *Average main: $15* ⊠ *1408 Clement St., Richmond* ☎ *415/349–0969* ⊕ *www.breadbellysf.com* ⊗ *Closed Tues. and Wed. No dinner.*

▼ Nightlife

The nightlife in these practical, comfy neighborhoods centers more on reasonably priced restaurants than on bars and nightclubs. What bar scene there is, you'll find low-key and welcoming.

MUSIC CLUBS

The Plough and the Stars

LIVE MUSIC | A decidedly unglamorous pub where old-timers swap stories over pints of Guinness, this is your best bet for traditional Irish music. Bay Area musicians (and, once in a while, big-name bands) perform every night except Monday and Tuesday. Talented locals gather for *seisiúns,* informal sessions where musicians sit around a table and drink and eat while chiming in; anyone skilled at Irish traditional music can play. ⊠ *116 Clement St., at 2nd Ave., Richmond* ☎ *415/751–1122* ⊕ *theploughandstars.com.*

🛍 Shopping

The Richmond is known for its Asian and other markets. Geary Boulevard is the main drag, but some of the neighborhood's most interesting shops can be found in the dozen blocks of Clement Street west of Arguello, among them the much-loved Green Apple Books.

BOOKS
★ **Green Apple Books**

BOOKS | A local favorite with a huge used-book department also carries new books in every field. It's known for its history room and rare-books collection, as well as fiction CDs, DVDs, comic books, and graphic novels. ⊠ *506 Clement St., at 6th Ave., Richmond* ☎ *415/387–2272* ⊕ *www.greenapplebooks.com.*

GIFTS AND SOUVENIRS
Park Life

SOUVENIRS | An eclectic assortment of souvenirs, art, books, apparel, stationery, and prints tempts browsers at this design-centric hipster outpost. With a well-curated collection of School of Life philosophy books and non-touristy T-shirts to take back home, it's the perfect place to browse for a half hour while waiting for your table at Burma Superstar across the street. ⊠ *220 Clement St., Richmond* ☎ *415/386–7275* ⊕ *www.parklifestore. com.*

The Sunset District

Hugging the southern edge of Golden Gate Park and built atop the sand dunes that covered much of western San Francisco into the 19th century, the Sunset is made up of two distinct neighborhoods: the popular Inner Sunset, from Stanyan Street to 19th Avenue, and the foggy Outer Sunset, from 19th to the beach. The Inner Sunset is perhaps the perfect San Francisco "suburb": not too far from the center of things, reachable by public transit, and home to main streets—Irving

Street and 9th Avenue just off Golden Gate Park—packed with excellent dining options, with Asian food particularly well represented. Long the domain of surfers and others who love the laid-back beach vibe and the fog, the slow-paced Outer Sunset finds itself on the radar of locals, with high-quality cafés and restaurants and quirky shops springing up along Judah Street between 42nd and 46th Avenues. The San Francisco Zoo is the district's main tourist attraction.

◉ Sights

San Francisco Zoo & Gardens
ZOO | FAMILY | Occupying prime ocean-front property, the San Francisco Zoo touts itself as a wildlife-focused recreation center that inspires visitors to become conservationists. Integrated exhibits group different species of animals from the same geographic areas together in enclosures that don't look like cages. More than 2,000 animals and 250 species reside here, including endangered species such as the snow leopard, Sumatran tiger, and grizzly bear. The zoo's superstar exhibit is Grizzly Gulch, where orphaned grizzly bear sisters Kachina and Kiona enchant visitors with their frolicking and swimming. The Mexican Gray Wolf grotto houses the smallest gray wolf and the most endangered wolf subspecies in the world. The Lemur Forest has seven varieties of the bug-eyed, long-tailed primates from Madagascar and is the country's largest outdoor lemur habitat. African kikuyu grass carpets the circular outer area of the Jones Family Gorilla Preserve, one of the most natural gorilla habitats of any zoo in the world. Other popular exhibits include Penguin Island, Koala Crossing, and the African Savanna exhibit. The six-acre Children's Zoo has about 300 mammals, birds, and reptiles, plus a huge playground, a restored 1921 Dentzel carousel, and a mini–steam train. ⊠ Sloat Blvd. and 47th Ave., Sunset ☎ 415/753–7080 ⊕ www.sfzoo.org ✉ $25.

16th Avenue Tiled Steps
OTHER ATTRACTION | A community-based project dedicated in 2005, these 163 tiled steps have beautiful designs showing fish, shells, animals, starry skies, and other scenes. The steps are in a residential neighborhood, so enjoy the steps and the city views from the top quietly. ⊠ Moraga St., between 15th and 16th Ave., Sunset ⊕ www.16thavenuetiledsteps.com.

🍴 Restaurants

The Sunset has a surf-town vibe. It's known for its fog, yes, but also bargain eats (UC San Francisco is here) that range from pizzas and salads to Eritrean injera (flatbread) and Chinese dumplings, concentrated along Irving Street.

Beach Chalet
$$$ | AMERICAN | A perch on the second floor of a 1920s building provides first-rate looks at Ocean Beach across the Great Highway (it used to be a changing room for beachgoers). But the service is just okay, and the food is basic American—burgers, chowders, and steak. Known for: variable service; beach views; house-brewed beer. $ Average main: $33 ⊠ 1000 Great Hwy., Sunset ☎ 415/386–8439 ⊕ www.beachchalet.com.

★ Hook Fish Co
$ | SEAFOOD | Unpretentious yet undeniably chic, this neighborhood beach shack is famous for its simple, fresh seafood. The menu changes daily depending on the day's catch, so join hungry surfers and locals as they gobble up tacos, burritos, or fish-and-chips; wash your choice down with beer or wine. Known for: possibly the best fish-and-chips in San Francisco; blackboard oysters and specials; long lines. $ Average main: $16 ⊠ 4542 Irving St., Sunset ☎ 415/569–4984 ⊕ www.hookfishco.com.

Outerlands

$$ | MODERN AMERICAN | As infamous for its lines as it is famous for its brunch, this cozy, wood-paneled restaurant serves food that is thoroughly Northern California, from the granola with goat's milk yogurt to the avocado toast drizzled with Meyer lemon vinaigrette. The cast-iron grilled cheese sandwich is legendary, and dinner also offers plenty of charm: just make sure you have some time on your hands and layers to ward off the Sunset chill while you wait. **Known for:** high-quality ingredients; Dutch pancakes; house-made bread. $ *Average main: $25* ✉ *4001 Judah St., Sunset* ☎ *415/661–6140* ⊕ *outerlandssf.com* ⊘ *Closed Mon. and Tues. No lunch Wed. and Thurs.*

San Tung

$ | CHINESE | FAMILY | The food of China's northeastern province of Shandong is the draw at this bare-bones storefront restaurant where specialties include steamed dumplings—shrimp and leek dumplings are the most popular—and hand-pulled noodles in soup or stir-fried. Especially popular are the platters of excellent dry-fried chicken wings, a cult dish in the city. **Known for:** sautéed string beans; famous chicken wings; long waits. $ *Average main: $19* ✉ *1031 Irving St., Sunset* ☎ *415/242–0828* ⊕ *www. santung.net* ⊘ *Closed Tues. and Wed.*

Terra Cotta Warrior

$ | NORTHERN CHINESE | This family-owned restaurant is the best place in the city to sample hard-to-find Muslim Chinese cuisine from northwest China and to carb-load. Order classics like wide *biang biang* hand-pulled noodles with cumin lamb or *liangpi* cold noodles, and accompany them with pita bread soaked in flavorful lamb soup. **Known for:** homey appetizers; excellent value; Chinese hamburger. $ *Average main: $12* ✉ *2555 Judah St., Sunset* ☎ *415/681–3288* ⊕ *tcwus.com* ⊘ *Closed Mon. No lunch.*

☕ Coffee and Quick Bites

Andytown Coffee Roasters

$ | CAFÉ | A neighborhood cornerstone like surfing and frigid sunsets, this charming Outer Sunset roastery and café serves house-baked Irish soda bread, scones, and, of course, coffee drinks. A particular favorite is the Snowy Plover: espresso, simple syrup, sparkling water, and house-made whipped cream. **Known for:** excellent breakfast sandwiches; long lines; original Snowy Plover. $ *Average main: $6* ✉ *3655 Lawton St., Sunset* ⊕ *www. andytownsf.com* ⊘ *No dinner.*

Arizmendi Bakery

$ | BAKERY | FAMILY | A Bay Area worker-owned cooperative, this bakery lures passersby with liberal slogans and baked goodies displayed in its large storefront window. The menu changes daily, offering different types of bread, sweet treats like scones, and pizza. **Known for:** enthusiastic local following; one amazing pizza per day, always vegetarian; tough parking. $ *Average main: $6* ✉ *1331 9th Ave, Sunset* ☎ *415/566–3117* ⊕ *www. arizmendibakery.com* ⊘ *Closed Mon.*

★ Devil's Teeth Baking Company

$ | BAKERY | Folks line up on weekends for the amazing breakfast sandwiches here: fluffy eggs, thick bacon, pepper jack, avocado, and lemon-garlic aioli on a melt-in-your-mouth buttermilk biscuit. Made-to-order beignets are another favorite. **Known for:** donut muffins; loaded breakfast sandwiches on unforgettable biscuits; long weekend waits. $ *Average main: $12* ✉ *3876 Noriega St., Sunset* ☎ *415/683–5533* ⊕ *www.devilsteethbakingcompany.com* ⊘ *No dinner.*

☺ Nightlife

BARS

The Riptide

BARS | A cozy cabin bar that's the perfect finale for beachgoers, the Riptide is a surfer favorite, but you don't have to own a board to feel at home. You'll find classic beers and good food, all at wallet-friendly prices. There's live music most nights, often country, bluegrass, honky-tonk, and open mic. Many tourists fooled by San Francisco's version of summer end up warming their popsicle toes at the bar's fireplace. Sunday features a bacon Bloody Mary, great for hangovers. ⊠ 3639 Taraval St., Sunset ☎ 415/681–8433 ⊕ riptidesf.com.

☺ Performing Arts

Stern Grove Festival

CONCERTS | FAMILY | One of San Francisco's favorite summer events, this annual concert series in a picturesque meadow surrounded by redwood and eucalyptus trees attracts fans of all ages each Sunday between June and August. Performers are often nationally-known acts that have a Bay Area connection, and genres tremendously vary from rock to country to the San Francisco Symphony. Concerts are free but reservations are mandatory. ⊠ Wawona St., Sunset ☎ 415/252–6252 ⊕ www.sterngrove.org ⊠ Free.

Golden Gate Park

Jogging, cycling, skating, picnicking, going to a museum, checking out a concert, dozing in the sunshine … Golden Gate Park is the perfect playground for fast-paced types, laid-back dawdlers, and everyone in between. More than 1,000 acres, stretching from the Haight all the way to the windy Pacific coast, the park is a vast patchwork of woods, trails, lakes, lush gardens, sports facilities, museums—even a herd of bison. You can hit the highlights in a few hours, but it would literally take days to fully explore the entire park.

⇨ For more information about the park, see Chapter 11, Golden Gate Park.

☺ Activities

BOATING AND SAILING

Stow Lake

BOATING | FAMILY | If you prefer calm freshwater, you can rent rowboats and pedal boats at Stow Lake in Golden Gate Park. ■ TIP→The lake is open 10–5 on weekends and 11–4:30 on weekdays for boating; rentals stop one hour before closing. ⊠ Stow Lake Boathouse, 50 Stow Lake Dr. E, off John F. Kennedy Dr., Golden Gate Park ☎ 415/386–2531 ⊕ stowlakeboathouse.com ⊠ From $26 per hour for boat rentals.

HIKING

Golden Gate National Recreation Area (*GGNRA*)

HIKING & WALKING | FAMILY | This huge, protected area encompasses the San Francisco coastline, the Marin Headlands, and Point Reyes National Seashore, perhaps one of the most beautiful places on the planet. It's veined with hiking trails, including the spectacular Coastal Trail at Lands End in San Francisco (access this from the parking lot near the western end of Point Lobos Avenue), and guided walks are offered in some places. You can find current schedules at visitor centers at Lands End, in the Presidio, and in the Marin Headlands; they're also online. ⊠ San Francisco ☎ 415/561–4700 ⊕ www.nps.gov/goga.

Chapter 11

GOLDEN GATE PARK

Updated by
Denise M. Leto

A GREEN RETREAT

Stretching more than 1,000 acres from the ocean to the Haight, Golden Gate Park is a place to slow down and smell the eucalyptus. Stockbrokers and gadget-laden parents stroll the Music Concourse, while speedy tattooed cyclists and wobbly, training-wheeled kids cruise along shaded paths. Seniors and teenagers warm the garden benches, hikers search for waterfalls, and picnickers lounge in the Rhododendron Dell. San Franciscans love their city streets, but the park is where they come to breathe.

PLANNING A PARK VISIT

GETTING ORIENTED

The park breaks down naturally into three chunks. The eastern end attracts the biggest crowds with its cluster of blockbuster sights. It's also the easiest place to dip into the park for a quick trip. Water hobbyists come to the middle section's lake-speckled open space. Sporty types head west to the coastal end for its soccer fields, golf course, and archery range. This windswept western end is the park's least visited and most naturally landscaped part. ⏱ Daily 6 am–10 pm ⊕ www.sfrecpark.org.

WALKING TOURS

San Francisco Botanical Garden (☎ 415/661–1316) has botanical tours every day (free with general admission). Tours start near the main gate daily at 1:30 pm.

San Francisco City Guides (☎ 415/557–4266) offers free year-round tours of the eastern end and the western end of the park and two different tours of the Japanese Tea Garden.

BEST TIMES TO VISIT

Time of day: It's best to arrive early at the Conservatory of Flowers, the de Young Museum, and the Japanese Tea Garden to avoid crowds. At sunset, the only place to be is the park's western end, watching the sun dip into the Pacific.

Time of year: Visit during the week if you can. The long, late summer days of September and October are the warmest times to visit, and many special weekend events are held then.

Blooms: The rhododendrons bloom between February and May. The Queen Wilhelmina Tulip Garden blossoms in February and March. Cherry trees in the Japanese Tea Garden bloom in April, and the Rose Garden is at its best from mid-May to mid-June, in the beginning of July, and during September.

(opposite) Conservatory of Flowers (top left) The San Francisco Botanical Garden in bloom

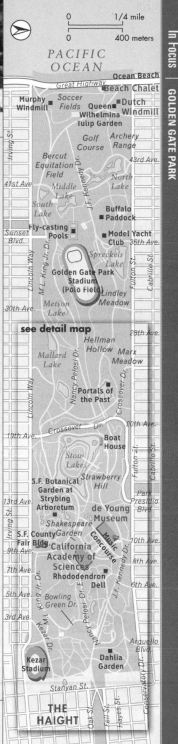

TIPS

■ Carry a map or check online (See ⊕ www.golden-gatepark.com)—the park's sightlines usually prevent you from using city landmarks as reference points. Posted maps are few and far between, and they're often out of date. Paths aren't always clear, so stick to well-marked trails.

■ In Golden Gate Park, free public restrooms are fairly common and mostly clean, especially around the eastern end's attractions. Facilities are available behind the Conservatory of Flowers or in the de Young Museum at the sculpture garden and café patio. Farther west, behind Stow Lake's boathouse and near the Koret Children's Quarter are facilities.

BEST WAYS TO SPEND YOUR TIME

The park stretches 3 miles east to west and is a half-mile wide, so it's possible to cover the whole thing in a day—by car, public transportation, bike, or even on foot. But to do so might feel more like a forced march than a pleasure jaunt. Weigh your time and your interests, choose your top picks, then leave at least an extra hour to just enjoy being outdoors.

Two hours: Swing by the exquisite Conservatory of Flowers for a 20-minute peek, then head to the de Young Museum. Spend a few minutes assessing its controversial exterior and perhaps glide through some of the galleries before heading to the observation tower for a panoramic view of the city. Cross the Music Concourse to the spectacular Academy of Sciences.

Half day: Spend a little extra time at the sights described above, then head to the nearby Japanese Tea Garden to enjoy its perfectionist landscape. Next, cross the street to the San Francisco Botanical Garden at Strybing Arboretum and check out the intriguing Primitive Garden. If you brought supplies, this is a great place for a picnic; you can also grab lunch at the de Young Café.

Full day: After the half-day tour (above) continue on to the children's playground if you have kids in tow. Once your little ones see the playground's tree house–like play structures and climbing opportunities, you may be here for the rest of the day. Alternatively, make your way to the serene National AIDS Memorial Grove. Then head west, stopping at Stow Lake to climb Strawberry Hill. Wind up at the Beach Chalet for a sunset drink.

(top) Amateur musicians entertain passersby. (middle) Sundays are ideal biking days. (bottom) The meandering paths are perfect for strolling.

GETTING AROUND THE PARK

WALKING
The most convenient entry point is on the eastern edge at Stanyan Street, continuing into the park on JFK Drive, which points you directly toward the Conservatory of Flowers. It's a 10-minute walk there; allow another 10–15 minutes to reach the California Academy of Sciences, de Young Museum, Japanese Tea Garden, and San Francisco Botanical Garden. Stow Lake is another 10 minutes west from these four sights.

BY BIKE OR SKATE
The park is fantastic for cycling and skating, with a car-free route end-to-end; east to west it runs down John F. Kennedy Drive to the center of the park, then Overlook, Middle, and Martin Luther King Junior Drives to the beach. Biking the park round-trip is about a 7-mile trip, which usually takes 1–2 hours. The route down John F. Kennedy Drive takes you past the prettiest, well-maintained sections of the park on a mostly flat circuit. The most popular route continues all the way to the beach. Keep in mind that the ride is downhill toward the ocean, uphill heading east. Skaters gravitate toward John F. Kennedy Drive, especially at Skatin' Place (off John F. Kennedy Drive at 6th Avenue), a free, dedicated outdoor gathering spot for enthusiasts of all ages, with a very San Francisco psychedelic mural.

BY CAR
If you have a car, you'll have no trouble hopping from sight to sight. (Visit sfrecpark.org for routes that avoid the car-free sections of John F. Kennedy, Overlook, Middle, and Martin Luther King Junior Drives.) Parking within the park is often free and is usually easy to find beyond the eastern end. On Sundays or anytime the eastern end is crowded, head for the residential streets north of the park or the underground parking lot; enter on 10th and Fulton (northern edge of the park) or MLK Drive and Concourse (in the park).

BY SHUTTLE
The free Golden Gate Park shuttle runs 12-6 on weekdays and 9-6 on weekends and holidays. It loops through the eastern half of the park every 15–20 minutes, stopping at 14 sights from McLaren Lodge to Stow Lake. Look for the green shuttle stop signs.

(top) Water lilies adorn the Japanese Tea Garden.

WHERE TO RENT

Parkwide Bike Rentals & Tours (☎ 415/671–8989). The only rental shop in the park is behind the band-shell on the music concourse. For an extra $10 you can return your bike to the Embarcadero/Ferry Building, the Marina, or Union Square. **Unlimited Biking** (✉ 1792 Haight St, ☎ 415/854-2222). Rent from this shop just east of the park and you can return your wheels to their other locations at Fisherman's Wharf or Union Square. San Francisco Bicycle Rentals. (✉ 425 Jefferson St. ☎ 415/922–4537). Customers rave about excellent service and good deals at this Fisherman's Wharf outfit. **Blazing Saddles** (✉ 2715 Hyde St ☎ 415/202–8888). This business operates out of Fisherman's Wharf and North Beach but you can take their bikes to the park, too.

BEST PLACES TO PICNIC ON WEEKENDS

- ■ Lawn in front of the Conservatory of Flowers
- ■ By the pond in the San Francisco Botanical Garden
- ■ The benches overlooking the Rustic Bridge at Stow Lake
- ■ Rhododendron Dell

DON'T-MISS SIGHTS

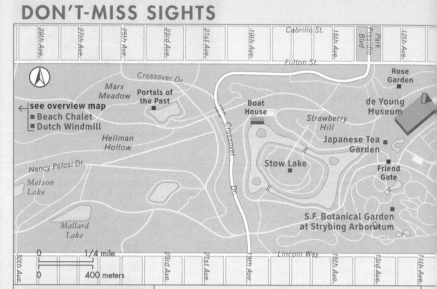

Marx Meadow
Portals of the Past
Crossover Dr.
Boat House
de Young Museum
Rose Garden
see overview map
■ Beach Chalet
■ Dutch Windmill
Hellman Hollow
Strawberry Hill
Japanese Tea Garden
Nancy Pelosi Dr.
Stow Lake
Friend Gate
Metson Lake
Mallard Lake
S.F. Botanical Garden at Strybing Arboretum
Lincoln Way

Conservatory of Flowers
✉ 100 John F. Kennedy Dr. at Conservatory Dr.
☎ 415/831-2090
💲 $11–13 Tues.–Thurs., $15 Fri.–Sun.
🕐 Tues.–Sun. 10–4:30
🌐 www.conservatoryof flowers.org

CONSERVATORY OF FLOWERS

Whatever you do, be sure to at least drive by the Conservatory of Flowers—it's just too darn pretty to miss. The gorgeous, white-framed, 1878 glass structure is topped with a 14-ton glass dome. Stepping inside the giant greenhouse is like taking a quick trip to the rainforest; it's humid, warm, and smells earthy. The undeniable highlight is the Aquatic Plants section, where lily pads float and carnivorous plants dine on bugs to the sounds of rushing water. On the east side of the conservatory (to the right as you face the building), cypress, pine, and redwood trees surround the **Dahlia Garden,** which blooms in summer and fall. To the west is the **Rhododendron Dell,** which contains 850 varieties, more than any other garden of its kind in the country. It's a favorite local Mother's Day picnic spot.

STOW LAKE

Russian seniors feed the pigeons, kids watch turtles sunning themselves, and joggers circle this placid body of water, Golden Gate Park's largest lake. Early park superintendent John McLaren may have snarked that manmade Stow Lake was "a shoestring around a watermelon," but for more than a century visitors have come to walk its paths and bridges, paddle boats, and climb Strawberry Hill (the "watermelon"). Cross one of the bridges—the 19th-century stone bridge on the southwest side is lovely—and ascend the hill; keep your eyes open for the waterfall and an elaborate Chinese Pavilion.

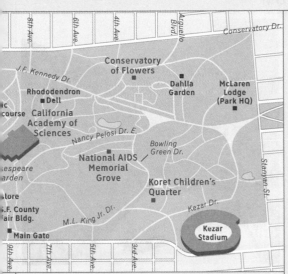

Stow Lake

✉ Off John F. Kennedy Dr.

☎ Boat rental 415/386–2531

🕐 Boat rentals 11–4 weekdays, 10–5 weekends

🌐 www.stowlakeboathouse.com

San Francisco Japanese Tea Garden

✉ 75 Hagiwara Tea Garden Dr.

☎ 415/752–1171

💲 $13

🕐 Mar.–Oct., daily 9–5:45; Nov.–Feb., daily 9–4:45

🌐 www.japaneseteagardensf.com

Koret Children's Quarter

✉ Bowling Green Dr., off Martin Luther King Jr. Dr

☎ 415/861–0778

💲 Playground free, carousel $2

🕐 Playground daily dawn–dusk; carousel Memorial Day–Labor Day, weekdays 10:30–5, weekends 10–6, Labor Day–Memorial Day, weekends 10–4.

🌐 www.sfrec.org

SAN FRANCISCO JAPANESE TEA GARDEN

As you amble through the manicured landscape, past Japanese sculptures and perfect miniature pagodas, over ponds of huge carp, you may be transported to a more peaceful plane. Or maybe the shrieks of kids clambering over the almost vertical "humpback" bridges will keep you firmly in the here and now. Either way, this garden is one of those tourist spots that's truly worth a stop (a half-hour will do). And at 5 acres, it's large enough that you'll always be able to find a bit of serenity, even when the tour buses drop by.

■ TIP→ The garden is especially lovely in April, when the cherry blossoms are in bloom.

KORET CHILDREN'S QUARTER

Founded in 1888 and impressively renovated, the country's first public children's playground has wave-shaped climbing walls, old-fashioned cement slides, and a 20-plus-foot rope climbing structure that kids love and parents fear. Thankfully, one holdover is the beautiful, handcrafted 1912 Herschell-Spillman Carousel. The lovely stone Sharon Building, next to the playground, offers kids' art classes. Bring a picnic or pick up grub nearby on 9th Avenue and you could spend the entire day here. Be aware that the playground, which has separate areas for toddlers and bigger kids, is unenclosed and sightlines can be obstructed.

DE YOUNG MUSEUM

- ✉ 50 Hagiwara Tea Garden Dr.
- ☎ 415/750–3600
- 🌐 www.deyoung.famsf.org
- 💲 $15; free first Tues. of month
- 🕐 Tues.–Sun. 9:30–5:15

TIPS

■ Admission at the de Young is good for same-day admission to the Legion of Honor and vice-versa.

■ The de Young is famous these days first and foremost for its striking and controversial building and tree-topping tower. These are accessible to the public for free, so if it's not the art you're interested in seeing, save the cost of admission and head up the elevator to 360-degree views from the glass-walled observation floor.

■ When it's time for a nosh, head to the de Young Café and dine in the lovely outdoor sculpture garden.

Everyone in town has a strong opinion about the de Young. Some adore the striking copper facade, while others grimace and hope that the green patina of age will mellow the effect. The building almost overshadows the museum's respected collection of American, African, and Oceanic art.

HIGHLIGHTS

Head through the sprawling concourse level and begin your visit on the upper level, where you'll find textiles; art from Africa, Oceana, and New Guinea; and highlights of the 20th-century American painting collection (such as Wayne Thiebaud, John Singer Sargent, Winslow Homer, and Richard Diebenkorn). These are the don't-miss items, so take your time. Then head back downstairs to see art from the Americas and contemporary work.

The de Young has had some major international coups, scoring exhibits such as *Tutankhamun and the Golden Age of the Pharoahs*; *Van Gogh, Gaugin, Cezanne*, and *Beyond: Post-Impressionist Masterpieces* from the Musée d'Orsay; and *Picasso: Masterpieces from the Musée National Picasso, Paris*. Be sure to check for traveling exhibits while you're visiting (extra fees apply).

CALIFORNIA ACADEMY OF SCIENCES

⊠ 55 Music Concourse Dr.

☎ 415/379–8000

⊕ www.calacademy.org

💳 $37–$45, $3 off for visitors who walk, bike, or take public transit.

🕐 Mon.–Sat. 9:30–5, Sun. 11–5

TIPS

■ The academy often hosts gaggles of schoolchildren. Arrive early and allow plenty of time to wait in line.

■ Plan ahead: check Planetarium show times, animal feeding times, etc, before you arrive.

■ Visitors complain about the high cost of food here; consider bringing a picnic.

■ Free days are tempting, but the tradeoff includes extremely long lines and the possibility that you won't get in.

■ With antsy kids, visit Early Explorers Cove and use the academy's in-and-out privileges to run around outside.

■ Take time to examine the structure itself, from denim insulation to weather sensors.

With its native plant–covered living roof, retractable ceiling, three-story rain forest, gigantic planetarium, living coral reef, and frolicking penguins, the Cal Academy is one of the city's most spectacular treasures. Dramatically designed by Renzo Piano, it's an eco-friendly, energy-efficient adventure in biodiversity and green architecture. The roof's large mounds and hills mirror the local topography, and Piano's audacious design completes the dramatic transformation of the park's Music Concourse. Moving away from a restrictive role as a backward-looking museum that catalogued natural history, the new academy is all about sustainability and the future, but you'll still find those beloved dioramas in African Hall.

HIGHLIGHTS

By the time you arrive, hopefully you've decided which shows and programs to attend, looked at the academy's floor plan, and designed a plan to cover it all in the time you have. And if not, here's the quick version: Head left from the entrance to the wooden walkway over otherworldly rays in the Philippine Coral Reef, then continue to the Swamp to see Claude, the famous albino alligator. Swing through African Hall and view the penguins, take the elevator up to the living roof, then return to the main floor and get in line to explore the Rainforests of the World, ducking free-flying butterflies and watching for other live surprises. You'll end up below ground in the Amazonian Flooded Rainforest, where you can explore the academy's other aquarium exhibits. Phew.

ALSO WORTH SEEING

San Francisco Botanical Garden at Strybing Arboretum

SAN FRANCISCO BOTANICAL GARDEN AT STRYBING ARBORETUM

One of the best picnic spots in a very picnic-friendly park, the 55-acre arboretum specializes in plants from areas with climates similar to that of the Bay Area. Walk the Eastern Australian garden to see tough, pokey shrubs and plants with cartoon-like names, such as the hilly-pilly tree. Kids gravitate toward the large shallow fountain and the pond with ducks, turtles, and egrets. Free tours meet at the main gate daily at 1:30.
⊠ *Enter park at 9th Ave. at Lincoln Way* ☎ *415/661–1316* ⊕ *www.sfbg.org* ✍ *$13 Feb.-Oct., $10 Nov.-Jan.; Free daily 7:30–9* ☯ *Mar.–Sept., daily 7:30–6; Oct.–early Nov. and Feb.–Mar., daily 7:30–5. Nov.–Jan., daily 7:30–4.*

NATIONAL AIDS MEMORIAL GROVE

This lush, serene 7-acre grove was conceived as a living memorial to the disease's victims. Coast live oaks, Monterey pines, coast redwoods, and other trees flank the grove. There are also two stone circles, one recording the names of the dead and their loved ones, the other engraved with a poem. Free self-guided tours are available to download on any mobile device.
⊠ *Middle Dr. E, west of tennis courts* ☎ *415/765–0498* ⊕ *www.aidsmemorial.org.*

Beach Chalet

BEACH CHALET

Hugging the park's western border, this 1925 Willis Polk–designed structure houses gorgeous Depression-era murals of familiar San Francisco scenes by Lucien Adolphe Labaudt, while verses by local poets adorn niches here and there. Stop by the ground-floor visitors center on your way to indulge in a microbrew upstairs, ideally at sunset.
⊠ *1000 Great Hwy.* ☎ *415/386–8439 restaurant* ⊕ *www.beachchalet.com* ☯ *Restaurant weekdays 11–9, weekends 10–9.*

DUTCH WINDMILL

It may not pump water anymore, but this carefully restored windmill, built in 1903 to irrigate the park, continues to enchant visitors. The Queen Wilhelmina Tulip Garden here is a welcoming respite, particularly lovely during its February and March bloom. The Murphy Windmill is just south of the Dutch Windmill and has a refurbished copper dome; swing by for an interesting comparison.
⊠ *1691 John F. Kennedy Dr., 1/2 block east of Great Hwy., northwest corner of park* ☎ *No phone* ☯ *Dawn–dusk daily.*

Dutch Windmill

Chapter 12

THE HAIGHT, THE CASTRO, HAYES VALLEY, AND NOE VALLEY

Updated by
Denise Leto

● Sights	🍴 Restaurants	🛏 Hotels	🛍 Shopping	🍸 Nightlife
★☆☆☆☆	★★★☆☆	★☆☆☆☆	★★★☆☆	★★★☆☆

NEIGHBORHOOD SNAPSHOT

TOP EXPERIENCES

■ **Castro Theatre:** Take in a film at this gorgeous throwback and join the audience shouting out lines, commentary, and songs. Come early and let the Wurlitzer set the mood.

■ **Vintage shopping in the Haight:** Find the perfect 1930s afternoon dress at Relic Vintage, a pristine faux-leopard coat at Held Over, or the motorcycle jacket of your dreams at Buffalo Exchange.

■ **Browsing and noshing in Hayes Valley:** Window shop and sip wine along the few packed blocks of Hayes Street between Patricia's Green park and Laguna Street.

■ **24th Street stroll:** Ramble along Noe Valley's main drag, lined with cafés, comfy eateries, and cute shops.

■ **SFJAZZ Center:** Experience the amazing acoustics at Hayes Valley's intimate temple to jazz.

GETTING HERE

■ F-line trolleys serve the Castro. Muni light-rail K–Ingleside and M–Ocean View trains stop at Castro station, and the J–Church serves the Castro and Noe Valley. The 6–Haight/Parnassus and 7–Haight/Noriega buses serve the Haight from Market Street. If on foot, know that the hill between the Castro and Noe Valley is steep. For Hayes Valley, take Muni light rail line J–Church, K–Ingleside, or M–Ocean View to Van Ness Avenue or BART to Civic Center and walk (avoid this walk after dark).

PLANNING YOUR TIME

The Upper Haight is only a few blocks long; an hour or so should be enough unless you're into vintage shopping. Many restaurants cater to the morning-after crowd, so this is a great place for brunch. You'll be most comfortable here during the daytime.

The Castro, with its fun, adult-theme storefronts, invites unhurried exploration; allot at least an hour. Visit in the evening for the lively nightlife, or in the late morning—especially on weekends—when the street scene is hopping.

A loop through Noe Valley takes about an hour. With its popular breakfast spots and cafés, this neighborhood is a good place for a morning stroll. After you've filled up, browse the shops along 24th and Church Streets.

Hayes Valley is best visited during business hours to browse its unique shops; allow an hour or so to explore. Consider a late-afternoon visit followed by dinner at one of the neighborhood's many trendy restaurants, topped off by a glass at one of its inviting wine bars.

VIEWFINDER

■ San Francisco has plenty of famous vista points— Twin Peaks and Coit Tower come immediately to mind. To enjoy sweeping, totally unobstructed views of the city all the way to the bay without the tour buses, head to Kite Hill Park, a lesser-known perch in the Castro. A grass-topped neighborhood gem popular with dog owners, this open space is accessible at the end of Corwin Street, the end of Grand View Terrace, and near the intersection of Eagle and Yukon Streets. There are benches to rest on after the climb, but bring a jacket—it gets windy up here.

These neighborhoods wear their personalities large and proud, and are perfect for strolling around. Like a slide show of San Francisco's history, you can move from the Haight's residue of 1960s counterculture, to the Castro's connection to '70s and '80s gay life, to '90s gentrification in Noe Valley and Hayes Valley.

Although historic events thrust the Haight and the Castro onto the international stage, both are anything but stagnant—they're still dynamic areas well worth exploring.

The Haight

During the 1960s, the siren song of free love, peace, and mind-altering substances lured thousands of young people to the Haight, just east of Golden Gate Park. By 1966 the area had become a hot spot for rock artists, including the Grateful Dead, Jefferson Airplane, and Janis Joplin. Some of the most infamous flower children, including Charles Manson and People's Temple founder Jim Jones, also called the Haight home.

Today the '60s message of peace, civil rights, and higher consciousness has been distilled into a successful blend of commercialism and progressive causes: the Haight Ashbury Free Clinic, founded in 1967, survives at the corner of Haight and Clayton Streets, while throwbacks like Bound Together Bookstore (an anarchist book collective), the head shop Pipe Dreams, and a bevy of tie-dye shops all keep the Summer of Love alive in their own way. The Haight's famous political spirit—it was the first neighborhood in the nation to lead a freeway revolt, and it continues to resist chain stores—survives alongside some of the finest Victorian-lined streets in the city.

The Haight is actually composed of two distinct neighborhoods: the Lower Haight runs from Divisadero to Webster; the Upper Haight, immediately east of Golden Gate Park, is the part people tend to call Haight-Ashbury. San Franciscans come to the Upper Haight for the myriad vintage clothing stores concentrated in its few blocks, bars with character, restaurants where huge breakfast portions take the edge off a hangover, and Amoeba Music, the best place in town for new and used CDs and vinyl. The Lower Haight is an equally lively stretch with several well-loved pubs and a smattering of niche music shops.

⊙ Sights

Buena Vista Park
CITY PARK | The reward for the steep climb to get here is this eucalyptus-filled space with great city views. Dog walkers and

Hippie History

The eternal lure for twentysome-things—cheap rent—helped spawn an indelible part of SF's history and public image. In the early 1960s, young people started streaming into the sprawling, inexpensive Victorian houses in the area around the University of San Francisco, earnestly seeking a new era of communal living, individual empowerment, and expanded consciousness.

Golden Gate Park's Panhandle, a green strip on the Haight's northern edge, was their gathering spot—the site of protests, concerts, food giveaways, and general hanging out. In 1967, George Harrison strolled up the park's Hippie Hill, borrowed a guitar, and played for a while before being recognized. He led the crowd, Pied Piper–style, into the Haight.

A Hippie State of Mind

At first the counterculture was all about sharing and taking care of one another—a good thing, considering most hippies were either broke or had renounced money. The daily free "feeds" in the Panhandle were a staple for many. The Diggers, an anarchist street-theater group, were known for handing out bread shaped like the big coffee cans they baked it in.

At the time, the U.S. government, Harvard professor Timothy Leary, a Stanford student named Ken Kesey, and the kids in the Haight were all experimenting with LSD. Acid was legal, widely available, and usually given away for free. At Kesey's all-night parties, called "acid tests," a buck got you a cup of "electric" Kool-Aid, a preview of psychedelic art, and an earful of the house band, the Grateful Dead. When LSD was made illegal in 1966, the kids responded by staging a Love Pageant Rally, where they dropped acid tabs en masse and rocked out to Janis Joplin and the Dead.

The Peak of the Party

Things crested early in 1967, when between 10,000 and 50,000 people ("depending on whether you were a policeman or a hippie," according to one hippie) gathered at the Polo Field in Golden Gate Park for the "Human Be-In: A Gathering of the Tribes." Poet Allen Ginsberg and Timothy Leary spoke, the Dead and Jefferson Airplane played, and people adorned in beads and feathers waved flags, clanged cymbals, and beat drums. A parachutist dropped onto the field, tossing fistfuls of acid tabs to the crowd. America watched via satellite, gape-mouthed—it was every conservative parent's nightmare.

Burn Out

Later that year, thousands heeded Scott McKenzie's song "San Francisco," which promised, "For those who come to San Francisco, summertime will be a love-in there." The Summer of Love swelled the Haight's population from 7,000 to 75,000; people came to join in and to ogle. But less positive forces soon joined the gentle people, heroin replaced LSD, crime became rampant, and the Haight began a fast slide.

Hippies will tell you the Human Be-In was the pinnacle of their scene, while the Summer of Love was a media creation that turned their movement into a monster. Still, the idea of that fictional summer lingers, and to this day draws pilgrims from all over the world.

homeless folks make good use of the park, and the playground at the top is popular with kids and adults alike. Be sure to scan the stone rain gutters lining many of the walkways for inscribed names and dates; these are the remains of gravestones left unclaimed when the city closed the Laurel Hill cemetery around 1940. A pit stop includes a portable toilet and disposal for used needles and condoms; definitely avoid the park after dark, when these items are left behind. ✉ *Haight St. between Lyon St. and Buena Vista Ave. W, Haight* 🌐 *sfrecpark.org/770/golden-gate-park.*

Grateful Dead House
HISTORIC HOME | On the outside, this is just one more well-kept Victorian on a street that's full of them, but true fans of the Dead may find some inspiration looking at this legendary structure. The three-story house (closed to the public) is tastefully painted in sedate mauves, tans, and teals—no bright tie-dye colors here. ✉ *710 Ashbury St., Haight.*

Haight-Ashbury Intersection
STREET | On October 6, 1967, hippies took over the intersection of Haight and Ashbury Streets to proclaim the "Death of Hip." If they thought hip was dead then, they'd find absolute confirmation of it today—the only tie-dye in sight on the famed corner is a Ben & Jerry's storefront. ✉ *Haight.*

🍴 Restaurants

Haight-Ashbury was home base for the country's famed 1960s counterculture, and its café scene still reflects that colorful past.

Over time, the Haight has become two distinct neighborhoods. The Upper Haight is an energetic commercial stretch from Masonic Avenue to Stanyan Street, where head shops and tofu-burger joints still thrive. Meanwhile, the modestly gritty Lower Haight has emerged as a lively bohemian quarter of sorts, with mostly international eateries lining the blocks between Webster and Pierce Streets.

Cha Cha Cha
$$ | CARIBBEAN | This boisterous institution serves island cuisine—a mix of Cajun, Southwestern, and Caribbean influences—tapas style, in a setting with Technicolor tropical plastic decor. The food is hot and spicy: try the fried calamari or chili-spiked Cajun shrimp, and wash everything down with a pitcher of Cha Cha Cha's signature sangria. **Known for:** worthy ceviche and paella mixta; ropa vieja (stewed shredded beef and vegetables); long but quick-moving lines;. [$] *Average main: $25* ✉ *1801 Haight St., Haight* ☎ *415/386–7670* 🌐 *chachachasf.com.*

Parada 22
$ | PUERTO RICAN | A small, colorful space, Parada 22 serves up heaping plates of home-style Puerto Rican cuisine—think plantains, seafood, and slow-roasted pork. There's also plenty of vegetarian fare on offer. **Known for:** delicious yuca fries; marinated meats and vegetables; lunch specials. [$] *Average main: $17* ✉ *1805 Haight St., Haight* ☎ *415/750–1111* 🌐 *www.paradasf.com.*

Uva Enoteca
$$ | ITALIAN | This casual Italian wine bar hits all the right notes: the mood is convivial, the food is solid, and there's plenty of wine—more than 10 by the glass and a long list of bottles. The menu is straightforward, with assortments of Italian cured meats and cheeses, a selection of salads and vegetable dishes, and a roster of pastas and pizzas. **Known for:** simple but delicious food; good gelato; friendly staff. [$] *Average main: $21* ✉ *568 Haight St., Haight* ☎ *415/829–2024* 🌐 *www.uvaenoteca.com* ⏰ *No lunch.*

☕ Coffee and Quick Bites

Flywheel Coffee Roasters
$ | CAFÉ | Family-owned, this light-filled café with a view of Golden Gate Park roasts its beans in-house for a great

The Haight,
the Castro, Hayes Valley
and Noe Valley

cuppa. The cold brew is very good, and the food includes vegan options. **Known for:** location overlooking the park; airy, artsy-rustic space; cold brew and siphon coffee. $ *Average main: $7* ⊠ *672 Stanyan St., Haight* ⊕ *flywheelcoffee.com.*

 Hotels

★ The Metro Hotel

$ | **HOTEL** | These tiny rooms, with simple yet modern decor and private bathrooms, are within walking distance to the lively Haight, Hayes Valley, and Castro neighborhoods. **Pros:** unbeatable price; out-of-downtown location; friendly staffers. **Cons:** small rooms and bathrooms; street noise; no elevator. $ *Rooms from: $195* ⊠ *319 Divisadero St., Haight* ☎ *415/861–5364* ⊕ *www.metrohotelsf.com* ⏥ *24 rooms* ⚭ *No Meals.*

⏦ Nightlife

The hippie joints that made the Haight famous may be long gone, but this neighborhood retains a counterculture vibe. Beer connoisseurs should head directly to the Toronado or Magnolia.

BARS

The Alembic

COCKTAIL LOUNGES | This dark-wood, low-lit space has a certain swagger that's at once charming and classy. It serves full meals but is also a good choice for cocktails and small plates—the polenta fries, Scotch egg, and seasonal salad are all winners. ⊠ *1725 Haight St., Haight* ☎ *415/666–0822* ⊕ *alembicsf.com.*

Magnolia Brewing Company

BREWPUBS | Known for its food as much as its beers, Magnolia is a San Francisco institution, thanks in part to its prime location near the Haight-Ashbury intersection. Come for the smoked trout croquettes, falafel salad, and famed burgers, or just grab any one of the dozen-plus beers on tap, many brewed in-house. The brewpub occupies the site of The

Drugstore Cafe, one of the first hippie hangouts in the Haight in the 1960s. ⊠ *1398 Haight St., Haight* ☎ *415/864–7468* ⊕ *magnoliabrewing.com.*

Noc Noc

BARS | A cross between a Tim Burton film and an Oingo Boingo album, this funky, cavelike bar makes every day Halloween. Noc Noc's bartenders serve up about 20 or so beers on tap, sake (even unfiltered), and unique twists on traditional drinks, like the Snake Bite, a blend of lager and cider. The house DJ plays acid jazz, industrial, and ambient music. ⊠ *557 Haight St., Haight* ☎ *415/861–5811* ⊕ *www.nocnocs.com.*

★ Toronado Pub

BARS | You come to one of the city's most popular dive bars for one thing and one thing only: the reasonably priced beers, about four dozen of them on tap. The Toronado opens in the late morning and has a good-size crowd by early afternoon, so show up early to sit at one of the highly coveted tables. Just make sure to bring cash, as they don't accept credit cards. ⊠ *547 Haight St., Haight* ☎ *415/863–2276* ⊕ *www.toronado.com.*

LGBTQ+ NIGHTLIFE

Trax Bar

BARS | "Laid-back" would be an understatement. Once inside Trax, you won't feel like you're in a gay bar—or in San Francisco—and that's the way the regulars like it. Cheap beer specials draw all types, and though you don't have to don your cruise wear for this place, it's still social. ⊠ *1437 Haight St., Haight* ☎ *415/864–4213* ⊕ *traxbarsf.com.*

⏦ Performing Arts

SPOKEN WORD AND READINGS

Cafe International

MUSIC | It's a chill café during the day and a performance venue at night. Weekends bring live jazz, open-mic sessions, and acoustic musical acts. ⊠ *508 Haight St.,*

Haight ☎ 415/552–7390 ⊕ www.face-book.com/cafeinternational.

🛍 Shopping

Largely free of chain stores and big companies, Haight Street is *the* place to find high-quality vintage clothing, funky shoes, folk art from around the world, and used records and CDs.

BOOKS

Booksmith

BOOKS | FAMILY | This fine bookshop sells current releases, children's titles, and offbeat periodicals. Authors passing through town often make a stop at this neighborhood institution. ⊠ 1644 Haight St., Haight ☎ 415/863–8688 ⊕ www. booksmith.com.

Bound Together Bookstore

BOOKS | This old-school collective, around since 1976, stocks books on anarchist theory and practice, as well as titles about gender issues, radicalism, and various other left-leaning topics. A portion of the revenue supports anarchist projects and the Prisoners Literature Project. ⊠ 1369 Haight St., Haight ☎ 415/431–8355 ⊕ boundtogether.org.

CLOTHING

Buffalo Exchange

MIXED CLOTHING | Men and women can find fashionable, high-quality, used clothing at this national chain. Among the items are Levi's, leather jackets, sunglasses, and novelty jewelry. It's also known for its costume offerings and more offbeat merchandise. ⊠ 1555 Haight St., Haight ☎ 415/431–7733 ⊕ buffaloexchange.com.

★ Held Over

MIXED CLOTHING | The extensive collection of clothing from the 1920s through the 1980s in this vintage store is organized by decade, saving those looking for flapper dresses from having to wade through lime-green '70s polyester sundresses. Shoes, hats, handbags, and jewelry

complete the different looks. ⊠ 1543 Haight St., Haight ☎ 415/864–0818.

Relic Vintage

MIXED CLOTHING | Offering well-curated clothing, accessories, and jewelry from the roaring '20s to the hippie '60s, this premier vintage shop has a loyal following among retro-conscious gals and pals. Patrons have fun turning back the clock in the well-organized yet funky interior with Hawaiian-theme dressing rooms and a leopard-print chaise lounge. ⊠ 1475 Haight St., Haight ☎ 415/255–7460 ⊕ www.relicvintagesf.com.

MUSIC

★ Amoeba Music

MUSIC | With well over a million new and used CDs, DVDs, and records at bargain prices, this warehouse-like offshoot of the Berkeley original carries titles you won't find on Amazon. No niche is ignored—from electronica and hip-hop to jazz and classical—and the stock changes frequently. In-store performances attract large crowds. ⊠ 1855 Haight St., Haight ☎ 415/831–1200 ⊕ www.amoeba. com.

SHOES

John Fluevog

SHOES | The trendy but sturdily made and utterly unique footwear for men and women is among the best in the city. Club girls go gaga over the wacky heels, handing over a pretty penny, and everyone loves the sweet messages of affirmation, like "No one can fill your shoes." ⊠ 1697 Haight St., Haight ☎ 415/436–9784 ⊕ www.fluevog.com.

SOUVENIRS

San Francisco Mercantile

SOUVENIRS | This sweet, airy space offers city mementos more than a few standard deviations above the usual Fisherman's Wharf or Chinatown souvenirs. High-quality San Francisco–themed wares include graphic tees, sweatshirts, and beanies, as well as cute onesies and other items for kids. Beautiful books, housewares, and glassware by local artists make excellent souvenirs and gifts. ✉ *1698 Haight St., Haight* ☎ *415/757–0677* ⊕ *www.shopsfmercantile.com.*

The Castro

The brash and sassy Castro district—the social, political, and cultural center of San Francisco's thriving LGBTQ+ community—stands at the western end of Market Street. This neighborhood is one of the city's liveliest and most welcoming, especially on weekends. Streets teem with folks out shopping, pushing political causes, heading to art films, and lingering in bars and cafés. It's also one of the city's most expensive neighborhoods to live in, with an influx of tech money exacerbating an identity crisis that's been simmering for decades. But you'll still see hard-bodied men in painted-on T-shirts cruising the cutting-edge clothing and novelty stores and pairs of all genders and sexual persuasions holding hands. Brightly painted, intricately restored Victorian houses line the streets, making the Castro a good place to view striking examples of the architecture San Francisco is famous for.

◉ Sights

★ Castro Theatre

PERFORMANCE VENUE | Here's a classic way to join in a beloved Castro tradition: grab some popcorn and catch a flick at this 1,500-seat art-deco theater built in 1922, the grandest of San Francisco's few remaining movie palaces. The neon marquee, which stands at the top of the Castro strip, is the neighborhood's great landmark. The Castro was the fitting host of 2008's red-carpet preview of Gus Van Sant's film *Milk*, starring Sean Penn as openly gay San Francisco supervisor Harvey Milk. The theater's elaborate Spanish baroque interior is fairly well preserved. Before many shows, the theater's pipe organ rises from the orchestra pit and an organist plays pop and movie tunes, usually ending with the Jeanette MacDonald standard "San Francisco" (go ahead, sing along). The crowd can be enthusiastic and vocal, talking back to the screen as loudly as it talks to them. ⚠ **The theater's management is making renovation plans that may change the nature of theater's offerings. Check online for updates before planning your trip.** ✉ *429 Castro St., Castro* ☎ *415/621–6120* ⊕ *www.castrotheatre.com* 🎟 *$14.*

GLBT Historical Society Museum

HISTORY MUSEUM | The small, two-gallery Gay, Lesbian, Bisexual, and Transgender (GLBT) Historical Society Museum, the first of its kind in the United States, presents multimedia exhibits from its vast holdings covering San Francisco's queer history. In the main gallery, you might hear the audiotape Harvey Milk made for the community in the event of his assassination; explore artifacts from "Gayborhoods," lost landmarks of the city's gay past; or flip through a memory book with pictures and thoughts on some of the more than 20,000 San Franciscans lost to AIDS. Though perhaps not for everyone (those offended by sex toys and photos of lustily frolicking naked people may, well, be offended), the museum offers an inside look at these communities so integral to the fabric of San Francisco life. ✉ *4127 18th St., Castro* ☎ *415/621–1107* ⊕ *www.glbthistory.org* 🎟 *$10* ⊗ *Closed Sun. and Mon.*

Harvey Milk Plaza

PLAZA/SQUARE | An 18-foot-long rainbow flag flies above this plaza named for the man who electrified the city in 1977 by being elected to its Board of Supervisors as an openly gay candidate. In the early 1970s, Milk's camera store on Castro Street became the center for his campaign to open San Francisco's social and political life to gays and lesbians.

Milk hadn't served a full year of his term before he and Mayor George Moscone

The History of Gay San Francisco

San Francisco's gay community has been a part of the city since its origins. As a port town and a hub of the gold rush, San Francisco became known for its sexual openness and other liberalities.

Stationed in Sodom

During World War II, hundreds of thousands of servicemen cycled through "Sodom by the Sea," and for most, San Francisco's permissive atmosphere was an eye-opening experience. The army's lists of forbidden establishments unintentionally pointed the way to the city's gay bars.

Many soldiers who were dishonorably discharged for homosexual activity stayed and found homes in Eureka Valley. When the war ended, many families in that neighborhood moved out to the burbs, and the new arrivals snapped up the Victorians on Castro Street.

Beginning of the Movement

In the 1950s, San Francisco's police chief vowed to crack down on "perverts," and the city's queer residents lived in fear of raids. (Arrest meant being outed in the morning paper.) But harassment galvanized the community. The Daughters of Bilitis lesbian organization was founded in the city in 1955; the gay male Mattachine Society, started in Los Angeles in 1950, followed suit with a San Francisco branch.

The Tide Begins to Turn

In the 1960s, these clashes gave the gay population a national profile. In 1965 police dramatically raided a New Year's benefit event, and public opinion began to turn. The police were forced to appoint a liaison to the gay community, and gay organizations began to lobby openly. As one participant noted, "We didn't go back into the woodwork."

The 1970s

The 1970s—thumping disco, raucous street parties, and gay bashing—were a tumultuous time. Eureka Valley had more than 60 gay bars, the bathhouse scene in SoMa was thriving, and graffiti around town read "Save San Francisco—Kill a Fag." When the Eureka Valley Merchants Association refused to admit gay-owned businesses in 1974, camera-shop owner Harvey Milk founded the Castro Valley Association, and the neighborhood's new moniker was born.

The AIDS Crisis

The gay community thrived, but in 1981 reports of a dangerous new disease surfaced. A notice in a Castro pharmacy's window warned about "the gay cancer." By 1990 the disease had killed 10,000 San Franciscans.

Gay activists were quick to mobilize, starting foundations to care for the sick, lobby for faster drug development, and raise awareness nationwide. The city's network of volunteer organizations has since been recognized as one of the best global models for combating the disease.

Today's Castro

While Castro is still the heart of San Francisco's gay life, its character (like that of many other neighborhoods) has become diluted by an influx of tech workers. But the legacy remains, evident in the rainbow flag above Castro and Market Streets and the Harvey Milk bust in City Hall.

were shot to death in November 1978 at City Hall. The murderer was a conservative ex-supervisor named Dan White, who had resigned his post and then became enraged when Moscone wouldn't reinstate him. Milk and White had often been at odds on the board. The gay community became infuriated when the "Twinkie defense"—that junk food had led to diminished mental capacity—resulted in only a manslaughter verdict for White. During the so-called White Night Riot of May 21, 1979, gays and their allies stormed City Hall, torching its lobby.

Milk, who had feared assassination, left behind a tape recording in which he urged the community to continue his work. His legacy is the high visibility of gay people throughout city government; a bust of him was unveiled at City Hall in 2008, and the 2008 film *Milk* gives insight into his life. Keep your visiting expectations in check: this is more of a historical site than an Instagrammable spot. ✉ *Southwest corner of Castro and Market Sts., Castro.*

Pink Triangle Park
MONUMENT | On a median near the Castro's huge rainbow flag stands this memorial to the people forced by the Nazis to wear pink triangles. Fifteen triangular granite columns, one for every 1,000 gay, lesbian, bisexual, and transgender people estimated to have been killed during and after the Holocaust, stand in a grassy triangle—a reminder of the gay community's past and ongoing struggle for civil rights. ✉ *Corner of Market, Castro, and 17th Sts., Castro.*

Randall Museum
SCIENCE MUSEUM | **FAMILY** | Younger kids who are still excited about petting a rabbit, touching a snakeskin, or seeing a live hawk will enjoy a trip to this nature museum. The museum sits beneath a hill variously known as Red Rock, Museum Hill, and, correctly, Corona Heights; hike up the steep but short trail for great, unobstructed city views. Just be sure to bring a windbreaker. ✉ *199 Museum Way, Castro* ☎ *415/554–9600* 🌐 *randallmuseum.org* 🎫 *Free* 🕒 *Closed Sun. and Mon.*

🍴 Restaurants

The Castro is chockablock with restaurants and bars. Market Street between Church and Castro Streets is a great stretch for café- or bistro-hopping.

Frances
$$$$ | **MODERN AMERICAN** | One of the hottest tickets in town, chef Melissa Perello's simple, sublime restaurant is a consummate date-night destination. Perello's seasonal California-French cooking is its own enduring love affair, with standouts including the savory bavette steak, grilled Sakura pork chop, and *panisse frites*. **Known for:** lumberjack cake; neighborhood gem; reasonably priced tasting menu. [$] *Average main: $86* ✉ *3870 17th St., Castro* ☎ *415/621–3870* 🌐 *www.frances-sf.com* 🕒 *Closed Sun. and Mon. No lunch.*

Woodhouse Fish Co.
$$ | **SEAFOOD** | **FAMILY** | New Englanders or anyone else hungry for a lobster roll fix need look no further than this super-friendly spot, where the rolls are utterly authentic and accompanied with slaw and fries. Seafood fans will find plenty else to love on the menu, which is stocked with everything from cioppino to crab melts. **Known for:** beer-battered fish-and-chips; $1.25 oysters on Tuesday; nautical decor. [$] *Average main: $26* ✉ *2073 Market St., Castro* ☎ *415/437–2722* 🌐 *www.woodhousefish.com.*

☕ Coffee and Quick Bites

Castro Coffee Company
$ | **CAFÉ** | The knowledgeable staff at this small storefront pours a perfect latte, Turkish coffee, or French roast. It's the best place in the neighborhood to grab a pound of beans or a cup of quality

coffee to go. **Known for:** friendly service; reasonable prices; solid variety of excellent coffee drinks. [$] *Average main: $5* ✉ *427 Castro St., Castro* ☎ *415/552–6676* 🌐 *www.castro-coffee.com.*

Dinosaurs

$ | **VIETNAMESE** | This small Castro storefront serves up exceptionally fresh banh mi and rockin' spring rolls. Service is quick, and a couple of tables take in the scene on Market Street. **Known for:** special banh mi with three kinds of pork; vegetarian options; smoothies and Vietnamese iced coffee. [$] *Average main: $12* ✉ *2275 Market St., Castro* ☎ *415/503–1421* 🌐 *www.eatdinosaurs.com.*

Poesia Café

$ | **ITALIAN** | An offshoot of the restaurant Poesia next door, the name means "poetry" in Italian, and the pastries, desserts, and savory sandwiches at this cafe live up to the name. You can't go wrong with anything on the house-made cornetti or focaccia, or for that matter any of the wide variety of Italian pastries. **Known for:** inspiring impulsive "just one more" purchases; warm service; Italian cornetti sandwiches. [$] *Average main: $10* ✉ *4076 18th St., Castro* 🌐 *www.poesiasf.com* 🕒 *No dinner.*

Hotels

Beck's Motor Lodge

$ | **MOTEL** | A handy Castro location, reasonable prices, and the holy grail of San Francisco lodging—free parking—make this courtyard-style motel with cool mid-century vibes a favorite. **Pros:** splashy mid-century update; comfortable, spacious guest rooms; free parking. **Cons:** some street noise; not near blockbuster sights; no breakfast. [$] *Rooms from: $185* ✉ *2222 Market St., Castro* ☎ *415/241–0435, 415/621–8212* 🌐 *becksmotorlodge.com* 🛏 *58 rooms* 🍴 *No Meals.*

Hotel Castro

$$ | **HOTEL** | The Castro has been waiting for this brand-new, 12-room hotel, designed for travelers who appreciate smart design and embrace self-service. **Pros:** lobby restocking cabinet with extra tea, coffee, toilet paper; fantastic Castro location convenient to public transit; assistance available 24/7 via text, chat, and email. **Cons:** rooms are small; lack of on-site staff not for everyone; no daily housekeeping or luggage storage. [$] *Rooms from: $295* ✉ *4230 18th St., Castro* ☎ *415/854–9029* 🌐 *thehotelcastro.com* 🛏 *12 rooms* 🍴 *No Meals.*

Nightlife

The gay district is as outrageous as one might expect. Leather daddies, costumed club kids, and those who defy "no nudity" laws are among the characters you'll stumble across day or night.

BARS

Blackbird

COCKTAIL LOUNGES | This neighborhood hangout blends industrial chic and old-world charm. The crowd is less casual than others in the Castro, though no one will judge you for wearing Chuck Taylors. Blackbird serves up a good selection of craft beers, along with seasonal cocktails. ✉ *2124 Market St., Castro* ☎ *415/872–5310* 🌐 *www.blackbirdbar.com.*

LGBTQ+ NIGHTLIFE

Midnight Sun

COCKTAIL LOUNGES | One of the Castro's longest-running bars—open since 1971—is popular with the polo-shirt-and-khakis crowd. Giant video screens play the latest music videos as well as episodes of shows like *Will & Grace* and *Queer Eye.* ✉ *4067 18th St., Castro* ☎ *415/861–4186* 🌐 *www.midnightsunsf.com.*

Moby Dick

BARS | This quintessential neighborhood watering hole outfitted with a pool table and pinball machines has TV screens

Gay and Lesbian Nightlife

In the days before the gay liberation movement, bars were more than mere watering holes—they also served as community centers where members of a mostly underground minority could network and socialize. In the 1960s, the bars became hotbeds of political activity; by the 1970s, other social opportunities had become available to gay men and lesbians and the bars' importance as centers of activity decreased.

Old-timers may wax nostalgic about the vibrancy of pre-AIDS, 1970s bar life, but you can still have plenty of fun. A major difference is the one-night-a-week operation of some of the best clubs, which may cater to a different (sometimes straight) clientele on other nights. This type of club tends to come and go, so it's best

to pick up one of the two main gay papers to check the latest happenings.

Bay Area Reporter. The weekly *Bay Area Reporter* (⊕ www.ebar. com) covers LGBTQ+ events in its entertainment pages and calendar and has a nightlife section on its website (⊕ www.ebar.com/events/ nightlife_events).

San Francisco Bay Times. The biweekly *Bay Times* (⊕ sfbaytimes. com) runs features and provides extensive calendar listings of LGBTQ+ events.

For a place known as a gay mecca, San Francisco has a surprising drought of lesbian bars. You'll find queer gals (and many more queer guys) at the Mint, but lesbians looking for nightlife should head to the Bernal Heights neighborhood.

playing pop videos and music. A giant fish tank sits over the bar, giving shy types a place to rest their gaze while taking a shot of liquid courage. Casually dressed couples and guys with nothing to prove frequent this place, but there's pickup potential, too. Like many smaller dive bars, it's cash only. ⊠ *4049 18th St., Castro* ☎ *415/294–0731.*

Pilsner Inn

BARS | Casual and comfortable—yet still hip and cruise-y—this is the type of neighborhood joint you quickly claim as your own. Kick back with a pint on the fantastic year-round patio and enjoy eye candy of the thirtysomething variety (ranging from conservative yuppie guys to Mission emo boys). The Pilsner is technically a sports bar, which means it has a pool table and TVs tuned to local games. ⊠ *225 Church St., Castro* ☎ *415/621–7058* ⊕ *www.pilsnerinn.com.*

WINE BARS
Blush! Wine Bar

WINE BARS | A cozy, casual date spot, Blush! serves wines paired with tapas, charcuterie boards, and grilled cheese sandwiches. Sit at the counter for a nice chat with the friendly bartender, and pick a glass or bottle of bubbly or white, rosé, or red wine from its well-curated collection. This place always buzzes on weekends, so reserve in advance. ⊠ *476 Castro St., Castro* ☎ *415/558–0893* ⊕ *www.blushwinebar.com.*

🛍 Shopping

The "gay capital of the world" is also a major shopping destination for all travelers. It has several men's clothing boutiques and home-accessories stores. And if you're looking for something kitschy to shock your Aunt Martha back home, you've come to the right place.

CLOTHING

Rolo

MEN'S CLOTHING | Selling hard-to-find denim, sportswear, shoes, and accessories with a European influence, this store includes clothes designed by Fred Perry, G-Star RAW, and Benson. R by Rolo, down the street at 2267 Market Street, has high-quality gym- and sportswear. ✉ *2351 Market St., Castro* ☎ *415/431–4545* 🌐 *www.rolo.com.*

COSMETICS AND FRAGRANCES

ZGO Perfumery

PERFUME | Carrying a unique collection of high-end perfumes, lotions, diffusers, scented candles, and even Mariage Frères teas, this upscale shop is an abiding favorite among discriminating Castro noses. Shop clerks are knowledgeable and can suggest the perfect gift for yourself or any lucky recipient. ✉ *600 Castro St., Castro* ☎ *888/789–4753* 🌐 *www.zgoperfumery.com.*

JEWELRY AND COLLECTIBLES

Brand X Antiques

JEWELRY & WATCHES | The vintage jewelry here, mostly from the early part of the 20th century, includes a wide selection of estate pieces and objets d'art. With rings that range in price from $5 to a couple thousand, there's something for everyone. Hours can vary, so it's best to call ahead before visiting. ✉ *570 Castro St., Castro* ☎ *415/626–8908.*

SOUVENIRS

Local Take

SOUVENIRS | More than 100 local artists contribute their wares to this thoughtfully curated shop, the best place in the neighborhood for San Francisco gifts and souvenirs. The inventory changes but might include anything from laser-cut metal city maps and a good selection of jewelry to high-quality knitwear and graphic T-shirts. ✉ *4122 18th St., Castro* ☎ *415/556–5300* 🌐 *www.localtakesf.com.*

Hayes Valley

A chic neighborhood due west of Civic Center, Hayes Valley has terrific eateries, cool watering holes, and great browsing in its funky clothing, home-decor, and design boutiques. Locals love this quarter, but without any big-name draws it remains off the radar for many visitors.

👁 Sights

San Francisco LGBT Center

ARTS CENTER | Night and day, the center hosts many social activities, from mixers and youth game nights to holiday parties and slam poetry performances. ✉ *1800 Market St., Hayes Valley* ☎ *415/865–5555* 🌐 *www.sfcenter.org.*

🍴 Restaurants

Hayes Valley is home to several hip and haute dining destinations, centered around Hayes Street, perfect for pre-theater dining. The low-key vibe in the wine bars and cafés makes it easy to feel like a local.

Hayes Street Grill

$$$ | **SEAFOOD** | You'll snag a table if you arrive at this longtime (since 1979) standby just as music lovers are folding their napkins and heading off for a show at the nearby Opera House or SFJAZZ Center. Fresh, sustainable, often local seafood lures the faithful here, as well as peak seasonal produce from the nearby region. **Known for:** simple yet excellent fish preparations; choice of sauces; white-tablecloth dining in timeless atmosphere. [$] *Average main: $36* ✉ *320 Hayes St., Hayes Valley* ☎ *415/863–5545* 🌐 *www.hayesstreetgrill.com* 🕓 *Closed most Mon.–Wed. except opera and symphony performance days.*

★ Nightbird

$$$$ | **MODERN AMERICAN** | Chef-owner Kim Alter's solo debut is this small, charming, seasonally focused tasting-menu destination that is an oasis of calm away from the frantic traffic of Gough Street. The five-course-plus-five-bite menus are beautifully orchestrated, served by a staff that seems to always anticipate the next question or request, making this one of the more relaxed splurges of San Francisco's gastronomic elite restaurants. **Known for:** quail egg amuse-bouche; tiny art-deco adjacent bar, Linden Room; timing adjusted for diners with tickets to a show. $ Average main: $185 ⊠ 330 Gough St., Hayes Valley ☎ 415/829–7565 ⊕ www.nightbirdrestaurant.com ⊘ Closed Sun. and Mon. No lunch.

★ Rich Table

$$$ | **MODERN AMERICAN** | Sardine chips and porcini doughnuts are popular bites at co-chef Evan and Sarah Rich's lively, creative restaurant; mains are also clever stunners, including pastas like the sea urchin cacio e pepe. The room's weathered-wood wallboards, repurposed from a Northern California sawmill, give it a homey vibe. **Known for:** tough-to-get reservations; freshly baked bread; seasonal ingredients. $ Average main: $34 ⊠ 199 Gough St., Hayes Valley ☎ 415/355–9085 ⊕ www.richtablesf.com ⊘ Closed Sun. and Mon. No lunch.

Robin

$$$$ | **SUSHI** | The classic Japanese omakase experience (the chefs select the sushi and other small bites) gets a seasonal Californian influence at Adam Tortosa's hip, modern restaurant. The raw fish preparations are magnificent, and it's a relative deal where diners can name the price between $109 and $209, depending on their desire to splurge. **Known for:** exquisite nigiri with creative garnishes; caviar–potato chip bite; strong sake and wine lists. $ Average main: $120 ⊠ 620 Gough St., Hayes Valley ☎ 415/448–7372 text only ⊕ www.robinsanfrancisco.com ⊘ Closed Mon. and Tues. No lunch.

Souvla

$ | **GREEK** | Join the lines, get ready to Instagram, and enjoy the superb Cali-Greek pita sandwiches and salads at the flagship of this fast-casual (or self-described "fast-fine") concept. The menu keeps it simple with four proteins (roasted white sweet potato or a trio of spit-roasted meats), but the secret to the magic is how each protein is pre-partnered with captivating sauces and fresh garnishes, turning a simple-sounding white sweet potato sandwich into a stellar meal. **Known for:** lamb leg with harissa-spiked yogurt; Greek frozen yogurt with baklava crumbles; prime location for picking up a picnic for Patricia's Green or Alamo Square Park. $ Average main: $16 ⊠ 517 Hayes St., Hayes Valley ☎ 415/400–5458 ⊕ www.souvla.com.

Suppenküche

$$ | **GERMAN** | Nobody goes hungry—and no beer drinker goes thirsty—at this lively, hip outpost of simple German cooking. The hearty food—bratwurst and sauerkraut, potato pancakes with house-made applesauce, meat loaf, braised beef, pork loin, schnitzel, spaetzle—is tasty and kind to your wallet, and the imported brews are first-rate. **Known for:** seating at common tables; variety of sausages; quick service. $ Average main: $26 ⊠ 525 Laguna St., Hayes Valley ☎ 415/252–9289 ⊕ www.suppenkuche.com ⊘ Closed Mon. No lunch weekdays.

★ Zuni Café

$$$ | **MODERN AMERICAN** | After one bite of Zuni's succulent brick-oven-roasted whole chicken with warm bread salad, you'll understand why the two-floor café is a perennial star. Its long copper bar is a hub for a disparate mix of patrons who commune over oysters on the half shell and cocktails and wine. **Known for:** seasonal Californian cooking at its best; under-the-radar lunch and late-night burger; beloved margarita. $ Average main: $39 ⊠ 1658 Market St., Hayes

Valley ☎ *415/552–2522* 🌐 *zunicafe.com* 🕒 *Closed Mon. and Tues.*

Coffee and Quick Bites

Blue Bottle Coffee

$ | **CAFÉ** | Hidden away on a side street by Patricia's Green is this modest kiosk where the organic beans are ground for each cup and the espresso is automatically *ristretto*—a short shot. While Blue Bottle is now a global juggernaut (the blue, boutique equivalent of the green mermaid chain, as locals like to say), Linden Street was the first brick-and-mortar shop, and it's still a San Francisco coffee lover's favorite. **Known for:** must-stop on a Hayes Valley tour; intense dedication to quality coffee; where it all started. [$] *Average main: $6* ✉ *315 Linden St., Hayes Valley* 🌐 *bluebottlecoffee.com.*

Loquat

$ | **BAKERY** | This charming bakery, done in pinks and pressed tin, features treats by Tartine Bakery alum Kristina Costa that reflect the Jewish diaspora. With tempting cakes lining the marble counter and display cases full of tarts, cookies, babka, and other pastries, you'll be hard-pressed to get away without trying more than one. **Known for:** savory bourekas, great for picnics; to-die-for cinnamon date sugar babka; long lines. [$] *Average main: $6* ✉ *198 Gough St., Hayes Valley* ☎ *415/994–6594* 🌐 *loquatsf.com* 🕒 *Closed Tues. and Wed. No dinner.*

Hotels

Hayes Valley should be called Hip Valley. Head-turning urbanites stroll past the boutiques, cafés, and high-end eateries day and night. But this wasn't always the case, and there still is a dodgy element to the streets off the main drag. Travelers can find a couple modest inns.

Inn at the Opera

$$ | **B&B/INN** | Within walking distance of Davies Symphony Hall and the War Memorial Opera House, this inn with small rooms with dark wood furnishings caters to season-ticket holders for the opera, ballet, and symphony; it's also been the choice for stars from Luciano Pavarotti to Mikhail Baryshnikov. **Pros:** staff goes the extra mile; prime location but a quiet block; good nearby dining. **Cons:** no air-conditioning; sold out far in advance during opera season; difficult parking. [$] *Rooms from: $249* ✉ *333 Fulton St., Hayes Valley* ☎ *415/863–8400* 🌐 *www.extraholidays.com/san-francisco-california/inn-at-the-opera* 🛏 *48 rooms* 🍴 *No Meals.*

★ **The Parsonage**

$$ | **B&B/INN** | The owners of this 1883 Victorian house, a historic landmark, have created a one-of-a-kind bed-and-breakfast steps from the lower Haight and Hayes Valley, with many of the original mantelpieces, fireplaces, and mirrors, as well as the ornate ceiling molding, still intact. **Pros:** handmade McRoskey mattresses; relaxed, welcoming atmosphere; superior breakfasts. **Cons:** street parking only; bygone-era feel not for everyone; two-night minimum. [$] *Rooms from: $260* ✉ *198 Haight St., Hayes Valley* ☎ *415/863–3699* 🌐 *theparsonage.com* 🛏 *5 rooms* 🍴 *Free Breakfast.*

Nightlife

Chic Hayes Valley is known for its wine and cocktail lounges with dark lighting and plenty of atmosphere, making it easy to spend a pleasant evening moving from bar to bar and having small bites.

BARS

Absinthe Brasserie & Bar

COCKTAIL LOUNGES | The popular restaurant's nearly two dozen specialty cocktails make a trip just to the bar worthwhile. The classic but modern French cuisine, California and French wines, and vintage bistro decor are terrific, too, so pair a cocktail with a few bites before or after a show. ⊠ *398 Hayes St., Hayes Valley* ☎ *415/551–1590* ⊕ *absinthe.com.*

Anina

COCKTAIL LOUNGES | This floral-and-tropics-themed bar boasts one of the prime patios in San Francisco, plus excellent, non-fussy craft cocktails. ⊠ *482 Hayes St., Hayes Valley* ⊕ *www.aninasf.com.*

Birba

WINE BARS | With a charming rear garden and an excellent selection of lesser-known European vintages, this wine bar is a local favorite for a leisurely happy hour or date night. It's a little removed from the main Hayes Valley action, so the crowd tends to be regulars, who come in frequently to try a new Greek rosé or a Touriga from Portugal. Bites are limited to mostly cheese, charcuterie, and smoked or tinned fish, but everything is beautifully composed. ⊠ *458 Grove St., Hayes Valley* ⊕ *www.birbawine.com.*

Fig & Thistle

WINE BARS | The Golden State's wines are the specialty at this relaxed, rustic-feeling bar. Natural and biodynamic wines from the greater West Coast and around the world are also poured, pairing nicely with cheese selections. Their eponymous and popular cannabis dispensary is just around the corner. ⊠ *429 Gough St., Hayes Valley* ☎ *415/651–9905* ⊕ *www.figandthistlesf.com.*

Hôtel Biron Wine Bar and Art Gallery

WINE BARS | This tiny, cave-like (in a good way) spot displays the work of local artists on its brick walls. The well-behaved twenty- to thirtysomething clientele enjoys the off-the-beaten-path quarters, the wines from around the world, the soft lighting, and the hip music. ⊠ *45 Rose St., Hayes Valley* ☎ *415/780–5366* ⊕ *hotelbironwinebar.com.*

The Mint Karaoke Lounge

THEMED ENTERTAINMENT | A mixed gay-straight crowd that's drop-dead serious about its karaoke—to the point where you'd think an *American Idol* casting

agent was in attendance—comes here seven nights a week. Do *not* walk onstage unprepared! Cash only. ⊠ *1942 Market St., Hayes Valley* ☎ *415/626–4726* ⊕ *themint.net.*

★ Smuggler's Cove

COCKTAIL LOUNGES | With the decor of a pirate ship and a slew of rum-based cocktails, you half expect Captain Jack Sparrow to sidle up next to you at this offbeat, Disney-esque hangout. But the folks at Smuggler's Cove take rum so seriously they've even had it made for them from distillers around the world, which you can sample along with more than 550 other offerings. ⊠ *650 Gough St., Hayes Valley* ☎ *415/869–1900* ⊕ *www.smugglerscovesf.com.*

🎫 Performing Arts

DANCE
RAWdance CONCEPT Series

MODERN DANCE | This modern-day salon is made for both dance aficionados and those just ballet-curious. The choreography is colorful and "outside the lines" of your usual dance troupe. In true bohemian spirit, admission is pay-what-you-can (suggested donation is $10–$30) and sometimes food is served as well. ⊠ *1446 Market St., Hayes Valley* ☎ *415/729–3959* ⊕ *rawdance.org.*

MUSIC
★ SFJAZZ Center

MUSIC | Jazz legends Branford Marsalis and Herbie Hancock have performed at the snazzy center, as have Rosanne Cash, Dianne Reeves, and world-music favorite Esperanza Spalding. The sight lines and acoustics here are impressive, as are the second-floor tile murals. ⊠ *201 Franklin St., Hayes Valley* ☎ *866/920–5299* ⊕ *www.sfjazz.org.*

🛍 Shopping

A community park called Patricia's Green breaks up a crowd of cool shops just west of Civic Center. Art galleries and stores selling hip home decor, clothing, shoes, and handcrafted jewelry predominate. The density of unique shops and the absence of chains make Hayes Valley a favorite destination for local shoppers.

BOOKS

The Green Arcade

BOOKS | For environmental, political, and sustainable books, look no further. With deep roots in the community, energetic artwork, and an atmosphere that encourages reading, this is a good place to hide away. ⊠ *1680 Market St., Hayes Valley* ☎ *415/431–6800* ⊕ *thegreenarcade.com.*

Isotope Comic Book Lounge

BOOKS | For full-frontal nerdity in a chic modern setting, visit SF's premier comic book hangout. You'll find a great selection of graphic novels and artwork by popular and local artists, as well as lively after-hours events. ⊠ *326 Fell St., Hayes Valley* ☎ *415/621–6543* ⊕ *www.isotopecomics. com* ☉ *Closed Sun. and Mon.*

FOOD AND DRINK

Arlequin Wine Merchant

WINE/SPIRITS | If you like the wine list at Absinthe Brasserie & Bar, you can walk next door and pick up a few bottles from its joint establishment. This unintimidating shop carries hard-to-find wines from small producers. Why wait to taste? Crack open a bottle on the patio of sibling restaurant Arbor out back. ⊠ *384 Hayes St., Hayes Valley* ☎ *415/863–1104* ⊕ *www.arlequinwinemerchant.com.*

Miette Patisserie & Confiserie

CANDY | There is truly nothing sweeter than a cellophane bag tied with colorful ribbon and filled with malt balls or floral meringues from this Insta-friendly candy and pastry store. Grab a gingerbread cupcake or a tantalizing macaron or some shortbread. The pastel-color cake stands make even window shopping a treat. ⊠ *449 Octavia Blvd., Hayes Valley* ☎ *415/626–6221* ⊕ *www.miette.com.*

True Sake

WINE/SPIRITS | At the first store in the United States dedicated entirely to sake, each of the many sakes is displayed with a label describing the drink's qualities, with food-pairing suggestions. ⊠ *560 Hayes St., Hayes Valley* ☎ *415/355–9555* ⊕ *www.truesake.com.*

HANDICRAFTS AND FOLK ART

F. Dorian

CRAFTS | In addition to scarves, jewelry, and other crafts from around the world, this decorative-arts store carries brightly colored glass and ceramic works by local and international artisans, plus beautiful votive candles. ⊠ *370 Hayes St., Hayes Valley* ☎ *415/861–3191.*

JEWELRY AND ACCESSORIES

Métier

JEWELRY & WATCHES | For boutique shopping that's anything but hit or miss, browse through this unusual selection of jewelry by artists like Gabriella Kiss, Harwell Godfrey, and Gillian Conroy. The one-of-a-kind rings, charms, and pendants have won this boutique a loyal following. ⊠ *575 Hayes St., Hayes Valley* ☎ *415/590–2998* ⊕ *www.metiersf.com.*

SHOES

Paolo Shoes

SHOES | This is *the* place in San Francisco to find gorgeous handcrafted Italian leather shoes. From knee-high boots to contoured heel pumps, Paolo Iantorno's selection will make your heart miss a beat. ⊠ *524 Hayes St., Hayes Valley* ☎ *415/552–4580* ⊕ *paoloshoes.com.*

Noe Valley

This upscale but relaxed enclave just south of the Castro is among the city's most desirable places to live, with laid-back cafés, kid-friendly restaurants, and

A popular photo stop, windswept Twin Peaks has expansive views of the city and nearby counties.

old-timey shops along Church Street and 24th Street. It was spared the fire that followed the 1906 earthquake and has a large number of pre-quake homes. You can also see remnants of Noe Valley's agricultural beginnings: Billy Goat Hill (at Castro and 30th Streets), a wild-grass hill often draped in fog and topped by one of the city's best rope-swinging trees, is named for the goats that grazed here right into the 20th century.

👁 Sights

Seward Street Slides

CITY PARK | FAMILY | A teenager designed these two long, concrete slides back in 1973, saving this mini park from development. Aimed at older kids and adults rather than little ones, the slides offer a fun, steep ride down, so wear sturdy pants. ⊠ *Seward Mini Park, 30 Seward St., Noe Valley* ⊕ *www.sfrecpark.org* ⊗ *Closed Mon.*

★ Twin Peaks

VIEWPOINT | Windswept and desolate, Twin Peaks yields sweeping vistas of San Francisco and the neighboring counties. At a hilltop park 922 feet above sea level, you can get a real feel for the city's layout, but you'll share it with busloads of other admirers; in summer, arrive before the late-afternoon fog turns the view into pea soup. To drive here, head west from Castro Street up Market Street, which eventually becomes Portola Drive. Turn right (north) on Twin Peaks Boulevard and follow the signs to the top. Muni bus 37–Corbett heads west to Twin Peaks from Market Street. Catch this bus above the Castro Street Muni light-rail station on the island west of Castro at Market Street. ⊠ *Twin Peaks Blvd., Noe Valley.*

🍽 Restaurants

★ La Ciccia

$$ | ITALIAN | This charming neighborhood trattoria is the only restaurant in the city exclusively serving Sardinian food. The island's classics are all

represented—octopus stew in a spicy tomato sauce; spaghetti with *bottariga* (cured roe); and macaroni with sea urchin and cured tuna heart. **Known for:** romantic patio dining; restaurant industry favorite; extensive wine list including Sardinian wines. $ *Average main: $30 ⊠ 291 30th St., Noe Valley ☎ 415/550–8114 ⊕ www. laciccia.com ⊘ Closed Sun. and Mon. No lunch.*

☕ Coffee and Quick Bites

Lovejoy's Tea Room
$$ | BRITISH | The tearoom is a homey jumble, with its lace-covered tables, couches, and mismatched chairs set among the antiques for sale. High tea and cream tea are served, along with traditional English-tearoom "fayre," such as crustless sandwiches, scones, crumpets, and shepherd's pie. **Known for:** Lovejoy's Antiques, across the street; classic English high tea; comfy-chic vibe. $ *Average main: $28 ⊠ 1351 Church St., Noe Valley ⊕ www.lovejoystearoom.com ⊘ Closed Mon.–Wed. No dinner.*

🛍 Shopping

Noe Valley is an enclave of fancy-food stores, bookshops, clothing boutiques, and specialty gift stores.

BOOKS
Omnivore Books on Food
BOOKS | Love to eat? Love to read? Then this place is paradise. The shelves are bursting with books on growing and cooking food. The store stocks cookbooks on such diverse subjects as the cuisine of colonial Jamaica or 1940s creole cooking. And if you're after a signed first edition by Julia Child or James Beard, you'll find that, too. The shop frequently hosts fun conversations with cookbook authors and chefs. ⊠ *3885 Cesar Chavez St., Noe Valley ☎ 415/282–4712 ⊕ omnivorebooks.com.*

CLOTHING
Small Frys
CHILDREN'S CLOTHING | FAMILY | The colorful cottons carried here are mainly for infants, with some articles for older children. Brands include many Californian and European labels, including Petite Lem, Kanz, and 3 Pommes. There's a sizable section of San Francisco–theme gear and books, and a few shelves of organic and eco-friendly toys as well as whimsical finger puppets round out the selection. ⊠ *3985 24th St., Noe Valley ☎ 415/648–3954 ⊕ www.smallfrys.com.*

Two Birds
WOMEN'S CLOTHING | A fresh place to find a lacy top or a soft pair of jeans, Two Birds stocks Frēda Salvador, Ulla Johnson, and Smythe. You'll also find sleek jewelry, handbags, and dresses by local designers. ⊠ *1309 Castro St., Noe Valley ☎ 415/285–1840 ⊕ www.2birds1store. com.*

HANDICRAFTS AND FOLK ART
Xela Imports
CRAFTS | Africa, Southeast Asia, Europe, and Central America are the sources for the handicrafts sold at Xela (pronounced *shay*-la). They include jewelry, masks, religious icons, and decorative wall hangings. ⊠ *3925 24th St., Noe Valley ☎ 415/695–1323 ⊕ xelaimports.com.*

Chapter 13

MISSION DISTRICT, BERNAL HEIGHTS, AND POTRERO HILL

Updated by
Trevor Felch

◉ Sights	🍴 Restaurants	🛏 Hotels	🛍 Shopping	🍸 Nightlife
★★☆☆☆	★★★★★	★☆☆☆☆	★★★☆☆	★★★★★

NEIGHBORHOOD SNAPSHOT

TOP EXPERIENCES

■ **Vivid murals:** Check out dozens of energetic, colorful public artworks in alleyways and on building exteriors.

■ **Dolores Park:** Join Mission locals and their dogs on this hilly expanse of green that has a glorious view of downtown and, if you're lucky, the Bay Bridge. On sunny days, the whole neighborhood comes out to play.

■ **Phenomenal global food:** Keen appetites and thin wallets will meet their match here. Decide between deliciously fresh burritos, garlicky falafel, thin-crust pizza, savory samosas, and more.

■ **Barhopping:** Embrace your inner hipster: grab a cocktail at Trick Dog, whose mixologists serve some of the Mission's finest drinks, then peruse the small and mighty menu at the retro-chic Beehive or stop by Elixir, where San Francisco history meets craft cocktails.

■ **One-of-a-kind shopping:** From trendy clothing to pirate supplies (it's true), the Mission is one of the city's prime shopping neighborhoods, especially on perennially hip Valencia Street.

PLANNING YOUR TIME

A walk that includes Mission Dolores and the neighborhood's murals takes about two hours. If you plan to go on a mural tour with the Precita Eyes organization, or if you're a window-shopper, add at least another hour. The Mission is a neighborhood that sleeps in. In the afternoon and evening, the main drags—Mission, Valencia, and 24th Streets—really come to life.

From Sunday through Tuesday, it's relatively quiet here, especially in the evening—a great time to get a café table with no wait. Dogpatch is liveliest during the week, midday to evening, when businesses are hopping. On weekends, this neighborhood relaxes at home.

GETTING HERE

■ The Mission is welcomingly flat, and BART's two Mission District stations drop you in the heart of the action. Get off at 16th Street for Mission Dolores and the shopping, nightlife, and restaurants of the Valencia Corridor or 24th Street to see the neighborhood murals and the increasingly trendy Calle 24 district. Parking is difficult, so take a taxi or rideshare. Bernal Heights and Potrero Hill have slightly easier parking situations (though prepare for steep street-parking angles) and are connected to the Mission by Muni bus lines.

VIEWFINDER

■ Visitors often wish for a gondola or chair lift to the top of Bernal Heights Park. However, the reward for the short and steep hike is the rare San Francisco viewpoint that is striking in every direction for miles (usually there's another nearby hill blocking some direction). And, unlike its peers such as Twin Peaks and Dolores Park, the park is still rarely, if ever crowded—and almost entirely locals out for a workout or dog walk. It's the perfect downtown skyline photo vantage point and gives a terrific overview of the city and general Bay Area's unique layout.

The Mission has a number of distinct personalities: it's a Latino neighborhood where working-class folks raise families; it's a hipster hood where the tattooed and pierced hold court; it's a culinary epicenter, with destination restaurants and affordable global cuisines; it's the face of gentrification, where tech money prices out longtime renters; and it's an artists' quarter, where murals adorn walls long after their creators have moved to cheaper digs.

It's also the city's equivalent of the Sunshine State—this neighborhood's always one of the last to succumb to fog.

While the Mission is diverse and lively, Bernal Heights and Potrero Hill are decidedly subdued in comparison, almost like pleasant suburban neighborhoods in an urban setting. As the names suggest, both areas feature a signature steep hill with sweeping views. And, both areas have a charming central business street (Cortland Avenue for Bernal and 18th Street for Potrero) that feels as cute and quaint Main Street USA as you'll find anywhere in San Francisco.

Mission District

Packed with destination restaurants, hole-in-the-wall eateries representing dozens of cuisines, and hip watering holes—plus taquerias, *pupuserías* (places selling thick, filled tortillas), and produce markets—one of the city's hottest hoods strikes an increasingly precarious balance between cutting-edge hot spot and working-class enclave. With longtime businesses being forced out by astronomical rents and city agencies coming together with community groups to create an action plan to reverse gentrification in the neighborhood, the Mission is in flux once again.

The eight blocks of Valencia Street between 16th and 24th Streets—what's become known as the Valencia Corridor—typify the Mission District's diversity. Businesses on the block between 16th and 17th Streets, for instance, include a bustling Peruvian restaurant, funky home-decor stores, a hip cocktail destination, a sushi bar, an upscale matcha-focused café, and bargain and pricey thrift shops. As prices rise, this strip has lost some of its edge as even international publications proclaim its hipness. At the same time, nearby Mission

Street is slowly morphing from a row of check-cashing parlors, dollar stores, and residential hotels into overflow for the Valencia Corridor's restaurant explosion. Meanwhile, 24th Street has become the Calle 24 Latino Cultural District in an attempt to protect the mostly Latino-owned businesses that have served this thriving neighborhood for decades.

Italian and Irish in the early 20th century, the Mission became heavily Latino in the late 1960s, when immigrants from Mexico and Central America began arriving. Since the 1970s, groups of muralists have transformed walls and storefronts into canvases, creating art accessible to everyone. Following the example set by the Mexican artist and muralist Diego Rivera, many artists address political and social justice issues in their murals.

The conversations you'll hear on the street these days might unfold in Chinese, Vietnamese, Arabic, and other tongues of the immigrants who began settling in the Mission in the 1980s and 1990s along with a young bohemian crowd enticed by cheap rents and the burgeoning arts-and-nightlife scene. These newer arrivals made a diverse and lively neighborhood even more so, setting the stage for the Mission's current hipster cachet. With the neighborhood flourishing, rents have gone through the roof, but the Mission remains scruffy in patches, so as you plan your explorations, take into account your comfort zone.

⚠ **Be prepared for homelessness and drug use around the BART stations, prostitution along Capp Street, and raucous barhoppers along the Valencia Corridor.**

Tours

Avital Tours
FOOD AND DRINK TOURS | The sheer volume of tempting culinary choices in the Mission District can be overwhelming. For food-focused visitors, there's no better tour in the city than joining the insightful guides of this boutique company. Each walk-eat-repeat experience is a delicious, educational few hours mixing a few dining stops with sights (like the Mission murals and Dolores Park) and history lessons. Tours are held each Sunday at 11 am and start at various places within three blocks of the 16th Street BART station. (A similar North Beach tour is offered as well.) ✉ *2000 Mission St., Mission District* ☎ *415/355–4044* ⊕ *avital-tours.com* ✒ *From $99.*

⊙ Sights

Balmy Alley
PUBLIC ART | Mission District artists have transformed the walls of their neighborhood with paintings, and Balmy Alley is one of the best-executed examples. Many murals adorn the one-block alley, with newer ones continually filling in the blank spaces. In 1971, artists began teaming with local children to create a space to promote peace in Central America, community spirit, and (later) AIDS awareness; since then dozens of muralists have added their vibrant works. The alley's longtime popularity has grown exponentially thanks to its Instagram appeal. Once you're done at Balmy Alley, head a couple blocks west on 24th Street to another prominent alley of murals on Cypress Street (also between 24th and 25th Streets). ⚠ **Be alert here: the 25th Street end of the alley adjoins a somewhat dangerous area.** ✉ *24th St. between and parallel to Harrison and Treat Sts., alley runs south to 25th St., Mission District* ⊕ *balmyalley.org.*

Clarion Alley
PUBLIC ART | Inspired by the work in Balmy Alley, a new generation of muralists began creating a fresh alley-cum-gallery here in 1992, offering a quick but dense glimpse at the Mission's contemporary art scene. The works by the loosely connected artists of the Clarion Alley Mural Project (CAMP) represent a broad range

Did You Know?

San Francisco is chockablock with murals—around 2,000—and the Mission District is the epicenter of all the artistic fervor.

The Mission District, Bernal Heights, and Potrero Hill

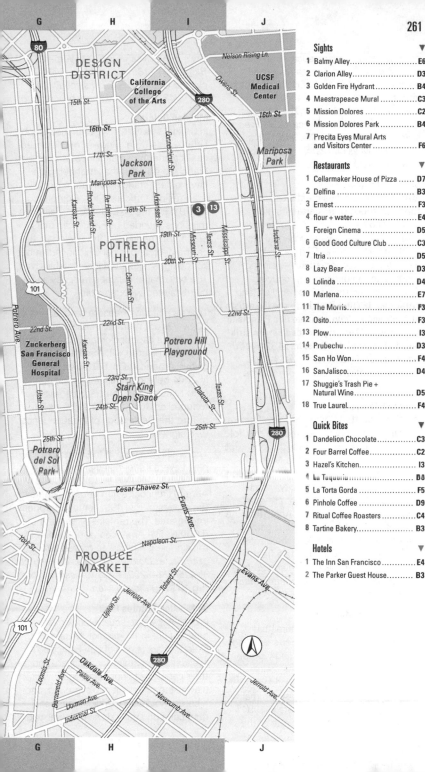

Sights ▼

1	Balmy Alley	E6
2	Clarion Alley	D3
3	Golden Fire Hydrant	B4
4	Maestrapeace Mural	C3
5	Mission Dolores	C2
6	Mission Dolores Park	B4
7	Precita Eyes Mural Arts and Visitors Center	F6

Restaurants ▼

1	Cellarmaker House of Pizza	D7
2	Delfina	B3
3	Ernest	F3
4	flour + water	E4
5	Foreign Cinema	D5
6	Good Good Culture Club	C3
7	Itria	D5
8	Lazy Bear	D3
9	Lolinda	D4
10	Marlena	E7
11	The Morris	F3
12	Osito	F3
13	Plow	I3
14	Prubechu	D3
15	San Ho Won	F4
16	SanJalisco	D4
17	Shuggie's Trash Pie + Natural Wine	D5
18	True Laurel	F4

Quick Bites ▼

1	Dandelion Chocolate	C3
2	Four Barrel Coffee	C2
3	Hazel's Kitchen	I3
4	La Taqueria	D6
5	La Torta Gorda	F5
6	Pinhole Coffee	D9
7	Ritual Coffee Roasters	C4
8	Tartine Bakery	B3

Hotels ▼

1	The Inn San Francisco	E4
2	The Parker Guest House	B3

of styles and imagery, such as an exuberant, flowery exhortation to Tax the Rich, several colorful and powerful messages about hot-button political topics, and poignant murals honoring the legacies of George Floyd and Prince. ⊠ *Between Valencia and Mission Sts. and 17th and 18th Sts., Mission District* ⊕ *www.clarionalleymuralproject.org.*

Creativity Explored

ARTS CENTER | Joyous creativity pervades the workshops of this art-education center and gallery for developmentally disabled adults. Several dozen adults work at the center each day—guided by a staff of working artists—painting, working in the darkroom, producing videos, and crafting prints, textiles, and ceramics. ■ TIP→ **Drop by to see the artists at work and pick up a unique San Francisco masterpiece. The art produced here is striking, and some of it is for sale.** ⊠ *3245 16th St., Mission District* ☎ *415/863–2108* ⊕ *www.creativityexplored.org* ⌷ *Free* ☉ *Closed Sun.–Wed.*

Golden Fire Hydrant

OTHER ATTRACTION | When all the other fire hydrants went dry during the fire that followed the 1906 earthquake, this one kept pumping. Noe Valley and the Mission District were thus spared the devastation wrought elsewhere in the city, which explains the large number of pre-quake homes here. Every year on April 18th (the anniversary of the quake), folks gather here to share stories about the disaster, and the famous hydrant gets a fresh coat of gold paint. ⊠ *Church and 20th Sts., southeastern corner of intersection, across from Dolores Park, Mission.*

Maestrapeace Mural

PUBLIC ART | The towering mural that seems to enclose the Women's Building, a community space supporting women and community organizations, celebrates women around the world who work for peace. Created by seven main artists and almost 100 helpers in 1994, this five-story-tall artwork is one of the city's don't-miss murals. ⊠ *Women's Bldg., 3543 18th St., between Valencia and Guerrero Sts., Mission District* ☎ *415/431–1180* ⊕ *womensbuilding.org.*

Mission Dolores

RELIGIOUS BUILDING | Two churches stand side by side here: a newer multi-domed basilica and the small adobe Mission San Francisco de Asís, the latter being the city's oldest standing structure along with the Presidio Officers' Club. Completed in 1791, it's the sixth of the 21 California missions founded by Franciscan friars in the 18th and early 19th centuries. Its ceiling depicts original Ohlone Indian basket designs, executed in vegetable dyes. The tiny chapel includes frescoes and a hand-painted wooden altar.

There's a hidden treasure here: a 20-by-22-foot mural with images including a dagger-pierced Sacred Heart of Jesus, painted with natural dyes by Native Americans in 1791, was found in 2004 behind the altar. Interesting fact: Mission San Francisco de Asís was founded on June 29, 1776, five days before the Declaration of Independence was signed.

The small museum in the mission complex covers its founding and history, and the pretty cemetery—which appears in Alfred Hitchcock's film *Vertigo*—contains the graves of mid-19th-century European immigrants. The remains of an estimated 5,000 Native Americans who died at the mission lie in unmarked graves. ⊠ *3321 16th St., at Dolores St., Mission District* ☎ *415/621–8203* ⊕ *www.missiondolores.org* ⌷ *$7* ☉ *Closed Mon.*

★ Mission Dolores Park

CITY PARK | A two-square-block microcosm of life in the district, Mission Dolores Park is one of San Francisco's liveliest green spaces: dog lovers and their pampered pups congregate, kids play at the extravagant playground, and hipsters hold court, drinking beer and rosé cans on sunny days. (Fair warning:

Lively Dolores Park in the Mission is popular for its playground, special events, and city views.

if it's over 70°F, the place can get packed like traffic at rush hour for picnic-blanket space.) During the summer, Dolores Park hosts movie nights, performances by the San Francisco Mime Troupe, and pop-up events and impromptu parties. Spend a warm day here—maybe sitting at the top of the park with a view of the city and the Bay Bridge—surrounded by locals and that laid-back, still-abundant San Francisco energy, and you may well find yourself plotting your move to the city. The best views are in the southwest corner, near the historic golden fire hydrant that saved the neighborhood after the 1906 earthquake. ⊠ *Between 18th and 20th Sts. and Dolores and Church Sts., Mission District* ⊕ *sfrecpark.org.*

Precita Eyes Mural Arts and Visitors Center
ARTS CENTER | The muralists of this nonprofit design and create murals and lead guided walks. Tours are given on most Saturdays and cover several murals throughout the neighborhood, along with providing insightful historical context to the outdoor art. You can pick up a map

of 24th Street's murals at the center and buy art supplies, books, T-shirts, postcards, and other mural-related items. ⊠ *2981 24th St., Mission District* ☎ *415/285–2287* ⊕ *www.precitaeyes.org* 🎫 *Center free, tours $20* 🕐 *Closed Sun.*

🍴 Restaurants

You'll never go hungry here, in San Francisco's most jam-packed restaurant neighborhood. From bargain taquerias to hip *izakayas* (a kind of Japanese bar serving small plates and snacks with the drinks), city dwellers know this sector as the go-to area for a great meal. The Valencia Street corridor has been particularly hot, opening new restaurants at a breakneck pace, with many locals declaring it the best food neighborhood in the city.

★ Delfina
$$ | **ITALIAN** | Crowds are a constant fixture at Craig and Annie Stoll's cultishly adored northern Italian spot. Deceptively simple, exquisitely flavored dishes include excellent pastas and the city's

Mission Festivals

Cinco de Mayo is an important event in the Mission: music, dance, and many parties commemorate the victory, on May 5, 1862, of Mexicans over French troops who had invaded their country.

On Memorial Day weekend the revelers come out in earnest, when Carnaval transforms the neighborhood into a northern Rio de Janeiro for two days. Festivities close down several blocks (usually of Harrison Street), where musicians and dancers perform and crafts and food booths are set up. The Grand Carnaval Parade, along 24th, Mission, and 17th Streets, caps the celebration.

Each fall, a festival of the altars for Día de los Muertos (Day of the Dead) is held at the southeastern edge of the Mission at Potrero del Sol Park, followed by a procession around the Mission starting from Bryant and 22nd Streets.

greatest panna cotta. **Known for:** signature spaghetti with plum tomatoes; hard to get reservations; Monterey Bay calamari with white bean salad. $ *Average main: $28* ⊠ *3621 18th St., Mission District* ☎ *415/552–4055* ⊕ *www.delfinasf.com* ⊗ *Closed Tues. No lunch.*

Ernest

$$$ | **CONTEMPORARY** | After several years as the chef de cuisine at Rich Table, Brandon Rice set off on his own with this creative restaurant, and it's been wildly successful. Rice's cooking emphasizes local ingredients and is inspired by many cuisines, yet always has a few curveballs involved, like pork tonkotsu inspired by Nashville hot chicken and sushi rice topped with salmon roe and raw beef. **Known for:** caviar and homemade tater tots; "let the kitchen cook for you" menu; "magic shell" soft-serve sundae. $ *Average main: $35* ⊠ *1890 Bryant St., Suite 100, Mission District* ☎ *829–2961* ⊕ *ernestsf.com* ⊗ *Closed Mon. and Tues. No lunch.*

★ flour + water

$$ | **MODERN ITALIAN** | This handsome and boisterous hot spot with a tiny bar and a sleek yet rustic dining room is synonymous with pasta. The grand experience here is the seven-course pasta-tasting menu (extra charge for wine pairings) with seasonally changing dishes (the one standby is a meatless Taleggio scarpinocc with aged balsamic drizzled over the bow tie–shaped pasta). **Known for:** difficult-to-get reservations; rarely seen pasta shapes; Italian wines from small producers. $ *Average main: $28* ⊠ *2401 Harrison St., Mission District* ☎ *415/826–7000* ⊕ *www.flourandwater. com* ⊗ *No lunch.*

Foreign Cinema

$$$ | **MODERN AMERICAN** | Classic films are projected on the wall of a large inner courtyard in this hip, loftlike space while you're served stellar seasonal California cooking, and weekend brunch brings throngs fighting for a spot on the patio for some of the city's best egg dishes and Bloody Marys. The majestic atmosphere enhances plates of perfectly shucked oysters on the half shell and sesame fried chicken. **Known for:** warm brandade appetizer; excellent cocktails at the restaurant and adjacent Laszlo Bar; pop tarts and croque madame at brunch. $ *Average main: $35* ⊠ *2534 Mission St., Mission District* ☎ *415/648–7600* ⊕ *www.foreigncinema.com* ⊗ *No lunch weekdays.*

Good Good Culture Club

$$ | ASIAN FUSION | The Liholiho Yacht Club team opened this concept driven by diversity, equality, and inclusion that emphasizes healthy working conditions and fair wages in an industry that unfortunately isn't known for either. The AAPI heritage–inspired menu is divided between starters like a chicken wing stuffed with egg roll filling, and larger courses meant for sharing. **Known for:** pandan bibingka, a steamed rice dessert; beautiful upstairs patio; smoked beef belly steam bun. $ *Average main: $28 ✉ 3560 18th St., Mission District ⊕ goodgoodcultureclub.com ⊗ Closed Sun. and Mon. No lunch.*

Itria

$$ | MODERN ITALIAN | A former chef from the Mission District's acclaimed Al's Place (which sadly closed in 2022) is the culinary talent at this fantastic, dimly lit oasis near the hectic 24th St.-Mission BART station. The menu's focus is on two trendy Italian cuisine items—pasta and fish crudo—that might be hip clichés now, but this kitchen does them as well as anyone in town and always with a unique spin. **Known for:** incredible rosemary focaccia with garlic-anchovy oil; spaghetti with shellfish ragu; a unique tiramisu interpretation. $ *Average main: $26 ✉ 3266 24th St., Mission District ☎ 874–9821 ⊕ itriasf.com ⊗ Closed Mon. and Tues. No lunch.*

★ Lazy Bear

$$$$ | MODERN AMERICAN | There's no end to the buzz around chef David Barzelay's 12-plus-course prix-fixe seasonal and imagination-driven dinners, which might include guinea hen with English peas and morel mushrooms or delicate "sandwiches" of Wagyu 'nduja pimento cheese and fried green heirloom tomatoes. An ode to the Western lodge, the high-ceilinged, spacious dining room includes a fireplace, charred wood walls, and wooden rafters. **Known for:** freshly baked rolls with butter cultured in-house; sensational friendly yet formal service; stellar beverage program. $ *Average main: $275 ✉ 3416 19th St., Mission District ☎ 415/874–9921 ⊕ www.lazybearsf. com ⊗ Closed Sun. and Mon. No lunch.*

Lolinda

$$ | ARGENTINE | Argentine fare, a convivial atmosphere, and talented bartenders help explain the long-running appeal of this contemporary steak house in a sceney two-level space with two bars and a rooftop neighbor (El Techo) that offers captivating views—it's no surprise that the crowd sometimes swings young and noisy. While beef is deservedly the headliner, make sure not to miss the chicken empanadas, with flaky pastry and a slight sweetness. **Known for:** wood-fire-grilled meats; lines on Mission Street for El Techo; an epic burger on the bar menu. $ *Average main: $25 ✉ 2518 Mission St., Mission District ☎ 415/550–6970 ⊕ www.lolindasf.com ⊗ Closed Mon. No lunch.*

The Morris

$$$ | MODERN AMERICAN | The eastern Mission's seasonal Californian charmer is a delightful stop for a concise menu of "won't ever leave the menu" dishes, plus a few always-changing farmers' market–driven creations. Owner Paul Einbund is one of the city's top sommeliers, so, on cue, the wine list is particularly impressive, and so is the industrial yet cheery dining room and impressive parklet. **Known for:** signature smoked duck; Chartreuse and Madeira collection; buckwheat doughnuts. $ *Average main: $36 ✉ 2501 Mariposa St., Mission District ☎ 415/612–8480 ⊕ themorris-sf.com ⊗ Closed Sun. No lunch.*

Osito

$$$$ | MODERN AMERICAN | In an immaculate setting boasting a long communal table, firewood as decor, and an enormous open kitchen, chef-owner Seth Stowaway's complex and invigorating tasting menus change their concept every few weeks. However, the firewood is a hint at the overarching theme of every experience: live-fire cooking incorporated into every dish. **Known for:** great cocktails and more casual, still live-fire driven bites at adjacent bar, Liliana; unique fine dining concept; friendly, impeccable service. $ *Average main: $250* ⊠ *2875 18th St., Mission District* ☎ *817–1585* ⊕ *ositosf.co* ⊘ *Closed Sun. and Mon. No lunch.*

Prubechu

$$ | SOUTH PACIFIC | San Francisco's only Guam-inspired restaurant is always an outdoor party with a South Pacific evoking, picnic table–filled patio in an old parking lot. The extensive, contemporary Guam-Californian menu can be a little overwhelming but is always satisfying. **Known for:** "fiesta table" shared tasting menu; dry-spiced fried chicken wings; interesting natural wines. $ *Average main: $30* ⊠ *2224 Mission St., Mission District* ☎ *853–0671* ⊕ *prubechu.com* ⊘ *Closed Mon. and Tues. No dinner Sun.*

San Ho Won

$$$$ | KOREAN | A lychee wood charcoal grill in the open kitchen is the star of this excellent contemporary Korean dining destination. Most of the menu is similar to its Korean barbecue peers but given a little twist—homemade *soondae* (blood sausage) adorns green-onion pancakes and unique *banchan* (pickled items) like jellyfish and hot mustard. **Known for:** savory egg soufflé; barbecue galbi short rib; soju selection. $ *Average main: $42* ⊠ *2170 Bryant St., Mission District* ☎ *868–4479* ⊕ *sanhowon.com* ⊘ *Closed Mon. and Tues. No lunch.*

SanJalisco

$ | MEXICAN | FAMILY | This sun-filled, family-run restaurant has been a neighborhood favorite since 1988, and not only because it serves breakfast all day—though the hearty chilaquiles always hits the spot. On weekends, regulars opt for *birria*, a spicy barbecued goat stew, or *menudo*, a tongue-searing soup made from beef tripe, complemented by

beer and sangria. **Known for:** chilaquiles; soups change based on day of the week; friendly service. $ *Average main: $16* ⊠ *901 S. Van Ness Ave., Mission District* ☎ *415/648–8383* ⊕ *www.sanjaliscorestaurant.com.*

Shuggie's Trash Pie + Natural Wine

$$ | PIZZA | It's never pleasant to think about food waste, but it's an unfortunate reality in our world today—there is an enormous amount of perfectly fine food thrown away. This colorful, quirky, purposefully over the top restaurant embraces the concept of food waste as a key centerpiece of a pizza-centric menu (the crust is made of discarded whey and oat flour). **Known for:** funky but delightful wines; "Sausage Party" pizza with grape must; chairs made of giant Hulk-like green hands. $ *Average main: $24* ⊠ *3349 23rd St., Mission District* ☎ *655–3051* ⊕ *shuggiespizza.com* ⊘ *No lunch.*

★ True Laurel

$ | MODERN AMERICAN | Hardly just a plan B for those who didn't score a table at its sibling, Lazy Bear, this excellent cocktail bar and creative small-plates restaurant by the same people offers intriguing combinations and endless conversation starters in a cool modern setting. Menu standouts include California halibut ceviche and fried hen-of-the-woods mushrooms. **Known for:** patty melt; inventive cocktails using seasonal produce; excellent weekend brunch. $ *Average main: $18* ⊠ *753 Alabama St., Mission District* ☎ *415/341–0020* ⊕ *www.truelaurelsf.com* ⊘ *Closed Mon. No lunch weekdays.*

☕ Coffee and Quick Bites

Dandelion Chocolate

$ | DESSERTS | FAMILY | San Francisco's real life Willy Wonka factory is the fascinating and delicious home of this "bean to bar" chocolatier. Of course, chocolate in many forms is the highlight for guests, whether it's in pure chocolate bars, in drinks, or as a subtle ingredient in some of the city's most inventive pastries. **Known for:** made-to-order s'mores; outrageously great hot chocolate; chocolate canelé pastries. $ *Average main: $6* ✉ *2600 16th St., Mission District* ☎ *349–0942* ⊕ *dandelionchocolate.com* ⊘ *No dinner.*

Four Barrel Coffee

$ | **CAFÉ** | Coffee aficionados should head down Valencia Street to Four Barrel Coffee for excellent house-roasted coffee in a fun and funky space, packed with Mission hipsters, cyclists, and artists (be sure to look at the selection of Mission counterpart Dynamo doughnuts as well). **Known for:** locally owned business; fun space; high-quality roasting. $ *Average main: $5* ✉ *375 Valencia St, Mission District* ⊕ *www.fourbarrelcoffee.com.*

La Taqueria

$ | **MEXICAN** | The most well-known—and quite possibly the best—of the burrito choices around town forgoes rice in the filling (almost all burritos in the Mission include rice) to focus on tender meats. The carne asada is the house favorite, but you can't go wrong with the carnitas either. **Known for:** long lines; off menu crispy "dorado-style" burrito; outstanding salsas. $ *Average main: $13* ✉ *2889 Mission St., Mission District* ☎ *285–7117* ⊘ *Closed Mon. and Tues.*

La Torta Gorda

$ | **MEXICAN** | Enormous tortas (Mexican sandwiches with meat, avocado, queso fresco, and refried beans on a soft-interior/crunchy-exterior roll) are a culinary specialty of the state of Puebla in Mexico, and they're also the signature item of this Mission District daytime favorite. The tortas come in two sizes (you likely only need the smaller one). **Known for:** wonderful quesadillas; Mega Cubana torta with several kinds of meat; pleasant outdoor patio. $ *Average main: $14* ✉ *2833 24th St., Mission District* ☎ *642–9600* ⊕ *latortagorda.com* ⊘ *No dinner.*

Ritual Coffee Roasters

$ | **CAFÉ** | In the Mission District, the owners of the popular Ritual Coffee Roasters have plunked their roaster in the back of the café, so you know where your beans—usually single-origin, rather than a blend—were roasted when you order your espresso or drip coffee. **Known for:** seasonal espresso blends; small-batch roasting; independent, woman-owned business. $ *Average main: $5* ✉ *1026 Valencia St., Mission District* ⊕ *ritualcoffee.com.*

★ Tartine Bakery

$ | **BAKERY** | **FAMILY** | Chad Robertson is America's first modern cult baker, and this tiny Mission District outpost (along with the larger Tartine Manufactory on the eastern side of the neighborhood) is where you'll find his famed loaves of tangy country bread and beloved pastries like croissants and morning buns. You'll also find near-constant lines out the door; they're longest in the morning when locals (and plenty of tourists) need a pastry punch to start the day, and later in the afternoon when the famed loaves emerge freshly baked. **Known for:** anything bread-related; chocolate soufflé cake; fresh pastries. $ *Average main: $16* ✉ *600 Guerrero St., Mission District* ☎ *415/487–2600* ⊕ *tartinebakery.com* ⊘ *No dinner.*

Hotels

The vibrant Mission has slim choices in the hotel department, but travelers can find vacation rentals as well as under-the-radar B&Bs. The Mission is iffy for wandering around late at night.

The Inn San Francisco

$$ | **B&B/INN** | For decades this Italianate Victorian mansion decked out in ornate poster beds, opulent area rugs, and precious Victorian artifacts has welcomed visitors to the Mission District. **Pros:** charming antiques; garden and sundeck; oozes charm. **Cons:** neighborhood can

be sketchy at night; old-fashioned decor; a couple rooms lack a private bath. [$] *Rooms from: $205* ✉ *943 S. Van Ness Ave., Mission District* ☎ *415/641–0188, 800/359–0913 reservations only* 🌐 *www.innsf.com* 🛏 *21 rooms* 🍴 *Free Breakfast.*

★ The Parker Guest House

$$ | **B&B/INN** | Two yellow 1909 Edwardian houses enchant travelers wanting an authentic San Francisco experience; dark hallways and steep staircases lead to bright, earth-toned rooms with tiled baths (most with tubs), comfortable sitting areas, and cozy linens. **Pros:** handsomely designed, affordable rooms; close to the Castro and Dolores Park; evening wine social hour. **Cons:** long walk or short car ride from the main Mission nightlife; economy rooms have private baths in a hallway; standard rooms are a little tight. [$] *Rooms from: $209* ✉ *520 Church St., Mission District* ☎ *415/621–3222* 🌐 *www.parkerguesthouse.com* 🛏 *19 rooms* 🍴 *Free Breakfast.*

Nightlife

Once a vibrant mix of Latino street culture and twentysomething dot-com action, the Mission is defined these days by its hipster crowd. This neighborhood rarely sleeps.

BARS

ABV

BARS | One of the city's top cocktail bars offers elevated small plates (the burger has a devoted following) late into the night to pair with the excellent cocktail menu, which includes such favorites as a Mumbai Mule with saffron vodka. A knowledgeable and friendly staff serves a diverse, energetic crowd in a smart modern setting. ✉ *3174 16th St., Mission District* ☎ *415/294–1871* 🌐 *www.abvsf.com.*

The Beehive

COCKTAIL LOUNGES | The groovy 1960s are the inspiration for the gorgeous setting of this cocktail destination with a busy bar up front and a more relaxed, lounge-style atmosphere in the back. However, the cocktails are straight-up modern excellence, always mixing a superb balance of high-quality spirits and homemade ingredients. The glassware and garnishes are gorgeous. ✉ *842 Valencia St., Mission District* ☎ *415/306–8209* 🌐 *www.thebeehivesf.com* 🕒 *Closed Mon.*

★ Elixir

BARS | The cocktails are well crafted and affordable at the city's second-oldest saloon location—various watering holes have operated on this site since 1858. It's San Francisco's best example of a vintage neighborhood favorite with the finest elements of a modern, ingredient-focused cocktail bar. Cocktail geeks and sports fans mingle in the same room. Don't miss the holiday cocktails in December. ✉ *3200 16th St., Mission District* ☎ *415/552–1633* 🌐 *www.elixirsf.com.*

El Rio

BARS | A dive bar in the best sense, El Rio has a calendar chock-full of events, from free bands and films to Salsa Sunday (every fourth Sunday), all of which keep Mission kids coming back. No matter what day you attend, expect to find a diverse gay and straight crowd enjoying local beers and margaritas. When the weather's warm, the large patio out back is especially popular, and the midday dance parties are the place to be. ✉ *3158 Mission St., Mission District* ☎ *415/282–3325* 🌐 *www.elriosf.com* 🕒 *Closed Mon. and Tues.*

Lone Palm

BARS | In a sea of hip craft cocktail bars, this slightly off-the-beaten-path neighborhood icon (you can't miss the namesake palm tree outside) is a refreshing throw-back. There is no cocktail menu; this is a place for martinis, Negronis, and other classic cocktails. This is the rare locals' joint that feels both divey and strangely refined—tables have white tablecloths and the soundtrack tends to be cheery '80's pop. ⊠ 3394 22nd St., Mission District ☎ 648–0109.

The Monk's Kettle

PUBS | Choosing the city's "best beer bar" is an impossible task, but there is no doubt that this intimate, friendly des-tination is one of them. The tap list cap-tivates the most ardent beer geeks, the bottle list is as deep as many fine-dining restaurants' wine lists, and the gastropub cuisine is particularly impressive. ⊠ 3141 16th St., Mission District ☎ 415/865–9523 ⊕ monkskettle.com.

Rite Spot Cafe

CAFÉS | A Mission tradition, this classy and casual charmer is like a cabaret club in an aging mobster's garage—it's almost hard to believe you're in 2020s San Francisco. Quirky lounge singers and other musicians entertain most nights. A small menu of affordable sandwiches and Italian food beats your average bar fare. ⊠ 2000 Folsom St., Mission District ☎ 415/552–6066 ⊕ www.ritespotcafe.net ⊗ Closed Sun. and Mon.

★ Trick Dog

BARS | At San Francisco's most talked about (and arguably most innovative) craft cocktail bar, every drink has at least one "huh?" ingredient. But no worries, you're in the hands of some of the most capable bartenders that you'll ever have the honor of enjoying a drink from. It gets very crowded, both for the drinks and for the outstanding hot dog–shaped burger and beloved kale salad. ⊠ 3010 20th St., Mission District ☎ 415/471–2999 ⊕ www.trickdogbar.com.

★ Zeitgeist

BEER GARDENS | It's a dive but one of the city's best beer bars—there are almost 50 on tap—and a great place to relax with a cold one or an ever-popular Bloody Mary in the large "garden" (there's not much greenery) on a sunny day. Burgers and brats are available, and if you own a trucker hat, a pair of Vans, and a Pabst Blue Ribbon T-shirt, you'll fit right in. ⊠ 199 Valencia St., Mission District ☎ 415/255–7505 ⊕ www.zeitgeistsf.com.

BREWPUBS

Fort Point Valencia

BREWPUBS | Most San Francisco brew-ery taprooms are lacking in decor since they're usually just part of a warehouse-like brewing complex. That isn't the case with this sleek, beauti-fully designed bar-restaurant serving approachable, fun beers from a brewery next to Crissy Field. This is also the rare San Francisco brewery with a notable food menu. Here, San Francisco's deep seafood history is featured, led by the terrific Dungeness crab roll, and nicely accompanies the IPAs and KSA Kölsch. ⊠ 742 Valencia St., Mission District ☎ 415/361–7001 ⊕ fortpointbeer.com.

LGBTQ+ NIGHTLIFE

Martuni's

PIANO BARS | A mixed crowd enjoys cocktails in the semi-refined environment of this piano bar where the Castro, the Mission, and Hayes Valley intersect; variations on the martini and different fruit-flavored lemon drops are a special-ty. This is not the place for innovative mixology. In the intimate back room a pianist plays nightly, and patrons take turns boisterously singing show tunes. Martuni's often gets busy after sympho-ny and opera performances—Davies Hall and the Opera House are both within walking distance. ⊠ 4 Valencia St., Mis-sion District ☎ 415/241–0205.

THEMED ENTERTAINMENT
Urban Putt

THEMED ENTERTAINMENT | It's kid-friendly during the day, but this 14-hole indoor miniature golf course really lights up at night when you can enjoy a quality cocktail or beer and putt through the Transamerica Pyramid and those famous Painted Ladies. It's one of the city's favorite spots for a first or second date. ⊠ *1096 S. Van Ness Ave., Mission District* ☎ *415/341–1080* ⊕ *www.urbanputt.com* ⊗ *Closed Mon.*

Performing Arts

Joe Goode Performance Group

MODERN DANCE | Physicality and high-flying style are the hallmarks of this original group, a blend of modern dance and theater. Works include narrative, video projections, and song, and they succeed at being both poignant and funny. ⊠ *401 Alabama St., Mission* ☎ *415/561–6565* ⊕ *www.joegoode.org.*

Shopping

The aesthetic of the hipsters and artist types who reside in the Mission contributes to the individuality of shopping here. These night owls keep the city's best thrift stores, vintage-furniture shops, alternative bookstores, and small clothing boutiques afloat. As the Mission gentrifies, though, bargain hunters find themselves trekking farther afield in search of truly local flavor.

BOOKS
Dog-Eared Books

BOOKS | An eclectic group of shoppers wanders the aisles of this pleasantly ramshackle bookstore. The diverse stock is mostly used and unique, including quirky selections like local zines, vintage children's books, and remaindered art books. There are also paintings from local artists on sale. ⊠ *900 Valencia St.,* *Mission District* ☎ *415/282–1901* ⊕ *www. dogearedbooks.com.*

CLOTHING
Lemon Twist

WOMEN'S CLOTHING | Danette Scheib's smart, sharp designs make this one of SF's leading of-the-moment clothing boutiques. Caftans, wrap dresses, and leisure suit jackets are both comfortable and savvy enough for a night out or a business meeting. ⊠ *3418 25th St., Mission District* ☎ *415/297–2423* ⊕ *www. lemontwist.net.*

FOOD AND DRINK
★ Bi-Rite Market

FOOD | San Francisco is one of the culinary centers of the world, and this universally adored grocery store is its beating heart. It's a farmers' market every day inside and well worth browsing around to see the bounty of Northern California, from peak summer tomatoes to local king salmon, plus all kinds of goodies from small producers. Buy a local peach or blood orange to snack on before strolling across the street for a scoop of salted caramel ice cream from Bi-Rite's equally beloved creamery. ⊠ *3639 18th St., Mission District* ☎ *415/241–9760* ⊕ *birite-market.com.*

HOUSEWARES AND GIFTS
★ Heath Ceramics

CERAMICS | Heath designs and produces sleek, glossy tiles for the home and newly spun bowls, plates, and cups in rich earth colors to decorate kitchens. You'll also find locally inspired cookbooks and high-quality furniture and silverware from trendy peers throughout Heath's immaculately arranged factory showroom. The company's designs can be found at many of San Francisco's top restaurants and cafés, including the adjacent Tartine Manufactory. ⊠ *2900 18th St., Mission District* ☎ *415/361–5552* ⊕ *www.heath-ceramics.com* ⊗ *Closed Sun. and Mon.*

Paxton Gate

SOUVENIRS | Elevating gardening to an art, this serene shop offers beautiful vases, succulents, decorative garden items, and coffee table books. The collection of taxidermy and preserved bugs provides more unusual gift ideas. A couple storefronts away is too-cute Paxton Gate Curiosities for Kids, jam-packed with retro toys, books, and other stellar finds. ⊠ *824 Valencia St., Mission District* ☏ *415/824–1872* ⊕ *paxtongate.com.*

Therapy

SOUVENIRS | In addition to fun housewares, books, wellness items, and stationery that leans toward retro charm, this local company sells smart decor, linens, and accessories with San Francisco and California themes. ⊠ *545 Valencia St., Mission District* ☏ *415/865–0981* ⊕ *therapystores.com.*

TOYS AND GADGETS

826 Valencia

TOYS | FAMILY | The brainchild of local author Dave Eggers is primarily a center established to help kids with their writing skills via writing programs, tutoring, and storytelling events. But the storefront is also "San Francisco's only independent pirate supply store," a quirky space filled with eye patches, spyglasses, and other pirate-themed paraphernalia. Eggers's quarterly journal, *McSweeney's*, and other publications are available here. Proceeds benefit the writing center.

On the center's storefront is an intricate mural designed by graphic novelist Chris Ware as a meditation on the evolution of human communication. ⊠ *826 Valencia St., Mission District* ☏ *415/642–5905* ⊕ *826valencia.org.*

Bernal Heights

A neighborhood with a small-town vibe that's home to young families, dog lovers, and a visible lesbian contingent, Bernal Heights draws some locals for its handful of good restaurants and the 360-degree views from the top of Bernal Hill. Less hipster than the neighboring Mission (to the north) and less saturated with the tech money set than Noe Valley (to the west), Bernal Heights feels like a throwback to another time, with a rarely found classic butcher shop (Avedano's), a beloved community garden, the annual Hillwide Garage Sale, one of the city's most adorable tiny coffee shops (Pinhole Coffee), and hardly a chain store in sight.

Take a stroll down Cortland Avenue, climb the hill at Bernal Heights Park for one of the city's definitive skyline views (and get a photo sitting in the swing), or explore the stairways in one of San Francisco's lowest-key neighborhoods. The northern part of Bernal Heights, which borders the Mission, is defined by flat, grass-filled Precita Park, a perfect spot for a picnic or game of Frisbee (unlike the very windy, steep Bernal Heights Park). Precita Park is also next to one of the city's most exciting seasonal modern Californian restaurants, Marlena.

🍴 Restaurants

Cellarmaker House of Pizza

$$ | PIZZA | There are several excellent pizzerias and many terrific small breweries in town, but it almost seems unfair that quite possibly the best of both genres is one place located where the Mission blurs into Bernal Heights. Cellarmaker is known for its ultra-hoppy beers and unique Coffee & Cigarettes smoked coffee porter; the pizza side focuses on perfect renditions of thick, crispy-edged Detroit-style square slices. **Known for:**

frequently changing IPA beers; market-special Detroit-style pizza; constant stream of beer geeks. $ *Average main: $23* ⊠ *3193 Mission St., Bernal Heights* ☎ *415/296–6351* ⊕ *cellarmakerbrewing. com* ☾ *No lunch weekdays.*

Marlena

$$$$ | MODERN AMERICAN | A husband-and-wife team (he does the savory cooking, she's the pastry chef) crafts approachable yet exciting multi-course menus at this charming spot overlooking Precita Park. All diners enjoy four courses with at least two choices in each category. **Known for:** excellent wine list; seasonal pasta creations; impressive desserts. $ *Average main: $75* ⊠ *300 Precita Ave., Bernal Heights* ☎ *415/400–5997* ⊕ *marlenarestaurant.com* ☾ *No lunch.*

☕ Coffee and Quick Bites

Pinhole Coffee

$ | CAFÉ | FAMILY | This tiny, beautifully designed coffee shop might be the most adorable in this city full of cute cafés. Families, longtime Bernal Heights residents, and coffee lovers from around the city gather here every morning for perfect cappuccinos and teas from various local purveyors. **Known for:** delightful chai latte; excellent espresso drinks; adorable tree stump tables. $ *Average main: $5* ⊠ *231 Cortland Ave., Bernal Heights* ☎ *415/364–8257* ⊕ *pinholecoffee.com.*

Potrero Hill

Tucked between two freeways east of the Mission and south of SoMa, warm and sunny Potrero Hill is a laid-back, family-friendly neighborhood that can feel like a place apart from the rest of the city. Most of the action happens around 18th and Connecticut Streets. With fantastic views from its slopes, and some good

Vermont Street ⊙

With its series of switchbacks, this Potrero Hill roadway is a kind of low-key Lombard Street, minus the throngs (and the spectacular gardens and views). It's on the east side of the 101 from the Mission. To check it out, head down 24th Street to the end, go left on Vermont, right on 23rd Street past the freeway, left on Rhode Island Street, left on 20th Street, and finally head left down the curvy stretch of Vermont that is adjacent to the McKinley Square park area.

shops, restaurants, and bars, Potrero Hill is a neighborhood attractive to locals but still off the tourist radar.

🍴 Restaurants

Plow

$$ | AMERICAN | FAMILY | Weekend or weekday, the brunch lines are as constant as the excellent scrambles, biscuits, and fluffy lemon-ricotta pancakes. The atmosphere is also winning—bright and pastoral, with rustic wood floors and huge windows—and the Little Plowers menu dishes out smaller-portioned pancakes, French toast, and grilled cheese for younger brunch-loving guests. **Known for:** Plow potatoes; soft scrambled eggs with peak seasonal produce; happiest place in San Francisco at 10 am. $ *Average main: $22* ⊠ *1299 18th St., Potrero Hill* ☎ *415/821–7569* ⊕ *www.eatatplow. com* ☾ *No dinner.*

☕ Coffee and Quick Bites

Farley's

$ | CAFÉ | While you're sipping your inky strong cup at friendly Farley's, a neighborhood institution on sunny Potrero Hill, you can play chess, check out the eclectic magazine selection, or catch up on the local gossip. There are a few pastries and usually empanadas for a light breakfast or a snack, but it's really all about coffee and tea here. **Known for:** coffee roasted in-house; feels like the neighborhood meeting center; maple latte. $ *Average main: $6* ⊠ *1315 18th St., Potrero Hill* ☎ *415/648–1545* ⊕ *farleyscoffee.com.*

Hazel's Kitchen

$ | SANDWICHES | Sandwich lovers build up their appetite with a hike up the steep hill and then are greeted with some of the city's consistently excellent sandwiches at this small, friendly shop where the menu seems bigger than the actual space. If you're not in a sandwich mood, there are also a few other items like breakfast scrambles, fish tacos, and salads. **Known for:** tuna salad and cheddar sandwich; breakfast burritos; any of the gooey melts. $ *Average main: $13* ⊠ *1319 18th St., Potrero Hill* ☎ *415/647–7941* ⊕ *hazelskitchen.com* ⊗ *No dinner*

▼ Nightlife

One of the city's less walkable neighborhoods is far from the center of the nightlife scene and sometimes feels downright sleepy. But a strip of 18th Street near Connecticut Street has good food and drinks, and the bottom of the hill is home to the beloved sports bar Connecticut Yankee, plus a pair of notable live music bars: Thee Parkside and the aptly named Bottom of the Hill.

BREWPUBS AND BEER GARDENS
Anchor Brewing

BREWPUBS | Mention "San Francisco" and "beer" and most locals and tourists will immediately think about Anchor Steam. It's a core part of the city's culture—it's what San Franciscans drink when the Giants win or after a tough day at work. Anchor started in 1896 and moved to its iconic Potrero Hill home in 1977, where the smell of brewing yeasts, hops, and barley greets the area on most days. The brewery tour and tasting is always a hot ticket (and well worth the time to see the historic copper kettles), but it's much easier to grab a flight or pint at their Public Taps bar next door. While you're there, make sure to order some of the unique Californian-Mexican cooking. ⊠ *495 De Haro St., Potrero Hill* ☎ *415/863–8350* ⊕ *www.anchorbrewing.com* ⊗ *Closed Mon.*

MUSIC CLUBS
Bottom of the Hill

LIVE MUSIC | This is a great live-music dive—in the best sense of the word—and truly the epicenter of Bay Area indie rock. The club has hosted some great acts over the years, including the Strokes and Throwing Muses. Country and hip-hop acts occasionally make it to the stage. ⊠ *1233 17th St., Potrero Hill* ☎ *415/626–4455* ⊕ *www.bottomofthehill.com.*

Thee Parkside

LIVE MUSIC | There's a fun event practically every night at one of the city's leading indoor-outdoor venues. Part bar, part music club, part beer garden, it rotates vibes from a relaxed patio setting to one of the city's leading stages for punk and metal acts. Some nights swap shows for movies or karaoke. There's a small coffee kiosk in the bar during the morning and early afternoon hours that serves some of the neighborhood's greatest espres-so-based drinks. ⊠ *1600 17th St., Potrero Hill* ☏ *415/252–1330* ⊕ *www.theeparkside.com.*

🛍 Shopping

ART GALLERIES
Catharine Clark Gallery

ART GALLERIES | Although nationally known artists—like Masami Teraoka and Ana Teresa Fernández—display their modern sculptures, paintings, photographs, and installation artwork here, emerging Bay Area artists get a spotlight too. The gallery's BOXBLUR space showcases contemporary art both in visual exhibitions and performances. ⊠ *248 Utah St., Potrero Hill* ☏ *415/399–1439* ⊕ *cclarkgallery.com* ⊗ *Closed Sun. and Mon.*

Chapter 14

THE BAY AREA

14

Updated by
Trevor Felch

⊙ Sights	🍽 Restaurants	🛏 Hotels	🛍 Shopping	🍸 Nightlife
★★★★☆	★★★★☆	★★★☆☆	★★☆☆☆	★★★★☆

WELCOME TO THE BAY AREA

TOP REASONS TO GO

★ **Berkeley's culinary mecca:** Eat your way through North Berkeley, starting with a slice of perfect pizza from Cheese Board Pizza.

★ **Point Reyes National Seashore:** Hike beautifully rugged—and often deserted—beaches at one of the most beautiful places on Earth.

★ **Sitting on a dock by the Bay:** Admire the beauty of the Bay from the rocky shores of Sausalito or Tiburon.

★ **"Beer-hopping" in Oakland's hippest hoods:** Discover the wealth of unique brewers along the Oakland Ale Trail.

★ **Giant redwoods:** Walking into Muir Woods National Monument is like entering a cathedral of nature.

★ **Elephant seals:** Few sights are as spectacular as seeing thousands of elephant seals breeding and resting on the beach at Año Nuevo State Park.

★ **Palm Drive:** The drive toward Stanford University and the Santa Cruz Mountains is postcard-perfect.

1 Berkeley. Hip college town.

2 Oakland. Diverse city with lively arts, nightlife, and food.

3 The Marin Headlands. Spectacular vistas.

4 Sausalito. Views and bohemian vibes.

5 Tiburon. A quaint, scenic town.

6 Mill Valley. Gateway to incredible nature.

7 Muir Beach. Quiet beach with a local feel.

8 Stinson Beach. Beach town with a surfer vibe.

9 Point Reyes National Seashore. Dramatic coastline with sandy beaches.

10 Palo Alto. A residential city for Big Tech.

11 Menlo Park. Home of Meta.

12 Stanford. Beautiful academic hotspot.

13 Sunnyvale and Mountain View. The hip heart of Silicon Valley.

14 San Jose. A dynamic and intriguing city.

15 Santa Cruz Mountains AVA. Redwood forests and pinot noirs.

16 Peninsular Coastline. Whales, elephant seals, and huge waves.

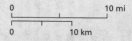

It's rare for a metropolis to compete with its suburbs for visitors, but the view from any of San Francisco's hilltops shows that the Bay Area's temptations extend far beyond the city limits.

MAJOR REGIONS

East of the city are the energetic urban centers of Berkeley and Oakland. Berkeley is famously radical yet sophisticated, while Oakland has an arts and restaurant scene so hip that it pulls San Franciscans across the bay. To the north is Marin County with its dramatic coastal beauty and chic, affluent villages.

The East Bay. The college town of Berkeley has long been known for its liberal ethos, stimulating university community (and perhaps even more stimulating coffee shops), and activist streak. But these days, the lively restaurant and arts scenes are luring even those who wouldn't be caught dead in Birkenstocks. Meanwhile, life in the diverse, harborfront city of Oakland is strongly defined by a turbulent history. Today, progressive Oakland is an incubator for artisans of all kinds, and the thriving culinary and creative scenes are taking off.

Marin County. Marin is the prettiest of the Bay Area counties, primarily because of its wealth of open space. Anchored by water on three sides, the county is mostly parkland, including long stretches of undeveloped coastline along the Marin Headlands, recognizable by the distinguished peak of Mt. Tamalpais. The coastal treasures of Muir Woods National Monument, "Mt. Tam," Stinson and Muir Beaches, and the entire Point Reyes National Seashore are among the country's greatest natural beauties. It's no wonder that the picturesque small towns

here—Sausalito, Tiburon, Mill Valley, and Bolinas among them—may sometimes look rustic, but most are home to a dizzyingly high tax bracket.

The Peninsula and South Bay. Home to Silicon Valley, Stanford University, the Santa Cruz Mountains and a spectacular coastline, this is an incredibly diverse region of the Bay Area—the technology campuses and tranquil redwood forests are just minutes apart from each other. San Jose is the largest city in the region and has several interesting museums worth visiting. The Santa Cruz Mountains are home to some of the Bay Area's greatest vineyards and hiking trails.

Planning

When to Go

You can visit the rest of the Bay Area any time of year, though it's especially nice in late spring and fall. Unlike San Francisco, the surrounding areas are reliably sunny in summer—it gets hotter as you head inland. Even the rainy season has its charms, as otherwise golden hills turn a rich green and wildflowers become plentiful. Precipitation is usually the heaviest between November and March. Berkeley is a university town, so it's easier to navigate the streets and find parking near the university between semesters, but there's also less buzz around town then. The Marin County and

Peninsular coastlines are well known for their frequent fog and fierce winds throughout the year, but a few days each month they'll have surprisingly sunny and mild conditions.

Getting Here and Around

Seamless travel from train to ferry to bus with one fare card is possible—and often preferable to driving on congested freeways and over toll bridges. For trips from one city to the next across the bay, save time and money with a Clipper card. They work with BART, Muni, buses, and ferries. Order a Clipper card before you travel at ⊕ www.clippercard.com.

BART

Using public transportation to reach Berkeley or Oakland is ideal. The under- and aboveground BART (Bay Area Rapid Transit) trains make stops in both cities as well as other East Bay destinations. Trips to either take about a half hour one-way from the center of San Francisco. Trains also take passengers from the city directly to San Francisco International Airport and from the East Bay to North San Jose. BART does not serve Downtown San Jose, Marin County, or the Peninsula. ■TIP→ Check ahead for safety measures and service advisories.

CONTACTS BART. ☎ 510/465–2278 ⊕ www.bart.gov.

BOAT AND FERRY

For sheer romance, nothing beats the ferry; there's service from San Francisco to Sausalito, Tiburon, and Larkspur in Marin County, and to Alameda and Oakland in the East Bay.

The Golden Gate Ferry crosses the bay to Larkspur and Sausalito from San Francisco's Ferry Building. Blue & Gold Fleet ferries depart daily for Sausalito from Pier 41 at Fisherman's Wharf; weekday commuter ferries leave from the Ferry Building for Tiburon. The trip takes from 25 minutes to an hour. Purchase tickets from terminal vending machines.

The Angel Island–Tiburon Ferry sails to the island Wednesday–Sunday from April through October and on weekends the rest of the year. Call ahead to book and to check schedules.

The San Francisco Bay Ferry runs several times daily between San Francisco's Ferry Building and Oakland's Jack London Square, by way of Alameda. The trip lasts from 25 to 45 minutes and leads to Oakland's waterfront shopping and restaurant district. Purchase tickets on the Clipper Card app or at terminals or on board.

CONTACTS Angel Island–Tiburon Ferry. ☎ 415/435–2131 ⊕ angelislandferry. com. Blue & Gold Fleet. ☎ 415/705–8200 ⊕ www.blueandgoldfleet.com. Golden Gate Ferry. ☎ 415/921–5858 ⊕ www. goldengate.org. San Francisco Bay Ferry. ☎ 707/643–3779, 877/643–3779 ⊕ sanfranciscobayferry.com.

BUS

Golden Gate Transit buses travel north to Sausalito, Tiburon, and elsewhere in Marin County from the Financial District and SoMa in San Francisco. For Mt. Tamalpais State Park and West Marin (Stinson Beach, Bolinas, and Point Reyes Station), take any route to Marin City and then transfer to the West Marin Stagecoach. San Francisco Muni buses primarily serve the city.

■TIP→ Several other bus options exist for local and regional travel throughout the Bay Area, including Amtrak and Greyhound.

Though less speedy than BART, AC Transit bus lines serve Oakland, Berkeley, and all of Alameda County. The Peninsula is served by VTA and Samtrans bus lines.

CONTACTS AC Transit. ☎ 510/891–4777 ⊕ www.actransit.org. Golden Gate Transit. ☎ 511 ⊕ www.goldengate.org. SamTrans. ☎ 800/660–4287 ⊕ www.samtrans. com. San Francisco Muni. ☎ 311 ⊕ www.

sfmta.com. **West Marin Stagecoach.** ☎ 511 ⊕ marintransit.org/stagecoach.

CAR

To reach the East Bay, take Interstate 80 East across the San Francisco–Oakland Bay Bridge. For U.C. Berkeley, merge onto I–580 West and take Exit 11 for University Avenue. For Oakland, merge onto I–580 East. To reach downtown Oakland, take I–980 West from Interstate 580 East and exit at 14th Street. Travel time varies depending on traffic but should take about 30 minutes (or more than an hour if it's rush hour).

For all points in Marin, head north on U.S. 101 and cross the Golden Gate Bridge. Sausalito, Tiburon, the Marin Headlands, and Point Reyes National Seashore are all accessed off U.S. 101. The scenic coastal route, Highway 1, also called Shoreline Highway (and briefly, Panoramic Highway) for certain stretches, can be accessed off U.S. 101 as well. Follow this road to Muir Woods, Mt. Tamalpais State Park, Muir Beach, Stinson Beach, and Bolinas. From Bolinas, you can continue north on Highway 1 to Point Reyes.

From San Francisco, U.S. 101 and I–280 go straight down the Peninsula. The former is the more congested artery near the bay; the latter is closer to the Coastal Range. Both end up in San Jose.

Hotels

With a few exceptions, hotels in Berkeley and Oakland tend to be standard-issue, but many Marin hotels package themselves as cozy retreats. Summer in Marin is often booked well in advance, despite weather that can be downright chilly. Check for special packages during this season. Peninsula hotels wildly vary from basic chains on busy roads to some of the splashiest resorts in Northern California. Prices are always much steeper on weekdays here year-round, while it's the opposite on the coast.

⇨ Restaurant and hotel reviews have been shortened. For full information, visit Fodors.com. Restaurant prices are the average cost of a main course at dinner or, if dinner is not served, at lunch. Hotel prices are the lowest cost of a standard double room in high season.

What It Costs in U.S. Dollars			
$	$$	$$$	$$$$
RESTAURANTS			
under $20	$20–$30	$31–$40	over $40
HOTELS			
under $200	$200–$350	$351–$500	over $500

Restaurants

The Bay Area is home to many innovative restaurants, such as Chez Panisse in Berkeley and Commis in Oakland—for which reservations must be made well in advance. There are also many casual but equally tasty eateries to test out; expect an emphasis on organic seasonal produce, locally raised meats, craft cocktails, and curated wine menus. Marin and the Peninsula's dining scene trends toward the sleepy side, so check hours ahead of time. One of the best things about the region is that no matter where you are, there will surely be a terrific restaurant within a few minutes.

Berkeley

2 miles northeast of Bay Bridge.

Berkeley is the birthplace of the Free Speech Movement, the radical hub of the 1960s, the home of arguably the nation's top public university, and a frequent site of protests and political movements. The city of 103,000 is also a culturally diverse breeding ground for social trends, a bastion of the counterculture, and an important center for Bay Area writers, artists, and musicians. Berkeley residents, students, and faculty spend hours nursing coffee concoctions while they read, discuss, and debate at the dozens of cafés that surround campus. It's the quintessential university town, with numerous independent bookstores, countless casual eateries, myriad meet-ups, and thousands of cyclists.

Oakland may have the edge over Berkeley when it comes to ethnic diversity and cutting-edge arts, but unless you're accustomed to sipping hemp-milk lattes while taking in a spontaneous street performance prior to yoga, you'll likely find Berkeley charmingly offbeat.

GETTING HERE AND AROUND
BART is the easiest way to get to Berkeley from San Francisco. Exit at the Downtown Berkeley Station, and walk a block up Center Street to get to the western edge of campus. AC Transit buses F and FS lines stop near the university and Fourth Street shopping. By car, take I–80 East across the Bay Bridge, merge onto I–580 West, and take the University Avenue exit through downtown Berkeley or take the Ashby Avenue exit and turn left on Telegraph Avenue. Once you arrive, explore on foot. Berkeley is very pedestrian-friendly.

TOURS
Edible Excursions
FOOD AND DRINK TOURS | For an unforgettable foodie experience in Berkeley, book a culinary walking tour, maybe one of North Berkeley or a Downtown Berkeley brunch stroll. Come hungry for knowledge and noshing. Tours take place on weekends. The company also offers tours of San Francisco and Oakland. ⌂ *Berkeley* ☎ *415/806–5970* ⊕ *www.edibleexcursions.net* ⤢ *From $120.*

ESSENTIALS
Koret Visitor Center. ⌂ *2227 Piedmont Ave., at California Memorial Stadium, Downtown* ☎ *510/642–5215* ⊕ *visit.*

berkeley.edu. **Visit Berkeley.** ⌂ *2030 Addison St., Suite 102, Downtown* ☎ *510/549–7040* ⊕ *www.visitberkeley.com.*

◉ Sights

★ BAMPFA (Berkeley Art Museum and Pacific Film Archive)
ART MUSEUM | This combined art museum, repertory movie theater, and film archive, known for its extensive collection of 28,000 works of art and 18,000 films and videos, is also home to the world's largest collection of African American quilts. Artworks span five centuries and include modernist notables Mark Rothko, Jackson Pollock, David Smith, and Hans Hofmann. The Pacific Film Archive includes the largest selection of Japanese films outside Japan and specializes in international films, offering regular screenings and performances. ⌂ *2155 Center St., Berkeley* ☎ *510/642–0808* ⊕ *bampfa.org* ⤢ *$14; free 1st Thurs. of month* ⊙ *Closed Mon. and Tues.*

Fourth Street
NEIGHBORHOOD | Once an industrial area, this walkable stretch of Fourth Street north of University Avenue has transformed into the busiest few blocks of refined shopping and eating in Berkeley. A perfect stop for lovers of design, curated taste experiences, artful living, and fashion, the vibrant district boasts more than 70 shops, specialty stores, cafés, and restaurants. Find inspiration at Castle in the Air, Builders Booksource, and Stained Glass Garden, or sip a perfect drip coffee at Artís, where you can watch small-batch coffee roasting in progress—one pound at a time. ⌂ *4th St. between University Ave. and Virginia St., Berkeley* ⊕ *www.fourthstreet.com.*

★ Shattuck & Vine Street Neighborhood
NEIGHBORHOOD | The success of Alice Waters's Chez Panisse defined California cuisine and attracted countless food-related enterprises to a stretch of Shattuck

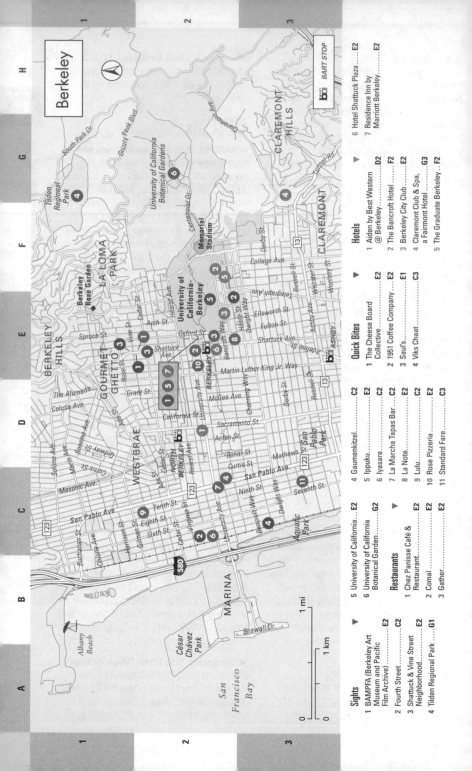

Berkeley

BART STOP

Sights
1 BAMPFA (Berkeley Art Museum and Pacific Film Archive)....... E2
2 Fourth Street.................. C2
3 Shattuck & Vine Street Neighborhood.......... E2
4 Tilden Regional Park...... G1
5 University of California... E2
6 University of California Botanical Garden.......... G2

Restaurants
1 Chez Panisse Café & Restaurant.................. E2
2 Comal........................... E2
3 Gather.......................... E2
4 Gaumenkitzel................. E2
5 Ippuku........................... E2
6 Iyasare.......................... C2
7 La Marcha Tapas Bar.... C2
8 La Note.......................... E2
9 Lulu............................... C2
10 Rose Pizzeria................. E2
11 Standard Fare............... C3

Quick Bites
1 The Cheese Board Collective.................... E2
2 1951 Coffee Company.... E2
3 Saul's........................... E1
4 Viks Chaat.................... C3

Hotels
1 Aiden by Best Western @ Berkeley.................. D2
2 The Bancroft Hotel........ F2
3 Berkeley City Club........ E2
4 Claremont Club & Spa, a Fairmont Hotel.......... G3
5 The Graduate Berkeley... F2
6 Hotel Shattuck Plaza..... E2
7 Residence Inn by Marriott Berkeley........ E2

Avenue. Foodies will do well here poking around the shops, grabbing a quick bite, or indulging in a feast. **Tigerlily** (⌂ *1513 Shattuck Ave.*) dishes up authentic modern Indian cuisine along with signature cocktails and light fare on the patio. Neighboring **Epicurious Garden** (⌂ *1511 Shattuck Ave.*) food stands sell everything from sushi to gelato.

Across Vine Street, the **Vintage Berkeley** (⌂ *2113 Vine St.*) wine shop offers tastings and reasonably priced bottles within a historic former pump house. Coffee lovers can head to the original Peet's Coffee & Tea at the corner of **Walnut and Vine** (⌂ *2124 Vine St.*).

South of Cedar Street, **The Local Butcher Shop** (⌂ *1600 Cedar St.*) sells locally sourced meat and hearty sandwiches of the day. For high-end food at takeout prices, try the salads, sandwiches, and signature potato puffs at **Grégoire** (⌂ *2109 Cedar St.*). **Masse's Pastries** (⌂ *1469 Shattuck Ave.*) is a museum of edible artwork. We could go on, but you get the idea. ⌂ *Shattuck Ave. between Delaware and Rose Sts., Berkeley* ⊕ *www.northshattuckassociation.org.*

★ Tilden Regional Park

CITY PARK | FAMILY | Stunning bay views, a scaled-down steam train, and a botanical garden with the nation's most complete collection of California plant life are the hallmarks of this 2,077-acre park in the hills just east of the UC Berkeley campus. The garden's visitor center offers weekend lectures about its plants and information about Tilden's other attractions, including its picnic spots, Lake Anza swimming site, golf course, and hiking trails (the paved Nimitz Way, at Inspiration Point, is a popular hike with wonderful sunset views). ■TIP→ Children love Tilden's interactive Little Farm and vintage carousel. ⌂ *Tilden Regional Park, 2501 Grizzly Peak Blvd., Berkeley* ☎ *510/544–2747* ⊕ *www.ebparks.org* ⌂ *Free parking and botanic garden.*

University of California

COLLEGE | Known simply as "Cal," the founding campus of California's university system is one of the leading intellectual centers in the United States and a major site for scientific research. Chartered in 1868, the university sits on 178 oak-covered acres split by Strawberry Creek. Campus highlights include bustling and historic **Sproul Plaza** (⌂ *Bancroft Way and Sather Rd.*), the seven floors and 61-bell carillon of **Sather Tower** (⌂ *Campanile Esplanade*), hands-on **Lawrence Hall of Science** (⌂ *1 Centennial Dr.*), the vibrant 34-acre **Botanical Gardens** (⌂ *200 Centennial Dr.*), and the historic **Hearst Greek Theatre** (⌂ *2001 Gayley Rd.*), the classic outdoor amphitheater designed by John Galen Howard. ⌂ *Berkeley* ☎ *510/642–6000* ⊕ *www.berkeley.edu.*

University of California Botanical Garden

GARDEN | FAMILY | Thanks to Berkeley's temperate climate, more than 10,000 types of plants from all corners of the world flourish in the 34-acre University of California Botanical Garden. Free garden tours are given regularly with paid admission. Benches and shady picnic tables make this a relaxing place for a snack with a breathtaking view. Call or go online before you travel to reserve your visit. ⌂ *200 Centennial Dr., Berkeley* ☎ *510/643–2755* ⊕ *botanicalgarden.berkeley.edu* ⌂ *$15* ⊙ *Closed 1st and 3rd Tues. every month.*

🍴 Restaurants

Dining in Berkeley may be low-key when it comes to dress, but it's top-of-class in quality, even in less fancy spaces. Late diners beware: Berkeley is an "early to bed" kind of town.

★ Chez Panisse Café & Restaurant

$$$$ | MODERN AMERICAN | Alice Waters's legendary eatery, the birthplace of California cuisine, first opened its doors in 1971. It's still known for a passionate dedication to locally sourced heirloom

The University of California is the epicenter of Berkeley's energy and activism.

varieties of fruits and vegetables, heritage breeds, and ethically farmed or foraged ingredients. **Known for:** sustainably sourced meats; attention to detail; pizzas and fruit galettes upstairs. $ *Average main: $175 ⊠ 1517 Shattuck Ave., Berkeley ☎ 510/548–5525 restaurant, 510/548–5049 café ⊕ www.chezpanisse. com ⊗ Closed Sun. and Mon. No lunch in restaurant. No lunch Tues.–Thurs. in café.*

Comal

$ | **MODERN MEXICAN** | Relaxed yet trendy, Comal's cavernous indoor dining space and intimate back patio and firepit draw a diverse, casual crowd for creative Oaxacan-inspired fare and well-crafted cocktails. The modern Mexican menu centers on small dishes that lend themselves to sharing and are offered alongside more than 100 tequilas and mezcals. **Known for:** margaritas and mezcal; house-made chicharróns; wood-fired entrées. $ *Average main: $16 ⊠ 2020 Shattuck Ave., Berkeley ☎ 510/926–6300 ⊕ www. comalberkeley.com ⊗ No lunch.*

Gather

$$ | **MODERN AMERICAN** | All things local, organic, seasonal, and sustainable harmonize at Gather. This haven for vegans, vegetarians, and carnivores alike serves up market and grain salads, shareable grilled local vegetables or cheese plates, roast chicken, and more in a vibrant, well-lit space that boasts funky light fixtures, shiny wood furnishings, and banquettes made of recycled leather belts. **Known for:** falafel burger; wood-fired pizzas; compelling cocktails. $ *Average main: $26 ⊠ 2200 Oxford St., Berkeley ☎ 510/809–0400 ⊕ www.gatherberkeley. com ⊗ Closed Mon. and Tues.*

Gaumenkitzel

$$ | **GERMAN** | **FAMILY** | This award-winning, convivial locale for organic, slow-food German fare has the Bay Area's best variety of German beers. With dishes like spätzle and caramelized onions, house-made brezel with bratwurst, jägerschnitzel with braised red cabbage, and panfried catch of the day, the kitchen puts a fresh stamp on traditional

An Urban Winery Walk 🍴

The industrial area of Berkeley near I-80 and the Fourth Street shopping district doesn't exactly have the bucolic rolling hills and sweeping vineyards of Napa and Sonoma. However, there are some terrific wineries located here, often operated by younger winemakers avoiding the exorbitant real estate farther north and not having to follow the rules of only producing wines from certain varietals.

Donkey & Goat (🌐 *donkeyandgoat.com*) was the longtime gold standard as a pioneer of low-intervention "natural wine," but now it's in the middle of the Berkeley pack. Maître de Chai (🌐 *mdc.wine*) and Vinca Minor (🌐 *vincaminorwine.com*) are two newer standouts. Lusu Cellars (*lusucellars.com*) offers a wide range of varieties from around California. Hammerling Wines (🌐 *hammerling-wines.co*) specializes in cool climate Golden State sparkling wines. At the northern end of the group, Broc Cellars (🌐 *broccellars.com*) continues to be a Bay Area–wide favorite for natural wines that tend to taste fresh and juicy instead of funky.

German favorites. **Known for:** German wine and beer selection; house-made German breads; grass-fed beef goulash. [$] *Average main: $22* ✉ *2121 San Pablo Ave., Berkeley* ☎ *510/647–5016* 🌐 *www.gaumenkitzel.net* 🕒 *Closed Mon. and Tues. No lunch Wed.–Fri.*

Ippuku

$ | JAPANESE | More Tokyo street chic than standard sushi house, this *izakaya*—the Japanese equivalent of a bar with appetizers—is decked with bamboo-screen booths. Servers pour an impressive array of sakes and shōchū and serve up satisfying fare. **Known for:** bacon-wrapped mochi; charcoal-grilled yakitori skewers; tempura vegetables. [$] *Average main: $18* ✉ *2130 Center St., Berkeley* ☎ *510/665–1969* 🌐 *ippukuberkeley.com* 🕒 *Closed Mon. and Tues. No lunch.*

Iyasare

$$ | JAPANESE | Reservations are recommended at this hot spot where the outdoor seating is ideal for people-watching and the Japanese country food is uniquely prepared. Locals come for seasonally changing, eclectic dishes made with a blend of local ingredients, such as burdock root tempura and tamari-kombu cured salmon or a wonderful salad combining various kinds of sashimi with a spicy miso dressing. **Known for:** sushi omakase; donburi (rice-bowl dishes) and small plates; ramen. [$] *Average main: $27* ✉ *1830 4th St., Berkeley* ☎ *510/845–8100* 🌐 *iyasare-berkeley.com.*

La Marcha Tapas Bar

$ | SPANISH | Delectable samplings of Spanish cuisine and a lively setting with expanded outdoor seating (Thurs.–Sun. only) keep this tapas bar brimming with energy amid savory smells of seafood dishes and small plates of peel-and-eat prawns, cumin lamb sliders, or goat cheese–stuffed piquillos rellenos. The bar's passion for Spanish cuisine and culture is evident in the wines, the Mediterranean flavors, and the cozy setting with tile mosaics. **Known for:** paella varieties; happy hour specials; churros con chocolate.. [$] *Average main: $17* ✉ *2026 San Pablo Ave., Berkeley* ☎ *510/647–9525* 🌐 *www.lamarchaberkeley.com.*

La Note

$ | FRENCH | A charming taste of Provence in a 19th-century locale with stone floors, country tables, and a seasonal flowering patio, La Note serves thoughtfully prepared rustic food. Enjoy breakfast and lunch outdoors with fresh, crusty breads and pastries, eggs Lucas with house-roasted tomatoes, and lemon gingerbread pancakes. **Known for:** rustic sandwiches; tempting egg preparations; brioche pain perdu. $ *Average main: $18* ⊠ *2377 Shattuck Ave., Berkeley* ☎ *510/843–1525* ⊕ *www.lanoterestaurant.com* ⊘ *No dinner.*

Lulu

$ | **MIDDLE EASTERN** | Chef-owner Mona Leena Michael channels her heritage as a first-generation Palestinian in California. Breakfast, lunch, and Friday-to-Sunday brunch are the main events here, in particular the reservation-only, prix-fixe brunch affair that might feature eight to ten compelling *mezze* (small plates). **Known for:** outstanding freshly baked pastries; Turkish eggs with house chili crisp and fresh pita; rose brûlée cappuccino. $ *Average main: $18* ⊠ *1019 Camelia St., Berkeley* ☎ *510/529–4300* ⊕ *luluberkeley.com* ⊘ *Closed Mon. No dinner.*

Rose Pizzeria

$$ | **PIZZA** | The East Bay is saturated with excellent pizzerias, but arguably the best of the esteemed group is hiding in plain sight on busy University Avenue, right by the heart of downtown Berkeley. Day and night, diners enjoy whole pies (no slices) in the cozy dining room and pleasant back patio. **Known for:** creative pizzas with several tempting vegetarian options; spicy Caesar salad; notable roster of natural wines. $ *Average main: $22* ⊠ *1960 University Ave., Berkeley* ⊕ *rosepizzeria.com* ⊘ *Closed Mon. and Tues.*

★ Standard Fare

$ | **AMERICAN** | Just look for the hungry crowds and the smell of freshly baked muffins; breakfast-lunch-brunch paradise is here in a far-flung corner of Berkeley. Kelsie Kerr's daytime-only restaurant/bakery started in 2014 and has been a sensation ever since. **Known for:** house-made hummus plate; brunch salads anchored by organic pasture-raised eggs; sourdough waffle with seasonal fruit and house-cured bacon. $ *Average main: $15* ⊠ *2701 Eighth St., Berkeley* ☎ *510/356–2261* ⊕ *standardfareberkeley.com* ⊘ *Closed Sun. and Mon. No dinner.*

☕ Coffee and Quick Bites

★ The Cheese Board Collective

$ | **PIZZA** | A jazz combo often entertains the line that snakes down the block outside Cheese Board Pizza; it's that good. The cooperatively owned vegetarian and vegan takeout spot and restaurant draws devoted customers with the smell of just-baked garlic on the pie of the day. **Known for:** cheese varieties; green sauce; daily changing toppings. $ *Average main: $12* ⊠ *1504–1512 Shattuck Ave., Berkeley* ☎ *510/549–3183* ⊕ *cheeseboardcollective.coop/pizza* ⊘ *Closed Sun.–Tues. Pizza: no lunch; bakery: no dinner.*

1951 Coffee Company

$ | **CAFÉ** | Taking its name from the 1951 UN Refugee Convention, this nonprofit coffee shop is inspired and powered by refugees. In addition to serving high-caliber coffee drinks, local pastries, and savory bites, the colorful café also serves as an advocacy space and barista training center for refugees. **Known for:** hand-roasted blends; excellent local pastries; matcha lattes. $ *Average main: $6* ⊠ *2410 Channing Way, Berkeley* ☎ *510/280–6171* ⊕ *www.1951coffee.com.*

Saul's

$$ | **JEWISH DELI** | **FAMILY** | High ceilings and red-leather booths add to the friendly, retro atmosphere of Saul's deli, a Berkeley institution that is well known for its house-made sodas and enormous sandwiches made with Acme bread. Locals swear by the pastrami Reubens, stuffed-cabbage rolls, and challah French toast. **Known for:** hand-rolled organic bagels; chicken schnitzel; deli hash with pastrami, corned beef, and poached eggs. $ *Average main: $22* ⊠ *1475*

Shattuck Ave., Berkeley ☎ *510/848–3354* 🌐 *www.saulsdeli.com.*

Viks Chaat

$ | **INDIAN** | The Chopra family has been selling excellent chaat (Indian street food snacks) to East Bay diners since 1989. It's part market, part bustling fast-casual restaurant with more substantial meat dishes and daily specials, dosas, and the staple homemade chaat that tend to be crunchy and/or fried (like samosas or puffed puri shells filled with mint water). **Known for:** weekend tandoori chicken; bhel puri (rice puffs, potato, and chutney); warehouse atmosphere with long waits at peak times. [$] *Average main: $14* ✉ *2390 Fourth St., Berkeley* ☎ *510/644–4432* 🌐 *vikschaat.com.*

Hotels

For inexpensive lodging, investigate University Avenue, west of campus. The area can be noisy, congested, and somewhat dilapidated, but it does include a few decent motels and chain properties. All Berkeley lodgings are strictly mid-range.

Aiden by Best Western @ Berkeley

$$ | **HOTEL** | Within a mile of campus and the heart of downtown, the Aiden celebrates the culture of Berkeley with wall art showcasing the campus life and spirit the town is known for. **Pros:** private parking; rooftop terrace with firepits and Bay views; good blackout curtains. **Cons:** some rooms get street noise; rough walk to downtown and the university; not a good value for the location. [$] *Rooms from: $250* ✉ *1499 University Ave., Berkeley* ☎ *510/898–2650* 🌐 *www.bestwestern.com* 🛏 *39 rooms* 🍴 *No Meals.*

The Bancroft Hotel

$ | **HOTEL** | This eco-friendly boutique hotel—across from the U.C. campus—is quaint, charming, and completely green. **Pros:** closest hotel to U.C. campus; friendly staff; many rooms have good views. **Cons:** some rooms are quite small; thin walls; no elevator. [$] *Rooms from: $189* ✉ *2680 Bancroft Way, Berkeley* ☎ *510/549–1000* 🌐 *bancrofthotel.com* 🛏 *22 rooms* 🍴 *Free Breakfast.*

Berkeley City Club

$$ | **HOTEL** | Moorish design and Gothic architecture join with modern amenities at this historic locale steps from the campus, arts venues, and eateries. **Pros:** art gallery and courtyard seating; laundry facilities; bocce court. **Cons:** tiny standard rooms; old-fashioned design; no TVs in rooms. [$] *Rooms from: $235* ✉ *2315 Durant Ave., Berkeley* ☎ *510/848–7800* 🌐 *www.berkeleycityclub.com* 🛏 *38 rooms* 🍴 *Free Breakfast.*

★ Claremont Club & Spa, a Fairmont Hotel

$$$ | **HOTEL** | **FAMILY** | Straddling the Oakland–Berkeley border, this amenities-rich property dating from 1915 beckons like a gleaming white castle in the hills. **Pros:** excellent restaurant and lounge for sunset views; daily events and special programs for children; gorgeous, sharply designed rooms. **Cons:** steep resort fee; smallest rooms are truly compact; remote location. [$] *Rooms from: $369* ✉ *41 Tunnel Rd., Berkeley* ☎ *510/843–3000, 888/560–4455 reservations* 🌐 *www.fairmont.com/claremont-berkeley* 🛏 *276 rooms* 🍴 *No Meals.*

The Graduate Berkeley

$$ | **HOTEL** | Fresh, colorful design and Bohemian flair set the tone at this hotel in one of Berkeley's registered historic places, just steps from campus and downtown eating, shopping, and entertainment. **Pros:** convenient location; fun atmosphere; warm, nicely decorated rooms. **Cons:** rooms can be noisy; rooms can be small; restaurant isn't open every evening. [$] *Rooms from: $245* ✉ *2600 Durant Ave., Berkeley* ☎ *510/845–8981* 🌐 *www.graduatehotels.com/berkeley* 🛏 *144 rooms* 🍴 *No Meals.*

Hotel Shattuck Plaza

$$ | **HOTEL** | This historic boutique hotel sits amid Berkeley's downtown arts district, just steps from the U.C. campus

and a short walk from North Berkeley's best bites. **Pros:** central location; special date night and B&B packages; excellent remote work desk setup. **Cons:** public and street parking only; limited on-site fitness center; street-facing rooms may be noisy. [$] *Rooms from: $229* ✉ *2086 Allston Way, Berkeley* ☎ *510/845–7300* 🌐 *www.hotelshattuckplaza.com* 🛏 *199 rooms* 🍴 *No Meals.*

Residence Inn by Marriott Berkeley

$$ | **HOTEL** | **FAMILY** | This new hotel in the heart of the city's arts and cultural district reflects the community's dedication to green living, as evident in its Gold LEED certification, use of recycled materials, and organic design. **Pros:** views from bar and terrace on 12th floor; steps from campus, arts, fine dining, and sights; enormous suites. **Cons:** hefty pet fee; expensive parking; traffic congestion. [$] *Rooms from: $283* ✉ *2121 Center St., Berkeley* ☎ *510/982–2100* 🌐 *www.marriott.com* 🛏 *331 suites* 🍴 *Free Breakfast.*

Nightlife

East Bay Spice Company

BARS | This creative establishment pairs Indian food with excellent cocktails that are given a fun twist, often with atypical spices, liqueurs, and spirits. Try the "East Bay Indica" which partners mezcal and tequila with lemon and tamarind syrup. ✉ *2134 Oxford St., Berkeley* 🌐 *eastbayspiceco.com.*

★ The Freight & Salvage Coffeehouse

LIVE MUSIC | Since 1968, the Freight has been a venue for some of the world's finest practitioners of folk, jazz, gospel, blues, world-beat, bluegrass, and storytelling. The nonprofit grew from an 87-seat coffee house to a thriving, nearly 500-seat venue in the heart of Berkeley's Arts District. Many tickets cost less than $30. ✉ *2020 Addison St., Berkeley* ☎ *510/644–2020* 🌐 *thefreight.org.*

Tupper & Reed

BARS | Housed in the former music shop of John C. Tupper and Lawrence Reed, this cocktail haven presents a symphony of carefully crafted libations, which are mixed with live music performed by local musicians. The historic 1925 building features a balcony bar, cozy nooks, antique fixtures, a pool table, and romantic fireplaces. ✉ *2271 Shattuck Ave., Berkeley* ☎ *510/859–4472* 🌐 *www.tupperandreed.com* 🕒 *Closed Mon.*

Performing Arts

More than a hundred arts and cultural organizations championing local artists and musicians contribute to Berkeley's happening scene. Many venues have small playhouses and performance spaces, allowing for great sightlines and intimate listening experiences.

Aurora Theatre Company

THEATER | Known for critically acclaimed productions like David Mamet's *American Buffalo* and Toni Morrison's *The Bluest Eye* and frequently launching world premieres of new plays, the Aurora is at the heart of Berkeley storytelling and community engagement. The theater's Alafi Auditorium seats 150 on three sides of the stage for premium viewing, and the smaller Harry's UpStage offers a more intimate experience for 49. Beyond the stage, the company has a monthly online broadcast with members of the community and its artists. ✉ *2081 Addison St., Berkeley* ☎ *510/843–4822* 🌐 *www.auroratheatre.org.*

★ Berkeley Repertory Theatre

THEATER | One of the region's most highly respected and innovative repertory theaters, Berkeley Rep performs the work of classic and contemporary playwrights. Well-known pieces mix with world premieres and edgier fare. The theater's complex, which includes the 400-seat Peet's Theatre and the 600-seat Roda Theatre, is in the heart of downtown

Berkeley's arts district, near BART's Downtown Berkeley station. ✉ *2025 Addison St., Berkeley* ☎ *510/647–2949* ⊕ *www.berkeleyrep.org.*

★ California Jazz Conservatory

MUSIC | What started as a music education program in 1977, offering classes with the Bay Area's best jazz players, has become the area's top concert venue for the freshest sounds in jazz from around the world. Two 100-seat performance venues across the street from each other, Hardymon Hall (✉ *2087 Addison St.*) and Rendon Hall (✉ *2040 Addison St.*), offer intimate viewing of some of the world's most influential musicians. Classes and workshops continue to serve as the foundation of the conservatory, with regular, affordably priced concerts each week for the public. ✉ *2087 Addison St., Berkeley* ☎ *510/845–5373* ⊕ *cjc.edu.*

The UC Theatre Taube Family Music Hall

MUSIC | One of Berkeley's oldest theaters opened its doors in 1917 as a first-run movie house with seating for 1,466 filmgoers. For years it served as a famous venue for foreign and domestic classics, closing in 2001. The theater's programming is now run by the nonprofit Berkeley Music Group, dedicated to bringing local, national, and international talent to Berkeley's arts district. Limited outdoor drinks and dining are available at the street bar, Out Front at the UC. ✉ *2036 University Ave., Berkeley* ☎ *510/356–4000* ⊕ *theuctheatre.org.*

🛍 Shopping

★ ACCI Gallery

ART GALLERIES | The Arts & Crafts Cooperative, Inc., a collective of Berkeley artists and artisans, has been a stalwart gallery and store showcasing ceramics, textiles, paintings, photography, jewelry, and various media since 1957. Explore the amazing range of local talent in a well-lit historic space, and find truly one-of-a-kind gems to take home. The gallery also hosts special events featuring artists explaining their works. ✉ *1652 Shattuck Ave., Berkeley* ☎ *510/843–2527* ⊕ *www.accigallery.com.*

★ Amoeba Music

MUSIC | Heaven for audiophiles and movie collectors, this legendary shop is *the* place for new and used CDs, vinyl, cassettes, VHS tapes, Blu-ray discs, and DVDs. The massive and ever-changing stock includes thousands of titles for all music tastes. ✉ *2455 Telegraph Ave., Berkeley* ☎ *510/549–1125* ⊕ *www.amoeba.com* ⊘ *Closed Mon. and Tues.*

★ Moe's Books

BOOKS | The spirit of Moe—the creative, cantankerous late proprietor—lives on in this world-famous house full of new and used books. Since it first opened in 1959, students and professors have flocked here to browse the large selection of literary and cultural criticism, art titles, and literature in foreign languages. ✉ *2476 Telegraph Ave., Berkeley* ☎ *510/849–2087* ⊕ *www.moesbooks.com.*

Oakland

9 miles from San Francisco via Bay Bridge.

In contrast to San Francisco's buzz and Berkeley's storied counterculture, Oakland's allure lies in its amazing diversity. Here you can find a Nigerian clothing store, a Gothic revival skyscraper, a Buddhist meditation center, and a lively salsa club, all within the same block.

Oakland's multifaceted nature reflects its colorful and tumultuous history. Once a cluster of Mediterranean-style homes and gardens that served as a bedroom community for San Francisco, the town had a major rail terminal and port by the turn of the 20th century. Already a hub of manufacturing, Oakland became a center for shipbuilding and industry when the United States entered World War II. New jobs in the city's shipyards, railroads, and factories attracted thousands of laborers from across the country, including sharecroppers from the Deep South, Mexican Americans from the Southwest, and some of the nation's first female welders. Neighborhoods were imbued with a proud but gritty spirit, along with heightened racial tension. In the wake of the civil rights movement, racial pride gave rise to militant groups like the Black Panther Party, but they were little match for the economic hardships and racial tensions that plagued Oakland. In many neighborhoods the reality was widespread poverty and gang violence—subjects that dominated the songs of such Oakland-bred rappers as the late Tupac Shakur. The protests of the Occupy Oakland movement in 2011 and 2012 and the Black Lives Matter movement more recently illustrate just how much Oakland remains a mosaic of its past.

Oakland's affluent reside in hillside homes and wooded enclaves like Claremont, Piedmont, and Montclair, which provide a warmer, more spacious alternative to San Francisco. A constant flow of newcomers ensures diversity, vitality, and growing pains. Neighborhoods west and south of the city center show signs of gentrification as the renovated downtown and vibrant arts scene inject new life into the city. Even San Franciscans come to Uptown and Temescal for the nightlife, arts, and restaurants. However, much of West Oakland, East Oakland (including the area surrounding the Oakland Coliseum) and the long stretch of International Boulevard remain very dicey, so it's best to avoid walking in them.

Everyday life here revolves around the neighborhood. In some areas, such as Piedmont and Rockridge, you'd swear you were in Berkeley or Noe Valley. Along Telegraph Avenue just south of 51st Street, Temescal is littered with hipsters and pulsing with creative culinary and design energy. These are perfect places for browsing, eating, or relaxing between sightseeing trips to Oakland's architectural gems, rejuvenated waterfront, and numerous green spaces.

GETTING HERE AND AROUND

From San Francisco, take I–80 East across the Bay Bridge, then take I–580 East to the Grand Avenue exit for Lake Merritt. To reach downtown and the waterfront, take I–980 West from I–580 East and exit at 12th Street; exit at 18th Street for Uptown. For Temescal, take I–580 East to Highway 24 and exit at 51st Street.

By BART, use the Lake Merritt Station for the Oakland Museum and southern Lake Merritt; the Oakland City Center–12th Street Station for downtown, Chinatown, and Old Oakland; and the 19th Street Station for Uptown, the Paramount Theatre, and the north side of Lake Merritt.

By bus, take the AC Transit's C and P lines to get to Piedmont in Oakland. The O bus stops at the edge of Chinatown near downtown Oakland.

Oakland's Jack London Square is an easy hop on the ferry from San Francisco. Those without cars can take advantage of the free Broadway Shuttle, which runs from Jack London Square to Grand Avenue weekdays, with continued service to 27th Street weeknights from 7 to 10 pm. There's no weekend service.

Be aware of how quickly neighborhoods can change. Walking is generally safe downtown and in the Piedmont and Rockridge areas, but be mindful when walking west and southeast of downtown, especially at night.

ESSENTIALS

Visit Oakland. ⊠ *481 Water St., Jack London Square* ☎ *510/839–9000* ⊕ *www. visitoakland.com.*

Oakland's Lake Merritt provides opportunities for jogging, biking, boating, bird-watching, and otherwise relaxing in the midst of this dynamic city.

👁 Sights

Lake Merritt

CITY PARK | In the center of Oakland just east of downtown, this tidal lagoon with its unique habitat for more than 100 bird species became the country's first wildlife refuge in 1870. Today the three-mile path around the lake is a refuge for walkers, bikers, joggers, and nature lovers. **Lakeside Park** has **Children's Fairyland** (✉ 699 Bellevue Ave.) and the **Rotary Nature Center** (✉ 600 Bellevue Ave.). The **Lake Merritt Boating Center** (✉ 568 Bellevue Ave.) rents kayaks and rowboats (from $18; cash only).

On the lake's south side, the **Cam-ron-Stanford House** (✉ 1418 Lakeside Dr.) is the last of the grand Victorians that once dominated the area; it's open Sundays for tours. Nearby, bold **Oakland mural art** offers a more modern feast for the eyes (✉ Between Madison and Webster Sts. and 7th and 11th Sts.).

The lake's necklace of lights adds allure for diners heading to **Lake Chalet** (✉ 1520 Lakeside Dr.), as well as to a host of tasty options along Grand Avenue, from Ethiopian cuisine at **Enssaro** (✉ 357A Grand Ave.) and Korean barbecue at **Jong Ga House** (✉ 372 Grand Ave.) to comfort gourmet at **Grand Lake Kitchen** (✉ 576 Grand Ave.). ✉ Lake Merritt 🚇 Free.

★ **Oakland Museum of California** (OMCA)
OTHER MUSEUM | FAMILY | Designed by Kevin Roche, this museum is a quintessential example of mid-century modern architecture and home to a capacious collection of nearly two million objects in three distinct galleries celebrating California's history, natural sciences, and art. Listen to native species and environmental soundscapes in the Library of Natural Sounds and engage in stories of the state's past and future, from Ohlone basket making to emerging technologies. Don't miss the photographs from Dorothea Lange's personal archive and a worthy collection of Bay Area figurative painters, including David Park and Joan Brown. Stay for lunch at the Town Fare café, where chef Michele McQueen

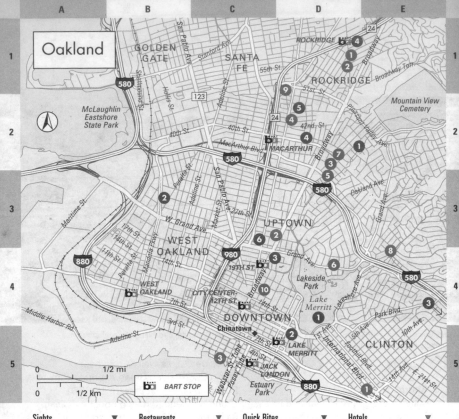

Oakland

Sights ▼
1 Lake Merritt	**D4**
2 Oakland Museum of California	**D5**
3 Oakland Zoo	**E4**
4 Rockridge	**D1**
5 Temescal	**D2**
6 Uptown/KONO	**C3**

Restaurants ▼
1 À Côté	**D1**
2 Belotti Ristorante e Bottega	**D1**
3 Commis	**D2**
4 Daytrip	**D2**
5 Mägo	**D3**
6 Mama Oakland	**D4**
7 Pomet	**D2**
8 Shakewell	**E4**
9 Snail Bar	**D1**
10 Sobre Mesa	**C4**

Quick Bites ▼
1 Fentons Creamery	**D2**
2 Horn BBQ	**B3**
3 Shawarmaji	**C4**
4 Tacos Oscar	**D2**

Hotels ▼
1 Best Western Plus Bayside Hotel	**E5**
2 Kissel Uptown Oakland	**C3**
3 Waterfront Hotel	**C5**

serves California-soul food dishes like Low Country shrimp and cheddar grits.
■ TIP→ **On Friday evening, the museum bustles with live music, food trucks, and after-hours gallery access.** ✉ *1000 Oak St., Downtown* ☎ *510/318–8400* ⊕ *museumca.org* 🎫 *$19; free 1st Sun. of month* 🕐 *Closed Mon. and Tues.*

Oakland Zoo

ZOO | FAMILY | One of the West Coast's leading zoos resides in the rolling hills of southeast Oakland. More than 750 animals from near and far live here, often putting on quite a show for the human visitors. The children's zoo and the California Trail are notable areas, with the latter featuring two of the most iconic animals in the Golden State: California condors and grizzly bears. The zoo has a handful of entertaining rides, but the main non-animal highlight for most guests is the Sky Ride gondola that offers incredible Bay Area views. ✉ *9777 Golf Links Rd., Oakland* ☎ *510/632–9525* ⊕ *oaklandzoo.org* 🎫 *$24.*

Rockridge

NEIGHBORHOOD | FAMILY | One of Oakland's most desirable places to live is this fashionable, upscale neighborhood. Explore the tree-lined streets that radiate out from College Avenue, just north and south of the Rockridge BART station for a look at California Craftsman bungalows at their finest. By day, College Avenue between Broadway and Alcatraz Avenue is crowded with shoppers buying fresh flowers, used books, and clothing; by night, the same folks are back for satisfying meals filled with fresh local ingredients, artisanal wines, and locally brewed ales. There's even a cider bar, one of the few in the Bay Area (**Redfield Cider Bar & Bottle Shop,** ✉ *5815 College Ave.*) With its specialty food shops and quick bites to go, **Market Hall**, an airy European-style marketplace at Shafter Avenue, is a hub of culinary activity, including the wonderful Californian-Mediterranean cooking of the attached **Acre Kitchen & Bar** (✉ *5655*

College Ave.). ✉ *Rockridge* ⊕ *www.rockridgedistrict.com.*

★ Temescal

NEIGHBORHOOD | Centering on Telegraph Avenue between 40th and 51st Streets, Temescal (the Aztec term for "sweat house") is a low-pretension, mon-eyed-hipster hood with young families and middle-aged folks in the mix. Protected bike lanes, bus islands, and a pedestrian plaza add to the vibrancy of this neighborhood. A critical mass of excellent eateries draws diners from around the Bay Area; there are newer favorites like excellent Filipino eats at **FOB Kitchen** (✉ *5179 Telegraph Ave.*) and **Smokin Woods BBQ** (✉ *4307 Telegraph Ave.*), as well as standbys like the fantastic fish tacos of **Cholita Linda** (✉ *4923 Telegraph Ave.*) and the unusually refined café-brewery **Rose's Taproom** (✉ *4930 Telegraph Ave.*). Old-timey dive bars and smog-check stations share space with public art installations of murals, sculptures, and mosaic trash cans.

Temescal Alley (✉ *Off 49th St.*), a tucked-away lane of tiny storefronts, crackles with creative energy. Get an old-fashioned straight-edge shave at **Temescal Alley Barber Shop** (✉ *470 49th St., Suite B*). Don't miss grabbing a sweet scoop at **Curbside Creamery** (✉ *482 49th St.*). ✉ *Telegraph Ave. between 40th and 51st Sts., Temescal* ⊕ *www.temescaldistrict.org.*

Uptown/KONO

NEIGHBORHOOD | Uptown and KONO (Koreatown/Northgate) is where nightlife and cutting-edge art merge. Dozens of galleries cluster around Telegraph Avenue and north of Grand Avenue into KONO, exhibiting everything from photography and installations to glasswork and fiber arts. The first Friday of each month, thousands of people descend for **Art Murmur** (⊕ *oaklandartmurmur.org*), a late-night gallery event that has expanded into **First Fridays** (⊕ www.oaklandfirstfridays.org), a festival of food trucks, street vendors, and live music along Telegraph Avenue.

14

The Bay Area OAKLAND

Restaurants with a distinctly urban vibe make Uptown/KONO a dining destination every night of the week. Favorites include eclectic Japanese-inspired fare at **Hopscotch** (✉ *1915 San Pablo Ave.*), ramen and izakaya offerings at **Shinmai** (✉ *1825–3 San Pablo Ave.*), the terrific Jamaican cooking of **Kingston 11** (✉ *2270 Telegraph Ave.*), fantastic Spanish tapas and paella from celebrated chef Paul Canales at **Duende** (✉ *468 19th St.*), and sushi hand rolls offered by **Yonsei Handrolls** (✉ *1738 Telegraph Ave.*).

Toss in the bevy of bars and there's plenty within walking distance to keep you busy all evening, such as **Drake's Dealership** (✉ *2325 Broadway*), with its spacious, hipster-friendly beer garden; fantastic cocktails paired with eclectic eats and a stunning art-deco atmosphere at **Palmetto** (✉ *1900 Telegraph Ave.*); and **Somar** (✉ *1727 Telegraph Ave.*), a bar, music lounge, and art gallery in one. ✉ *Telegraph Ave. and Broadway from 14th to 27th Sts., Uptown.*

🍴 Restaurants

À Côté

$$ | MEDITERRANEAN | This hot spot is all about seasonal and globe-spanning small plates, family-style eating, and excellent drinks. Intimate dining nooks, natural light, and a heated patio make this an ideal destination for couples, families, and the after-work crowd. **Known for:** Pernod mussels cooked in the wood oven; flatbreads; global and regional wine list. [$] *Average main: $26* ✉ *5478 College Ave., Rockridge* ☎ *510/655–6469* 🌐 *www.acoterestaurant.com* 🕑 *Closed Sun. and Mon. No lunch.*

Belotti Ristorante e Bottega

$$ | ITALIAN | Bay Area residents could debate for days about who truly makes the region's greatest pasta, but this Rockridge shop and restaurant from pasta whisperer Michele Belotti is more often than not on that short list. It's a perfect blend of traditional and comforting with modern influences. **Known for:** strong Italian wines roster; vitello tonnato (beef with Sicilian tuna sauce); tortellini in brodo. [$] *Average main: $22* ✉ *5403 College Ave., Oakland* ☎ *510/788–7890* 🌐 *belottirb.com* 🕑 *Closed Sun.*

★ Commis

$$$$ | AMERICAN | A slender, unassuming storefront houses the first East Bay restaurant with a Michelin star (two of them, in fact). The room is minimalist and polished: nothing distracts from the artistry of chef James Syhabout, who creates a multicourse prix-fixe experience based on the season and his distinctive vision of modern and classic creations. **Known for:** inventive tasting menu; fantastic wine collection; excellent bar next door with its own menu. [$] *Average main: $225* ✉ *3859 Piedmont Ave., Piedmont* ☎ *510/653–3902* 🌐 *commisrestaurant.com* 🕑 *Closed Sun. and Mon. No lunch.*

Daytrip

$$ | MODERN AMERICAN | A "fermentation-driven" restaurant sounds a bit odd, but you'll find a thrilling, umami-packed experience at this compact Temescal spot. With a disco ball overhead, you expect somebody to get up and dance with how groovy the vibe is. **Known for:** miso butter pasta; colorful wall mural and Rubik's cube–like counter; signature celery salad. [$] *Average main: $22* ✉ *4316 Telegraph Ave., Oakland* 🌐 *thisisdaytrip.com* 🕑 *No lunch weekdays.*

Mägo

$$$$ | SOUTH AMERICAN | After several years as a leading chef in San Francisco, Mark Liberman crossed the Bay Bridge to open this deeply personal restaurant that channels his Colombian heritage in a contemporary way. There are two tasting menus available—a long and a short. **Known for:** beautiful, colorful place with big open kitchen; lively bar; affordable tasting menu. [$] *Average main: $75* ✉ *3762 Piedmont Ave., Oakland*

☎ *510/344–7214* 🌐 *magorestaurant.com* 🕒 *Closed Sun.–Tues. No lunch.*

Mama Oakland

$$$ | MODERN ITALIAN | This classic Italian meets Californian menu is a stellar value where three courses clock in at less than $40 (the optional supplements are worth adding on). The quality is sky high, with no corners cut. **Known for:** homemade focaccia; stellar wine list; signature meatballs. [$] *Average main: $36* ✉ *388 Grand Ave., Oakland* ☎ *510/974–6372* 🌐 *mama-oakland.com* 🕒 *No lunch.*

Pomet

$$ | MODERN AMERICAN | Many restaurants have direct relationships between nearby farms and the kitchen, but very few are truly co-owned. Here, with chef Alan Hsu at the helm in the kitchen, top-tier local produce is showcased in excellent contemporary Californian dishes. **Known for:** warm, quaint setting with a large open kitchen; salt-and-pepper quail; "ugly mushroom" pasta with locally made miso butter. [$] *Average main: $30* ✉ *4029 Piedmont Ave., Oakland* ☎ *510/450–2541* 🌐 *pomet-oakland.com* 🕒 *Closed Mon. and Tues. No lunch.*

★ Shakewell

$$ | MEDITERRANEAN | Two *Top Chef* vets opened this stylish restaurant, which serves creative and memorable Mediterranean small plates in a lively setting with an open kitchen, wood-fired oven, communal tables, and snug seating. As the name implies, well-crafted cocktails are shaken (or stirred) and poured with panache. **Known for:** wood-oven paella; fried chicken with fenugreek yogurt; vegetarian options. [$] *Average main: $29* ✉ *3407 Lakeshore Ave., Grand Lake* ☎ *510/251–0329* 🌐 *www.shakewelloakland.com* 🕒 *Closed Mon. No dinner Sun. No lunch Tues.–Fri.*

★ Snail Bar

$$ | MODERN FRENCH | The Temescal neighborhood's dining anchor is a quirky wine bar with a powerful food program. At least half of the seating is outside, lending a Parisian indoor-outdoor café vibe to the air of this appropriately named spot with a signature escargots and cashew miso dish. **Known for:** raw seafood preparations; fish and avocado tostadas; unique wines from small producers. [$] *Average main: $20* ✉ *4935 Shattuck Ave., Oakland* ☎ *510/879–7678* 🌐 *snailbaroakland.com* 🕒 *No lunch.*

Sobre Mesa

$ | LATIN AMERICAN | A unique blend of African culinary influences along with flavors from various Latin American countries are the draw at chef Nelson German's restaurant. Each tapa is compelling (there are no main courses, though there are more than enough tempting dishes to satisfy a group) and nicely ties together the two geographic regions. **Known for:** the namesake cocktail with two kinds of rum; unique take on tostones; ground steak picadillo empanadas. [$] *Average main: $17* ✉ *1618 Franklin St., Oakland* ☎ *510/858–7544* 🌐 *sobremesaoak.com* 🕒 *Closed Mon. No lunch.*

Coffee and Quick Bites

★ Fentons Creamery

$ | AMERICAN | FAMILY | Beloved by the Bay since 1922 and featured in the Pixar film *Up*, this is the leading name locally for ice cream sundaes and good old-fashioned soda fountain fare. Kids of all ages adore the signature black-and-tan sundae with toasted almond and vanilla ice creams layered with caramel and chocolate sauces. **Known for:** ice cream sundaes; nostalgic atmosphere; tuna melt. [$] *Average main: $18* ✉ *4226 Piedmont Ave., Oakland* ☎ *510/658–7000* 🌐 *fentonscreamery.com.*

Horn BBQ

$$ | BARBECUE | It's hard to keep track of how many awards pitmaster Matt Horn has won at this point. After roving around the Bay Area for years as a pop-up with his smoker "Lucille," Horn set up shop permanently in West Oakland and has had lines out the door ever since. **Known for:** must-order pit beans on the side; best-in-class banana pudding; tender, irresistible smoked meats and sausages. $ *Average main: $20* ✉ *2534 Mandela Pkwy., Oakland* ☎ *510/225–6101* ⊕ *horn-barbecue.com* ⊘ *Closed Mon.–Wed.*

Shawarmaji

$ | **MIDDLE EASTERN** | Jordan-inspired street food is not easy to find in the Bay Area. The unique Californian catch here is the use of flour tortillas, which are better for the foot-long, narrow wraps that are pressed on the flat top for an extra level of caramelized delight to each bite. **Known for:** shawarma fries; shawarma wraps with homemade pickles and toum sauce; fresh side salads. $ *Average main: $14* ✉ *2123 Franklin St., Oakland* ☎ *510/397–9817* ⊕ *theshawarmaji.com.*

★ Tacos Oscar

$ | **MEXICAN** | Arguably the most talked-about tacos in the entire Bay Area are at this colorful, cheery spot in an alley in between Uptown, Temescal, and Piedmont Ave. The fresh corn tortillas are so tender—almost a revelation. Fillings are always packed with flavor, complemented by dialed-in salsas like a peanut-arbol chile one with carefully charred broccoli. **Known for:** truly exciting bean and cheese taco; fun courtyard seating; pork chile verde taco. $ *Average main: $5* ✉ *420 40th St., Oakland* ⊕ *tacososcar.com* ⊘ *Closed Tues. and Wed. No lunch.*

🛏 Hotels

Best Western Plus Bayside Hotel

$$ | **HOTEL** | This relatively small-sized property has pleasant accommodations with balconies or patios, many overlooking the water and Alameda island. **Pros:** spacious rooms; no destination or amenity fees; easy access to and from airport, Jack London Square, and downtown. **Cons:** few shops or restaurants in walking distance; freeway-side rooms

can be noisy; surprisingly high prices for location. $ *Rooms from: $209* ✉ *1717 Embarcadero, Oakland* ☎ *510/356–2450* ⊕ *www.bestwestern.com* 🛏 *81 rooms* ⦿ *Free Breakfast.*

Kissel Uptown Oakland

$$ | **HOTEL** | For years, Uptown Oakland was a hip neighborhood with outstanding restaurants and bars and nowhere to stay—until this ultra-chic Hyatt-flagged property came along. **Pros:** walking distance to all kinds of places; beautiful art and decorations; rooftop bar High 5ive. **Cons:** smallest rooms are a bit tight; dicey neighborhood; can be too hip of a scene. $ *Rooms from: $229* ✉ *2455 Broadway, Oakland* ☎ *510/216–1500* ⊕ *hyatt.com* 🛏 *168 rooms* ⦿ *No Meals.*

Waterfront Hotel

$ | **HOTEL** | **FAMILY** | Thoroughly modern and pleasantly appointed, this JdV by Hyatt hotel sits among the many breweries and restaurants of Jack London Square and is both a favorite place for locals' family members and a sweet spot for business travelers with its proximity to the square and downtown. **Pros:** outdoor dining in Jack London Square; lovely views, including some water views; outdoor pool. **Cons:** passing trains can be noisy on the city side; parking is pricey; long, dicey walk to downtown. $ *Rooms from: $172* ✉ *10 Washington St., Jack London Square* ☎ *510/836–3800 front desk* ⊕ *jdvhotels.com* 🛏 *145 rooms* ⦿ *No Meals.*

▶ Nightlife

BARS

★ Café Van Kleef

BARS | Long before Uptown got hot, the late Peter Van Kleef was serving stiff fresh-squeezed Greyhounds and booking live music at this funky café-bar that crackles with creative energy—there's still live music every weekend. ✉ *1621 Telegraph Ave., Uptown* ☎ *510/763–7711* ⊕ *cafevankleef.com* ⊘ *Closed Sun. and Mon.*

Friends & Family

BARS | This fantastic woman- and queer-owned bar-restaurant has an excellent compact food menu, standout cocktails, a chic interior design, and one of the best patios in the city. The house margarita is an intriguing must-try drink with mezcal and lemon instead of lime and tequila. Other drinks have eyebrow-raising elements that truly work like melon-infused gin or a coconut water popsicle. The grilled cheese and carrot cake are best in class for those comfort food staples. ✉ 468 25th St., Oakland ☎ 510/225–0469 ⊕ friendsandfamilybar.com.

★ Heinold's First and Last Chance Saloon

BARS | Arguably California's longest continuously active saloon since it opened in 1884, this watering hole, built from the hull of a flat-bottomed stern-wheeler, is where young Jack London got his start as a writer. Historic photos and artifacts hang from the crooked walls and ceilings, which have been atilt since the 1906 earthquake. Get a peek at the slanted bar, where beers on tap and bottomless stories of Oakland history abound. ✉ 48 Webster St., Jack London Square ☎ 510/839–6761 ⊕ www.heinoldsfirstandlastchance.com.

Low Bar

BARS | Unique cocktails; casual eats; and a fun space with plants and lots of natural light makes this one of the most compelling bars in Uptown Oakland. Cocktails have creative elements, like a spiced grapefruit cordial in the mezcal-based Deadbeat Summer. ✉ 2300 Webster St., Oakland ⊕ lowbaroakland.com.

★ Viridian

BARS | Some of the most innovative, pristine cocktails in the Bay Area are at this neon-lit, energetic bar. Bar Director William Tsui previously worked at fine dining juggernaut Lazy Bear in San Francisco, and that high level of meticulous technicality and ingredient sourcing is abundantly clear here across the bay. It's almost unfair that the food menu, nodding to several Asian cuisine elements with a California touch, is so great as well. The narrow space gets packed quickly. ✉ 2216 Broadway, Oakland ⊕ viridianbar.com.

BREWPUBS AND BEER GARDENS

Buck Wild Brewing

BREWPUBS | This chic taproom is California's first 100%-gluten-free brewery, specializing in craft beers made without rye, wheat, or barley. The brewery also has tempting gluten-free fare such as quesadillas and fish tacos. ✉ 401 Jackson St., Jack London Square ☎ 510/350–7938 ⊕ www.buckwildbrew.com ⊗ Closed Mon. and Tues.

Federation Brewing Company

BREWPUBS | Part of Oakland's Ale Trail, the brewery has a convivial tasting room in the Jack London District with plenty of games for extended sipping of their pilsners, saisons, sours, and hoppy IPAs. Their outdoor seating area includes booth areas made of repurposed shipping containers. The taproom hosts live music and events a few nights a month, so make sure to check their calendar. ✉ 420 3rd St., Jack London Square ☎ 510/496–4228 ⊕ www.federationbrewing.com.

Line 51 Brewing—The Terminal Taproom

BREWPUBS | This bright, airy, 7,500-square-foot brewery and taproom is a tribute to its early history, when the brewers hauled their kegs on public transit line 51 to their warehouse. Now, Oakland Ale Trail explorers can enjoy freshly tapped beer from a vintage 1971 AC transit bus that serves as a refrigeration unit for their brews. Fermentation tanks are on full display: the owners are passionate about their Red Death ale, IPAs, Short Dog ale, and porters. ✉ 303 Castro St., Jack London Square ☎ 510/985–4181 ⊕ www.line51beer.com ⊗ Closed Mon. and Tues.

Original Pattern Brewing

BREWPUBS | The love for beer of all varieties is evident in the selection of award-winners at this employee-owned brewery. Original Pattern consistently produces the most satisfying and compelling offerings of any brewery in this beer-loving town. ⊠ *292 4th St., Jack London Square* ☎ *510/844–4833* ⊕ *www. originalpatternbeer.com.*

Sante Adairius Rustic Ales Oakland Arbor

BREWPUBS | In 2022, Sante Adairius opened a taproom in Old Oakland and the entire region rejoiced with plenty of barrel-aged saisons in tulip glasses and pints of intricate hazy IPAs. The intimate, refined saloon space also has a great rear patio. Even though the brews come from an hour away, no visit to Oakland for beer lovers is complete without a stop here. ⊠ *460 8th St., Oakland* ⊕ *rusticales.com.*

MUSIC VENUES

Fox Theater

LIVE MUSIC | This renovated 1928 theater is a remarkable feat of Mediterranean Moorish architecture and has seen the likes of Willie Nelson, the Magnetic Fields, and B.B. King. The venue boasts good sight lines, a state-of-the-art sound system, brilliant acoustics, and a bar with food. ⊠ *1807 Telegraph Ave., Uptown* ☎ *510/302–2250* ⊕ *thefoxoakland.com.*

Yoshi's

LIVE MUSIC | Opened in 1972 as a sushi bar, Yoshi's has evolved into one of the area's best jazz and live music venues. The full experience includes traditional Japanese and Asian fusion cuisine in the adjacent restaurant. ⊠ *510 Embarcadero W, Jack London Square* ☎ *510/238–9200* ⊕ *yoshis.com.*

🎭 Performing Arts

Paramount Theatre

ARTS CENTERS | A glorious art-deco specimen, the Paramount operates as a venue for performances of all kinds, from silent films with orchestras playing the soundtrack, to the Oakland Ballet and Oakland Symphony. Docent-led tours ($5), offered the first and third Saturday of the month, are fun and informative. ⊠ *2025 Broadway, Uptown* ☎ *510/465– 6400* ⊕ *paramountoakland.org.*

🛍 Shopping

Pop-up shops and stylish, locally focused stores are scattered throughout the funky alleys of Old Oakland, Uptown, and Temescal, along with Rockridge's College Ave. Meanwhile, the winding streets around Lake Merritt and Grand Lake offer more modest boutiques.

Bay-Made

SOUVENIRS | Owned and operated by women artists, this gift shop showcases the delightful works of more than 120 Oakland artisans and makers. Browse handcrafted paper and print art, collage art, chocolate, waxworks, jewelry, ceramics, herbs and oils, and quality art and printing supplies. A rotating gallery wall features the latest works from local artists. ⊠ *3295 Lakeshore Ave., Grand Lake* ☎ *510/520–4600* ⊕ *www.bay-made. com* ⊗ *Closed Mon. and Tues.*

Maison d'Etre

HOUSEWARES | This store epitomizes the Rockridge neighborhood's funky-chic shopping scene. Look for high-end housewares along with impulse buys like whimsical watches, imported fruit-tea blends, and funky slippers. ⊠ *5640 College Ave., Rockridge* ☎ *510/658–2801* ⊕ *www.maisondetre.com.*

★ Oaklandish

MIXED CLOTHING | The ultimate place for Oakland swag started in 2000 as a public art project of local pride and has become a celebrated brand around the bay, with clothing and accessories for men, women, and kids. A portion of the proceeds from hip T-shirts and accessories supports grassroots nonprofits committed to bettering the local community. It's good-looking stuff for a good cause. ⊠ *1444 Broadway, Uptown* ☎ *510/251– 9500* ⊕ *oaklandish.com.*

Ordinaire

WINE/SPIRITS | This Grand Lake stalwart deserves an enormous amount of credit for showcasing small-producer, low-intervention wines (what some like to call natural wines), and for making wine an approachable, hip subject. Whether you're enjoying a glass at the bar with some cheese or browsing the impressive selection of retail bottles, this is the local game-changer that made boutique wine as trendy as craft beer and cocktails. ✉ *3354 Grand Ave., Oakland* ☎ *510/350–7524* ⊕ *ordinairewine.com.*

🏃 Activities

Oakland Athletics

BASEBALL & SOFTBALL | FAMILY | Baseball's Oakland Athletics, also called the Oakland A's, has a loyal following among locals in the East Bay and enjoys a fierce rivalry with the San Francisco Giants across the bay. The team hopes to move from its Oakland Coliseum stadium to a proposed new waterfront ballpark at Jack London Square, but that project has repeatedly stalled and fans are discouraged that it might not happen. Major League Baseball is also allowing the team to consider relocating to another city; stay tuned. ✉ *Oakland Coliseum, 7000 Coliseum Way, Oakland* ☎ *877/638–4900* ⊕ *mlb.com/athletics.*

The Marin Headlands

Due west of the Golden Gate Bridge's northern end.

The term "Golden Gate" has become synonymous with the world-famous bridge, but it was first given to the narrow waterway that connects the Pacific and San Francisco Bay. To the north of the Golden Gate Strait lie the Marin Headlands, part of the Golden Gate National Recreation Area (GGNRA), with some of the area's most dramatic scenery.

GETTING HERE AND AROUND

Driving from San Francisco, head north on U.S. 101. Just after you cross the Golden Gate Bridge, take Exit 442 for Alexander Avenue. Keep left at the fork and follow signs for San Francisco/U.S. 101 South. Go through the tunnel under the freeway, and turn right up the hill.

👁 Sights

Marin Headlands

NATIONAL PARK | FAMILY | The stunning headlands stretch from the Golden Gate Bridge to Muir Beach, drawing photographers who perch on the southern heights for spectacular shots of the city and bridge. Equally remarkable are the views north along the coast and out to the ocean, where the Farallon Islands are visible on clear days. Hawk Hill (accessed from Conzelman Road) has a trail with panoramic views and is a great place to watch the fall raptor migration; it's also home to the mission blue butterfly.

The headlands' strategic position at the mouth of San Francisco Bay made them a logical site for military installations from 1890 through the Cold War. Today you can explore the crumbling concrete batteries where naval guns once protected the area. Main attractions are centered on Forts Barry and Cronkhite, which are separated by Rodeo Lagoon and Rodeo Beach, a dark stretch of sand that attracts sandcastle builders and dog owners. ✉ *Sausalito* ☎ *415/331–1540* ⊕ *www.nps.gov/goga* 💲 *Free.*

Sausalito

2 miles north of Golden Gate Bridge.

Bougainvillea-covered hillsides and an expansive yacht harbor give Sausalito the feel of an Adriatic resort. The town sits on the northwestern edge of San Francisco Bay, where it's sheltered from the ocean by the Marin Headlands; the mostly mild weather here is perfect for strolling and outdoor dining. Nevertheless, morning fog and afternoon winds can roll over the hills without warning, funneling through the central part of Sausalito once known as Hurricane Gulch.

South of Bridgeway, which snakes between the bay and the hills, a water-side esplanade is lined with restaurants on piers that lure diners with good seafood and even better views. Stairs along the west side of Bridgeway and throughout town climb into wooded hill-side neighborhoods filled with both rustic and opulent homes. Back on the northern portion of the shoreline, harbors shelter a community of more than 400 house-boats. As you amble along Bridgeway past shops and galleries, you'll notice the absence of basic services. Find them and more on Caledonia Street, which runs parallel to Bridgeway and inland a couple of blocks. While ferry-side shops flaunt kitschy souvenirs, smaller side streets and narrow alleyways offer eccentric jewelry and handmade crafts.

■ TIP → **The ferry is the best way to get to Sausalito from San Francisco; you get more romance (and less traffic) and disembark in the heart of downtown.**

First occupied by the Coast Miwok tribe and later visited by Spanish explorers who called the area Saucito (Little Willow) for the trees growing along its streams, Sausalito was developed as a ranch in 1838 under the ownership of English mariner William Richardson. It served as a port for whaling ships and became a major terminus for transport by rail, ferry, and, eventually, car. By the mid-1800s, wealthy San Franciscans had made Sausalito their getaway across the bay and built lavish Victorian summer homes in the hills. Meanwhile, an influx of hardworking, fun-loving merchants and working-class folk populated the waterfront area, which grew thick with saloons, gambling dens, and bordellos. Bootleggers flourished during Prohibition,

and shipyard workers swelled the town's population in the 1940s, at the height of World War II.

Sausalito developed its bohemian flair in the 1950s and '60s, when creative types, including artist Jean Varda, poet Shel Silverstein, and madam Sally Stanford, established an artists' colony and a houseboat community here (this is Otis Redding's "Dock of the Bay"). Both the spirit of the artists and the neighborhood of floating homes persist. For a close-up view of the quirky community, head north on Bridgeway, turn right on Gate Six Road, park where it dead-ends, and enter through the unlocked gates.

GETTING HERE AND AROUND

From San Francisco by car or bike, follow U.S. 101 North across the Golden Gate Bridge and take Exit 442 for Alexander Avenue, just past Vista Point; continue down the winding hill toward the water to where the road becomes Bridgeway. Golden Gate Transit's Bus 130 will drop you off in downtown Sausalito, and the ferries dock downtown as well. The center of town is flat, with plenty of sidewalks and bay views. It's a pleasure and a must to explore on foot.

ESSENTIALS

Sausalito Chamber of Commerce. ⊠ 1913 Bridgeway, Sausalito ☎ 415/331–7262 ⊕ www.sausalito.org.

◉ Sights

Bay Model Visitor Center

VISITOR CENTER | FAMILY | One of the Bay Area's most unique attractions is a model of itself. It's a giant—over an acre—hydraulic model of the San Francisco Bay–San Joaquin River Delta (Sacramento area) water systems by the US Army Corps of Engineers. For visitors and tourists alike, it's a fascinating place to learn about one of the most complex, diverse environmental regions in the country. ⊠ 2100 Bridgeway, Sausalito ☎ 415/289–3007 ⊕ www.spn.usace.

Marin County

0   5 mi

0   5 km

army.mil/missions/recreation/bay-model-visitor-center ⊠ Free ⊘ Closed Sun. and Mon

The Marine Mammal Center

COLLEGE | FAMILY | This hospital for distressed, sick, and injured marine animals is a leading center for ocean conservancy in the Bay Area and the largest rehabilitation center of its kind in the world. Dedicated to pioneering education, rehabilitation, and research, the center is free and open daily to the public. Tour the facilities and see how elephant seals, sea lions, and pups are cared for and meet the scientists who care for them. Bonus: you'll catch some of the best views of the Marin Headlands and San Francisco Bay along the way. ⊠ *2000 Bunker Rd., Sausalito* ☎ *415/653–1870* ⊕ *www. marinemammalcenter.org* ⊠ *Free* ☞ *Check website for tour times.*

Sally Stanford Drinking Fountain

FOUNTAIN | There's an unusual historic landmark on the Sausalito Ferry Pier—a drinking fountain inscribed "Have a drink on Sally" in remembrance of Sally Stanford, the former San Francisco brothel madam who became Sausalito's mayor in the 1970s. Sassy Sally would have appreciated the fountain's eccentric attachment: a knee-level basin with the inscription "Have a drink on Leland," in memory of her beloved dog. ⊠ *Sausalito Ferry Pier, Anchor St. at Humboldt St., off southwest corner of Gabrielson Park, Sausalito* ⊕ *www.oursausalito.com.*

Viña del Mar Plaza and Park

PLAZA/SQUARE | The landmark Plaza Viña del Mar, named for Sausalito's sister city in Chile, marks the center of town. Adjacent to the parking lot and ferry pier, the plaza is flanked by two 14-foot-tall statues of elephants, which were created for the Panama–Pacific International Exposition World's Fair held in San Francisco in 1915. A picture-perfect fountain here is great for people-watching. ✉ *Bridgeway and El Portal St., Sausalito* 🌐 *www.oursausalito.com.*

🍴 Restaurants

The Joinery

$ | **AMERICAN** | Sausalito's popular beer hall and rotisserie offers ample, open, airy indoor seating at long tables and expanded outdoor deck dining with exceptional views of the bay. It's a relaxing spot to enjoy burgers, sandwiches, soups, and salads along with a selection of Belgian beers, IPAs, lagers, and ciders on tap. **Known for:** fried chicken sandwich and grilled cheese; Joinery burger with special sauce; dirty fries and fried Brussels sprouts. [$] *Average main: $14* ✉ *300 Turney St., Sausalito* ☎ *415/766–8999* 🌐 *www.joineryca.com.*

Le Garage

$$$ | **FRENCH** | Brittany-born Olivier Souvestre serves traditional French bistro fare in a relaxed, bayside setting that feels more sidewalk café than the converted garage that it is. The restaurant seats only 35 inside and 15 outside, so make reservations or arrive early. **Known for:** PEI mussels and house-cut fries; popular weekend brunch; outstanding bouillabaisse. [$] *Average main: $34* ✉ *85 Liberty Ship Way, Suite 109, Sausalito* ☎ *415/332–5625* 🌐 *www.legaragesausalito.com* 🕘 *Closed Mon. No dinner Sun.*

Poggio

$$ | **MODERN ITALIAN** | Poggio serves modern Tuscan comfort food in a handsome, old world–inspired space. An extensive and ever-changing menu, with ingredients sourced from the restaurant's garden and local farms, features local and Italian wines, fresh fish, and wood-fired pizzas. **Known for:** burrata; grilled half chicken with brown butter; spaghetti carbonara. [$] *Average main: $27* ✉ *777 Bridgeway, at Bay St., Sausalito* ☎ *415/332–7771* 🌐 *www.poggiotrattoria.com.*

Sausalito Seahorse

$$ | **ITALIAN** | Live music and dancing complement Tuscan seafood and pasta specialties here and make the Seahorse one of Sausalito's most spirited supper clubs. Sample an abundant antipasti menu and homemade gnocchi on outdoor patios or enjoy the band inside with a seafood pasta or lasagna classica. **Known for:** seafood stew; schiacciata (a type of Tuscan bread) panini; fun atmosphere. [$] *Average main: $25* ✉ *305 Harbor Dr., Sausalito* ☎ *415/331–2899* 🌐 *www.sausalitoseahorse.com* 🕘 *No dinner Mon.*

★ Sushi Ran

$$$ | **JAPANESE** | Sushi aficionados swear that this tiny, stylish restaurant is the Bay Area's finest option for raw fish, but don't overlook the excellent Pacific Rim fusions, a melding of Japanese ingredients and French techniques. Book in advance or expect a wait, which you can soften by sipping one of the bar's 30 by-the-glass sakes. **Known for:** glorious pristine raw fish preparations; local miso-glazed black cod; outstanding sake and wine list. [$] *Average main: $35* ✉ *107 Caledonia St., at Pine St., Sausalito* ☎ *415/332–3620* 🌐 *sushiran.com* 🕘 *No lunch Mon.–Thurs.*

☕ Coffee and Quick Bites

★ Fish

$$ | **SEAFOOD** | **FAMILY** | Unsurprisingly, fish—specifically, fresh, sustainably caught fish—is the focus at this gleaming dockside fish house a mile north of downtown. Order at the counter and then grab a seat by the floor-to-ceiling windows or at a picnic table on the pier, overlooking the yachts and fishing boats. **Known for:** fish taco plate; fish reuben sandwich; local tuna poke. [$] *Average main: $23* ✉ *350 Harbor Dr., at Gate 5*

Rd., off Bridgeway, Sausalito ☎ *415/331–3474* 🌐 *www.331fish.com.*

Salsalito Taco Shop

$ | **MEXICAN** | This breezy spot has been a locals' go-to for Baja Mexico–style tacos with distinct Californian influences since the early 2000s. Diners tend to choose two or three kinds of tacos for a meal, perhaps free-range chicken roasted in achiote and sautéed shrimp. **Known for:** tequila-free margaritas with agave wine; fish tacos; colorful, beach-like vibe inside and outside. [$] *Average main: $15* ✉ *1115 Bridgeway, Sausalito* ☎ *415/331–5595* 🌐 *salsalitotacoshop.com* 🕒 *Hrs and closures vary seasonally.*

Hotels

Cavallo Point

$$$ | **HOTEL** | With a striking setting almost at the foot of the Golden Gate Bridge, this refined, upscale destination is truly the closest countryside getaway to San Francisco. **Pros:** can't beat the setting and urban proximity combination; excellent restaurant, bar, and spa; activities like guided hikes and yoga classes. **Cons:** not as luxurious as some of its peers; very hard to get rideshares; long walk to anything. [$] *Rooms from: $425* ✉ *601 Murray Circle, Sausalito* ☎ *888/651–2003, 415/339–4700* 🌐 *cavallopoint.com* 🛏 *142 rooms* 🍴 *No Meals.*

The Inn Above Tide

$$$ | **B&B/INN** | The balconies at the inn literally hang over the water, and each of its rooms has a "perfect 10" view that takes in wild Angel Island as well as the city lights across the bay. **Pros:** generous continental breakfast; walking distance to lots of sights and restaurants; beautiful beach meets urbane room decor. **Cons:** expensive; some rooms are on the small side; ferry-side rooms can be noisy. [$] *Rooms from: $465* ✉ *30 El Portal, Sausalito* ☎ *415/332–9535, 800/893–8433* 🌐 *www.innabovetide.com* 🛏 *33 rooms* 🍴 *Free Breakfast.*

Tiburon

7 miles north of Sausalito, 11 miles north of Golden Gate Bridge.

On a peninsula that was named Punta de Tiburón (Shark Point) by 18th-century Spanish explorers, this beautiful Marin County community retains the feel of a village—it's more low-key than Sausalito—despite the encroachment of commercial establishments from the downtown area. The harbor faces Angel Island across Raccoon Strait, and San Francisco is directly south across the bay, making the views from the decks of harbor restaurants major attractions. Since 1884, when the San Francisco and North Pacific Railroad relocated their ferry terminal facilities to the harbor town, Tiburon has centered on the waterfront. The ferry is the most relaxing (and fastest) way to get here and allows you to skip traffic and parking problems.

One of the bay's best secrets in plain sight, Angel Island State Park (🌐 *www.parks.ca.gov*) offers 13 miles of roads and trails from the perimeter up to Mt. Livermore (788 feet), with magnificent panoramic views. The 12-minute ferry ride to Angel Island from Tiburon (🎫 *$17.40 round-trip*) includes the cost of park admission.

■ **TIP→ To see the sites by bike, rent on the island (🌐 *www.angelisland.com/bike-rentals*).**

GETTING HERE AND AROUND

The Golden Gate Ferry travels between San Francisco and Tiburon daily. By car, head north from San Francisco on U.S. 101 and get off at CA 131/Tiburon Boulevard/East Blithedale Avenue (Exit 447). Turn right onto Tiburon Boulevard and drive just over 4 miles to downtown. Note that there is no bus service directly to Tiburon; ferry is the only public transit available. Tiburon's Main Street is perfect for wandering, as are the footpaths that frame the water's edge.

ESSENTIALS

destination: Tiburon. ✉ *Town Hall, 1505 Tiburon Blvd., Tiburon* ☎ *415/435–2298* 🌐 *www.destinationtiburon.org.*

Sights

Ark Row

STREET | The historic second block of Main Street is known as Ark Row and has a tree-shaded walk lined with antiques shops, restaurants, and specialty stores. The quaint stretch gets its name from the 19th-century ark houseboats that floated in Belvedere Cove before being beached and transformed into stores. **■ TIP→ If you're curious about architectural history, the Tiburon Heritage & Arts Commission has a self-guided walking-tour map, available online and at local businesses.** ✉ *Ark Row, Main St., south of Juanita La., Tiburon* 🌐 *www.townoftiburon.org.*

Old St. Hilary's Landmark and John Thomas Howell Wildflower Preserve

CHURCH | The architectural centerpiece here is a stark-white 1888 Carpenter Gothic church that overlooks the town and the bay from its hillside perch. Surrounding the church, which was dedicated as a historical monument in 1959, is a wildflower preserve that's spectacular in May and June, when the rare Tiburon paintbrush and Tiburon black jewel flower bloom. Expect a steep walk uphill to reach the preserve. The Landmarks Society arranges guided tours by appointment. **■ TIP→ The hiking trails behind the landmark wind up to a peak that has views of the entire Bay Area.** ✉ *201 Esperanza St., Tiburon* ☎ *415/435–1853* 🌐 *landmarkssociety.com* 🕒 *Church closed Mon.–Sat. and Nov.–Mar.*

Railroad & Ferry Depot Museum

HISTORY MUSEUM | A short waterfront walk from the ferry landing, this free museum in Shoreline Park is a well-preserved time capsule of the city's industrial history, complete with working trains. The landmark building has a detailed scale model of Tiburon and its 43-acre rail yard at the turn of the 20th century, when the city served as a major railroad and ferry hub for San Francisco Bay. The Depot House Museum on the second floor showcases a restoration of the stationmaster's living quarters. ✉ *1920 Paradise Dr., Tiburon* ☎ *415/435–1853* 🌐 *landmarkssociety.com* 🕒 *Closed Mon.–Sat. and Oct.–Apr.*

Restaurants

Bungalow Kitchen

$$$ | MODERN AMERICAN | Tiburon's low-key, mostly casual dining scene received a jolt of energy when celebrity chef Michael Mina and partner Brent Bolthouse opened this hip restaurant right next to the ferry dock in 2021. It's certainly a scene and a place to dress up, yet it's also a compelling destination for terrific eats that don't adhere to many rules or cuisines other than high-quality ingredients. **Known for:** festive, prix-fixe weekend brunch; tuna tartare and yellowtail sashimi preparations; the rare Marin restaurant with food on weekends until midnight. [$] *Average main: $39* ✉ *5 Main St., Tiburon* ☎ *415/366–4088* 🌐 *bungalowkitchen.com* 🕒 *Closed Mon. and Tues. No lunch weekdays.*

★ Luna Blu

$$$ | SICILIAN | Friendly, informative staff serve Sicilian-inspired seafood in this lively Italian restaurant just a stone's throw from the ferry. Enjoy views on the expansive heated patio overlooking the bay, or cozy up with friends on one of the high-sided booths near the bar. **Known for:** sustainably caught seafood and local, organic ingredients; homemade pastas; rock crab bisque. [$] *Average main: $35* ✉ *35 Main St., Tiburon* ☎ *415/789–5844* 🌐 *lunablurestaurant.com* 🕒 *Closed Tues. No lunch weekdays.*

Salt & Pepper

$$ | AMERICAN | FAMILY | Bright and welcoming, this American bistro on Ark Row is known for its seafood starters (oyster poppers, crab stacks, scallops, and steamers) and salads as well as shareable dishes and burgers, chops, and ribs. The airy, rustic space has a pleasant café-like atmosphere that makes it easy to stay and even consider returning for a breakfast of Dungeness crab omelet or ricotta pancakes. **Known for:** clam chowder; kabocha squash and vegetable curry; Mongolian pork chops and rib-eye steaks. $ *Average main: $27* ⊠ *38 Main St., Tiburon* 🕾 *415/435–3594* ⊕ *www. saltandpeppertiburon.com.*

★ Sam's Anchor Cafe

$$ | **AMERICAN** | Open since 1920, this beloved dockside restaurant is the town's most famous eatery, and after 99 years, a bright remodel includes floor-to-ceiling sliding-glass doors and an 80-foot heated bench for deck views on cool days. Remnants of Sam's history are evident in some vintage decor, the hamburger and Champagne specials, and the free popcorn. **Known for:** excellent raw bar; pink lemonade and margarita "bowls"; Dungeness crab Louie. $ *Average main: $26* ⊠ *27 Main St., Tiburon* 🕾 *415/435– 4527* ⊕ *samscafe.com.*

☕ Coffee and Quick Bites

Waypoint Pizza

$ | **PIZZA** | **FAMILY** | A nautical theme and a tasty "between the sheets" pizza-style sandwich are signatures of this creative pizzeria, which is housed in the 19th-century landmark building that was once home to the Pioneer Boathouse. Indoor deck chairs and a picnic table complete with umbrella add a playful air. **Known for:** pizza-style sandwiches; wild shrimp pesto pizza; soft-serve organic ice cream. $ *Average main: $15* ⊠ *15 Main St., Tiburon* 🕾 *415/435–3440* ⊕ *www. waypointpizza.com.*

🛏 Hotels

Waters Edge Hotel

$$ | **B&B/INN** | This stylish downtown hotel feels like an inviting retreat by the water—the views are stunning, and the lighting is perfect. **Pros:** complimentary wine and cheese every evening; restaurants and sights are steps away; free bike rentals. **Cons:** downstairs rooms lack privacy and balconies; paid self-parking; two-night minimum weekends, three-night minimum holidays. $ *Rooms from: $319* ⊠ *25 Main St., Tiburon* 🕾 *415/789– 5999* ⊕ *watersedgehotel.com* ⇥ *23 rooms* ⦿⧉ *Free Breakfast.*

👜 Shopping

Local Spicery

FOOD | This is the place for spices of all varieties from around the world, from aji amarillo chili to za'atar. The apothecary-like storefront features an aromatic library of loose teas and spices milled in small quantities and prepared in small-batch hand blends to obtain maximum freshness and quality. ⊠ *80 Main St., Tiburon* 🕾 *415/435–1100* ⊕ *www.local-spicery.com* ⊗ *Closed Tues. and Wed.*

Schoenberg Guitars

MUSIC | Chockablock with handmade guitars alongside vintage classics, this shop is a treat even for those who don't play music. Dozens of guitars varying in size, shape, and color hang from the walls and stand against the polished wood floor. There's an organized beauty to the layout and a comforting sense of musical harmony. You may even enjoy an impromptu concert or workshop. ⊠ *Ark Row Shopping Center, 106 Main St., Tiburon* 🕾 *415/789–0846* ⊕ *www.om28. com* ⊗ *Closed Sun. and Mon.*

Tiburon Wine

WINE/SPIRITS | Some 200 regional and international wines as well as local Skywalker wines (from George Lucas's ranch) line the walls of this cozy shop, which has an indoor tasting room and outdoor seating for sipping by the glass or bottle. ⊠ *84 Main St., Tiburon* ☎ *415/435–3499* ⊕ *tiburonwine.net.*

Mill Valley

2 miles north of Sausalito, 4 miles north of Golden Gate Bridge.

Chic and woodsy Mill Valley has a dual personality. Here, as elsewhere in the county, the foundation is a superb natural setting. Virtually surrounded by parkland, the town lies at the base of Mt. Tamalpais and contains dense redwood groves traversed by countless creeks. But this is no lumber camp. Smart restaurants and chichi boutiques line streets that have been roamed by more rock stars than one might suspect.

The rustic village flavor is a holdover from the town's early days as a center for the lumber industry. In 1896, the Mt. Tamalpais Scenic Railroad—dubbed the "Crookedest Railroad in the World" because of its curvy tracks—began transporting visitors from Mill Valley to the top of Mt. Tam and down to Muir Woods, and the town soon became a vacation retreat for city slickers. The trains stopped running in the 1930s as cars became more popular, but the old railway depot still serves as the center of town: the 1929 building has been transformed into the popular Depot Café & Bookstore, at ⊠ *87 Throckmorton Avenue.*

The small downtown area has the constant bustle of a leisure community; even on weekdays people are out shopping for fancy cookware, eco-friendly home furnishings, and boutique clothing.

GETTING HERE AND AROUND
By car from San Francisco, head north on U.S. 101 and get off at CA 131/Tiburon Boulevard/East Blithedale Avenue (Exit 447). Turn left onto East Blithedale Avenue and continue west to Throckmorton

Avenue; turn left to reach Depot Plaza, then park. Golden Gate Transit buses serve Mill Valley from San Francisco. Once here, explore the town on foot.

ESSENTIALS
Mill Valley Chamber of Commerce & Visitor Center. ⊠ *85 Throckmorton Ave., Mill Valley* ☎ *415/388–9700* ⊕ *www.millvalley. org.*

◉ Sights

Lytton Square
PLAZA/SQUARE | FAMILY | Mill Valley locals congregate on weekends to socialize in the coffeehouses and cafés near the town's central square, but it's buzzing most of any day of the week with the lunchtime crowd, tourists, and Marin residents running errands. The Mill Valley Depot Café & Bookstore at the hub of it all is the place to grab a coffee and sweet treat while reading or playing a game of chess. Shops, restaurants, and cultural venues line the nearby streets. ⊠ *Miller and Throckmorton Aves., Mill Valley.*

★ Marin County Civic Center
NOTABLE BUILDING | A wonder of arches, circles, skylights, and an eye-catching blue roof just 10 miles north of Mill Valley, the Civic Center was Frank Lloyd Wright's largest public project (and his final commission) and has been designated a national and state historic landmark. It's a performance venue and is adjacent to where the always-fun Marin County Fair is held each summer. Ninety-minute docent-led tours begin Friday mornings at 10:30 am. ⊠ *3501 Civic Center Dr., San Rafael* ☎ *415/473–6400 Cultural Services department* ⊕ *www.marincounty.org* 🎟 *Free; tour $12* 🕙 *Closed weekends.*

Mill Valley Lumber Yard
NEIGHBORHOOD | FAMILY | The lumber yard, once a vital center of the region's logging industry, is now a vibrant micro-village of craftsfolk, bread bakers, textile makers, and lifestyle designers, and their boutiques and restaurants. You'll even find a

Did You Know?

The gorgeous old-growth redwood trees in Muir Woods are often enveloped in fog, which provides the moisture to help them survive the dry summers.

chocolate art studio where custom-designed chocolates and truffles may look almost too good to eat. The preserved brick-red historic structures are hard to miss along Miller Avenue, and with plenty of parking in the area, plus picnic tables and outdoor space, it's well worth a visit. ⊠ *129 Miller Ave., Mill Valley* ⊕ *www.millvalleylumberyard.com.*

★ Mt. Tamalpais State Park

MOUNTAIN | FAMILY | The view of Mt. Tamalpais from all around the bay can be a beauty, but that's nothing compared to the views from the mountain, which take in San Francisco, the East Bay, the coast, and beyond. Although the summit of Mt. Tamalpais is only 2,571 feet high, the mountain rises practically from sea level, dominating the topography of Marin County. For years the 6,300-acre park has been a favorite destination for hikers, with more than 200 miles of trails. The park's major thoroughfare, Panoramic Highway, snakes its way up from U.S. 101 to the Pantoll Ranger Station and down to Stinson Beach. Parking is free along the roadside, but there's an $8 fee (cash or check only) at the ranger station and additional charges for walk-in campsites and group use.

The Mountain Theater, also known as the Cushing Memorial Amphitheatre, is a natural 3,750-seat amphitheater that has showcased summer Mountain Plays since 1913. The Rock Spring Trail starts at the Mountain Theater and gently climbs for 1½ miles to the West Point Inn, where you can relax at picnic tables before forging ahead via Old Railroad Grade Fire Road and the Miller Trail to Mt. Tam's Middle Peak.

From the Pantoll Ranger Station, the precipitous Steep Ravine Trail brings you past stands of coastal redwoods. Hike the connecting Dipsea Trail to reach Stinson Beach. ■TIP→ **If you're too weary to make the 3½-mile trek back up, Marin Transit Bus 61 takes you from Stinson Beach back to the ranger station.** ⊠ *Pantoll Ranger Station, 3801 Panoramic Hwy., Mill Valley* ☎ *415/388–2070* ⊕ *www.parks.ca.gov.*

★ Muir Woods National Monument

NATIONAL PARK | FAMILY | One of the last old-growth stands of redwood (*Sequoia sempervirens*) giants, Muir Woods is nature's cathedral: awe-inspiring and not to be missed. The nearly 560 acres of Muir Woods National Monument contain some of the most majestic redwoods in the world—some more than 250 feet tall.

Part of the Golden Gate National Recreation Area, Muir Woods is a pedestrian's park. The popular two-mile main trail begins at the park headquarters and provides easy access to streams, ferns, azaleas, and redwood groves. Summer weekends can prove busy, so consider taking a more challenging route, such as the Dipsea Trail, which climbs west from the forest floor to soothing views of the ocean and the Golden Gate Bridge.

Picnicking and camping aren't allowed, and neither are pets. Crowds can be large, especially from May through October, so come early in the morning or late in the afternoon. The Muir Woods Visitor Center has books and exhibits about redwood trees and the woods' history as well as the latest info on trail conditions; the Muir Woods Trading Company serves hot food, organic pastries, and other tasty snacks, and the gift shop offers plenty of souvenirs.

■TIP→ **Muir Woods has no cell service or Wi-Fi, so plan directions and communication ahead of time.**

For parking reservations (required) and shuttle information, visit ⊕ *gomuirwoods. com.* To drive directly from San Francisco, take U.S. 101 North across the Golden Gate Bridge to Exit 445B for Mill Valley/Stinson Beach, then follow signs for Highway 1 North and Muir Woods. ⊠ *1 Muir Woods Rd., off Panoramic Hwy., Mill Valley* ☎ *415/561–2850 park reservations* ⊕ *www.nps.gov/muwo* ⊠ *$15.*

Old Mill Park

CITY PARK | FAMILY | To see one of the outdoor oases that make Mill Valley so appealing, follow Throckmorton Avenue west from Lytton Square to Old Mill Park, a shady patch of redwoods that shelters a playground and reconstructed sawmill. The park also hosts September's annual Mill Valley Fall Arts Festival. From the park, Cascade Way winds its way past creek-side homes to the trailheads of several forest paths. ⊠ *Throckmorton Ave. and Cascade Dr., Mill Valley* ☎ *415/383–1370 for rental information* ⊕ *www.millvalleyrecreation.org.*

🍴 Restaurants

Buckeye Roadhouse

$$ | AMERICAN | House-smoked meats and fish, grilled steaks, classic salads, and decadent desserts bring locals and visitors back again and again to this 1937 lodge-style roadhouse. Enjoy a Marin martini at the cozy bar or sip local wine beside the river-rock fireplace. **Known for:** oysters bingo; chili-lime "brick" chicken; ribs and chops. Ⓢ *Average main: $30* ⊠ *15 Shoreline Hwy., Mill Valley* ☎ *415/331–2600* ⊕ *www.buckeyeroadhouse.com* ⊙ *No lunch weekdays.*

Bungalow 44

$$ | MODERN AMERICAN | An open, well-lit space with booths and countertop seating from which diners can watch the cooks in action sets the scene at this lively eatery, which serves contemporary California cuisine and inventive cocktails. The menu focuses on locally sourced veggies and seafood. **Known for:** $1 oyster happy hour; root beer–braised short rib; kickin' fried chicken. Ⓢ *Average main: $27* ⊠ *44 E. Blithedale Ave., Mill Valley* ☎ *415/381–2500* ⊕ *www.bungalow44.com* ⊙ *No lunch.*

La Ginestra

$$ | ITALIAN | FAMILY | In business since 1964, La Ginestra—named for the flowers that grow on Mt. Vesuvius, in the owners' homeland—is a Mill Valley institution renowned for its no-pretense, family-style Italian meals and impressive wine list. The Sorrento Bar, off the dining room, serves up a delectable array of bar bites, pizzas, and sweets to enjoy while sipping wines and cocktails. **Known for:** handmade pasta and gnocchi; excellent ravioli; daily fish and small plates. Ⓢ *Average main: $24* ⊠ *127 Throckmorton Ave., Mill Valley* ☎ *415/388–0224* ⊕ *www.laginestramv.com* ⊙ *Closed Mon. and Tues. No lunch.*

Paseo: A California Bistro

$$$ | MODERN AMERICAN | In a cozy setting down a quiet alley with a beautiful brick-walled courtyard, peak seasonal produce and Northern California farms and artisans are highlighted on chef Brandon Breazeale. Start with one of the beautifully fresh salads before continuing on to a rustic yet refined main like duck breast with yellow mole and squash blossom tamale. **Known for:** fantastic selection of wines and cocktails; locally rooted menu with exciting global influences; weekend brunch dishes like huevos rancheros with homemade chorizo. Ⓢ *Average main: $36* ⊠ *17 Throckmorton Ave., Mill Valley* ☎ *415/888–3907* ⊕ *paseobistro.com* ⊙ *Closed Mon. No lunch weekdays.*

Piazza D'Angelo

$$ | ITALIAN | FAMILY | Busy D'Angelo's is known for its authentic and fresh pastas; there are even gluten-free options. Another draw is the scene, especially in the lounge area, which hosts a lively cocktail hour in a traditional trattoria setting. **Known for:** fresh seafood; homemade pasta; top-notch tiramisu. Ⓢ *Average main: $23* ⊠ *22 Miller Ave., Mill Valley* ☎ *415/388–2000* ⊕ *www.piazzadangelo.com* ⊙ *No lunch Mon.–Thurs.*

Playa

$ | MODERN MEXICAN | Modern Mexican farm-to-table creations and inspired cocktails are the focus of this festive indoor-outdoor space that's popular for its firepit, made-to-order masa station, and happy hour. An open kitchen serves up locally sourced, organic, and sustainable dishes like ceviche and flautas, grilled fresh fish tacos, and braised pork tortas. **Known for:** tacos with creative fillings like scallops; rare tequilas and mezcals; moles and salsas. $ *Average main: $18 ⌧ 41 Throckmorton Ave., Mill Valley ☎ 415/384–8871 ⊕ www.playamv.com ⊘ Closed Mon. No lunch Tues.–Thurs.*

☕ Coffee and Quick Bites

Avatar's Restaurant

$ | **INDIAN** | The lines can get long at this hole-in-the-wall, no-frills kitchen, where Indian curries are served burrito-style while you wait. Punjabi burritos or rice plates come with savory lamb, chicken, fish, vegetarian, and vegan ingredients flavored with seasonal fruit chutneys, tamarind sauce, and aromatic blends. **Known for:** curried pumpkin; smoked eggplant; Avatar's Dream fusion dessert. $ *Average main: $12 ⌧ 15 Madrona St., Mill Valley ☎ 415/381–8293 ⊕ avatarsrestaurant.square.site ▭ No credit cards.*

Equator Coffees

$ | **CAFÉ** | This is the prime spot for a pick-me-up over a picturesque view of downtown Mill Valley and Mt. Tam. The owners are as serious about coffee as they are about social responsibility, from their fair-chain single-origin beans and organic loose teas down to the locally recycled wood and metal decor. **Known for:** espresso and cappuccino drinks; breakfast sandwiches; strawberry and chocolate waffles. $ *Average main: $9 ⌧ 2 Miller Ave., Mill Valley ☎ 415/383–1651 ⊕ www.equatorcoffees.com ⊘ No dinner.*

Hotels

Acqua Hotel

$$ | **HOTEL** | Alongside Richardson Bay, this stylish boutique hotel has modern, elegant rooms decorated in soft Zen-like color schemes. **Pros:** evening wine service; free parking and easy to get to San Francisco; hearty breakfast buffet. **Cons:** next to freeway; traffic audible in rooms facing east; several rooms are truly cramped. $ *Rooms from: $289 ⌧ 555 Redwood Hwy., Mill Valley ☎ 415/380–0400 ⊕ acquahotel.com ⇄ 49 rooms ⦿ Free Breakfast.*

Mill Valley Inn

$$ | **B&B/INN** | The only hotel in downtown Mill Valley comprises one of the area's first homes, the Creek House, which has smart-looking Victorian rooms, and two small cottages nestled in a grove beyond a creek. **Pros:** unique rooms in private yet central location; some rooms have balconies, soaking tubs, and fireplaces; free mountain bikes. **Cons:** some rooms feel dated; dark in winter; no attached restaurant. $ *Rooms from: $349 ⌧ 165 Throckmorton Ave., Mill Valley ☎ 415/389–6608 ⊕ millvalleyinn.com ⇄ 25 rooms ⦿ Free Breakfast.*

Mountain Home Inn

$$ | **B&B/INN** | Abutting 40,000 acres of state and national parks, this airy wooden inn sits on the skirt of Mt. Tamalpais, where you can follow hiking trails all the way to Stinson Beach. **Pros:** amazing terrace and views; peaceful, remote setting; handsome, rustic room design. **Cons:** nearest town is a 12-minute drive away; restaurant can get crowded on sunny weekend days; some rooms are tiny and have no TVs. $ *Rooms from: $228 ⌧ 810 Panoramic Hwy., Mill Valley ☎ 415/381–9000 ⊕ www.mtnhomeinn.com ⇄ 10 rooms ⦿ Free Breakfast.*

☒ Nightlife

BREWPUBS AND BEER GARDENS

The Junction Beer Garden & Bottle Shop

BEER GARDENS | With more than a hundred styles of canned and bottled beers and 30 beers on tap, plus wine and hard kombucha, this enormous indoor and outdoor beer garden is perfectly situated along the Dipsea Trail for a visit before or after a Mt. Tam hike or Tennessee Valley beach visit. The brewers partnered with PizzaHacker, a cult-favorite pizzeria in San Francisco's Bernal Heights, to provide classic pies like their "top-shelf" Margherita, as well as salads and meatballs. The landscaped outdoor space is lined with picnic tables, Adirondack chairs, and firepits. ⊠ *226 Shoreline Hwy., Mill Valley* ☎ *415/888–3544* ⊕ *thejunc.com.*

MUSIC VENUES
Sweetwater Music Hall
LIVE MUSIC | With the gracious help of Bob Weir of the Grateful Dead, this renowned nightclub and café reopened in a historic Masonic Hall in 2012. Famous and up-and-coming bands play on most nights, and local stars such as Bonnie Raitt and Huey Lewis sometimes stop in for a pickup session. ⊠ *19 Corte Madera Ave., Mill Valley* ☎ *415/388–3850* ⊕ *sweetwatermusichall.com.*

Performing Arts

★ Throckmorton Theatre
ARTS CENTERS | A vibrant cultural hub in the region, the restored cinema and vaudeville house in Mill Valley is known for fostering exceptional arts and education. The darling playhouse seats upward of 260 and features live theater, comedy, and concerts. Two smaller street-side halls, the Tivoli and Crescendo, feature Tuesday night comedy shows, along with improvisation workshops, jazz performances, and new art exhibits every month. ⊠ *142 Throckmorton Ave., Mill Valley* ☎ *415/383–9600* ⊕ *www.throckmortontheatre.org* ⟟ *Tickets from $20.*

Shopping

Mill Valley Market
FOOD | This family-owned market is the go-to stop for specialty foods, groceries, deli items, and hot food. Known for the notable beer and wine selection alongside local and organic produce and healthy grab-and-go foods, this is an ideal place to prepare for a picnic or seek out gourmet gifts, like imported chocolates and 100-year-old balsamic vinegars. ⊠ *12 Corte Madera Ave., Mill Valley* ☎ *415/388–3222* ⊕ *millvalleymarket.com.*

Muir Beach

12 miles northwest of Golden Gate Bridge, 6 miles southwest of Mill Valley.

Except on the sunniest of weekends, Muir Beach is relatively quiet, but the drive to this community and beach is a scenic adventure.

GETTING HERE AND AROUND
A car is the best way to reach Muir Beach. From Highway 1, follow Pacific Way southwest a quarter mile.

 ## Beaches

Muir Beach
BEACH | FAMILY | Small but scenic, this beach—a rocky patch of shoreline off Highway 1—is a good place to stretch your legs and gaze out at the Pacific Ocean. Locals often walk their dogs here; families and cuddling couples come for picnicking and sunbathing. At the northern end of the beach are waterfront homes (and occasional nude sunbathers), and at the other are the bluffs of the Golden Gate National Recreation Area. A land bridge connects directly from the parking lot to the beach, as well as to a short trail that leads to a scenic overlook and connects to other coastal paths. There are no lifeguards on duty and the currents can be challenging, so swimming is not advised. **Amenities:** parking (free); toilets. **Best for:** solitude; sunset; walking. ⊠ *100 Pacific Way, off Shoreline Hwy., Muir Beach* ☎ *415/561–4700* ⊕ *www.nps.gov/goga.*

🛏 Hotels

The Pelican Inn
$$ | **B&B/INN** | From its slate roof to its whitewashed plaster walls, this Tudor-style inn built in the 1970s is English to the core, with its cozy upstairs guest rooms (no elevator) and draped half-tester beds, a sun-filled solarium, and bangers and grilled tomatoes for breakfast. **Pros:** five-minute walk to the beach; great bar and restaurant; peaceful setting with a fun personality. **Cons:** 20-minute drive to nearby attractions; rooms are quite small and rustic; prices are as steep as more luxurious destinations. [$] *Rooms from: $285* ✉ *10 Pacific Way, off Hwy. 1, Muir Beach* ☎ *415/383–6000* 🌐 *www.pelican-inn.com* 🛏 *7 rooms* 🍴 *Free Breakfast.*

Stinson Beach

20 miles northwest of Golden Gate Bridge.

This laid-back hamlet is all about the beach, and folks come from all over the Bay Area to walk its sandy, often windswept shore. An ideal day trip would include a morning hike at Mt. Tamalpais followed by lunch at one of Stinson's unassuming eateries and a leisurely beach stroll.

GETTING HERE AND AROUND

If you're driving, take U.S. 101 to the Mill Valley/Stinson Beach/Highway 1 exit and follow the road west and then north. By bus, take Golden Gate Transit to Marin City and then transfer to the West Marin Stagecoach (61) for Bolinas.

⛱ Beaches

Stinson Beach
BEACH | **FAMILY** | When the fog hasn't rolled in, this expansive stretch of sand is about as close as you can get in Marin to the stereotypical feel of a Southern California beach. There are several clothing-optional areas, among them a section south of Stinson Beach called Red Rock Beach. Pets are not allowed on the national park section of the beach.

⚠ **Swimming at Stinson Beach can be dangerous; the undertow is strong, and shark sightings, though infrequent, have occurred. Lifeguards are on duty July–September.**

On any hot summer weekend, roads to Stinson are packed and the parking lot fills, so factor this into your plans. The town itself—population 600, give or take—has a nonchalant surfer vibe, with a few good eating options and pleasant hippie-craftsy browsing. **Amenities:** food and drink; lifeguards (summer); parking (free); showers; toilets. **Best for:** nudists; sunset; surfing; swimming; walking, windsurfing. ✉ *Hwy. 1, 1 Calle Del Sierra, Stinson Beach* ☎ *415/561–4700* 🌐 *www.nps.gov/goga.*

🍴 Restaurants

★ Parkside Cafe
$$ | **AMERICAN** | **FAMILY** | Though this place is popular for its 1950s beachfront snack bar, the adjoining café, coffee bar, marketplace, and bakery shouldn't be missed either. The full menu serves up fresh ingredients, local seafood, and wood-fired pizzas. **Known for:** espresso and pastry bar; tasty fish-and-chips; rustic house-made breads. [$] *Average main: $28* ✉ *43 Arenal Ave., Stinson Beach* ☎ *415/868–1272* 🌐 *www.parksidecafe.com.*

Stinson Beach Breakers Cafe
$$ | **AMERICAN** | Hard to miss along the tiny stretch of Main Street, this café is an easy destination for a pre-beach sandwich or post-surf bar bites and cocktails on the heated patio in the afternoon. Beach-cottage hardwood floors and a woodstove add to the warmth of the rustic seaside interior, while a mountain view and firepit enhance the deck. **Known for:** Dungeness crab melt; fresh oysters; crispy fish tacos. [$] *Average*

main: $22 ✉ 3465 Hwy. 1, Stinson Beach ☎ 415/868–2002 🌐 stinsonbeachbreakerscafe.com 🕒 Closed Tues. and Wed.

Hotels

Sandpiper Lodging

$$ | B&B/INN | FAMILY | Recharge, rest, and enjoy the local scenery at this ultrapopular lodging that books up months in advance. **Pros:** beach chairs, towels, and toys provided; lush garden with grill; minutes from the beach and town. **Cons:** thin walls; limited amenities; charge for rollaway beds. [$] *Rooms from: $220 ✉ 1 Marine Way, Stinson Beach ☎ 415/868–1632 🌐 www.sandpiperstinsonbeach.com 🛏 11 rooms 🍴 No Meals.*

Point Reyes National Seashore

Bear Valley Visitor Center is 14 miles north of Stinson Beach.

With sandy beaches stretching for miles, a dramatic rocky coastline, a spectacular lighthouse, and idyllic, century-old dairy farms, Point Reyes National Seashore is one of the most varied and strikingly beautiful corners of the Bay Area.

GETTING HERE AND AROUND

From San Francisco, take U.S. 101 North, head west at Sir Francis Drake Boulevard (Exit 450B) toward San Anselmo, and follow the road just under 20 miles to Bear Valley Road. From Stinson Beach or Bolinas, drive north on Highway 1 and turn left on Bear Valley Road. If you're going by bus, the West Marin Stagecoach takes riders to Bolinas from Marin City via the 61 bus and to Point Reyes Station and Inverness via the 68 bus.

Sights

Bear Valley Visitor Center

VISITOR CENTER | FAMILY | Tucked in the Olema Valley, this welcoming center is a perfect point of orientation for trails and roads throughout the region's unique and diverse ecosystem. It offers a rich glimpse of local cultural and natural heritage with engaging exhibits about the wildlife, history, and ecology of the Point Reyes National Seashore. The rangers at the barnlike facility share their in-depth knowledge about beaches, whale-watching, hiking trails, and camping. Restrooms are available, as well as trailhead parking and a picnic area. Hours vary seasonally; call or check the website for details. *✉ Bear Valley Visitor Center, 1 Bear Valley Rd., Point Reyes Station ☎ 415/464–5100 🌐 www.nps.gov/pore.*

★ Duxbury Reef

NATURE PRESERVE | FAMILY | Excellent tide-pooling can be had along the three-mile shoreline of Duxbury Reef; it's one of the largest shale intertidal reefs in North America. Look for sea stars, barnacles, sea anemones, purple urchins, limpets, sea mussels, and the occasional abalone. But check a tide table (🌐 *usharbors.com*) or the local papers if you plan to explore the reef—it's accessible only at low tide. The reef is a 30-minute drive from the Bear Valley Visitor Center. Take Highway 1 South from the center, turn right at Olema Bolinas Road (keep an eye peeled; the road is easy to miss), left on Horseshoe Hill Road, right on Mesa Road, left on Overlook Drive, and then right on Elm Road, which dead-ends at the Agate Beach County Park parking lot. **⚠ Avoid areas rich with fragile Monterey shale, which are prone to erosion from human disturbance. It is illegal to collect anything from this protected marine area.** *✉ Bolinas ✣ At Duxbury Point, 1 mile west of Bolinas 🌐 wildlife.ca.gov 🎟 Free.*

Heidrun Meadery

WINERY | Northern California is known for wine, but it's a different buzz at this meadery situated just outside the center of Point Reyes Station. All of the meads are sparkling, made in the Champagne production style. The honey comes from local hives owned by the meadery and from hives around the country and the world. Flavors can vary from Tanzanian miombo wildflower to Oregon radish blossom. The tasting room is open daily. ⊠ *11925 Rte. 1, Point Reyes Station* ⊕ *heidrunmeadery.com* ⊟ *Tastings $25.*

Point Reyes Bird Observatory

WILDLIFE REFUGE | **FAMILY** | Birders adore Point Blue Conservation Science, which maintains the Point Reyes Bird Observatory, located in the southernmost part of Point Reyes National Seashore. The surrounding woods harbor some 200 bird species. As you hike the quiet trails through forest and along ocean cliffs, you're likely to see biologists banding birds to aid in the study of their life cycles. ■TIP→ **Visit Point Blue's website for detailed directions and to find out how to make an appointment to attend a banding demonstration.** ⊠ *999 Mesa Rd., Bolinas* ☎ *415/868–0655 field station* ⊕ *www. pointblue.org.*

★ Point Reyes Lighthouse & Visitor Center

LIGHTHOUSE | **FAMILY** | This decommissioned lighthouse occupies the tip of Point Reyes, 21 miles from the Bear Valley Visitor Center, a scenic 40-minute drive over hills scattered with dairy farms. Today it's one of the best spots on the coast for watching gray whales. On both legs of their annual migration, the magnificent animals pass close enough to see with the naked eye. Southern migration peaks in mid-January, and the whales head back north in March. Parking is limited, and there's a quarter-mile one-way path from the parking lot to the visitor center. The lighthouse steps are open only during visitor center hours. Winds can be chilly, and food, water, gas,

and other resources are scarce, so come prepared. ⊠ *Lighthouse Visitor Center, 27000 Sir Francis Drake Blvd., Inverness* ☎ *415/669–1534 visitor center* ⊕ *www. nps.gov/pore/planyourvisit/lighthouse. htm* ⊗ *Closed Mon.–Thurs.*

★ Point Reyes National Seashore

NATIONAL PARK | **FAMILY** | One of the Bay Area's most spectacular treasures, the 71,000-acre Point Reyes National Seashore encompasses hiking trails, secluded beaches, and rugged grasslands, as well as Point Reyes itself, a triangular peninsula that juts into the Pacific. The infamous San Andreas Fault runs along the park's eastern edge; take the Earthquake Trail from the visitor center to see the impact near the epicenter of the 1906 earthquake that devastated San Francisco. A half-mile path from the visitor center leads to Kule Loklo, a reconstructed Miwok village of the region's first known inhabitants. You can experience the diversity of Point Reyes's ecosystems on the scenic Coast Trail through eucalyptus groves and pine forests and along seaside cliffs to beautiful and tiny Bass Lake. The 4.7-mile-long (one-way) Tomales Point Trail follows the spine of the park's northernmost finger of land through the Tule Elk Preserve, providing spectacular ocean views from high bluffs. ⊠ *Bear Valley Visitor Center, 1 Bear Valley Rd., Point Reyes Station* ⊹ *West of Hwy. 1* ☎ *415/464–5100* ⊕ *www.nps.gov/ pore* ⊟ *Free.*

🍴 Restaurants

Due West

$$ | **AMERICAN** | A convivial atmosphere and local, sustainable culinary provisions make this classic Point Reyes tavern a favorite stop among locals. Refurbished and modernized since its days as a horse-and-wagon stop in the 1860s, it now has a farm-to-fork seasonal menu including American classics from burgers and brick-roasted chicken to seafood specialties like cioppino and fish and

Did You Know?

The majestic Point Reyes
National Seashore offers
many attractions for
nature lovers: hiking,
bird-watching, camping,
or whale-watching,
depending on the season.
But flower picking isn't
an approved activity;
the wildflowers here are
protected.

chips. **Known for:** fried chicken sandwich; steak frites; excellent wine list including the hotel's own label. $ *Average main: $27* ✉ *10005 Coastal Hwy. 1, Olema* ☎ *415/663–1264* ⊕ *olemahouse.com/ due-west-restaurant* ⊗ *Closed Mon.*

Eleven

$ | **WINE BAR** | For a true taste of local culture, this sisters-owned venture welcomes you to relax, sip some wine, and enjoy the flavors and scene Bolinas is known for, from the town's laid-back lifestyle and quirky decor to the natural beauty and the fresh coastal air. The wine bar and bistro's short but ever-changing creative and thoughtful Californian-Italian menus change daily and reflect the richness of this region's foodshed—considered one of the nation's most diverse. **Known for:** house-made, locally sourced ingredients; natural wine selections; pizzas and oysters. $ *Average main: $17* ✉ *11 Wharf Rd., Bolinas* ☎ *415/868–1133* ⊕ *www.11wharfroad.com* ⊗ *Closed Sun.–Wed. No lunch.*

★ Hog Island Oyster Co. Marshall Oyster Farm and the Boat Oyster Bar

$$ | **SEAFOOD** | **FAMILY** | Take a short trek north on Highway 1 to the gritty mecca of Bay Area oysters—the Hog Island Marshall Oyster Farm. Here, the Boat Oyster Bar is an informal outdoor café that serves raw and grilled oysters, local snacks, and tasty beverages. **Known for:** fresh, raw, and grilled oysters; local fish crudo; Hog Shack shellfish to go. $ *Average main: $21* ✉ *20215 Shoreline Hwy., Marshall* ☎ *415/663–9218* ⊕ *hogislandoysters.com* ⊗ *Oyster Bar closed Tues. No dinner.*

Inverness Park Market & Tap Room

$ | **AMERICAN** | An organic oasis, this deli, restaurant, and taproom offers a true taste of the Point Reyes foodshed. Classic sandwiches, breakfast bites, burritos, grilled Niman Ranch beef, wild-caught salmon, and vegan burgers are all prepared with fresh local ingredients. **Known for:** Wednesday sushi and Thursday Thai specials; breads, pies, and morning pastries baked in-house; grilled oysters. $ *Average main: $19* ✉ *12301 Sir Francis Drake Blvd., Inverness Park* ☎ *415/663–1491* ⊕ *invernessparkmarket. com* ⊗ *Closed Sun. Taproom closed Mon. No lunch.*

★ The Marshall Store

$ | **SEAFOOD** | It's oyster bliss at this very friendly daytime restaurant along Tomales Bay. There are a few indoor seats, but the in-demand spots are on the outside deck, where heaters keep guests somewhat warm even on the chilliest days. **Known for:** chorizo fish stew and clam chowder; local bread, cheeses, and dairy soft-serve; pristine Pacific Preston Point oysters. $ *Average main: $18* ✉ *19225 Highway 1, Point Reyes Station* ☎ *415/663–1339* ⊕ *themarshallstore.com* ⊗ *Closed Tues.–Thurs. No dinner.*

Saltwater Oyster Depot

$$ | **SEAFOOD** | Oysters shucked moments after they're taken out of Tomales Bay and French and California wines sourced from minimal-intervention small producers are the keystones of this neighborhood oyster bar. With indoor and outdoor patio seating and a creative menu, this spot makes for a welcome post-hike or post-beach indulgence. **Known for:** broiled and raw oysters; unique rendition of clam chowder; local fish and seafood. $ *Average main: $23* ✉ *12781 Sir Francis Drake Blvd., Inverness* ☎ *415/669–1244* ⊕ *saltwateroysterdepot.com* ⊗ *Closed Tues.–Thurs. No lunch Mon.*

★ Side Street Kitchen

$ | **AMERICAN** | **FAMILY** | Rotisserie meats and veggies sourced from local farms steal the show at this former mid-20th-century truck stop and diner. It's a go-to for tri-tip and pork belly sandwiches or house-seasoned roasted chicken, best eaten with a host of sides, sips, and sweets, like crispy Parmesan Brussels sprouts, New Orleans–style cold brew coffee, and butterscotch pudding. **Known for:** rotisserie chicken and lots of vegetarian dishes; dog-friendly outdoor patio; apple fritters. $ *Average main: $18* ⌗ *60 4th St., Point Reyes Station* ☎ *415/663–0303* ⊕ *sidestreet-prs. com* ⊘ *Closed Mon. and Tues. No dinner after 6 pm.*

★ Station House Café

$ | AMERICAN | The Station House Café has been a stalwart venue for local music and a staunch supporter of local farms and food artisans. The community-centric eatery serves a blend of modern and classic California dishes comprised of organic seasonal ingredients, sustainable hormone-free meats, and wild-caught seafood. **Known for:** signature popovers; special weekend brunch items; fresh local seafood. $ *Average main: $19* ⌗ *11180 Hwy. 1, at 3rd St., Point Reyes Station* ☎ *415/663–1515* ⊕ *stationhouse-cafe.com* ⊘ *Closed Wed. and Thurs.*

Hotels

Nick's Cove

$$$ | HOTEL | On the shore of Tomales Bay, these cottage (some are quite grand, others are typical hotel room–sized) are warm and homey with wooden stoves and a decor that nicely balances an old maritime aesthetic with a contemporary edge. **Pros:** tons of nearby activities including kayaking on-site; bucolic setting; rural luxury. **Cons:** hefty prices; can't walk to anything; restaurant closes early. $ *Rooms from: $455* ⌗ *23240 Hwy. 1* ☎ *415/663–1033* ⊕ *nickscove.com* 🍽 *12 rooms* ⦿ *No Meals.*

★ Olema House

$$ | B&B/INN | FAMILY | Once a historic 1860s stagecoach stopover, this luxurious getaway offers as many reasons to stay on-property—with its views of Mt. Wittenberg and garden setting—as to explore the 71,000 acres of national seashore just steps away. **Pros:** steps from trails; convenient parking and horse hitching; friendly and informative staff. **Cons:** steps to some rooms are steep;

street-facing rooms may be noisy; spotty Wi-Fi and cell service. $ *Rooms from: $328* ⌗ *10021 Coastal Hwy. 1, Olema* ☎ *415/663–9000* ⊕ *olemahouse.com* 🍽 *25 rooms* ⦿ *No Meals.*

⬛ Shopping

Gospel Flat Farm Stand

FOOD | This combination art gallery, farm stand, and flower shop captures the true essence of the area, with its dedication to community arts and a bounty of local organic vegetables, fruits, and eggs. The colorful self-serve site is open 24 hours, but what makes it truly special is that the entire stand operates on the honor system. Weigh and log your produce, and slip your payment (cash or check) in the box. The ever-rotating local art on exhibit adds to the allure. ⌗ *140 Olema-Bolinas Rd., Bolinas.*

★ Toby's Feed Barn

OTHER SPECIALTY STORE | The heart of the community since 1942, the barn has a bounty of local gifts and produce, plus an art gallery, yoga studio, and Toby's Coffee Bar for espresso drinks and sell-out pastries. See and hear what's happening locally, catch a live band or literary event, and explore the garden. The internationally renowned all-local, all-organic Point Reyes Farmers' Market is held here on Saturdays during the growing season (even King Charles and Queen Camilla visited it in 2005). ⌗ *11250 Hwy. 1, Point Reyes Station* ☎ *415/663–1223* ⊕ *www. tobysfeedbarn.com.*

Palo Alto

33 miles south of San Francisco.

Despite being a midsized residential community, Palo Alto enjoys an outsized reputation as one of the premier cities to live and work in—with eye-popping real estate figures to complement that. It's the home of many tech companies and neighbor to that great bastion of research and learning, Stanford University. Palo Alto is somewhat split between its historic northern half, anchored by the always exciting University Avenue. The "other downtown" centers on California Avenue, where most of the city's science and technology offices are located. Throughout the city, there are pleasant little parks and a variety of homes from modern mansions, to quirky bungalows, to the unique mid-century Eichlers that are like large suburban cabins.

It's a progressive, environmentally-centered city where bikes, electric cars and hybrid cars seem to outnumber regular cars. That green focus possibly dates back to the city's namesake, a giant redwood tree that still stands proudly and quietly in a little forest by the San Francisquito Creek.

GETTING HERE AND AROUND
From San Francisco, drivers can take U.S. 101 South to a trio of different exits: University Avenue, Embarcadero Road, and Oregon Expressway. Alternatively, the more scenic route takes I–280 to the Page Mill Road exit.

By Caltrain, it's roughly 45 minutes to an hour (depending on if it's an express or a local train) to Palo Alto's downtown station and California Avenue station.

ESSENTIALS
Destination Palo Alto. ⊕ *destinationpaloalto.com.* **City of Palo Alto.** ⊕ *cityofpaloalto.org.*

◉ Sights

California Avenue
STREET | FAMILY | Palo Alto's "second downtown" actually was its own town named Mayfield until it joined the neighboring city in 1925. Back then, the main difference between the towns was that Palo Alto was dry and Mayfield was predominantly saloons. Things are quite different a century later; the old Mayfield's main thoroughfare, California Avenue, is now a favorite dining and shopping destination for the nearby Page Mill Road tech workers and Stanford students.

Térun's (✉ *448 California Ave.*) Neapolitan pizzas are among the best on the Peninsula, while the Latin cuisine and rum cocktails at **La Bodeguita del Medio** (✉ *463 California Ave.*), named for Ernest Hemingway's favorite bar in Havana, have a devoted following. **Bistro Elan** (✉ *2363 Birch St.*) and **Protégé** (✉ *250 California Ave.*) are the two fine-dining standard bearers on the street. **Mediterranean Wraps's** (✉ *443 California Ave.*) lamb and beef shawarma plates and falafel wraps are a popular choice for the lunchtime crowds. A pair of coffee shops are the morning heart of the corridor, with **Backyard Brew** (✉ *444 California Ave.*) serving excellent coffees in a hidden garden setting, and the quirky **Zombie Runner** (✉ *344 California Ave.*) producing a terrific chai tea in addition to coffee from beans roasted by the café (it was previously a running shoe store with a small coffee kiosk, then fully switched and no longer sells shoes). California Avenue really shines every Saturday morning when it hosts what most residents consider the Peninsula's most impressive farmers' market. And every day of the week, there's a fun European vibe because it's now permanently pedestrian-only to expand restaurants' outdoor seating options. ✉ *California Ave., between El Camino Real and Park Blvd., Palo Alto* ⊕ *destinationpaloalto.com/california-avenue.*

University Avenue
STREET | Downtown Palo Alto's main street is a continuation of Stanford's Palm Drive after the university stretch reaches the Caltrain station. Shops, restaurants, and an always popular Apple Store (it's no different than other stores but considered special since Steve Jobs lived nearby) line the blocks of the street until it becomes residential.

Understanding Silicon Valley 👁

It's remarkable that world-famous Silicon Valley's "birthplace" is a humble garage behind a California shingle-style home on a residential street in Palo Alto. This was where Bill Hewlett and Dave Packard went to work in 1938 on their new technology business that quickly grew into the global icon, Hewlett Packard. The garage itself is not open to the public, though it's a popular choice for visitors to swing by for a photo from the sidewalk (please be respectful of the garage's neighbors). Like the garage, the major Silicon Valley companies such as Google (Mountain View), Apple (Cupertino), and Meta (Menlo Park) are not open to the public and visits are pretty much limited to photos with a sign.

However, for visitors looking for a more in-depth look at the technologies and history that makes Silicon Valley what it is today, the region has a pair of notable museums worth stopping at. Right by Google's campus, the **Computer History Museum** (⊕ computerhistory.org) looks at technology from 2,000 years ago, to the early Apple Macintosh days, to the first days of the internet, and finally to today's astonishing innovations. It's a very hands-on, interactive museum: not surprising given the subject.

In the heart of downtown San Jose along the Plaza de Cesar Chavez, **The Tech Interactive** (⊕ thetech.org) is hard to miss with its orange exterior and purple rotunda on top (home to a massive IMAX movie theater). The science and technology exhibits were innovative when it opened more than three decades ago, and it still remains cutting-edge today. It's really more of a hands-on educational facility than a museum. This is the place to interact with robots, try to solve real-world environmental problems, and learn about genetics and new advances in biotechnology in the BioTinkering Lab. The highlight for many visitors are the nature films on the massive IMAX screen, the largest IMAX dome screen on the West Coast.

The crown jewel is the **Stanford Theatre** (✉ 221 University Ave.), a magnificent ode to classic Hollywood. Across the street is **Lytton Plaza**, a spacious, eclectic gathering place where surely somebody will be putting on an impromptu concert or protest. Toward the eastern end of the downtown area is what previously was another Hollywood Golden Age cinema, the **Varsity Theatre**. Its classic Colonial Spanish and Mission Revival–influenced architecture is still stunning as a tech shared workspace and a **Blue Bottle Coffee** café (✉ 456 University Ave.).

There are dining highlights up and down University Avenue, led by contemporary Vietnamese stalwart **Tamarine** (✉ 546 University Ave.) and the silky hummus specialty at **Oren's Hummus** (✉ 261 University Ave.). The quieter side streets off University Avenue also feature several standout restaurants including **Ramen Nagi** (✉ 541 Bryant St.), the Georgian cooking of **Bevri** (✉ 530 Bryant St.), craft cocktails with excellent French bistro fare at **Zola** and **BarZola** (✉ 565 and 585 Bryant St.), contemporary Indian cuisine in lavish surroundings at **Ettan** (✉ 518 Bryant St.), **Taverna's** (✉ 800 Emerson St.) excellent modern and rustic Greek dishes, and **Bird Dog's** (✉ 420 Ramona St.) captivating contemporary Californian menu. ✉ University Avenue, between El

Camino Real and Middlefield Rd., Palo Alto 🌐 *destinationpaloalto.com.*

🍴 Restaurants

Bevri

$$ | EASTERN EUROPEAN | As one of the few Georgian restaurants in the Bay Area, many diners from around the region come to this small, cheery spot to learn all about the Caucasus Mountains–region country's important culinary heritage. Every table has an order of the two iconic dishes from Georgia: *kinkhali* (juicy dumplings filled with various meats) and the "cheese boat" of *khachapuri*, which is a trapezoid-shaped, ultra-moist, somewhat puffy bread with cheese in the center and an egg yolk. **Known for:** extensive Georgian wine list; grilled whole rainbow trout; kebabs and hand-chopped beet and spinach "pkhali" dips. [$] *Average main: $23* ✉ *530 Bryant St., Palo Alto* ☎ *650/600–0433* 🌐 *bevri.com* 🕒 *Closed Mon. and Tues.*

Bird Dog

$$ | MODERN AMERICAN | It's a little strange for a chic, contemporary-minded restaurant to be best known for an avocado dish. However, that's the case at chef Robbie Wilson's suave downtown restaurant where the delicately grilled avocado has its own devoted following. **Known for:** inventive dishes with unique spices and sauces; best cocktails in town; fish crudo. [$] *Average main: $27* ✉ *420 Ramona St., Palo Alto* ☎ *650/656–8180* 🌐 *birddogpa.com* 🕒 *Closed Sun.–Mon. No lunch.*

Bistro Elan

$$$ | MODERN FRENCH | One of the Peninsula's leading examples of a small, farm-to-table driven, local ingredients–centric establishment is this homey dining room with sidewalk seating just off California Avenue. For more than 25 years, Bistro Elan has been the understated gathering place for many business and celebratory meals, where professors, CEOs, and longtime residents enjoy the signature potato waffle with smoked salmon and a smartly curated wine list. **Known for:** tiny dining room; cast iron–seared steak frites; exquisite almond cake. [$] *Average main: $37* ✉ *2363A Birch St., Palo Alto* ☎ *650/327–0284* 🌐 *bistroelan.com.*

★ Protégé

$$$$ | MODERN AMERICAN | A pair of French Laundry alums—protégés of some of the culinary world's greatest chefs—are the driving forces of this fine-dining standout near the train station on California Avenue. The restaurant is split into two parts: the main formal restaurant with an elaborate tasting menu at a high price point; and the sleek lounge area where the menu is à la carte. **Known for:** unique "fish and chips" dish; sleek design; cocktails that are as notable as the wine list. [$] *Average main: $225* ✉ *250 California Ave., Palo Alto* 🌐 *protegepaloalto.com* 🕒 *Closed Sun. and Mon. No lunch.*

Sundance The Steakhouse

$$$$ | STEAKHOUSE | It's almost a rite of passage for Stanford students and visiting families to visit this steak-house stalwart. Since 1974, it's been the place to go for shrimp cocktail followed by juicy prime rib. **Known for:** steaks with loaded baked potatoes; martinis and margaritas; Dungeness crab cakes and oysters Rockefeller. [$] *Average main: $48* ✉ *1921 El Camino Real, Palo Alto* ☎ *650/321–6798* 🌐 *sundancethesteakhouse.com* 🕒 *No lunch weekends.*

Vina Enoteca

$$ | MODERN ITALIAN | Palo Alto is filled with Italian restaurants, but the best in town resides in Leland Stanford's old brick barn (where Stanford's own wines were produced), on the edge of campus. Homemade pastas are served with an idyllic toothsome al dente texture. **Known for:** mezze maniche pasta cacio e pepe; excellent global wine list; daytime Italian market. [$] *Average main: $25* ✉ *700 Welch Rd., Suite 110, Palo Alto* ☎ *650/646–3477* 🌐 *vinaenoteca.com* 🕒 *Closed Sun. and Mon. No lunch.*

Coffee and Quick Bites

Backyard Brew

$ | **CAFÉ** | Palo Alto's eclectic past meets its digital present at California Avenue's outdoor-only coffee shop/roaster that is hidden from the main street by a narrow alleyway. With plenty of mismatched tables, lo-fi jazz on the stereo, and flowers growing on a wall next to a wall with drawings of its many regular dog visitors, it's easy to feel Palo Alto's old bohemian personality alive and well here. **Known for:** Nutella latte; single-origin drip coffees; beautiful setting. [$] *Average main: $6* ✉ *444 California Ave., Palo Alto* ☎ *650/704–7785* 🌐 *backyardbrew.com.*

Hotels

Hotels in Palo Alto vary dramatically, from some of the most glamorous accommodations anywhere in the Bay Area, to quiet chain hotels on nondescript blocks of El Camino Real. A Westin and a Sheraton reside by downtown's Caltrain station, but the few hotels within the main downtown area are smaller boutique hotels.

The Clement Palo Alto

$$$$ | **ALL-INCLUSIVE** | Palo Alto doesn't exactly strike travelers as an all-inclusive luxury getaway like Cancun, but that's what this impeccable hotel offers. **Pros:** rooftop pool and hot tub; beautifully designed, spacious rooms; outstanding food program. **Cons:** not a great business model for encouraging city exploration; only some rooms have great views; limited dining options. [$] *Rooms from: $854* ✉ *711 El Camino Real, Palo Alto* ☎ *650/322–7111* 🌐 *theclementpaloalto.com* 🛏 *23 suites* 🍴 *All-Inclusive.*

★ El Prado Hotel

$$$ | **HOTEL** | This elegant boutique hotel is an extremely welcome breath of fresh air of non-gimmicky, non tech oriented space. **Pros:** unique design; great cocktails and bites in the tapas bar; sharp, friendly service. **Cons:** noise from courtyard; no in-room coffee; rooms aren't as luxurious as the public spaces. [$] *Rooms from: $365* ✉ *520 Cowper St., Palo Alto* ☎ *650/322–9000* 🌐 *elpradopaloalto.com* 🛏 *62 rooms* 🍴 *No Meals.*

Four Seasons Hotel Silicon Valley at East Palo Alto

$$$ | **HOTEL** | There is luxury at every turn in this stalwart accommodation for the Silicon Valley power players from the prestigious global brand. **Pros:** outstanding attention to detail everywhere; great bar and Quattro Restaurant; quiet, spacious rooms with comfortable beds. **Cons:** can't walk to anything; pool needs a renovation; uninspiring views. [$] *Rooms from: $475* ✉ *2050 University Ave., Palo Alto* ☎ *650/566–1200* 🌐 *fourseasons.com* 🛏 *200 rooms* 🍴 *No Meals.*

Graduate Palo Alto

$$ | **HOTEL** | There are many hotels with bland, corporate décor—and then there's the Graduate Palo Alto, where every square inch of space seems to have some form of elaborate design or decoration. **Pros:** outstanding rooftop bar; great blend of past and modern architecture; excellent Lou & Herbert's café. **Cons:** cluttered and over-designed; some rooms feel small; hectic lobby. [$] *Rooms from: $295* ✉ *400 University Ave., Palo Alto* ☎ *650/843–9755* 🌐 *graduatehotels.com* 🛏 *100 rooms* 🍴 *No Meals.*

Nobu Hotel Palo Alto

$$$$ | **HOTEL** | When Silicon Valley tech money meets the country's biggest celebrity sushi chef, you get this ultra-contemporary luxury hotel with, of course, a Nobu restaurant included. **Pros:** top-quality in-house restaurant; beautifully designed rooms; some rooms have balconies facing the Santa Cruz Mountains. **Cons:** relatively small rooms; feels more like Vegas than Palo Alto; comparatively limited amenities. [$] *Rooms from: $503* ✉ *180 Hamilton Ave., Palo Alto* ☎ *650/531–8888* 🌐 *paloalto.nobuhotels.com* 🛏 *73 rooms* 🍴 *No Meals.*

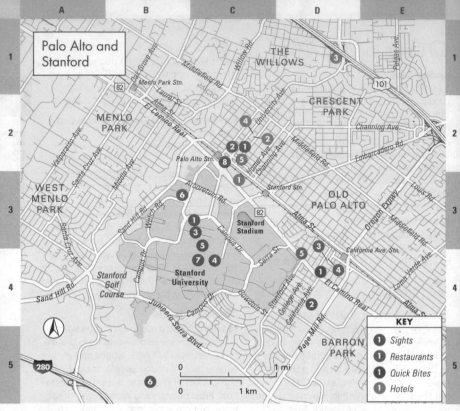

Palo Alto and Stanford

Sights ▼

1 Anderson Collection at
Stanford University......**C3**

2 California Avenue.......**D4**

3 Cantor Arts Center at
Stanford University......**C3**

4 Hoover Tower.............**C4**

5 Palm Drive and
the Oval...................**C3**

6 Stanford Dish...........**B5**

7 Stanford University
Main Quad................**C4**

8 University Avenue.......**C2**

Restaurants ▼

1 Bevri........................**C2**

2 Bird Dog...................**C2**

3 Bistro Elan...............**D4**

4 Protégé....................**D4**

5 Sundance
The Steakhouse.........**D4**

6 Vina Enoteca.............**B3**

Quick Bites ▼

1 Backyard Brew..........**D4**

Hotels ▼

1 The Clement
Palo Alto..................**C3**

2 El Prado Hotel............**C2**

3 Four Seasons
Hotel Silicon Valley
at East Palo Alto........**D1**

4 Graduate
Palo Alto..................**C2**

5 Nobu Hotel
Palo Alto..................**C2**

Nightlife

The Rose & Crown

PUBS | A true English pub, this is Palo Alto's best place for a proper pint of Old Speckled Hen or a pour of a locally-produced double IPA. Evenings bring tech workers and graduate students out to play darts and have lively conversations at the wooden tables inside or at the picnic benches on the narrow patio. Trivia nights are particularly popular in this scholarly area. ✉ *547 Emerson St., Palo Alto* ☎ *650/327–7673* ⊕ *therosepa.com.*

The Wine Room

WINE BARS | Palo Alto's favorite gathering spot for wines from around the world is this cozy, quirky cottage that looks as if it was lifted out of the Cotswolds. Seating arrangements include several comfortable couches that are popular with date nights. The staff is very knowledgeable about the wines and happy to offer recommendations since the extensive menu can be wonderfully intimidating. ✉ *520 Ramona St., Palo Alto* ☎ *650/462–1968* ⊕ *thepawineroom.com.*

Performing Arts

CINEMA

★ **Stanford Theatre**

FILM | **FAMILY** | A cinematic treasure since 1925, University Avenue's grande dame is a time-traveling spectacle not to be missed—an oasis of Hollywood Golden Age glamour in the center of this relentlessly future-minded region. Everything here is majestic: the grand marquee, the bi-level interior, the intricate interior architecture and chandeliers, and the crisp screen and audio quality often showing black-and-white films still in mint condition. Films are often shown as a themed double-feature, perhaps Fred Astaire and Ginger Rogers or 1929 silent films. Arguably the highlight for any night is when the Mighty Wurlitzer organ player strikes a tune during the intermission between films. ✉ *221 University Ave., Palo Alto* ☎ *650/324–3700* ⊕ *stanfordtheatre.org.*

Stanford

34 miles from San Francisco.

Few names are as recognizable in higher education as Stanford University—or technically Leland Stanford Jr. University, named for the deceased son of its founder, a railroad tycoon and former California governor. Stanford's campus resides on 8,180 acres, one of the largest universities in terms of land size in the entire country. Its academic specialties are too numerous to count and its alums have gone on to make a tremendous impact on the world across dozens of disciplines. There are athletes like Tiger Woods, John Elway, and John McEnroe. Former President Herbert Hoover graduated from here, as did Sandra Day O'Connor and Rishi Sunak. In business, science, and technology, there are alums including Sally Ride, Phil Knight, Sergey Brin, and Charles Schwab.

It's commonly referred to as "The Farm" since it resides on what was Leland Stanford's farm before the university was founded in 1885. Today, the old red horse barn is still used by the equestrian team and the other brick "barn" (back then a wine-making facility) now houses restaurants and offices. Even though Stanford is renowned for its serious academic prowess, students also definitely know how to have fun. The Stanford Band is famous (and sometimes maligned) for its free-wheeling style, complemented by a dancing redwood tree mascot (the school's mascot is the Cardinal—the color, not the bird).

The university is an architectural and natural marvel. Its signature style is a unique mix of Mission and Romanesque styles called Richardsonian Romanesque, named for Henry Hobson Richardson whose protégé, Charles Allerton

Coolidge, was the primary architect. Its defining characteristics are dramatic arched hallways connected with textured sandstone buildings and eye-catching red-tiled roofs. Spend just one minute in the Main Quad and it's easy to understand the style.

GETTING HERE AND AROUND

Stanford's campus can be reached from San Francisco via Highway 101's University Avenue exit, which drives across Palo Alto and becomes Palm Drive once it reaches the university. From Interstate 280, use the Alpine Road or Sand Hill Road exits.

Caltrain's University Avenue station in Downtown Palo Alto is the closest stop. VTA buses and SamTrans also stop here (known as the Palo Alto Transit Center).

Stanford's campus is huge, so most students bike here. The university has a free shuttle running several routes around campus known as the Marguerite. Note that parking is extremely restricted around the Stanford campus. Most visitor parking is in select garages or paid parking near the art museums and the Oval.

ESSENTIALS

Visit Stanford. ✉ 295 Galvez St., Stanford ⊕ visit.stanford.edu.

⊙ Sights

Anderson Collection at Stanford University

ART MUSEUM | Modern, post–World War II art shines at the neighbor to the Cantor Arts Center, where the impressive collection from Harry W. and Mary Margaret Anderson and Mary Patricia Anderson Pence is displayed. Marquee mid-century artists including Richard Diebenkorn, Jackson Pollock, and Ellsworth Kelly are showcased in a gleaming concrete and glass-heavy building that smartly reflects the contemporary ethos of the artwork inside. ✉ 314 Lomita Dr., Stanford ☎ 650/721–6055 ⊕ anderson.stanford. edu ➟ Free ⊙ Closed Mon. and Tues.

Cantor Arts Center at Stanford University

ART MUSEUM | Stanford's main art museum is a wonderful indoor-outdoor mix, where it's easy to linger for two or three hours. Outside is the acclaimed Rodin Sculpture Garden, home to the one of the largest collections of the legendary French sculptor's works in the U.S. Inside, beyond the ornate opening steps and grand entry hall are two levels of galleries that mix modern works with rotating exhibitions, indigenous American art, and classical European and American paintings. ✉ 328 Lomita Dr., Stanford ☎ 650/723–4177 ⊕ museum.stanford. edu ➟ Free ⊙ Closed Mon. and Tues.

Hoover Tower

NOTABLE BUILDING | It's hard to miss Stanford's iconic building named for the 31st President of the United States and class of 1895 alum, Herbert Hoover. At 285-feet tall, it's the closest thing the Peninsula has to a skyscraper. The domed red-tile roof with a Belgian carillon underneath it can be seen for miles. Visitors of Stanford-affiliated individuals can take the elevator up to the top for a panoramic view from San Francisco, to the bay and East Bay Hills, to the Santa Cruz Mountains. Unfortunately, the general public can only visit the exhibition galleries at the base of the tower. ✉ 550 Jane Stanford Way, Stanford ☎ 650/723–3563 ⊕ hoover.org.

★ Palm Drive and the Oval

STREET | FAMILY | Few streets in the Bay Area can match the dramatic scenery of Stanford's entrance from downtown Palo Alto. For about 2/3 mile, palm trees line the street, which runs in a direct straight line towards Memorial Church. The Santa Cruz Mountains emerge on the horizon, and it all looks as if it was framed intentionally for postcards. Palm Drive runs into a giant grass area called the Oval, named for its distinct shape, which revolves around flower plantings shaped as an "S" for Stanford. On sunny days, Stanford students are always out in force studying on the grass or playing Frisbee. It can appear like a university admissions brochure in real life. ✉ *The Oval, 20 Palm Dr., Stanford.*

Stanford Dish

NATURE PRESERVE | FAMILY | Known by locals as The Dish, this radio telescope has served many purposes over the years, including some for the government; it's run by a local research institute, not the university itself. The main reason that everyone comes to The Dish is because of its series of hiking and jogging trails that wind their way around the classic Northern California landscape full of oak trees, poppy flowers, and local wildlife, rewarding each workout with stellar views. ✉ *Stanford ⊹ Trailhead at Stanford Ave. and Junipero Serra Blvd.* ⊕ *dish.stanford.edu.*

★ Stanford University Main Quad

COLLEGE CAMPUS | The heart of the Stanford University campus is its distinct Richardsonian Romanesque quad. Stanford's signature look revolves around red-tiled roofs and palm trees. The focal point of the quad is Memorial Church, a striking memorial built by Jane Stanford to her late husband Leland. The interior boasts stunning mosaics and stained-glass windows. There was originally a bell and clock tower, but that was destroyed by the powerful 1906 earthquake, just three years after the church completed construction. Docent-led tours of the church are held Friday mornings at 11. ✉ *Bldg. 500, 450 Jane Stanford Way, Stanford* ☎ *650/723–1762* ⊕ *orsl.stanford. edu* 🎟 *Free.*

🎭 Performing Arts

Bing Concert Hall

CONCERTS | Stanford's stunning main performing arts center is a wonder of distinct curves, sharp modern design, and top-notch acoustics; it's pleasing both to eyes and ears. Concerts are split between various Stanford orchestras,

symphonies, and other groups, and musicians visiting from outside the university. ✉ *327 Lasuen St., Stanford* ☎ *650/724–2464* ⊕ *live.stanford.edu.*

Menlo Park

30 miles south of San Francisco.

Not to be confused with lightbulb inventor Thomas Edison's New Jersey hometown, this bedroom community centers on a small downtown strip of restaurants and shops on Santa Cruz Avenue. Menlo Park's global profile received an enormous boost in 2015 when Facebook (now Meta) opened its headquarters at the edge of the city (with the help of legendary architect Frank Gehry). The campus is actually not close to Downtown Menlo Park, but the residual effect can certainly be felt in the real estate prices and enormous amount of construction closer to town. Sand Hill Road lies along the edge of the city with Stanford's campus and Palo Alto, and its name is synonymous with the powerful venture capitalist firms that call it home. Woodside is Menlo Park's mostly pastoral northern home, where there are a couple excellent destination-worthy restaurants and the lavish Filoli Estate's mansion and gardens.

👁 Sights

Allied Arts Guild

ARTS CENTER | A popular site for photo shoots, weddings, and events, this landmark built in 1929 is known for its gardens, gorgeous Colonial Spanish architecture, and artist studios, where you can buy directly from the artists. The main Artisan Shop continues the guild's mission to help the community, with profits going to the children's hospital at Stanford. Docent tours are given six days a week, and the on-site Café Wisteria is a picturesque choice for a leisurely lunch. ✉ *75 Arbor Rd., Menlo Park*

Sights

1 Allied Arts Guild......... **C3**

2 Filoli **A2**

Restaurants

1 Buck's of Woodside... **A3**

2 Camper...... **C2**

3 Flea Street.. **C3**

4 Rossotti's · Alpine Inn... **C5**

5 Selby's **C2**

6 The Village Pub **A3**

Hotels

1 Hotel Nia.... **C1**

2 Park James Hotel......... **C2**

3 Rosewood Sand Hill **B4**

4 The Stanford Park Hotel .. **D2**

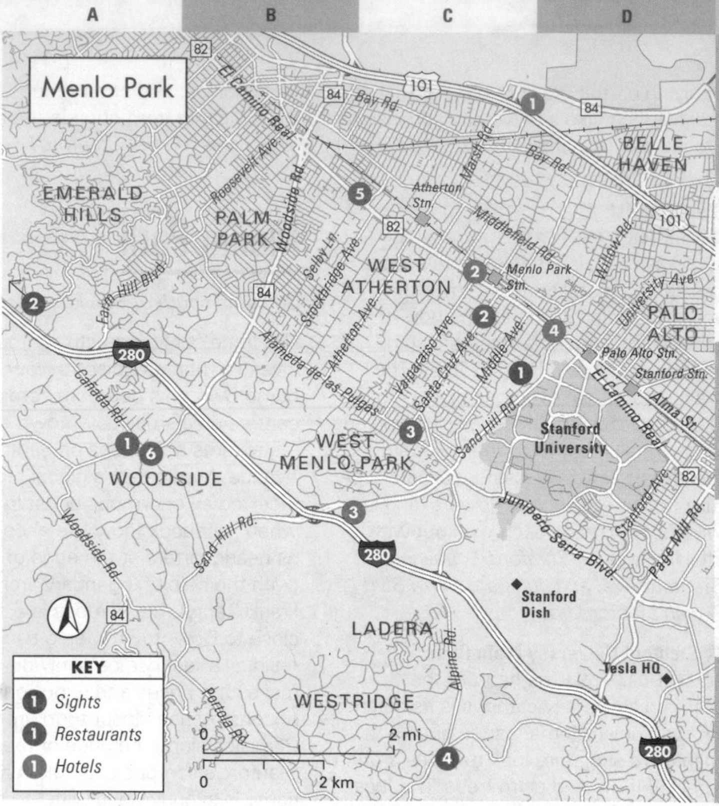

☎ *650/322–2405* 🌐 *alliedartsguild.org*
⏲ *Closed Sun.*

★ Filoli

HISTORIC HOME | **FAMILY** | The Bay Area's definitive early-20-century mansion and gardens reside in a quiet area along the beautiful Crystal Springs Reservoir at the base of the Santa Cruz Mountains, just a short drive from Menlo Park on I–280. Part of the National Trust for Historic Preservation, Filoli dates back to 1917 when it was built for the Bourn family based on a fortune from gold mining. Across 654 acres, the estate features several beautiful gardens, farmland, different ecosystems, and even crosses the San Andreas Fault (the source of many Northern California earthquakes). A mile-long trail gives a good general overview of the estate. For most visitors, the enchanting gardens are the highlights, particularly in spring when the daffodils and myriad other flowers are in full bloom. ✉ *86 Cañada Rd., Woodside* ☎ *650/364–8300* 🌐 *filoli.org* 🎟 *$34.*

🍴 Restaurants

Buck's of Woodside

$ | **AMERICAN** | **FAMILY** | One of the Peninsula's best-known restaurants is this funky, family-friendly brunch specialist in the heart of tiny downtown Woodside. The restaurant is a gathering spot for the tech company executives and venture capitalists who live nearby, but it's ultimately a blend of a saloon and a diner, where many hungry locals come looking for omelets and tuna melts. **Known for:** smash burger; coffee cake; eclectic decor. [$] *Average main: $19* ✉ *3062 Woodside Rd., Woodside* ☎ *650/851–8010* 🌐 *buckswoodside.com.*

★ Camper

$$$ | MODERN AMERICAN | If there's such a genre as refined camping fare, then that is what chef Greg Kuzia-Carmel offers guests at his warm, bustling restaurant. Local fish, meats, and produce are highlighted, with dishes that beautifully blend pastoral with contemporary. **Known for:** smoked half chicken from Petaluma; cast-iron buttermilk cornbread; excellent wine list. [$] *Average main: $34* ✉ *898 Santa Cruz Ave., Menlo Park* ☎ *650/321–8980* 🌐 *campermp.com* 🕑 *Closed Sun. No lunch.*

Flea Street

$$$ | MODERN AMERICAN | Restaurants in Berkeley and San Francisco tend to get most of the credit for launching the local ingredient–focused farm-to-table California cuisine movement in the 1970s and 1980s. However, chef Jesse Cool played an enormous role in that as well when she opened this venerable restaurant in 1980. **Known for:** strong local-centric wine list; grass-fed slow-braised short ribs; local-ingredient salads. [$] *Average main: $38* ✉ *3607 Alameda de las Pulgas, Menlo Park* ☎ *650/854–1226* 🌐 *cooleatz.com* 🕑 *Closed Sun. and Mon. No lunch.*

Rossotti's Alpine Inn

$ | AMERICAN | FAMILY | On sunny weekend afternoons, the enormous tree-covered, creekside beer garden of this countryside dining icon feels like the epicenter of Silicon Valley. It's a popular destination for professors and graduate students to enjoy brews and sandwiches, located just beyond campus in the pastoral town of Portola Valley. **Known for:** barbecue sandwiches; fun, bucolic setting; wood-fired pizzas. [$] *Average main: $15* ✉ *3915 Alpine Rd., Menlo Park* ☎ *650/854–4004* 🌐 *alpineinnpv.com* 🕑 *Closed Mon.*

Selby's

$$$$ | MODERN AMERICAN | It's a trip back in time at this elegant retro sibling to the Village Pub. Dishes are grand and elaborate, often with luxurious flourishes, yet deeply rooted in the seasonal focus that is the hallmark of California cuisine. **Known for:** divine midnight chocolate cake; polished design; crisp, stiff martinis. [$] *Average main: $98* ✉ *3001 El Camino Real, Redwood City* ☎ *650/546–7700* 🌐 *selbysrestaurant.com* 🕑 *No lunch.*

★ The Village Pub

$$$$ | MODERN AMERICAN | This Woodside institution actually is a Michelin-starred fine dining destination; the only similarity with an actual pub is that the bar has its own casual menu (the main dining room is prix-fixe with multiple choices per each course) and is frequently a gathering place for well-heeled regulars. The suave dining room with red velvet chairs and booths is a beautiful backdrop for intricate dishes that often feature produce from the nearby organic SMIP Ranch. **Known for:** deep wine list; pub burger on an English muffin; chocolate soufflé. [$] *Average main: $100* ✉ *2967 Woodside Rd., Woodside* ☎ *650/851–9888* 🌐 *thevillagepub.net* 🕑 *No lunch Mon.–Thurs.*

Hotels

Hotel Nia

$$ | HOTEL | One of the first of the new wave Silicon Valley hotels, this Autograph Collection property is the closest place to stay near Meta's campus. **Pros:** wonderfully incorporates nature into indoor and outdoor design; large rooms; on-site Porta Blu restaurant. **Cons:** substantial drive to sights and restaurants; hard to reach at rush hour; rooms facing highway don't block out all noise. [$] *Rooms from: $256* ✉ *200 Independence Dr., Menlo Park* ☎ *650/900–3434* 🌐 *hotelnia.com* 🛏 *250 rooms* 🍴 *No Meals.*

Park James Hotel

$$ | HOTEL | There's an exciting energy in the courtyard of this charming boutique hotel. **Pros:** terrific restaurant and bar; great beds and work space; enthusiastic, helpful staff. **Cons:** bare room design; small bathrooms; not a pleasant walk to train station and downtown. $ *Rooms from: $262* ✉ *1400 El Camino Real, Menlo Park* ☎ *650/304–3880* ⊕ *parkjames. com* ⇥ *61 rooms* ❌ *No Meals.*

Rosewood Sand Hill

$$$$ | **HOTEL** | Synonymous with the relentless pursuit of exquisite luxury and exorbitant prices, few hotels in Northern California can match the gravitas and sheer delight of this gem near the northeastern base of the Santa Cruz Mountains. **Pros:** terrific upscale California cuisine at Madera restaurant; enormous, well-appointed rooms that all have balconies; beautiful grounds and views. **Cons:** hard to rationalize the price tag; the location is an office park at a highway exit; rooms don't always block out exterior noise. $ *Rooms from: $1,030* ✉ *2825 Sand Hill Rd., Menlo Park* ☎ *650/561–1500* ⊕ *rosewoodhotels.com* ⇥ *121 rooms* ❌ *No Meals.*

★ The Stanford Park Hotel

$$$ | **HOTEL** | With the university in its name and images of esteemed alums throughout the hallways, it's clear why many guests stay at this upscale boutique stalwart. **Pros:** oozes charm and personality; excellent outdoor pool and fitness center; large, nicely decorated rooms. **Cons:** have to drive to everything except shopping center; annoying noise from adjacent train tracks; rooms have small windows. $ *Rooms from: $399* ✉ *100 El Camino Real, Menlo Park* ☎ *650/322–1234* ⊕ *stanfordparkhotel. com* ⇥ *162 rooms* ❌ *No Meals.*

ⓨ Nightlife

Dutch Goose

BEER GARDENS | For a true taste of Peninsula life, visit this longtime locals' favorite for burgers and beers on a fun patio or inside the well-worn restaurant space. There's always a lively game of pool going on and any Bay Area sports team will surely be on the TVs. Families, beer league softball teams, and many other

regulars (including several celebrities who live nearby) come by for fun parties or a quick pizza dinner. The deviled eggs are not to be missed. ✉ *3567 Alameda de las Pulgas, Menlo Park* ☎ *650/854–3245* ⊕ *dutchgoose.net.*

⌂ Shopping

Kepler's Books

BOOKS | **FAMILY** | Since 1955, this bookstore has been the heart of Menlo Park. The store has many mainstream books, yet also maintains the independent, intellectual side that made it popular with the Beat Generation and activists (even the Grateful Dead's Jerry Garcia would play his guitar here). Author talks are a big draw at what continues to be one of the Bay Area's definitive local bookstores. ✉ *1010 El Camino Real, Menlo Park* ☎ *650/324–4321* ⊕ *keplers.com.*

Sunnyvale and Mountain View

38 miles south of San Francisco.

Originally a stagecoach stop on the Peninsula for travelers between San Francisco and San Jose, Mountain View's technology certainly has evolved in the century and a half since its founding. Castro Street is the main downtown area, where bars, restaurants, coffee shops, and boutiques are frequented throughout the day. The iconic heart of the city, though, is out toward the Bay, where internet giant Google's sprawling campus and headquarters are located. It's located right next to the Shoreline Amphitheatre (a popular concert venue) and the NASA Ames Research Center that opened in 1939, three decades before Neil Armstrong first set foot on the moon. Mountain View's neighbor is Sunnyvale, which is a quaint downtown stretch on Murphy Avenue by its Caltrain station but other than that is a quiet suburb with lots of tech company office parks. Together, these two cities are often considered the center of Silicon Valley since they reside in the geographic middle of the region.

GETTING HERE AND AROUND
From San Francisco, drivers can choose between U.S. 101 and I–280 for reaching Mountain View and Sunnyvale. Both routes will take between 45 minutes and a little over an hour depending on traffic.

Via U.S. 101, the main exits are Shoreline Boulevard and Rengstorff Avenue. From U.S. 280, El Monte Avenue is the primary exit. However, from both freeways, drivers often use Highway 85 to bisect Mountain View and exit at El Camino Real or Evelyn Avenue to reach downtown.

For Sunnyvale, use the Mathilda Avenue exit from U.S. 101 and the Sunnyvale-Saratoga Road exit from I–280.

Caltrain services stations in the heart of both cities' downtowns. Trains take between an hour and 1 hour 20 minutes depending on if it's an express train or a local train. Both cities also have light rail and bus service from the VTA.

ESSENTIALS
City of Mountain View. ⊕ *mountainview. gov.* **Mountain View Chamber of Commerce.** ⊕ *chambermv.org.* **City of Sunnyvale.** ⊕ *sunnyvale.ca.gov.* **Sunnyvale Chamber of Commerce.** ⊕ *svcoc.org.*

 Sights

Castro Street
STREET | The heart of Downtown Mountain View, this constantly bustling street runs from the Caltrain station (where a few blocks are pedestrian-only for outdoor dining because of the COVID-19 pandemic) to the City Hall complex that includes the Mountain View Center for the Performing Arts. Fast-casual restaurants and ramen shops tend to be the main destinations during the daytime, while the bar scene in the evening is

livelier than in any other city between San Jose and San Francisco.

A pair of excellent coffee shops anchor the ends of Castro Street: **Red Rock Coffee** (⊠ *201 Castro St.*) and **1 Oz Coffee** (⊠ *650 Castro St.*). Once you're caffeinated, make sure to try downtown's two premier French bakery/pastry shops: **Alexander's Patisserie** (⊠ *209 Castro St.*) and **Maison Alyzée** (⊠ *212 Castro St.*). **Doppio Zero** (⊠ *160 Castro St.*) is the best restaurant of the crowd directly on the street, serving superb Neapolitan pizzas with an irresistible soft, lightly charred crust. Just off Castro Street are a pair of dramatically different establishments, both worth a visit: **Steins Beer Garden & Restaurant** (⊠ *895 Villa St.*) and longtime fine-dining icon **Chez TJ** (⊠ *938 Villa St.*), where the careers of many top Bay Area chefs began. ⊠ *Mountain View ✛ Castro Street between Yosemite Ave. and Central Expy.* ☎ *650/968–8378* ⊕ *chambermv. org.*

Los Altos
TOWN | **FAMILY** | Arguably best known for its remaining apricot orchards, Mountain View's neighbor, Los Altos, is of the most charming, Main Street USA–evoking downtowns in the Bay Area—well worth a stroll and a lunch break. Anchored by a grand clock at the intersection of its two main streets, the small business area is split between Main Street and State Street, where both run for roughly five blocks. **Linden Tree Books** (⊠ *265 State St.*) is the signature boutique in town, and families drive from many miles away to browse the children's book selection and attend the book talks and other events a few days each month.

Popular breakfast and lunch spots along Main Street include **Red Berry Coffee** (⊠ *145 Main St.*), **Manresa Bread** (⊠ *271 State St.*), **Tal Palo** (⊠ *149 Main St.*) and **The American Italian Delicatessen** (⊠ *139 Main St.*). In the evening, crowds descend upon the contemporary farm-to-table cooking at **ASA** (⊠ *242 State St.*)

and **Cetrella** (✉ 400 Main St.), contemporary Indian cuisine at **Aurum** (✉ *132 State St.*), yakitori specialist **Sumika** (✉ *236 Plaza Central*), and craft cocktails at **Amandine Lounge** (✉ *235 1st St.*). A five-minute drive from downtown takes you to **Chef Chu's** (✉ *1067 N. San Antonio Rd., Suite 1300*), an institution for excellent Chinese cooking. ✉ *145 Main St., Los Altos* ☎ *650/949–5282* 🌐 *downtownlosaltos.org.*

Coffee and Quick Bites

Zareen's
$ | **INDIAN** | Serving a mix of contemporary Indian and Pakistani fare, this popular fast-casual restaurant started near Google in Mountain View in 2014 and now has two other Silicon Valley locations. Flavors are bold and riveting, whether it's a handheld lunch like a paratha roll filled with chicken *boti* (a spice-marinated kebab) or a comforting slow-cooked lamb stew. **Known for:** Peshawar-style beef chapli kebab as a burger; paneer cheese paratha roll; chicken biryani on Fridays. [$] *Average main: $15* ✉ *1477 Plymouth St., Mountain View* ☎ *650/628–6100* 🌐 *zareensrestaurant.com* 🕒 *Closed Mon.*

Hotels

★ The Ameswell Hotel
$$ | **HOTEL** | Just a freeway exit away from the NASA Ames Research Center and Google Headquarters, this fun, sharp hotel nicely balances being a dressed-up business hotel with a playful side. **Pros:** outdoor airstream bar; great wellness focus with spa and fitness center; comfortable, nicely designed rooms. **Cons:** mediocre coffee at café; sinks are weirdly designed; not walking distance to anything. [$] *Rooms from: $209* ✉ *800 Moffett Blvd., Mountain View* ☎ *650/880–1000* 🌐 *theameswellhotel.com* 🔑 *255 rooms* 🍴 *No Meals.*

Shashi Hotel Mountain View
$$ | **HOTEL** | The closest hotel to Google's campus feels more like Palm Springs than Silicon Valley. **Pros:** plenty of great amenities and dining options; short drive to Silicon Valley offices and attractions; hip, relaxed vibe. **Cons:** room prices soar on weekdays; pool almost never sees sunlight; hardwood floors in rooms. [$] *Rooms from: $299* ✉ *1625 N. Shoreline Blvd., Mountain View* ☎ *650/420–2600* 🌐 *shashihotel.com* 🔑 *200 rooms* 🍴 *No Meals.*

Tetra Hotel, Autograph Collection
$$ | **HOTEL** | With a sleek Japanese-inspired modern design, this is definitely one of Silicon Valley's top hotel destinations. **Pros:** spacious rooms; Adrestia restaurant on-site is the best in Sunnyvale; nice architecture. **Cons:** surrounded by office parks; beds could be more comfortable; minimalist aesthetic. [$] *Rooms from: $259* ✉ *400 W. Java Dr., Sunnyvale* ☎ *408/734–2300* 🌐 *marriott.com* 🔑 *200 rooms* 🍴 *No Meals.*

Performing Arts

TheatreWorks Silicon Valley
THEATER | Bay Area theater legend Robert Kelley founded this company in 1970, and today it continues to be one of the most thrilling performing arts destinations in the region. Performances are split between the intimate Lucie Stern Theatre in Palo Alto and the grander, newer Mountain View Center for the Performing Arts. The fare is never overly edgy yet is always full of innovative touches. The cast and set designs are consistently top-tier. ✉ *500 Castro St., Mountain View* ☎ *877/662–8978* 🌐 *theatreworks.org* 🎟 *From $30.*

San Jose

55 miles south of San Francisco.

California's third-largest city, San Jose is often thought of as a smaller Los Angeles because of its relentless sprawl and valley setting surrounded by mountains and water. However, there is really nothing small about San Jose. It has a large downtown area that is home to the Plaza de Cesar Chavez, San Jose State University, and several small but enjoyable museums, including the San Jose Museum of Art and Children's Discovery Museum. About a 10-minute drive from downtown is a charming residential area that includes the Municipal Rose Garden (one of the best in the region when it's in bloom) and the Rosicrucian Egyptian Museum, both popular with families from around the South Bay and Peninsula. While San Jose doesn't have the iconic tourist sights and fascinating topography of its friendly rival to the north San Francisco, it has a lot of unique neighborhoods and an energetic vibe that reflects its position as the largest city (and the southern end) of Silicon Valley.

GETTING HERE AND AROUND

From San Francisco, both Highway 101 and Interstate 280 go directly to San Jose. To reach the heart of downtown from either 101 or 280, take the Highway 87/Guadalupe Parkway exit, which runs parallel to the river that the highway is named after. Then take the exit for W Santa Clara Street, and that approach will land you in the center of downtown San Jose.

Caltrain connects San Francisco to San Jose at the San Jose Diridon station. the journey is 1 hour 16 minutes on an express train or 1 hour 39 minutes on a local train. VTA Light Rail and bus lines serve neighborhoods across San Jose.

ESSENTIALS

City of San Jose. ⊠ *San Jose* ⊕ *sanjoseca.gov.* **Visit San Jose.** ⊠ *San Jose* 🕾 *800/726–5673* ⊕ *sanjose.org.*

 ## Sights

San Pedro Square Market

MARKET | There is something for everyone at this longtime Downtown favorite. Dating back to 1972, it's technically still a market (there are a handful of boutiques), but it's really a lively, vast food hall with over a dozen tempting choices and plenty of places to sit and watch sports on TVs or enjoy live music outside. ⊠ *87 N. San Pedro St., San Jose* ⊕ *sanpedrosquaremarket.com.*

Winchester Mystery House

HISTORIC HOME | One of the Bay Area's grandest and strangest attractions is the 24,000-square-foot, 160-room Victorian mansion once owned by Sarah Winchester, the heiress to a firearms manufacturing fortune. Much of its mystique centers around the tragedies that Winchester faced in her life, and the mystery of what drove her to build and live as a recluse in this sprawling mansion after the deaths of her husband and young daughter. The mystery name, though, came after she passed away and the famous magician Harry Houdini visited the home in 1924 to investigate the stories of ghostly visitors. Apparently even Houdini was spooked by the home, and so what was the Llanada Villa became known as the Winchester Mystery House. ⊠ *525 S. Winchester Blvd., San Jose* 🕾 *408/247–2000* ⊕ *winchestermysteryhouse.com* 🎫 *Tickets from $20.*

Restaurants

Adega

$$$$ | **PORTUGUESE** | San Jose's only Michelin-starred restaurant and the most ambitious destination for Portuguese-influenced cuisine in the Bay Area is this fantastic tasting menu-only spot.

Sights

1 San Pedro Square Market...... C3

2 Winchester Mystery House....... B3

Restaurants

1 Adega....... D3

2 Jubba Somali Restaurant.. C4

3 Le Papillon.. B3

Quick Bites

1 Slice of Homage Pizza......... C3

Hotels

1 Hotel Valencia Santana Row.......... B3

2 Signia by Hilton San Jose.... C3

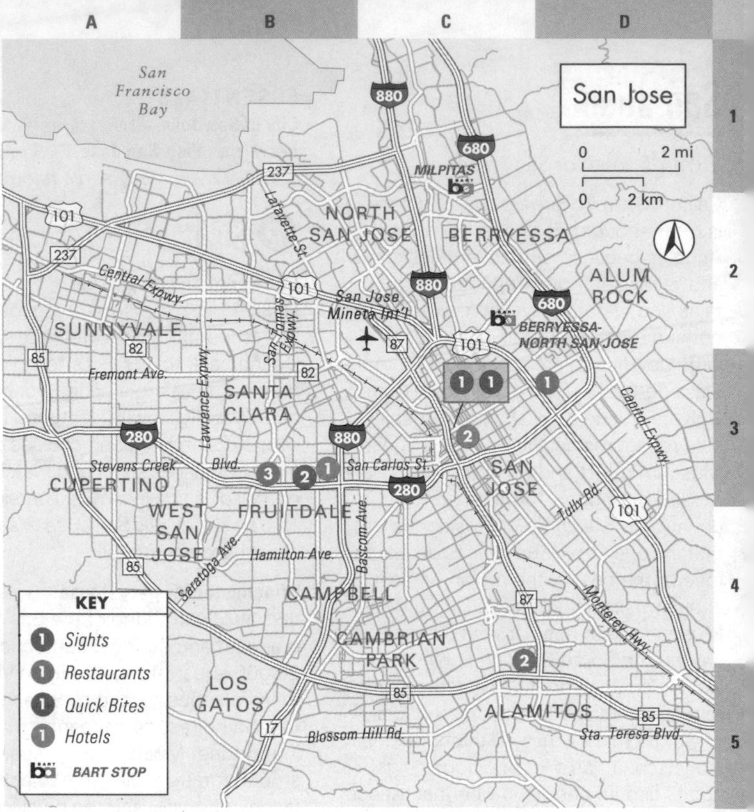

Seven-course dinners weave together meat and seafood plates, where the Portuguese fish staple of bacalhau (codfish) might be incorporated into a cannelloni, before leading to a delicately seared A5 Wagyu dish. **Known for:** fantastic pastries and desserts; enormous selection of Portuguese wines; San Jose's most ambitious restaurant. [$] *Average main: $229* ✉ *1614 Alum Rock Ave., San Jose* ☎ *408/926–9075* 🌐 *adegarest.com* 🕘 *Closed Mon. and Tues. No lunch.*

Jubba Somali Restaurant

$ | **AFRICAN** | Diners enjoy sampling the unique specialties presented by this friendly eatery, one of the few Somali restaurants in the Bay Area. The go-to dish is "kay kay," a sweet-and-savory stir-fry of chopped chapatti bread, spice-rubbed beef or chicken, African tea, onions, and bananas—and yes, you read that last one right. **Known for:** grilled spice-rubbed chicken suqaar; roast goat cutlet rice plate; wraps filled with beef, chicken, or fish. [$] *Average main: $19* ✉ *5330 Terner Way, San Jose* ☎ *408/440–1504* 🕘 *Closed Wed.*

Le Papillon

$$$$ | **MODERN FRENCH** | For those who think that French-influenced fine dining is passé, San Jose's gastronomic stalwart will change a few opinions. It's the best of both culinary worlds, where timeless luxury meets a contemporary approach. **Known for:** outstanding service; roast duck breast and pavé of leg; soufflés. [$] *Average main: $110* ✉ *410 Saratoga Ave., San Jose* ☎ *408/296–3730* 🌐 *lepapillon.com* 🕘 *Closed Mon. and Tues. No lunch* 👔 *Business casual.*

Coffee and Quick Bites

Slice of Homage Pizza

$$ | PIZZA | San Jose's most well-known dining destination might be this Detroit-style square pizza specialist that only found a full-time home in 2022 after being a pop-up in a nightclub. Now it's part of a multipurpose entertainment space called San Pedro Social, just a block away. **Known for:** three wings options; pepperoni pies; incredible caramelized crust for Detroit and Sicilian pies. [$] *Average main: $27* ✉ *163 W. Santa Clara St., San Jose* ☎ *408/490–4477* 🌐 *sohpizza.com* ⏲ *Closed Mon.*

Hotels

Hotel Valencia Santana Row

$$$ | HOTEL | This outpost of a Texas-based boutique hotel group is located in the glossy, Disneyland-ish Santana Row shopping area on the outskirts of San Jose. **Pros:** pedestrian-friendly; comfortable beds with soft Egyptian linens; unique architecture in public spaces. **Cons:** bar becomes a loud, crowded nightclub on weekends; lobby elevator is painfully slow; basic room decor. [$] *Rooms from: $419* ✉ *355 Santana Row, San Jose* ☎ *855/596–3396 reservations, 408/551–0010* 🌐 *hotelvalencia-santanarow.com* 🛏 *233 rooms* 🍴 *No Meals.*

Signia by Hilton San Jose

$$ | HOTEL | Downtown San Jose's massive signature hotel recently switched brands and underwent a renovation, changing from Fairmont to this Hilton label. **Pros:** fitness classes daily; beautiful marble bathrooms; great Japanese-Peruvian restaurant and classic steak house. **Cons:** area gets a little edgy at night; large and intimidating; high price for a downtown convention hotel. [$] *Rooms from: $342* ✉ *170 S. Market St., San Jose* ☎ *408/998–1900* 🌐 *hilton.com* 🛏 *541 rooms* 🍴 *No Meals.*

Nightlife

Haberdasher

BARS | This sharply dressed speakeasy is one of the South Bay's gold standards for craft cocktails. Drinks are intricate without being fussy, and the bartenders are always quick to offer insight into what cocktails might fit your taste. The cozy, low-ceilinged space is filled with velvet curtains and plush booths, continuing the 1920s feeling. ✉ *43 W. San Salvador St., San Jose* ☎ *408/792–7356* 🌐 *haberdashersj.com.*

★ Paper Plane

BARS | This cocktail bar with a stunning brick back bar easily competes with the best in the Bay Area. Cocktails are creative and compelling, frequently incorporating atypical ingredients like Thai tea or a syrup made of pepitas (pumpkin seeds). The short food menu revolving around spruced up comfort food is less inventive than the cocktails but far more interesting than standard bar grub. ✉ *72 S. 1st St., San Jose* ☎ *408/713–2625* 🌐 *paperplanesj.com.*

Activities

Levi's Stadium

FOOTBALL | The NFL's San Francisco 49ers don't actually play in San Francisco—in 2014, they relocated 40 miles south to this magnificent 68,500-seat stadium. In addition to Niners games each autumn, it's also the leading concert venue for the Bay Area, where stars like Beyoncé and Taylor Swift perform. Getting to games and events can be an enormous hassle, but the VTA Light Rail stops next to the stadium and connects with Caltrain at Mountain View. ✉ *4900 Marie P. DeBartolo Way, Santa Clara* ☎ *415/464–9377 box office* 🌐 *levisstadium.com.*

SAP Center at San Jose

HOCKEY | FAMILY | Known by fans as the Shark Tank, the South Bay's marquee arena is home to the NHL's San Jose

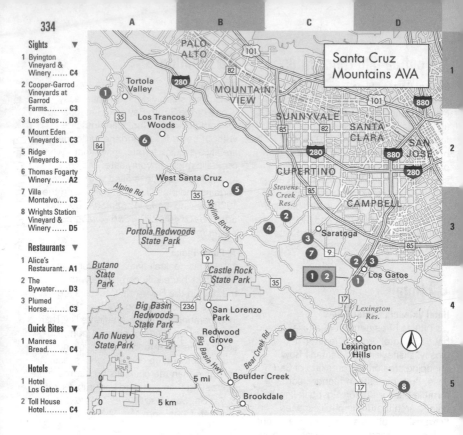

Sharks, in addition to being a major stop for concert tours. With a capacity of just over 17,000 hockey fans, it's one of the most exciting places to see the puck on ice in the country. Younger fans always enjoy meeting SJ Sharkie, the franchise's mascot. ✉ *525 W. Santa Clara St., San Jose* ☎ *408/287–7070* ⊕ *sapcenter.com.*

Santa Cruz Mountains AVA

Los Gatos is 50 miles south of San Francisco.

Napa Valley and Sonoma County might get most of the winery tourists, but the massive Santa Cruz Mountains AVA is often cited by locals and wine snobs alike as their favorite wine-growing region in the Bay Area. The vineyards here reside on steep, redwood tree–shaded mountains instead of in sun-drenched valleys, and are also much closer to the ocean.

The appellation is split between Santa Cruz County and Santa Clara County (and a tiny bit of San Mateo County) at the top of Highway 17 around Summit Road, an area best known as the epicenter of the 1989 Loma Prieta Earthquake. Skyline Boulevard, the main artery through the mountains, is full of hiking parking lots and panoramic viewpoints. At the base of the mountains are a pair of beautiful small towns, Los Gatos and Saratoga, full of great restaurants and a few tasting rooms. The mountains are much more narrow up the Peninsula, as the vineyards conclude in the terrain above the town of Woodside and then the mountain range fades into the ground several miles before San Francisco.

Santa Cruz Mountains Hiking

The Santa Cruz Mountains are a hiker's paradise full of spectacular trails. Hiking areas are split between county parks, state parks, and the Midpeninsula Regional Open Space District. The San Andreas Fault runs right through the Los Trancos Open Space Preserve, and a self-guided hike (⊕ openspace.org) there can show the power of the fault during earthquakes when plates collide with each other. Farther north, Windy Hill Preserve is another popular choice for moderate trails and gorgeous views. Towards the south, Castle Rock State Park is always a popular choice for hiking and camping, high above Saratoga and Los Gatos. By the Lexington Reservoir, just south of Los Gatos, the Priest Rock Trail is a steep, challenging choice but rewards hikers with one of the best overlooks of the Santa Cruz Mountains and the South Bay.

GETTING HERE AND AROUND

Don't rely on public transit or rideshares here. This is the wilderness—phone reception and internet are spotty at best. A car is all but necessary.

From San Francisco, take Interstate 280 either to Woodside Road to reach the northern part of the range, or continue to Highway 85 in Cupertino. From Highway 85, the exits for Saratoga Avenue or Highway 17 will take you towards the mountains. If you're driving the Highway 17 route, take the State Route 9/Saratoga-Los Gatos Road exit, which arrives directly into downtown Los Gatos. Alternatively, Highway 17 continues further south to the Summit Road exit, where several wineries reside at the summit of the Santa Cruz Mountains.

Skyline Boulevard/State Route 35 runs along the top of the mountain range from south to north with many thrilling curves. Saratoga-Los Gatos Road/State Route 9 connects the two most important cities at the base of the mountains.

ESSENTIALS

Santa Cruz Mountains Winegrowers Association. ☎ 831/685–8463 ⊕ winesofthesantacruzmountains.com. **Los Gatos.** ⊕ www.losgatosca.gov/3/visiting-los-gatos.

Saratoga Chamber of Commerce. ☎ 408/867–0753 ⊕ saratogachamber.org.

◉ Sights

Byington Vineyard & Winery

WINERY | About as isolated as it gets, this winery rewards visitors with outstanding pinot noirs from the eight acres of vineyards on property and views that can extend over the mountains to Monterey Bay on a clear day. You'll feel like you're on top of the world. Wines from the estate and much further afield are across the board enjoyable in the tastings. ✉ 21850 Bear Creek Rd., Los Gatos ☎ 408/354–1111 ⊕ byington.com 🍷 Tastings from $25 ⊗ Closed Mon.–Thurs.

★ Cooper-Garrod Vineyards at Garrod Farms

WINERY | Horseback riding and wine tasting makes a great combination for a day in the mountains; it's that duo that draws visitors to this longtime farm and winery above Saratoga. A former test pilot, George Cooper founded the winery in 1972 and all of the wine continues to be sourced exclusively from the 28 acres of vines on the estate. Don't miss the unique Test Pilot red blends and the quiet specialty of the winery: cabernet franc. ✉ 22645 Garrod Rd. ☎ 408/867–7116 ⊕ garrodfarms.com 🍷 Tastings form $22.

Los Gatos

TOWN | Situated at the southern end of the San Jose sprawl as the last city stop in the Bay Area before Santa Cruz and the gateway to the Santa Cruz Mountains, Los Gatos is a fun, exciting city that has also maintained its small-town vibe. The downtown area is almost L-shaped, where Santa Cruz Avenue connects with Main Street for two different thoroughfares that feel like one together. Along Santa Cruz, there's the beautifully renovated art-deco-style **Los Gatos Theatre** (⌧ *43 Santa Cruz Ave.*). Excellent cocktails and seasonal eats are served at **The Lexington House** (⌧ *40 Santa Cruz Ave.*); standout pizzas at **Oak & Rye** (⌧ *303 Santa Cruz Ave.*); notable pastas are offered at **The Pastaria & Market** (⌧ *27 Santa Cruz Ave.*); fantastic breads and pastries from **Manresa Bread** (⌧ *40 Santa Cruz Ave.*); and house-made brews are showcased at **Loma Brewing Company** (⌧ *130 Santa Cruz Ave.*). Elsewhere in downtown on the small side streets are creative cocktails from **Los Gatos Soda Works** (⌧ *21 College Ave.*), the unique gluten-free Italian cooking of **Polenteria** (⌧ *10 Victory La.*), and modern Spanish tapas at **Telefèric Barcelona** (⌧ *50 University Ave., Suite B270*).

Beyond downtown, Los Gatos is a residential city with a variety of neighborhoods and parks. **Vasona Lake** is a beautiful reservoir within a county park (⊕ *parks.sccgov.org*) that includes a children's railroad pulled by a steam engine and is a must-visit for families. At the far northern tip of the city is the headquarters of Netflix. ⌧ *40 Santa Cruz Ave., Los Gatos* ⊕ *visitlosgatosca.com.*

Mount Eden Vineyards

WINERY | This longtime producer above Saratoga is widely considered the region's pinot noir whisperer. Its vineyards date back to 1945 when one of the most iconic names in California wine, winery founder Martin Ray, planted them at an elevation of roughly 2,000 feet.

Mount Eden also produces outstanding estate chardonnay and cabernet sauvignon. Tastings on the veranda include three wines and are by appointment only. ⌧ *22020 Mount Eden Rd., Saratoga* ☎ *408/867–5832* ⊕ *mounteden.com* ✉ *Tastings $35* ⊙ *Closed weekends.*

★ Ridge Vineyards

WINERY | One of the most iconic names in American wine, Ridge's 1971 Monte Bello Cabernet Sauvignon participated in the famous 1976 Judgement of Paris tasting between French and Californian wines. See that celebrated Monte Bello Vineyard here, a stunning hillside of wine royalty with a mesmerizing view over the South Bay. Longtime winemaker Paul Draper was a visionary for prioritizing single-vineyard expressions and a minimal-intervention approach to crafting wines, and the winery continues that tradition. Visitors can usually purchase a taste of Ridge's signature Monte Bello wine (a red Bordeaux-style blend), but fair warning, it's one of the country's most expensive wines. ⌧ *17100 Montebello Rd., Cupertino* ☎ *408/868–1320* ⊕ *ridgewine.com* ✉ *Tastings $30.*

Thomas Fogarty Winery

WINERY | The northernmost winery open to the public in the Santa Cruz Mountains is named after its founder, a legendary heart surgeon. Pinot noir is the specialty here, but tastings often include a few wild cards like nebbiolo. The tasting room is surrounded by rolling vineyards, yet the real postcard views are in the adjacent area where weddings are held with a panoramic backdrop of what must be close to half of the Bay Area. ⌧ *19501 Skyline Blvd., Woodside* ☎ *650/851–6777* ⊕ *fogartywinery.com* ✉ *Tastings $35.*

Villa Montalvo

ARTS CENTERS | **FAMILY** | Tuscany meets Northern California at this nonprofit arts center and 166-acre park, where a beautiful villa stands proudly amidst a forest of redwood trees. It's a special place for a lawn picnic in the sunshine, and holds concerts in its hillside amphitheater. ✉ *15400 Montalvo Rd., Saratoga* ☎ *408/961–5800* 🌐 *montalvoarts.org.*

Wrights Station Vineyard & Winery
WINERY | Near Loma Prieta, as high as one can go in the Santa Cruz Mountains, this fun winery balances high-quality wines with a more laid-back atmosphere that encourages relaxing all afternoon. There's a bocce court, splendid vineyard views, and excellent estate chardonnay and pinot noir. Charcuterie boards are sold for hungry tasting groups, and once a month or so there's a food truck on hand. This is one of the few local wineries that welcomes both children and dogs. ✉ *24250 Loma Prieta Ave., Los Gatos* ☎ *408/560–9343* 🌐 *wrightsstation.com* 🎫 *Tastings $20* 🕒 *Closed Mon.–Thurs.*

🍴 Restaurants

Alice's Restaurant
$ | **AMERICAN** | At the prominent intersection of Skyline Boulevard and Highway 84, this indoor-outdoor restaurant is a landmark for weekend breakfast and lunch. Alice's is surrounded by redwood trees, so sitting outside at the picnic benches is beautiful but almost always on the chilly side. **Known for:** dog-friendly outdoor deck; French toast and blueberry pancakes; vast menu including several burgers. $ *Average main: $15* ✉ *17288 Skyline Blvd.* ☎ *650/851–0303* 🌐 *alicesrestaurant.com.*

The Bywater
$$ | **CAJUN** | Legendary farm-to-table fine dining chef David Kinch co-owns this casual restaurant. It's a loving ode to the good times and great cuisine of New Orleans. **Known for:** broiled oysters; shrimp and avocado remoulade; beignets covered in powdered sugar. $ *Average main: $21* ✉ *532 N. Santa Cruz Ave., Los Gatos* ☎ *408/560–9639* 🌐 *thebywaterca.com* 🕒 *Closed Tues.*

Plumed Horse
$$$$ | **MODERN AMERICAN** | Plumed Horse is a venerable institution for outstanding luxury mixed with the brightness and freshness of local ingredients. The posh, shimmering space is highlighted by a giant glass wine storage area. **Known for:** lively and well-heeled crowd; black pepper and Parmesan soufflé; incredible Champagne collection. $ *Average main: $54* ✉ *14555 Big Basin Way, Saratoga* ☎ *408/867–4711* 🌐 *plumedhorse.com* 🕒 *Closed Mon. and Tues. No lunch.*

☕ Coffee and Quick Bites

★ Manresa Bread
$ | **BAKERY** | **FAMILY** | In a region with several outstanding destinations for fresh baguettes and levain breads, the freshly baked loaves here deserve some of the highest praise. Everything in the display case and on the cooling racks is absolutely dialed in, from the *kouign-amann* (like a decadent glazed dessert version of a croissant) and cookies to slices of custardy quiche and simple avocado toast. **Known for:** almond croissant; excellent breakfast and lunch sandwiches; terrific locally roasted coffee and espresso drinks. $ *Average main: $14* ✉ *40 N. Santa Cruz Ave., Los Gatos* ☎ *408/402–5372* 🌐 *manresabread.com* 🕒 *No dinner.*

🛏 Hotels

Hotel Los Gatos
$$ | **HOTEL** | The Tuscan villa–inspired design is hard to miss at this very pleasant hotel, it's a welcome refuge from the sprawl and tech-centric culture of Silicon Valley. **Pros:** doesn't feel like a chain; great neighborhood with several restaurants; outdoor pool and Jacuzzi. **Cons:** no in-house breakfast option; over-the-top theme; not as luxurious as a villa should be. $ *Rooms from: $289* ✉ *210 E. Main St., Los Gatos* ☎ *408/335–1700* 🌐 *hotellosgatos.com* 🛏 *72 rooms* 🍴 *No Meals.*

Toll House Hotel

$$ | HOTEL | On the edge of downtown Los Gatos, this beautiful contemporary hotel is a great choice for wine-tasting weekenders or business travelers looking for a calmer, more charming locale than most of Silicon Valley. **Pros:** nice indoor-outdoor fitness center; spacious bathrooms; quiet but central location. **Cons:** lacks personality; destination fee; not many amenities. $ *Rooms from: $259* ⊠ *140 S. Santa Cruz Ave., Los Gatos* ☎ *800/238–6111* ⊕ *tollhousehotel. com* ⇆ *115 rooms* ⦿ *No Meals.*

ⓨ Nightlife

Loma Brewing Company

BREWPUBS | Many baseball fans make the trip to Los Gatos just to visit this brewery owned by former MLB infielder Kevin Youkilis. However, the brewery deserves many accolades in its own right for producing some of the top beers in the South Bay, such as the hops-packed Greek God of Hops, a double IPA that riffs on Youkilis' nickname in the book *Moneyball.* At this family-friendly brewpub, everyone can enjoy refined pub grub with or without the house beers. ⊠ *130 N. Santa Cruz Ave., Los Gatos* ☎ *408/560–9626* ⊕ *lomabrew.com.*

Mountain Winery

LIVE MUSIC | This gorgeous property is centered around the summer concert series at its beautiful amphitheater. Many notable musicians, often popular singers and groups from past decades, make a stop here. The winery was built by the iconic Paul Masson (one of the true pioneers of California wine in the late 19th century and early 20th century) and tastings are held each weekend. ⊠ *14831 Pierce Rd., Saratoga* ☎ *408/741–2822* ⊕ *mountainwinery.com.*

Sidecar Modern Tavern

BARS | A throwback atmosphere meets the modern craft cocktail movement at this excellent "tavern" that shows how much the concept of one has evolved. Cocktails might include a unique house-made tonic for a standout gin and tonic or a tiki drink incorporating aged rum, mango, and rooibos. ⊠ *25 E. Main St., Los Gatos* ☎ *408/399–5180* ⊕ *sidecar7. com.*

The Peninsular Coastline

Half Moon Bay is 24 miles south of San Francisco.

With steep, chiseled cliffs and frequently enormous waves that are popular with surfers and whales, the peninsular coastline is one of the great road trip destinations on the West Coast. Highway 1 winds up, down, and around tight curves and stunning viewpoints from Santa Cruz's beaches to the small bedroom communities of Half Moon Bay and Pacifica. Half Moon Bay is an artsy town, best known for its pumpkin festival and Halloween decorations and spirit. Pacifica is more of a surfing-centric town and home to many commuters making the short trek north to San Francisco on weekdays. The region is infamous for its near constant chilly temperatures (they rarely leave the 50s) and frequent fog, even in the summertime. These might be beaches, but nobody is going to linger for hours suntanning in a swimsuit on them.

GETTING HERE AND AROUND

SamTrans offers limited bus service to Half Moon Bay. Do not rely on public transportation when exploring the coastline. A car is essential.

Highway 1 is the main north-south thoroughfare along the coastline. From the Peninsula, take Highway 92 from San Mateo to Half Moon Bay. From San Francisco, Highway 1 connects with both Skyline Boulevard and I–280 at the southern border of San Francisco with Daly City, then flows into Pacifica.

No matter where you go, pack layers. Yes, it is a beach, but it will be chilly. Do not be fooled by potential sunshine. It is rarely above 60°F in Half Moon Bay and Pacifica.

ESSENTIALS

Half Moon Bay. ✉ *235 Main St., Half Moon Bay* ☎ *650/726–8380* 🌐 *visithalfmoonbay.org.* **Pacifica.** ☎ *650/355–4122* 🌐 *visitpacifica.com.*

Pacifica

🍴 Restaurants

Nick's Rockaway

$$ | AMERICAN | Dungeness crab, the Bay Area's favorite local seafood, is showcased in a consistently fantastic sandwich on grilled sourdough bread at this timeless Pacifica restaurant and lounge. It's an all-day restaurant attached to a motel right by the beach, with a vintage Americana atmosphere that looks like a blend of a coastal diner with maritime decor and a throwback martini bar with dim lighting, wood paneling, and tufted leather banquettes. **Known for:** always a fun scene; fresh seafood dishes; old-school favorites like prime rib and filet of sole. $ *Average main: $21* ✉ *100 Rockaway Beach Ave., Pacifica* ☎ *650/359–3900* 🌐 *nicksrestaurant.net* 🕒 *Closed Tues. and Wed.*

☕ Coffee and Quick Bites

Camelot Fish and Chips

$$ | BRITISH | Every coastal area needs a great fish-and-chips shop; for the peninsular coastline, it's this casual establishment that has been serving Pacifica diners since 1969. The batter for the fish is light and sports just the right crispy texture, while fries are of the thick, potato-forward style popular at classic English pubs. **Known for:** fish-and-chips paired with English ales; cozy interior; crispy shrimp and chips. $ *Average main: $20* ✉ *70 W. Manor Dr., Pacifica* ☎ *650/355–1555* 🌐 *camelotfishandchips.com* 🕒 *Closed Sun. and Mon.*

Soul Grind Coffee Roasters

$ | CAFÉ | With its frequent fog and ocean breeze chill, coffee is all but mandatory along the coastline. The best café in the region for your buzz is a lofty, garage-like roastery/café right by Pacifica's state beach with excellent espresso-based drinks and pour-overs from beans roasted in-house. **Known for:** single-origin pour-overs; any espresso-based drink; different kinds of quiche. $ *Average main: $12* ✉ *5400 Hwy. 1, Pacifica* ☎ *650/898–8660* 🌐 *soulgrindcoffee.com.*

America's Most Scenic Taco Bell 🍴

One of the quirkiest landmarks along the peninsular coastline is a Taco Bell. Yes, that's correct. It's a destination for many people to enjoy a cheesy gordita crunch while gazing out at the Pacifica State Beach waves right outside of this Taco Bell that fits into the landscape with its beach cabin appearance (✉ *5200 Hwy. 1*). There was even a wedding reception here in 2021. It's a little strange for a fast food giant to have this prime real estate, but it's also part of the folklore of this stretch of the California coast.

Activities

★ Devil's Slide

HIKING & WALKING | FAMILY | When the Tom Lantos Tunnels opened in 2013, the previously spine-tingling, white-knuckle-inducing cliff-top portion of Highway 1 between Pacifica and Montara was retired and became a delightful 1.3-mile-long trail. Locals can attest that it's much more relaxing to stroll or bike along the trail these days than it was to navigate its turns in a car. It's a popular spot for dog walking and presents splendid views of the rugged coastline and crashing waves. Keep an eye out for whales in the distance. ⊠ *Old Devil's Slide Hwy., Pacifica* ⊹ *Off Hwy. 1 between Pacifica and Montara* ⊕ *smcgov.org/parks/devils-slide-trail.*

Half Moon Bay

⊙ Sights

Half Moon Bay State Beach

BEACH | FAMILY | The peninsular coastline's signature beach is actually a collection of four smaller beaches. All of them are beautiful and all of them will definitely be too cold for swimming beyond a brisk dunk. Each of the beaches has its own facilities and they're connected by the Coastal Trail, a popular choice for joggers and cyclists. On a clear day, the beaches are absolutely magnificent with the tree-covered Santa Cruz Mountains looming tall behind you and the deep blue of the Pacific right in front of you. The appropriately named crescent-shaped beach has sand for roughly four miles, but its grand setting makes it feel much larger. For a good overview, hit the visitor's center at Francis Beach (open only on weekends). **Amenities:** restrooms, showers. **Best for:** walking, sunset. ⊠ *Francis Beach, Half Moon Bay* ☎ *650/726–8819* ⊕ *parks.ca.gov* ⊟ *Parking $10.*

Pillar Point Harbor and Mavericks Beach

NAUTICAL SIGHT | The second "downtown" area of Half Moon Bay, known as Princeton-by-the-Sea, surrounds this beautiful, calm harbor. It's the center of the seafood trade for the coast, and possibly the most important Bay Area fishing wharf other than San Francisco's Fisherman's Wharf. Stroll over to **Barbara's Fish Trap** (⊠ *281 Capistrano Rd.*) for some of that fresh catch. For pisco sours and fish in ceviche form, visit **La Costanera** (⊠ *260*

The World Pumpkin Capital ⊙

Charlie Brown must have visited Half Moon Bay, because every year, the coastal town crowns a giant pumpkin that can weigh more than 2,500 pounds. The annual Pumpkin Festival draws big crowds for all things pumpkin-related, from food, to pumpkin carving, to creative costumes. Lemos Farm (⊕ *lemosfarm.com*) is a popular amusement park with one of the area's most popular pumpkin patches. And it's always fun to make your own glass pumpkin at the Half Moon Bay Art Glass (⊕ *hmbartglass.com*).

Capistrano Rd.), one of the leading Peruvian restaurants in the Bay Area. Besides eating fish-and-chips and sand dabs, it's a great area for walking or kayaking.

At the edge of the harbor and around a corner resides Mavericks Beach, a somewhat hidden, world-famous surfing spot. Most of the time the waves aren't that notable. However, when the time is right, the best surfers in the world gather here for one of the most prestigious big wave competitions anywhere. Don't even think about trying to surf or swim here. ⊠ *1 Johnson Pier, Half Moon Bay.*

⊙ Restaurants

Pasta Moon

$$$$ | MODERN ITALIAN | Kim Levin's ode to rustic Italian cuisine in a lofty, natural light–filled space continues to thrill fervent regulars each week. Around 10 pastas are offered each evening, making it very difficult for diners to decide from the many tempting options. **Known for:** local Brussels sprouts chips; signature lasagna with housemade Sicilian sausage; pistachio chocolate cannoli. ⓢ *Average* *main: $42 ✉ 845 Main St., Half Moon Bay ☎ 650/726–5125 🌐 pastamoon.com ⏲ Closed Tues. No lunch.*

Sam's Chowder House

$$ | SEAFOOD | FAMILY | It's a little backwards to enjoy Maine lobster while gazing out at the Pacific, but when the crustacean meat is as wonderful as it is at this coastal icon, nobody cares what ocean is in the distance. Chowder may be in the name, but Sam's is all about that glorious lobster roll, served "naked" (warm with butter) or "dressed" (chilled with lemon aioli). **Known for:** local fresh catch preparations; patio overlooking the waves; possibly the Bay Area's best lobster roll. [$] *Average main: $30 ✉ 4210 N. Cabrillo Hwy., Half Moon Bay ☎ 650/712–0245 🌐 samschowderhouse.com.*

Coffee and Quick Bites

Breakwater Barbecue

$ | BARBECUE | The Peninsula's leading barbecue has only been grilling and smoking at its El Granada home since 2020, but it's already a favorite choice for Bay Area residents looking for an excellent hearty lunch on a coastal road trip day. All of the beef and pork is of very high quality and the sausage links are made in-house. **Known for:** massive platters with multiple meats, sides, and sauces; mac 'n' cheese with poblano peppers; smoked brisket tray. [$] *Average main: $15 ✉ 30 Avenue Portola, El Granada ☎ 650/713–5303 🌐 breakwaterbbq.com ⏲ Closed Mon.–Wed.*

★ **Dad's Luncheonette**

$ | AMERICAN | FAMILY | Talk about a career pivot—after years of cooking at San Francisco fine-dining standouts Saison and Benu, chef-owner Scott Clark traded in formal kitchens for a revamped caboose along the Half Moon Bay coast. Here, he opens for limited hours and serves a concise menu of outstanding hamburgers and mushroom sandwiches that are a perfect example of wholesome comfort food done with the careful technique and ingredient sourcing of a chef from a gastronomic background. **Known for:** homemade potato chips; hamburger sandwich with fresh oak lettuce and melted cheese; photogenic setting. [$] *Average main: $15 ✉ 225 Cabrillo Hwy. S, Half Moon Bay ☎ 650/560–9832 ⏲ Closed Mon.–Wed. No dinner.*

Hotels

Beach House Hotel

$$ | B&B/INN | With splendid ocean views and enormous junior suites throughout the property (each is more than 500 square feet), this appropriately named seaside getaway really does help travelers feel at home by the beach. **Pros:** can't beat the natural setting; massage treatments at the spa; fireplaces in each room. **Cons:** need to drive to downtown Half Moon Bay; nondescript room design; pool and hot tub could use renovation. [$] *Rooms from: $295 ✉ 4100 Cabrillo Hwy. N, Half Moon Bay ☎ 650/712–0220 🌐 beach-house.com 🛏 54 suites 🍴 Free Breakfast.*

Nantucket Whale Inn

$$ | B&B/INN | While most upscale hotels on the Peninsular coastline are indeed on the actual coast, this delightful bed and-breakfast resides right in the heart of Half Moon Bay's pleasant downtown. **Pros:** spacious rooms with lots of charm; unique zinc bed frames in most rooms; evening wine hour. **Cons:** smallest room's bathroom is private but accessed from hallway; some rooms only have a queen bed; thin walls. [$] *Rooms from: $200 ✉ 779 Main St., Half Moon Bay ☎ 650/726–1616 🌐 nantucketwhaleinn com 🛏 7 rooms 🍴 Free Breakfast.*

Oceano Hotel & Spa

$$ | HOTEL | Oceanside luxury is at its best at this venerable vacation favorite in the quaint Princeton-by-the-Sea area of Half Moon Bay. Every traveler to the coast knows about the fierce winds and fog in the area, so the fact that every guest room here has its own fireplace is an enormous asset. **Pros:** spacious, nicely decorated rooms; patios overlooking the ocean; fireplace in rooms. **Cons:** rooms can be noisy; inn rooms are on the smaller side; dated design. $ *Rooms from: $239* ⊠ *280 Capistrano Rd., Half Moon Bay* ☎ *650/726–5400* ⊕ *oceanohalfmoonbay.com* ⏎ *106 rooms* ⦿ *No Meals.*

The Ritz-Carlton, Half Moon Bay

$$$$ | **RESORT** | **FAMILY** | The grande dame of Northern California coastal hotels resides in its own little micro-community on a picturesque bluff. **Pros:** large, comfortable rooms with oceanic color theme; incredible setting and recreational opportunities; fantastic spa. **Cons:** excessive valet parking price; steep destination fee; can feel strangely hectic and stressful. $ *Rooms from: $795* ⊠ *1 Miramontes Point Rd., Half Moon Bay* ☎ *650/712–7000* ⊕ *ritzcarlton.com* ⏎ *261 rooms* ⦿ *No Meals.*

🍸 Nightlife

Half Moon Bay Brewing Company

BREWPUBS | This beloved gathering spot was one of the originals of the Bay Area craft beer scene and continues to be a popular spot for a pint or a full meal. Not surprisingly given the locale, there's a popular amber ale named for Mavericks, along with the Bay Area's favorite pumpkin ale in the fall. The food menu is definitely more exciting and seafood-focused than your average brewery fare. ⊠ *390 Capistrano Rd., Half Moon Bay* ☎ *650/728–2739* ⊕ *hmbbrewingco.com.*

Hop Dogma Brewing Co.

BREWPUBS | The coast has a small but impressive roster of craft breweries, and the best of them is this IPA specialist. The charming taproom and its front patio offer flights and full pours of the beers produced in-house. Beyond the hoppy beers, the brewery also serves a range of styles, from cucumber wheat beers to vanilla coffee stouts. ⊠ *270 Capistrano Rd., Suite 22, Half Moon Bay* ☎ *650/560–8729* ⊕ *hopdogma.com.*

🏃 Activities

Bike Works

BIKING | Half Moon Bay doesn't have Venice Beach or Santa Barbara's fame when it comes to biking along California boardwalks and coastal roads (Highway 1 is truly meant for cars), but this company's beach cruisers are perfect for a leisurely ride or a long workout along the Coastal Trail between Miramar Beach and the Ritz-Carlton. ⊠ *520 Kelly Ave., Half Moon Bay* ☎ *650/726–6708* ⊕ *bikeworkshmb.com* ⏎ *From $25 a day.*

Half Moon Bay Kayak Company

KAYAKING | Half Moon Bay is, after all, best explored by water. All paddles leave from Pillar Point Harbor, whether you're on your own or with a guide on a daytime, sunset, or nighttime exploration of the scenery and marine life. The most intense kayakers will enjoy the slightly more than a mile trek to the JV Fitzgerald Marine Reserve. ⊠ *2 Johnson Pier, Half Moon Bay* ☎ *650/773–6101* ⊕ *hmbkayak.com* ⏎ *From $30.*

🛍 Shopping

Mirada Art

ART GALLERIES | Like many quaint coastal communities, Half Moon Bay has a wonderful community of artists and galleries. This gallery in the heart of downtown is particularly special because visitors can interact with the artists whose works are on display. Paintings featuring nature and coastal beauty are usually a focus, but there's a wide variety of themes and artistic styles to see, including glass and jewelry. ⊠ *355 Main St., Half Moon Bay* ☎ *650/206–8722* ⊕ *mirada-art.com* ⏱ *Closed Mon.–Thurs.*

Año Nuevo State Park is a stunning destination for nature-lovers of all stripes.

Pescadero

👁 Sights

★ Año Nuevo State Park

NATURE PRESERVE | FAMILY | It's a seasonal ritual for California's elephant seals to come ashore here each winter—and a spectacular annual event for human visitors to watch these incredible marine mammals playing, flirting, breeding, and sometimes fighting in the chilly salt water and brisk sunshine. Guided tours (around three miles) are mandatory to keep the elephant seals safe and to protect this fragile ecosystem. ⊠ *1 New Years Creek Rd., Pescadero* 🕾 *650/879–2025* ⊕ *parks.ca.gov* 🗺 *Parking $10; tours $11* 🖉 *Reservations essential and book up quickly.*

Pescadero State Beach

BEACH | FAMILY | One of the most striking stretches of the peninsular coastline is where Highway 1 meets the road leading to the quaint town of Pescadero. On the other side of the highway is a marsh that is always a great spot for seeing local wildlife and birds. The mile-long beach almost appears like an amphitheater thanks to how the short, steep cliffs block any view of the highway above them. Stroll around and view the majestic rock arch and coves. **Amenities:** toilets, parking (free). **Best for:** walking. ⊠ *Pescadero State Beach, Pescadero* ✛ *Near Hwy. 1 and Pescadero Creek Rd.* 🕾 *650/726–8819* ⊕ *parks.ca.gov.*

Pigeon Point Lighthouse

LIGHTHOUSE | At 115 feet tall, it's impossible to miss this impressive lighthouse that is about halfway between Pescadero and the southern edge of San Mateo County. The lighthouse dates back to 1872, helping boats navigate through the ever-present local fog. The original lens is no longer used, but the Coast Guard still uses a much more modern LED light here to help guide those at sea. ⊠ *210 Pigeon Point Rd., Pescadero* 🕾 *650/879–2120* ⊕ *parks.ca.gov* 🗺 *Free.*

🍴 Restaurants

★ Duarte's Tavern

$$ | AMERICAN | Along with a stunning state beach, the tiny, adorable, largely agricultural community of Pescadero is known for this coastal dining legend. Dating back to the late 1800s, no other coastal restaurant comes close to the celebrity status of Duarte's. **Known for:** olallieberry pie; green chile and artichoke soup served together as half and half; a definitive cioppino. $ *Average main: $22 ✉ 202 Stage Rd., Pescadero ☎ 650/879–0464 ⊕ duartestavern.com ⏱ Closed Tues. No dinner Mon., Wed., and Thurs. Dinner ends at 6 pm Fri.–Sun.*

🏃 Activities

Harley Farms Goat Dairy

FOOD AND DRINK TOURS | FAMILY | One of the most bucolic corners of the peninsular coastal region is this farm, home of many adorable goats (last count: 108 baby goats). Tours introduce guests to the animal residents, including Jimmy the Guardian Alpaca. Goat's milk cheeses and other products are available in the shop. ✉ *205 North St., Pescadero ⊕ harleyfarms.com ⏱ Tours $55.*

Moss Beach

👁 Sights

JV Fitzgerald Marine Reserve

NATURE PRESERVE | FAMILY | Like the tide-pool section of an aquarium—except in real life—this protected area is on every must-visit list for school field trips and anyone interested in marine biology. This is one of the premier California coast places to see sea stars, crabs, and the other aquatic creatures who inhabit this unique marine ecosystem. Be careful walking around; tide pools are slippery and full of wildlife. There are trails for enjoying views from above. The reserve's website has a handy self-guided tour brochure. ✉ *200 Nevada Ave., Moss Beach ☎ 650/728–3584 ⊕ smcgov.org ⏱ Free.*

🍴 Restaurants

Moss Beach Distillery

$$ | AMERICAN | Every "best patio" article in the Bay Area features this oceanfront restaurant (and former speakeasy) with a beautiful view, whether it's sunny or foggy. The menu is always fresh and fun with a general emphasis on fish and seafood. **Known for:** Anchor Steam beer-battered artichoke hearts; seafood sliders; French onion soup and clam chowder. $ *Average main: $26 ✉ 140 Beach Way, Moss Beach ☎ 650/728–5595 ⊕ mossbeachdistillery.com.*

🛏 Hotels

Seal Cove Inn

$$$ | B&B/INN | It's impossible not to be charmed by this gorgeous European-inspired bed and breakfast surrounded by cypress trees in the small town of Moss Beach. **Pros:** small oceanside town getaway; free use of bikes for nearby trail; evening wine reception. **Cons:** isolated from most restaurants and shops; pricey rollaway beds if added to room; steep prices. $ *Rooms from: $364 ✉ 221 Cypress Ave., Moss Beach ☎ 650/728–4114 ⊕ sealcoveinn.com ⏱ 10 suites ⏱ Free Breakfast.*

NAPA AND SONOMA

15

Updated by
Daniel Mangin

Sights	Restaurants	Hotels	Shopping	Nightlife
★★★★★	★★★★★	★★★★☆	★★★☆☆	★★★☆☆

WELCOME TO NAPA AND SONOMA

TOP REASONS TO GO

★ **Touring wineries:** Let's face it: this is the reason you're here, and the range of excellent sips to sample would make any oeno-phile (or novice drinker, for that matter) giddy.

★ **Biking:** Gentle hills and vineyard-laced farmland make Napa and Sonoma perfect for combining lei-surely back-roads cycling with winery stops.

★ **Spa treatments:** Work-hard, play-hard types and inveterate sybarites flock to Wine Country spas for pampering.

★ **Fine dining:** A meal at a top-tier restaurant can be a revelation about the level of artistry intuitive chefs can achieve and how successfully quality wines pair with food.

★ **Viewing the art:** Several wineries, among them Napa Valley's Hall St. Helena and The Donum Estate in Sonoma dis-play museum-quality artworks indoors and on their grounds.

1 Napa. Good base, with tasting rooms, dining, shopping, nightlife.

2 Yountville. Walkable downtown, must-visit restaurants.

3 Oakville. Cabernet central.

4 Rutherford. Find out what "Rutherford dust" is.

5 St. Helena. Genteel downtown amid wineries.

6 Calistoga. Spas—from rustic to chic.

7 Sonoma. Anchored by a historic mission and plaza.

8 Glen Ellen. Creekside village with a rural flavor.

9 Kenwood. Top of Sonoma Valley.

10 Petaluma. Farming town, proud of it.

11 Healdsburg. Northern Sonoma's swank hub.

12 Geyserville. Alexander Valley wineries, fun downtown.

13 Forestville. Woodsy river enclave.

14 Guerneville. A Russian River vacation spot.

15 Sebastopol. West County's HQ.

16 Santa Rosa. Sonoma County's largest city.

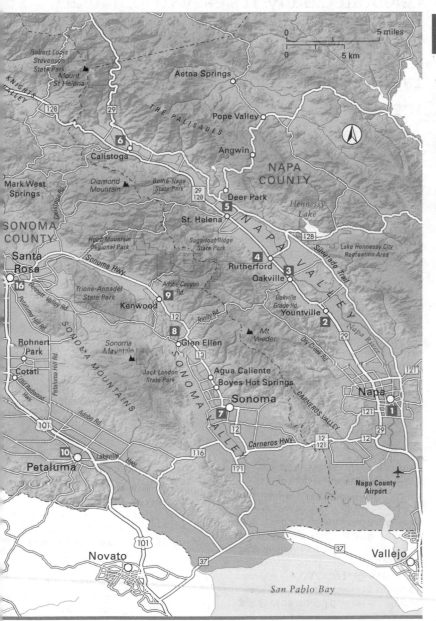

In California's premier wine region, the pleasures of eating and drinking are celebrated daily. It's easy to join in at famous wineries and rising newcomers off country roads, or at trendy in-town tasting rooms. Chefs transform local ingredients into feasts, and gourmet groceries sell perfect picnic fare.

Yountville, Healdsburg, and St. Helena have small-town charm as well as luxurious inns, hotels, and spas. Yet the natural setting is equally sublime, whether experienced from a canoe on the Russian River or the deck of a winery overlooking endless rows of vines.

The Wine Country is also rich in history. In Sonoma you can explore California's Spanish and Mexican pasts at the Sonoma Mission, and the origins of modern California wine making at Buena Vista Winery. Some wineries, among them St. Helena's Beringer and Rutherford's Inglenook, have cellars or tasting rooms dating to the late 1800s. Calistoga is a flurry of late-19th-century Steamboat Gothic architecture, though the town's oldest-looking building, the medieval-style Castello di Amorosa, is a 21st-century creation.

Visits to the Napa Valley's Beringer, Robert Mondavi, and Inglenook—and at Buena Vista in the Sonoma Valley—provide an entertaining overview of Wine Country history. Through the glass walls at Hall St. Helena's tasting room you may glimpse 21st-century wine-making technology in action, and over in Glen Ellen's Benziger Family Winery you can learn how its vineyard managers apply biodynamic farming principles to grape growing. At numerous facilities you can play winemaker at seminars in the fine art of blending wines. If that strikes you as too much effort, you can always pamper yourself at a luxury spa.

⇨ *To delve further into the fine art of Wine Country living, pick up a copy of Fodor's Napa and Sonoma.*

MAJOR REGIONS

Napa Valley. Practically speaking, the valley can be divided into its southern and northern parts. The southern Napa Valley encompasses cooler grape-growing areas and the tasting rooms, restaurants, and hotels of **Napa** and **Yountville**, along with slightly warmer **Oakville.** The northern valley begins around **Rutherford,** like Oakville blessed with Cabernet-friendly soils. Beyond it lies hotter **St. Helena,** whose downtown entices with boutiques, galleries, and restaurants. Warmer still is **Calistoga,** known for spas and hot springs.

Sonoma Valley and Petaluma. Modern California wine making began in Sonoma Valley. North of the tasting rooms, restaurants, and lodgings near Sonoma Plaza in downtown **Sonoma** lie the wineries of more pastoral **Glen Ellen** and **Kenwood.** To the valley's west, **Petaluma,** with a burgeoning dining scene, has come into its own as a Wine Country destination.

Northern Sonoma, Russian River, and West County. Its walkable downtown, swank hotels, and restaurant scene make **Healdsburg** the tourist hub of Sonoma County's northern section. North of Healdsburg, mostly rural **Geyserville** has a small, engaging downtown. The Russian River winds through or near **Forestville, Guerneville,** and **Sebastopol,** three West County towns where Chardonnay and Pinot Noir grow well. The county's largest city, **Santa Rosa,** contains nonwine attractions and affordable lodgings.

Planning

When to Go

High season extends from late May through October. In summer, expect the days to be hot and dry. Hotel rates are highest during the height of harvest, in September and October. Then and in summer, book lodgings well ahead. November, except for Thanksgiving week, and December before Christmas are less busy. The weather in Napa and Sonoma is pleasant nearly year-round. Daytime temperatures average from about 55°F during winter to the 80s and 90s (occasionally 100s) in summer. April, May, and October are milder but still warm. The rainiest months are usually from December through March.

Getting Here and Around

AIR

Wine Country regulars often bypass San Francisco and Oakland and fly into Santa Rosa's Charles M. Schulz Sonoma County Airport (STS), which receives direct flights from several western cities. The airport is 15 miles from Healdsburg.

■TIP➔ **Alaska Airlines allows passengers flying out of STS to check up to one case of wine for free.**

BUS

Bus travel is an inconvenient way to explore the Wine Country, though it is possible. Take Golden Gate Transit from San Francisco to connect with Sonoma County Transit buses. VINE connects with BART commuter trains in the East Bay and the San Francisco Bay Ferry in Vallejo. VINE buses serve the Napa Valley.

CAR

A car is the most convenient way to navigate Napa and Sonoma. If you're flying into the area, it's almost always easiest to pick up a car at the airport. You'll also find rental companies in major Wine Country towns. A few rules to note: smartphone use for any purpose is prohibited, including mapping applications unless the device is mounted to a car's windshield or dashboard and can be activated with a single swipe or finger tap. A right turn after stopping at a red light is legal unless posted otherwise.

Hotels

The fanciest accommodations are concentrated in the Napa Valley towns of Yountville, Rutherford, St. Helena, and Calistoga; Sonoma County's poshest lodgings are in Healdsburg. The cities of Napa, Petaluma, and Santa Rosa are the best bets for budget hotels and inns. On weekends, two- or even three-night minimum stays are commonly required at smaller lodgings. Book well ahead for stays at such places in summer or early fall. Some accommodations aren't suitable for kids, so ask before you book.

⇨ *Restaurant and hotel reviews have been shortened. For full information, visit Fodors.com. Restaurant prices are the average cost of a main course at dinner, or if dinner is not served, at lunch. Hotel prices are the lowest cost of a standard double room in high season.*

What It Costs in U.S. Dollars			
$	$$	$$$	$$$$
RESTAURANTS			
under $17	$17–$26	$27–$36	over $36
HOTELS			
under $200	$200–$300	$301–$400	over $400

Restaurants

Top Wine Country chefs tend to apply French and Italian techniques to dishes incorporating fresh, local products. Menus are often vegan- and vegetarian-friendly, with gluten-free options. At pricey restaurants you can save money by having lunch instead of dinner. With a few exceptions (noted in individual restaurant listings), dress is informal.

Napa

46 miles northeast of San Francisco.

After many years as a blue-collar burg detached from the Wine Country scene, the Napa Valley's largest town (population about 80,000) has evolved into its shining star. Masaharu Morimoto and other chefs of note operate restaurants here, swank hotels and inns can be found downtown and beyond, and the nightlife options include the West Coast edition of the famed Blue Note jazz club. A walkway that follows the Napa River has made downtown more pedestrian-friendly, and the Oxbow Public Market, a complex of high-end food purveyors, is popular with locals and tourists. The market is named for the nearby oxbow bend in the Napa River, a bit north of where Napa was founded in 1848. The first wood-frame building was a saloon, and the downtown area still projects an old-river-town vibe.

GETTING HERE AND AROUND

Downtown Napa lies a mile east of Highway 29—take the 1st Street exit and follow the signs. Ample parking, much of it free for the first three hours and some for the entire day, is available on or near Main Street. Several VINE buses serve downtown and beyond.

⊙ Sights

Arch & Tower

WINERY | While its Oakville winery undergoes renovations, a project expected to last from Summer 2023 to Summer 2025, the Robert Mondavi Winery will pour its wines (along with a few other luxury brands) in downtown Napa's 1877 Borreo Building. Erected using stone quarried a few miles away in Soda Canyon, the two-story Italian Renaissance–style building has large windows and an outdoor terrace with views west to Main Street. A tireless promoter of the Napa Valley as California's preeminent wine-growing region, the late Robert Mondavi elevated Sauvignon Blanc by labeling his bottlings with the more exotic name Fumé Blanc and made Bordeaux-style reds of renown from To Kalon Vineyard in Oakville. Visits to taste these and other selections, many of them winery exclusives, require a reservation. At time of writing, there was no plan to keep the Borreo Building location open after the Oakville winery reopens in 2025. ⊠ *930 3rd St., Napa* ✛ *At Soscol Ave.* ☎ *888/766–6328* ⊕ *robertmondaviwinery. com* ☜ *Tastings from $65.*

CIA at Copia

COLLEGE | Food fanatics and the merely curious achieve gastronomical bliss at the Culinary Institute of America's Oxbow District campus, its facade brightened by a wraparound mural inspired by the colorful garden that fronts the facility. You could easily spend a few hours checking out the wine and culinary options; visiting the well-curated shop, theme exhibitions, and Vintners Hall of Fame wall; or attending (book ahead) classes and demonstrations. Head upstairs to the Chuck Williams Culinary Arts Museum. Named for the Williams-Sonoma kitchenwares founder, it holds a fascinating collection of cooking, baking, and other food-related tools, tableware, gizmos, and gadgets, some dating back more than a century. ⊠ *500 1st St., Napa* ✛ *Near McKinstry St.* ☎ *707/967–2500* ⊕ *www.ciaatcopia.com* ✉ *Facility/museum free, class/demo fees vary.*

★ Domaine Carneros

WINERY | A visit to this majestic château is an opulent way to enjoy the Carneros District—especially in fine weather, when the vineyard views are spectacular. The château was modeled after an 18th-century French mansion owned by the Taittinger family. Carved into the hillside beneath the winery, the cellars produce sparkling wines reminiscent of those made by Taittinger, using only Los Carneros AVA grapes. Enjoy flights of sparkling wine or Pinot Noir with cheese and charcuterie plates, caviar, or smoked salmon. Tastings are by appointment only. ⊠ *1240 Duhig Rd., Napa* ✛ *At Hwy. 121* ☎ *707/257–0101, 800/716–2788* ⊕ *www.domainecarneros.com* ✉ *Tastings from $40.*

Etude Wines

WINERY | You're apt to see or hear hawks, egrets, Canada geese, and other wildlife on the grounds of Etude, known for sophisticated Pinot Noirs. Although the winery and its light-filled tasting room are in Napa County, the grapes for its flagship Carneros Estate Pinot Noir come from the Sonoma portion of Los Carneros, as do those for the rarer Heirloom Carneros Pinot Noir. Longtime winemaker Jon Priest also excels at single-vineyard Napa Valley Cabernets. In good weather, hosts pour Priest's reds, plus Chardonnay and Pinot Gris, on the patio outside the contemporary tasting room. Hosts of A Study of Pinot Noir, a private, seated experience, pour Pinot Noirs from

different areas to illustrate how soil, climate, and growing conditions affect the finished wines. ⊠ *1250 Cuttings Wharf Rd., Napa* ✛ *1 mile south of Hwy. 121* ☎ *707/257–5782* ⊕ *www.etudewines. com* ✉ *Tastings from $50.*

★ Fontanella Family Winery

WINERY | Six miles from the downtown Napa whirl, husband-and-wife Jeff and Karen Fontanella's hillside spread seems a world apart. In addition to his formal studies, Jeff learned about wine making at three prestigious wineries before he and Karen, a lawyer, established their own operation on 81 south-facing Mt. Veeder acres. The couple braved an economic recession, an earthquake, and wildfires in the first decade but emerged tougher, if no less gracious to guests lucky enough to find themselves tasting Viognier, Chardonnay, Zinfandel, and Cabernet Sauvignon on the patio here. Tastings often end with a Zinfandel-based port-style wine. ■TIP→ **Weather permitting, the reserve tasting includes the opportunity to stroll the estate, whose views south to San Francisco and east to Atlas Peak are terrific.** ⊠ *1721 Partrick Rd., Napa* ✛ *1st St. to Browns Valley Rd. west of Hwy. 29* ☎ *707/252–1017* ⊕ *www.fontanellawinery.com* ✉ *Tastings from $65.*

★ Mayacamas Downtown

WINERY | Cabernets from Mayacamas Vineyards placed second and fifth respectively on *Wine Spectator* magazine's 2019 and 2020 "Top 100" lists of the world's best wines, two accolades among many for this winery founded atop Mt. Veeder in 1889. One of Napa's leading viticulturists, Annie Favia farms the organic vineyards, elevation 2,000-plus feet, without irrigation; her husband, Andy Erickson, is the consulting winemaker. The grapes for the Chardonnay come from 40-year-old vines. Aged in mostly neutral (previously used) French oak barrels to accentuate mountain minerality, the wine is a Napa Valley marvel. The Cabernet Sauvignon

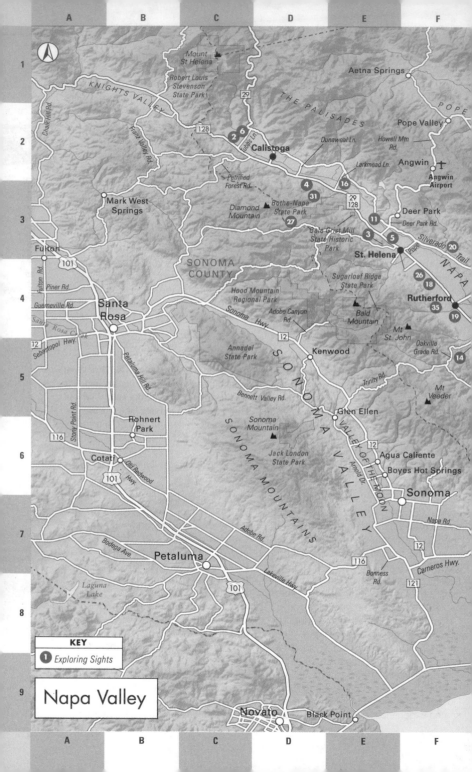

Napa Valley

KEY

1 *Exploring Sights*

Sights ▼

ages for three years, spending part of the time in oak barrels more than a century old. Erin Martin, a Napa Valley resident with a hip international reputation, designed the light-filled storefront tasting space. ■TIP→ **Experiencing these magnificent wines downtown—white wines-only and red wines-only tastings possible—may entice you to visit the estate.** ⊠ *First Street Napa, 1256 1st St., Napa ⊹ At Randolph St.* ☎ *707/294–1433* ⊕ *www.mayacamas. com* ⊞ *Tastings from $35* ⊙ *Closed Mon. and Tues.*

Napa Valley Wine Train

TRAIN/TRAIN STATION | Guests on this Napa Valley fixture travel the corridor established in 1864 to transport passengers as far north as Calistoga's spas. The rolling stock includes restored Pullman cars and a two-story Vista Dome coach with a curved glass roof. The train travels a leisurely, scenic route between Napa and St. Helena. Patrons on some tours enjoy a multicourse meal and tastings at one or more wineries. Some rides involve no winery stops, and themed trips are occasionally scheduled. ■TIP→ **It's best to make this trip during the day, when you can enjoy the vineyard views.** ⊠ *1275 McKinstry St., Napa ⊹ Off 1st St.* ☎ *707/253–2111, 800/427–4124* ⊕ *www.winetrain. com* ⊞ *From $225.*

★ Oxbow Public Market

MARKET | The 40,000-square-foot market's two dozen stands provide an introduction to Northern California's diverse artisanal food products. Swoon over decadent charcuterie at the Fatted Calf (great sandwiches, too), slurp oysters at Hog Island, enjoy empanadas at El Porteño, or chow down on Moroccan street food at Moro. Sample wine (and cheese) at the Oxbow Cheese & Wine Merchant, ales at Fieldwork Brewing's taproom (at ⊠ *1046 McKinstry, near Fatted Calf*), and barrel-aged cocktails at the Napa Valley Distillery. The owner of Kara's Cupcakes operates the adjacent Bar Lucia for (mostly) sparkling wines and rosés. Milestone Provisions is a combination butchery, restaurant (California country cuisine including sublime fried-chicken sandwiches), and creamery known for velvety ice cream. Among the few nonfood vendors here is Napa Bookmine, which also operates a larger store elsewhere downtown. ⊠ *610 and 644 1st St., Napa ⊹ At McKinstry St.* ☎ *No phone* ⊕ *www.oxbowpublicmarket.com.*

★ Robert Biale Vineyards

WINERY | Here's a surprise: a highly respected Napa Valley winery that doesn't sell a lick of Cabernet. Zinfandel from heritage vineyards, some with vines more than 100 years old, holds the spotlight, with luscious Petite Sirahs in supporting roles. Nearly every pour comes with a fascinating backstory, starting with the flagship Black Chicken Zinfandel. In the 1940s, the Biale family sold eggs, walnuts, and other farm staples, with bootleg Zinfandel a lucrative sideline. Because neighbors could eavesdrop on party-line phone conversations, "black chicken" became code for a jug of Zin. These days the wines are produced on the up-and-up, steps from the 10-acre property's tasting area. A stone's throw from Zinfandel vines, with far-off views of two mountain ranges, the open-air space has a back-porch feel. Visits are by appointment; call ahead for same-day. ⊠ *4038 Big Ranch Rd., Napa ⊹ At Salvador Ave.* ☎ *707/257–7555* ⊕ *biale. com* ⊞ *Tastings from $50.*

★ Robert Craig Winery Tasting Salon

WINERY | Based way up Howell Mountain but with meticulously farmed hillside sources on both sides of the valley, Robert Craig has established a loyal following for its textured, full-flavored Cabernet Sauvignons. Hosts pour the wines inside a refurbished 1890s downtown Napa Folk Victorian and on its front porch and red-brick patio. Tastings, by appointment but usually possible on short notice, often begin with a Sonoma County Chardonnay or, while it lasts, La Fleur Craig Grenache Rosé from Howell Mountain. One trait all the wines share is how well they age. The Zinfandel from Howell Mountain's Black Sears Vineyard does its varietal proud. ✉ *1553 2nd St.* ✣ *At Church St.* ☎ *707/252–2250* 🌐 *robertcraigwine.com* 🎫 *Tastings from $35.*

Stag's Leap Wine Cellars
WINERY | A 1973 Stag's Leap Wine Cellars S.L.V. Cabernet Sauvignon put this winery and the Napa Valley on the enological map by placing first in the famous Judgment of Paris tasting of 1976. The grapes for that wine came from a vineyard visible from the stone-and-glass Fay Outlook & Visitor Center, which has broad views of a second fabled Cabernet vineyard (Fay) and the promontory that gives both the winery and the Stags Leap District AVA their names. The top of the-line Cabernets from these vineyards are poured at appointment-only tastings (call ahead for same-day visits), some of which include perceptive food pairings by the winery's executive chef. ■ **TIP→ When the weather's right, two patios with the same views as the tasting room fill up quickly.** ✉ *5766 Silverado Trail, Napa* ✣ *At Wappo Hill Rd.* ☎ *707/261–6410* 🌐 *www.stagsleapwine-cellars.com* 🎫 *Tastings from $75.*

★ Trefethen Family Vineyards
WINERY | Superior estate Chardonnay, dry Riesling, Cabernet Sauvignon, Merlot, Pinot Noir, and the Malbec-heavy Dragon's Tooth blend are the trademarks of this family-run winery founded in 1968. To find out how well Trefethen wines age, book a reserve tasting, which includes pours of limited-release wines and one or two older vintages. The terra-cotta-color historic winery on-site, built in 1886, was designed with a gravity flow system, with the third story for crushing, the second for fermenting the resulting juice, and the first for aging. The wooden building suffered severe damage in the 2014 Napa earthquake, but after extensive renovations it reopened as the main tasting room. The early-1900s Arts and Crafts–style Villa, situated amid gardens, hosts reserve and elevated tastings. All visits require a reservation. ✉ *1160 Oak Knoll Ave., Napa* ✣ *Off Hwy. 29* ☎ *707/255–7700* 🌐 *www.trefethen.com* 🎫 *Tastings from $50.*

🍴 Restaurants

★ Angèle
$$$$ | FRENCH | A vaulted wood-beamed ceiling and paper-topped tables set the scene for romance at this softly lit French bistro inside an 1890s boathouse. Look for clever variations on classic dishes such as croque monsieur (grilled Parisian ham and Gruyère) and salade niçoise for lunch, with veal sweetbreads, cassoulet, beef bourguignon, and, in season, steamed mussels for dinner. **Known for:** classic bistro cuisine; romantic setting; outdoor seating under bright-yellow umbrellas. [$] *Average main: $38* ✉ *540 Main St., Napa* ✣ *At 5th St.* ☎ *707/252–8115* 🌐 *www.angelerestaurant.com.*

Grace's Table
$$$ | ECLECTIC | A dependable, varied menu makes this modest corner restaurant occupying a brick-and-glass storefront many Napans' go-to choice for a simple meal. Empanadas and iron-skillet corn bread with lavender honey and butter show up at all hours, with buttermilk pancakes and chilaquiles scrambled eggs among the brunch staples and cassoulet and roasted heirloom chicken popular for dinner. **Known for:** congenial staffers; good beers on tap; eclectic menu focusing on France, Italy, and the Americas. [$] *Average main: $30* ✉ *1400 2nd St., Napa* ✣ *At Franklin St.* ☎ *707/226–6200* 🌐 *www.gracestable.net.*

★ Kitchen Door
$$ | ECLECTIC | Todd Humphries has overseen swank haute-cuisine kitchens in Manhattan, San Francisco, and the Napa Valley, but he focuses on multicultural comfort plates at his high-ceilinged

Continued on page 360

WINE TASTING *in* NAPA *and* SONOMA

Whether you're a serious wine collector making your annual pilgrimage to Northern California's Wine Country or a newbie who doesn't know the difference between a Merlot and Mourvèdre but is eager to learn, you can have a great time touring Napa and Sonoma wineries. Your gateway to the wine world is the tasting room, where staff members are happy to chat with curious guests.

(opposite page) Carneros vineyards in autumn, Napa Valley. (top) Pinot Gris grapes. (bottom) Bottles from Far Niente winery.

VISITING WINERIES

Tasting rooms range from the grand to the humble, offering everything from a few sips of wine to in-depth tours of facilities and vineyards. Some are open for drop-in visits, usually daily from around 10 or 11 am to 5 pm. Many require guests to make reservations. First-time visitors frequently enjoy the history-oriented focus at Charles Krug, Inglenook, and Buena Vista. The environments at some wineries reflect their owners' or founders' other interests: art at The Donum Estate and Hall St. Helena, movie making at Francis Ford Coppola, and medieval history at the Castello di Amorosa.

Many wineries describe their pourers as "wine educators," and indeed some of them have taken online or other classes and have passed an exam to prove basic knowledge of appellations, grape varietals, vineyards, and wine-making techniques. The one constant, however, is a deep, shared pleasure in the experience of wine tasting.

Fees. Most wineries charge for tasting. In the Napa Valley, expect to pay $35–$65 to sample current releases, $75–$100 or more for reserve, estate, or library wines. Sonoma County tastings generally cost $20–$40 for the former, $40–$75 for the latter. To experience wine making at its highest level, consider splurging for at least one special tasting.

Some wineries waive tasting fees if you join the wine club, purchase a few bottles, or spend a particular dollar amount. At others, the fees are "exclusive of purchase."

Tipping. Many guests tip out of instinct, but it isn't required. Instances when you might consider tipping include when your server has given a few extra pours or a discount on your purchases or has otherwise provided outstanding service. For a basic tasting, $5–$10 per couple will suffice; for a hosted seated tasting, $5–$10 per person, perhaps a little more for extra attention.

WINE TASTING 101

TAKE A GOOD LOOK.
Hold your glass by the stem, raise it to the light, and take a close look at the wine. Check for clarity and color. (This is easiest to do if you can hold the glass in front of a white background.) Any tinge of brown usually means that the wine is over the hill or has gone bad.

BREATHE DEEP.
1. Sniff the wine once or twice to see if you can identify any smells.

2. Swirl the wine gently in the glass. Aerating the wine this way releases more of its aromas. (It's called "volatilizing the esters," if you're trying to impress someone.)

3. Take another long sniff. You might notice that experienced wine tasters spend more time sniffing the wine than drinking it. This is because this step is where the magic happens. The number of scents you might detect is almost endless, from berries, apricots, honey, and wildflowers to leather, cedar, or even tar. Does the wine smell good to you? Do you detect any "off" flavors, like wet dog or sulfur?

AT LAST! TAKE A SIP.
1. Swirl the wine around your mouth so that it makes contact with all your taste buds and releases more of its aromas. Think about the way the wine feels in your mouth. Is it watery or rich? Is it crisp or silky? Does it have a bold flavor, or is it subtle? The weight and intensity of a wine are called its body.

2. Hold the wine in your mouth for a few seconds and see if you can identify any developing flavors. More complex wines will reveal many different flavors as you drink them.

SPIT OR SWALLOW.
The pros typically spit, since they want to preserve their palate (and sobriety) for the wines to come, but you'll find that swallowers far outnumber the spitters in the winery tasting rooms. Whether you spit or swallow, notice the flavor that remains after the wine is gone (the finish).

Swirl

Sniff

Sip

MAKE AN APPOINTMENT

Most Napa and Sonoma wineries accept visitors by appointment only to serve patrons better, though some welcome walk-ins if space is available. To avoid disappointment, make reservations at least a day or two ahead. In summer and early fall, try to visit on weekdays or before 11 am or so when it's less crowded. Also look for wineries off the main drags of Highway 29 in Napa and Highway 12 in Sonoma.

HOW WINE IS MADE

1. CRUSHING
Harvested grapes go into a stemmer-crusher, which separates stems from fruit and crushes the grapes to release "free-run" juice.

2. PRESSING
Remaining juice is gently extracted from grapes. Usually done by pressing grapes against the walls of a tank with an inflatable bladder.

3. FERMENTING
Extracted juice (and also grape skins and pulp, when making red wine) goes into stainless-steel tanks or oak barrels to ferment. During fermentation, sugars convert to alcohol.

4. AGING
Wine is stored in stainless-steel or oak casks or barrels, or sometimes in concrete vessels, to develop flavors.

5. RACKING
Wine is transferred to clean barrels; sediment is removed. Wine may be filtered and fined (clarified) to improve its clarity, color, and sometimes flavor.

6. BOTTLING
Wine is bottled either at the winery or at a special facility, then stored again for bottle-aging.

WHAT'S AN APPELLATION?

American Viticultural Area (AVA) or, more commonly, an appellation. What can be confusing is that some appellations encompass smaller subappellations. The Rutherford, Oakville, and Mt. Veeder AVAs, for instance, are among the Napa Valley AVA's 16 subappellations. Wineries often buy grapes from outside their AVA, so their labels might reference different appellations. A winery in the warmer Napa Valley, for instance, might source Pinot Noir grapes from the cooler Russian River Valley, where they grow better. The appellation listed on a label always refers to where a wine's grapes were grown, not to where the wine was made.

By law, if a label bears the name of an appellation, 85% of the grapes must come from it.

industrial-contemporary restaurant downtown. The signature dishes include a silky cream of mushroom soup, flatbreads, pho, Thai fisherman's stew, duck banh mi sandwiches (go for the voluptuous duck jus add-on), and sweet, spicy, and succulent chicken wings among many other crowd-pleasers that keep this place hopping even in the off-season. **Known for:** specialty cocktails (bar a casual hangout); seasonally changing apps and entrées; outdoor patio. $ *Average main: $25* ✉ *First Street Napa, 1300 1st St., Suite 272, Napa* ✛ *Near Clay St.* ☎ *707/226–1560* ⊕ *www.kitchendoornapa.com.*

★ La Toque

$$$$ | **MODERN AMERICAN** | Chef Ken Frank's La Toque is the complete package: his French-inspired cuisine, served in a formal dining space, is complemented by a wine lineup that consistently earns the restaurant a coveted *Wine Spectator* Grand Award. Ingredients appearing on the à la carte and prix-fixe tasting menus often include caviar, Alaskan halibut, Wagyu beef, and rich cheeses in dishes prepared and seasoned to pair with wines jointly chosen by the chefs and master sommelier. **Known for:** chef's tasting menu; astute wine pairings; vegetarian tasting menu. $ *Average main: $50* ✉ *Westin Verasa Napa, 1314 McKinstry St., Napa* ✛ *Off Soscol Ave.* ☎ *707/257–5157* ⊕ *www.latoque.com* ☾ *Closed Mon. and Tues. No lunch.*

Morimoto Napa

$$$$ | **JAPANESE** | *Iron Chef* star Masaharu Morimoto is the big name behind this downtown Napa restaurant where everything is delightfully over the top, including the desserts. Organic materials such as twisting grapevines above the bar and rough-hewn wooden tables seem simultaneously earthy and modern, creating a fitting setting for the gorgeously plated Japanese fare, from straightforward sashimi to more elaborate seafood, chicken, pork, and beef entrées. **Known for:** theatrical ambience;

gorgeous plating; cocktail and sake menu. $ *Average main: $55* ✉ *610 Main St., Napa* ✛ *At 5th St.* ☎ *707/252–1600* ⊕ *www.morimotonapa.com.*

Oenotri

$$ | **ITALIAN** | Often spotted at local farmers' markets and his restaurant's gardens, Oenotri's ebullient chef-owner and Napa native Tyler Rodde is ever on the lookout for fresh produce to incorporate into his rustic southern Italian cuisine. His restaurant, a brick-walled contemporary space with tall windows and wooden tables, is a lively spot to sample house-made *salumi* and pastas, thin-crust pizzas, and entrées that might include seared fresh fish or grilled rib eye. **Known for:** lively atmosphere; Margherita pizza with San Marzano tomatoes; desserts with flair. $ *Average main: $26* ✉ *1425 1st St., Napa* ✛ *At Franklin St.* ☎ *707/252–1022* ⊕ *www.oenotri.com* ☾ *Closed Mon. No lunch weekdays.*

★ Scala Osteria & Bar

$$$ | **ITALIAN** | The brightly lit dining room's mural map of the Naples coastline signals the chef's focus on *frutti di mare* (seafood) at this downtown homage to southern Italian cuisine the folks behind valley-fave Bistro Don Giovanni opened in 2023. Raw oysters, cooked whole fish, skillet-sautéed mussels, and halibut soup were among the early hits, along with pizzas hot out of a wood-fired oven. **Known for:** shareable plates and pasta dishes; Italian wine selection; late-night pizza, small bites, and desserts. $ *Average main: $30* ✉ *1141 1st St., Napa* ✛ *Near Coombs St.* ☎ *707/637–4380* ⊕ *scalaosteria.com.*

★ Torc

$$$$ | **MODERN AMERICAN** | *Torc* means "wild boar" in an early Celtic dialect, and owner-chef Sean O'Toole, who formerly helmed kitchens at top Manhattan, San Francisco, and Yountville establishments, occasionally incorporates the restaurant's namesake beast into his eclectic offerings. A recent menu featured tuna

tartare, squash risotto, three hand-cut pasta dishes, a side of mushrooms foraged by a local pro, and Maine diver scallops in a lobster emulsion, all prepared by O'Toole and his team with style and precision. **Known for:** jolly only-at-the-bar happy hour (4–6 pm, nine seats total); specialty cocktails; Bengali sweet-potato pakora and deviled-egg appetizers. $ *Average main: $42* ⊠ *1140 Main St., Napa* ⊕ *At Pearl St.* ☎ *707/252–3292* ⊕ *www.torcnapa.com* ⊗ *Closed Sun. and Mon. No lunch.*

★ ZuZu

$$$ | **SPANISH** | The owner of this four-storefront empire touts it as a "mid-block party": ZuZu for paella, tapas, and other northern Spanish favorites; next door a gin bar (the spirit is big in Spain); third, a takeout window; and finally La Taberna for beer, wine, and *pintxos* (bar bites). The anchor, which opened in 2002, is still drawing crowds, who come for shareable plates that might include flounder ceviche, tender wood-fired octopus, *jamón ibérico,* and lamb chops with Moroccan barbecue glaze. **Known for:** range of gin flavors and tonics; paella of the day with bomba rice, chorizo, and shellfish; energetic crowds at gin bar and La Taberna. $ *Average main: $35* ⊠ *829 Main St., Napa* ⊕ *Near 3rd St.* ☎ *707/224–8555* ⊕ *www.zuzunapa.com* ⊗ *Closed Mon. and Tues.*

🛏 Hotels

Andaz Napa

$$$$ | **HOTEL** | Part of the Hyatt family, this boutique hotel with an urban-hip vibe has spacious guest rooms with white-marble bathrooms stocked with high-quality products. **Pros:** casual-chic feel; proximity to downtown restaurants, theaters, and tasting rooms; cheery, attentive service. **Cons:** unremarkable views from some rooms; expensive on weekends in high season; renovations planned for 2023 so ask for a room not affected by them. $ *Rooms from: $458* ⊠ *1450 1st St.,*

Napa ☎ *707/687–1234* ⊕ *andaznapa.com* ⊗ *141 rooms* ⊚| *No Meals.*

★ Archer Hotel Napa

$$$$ | **HOTEL** | Ideal for travelers seeking design pizzazz, a see-and-be-seen atmosphere, and first-class amenities, this five-story downtown Napa property fuses New York City chic and Las Vegas glamour. **Pros:** restaurants by chef Charlie Palmer; Sky & Vine rooftop bar; great views from upper-floor rooms (especially south and west). **Cons:** not particularly rustic; expensive in high season; occasional service and hospitality lapses. $ *Rooms from: $459* ⊠ *1230 1st St., Napa* ☎ *707/690–9800, 855/200–9052* ⊕ *archerhotel.com/napa* ⊗ *183 rooms* ⊚| *No Meals.*

★ Carneros Resort and Spa

$$$$ | **RESORT** | A winning combination of glamour, service, and pastoral seclusion makes this resort with freestanding board-and-batten cottages the perfect getaway for active lovebirds or families and groups seeking to unwind. **Pros:** cottages have lots of privacy; views from hilltop pool and hot tub; heaters on private patios. **Cons:** long drive to upvalley destinations; least expensive accommodations pick up highway noise; pricey pretty much year-round. $ *Rooms from: $1,000* ⊠ *4048 Sonoma Hwy./Hwy. 121, Napa* ☎ *707/299–4900, 888/400–9000* ⊕ *www.carnerosresort.com* ⊗ *100 rooms* ⊚| *No Meals.*

★ The Inn on First

$$$$ | **B&B/INN** | Guests gush over the hospitality at this inn, where the painstakingly restored 1905 mansion facing 1st Street contains five rooms, with five additional accommodations, all suites, in a building behind a secluded patio and garden. **Pros:** full gourmet breakfast by hosts-with-the-most owners; gas fireplaces and whirlpool tubs in all rooms; away from downtown but not too far. **Cons:** no TVs; owners "respectfully request no children, no exceptions"; lacks pool, fitness center, and other amenities of

larger properties. $ *Rooms from: $430* ⊠ *1938 1st St., Napa* ☎ *707/253–1331* ⊕ *www.theinnonfirst.com* ⇥ *10 rooms* ⏉ *Free Breakfast.*

★ Inn on Randolph

$$$$ | B&B/INN | A few calm blocks from the downtown action on a nearly 1-acre lot with landscaped gardens, the Inn on Randolph—with a Gothic Revival–style main house and its five guest rooms plus five historic cottages out back—is a sophisticated haven celebrated for its gourmet gluten-free breakfasts and snacks. **Pros:** quiet residential neighborhood; spa tubs in cottages and two mainhouse rooms; romantic setting. **Cons:** a bit of a walk from downtown; expensive in-season; weekend minimum-stay requirement. $ *Rooms from: $420* ⊠ *411 Randolph St., Napa* ☎ *707/257–2886* ⊕ *www.innonrandolph.com* ⇥ *10 rooms* ⏉ *Free Breakfast.*

Nightlife

Blue Note Napa

LIVE MUSIC | The famed New York jazz room's intimate West Coast club hosts national headliners such as Kenny Garrett, KT Tunstall, and Jody Watley. At Locals Night on many Wednesdays, homegrown talent performs. There's a full bar, and you can order a meal or small bites from the kitchen. The larger JaM Cellars Ballroom upstairs books similar artists. ⊠ *Napa Valley Opera House, 1030 Main St., Napa* ✛ *At 1st St.* ☎ *707/880–2300* ⊕ *www.bluenotenapa.com.*

Cadet Wine + Beer Bar

WINE BARS | Cadet plays things urban-style cool with a long bar, high-top tables, and a low-lit, loungelike feel. California wines and beers predominate, but the lineup circles the globe. Artisanal tequilas in cocktails or on their own will be the focus of Chispa, a new bar a few blocks away on 1st Street the same owners plan to open in 2023. ⊠ *930 Franklin St., Napa* ✛ *At end of pedestrian alley between 1st and 2nd Sts.* ☎ *707/224–4400* ⊕ *www. cadetbeerandwinebar.com.*

🛍 Shopping

First Street Napa

MALL | The Archer Hotel Napa anchors this open-air downtown complex of mostly ground-level restaurants, tasting rooms, and national (Anthropologie, Lululemon) and homegrown (The Bennington Napa Valley, Habituate Lifestyle + Interiors, Napa Stäk) design, clothing, housewares, and culinary shops. Copperfield's Books and the Visit Napa Valley Welcome Center are also here, along with Milo and Friends for pet necessities and accessories. ⊠ *1300 1st St., Napa* ✛ *Between Franklin and Coombs Sts.* ☎ *707/257–6900* ⊕ *www.firststreetnapa. com.*

🏃 Activities

Napa Valley Gondola

ENTERTAINMENT CRUISE | Rides in authentic gondolas that seat up to six depart from downtown Napa's municipal dock. You'll never mistake the Napa River for the Grand Canal, but this is a diverting excursion that often includes a serenade. ⊠ *Main St. Boat Dock, 700 Main St., Napa* ✛ *Riverfront Promenade, south of 3rd St. Bridge* ☎ *707/373–2100* ⊕ *napavalleygondola.com* 🎫 *From $169 (up to 6 people).*

Yountville

9 miles north of the town of Napa.

Yountville (population 3,000) is something like Disneyland for food lovers. You could stay here several days and not exhaust all the options—a few of them owned by The French Laundry's Thomas Keller—and the tiny town is full of small inns and high-end hotels that cater to those who prefer to walk (not drive) after an extravagant meal. It's also well located for excursions to many big-name Napa wineries, especially those in the Stags Leap District, from which big, bold Cabernet Sauvignons helped make the Napa Valley's wine-making reputation.

GETTING HERE AND AROUND

Downtown Yountville sits just off Highway 29. Approaching from the south take the Yountville exit—from the north take Madison—and proceed to Washington Street, home to the major shops and restaurants. Yountville Cross Road connects downtown to the Silverado Trail, along which many noted wineries do business. The free Yountville Trolley serves the town daily 10 am–7 pm (on-call service until 11 pm except on Sunday).

◉ Sights

★ Cliff Lede Vineyards

WINERY | Inspired by his passion for classic rock, owner and construction magnate Cliff Lede named the blocks in his Stags Leap District vineyard after hits by the Grateful Dead and other bands. Two other Lede obsessions are rock memorabilia and contemporary art like Jim Dine's outdoor sculpture *Twin 6' Hearts,* a magnet for the Instagram set. The vibe at this efficient, high-tech winery is anything but laid-back, however. Cutting-edge agricultural and enological science informs the vineyard management and wine making here. Lede produces Sauvignon Blanc, Cabernet Sauvignon, and Bordeaux-style red blends; tastings often include sparkling wine, Chardonnay, Pinot Gris, or Pinot Noir from sister winery FEL. All the wines are well crafted, though the Cabs truly rock. ■TIP→ **Book a Backstage Tasting Lounge session to sip top-tier wines amid a rock music–related art exhibition.** ⊠ *1473 Yountville Cross Rd., Yountville* ✛ *Off Silverado Trail* ☎ *707/944–8642* ⊕ *clifflede vineyards.com* 🍷 *Tastings from $60.*

Cornerstone Cellars

WINERY | Inside Yountville's whitewashed 19th-century passenger train depot, Cornerstone shares a space with an apparel shop and displays contemporary art curated by Aerena Galleries. The winery, started on something of a whim more than three decades ago (a Howell Mountain grower offered the founders some excess fruit late in the 1991 season), produces Cabernet Sauvignon from the valley's benchland and mountain sections. Because each Cabernet receives similar treatment from winemaker Kari Auringer, the wines express what's unique about their subappellations, vineyard sources, and vintages. Cornerstone is a good place to find out what type of Napa Valley Cabernet you prefer—perhaps the smooth Benchlands blend, in recent years softened with Merlot and Cabernet Franc, or maybe the sturdier yet still lush Howell Mountain offering, usually 100% Cabernet or nearly so. ⊠ *6505 Washington St., Yountville* ☎ *707/945–0388* ⊕ *www.cornerstonecellars.com* 🍷 *Tastings from $40.*

★ Elyse Winery

WINERY | One of his colleagues likens Elyse's winemaker, Russell Bevan, to "a water witch without the walking stick" for his ability to assess a vineyard's weather, soil, and vine positioning and intuit how particular viticultural techniques will affect wines' flavors. Bevan farms judiciously during the growing season, striving later in the cellar to preserve what nature and his efforts have yielded rather than rely on heavy manipulation. Elyse makes highly praised small-lot single-vineyard Zinfandels and Cabernet Sauvignons. Red blends containing as many as five varietals are another strong suit. A country lane edged by vines leads to this unassuming winery, whose unhurried tastings, often outdoors, have a backyard-casual feel. ■TIP→ **Costing much less than the average Napa Valley Cab, Elyse's Holbrook Mitchell Cabernet Sauvignon holds its own against**

peers priced appreciably higher. ✉ *2100 Hoffman La., Napa* ✥ *1¾ miles south of central Yountville, off Hwy. 29 or Solano Ave.* ☎ *707/944–2900* 🌐 *elysewinery.com* 🎟 *Tastings from $55.*

★ Mira Winery

WINERY | A close encounter of the wine kind—California winemaker and political communications expert (in this instance, Jim "Bear" Dyke) strike up a conversation in a Washington, D.C., bar—led to the formation of this winery devoted to single-vineyard wines from southern Napa Valley vineyards. At the time, the winemaker, Gustavo A. Gonzalez, headed up the red-wine program at Robert Mondavi Winery. Scaling down at Mira (from the Latin root word for "miracle"), he contributed his knowledge, connections, but most of all wise, restrained approach to creating Pinot Noir, Merlot, Syrah, Cabernet Sauvignon, and a few others. These unshowy but powerful wines, plus whites that include Chardonnay and a Sauvignon Gris fermented in a rare egg-shaped oak vessel, are served at a stone and glass hospitality house adjoining the winery. The structure's tall windows and outdoor seating areas take full advantage of Mira's setting between the Mayacamas Mountains and Wappo Hill. ✉ *6170 Washington St., Yountville* ✥ *1 mile south of downtown Yountville* ☎ *707/945–0881* 🌐 *miranapa.com* 🎟 *Tastings from $50.*

RH Wine Vault

WINERY | Gargantuan crystal chandeliers, century-old olive trees, and strategically placed water features provide visual and aural continuity at Restoration Hardware's quadruple-threat food, wine, art, and design compound. An all-day café fronts two steel, glass, and concrete home-furnishings galleries, with a bluestone walkway connecting them to the wine salon. Centered on a two-story 1904 manor house constructed from Napa River stone, it's an excellent spot to learn about small-lot Napa and Sonoma wines, served by the glass, flight, or bottle. Collector-revered labels like Corison, Fisher, Lail, Matthiasson, Mayacamas, and Spottswoode are all represented, the wines in good weather poured in "outdoor living rooms" behind the stone structure. Oozing RH fabulousness as it does, the Wine Vault can feel like a scene on a busy day, but the wines are the real deal. All tastings are by appointment. ✉ *6725 Washington St., Yountville* ✥ *At Pedroni St.* ☎ *707/339–4654* 🌐 *rh.com/yountville/winevault* 🎟 *Tastings from $20 glass, $65 flight.*

🍴 Restaurants

Ad Hoc

$$$$ | **AMERICAN** | At this low-key dining room with zinc-top tables, superstar chef Thomas Keller offers a changing daily fixed-price menu that might include smoked beef short ribs with creamy herb rice and charred broccolini or sesame chicken with radish kimchi and fried rice (check the website for that day's offerings). Ad Hoc also serves a small but decadent Sunday brunch, and Keller's Addendum annex, in a separate small building behind the restaurant, sells boxed lunches to go (including moist buttermilk fried chicken) from Thursday to Saturday except in winter. **Known for:** casual cuisine; don't-miss buttermilk-fried-chicken night; good prices for a Thomas Keller restaurant. [$] *Average main: $64* ✉ *6476 Washington St., Yountville* ✥ *At Oak Circle* ☎ *707/944–2487* 🌐 *www.thomaskeller.com/adhoc* 🕒 *Closed Tues. and Wed. No lunch weekdays and Sat.*

★ Bistro Jeanty

$$$ | **FRENCH** | Escargots, cassoulet, steak *au poivre* (pepper steak), and other French classics are prepared with precision inside this tan-brick country bistro whose flower-filled window boxes, extra-wide shutters, and red-and-white-striped awning hint at the Old World flair and joie de vivre that infuse the place. Regulars often start with the rich tomato soup in a flaky puff pastry before proceeding to sole meunière or coq au vin, completing the French sojourn with crème brûlée *au chocolat* or another authentic dessert. **Known for:** traditional preparations; oh-so-French atmosphere; patio seating. $ *Average main: $34* ✉ *6510 Washington St., Yountville* ✚ *At Mulberry St.* ☎ *707/944–0103* ⊕ *www.bistrojeanty.com.*

Bottega

$$$ | **ITALIAN** | At his softly lit, exposed-redbrick downtown trattoria, which occupies sections of the 19th-century former Groezinger Winery, chef Michael Chiarello (Food Network, etc.) and his team transform local, seasonally changing ingredients into regional Italian cuisine. Staples like ricotta gnocchi with tomato sauce and smoked/braised short rib in espresso *agrodolce* (sweet-and-sour sauce) served with creamy ancient-grain polenta show the chef at his most rustic yet sophisticated. **Known for:** romantic setting; soulful craft cocktails; Italian and California wines. $ *Average main: $33* ✉ *6525 Washington St., Yountville* ✚ *Near Mulberry St.* ☎ *707/945–1050* ⊕ *www.botteganapavalley.com.*

★ Bouchon Bistro

$$$ | **FRENCH** | The team that created The French Laundry is also behind this place, where everything—the zinc-topped bar, antique sconces, suave waitstaff, and traditional French onion soup—could have come straight from a Parisian bistro. Pan-seared flat iron steak with caramelized shallots and mussels steamed with white wine, saffron, and Dijon mustard—both served with crispy, addictive fries—are among the perfectly executed entrées. **Known for:** bistro classics; raw bar; Bouchon Bakery next door. $ *Average main: $36* ✉ *6534 Washington St., Yountville* ✚ *Near Humboldt St.* ☎ *707/944–8037* ⊕ *thomaskeller.com/bouchonyountville.*

★ Coqueta Napa Valley

$$$ | **SPANISH** | From pintxos and paellas to Iberian cheeses and fish *à la plancha*

(flat-grilled), the chefs at this Wine Country offspring of Michael Chiarello's successful San Francisco restaurant Coqueta reimagine Spanish classics with a 21st-century farm-to-table sensibility. The frenetic pace in the flame-happy open kitchen, inside Yountville's redbrick former railroad depot, keeps the mood lively in the relatively small dining space, with the vibe on the patio out back even more so. **Known for:** sensual flavors; dynamic spicing; seasonal cocktails inspired by Spain and the Napa Valley. $ *Average main: $33* ✉ *6525 Washington St., Yountville* ✚ *Near Yount St.* ☎ *707/244–4350* ⊕ *www.coquetanv.com.*

★ The French Laundry

$$$$ | **AMERICAN** | Inside an ivy-laced old stone building and atop many a Napa Valley visitor's bucket list, chef Thomas Keller's destination restaurant lives up to the hype with intricate yet not overthought cuisine. Some courses on the two prix-fixe menus, one of which highlights vegetables, rely on luxe ingredients such as white quail; others take humble elements like carrots or fava beans and elevate them to art. **Known for:** signature starter "oysters and pearls"; "supplements" like white truffles, caviar, and Wagyu beef; superior wine list. $ *Average main: $400* ✉ *6640 Washington St., Yountville* ✚ *At Creek St.* ☎ *707/944–2380* ⊕ *www.frenchlaundry.com* ⊙ *No lunch Mon.–Thurs.* 👔 *Jacket required* ☞ *Reservations essential wks ahead.*

Mustards Grill

$$$ | **AMERICAN** | Cindy Pawlcyn's Mustards Grill fills day and night with fans of her hearty cuisine, equal parts updated renditions of traditional American dishes—what Pawlcyn dubs "deluxe truck stop classics"—and fanciful contemporary fare. Barbecued baby back pork ribs and a lemon-lime tart piled high with brown-sugar meringue fall squarely in the first category, and sweet corn tamales with tomatillo-avocado salsa and wild mushrooms represent the latter. **Known**

for: roadhouse setting; convivial mood; hoppin' bar. $ *Average main: $31* ⊠ *7399 St. Helena Hwy./Hwy. 29, Napa* ⊹ *1 mile north of Yountville* ☎ *707/944–2424* ⊕ *www.mustardsgrill.com.*

★ Regiis Ova Caviar & Champagne Lounge

$$$ | WINE BAR | Even restaurateurs as famous as Thomas Keller test out concepts via pop-ups, though in retrospect his pairing of mostly French sparkling wines with caviar from a company (Regiis Ova) the chef co-owns was always destined for permanent glory. Intended as a palate-cleansing pit stop between Cab tasting and dinner, the place, furnished in insouciant, faintly decadent style by Bay Area celeb designer Ken Fulk, tempts patrons to stay put, order more bubbly and roe, and call it a meal. **Known for:** live jazz most days; sommelier-selected French Champagnes; chilled oysters, tartares, and crudités. $ *Average main: $35* ⊠ *6480 Washington St., Yountville* ⊹ *At Oak Circle* ☎ *707/947–7181* ⊕ *regiisovalounge.com* ☾ *Closed Mon. and Wed. No lunch (but check).*

🛏 Hotels

★ Bardessono

$$$$ | RESORT | Tranquillity and luxury with a low carbon footprint are among the goals of this ultragreen wood, steel, and glass resortlike property in downtown Yountville, but there's nothing spartan about the accommodations, arranged around four landscaped courtyards. **Pros:** large rooftop lap pool; in-room spa treatments; three luxury villas for extra privacy. **Cons:** expensive year-round; limited view from some rooms; a bit of street traffic on hotel's west side. $ *Rooms from: $1,100* ⊠ *6526 Yount St., Yountville* ☎ *707/204–6000* ⊕ *www.bardessono. com* ☜ *65 rooms* ⓘ⃝ *No Meals.*

Maison Fleurie

$$ | B&B/INN | A stay at this comfortable, reasonably priced inn, said to be the oldest hotel in the Napa Valley, places

you within walking distance of Yountville's fine restaurants. **Pros:** smallest rooms a bargain; outdoor hot tub and pool; free bikes. **Cons:** lacks amenities of a full-service hotel; some rooms pick up noise from nearby Bouchon Bakery; hard to book in high season. $ *Rooms from: $260* ⊠ *6529 Yount St., Yountville* ☎ *707/944–2056* ⊕ *www.maisonfleurie-apa.com* ☜ *13 rooms* ⓘ⃝ *Free Breakfast.*

Napa Valley Lodge

$$$$ | HOTEL | Clean rooms in a convenient motel-style setting draw travelers willing to pay more than at comparable lodgings in the city of Napa to be within walking distance of Yountville's tasting rooms, restaurants, and shops. **Pros:** well-maintained rooms; vineyard-view rooms on north and west sides; large pool area. **Cons:** no elevator; nice enough but lacks panache; pricey on weekends in high season. $ *Rooms from: $450* ⊠ *2230 Madison St., Yountville* ☎ *707/944–2468, 888/944–3545* ⊕ *www.napavalleylodge. com* ☜ *55 rooms* ⓘ⃝ *Free Breakfast.*

★ North Block Hotel

$$$$ | HOTEL | A two-story boutique property near downtown Yountville's northern edge, the North Block attracts sophisticated travelers who appreciate the clever but unpretentious style and offhand luxury. **Pros:** extremely comfortable beds; personalized service; spacious bathrooms. **Cons:** outdoor areas get some traffic noise; weekend minimum-stay requirement; rates soar on high-season weekends. $ *Rooms from: $662* ⊠ *6757 Washington St., Yountville* ☎ *707/944–8080* ⊕ *northblockhotel.com* ☜ *20 rooms* ⓘ⃝ *No Meals.*

Vintage House

$$$$ | RESORT | Part of the 22-acre Estate Yountville complex—other sections include sister lodging Hotel Villagio, the 13,000-square-foot Spa at The Estate, and shops and restaurants—this downtown hotel consists of two-story brick buildings along verdant landscaped paths shaded by mature trees. **Pros:**

sthetically pleasing accommodations; private patios and balconies; secluded feeling yet near shops, tasting rooms, and restaurants. **Cons:** highway noise audible in some exterior rooms; very expensive on summer and fall weekends; weekend minimum-stay requirement. Ⓢ *Rooms from: $800* ✉ *6541 Washington St., Yountville* ☎ *707/927–2130, 877/351–1153* ⊕ *www.vintagehouse.com* ↪ *80 rooms* ⑩ *Free Breakfast.*

⛹ Activities

BALLOONING
Napa Valley Aloft
BALLOONING | Passengers soar over the Napa Valley in balloons that launch from downtown Yountville. Flights are from 40 minutes to an hour-plus, depending on the wind speed, with the entire experience taking from three to four hours. ✉ *The Estate Yountville, 6525 Washington St., Yountville* ✛ *Near Mulberry St.* ☎ *707/944–4400, 855/944–4408* ⊕ *www.nvaloft.com* 🎟 *From $295.*

BICYCLING
Napa Valley Bike Tours
BIKING | With dozens of wineries within 5 miles, this shop makes a fine starting point for guided and self-guided vineyard and wine-tasting excursions. Rental bikes are also available. ✉ *6500 Washington St., Yountville* ✛ *At Mulberry St.* ☎ *707/251–8687* ⊕ *www.napavalleybiketours.com* 🎟 *From $169.*

SPAS
The Spa at The Estate
SPAS | The joint 13,000-square-foot facility of Vintage House and the Hotel Villagio is a five-minute walk from the former's lobby, even less from the latter's. Private spa suites are popular with couples, who enjoy the separate relaxation areas, indoor and outdoor fireplaces, steam showers, saunas, and extra-large tubs. Therapists customize the signature Estate Massage based on clients' needs. Other massages and treatments involve hot stones, grape-seed extract, mud, magnesium, CBD, or aromatherapy. Several types of facials are offered as well. The ground-floor retail area, open to the public, is well stocked with beauty products. ✉ *The Estate Yountville, 6481 Washington St., Yountville* ✛ *At Oak Circle* ☎ *707/948–5050* ⊕ *www.theestateyountville.com/spa* 🎟 *Treatments from $225.*

Oakville

2 miles northwest of Yountville.

A large butte that runs east–west just north of Yountville blocks the cooling fogs from the south, facilitating the myriad microclimates of the Oakville AVA, home to several high-profile wineries.

GETTING HERE AND AROUND
Driving along Highway 29, you'll know you've reached Oakville when you see the Oakville Grocery on the east side of the road. You can reach Oakville from the Sonoma County town of Glen Ellen by heading east on Trinity Road from Highway 12. The twisting route, along the mountain range that divides Napa and Sonoma, eventually becomes the Oakville Grade. The views on this drive are breathtaking, though the continual curves make it unsuitable for those who suffer from motion sickness.

◉ Sights

Far Niente
WINERY | Hamden McIntyre, a prominent winery architect of his era also responsible for Inglenook and what's now the Culinary Institute of America at Greystone, designed the centerpiece 1885 stone winery here. Abandoned in the wake of Prohibition and only revived beginning in 1979, Far Niente now ranks as one of the Napa Valley's most beautiful properties. Guests participating in the Estate Tasting learn some of this history

Far Niente ages its Cabernets and Chardonnays in 40,000 square feet of caves.

while sipping the flagship wines, a Chardonnay and a Cabernet Sauvignon blend, along with Russian River Valley Pinot Noir from the affiliated EnRoute label and Dolce, a late-harvest white dessert wine. The Extended Estate Tasting takes in the winery and its aging caves, while the Cave Collection library tasting pairs older vintages with seasonal bites. ■TIP➔ Fall, **when nearly 200 ginkgo trees lining the driveway glow yellow, is a fine time to visit.** ✉ *1350 Acacia Dr., Oakville ✛ Off Oakville Grade Rd.* ☎ *707/944–2861* ⊕ *www. farniente.com* ✉ *Tastings from $100.*

★ Silver Oak

WINERY | The first review of this winery's Napa Valley Cabernet Sauvignon declared the debut 1972 vintage not all that good and overpriced at $6 a bottle. Oops. The now-celebrated Bordeaux-style blend, still the only Napa Valley Cab bearing the winery's label each year, evolved into a cult favorite, and founders Ray Duncan and Justin Meyer received worldwide recognition for their signature use of exclusively American oak to age the wines.

Tastings take place in a hospitality center constructed out of reclaimed stone and other materials from a 19th-century Kansas flour mill. The standard session includes sips of the current Napa Valley vintage, its counterpart from Silver Oak's Alexander Valley operation in Sonoma County, and a library wine. Hosts of vertical tastings pour six Cabernet vintages. All visits require an appointment. ✉ *915 Oakville Cross Rd., Oakville ✛ Off Hwy. 29* ☎ *707/942–7022* ⊕ *www.silveroak. com* ✉ *Tastings from $60.*

★ Turnbull Cellars

WINERY | It'd be easy to confuse this winery for its more famous neighbor to the north, Cakebread Cellars—William Turnbull designed the original buildings at each. Founded by the architect in 1979 and owned since 1993 by Patrick O'Dell, Turnbull produces richly textured Cabernets from Oakville and Calistoga vineyards. Winemaker Peter Heitz plays light with French oak or, in some cases, handmade Italian amphorae. Guests sip his estate wines indoors among curated hows of works from O'Dell's art and photography collection or outside on landscaped patios surrounded by vineyards. The hospitality exceeds millennials' expectations, and social media–friendly backdrops make for enticing shots, but there's an older-Napa gentility to this appointment-only winery that even many locals haven't gotten around to visiting. Beat them to the punch. This place is worth it. ✉ *8210 St. Helena Hwy., Oakville ✚ ¼ mile south of Glos La.* ☎ *707/963–5839* ⊕ *www.turnbullwines. com* 🍷 *Tastings from $65.*

Rutherford

2 miles northwest of Oakville.

With its singular microclimate and soil, Rutherford is an important viticultural center, with more big-name wineries than you can shake a corkscrew at. Cabernet Sauvignon is king here. The well-drained, loamy soil is ideal for those vines, and since this part of the valley gets plenty of sun, the grapes develop exceptionally intense flavors.

GETTING HERE AND AROUND
Wineries around Rutherford are dotted along Highway 29 and the parallel Silverado Trail north and south of Rutherford Road/Conn Creek Road, on which wineries can also be found.

⊙ Sights

★ Frog's Leap
WINERY | If you're a novice, the tour at eco-friendly Frog's Leap is a fun way to begin your education. Conducted by hosts with a sense of humor, the tour stops by a barn built in 1884, an acre of organic gardens, and a frog pond topped with lily pads. The winery produced its first vintage, small batches of Sauvignon Blanc and Zinfandel, in 1981, adding Chardonnay and Cabernet Sauvignon the next year. Merlot, Petite Sirah, and the

Heritage Blend of classic Napa Valley varietals including Charbono and Valdiguié are among the other reds these days. All visits require a reservation, but walk-ins are accommodated when possible. ■**TIP**➔ **The tour is recommended, but you can forgo it and taste on a garden-view porch.** ✉ *8815 Conn Creek Rd., Rutherford* ☎ *707/963–4704* ⊕ *www.frogsleap. com* 🍷 *Tastings from $45.*

★ Inglenook
WINERY | *Wine Enthusiast* magazine bestowed a lifetime-achievement award on vintner-filmmaker Francis Ford Coppola, whose wine-world contributions include resurrecting the historic Inglenook estate. Over the decades, he reunited the original property acquired by Inglenook founder Gustave Niebaum, remodeled Niebaum's ivy-covered 1880s château, and purchased the rights to the Inglenook name. Just in time for the 2022 harvest, the winery unveiled a 22,000-square-foot wine cave and production facility. The eco-friendly cave and Inglenook's place in Napa Valley history are among the topics discussed at tastings, some involving food pairings. Most sessions see a pour of the signature Rubicon, a Cabernet Sauvignon–based blend with a classic Rutherford profile. All visits require an appointment; call the winery or check at the visitor center for same-day availability. ■**TIP**➔ **In lieu of a tasting, you can book a table at The Bistro, a wine bar with a picturesque courtyard, to sip wine by the glass or bottle.** ✉ *1991 St. Helena Hwy./Hwy. 29, Rutherford ✚ At Hwy. 128* ☎ *707/968–1179* ⊕ *www.ingle-nook.com* 🍷 *Tastings from $75* ⊙ *Closed Tues. and Wed., except for bistro.*

Mumm Napa
WINERY | When Champagne Mumm of France set about establishing a California sparkling-wine outpost, its winemaker chose the Napa Valley, where today the winery sources grapes from more than 50 local producers. Made in the *méthode traditionnelle* style from Chardonnay,

Pinot Noir, Pinot Meunier, and occasionally Pinot Gris, the wines are all fermented in the bottle. Most guests enjoy them alfresco, by the glass or flight, on a patio above the surrounding vineyards or one at eye level. Book an Oak Terrace Tasting to sample top-of-the-line cuvées under the sprawling branches of a blue oak nearly two centuries old. Tasting is by appointment only, but walk-ins are accommodated when possible. ✉ *8445 Silverado Trail, Rutherford* ✥ *1 mile south of Rutherford Cross Rd.* ☎ *707/967–7700* 🌐 *www.mummnapa.com* 🎫 *Tastings from $40.*

ZD Wines

WINERY | Founded in 1969 and still run by the same family, this winery specializing in Chardonnay, Pinot Noir, and Cabernet Sauvignon is respected for its organic practices, local philanthropy, and Abacus blend. Made "solera-style," Abacus contains wine from every ZD Reserve Cabernet Sauvignon vintage since 1992. The Chardonnay and Pinot Noir come from a Carneros property, the Cabernet from the winery's Rutherford estate, where the wines are made and presented to the public. Appointment-only tastings (same-day often possible, but call ahead) take place in a second-floor space with broad valley views west to the Mayacamas Mountains. Book a current-release flight for an introduction to ZD and its wine-making philosophy. Barrel tastings, small bites, and small-batch reserve wines are all part of the Abacus Experience, which concludes with a current and older Abacus blend. ✉ *8383 Silverado Trail, Rutherford* ☎ *800/487–7757* 🌐 *www.zdwines.com* 🎫 *Tastings from $50.*

🍴 Restaurants

★ Restaurant at Auberge du Soleil

$$$$ | **AMERICAN** | Possibly the most romantic roost for brunch, lunch, or dinner in all the Wine Country is a terrace seat at the Auberge du Soleil resort's illustrious restaurant, and the Mediterranean-inflected cuisine more than matches the dramatic vineyard views. The prix-fixe dinner menu (three or four courses), relying mainly on local produce, might include caviar or diver scallop starters, delicately prepared fish or vegetable middle-course options, and mains like prime beef pavé with béarnaise, spiced lamb loin, or Japanese Wagyu A5. **Known for:** six-course chef's tasting menu; comprehensive wine list; special-occasion feel. [$] *Average main: $150* ✉ *Auberge du Soleil, 180 Rutherford Hill Rd., Rutherford* ✥ *Off Silverado Trail* ☎ *707/963–1211* 🌐 *www.aubergedusoleil.com* 🕒 *Closed Mon. and Tues.*

Rutherford Grill

$$$ | **AMERICAN** | Dark-wood walls, subdued lighting, and red-leather banquettes make for a perpetually clubby mood at this Rutherford hangout where the patio, popular for its bar, fireplace, and rocking chairs, opens for full meal service or drinks and appetizers when the weather's right. Many entrées—steaks, burgers, fish, rotisserie chicken, and barbecued pork ribs—emerge from an oak-fired grill operated by master technicians. **Known for:** iron-skillet corn bread direct from the oven; signature French dip sandwich; reasonably priced wine list. [$] *Average main: $29* ✉ *1180 Rutherford Rd., Rutherford* ✥ *At Hwy. 29* ☎ *707/963–1792* 🌐 *www.rutherfordgrill.com.*

🛏 Hotels

★ Auberge du Soleil

$$$$ | **RESORT** | Taking a cue from the olive-tree-studded landscape, this hotel with a renowned restaurant and spa cultivates a luxurious look that blends French and California style. **Pros:** stunning valley views; spectacular pool and spa areas; Deluxe-category suites fit for a superstar. **Cons:** stratospheric prices; least expensive rooms get some noise from the bar and restaurant; weekend minimum-stay

quirement. $ *Rooms from: $1,575*
180 Rutherford Hill Rd., Rutherford
707/963–1211, 800/348–5406 www.
aubergedusoleil.com *52 rooms*
Free Breakfast.

★ **Rancho Caymus Inn**

$$$$ | **HOTEL** | A romantic hacienda-away-from-home that off-season may be the Napa Valley's best value in its price range, this upscale-contemporary boutique hotel near Inglenook and the Rutherford Grill contains rooms whose decor and art-works evoke the area's Mexican heritage. **Pros:** courtyard pool area; smallest rooms are 400 square feet, with several 600 or more; well-trained staff. **Cons:** all rooms have only showers (albeit nice ones); king beds in all rooms (no sofa beds, though a few rollaways available); no spa or fitness center. $ *Rooms from: $475* ⊠ *1140 Rutherford Rd., Rutherford* ☎ *707/963–1777* ⊕ *www.ranchocaymusinn.com* *26 rooms* *Free Breakfast.*

St. Helena

2 miles northwest of Oakville.

Downtown St. Helena is the very picture of good living in the Wine Country: sycamore trees arch over Main Street (Highway 29), where visitors flit between boutiques, cafés, and storefront tasting rooms housed in sun-faded redbrick buildings. The genteel district pulls in rafts of tourists during the day, though like most Wine Country towns St. Helena more or less rolls up the sidewalks after dark.

The Napa Valley floor narrows between the Mayacamas and Vaca mountains around St. Helena. The slopes reflect heat onto the vineyards below, and since there's less fog and wind, things get pretty toasty. This is one of the valley's hottest AVAs, with midsummer temperatures often reaching the mid-90s. Bordeaux varietals are the most popular grapes grown here—especially Cabernet

Sauvignon but also Merlot, Cabernet Franc, and Sauvignon Blanc.

GETTING HERE AND AROUND

Downtown stretches along Highway 29, called Main Street here. Many wineries lie north and south of downtown along Highway 29. More can be found off Silverado Trail, and some of the most scenic spots are on Spring Mountain, which rises southwest of town.

⊙ Sights

Beringer Vineyards

WINERY | Brothers Frederick and Jacob Beringer opened the winery that still bears their name in 1876. One of California's earliest bonded wineries, it's the oldest one in the Napa Valley never to have missed a vintage—no mean feat, given Prohibition. Some tastings take place inside or on the veranda of Frederick's grand Rhine House Mansion, completed in 1886 and surrounded by mature landscaped gardens worth a stroll themselves. Beringer is known for several widely distributed wines, but many poured here are winery exclusives. The Legacy Tasting & Tour surveys Beringer's history; the tasting takes place where the brothers crafted their first vintage. The winery prefers that all guests make a reservation, but same-day visits are often possible when no food is involved. ⊠ *2000 Main St./Hwy. 29, St. Helena* ✛ *Near Pratt Ave.* ☎ *707/257–5771* ⊕ *www.beringer.com* *Tastings from $20 glass, $45 flight.*

Charles Krug Winery

WINERY | A historically sensitive renovation of its 1874 Redwood Cellar Building transformed the former production facility of the Napa Valley's oldest winery into an epic hospitality center. Charles Krug, a Prussian immigrant, established the winery in 1861 and ran it until his death in 1892. Italian immigrants Cesare Mondavi and his wife, Rosa, purchased Charles Krug in 1943, operating it with their sons Peter Sr. and Robert (who later opened his own winery). Still run by Peter Sr's family, Charles Krug specializes in small-lot Yountville and Howell Mountain Cabernet Sauvignons plus Sauvignon Blanc, Chardonnay, Merlot, and Pinot Noir. All visits are by appointment. ✉ *2800 Main St./Hwy. 29, St. Helena* ✚ *Across from Culinary Institute of America* ☎ *707/967–2229* ⊕ *www.charleskrug.com* 🍷 *Tastings from $50.*

Duckhorn Vineyards

WINERY | Merlot's moment in the sun may have passed, but you wouldn't know it at Duckhorn, whose Three Palms Merlot was crowned wine of the year by *Wine Spectator* as recently as 2017. Duckhorn also makes Cabernet Sauvignon, Cabernet Franc, Chardonnay, Sauvignon Blanc, and a few other wines you can sip in the high-ceilinged tasting room or on a fetching wraparound porch overlooking carefully tended vines. "Elevated" experiences, some not offered daily, include a tasting of estate and single-vineyard wines and private hosted tastings guests can customize to suit their preferences. All visits are by appointment. ✉ *1000 Lodi La., St. Helena* ✚ *At Silverado Trail N* ☎ *707/963–7108* ⊕ *www.duckhorn.com* 🍷 *Tastings from $60.*

Hall St. Helena

WINERY | The Cabernet Sauvignons produced here are works of art born of the latest in organic-farming science and wine-making technology. A glass-walled tasting room allows guests to see some of the high-tech equipment winemaker Megan Gunderson employs to craft wines that also include Merlot, Cabernet Franc, and Sauvignon Blanc. Looking westward from the second-floor tasting area, rows of neatly spaced Cabernet vines capture the eye, and beyond them the tree-studded Mayacamas Mountains. Hard to miss as you arrive along Highway 29, Lawrence Argent's 35-foot-tall *Bunny Foo Foo,* a stainless-steel sculpture of a rabbit leaping out of the vineyard, is one

of many museum-quality artworks on display at appointment-only Hall (call for same-day). The Art of Cabernet tasting provides a solid introduction to this prominent producer's output. Another worthwhile tour takes in the grounds and the artworks. ■**TIP**➜ **Sister winery Hall Rutherford hosts an exclusive wine-and-food pairing atop a Rutherford hillside.** ✉ *401 St. Helena Hwy./Hwy. 29, St. Helena* ✚ *Near White La.* ☎ *707/967–2626* ⊕ *www.hallwines.com* 🍷 *Tastings from $60.*

★ Joseph Phelps Vineyards

WINERY | In 2022, LVMH's Moet Hennessy division purchased the winery the late Joseph Phelps founded a half-century before, a changing of the guard that reinforced Napa's stature as an international luxury-lifestyle player. Phelps produces excellent whites, along with Pinot Noir from its Sonoma Coast vineyards, but the blockbusters are the Bordeaux reds, particularly the Cabernet Sauvignons and Insignia, a luscious-yet-subtle Cab-dominant blend. Insignia, which often receives high-90s scores from respected wine publications, is always among the current releases poured at the one-hour seated Terrace Tasting overlooking grapevines and oaks. Other experiences, including one involving food pairings, unfold inside the main redwood structure, a classic of 1970s Northern California architecture. Participants in the Insignia Retrospective Tasting, offered a few times a month, sample several vintages of the flagship wine. ✉ *200 Taplin Rd., St. Helena* ✚ *Off Silverado Trail* ☎ *707/963–2745, 800/707–5789* ⊕ *www.josephphelps.com* 🍷 *Tastings from $115.*

Prager Winery & Port Works

WINERY | "If door is locked, ring bell," reads a sign outside the weathered-redwood tasting shack at this family-run winery known for red, white, and tawny ports. The sign, the bell, and the thousands of dollar bills tacked to the walls and ceilings inside are your first dications that you're drifting back in me with the old-school Pragers, who have been making regular and fortified wines in St. Helena since 1979. Five members of the second generation run this homespun operation founded by Jim and Imogene Prager. In addition to ports, the winery makes Petite Sirah and Sweet Claire, a late-harvest Riesling dessert wine. Some tastings take place in a garden outside the tasting room or on the crush pad. Visits are by appointment; call for same-day. ✉ *1281 Lewelling La., St. Helena* ✣ *Off Hwy. 29* ☎ *707/963–7678* 🌐 *www.pragerport.com* 🎟 *Tastings $40 (includes glass).*

★ Pride Mountain Vineyards

WINERY | This winery 2,200 feet up Spring Mountain straddles Napa and Sonoma counties, confusing enough for visitors but even more complicated for the wine-making staff: government regulations require separate wineries and paperwork for each side of the property. It's one of several Pride Mountain quirks, but the winery's "big red wines," including a Cabernet Sauvignon that earned 100-point scores from a prominent wine critic two years in a row, are serious business. On a visit, by appointment only, you can learn about the farming and cellar strategies behind Pride's acclaimed Cabs. The winery also produces Syrah, a Cab-like Merlot, Claret, Cabernet Franc, and noteworthy Chardonnay and Viognier whites. **■TIP→ The views here are knock-your-socks-off gorgeous.** ✉ *4026 Spring Mountain Rd., St. Helena* ✣ *Off St. Helena Rd. (extension of Spring Mountain Rd. in Sonoma County)* ☎ *707/963–4949* 🌐 *www.pridewines.com* 🎟 *Tastings from $30* ⏲ *Closed Tues.*

★ Tres Sabores Winery

WINERY | A long, narrow lane with two sharp bends leads to workaday Tres Sabores, where the sight of sheep, golden retrievers, guinea hens, pomegranate and other trees and plants, a slew of birds and bees, and a heaping compost pile reinforces a simple point: despite the Napa Valley's penchant for glamour this is, first and foremost, farm country. Owner-winemaker Julie Johnson specializes in single-vineyard wines that include Cabernet Sauvignon and Zinfandel from estate-grown certified-organic Rutherford bench vines. She also excels with Petite Sirah from dry-farmed Calistoga fruit, Sauvignon Blanc, and the zippy ¿Por Qué No? (Why not?) red blend. *Tres sabores* is Spanish for "three flavors," which to Johnson represents the land, her vines, and, as she puts it, "the spirit of the company around the table." Tastings by appointment only are informal and usually held outside. ✉ *1620 S. Whitehall La., St. Helena* ✣ *West of Hwy. 29* ☎ *707/967–8027* 🌐 *www.tressabores.com* 🎟 *Tastings from $55.*

🍴 Restaurants

Brasswood Bar + Bakery + Kitchen

$$$ | **ITALIAN** | After Napa Valley fixture Tra Vigne lost its lease, many staffers regrouped a few miles north at the restaurant (the titular Kitchen) of the Brasswood complex, which also includes a bakery, shops, and a wine-tasting room. Along with dishes developed for the new location, the chefs incorporate Tra Vigne favorites such as mozzarella-stuffed arancini (rice balls) into the Mediterranean-leaning menu. **Known for:** mostly Napa-Sonoma wine list; bakery a good lunch stop for pizzas, salads, and sandwiches; patio seating. [$] *Average main: $33* ✉ *3111 St. Helena Hwy. N, St. Helena* ✣ *Near Ehlers La.* ☎ *707/302–5101* 🌐 *brasswood.com/brasswoodbarkitchen.*

The Charter Oak

$$$ | **MODERN AMERICAN** | Christopher Kostow's reputation rests on his swoon-worthy haute cuisine for the Meadowood resort, but he and his Charter Oak team adopt a more straightforward approach—fewer ingredients chosen for maximum effect—at this high-ceilinged, brown-brick downtown restaurant. With exceedingly fresh produce from Meadowood's nearby farm, this strategy might translate into dishes like red kuri squash with pickled peppers, almonds, and goat cheese; or pork collar with fermented pepper jam (or just go for the cheeseburger and thick hand-cut fries). **Known for:** monthly changing wings appetizer; patio dining in brick courtyard; weekday happy hour 2:30–5. [$] *Average main: $32* ✉ *1050 Charter Oak Ave., St. Helena* ✣ *At Hwy. 29* ☎ *707/302–6996* 🌐 *www.thecharteroak.com.*

★ Cook St. Helena

$$$ | **ITALIAN** | A curved marble bar spotlit by contemporary art-glass pendants adds a touch of style to this downtown restaurant whose northern Italian cuisine pleases with understated sophistication. Mussels with house-made sausage in a spicy tomato broth, chopped salad with pancetta and pecorino, and the daily changing risotto are among the dishes regulars revere. **Known for:** top-quality ingredients; reasonably priced local and international wines; intimate dining. [$] *Average main: $30* ✉ *1310 Main St., St. Helena* ✣ *Near Hunt Ave.* ☎ *707/963–7088* 🌐 *www.cooksthelena.com* 🕒 *Closed weekends.*

★ Farmstead at Long Meadow Ranch

$$$ | **AMERICAN** | In a high-ceilinged former barn with plenty of outside seating, Farmstead revolves around an open kitchen whose chefs prepare meals with grass-fed beef and lamb, fruits and vegetables, and eggs, olive oil, wine, honey, and other ingredients from nearby Long Meadow Ranch. Entrées might include wood-grilled trout with fennel and bacon-mustard vinaigrette; caramelized beets with goat cheese and chimichurri; or a wood-grilled heritage pork chop with jalapeño grits. **Known for:** heritage St. Louis–style ribs; Sunday brunch; on-site general store, café, and Long Meadow Wines tasting space. [$] *Average main: $33* ✉ *738 Main St., St. Helena* ✣ *At Charter Oak Ave.* ☎ *707/963–4555* 🌐 *www.longmeadowranch.com/eat-drink/restaurant.*

Goose & Gander

$$$$ | **AMERICAN** | A Craftsman bungalow whose 1920s owner reportedly used the cellar for bootlegging during Prohibition houses this restaurant where the pairing of food and drink is as likely to involve a craft cocktail as a sommelier-selected wine. Main courses such as wood-grilled chicken or salmon, wet-aged black Angus rib eye, and the grass-fed G&G burger with Gruyère follow starters that might include corn croquettes, sticky pig ears, and harissa sausage with fry bread and baba ghanoush. **Known for:** intimate main dining room with fireplace; alfresco patio dining; basement bar among Napa's best watering holes. [$] *Average main: $41* ✉ *1245 Spring St., St. Helena* ✣ *At Oak St.* ☎ *707/967–8779* 🌐 *www.gooseganderr.com* 🕒 *No lunch.*

Gott's Roadside

$ | **AMERICAN** | A 1950s-style outdoor hamburger stand goes upscale at this spot whose customers brave long lines to order breakfast sandwiches, juicy burgers, root-beer floats, and garlic fries. Choices not available a half century ago include ahi-tuna and Impossible burgers and kale and Vietnamese chicken salads. **Known for:** tasty 21st-century diner cuisine; shaded picnic tables (arrive early or late for lunch to get one); second branch at Napa's Oxbow Public Market. [$] *Average main: $16* ✉ *933 Main St./Hwy. 29, St. Helena* ✣ *Near Charter Oak Ave.* ☎ *707/963–3486* 🌐 *www.gotts.com.*

★ Press

$$$$ | **AMERICAN** | For years this cavernous casual-chic restaurant with a contempo-barn interior and wraparound patio steps from neighboring vineyards was northern Napans' preferred stop for a top-shelf cocktail, dry-aged steak, and high-90s-scoring local Cabernet. You can still order a tomahawk or New York strip, but chef Philip Tessier, formerly of Yountville's The French Laundry and Bouchon istro and New York City's Le Bernardin, has introduced more refined cuisine, much of whose produce is grown nearby. **Known for:** impressive craft cocktails for pairing with dozen-plus apps; Wine Spectator Grand Award for wide-ranging list; prix-fixe tasting menu highly recommended. [$] *Average main: $56* ✉ *587 St. Helena Hwy./Hwy. 29, St. Helena* ✣ *At White La.* ☎ *707/967–0550* 🌐 *www.pressnapavalley.com* ⏲ *No lunch.*

Hotels

★ Alila Napa Valley

$$$$ | HOTEL | An upscale-casual ultracontemporary adults-only resort formerly known as Las Alcobas Napa Valley but now in the Hyatt Alila brand's fold, this hillside gem sits adjacent to Beringer Vineyards six blocks north of Main Street shopping and dining. **Pros:** vineyard views from most rooms; Acacia House restaurant; pool, spa, and fitness center. **Cons:** expensive much of the year; hotel is only for guests 18-plus; sizable resort fee. [$] *Rooms from: $767* ✉ *1915 Main St., St. Helena* ☎ *707/963–7000* 🌐 *www.alilanapavalley.com* 🛏 *68 rooms* 🍴 *No Meals.*

El Bonita Motel

$$$ | MOTEL | A classic 1950s-style neon sign marks the driveway to this roadside motel that during the off-season offers solid value to budget-minded travelers. **Pros:** cheerful rooms; family friendly; microwaves and minirefrigerators. **Cons:** noise issues in roadside and ground-floor rooms; expensive in high season; lacks amenities of fancier properties. [$] *Rooms from: $339* ✉ *195 Main St./Hwy. 29, St. Helena* ☎ *707/963–3216* 🌐 *www.elbonita.com* 🛏 *52 rooms* 🍴 *Free Breakfast.*

Harvest Inn

$$$ | HOTEL | Although this inn sits just off Highway 29, its patrons remain mostly above the fray, strolling 8 acres of gardens, enjoying views of the vineyards adjoining the property, and drifting to sleep in beds adorned with fancy linens and down pillows. **Pros:** garden setting; spacious rooms; near choice wineries, restaurants, and shops. **Cons:** fair amount of wedding action; rooms could be nicer for the high-season price; occasional service lapses. [$] *Rooms from: $399* ✉ *1 Main St., St. Helena* ☎ *707/963–9463* 🌐 *www.harvestinn.com* 🛏 *81 rooms* 🍴 *No Meals.*

Meadowood Napa Valley

$$$$ | RESORT | This elite 250-acre resort's celebrated restaurant and more than half its accommodations were destroyed in the 2020 Glass Fire, but the spa, pools, tennis courts, fitness center, and a fair number of cottages in one part survived, with continuing reconstruction in other areas not expected to affect the guest experience. **Pros:** scrupulously maintained rooms; all-organic spa; gracious service. **Cons:** still recovering from fire; far from downtown St. Helena; weekend minimum-stay requirement. [$] *Rooms from: $1,025* ✉ *900 Meadowood La.* ☎ *707/531–4788* 🌐 *meadowood.com* 🛏 *36 rooms* 🍴 *No Meals.*

Wine Country Inn

$$$$ | B&B/INN | Vineyards flank the three buildings, containing 24 rooms and five cottages, of this pastoral retreat where blue oaks, maytens, and olive trees provide shade and gardens feature lantana (small butterflies love it) and lavender. **Pros:** no resort fee; good-size swimming pool; vineyard views from most rooms. **Cons:** some rooms let in noise from neighbors; expensive in high season; weekend minimum-stay requirement. [$] *Rooms from: $429* ✉ *1152 Lodi La., St. Helena* ✣ *East of Hwy. 29* ☎ *707/963–7077, 888/465–4608* 🌐 *www.winecountryinn.com* 🛏 *29 rooms* 🍴 *Free Breakfast.*

★ Wydown Hotel

$$$ | HOTEL | This smart boutique hotel near downtown shopping and dining delivers comfort with a heavy dose of style: the storefront lobby's high ceiling and earth tones, punctuated by rich-hued splashes of color, hint at the relaxed grandeur owner-hotelier Mark Hoffmeister and his design team achieved in the rooms upstairs. **Pros:** well run; eclectic decor; downtown location. **Cons:** lacks the amenities of larger properties; large corner rooms pick up some street noise; two-night minimum on weekends. *$ Rooms from: $374 ✉ 1424 Main St., St. Helena ☎ 707/963–5100 🌐 www.wydownhotel.com 🛏 12 rooms 🍴 No Meals.*

Nightlife

The Saint

WINE BARS | This high-ceilinged downtown wine bar occupies a stone-walled late-19th-century former bank. Lit by chandeliers and decked out in contemporary style with plush sofas and chairs and Lucite stools at the bar, it's a classy, loungelike space to expand your enological horizons. *✉ 1351 Main St., St. Helena ✥ Near Adams St. ☎ 707/302–5130 🌐 www.thesaintnapavalley.com 🕘 Closed Mon.*

Calistoga

3 miles northwest of St. Helena.

With false-fronted, Old West–style shops and 19th-century inns and hotels lining its main drag, Lincoln Avenue in Calistoga comes across as more down-to-earth than its more polished neighbors. Don't be fooled, though. On its outskirts lie some of the Wine Country's swankest (and priciest) resorts and its most fanciful piece of architecture, the medieval-style Castello di Amorosa winery.

Calistoga was developed as a spa-oriented getaway from the start. Sam Brannan, a gold rush–era entrepreneur, planned to use the area's natural hot springs as the centerpiece of a resort complex. His venture failed, but old-time hotels and bathhouses—along with some glorious new spas—still operate. You can come for an old-school mud bath, or go completely 21st century and experience lavish treatments based on the latest innovations in skin and body care.

GETTING HERE AND AROUND

Highway 29 heads east (turn right) at Calistoga, where in town it is signed as Lincoln Avenue. If arriving via the Silverado Trail, head west at Highway 29/Lincoln Avenue.

Sights

Bennett Lane Winery

WINERY | Winemaker Rob Hunter of Bennett Lane strives "to create the greatest Cabernet Sauvignon in the world." At this appointment-only winery's tastefully casual salon in the far northern Napa Valley, you can find out how close he and his team come. Although known for valley-floor Cabernet, Bennett Lane also produces Merlot and the Maximus Red Feasting Wine, a Cab-heavy red blend nicely priced considering the quality. On the lighter side are Chardonnay and the Maximus White Feasting Wine blend of Sauvignon Blanc, Chardonnay, and Muscat. The basic flight surveys current-release whites and reds. There's also a Cab-focused offering. Many tastings take place in a garden whose pergola frames vineyard and Calistoga Palisades views. *✉ 3340 Hwy. 128, Calistoga ✥ 3 miles north of downtown ☎ 707/942–6684 🌐 www.bennettlane.com 🎟 Tastings from $35.*

Castello di Amorosa

WINERY | An astounding medieval structure complete with drawbridge and moat, chapel, stables, and secret passageways, the Castello commands Diamond Mountain's lower eastern slope. Some of the 107 rooms contain artist Fabio Sanzogni's replicas of 13th-century frescoes (cheekily signed with his website address), and the dungeon has an

The astounding Castello di Amorosa has 107 rooms.

iron maiden from Nuremberg, Germany. You must pay for a tour to see most of Dario Sattui's extensive eight-level property, though with general admission you'll have access to part of the complex. Bottlings of note include Sangiovese and other Italian-style wines and Il Barone, a deliberately big Cab. All visits are by appointment. ⊠ 4045 N. St. Helena Hwy./ Hwy. 29, Calistoga ⊹ Near Maple La. ☎ 707/967–6272 ⊕ www.castellodiamorosa.com ⏦ Tastings from $55.

Chateau Montelena

WINERY | Set amid a bucolic northern Calistoga landscape, this stately winery whose stone winery building was erected in 1888 helped establish the Napa Valley's reputation for high-quality wine making. At the pivotal Paris tasting of 1976, the Chateau Montelena 1973 Chardonnay took first place, beating out four white Burgundies from France and five other California Chardonnays, an event immortalized (with some liberties taken) in the 2008 movie *Bottle Shock*. A 21st-century Napa Valley Chardonnay is always part of A Taste of Montelena—the winery also makes Sauvignon Blanc, Riesling, a fine estate Zinfandel, and Cabernet Sauvignon—or you can opt for the Montelena Estate Collection tasting of Cabernets from several vintages. All visits require a reservation. ⊠ 1429 Tubbs La., Calistoga ⊹ Off Hwy. 29 ☎ 707/942–5105 ⊕ www.montelena.com ⏦ Tastings from $60.

Frank Family Vineyards

WINERY | Former Disney film and television executive Rich Frank founded his namesake winery in 1992, but the wine-making history here dates to the 19th century—portions of an original 1884 structure, reclad in stone in 1906, remain standing today. From 1952 until 1990, Hanns Kornell made sparkling wines on this site. Frank Family, since 2022 part of the Treasury Wine Estates portfolio, also makes sparklers, but the high-profile wines are the Carneros Chardonnay and several Cabernet Sauvignons, particularly the Rutherford Reserve and the Winston Hill red blend.

Tastings, some held in the glass-walled, vineyard's-edge The Miller House hospitality barn, which debuted in 2023, are sit-down affairs, with reservations required. ⊠ *1091 Larkmead La., Calistoga* ⌖ *Off Hwy. 29* ☎ *707/942–0859* ⊕ *www. frankfamilyvineyards.com* ✉ *Tastings from $60.*

★ **Schramsberg**

WINERY | On a Diamond Mountain site the German-born Jacob Schram planted to grapes in the early 1860s, Schramsberg pours its esteemed *méthode tradition-nelle* sparkling wines. Author Robert Louis Stevenson was among Schram's early visitors. After the vintner's death in 1905, the winery closed and fell into disrepair, but in 1965 Jack and Jamie Davies purchased the 200-acre Schramsberg property and began restoring its buildings and caves. Chinese laborers dug some of the latter in the 1870s. In the 1990s, the family set about replanting the vineyard to Cabernet Sauvignon and other Bordeaux varietals for the Davies Vineyards label's still red wines. Tastings at Schramsberg can include pours of only sparkling wines, only still wines, or a combination of the two. All visits are by appointment. ⊠ *1400 Schramsberg Rd., Calistoga* ⌖ *Off Hwy. 29* ☎ *707/942–2469, 800/877–3623* ⊕ *www. schramsberg.com* ✉ *Tastings with cave tour from $80.*

🍴 Restaurants

★ **Lovina**

$$$$ | **MODERN AMERICAN** | A vintage-style neon sign outside this bungalow restaurant announces "Great Food," and the chefs deliver with well-plated dishes served in two buildings, one a Craftsman gem, or on street-side patios that are especially festive during weekend brunch. The offerings at women-owned and-run Lovina change often, but a recent menu's roasted Cornish hen, lobster and prawn risotto, and seared wild halibut with gnocchi and wild mushrooms are typical of the imaginative cuisine. **Known for:** no-tipping policy; varied brunch menu; Wine Wednesdays no corkage fee and discounts on wine list. Ⓢ *Average main: $45* ⊠ *1107 Cedar St., Calistoga* ⌖ *At Lincoln Ave.* ☎ *707/942–6500* ⊕ *www.lovinacalistoga.com* ⊗ *No lunch Mon.–Wed. and Fri.*

Sam's Social Club

$$$ | **AMERICAN** | Tourists, locals, and spa guests—some of the latter in bathrobes after treatments—assemble inside this casual resort restaurant or on its extensive patio for breakfast, lunch, bar snacks, or dinner. Lunch options include thin-crust pizzas, sandwiches, a cheddar burger, and entrées such as chicken paillard, with the burger reappearing for dinner along with fish, steak, the house-made pasta of the day, and similar fare. **Known for:** weekend slow-roasted prime rib; cocktail-friendly starters; hearty salads. Ⓢ *Average main: $36* ⊠ *Indian Springs Resort and Spa, 1712 Lincoln Ave., Calistoga* ⌖ *At Wappo Ave.* ☎ *707/942–4969* ⊕ *www.samssocialclub. com.*

★ **Solbar**

$$$$ | **AMERICAN** | The restaurant at Solage attracts the resort's clientele, upvalley locals, and guests of nearby lodgings for sophisticated farm-to-table cuisine served in the high-ceilinged dining area or alfresco on a sprawling patio warmed by shapely heaters and a mesmerizing fire pit. Dishes on the lighter side might include house-made pasta or sake-marinated fish, with duck breast, crispy pork, or a tomahawk steak among the heartier options. **Known for:** artisanal cocktails; festive patio; lunchtime salads and sandwiches. Ⓢ *Average main: $48* ⊠ *Solage, 755 Silverado Trail, Calistoga* ⌖ *At Rosedale Rd.* ☎ *707/226–0860* ⊕ *aubergeresorts.com/solage/dine.*

Coffee and Quick Bites

★ Calistoga Depot

$$ | **AMERICAN** | Calistoga's flashy 19th-century entrepreneur Sam Brannan built the depot in 1868 to receive spa patrons, but it was looking careworn until his 21st-century equivalent, Wine Country vintner-showman Jean-Charles Boisset, restored the wood-frame building and opened a combination gourmet grocery, café, wine shop, distillery, and wine and beer garden. As at Boisset's historic Oakville Grocery, salads, artisanal sandwiches, and wood-fired pizzas headline. **Known for:** wine and craft-beer selection; all-day breakfast; patio seating. *[$] Average main: $17 ✉ 1458 Lincoln Ave., Calistoga ✣ At Fair Way ☎ 707/963–6925 🌐 calistogadepot.com ⏲ No dinner.*

Hotels

Four Seasons Resort and Residences Napa Valley

$$$$ | **RESORT** | Opened in 2021, this suave luxury resort entices high rollers with farmhouse-eclectic interiors and amenities that include a spa, a destination restaurant, two pools, 7-plus acres of vines, and a working winery. **Pros:** estate villa and one-bedroom suites offer maximum luxury and privacy; casual dining at indoor-outdoor Truss and five-course tasting menu at Auro; on-site vineyard and winery. **Cons:** expensive year-round; casual-chic yet may feel too formal for some guests; minimum weekend stay requirement. *[$] Rooms from: $1,491 ✉ 400 Silverado Trail N, Calistoga ☎ 707/709–2100, 800/819–5053 for reservations 🌐 www.fourseasons.com/napavalley 🔑 83 rooms 🍴 No Meals.*

Indian Springs Calistoga

$$$ | **RESORT** | Palm-studded Indian Springs—operating as a spa since 1862—ably splits the difference between laid-back and chic in accommodations that include lodge rooms, suites, cottages, stand-alone bungalows, and two houses. **Pros:** sprawling grounds with outdoor seating areas; on-site Sam's Social Club restaurant; enormous mineral pool. **Cons:** lodge rooms are small; many rooms have showers but no tubs; two-night minimum on weekends (three with Monday holiday). *[$] Rooms from: $309 ✉ 1712 Lincoln Ave., Calistoga ☎ 707/709–8139 🌐 www.indianspringscalistoga.com 🔑 113 rooms 🍴 No Meals.*

★ Solage

$$$$ | **RESORT** | The aesthetic at this 22-acre property where health and wellness are priorities is Napa Valley barn meets San Francisco loft: guest rooms have high ceilings, sleek contemporary furniture, all-natural fabrics in soothingly muted colors, and an outdoor patio. **Pros:** great service; complimentary bikes; separate pools for kids and adults. **Cons:** scene might not suit everyone; longish walk from some lodgings to spa and fitness center; expensive in season. *[$] Rooms from: $749 ✉ 755 Silverado Trail, Calistoga ☎ 866/942–7442, 707/226–0800 🌐 www.solagecalistoga.com 🔑 89 rooms 🍴 No Meals.*

★ Brannan Cottage Inn

$$$ | **B&B/INN** | Stained oak floors, wainscoting, and retro bathroom fixtures recall Victorian times at this small inn whose centerpiece is an 1860s cottage from Calistoga's original spa era. **Pros:** short walk from downtown; helpful staff; Sam's General Store for coffee and light meals. **Cons:** noise from neighbors can be heard in some rooms; showers but no bathtubs in some rooms; lacks pool and other amenities of larger properties. *[$] Rooms from: $329 ✉ 109 Wappo Ave., Calistoga ✣ At Lincoln Ave. ☎ 707/942–4200 🌐 www.brannancottageinn.com 🔑 6 rooms 🍴 Free Breakfast.*

⚡ Activities

SPAS

Indian Springs Spa

SPAS | Even before Sam Brannan constructed a spa on this site in the 1860s, the Wappo Indians built sweat lodges over its thermal geysers. Treatments include a Calistoga-classic, pure volcanic-ash mud bath followed by a mineral bath and an infrared sauna, after which clients are wrapped in a flannel blanket for a 15-minute cool-down session or until called for a massage if they've booked one. Body scrubs—one with sea salt, the other with sugar—and facials are also popular. Before or following a treatment, guests unwind at the serene Buddha Pool, fed by one of the property's four geysers. ⊠ *1712 Lincoln Ave., Calistoga ✛ At Wappo Ave.* ☎ *707/709–8139* ⊕ *indianspringscalistoga.com/spa-overview* ⌨ *Treatments from $115.*

★ Spa Solage

SPAS | This 20,000-square-foot eco-conscious spa reinvented the traditional Calistoga mud-and-mineral-water regimen with the hour-long "Mudslide." The three-part treatment includes a mud body mask applied in a heated lounge, a soak in a thermal bath, and a power nap in a sound-vibration chair. The mud here, less gloppy than at other resorts, is a mix of clay, volcanic ash, and essential oils. Massage and other traditional services are available, along with hydration therapy, infrared saunas for exfoliation and relaxation, and wellness sessions. ⊠ *755 Silverado Trail, Calistoga ✛ At Rosedale Rd.* ☎ *855/790–6023* ⊕ *aubergeresorts. com/solage/wellness/spa* ⌨ *Treatments from $200.*

Sonoma

14 miles west of Napa, 45 miles north-east of San Francisco.

One of the few towns in the valley with multiple attractions unrelated to food and wine, Sonoma has plenty to keep you busy for a couple of hours before you head out to tour the wineries. And you needn't leave town to taste wine. About three dozen tasting rooms are within steps of tree-filled Sonoma Plaza. The valley's cultural center, Sonoma was founded in 1835 when California was still part of Mexico.

GETTING HERE AND AROUND

Highway 12 (signed as Broadway near Sonoma Plaza) heads north into Sonoma from Highway 121 and south from Santa Rosa into downtown Sonoma. Parking is relatively easy to find on or near the plaza, and you can walk to many restaurants, shops, and tasting rooms. Signs point the way to several wineries a mile or more east of the plaza. Sonoma County Transit buses serve the town.

👁 Sights

Buena Vista Winery

WINERY | A local actor in top hat and 19th-century garb sometimes greets guests as Count Agoston Haraszthy at this homage to the birthplace of modern California wine making. Haraszthy's rehabilitated former press house (used for pressing grapes into wine), completed in 1864, is the architectural focal point, with photos, banners, plaques, and artifacts providing historical context. Chardonnay, Pinot Noir, Cabernet Sauvignon, and several Bordeaux-style red blends are the strong suits among the several dozen wines produced. During appointment-only visits (weekday walk-ins generally possible), you can taste some of them solo or preorder a cheese plate or box lunch from the affiliated Oakville Grocery. ⊠ *18000 Old Winery Rd., Sonoma ✛ Off E. Napa*

St. ☎ 800/926–1266 ⊕ www.buenavistaw-inery.com ☒ Tastings from $30.

Corner 103

WINERY | After leading an effort to revive a local winery, Lloyd Davis, an African American financier and oenophile, turned his attention to making the experience of learning about wine and food-wine pairings less daunting. To that end he opened a light-filled space, diagonally across from Sonoma Plaza, for tastings of Sonoma County wines guests can pair with cheeses or small bites. The lineup includes a brut rosé sparkler, Chardonnay and Marsanne-Roussanne whites, a rosé of Pinot Noir, and several reds. Corner 103's welcoming atmosphere, which in recent years has earned it a ranking at or near the top of USA Today's Best Tasting Room list, makes it an excellent choice for wine novices seeking to expand their knowledge. Visits are by appointment, though hosts usually accommodate drop-ins seeking wine-only tastings. ☒ 103 W. Napa St., Sonoma ✛ At 1st St. W ☎ 707/931–6141 ⊕ www.corner103.com ☒ Tastings from $30.

★ The Donum Estate

WINERY | The team at this prominent Chardonnay and Pinot Noir producer prizes viticulture —selecting vineyards with superior soils and microclimates, planting compatible clones, and farming organically with rigor—over wine-making wizardry. Tasting areas that include a contemporary white board-and-batten structure and a pavilion with a conical multicolor glass canopy afford guests hilltop views of Los Carneros, San Pablo Bay, and beyond. The wines, from several Sonoma County appellations and one in Mendocino County, continue to exhibit the "power yet elegance" that sealed the winery's fame in the 2000s. Tastings are by appointment only (last-minute unlikely). The more than three dozen large-scale museum-quality contemporary sculptures placed amid the vines, including works by Ai Weiwei, Lynda Benglis, Louise Bourgeois, Keith Haring, and Anselm Kiefer, add a touch of high culture to a visit here. ☒ 24500 Ramal Rd., Sonoma ✛ Off Hwy. 121/12 ☎ 707/732–2200 ⊕ www.thedonu-mestate.com ☒ Tastings from $125.

Gloria Ferrer Caves and Vineyards

WINERY | On a clear day this Spanish hacienda-style winery's Vista Terrace lives up to its name as guests at seated tastings sip delicate sparkling wines while taking in east-facing views of Los Carneros AVA and beyond it San Pablo Bay. The Chardonnay and Pinot Noir grapes from the vineyards in the foreground are the product of old-world wine-making knowledge—generations of the founding Ferrer family made cava in Spain—but also contemporary soil management techniques and clonal research. Hosts well-acquainted with the winery's sustainability practices and history as the Carneros District's first sparkling-wine house serve the wines, either solo or accompanied by food that varies from cheese and charcuterie to caviar or a full lunch. Except on Wednesday, visits are by appointment. ■ TIP→ On Wednesday only, the winery is open for by-the-glass pours and bottle service (no flights), reservations not required. ☒ 23555 Carneros Hwy./Hwy. 121, Sonoma ☎ 707/933–1986 ⊕ www.gloriaferrer.com ☒ Tastings from $65 ☉ Closed Tues. No flights (only bottle and by the-glass service) Wed.

Hanson of Sonoma Distillery

DISTILLERY | The Hanson family makes grape-based organic vodkas, one traditional, the rest infused with cucumbers, ginger, mandarin oranges, Meyer lemons, or habañero and other chili peppers. A surprise to many visitors, the Hansons make a blended white wine before distilling it into vodka. The family pours its vodkas and a single-malt whiskey in an industrial-looking tasting room heavy on the steel, with wood reclaimed from Deep South smokehouses adding a rustic note. In good weather, some sessions take place on the landscaped shore of a

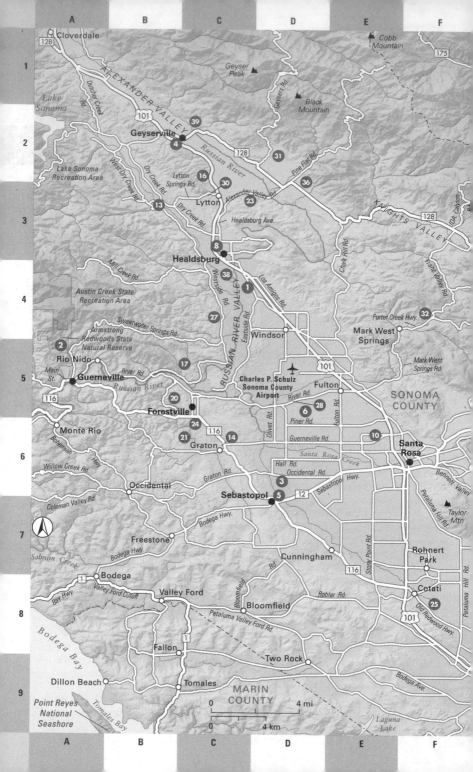

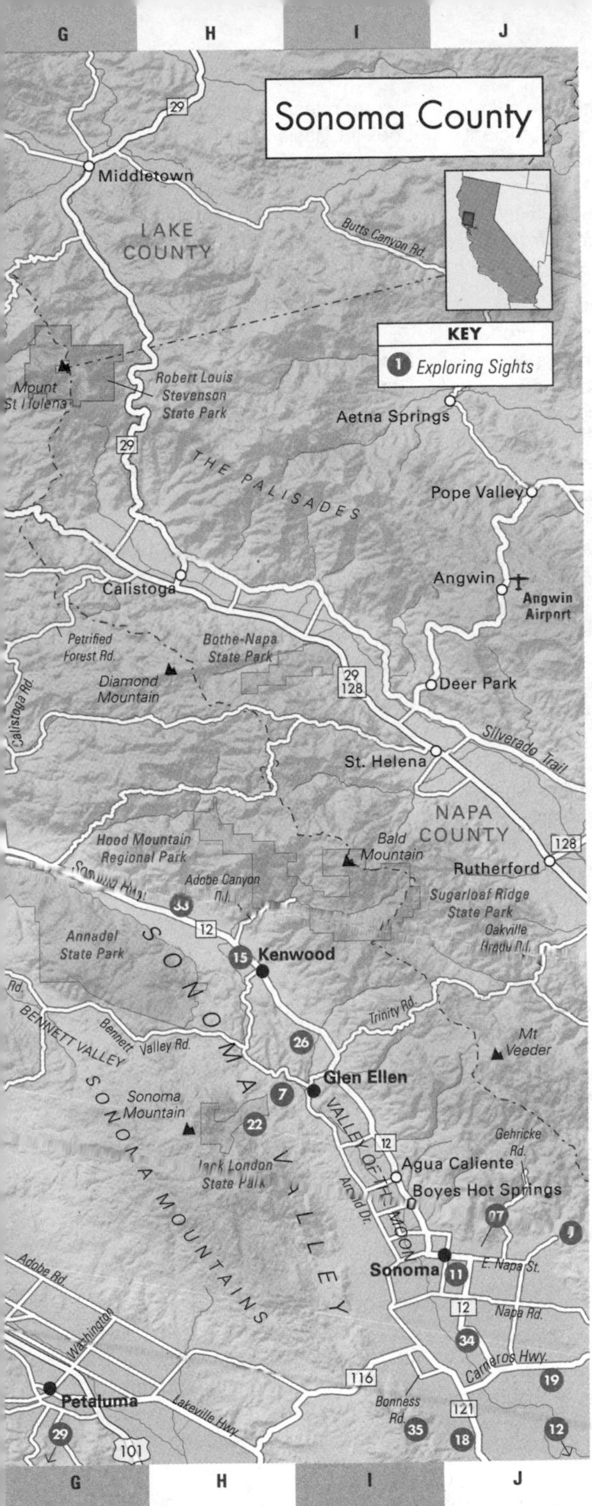

Sonoma County

KEY

1 Exploring Sights

small pond. Per state law, there's a limit to the amount poured, but it's sufficient to get to know the product. ✉ *22985 Burndale Rd., Sonoma ✛ At Carneros Hwy./Hwy. 121* ☎ *707/343–1805* ⊕ *hansonofsonoma.com* ✉ *Tastings from $35, tours from $75 (includes tasting).*

★ Sangiacomo Family Wines

WINERY | Several dozen wineries produce vineyard-designate Chardonnays and Pinot Noirs from grapes grown by the Sangiacomo family, whose Italian ancestors first started farming in Sonoma in 1927. The family didn't establish its own label until 2016, but its cool-climate wines and a Napa Valley Cabernet quickly earned critical plaudits. Chardonnay vines and the Carneros District's western hills form the backdrop for tastings, usually outdoors, at the 110-acre Home Ranch, the first of a dozen-plus vineyards the Sangiacomos acquired or lease. At appointment-only visits, you're apt to encounter one or more third-generation members, all of whom enjoy meeting guests and sharing their family's legacy. ■ TIP→ **On Friday from May through September, the winery hosts Sunset on the Terrace, with wines served by the glass, carafe, or bottle (no flights) from 3:30 pm until sundown.** ✉ *21545 Broadway, Sonoma ✛ 2½ miles south of Sonoma Plaza* ☎ *707/934–8445* ⊕ *www.sangiacomowines.com* ✉ *Tastings from $30.*

Schug Carneros Estate Winery

WINERY | As a young lad in Germany, the late Walter Schug made Pinot Noir, inspiring a lifelong preoccupation with the Burgundian varietal. The founding winemaker at Joseph Phelps, where he developed the flagship Insignia Bordeaux-style blend, in the 1980s he established his namesake winery in the far western reaches of Los Carneros AVA. His children continue his legacy, focusing on Chardonnay, Pinot Noir, Cabernet Sauvignon, and other Bordeaux varietals. There's also a wine from the St. Laurent grape, an offspring of Pinot. To sample current releases with a vineyard view, book a Classic Wine Tasting. The more comprehensive Cave Tour and Tasting includes a brief property walk, seasonal small bites, and current and library wines. ✉ *602 Bonneau Rd., Sonoma ✛ East off Hwy. 116 at Hwy. 121* ☎ *707/939–9363* ⊕ *schugwinery.com* ✉ *Tastings from $35* ☾ *Closed Mon.*

Sonoma Mission

CHURCH | The northernmost of the 21 missions established by Franciscan friars in California, Sonoma Mission was founded in 1823 as Mission San Francisco Solano. These days it serves as the centerpiece of Sonoma State Historic Park, which includes several other sites in Sonoma and nearby Petaluma. Some early mission structures fell into ruin, but all or part of several remaining buildings date to the era of Mexican rule over California. The Sonoma Barracks, a half block west of the mission at 20 East Spain Street, housed troops under the command of General Mariano Guadalupe Vallejo, who controlled vast tracts of land in the region. General Vallejo's Home, a Victorian-era structure, is a few blocks west. ✉ *114 E. Spain St., Sonoma ✛ At 1st St. E* ☎ *707/938–9560* ⊕ *www.parks.ca.gov* ✉ *$3, includes same-day admission to other historic sites.*

🍽 Restaurants

★ Cafe La Haye

$$$ | AMERICAN | In a postage-stamp-size open kitchen (the dining room, its white walls adorned with contemporary art, is nearly as compact), chef Jeffrey Lloyd turns out understated, sophisticated fare emphasizing seasonally available local ingredients. Meats, pastas, and seafood get deluxe treatment without fuss or fanfare—and the daily risotto special is always worth trying. **Known for:** Napa-Sonoma wine list with French complements; signature butterscotch pudding; owner Saul Gropman on hand to greet diners. Ⓢ *Average main: $27*

✉ *140 E. Napa St., Sonoma* ✢ *East of Sonoma Plaza* ☎ *707/935–5994* 🌐 *www.cafelahaye.com* 🕑 *Closed Sun. and Mon. No lunch.*

El Dorado Kitchen

$$$ | MODERN AMERICAN | This restaurant owes its visual appeal to its clean lines and svelte decor, but the eye inevitably drifts westward to the open kitchen, where longtime executive chef Armando Navarro's team crafts dishes full of subtle surprises. The menu might include ceviche or roasted maitake mushrooms as starters and pan-roasted salmon, fettuccine carbonara, or paella awash with seafood among the entrées. **Known for:** subtle tastes and textures; truffle-oil fries with Parmesan; takeout window for Mexican (plus the spicy burger). [$] *Average main: $29* ✉ *El Dorado Hotel, 405 1st St. W, Sonoma* ✢ *At W. Spain St.* ☎ *707/996–3030* 🌐 *eldoradokitchen.com.*

★ The Girl & the Fig

$$$ | FRENCH | At this hot spot for inventive French cooking inside the historic Sonoma Hotel bar, you can always find a dish with the signature figs on the menu, whether it's a fig-and-arugula salad or an aperitif blending sparkling wine with fig liqueur. Also look for duck confit, a burger with matchstick fries, and wild flounder meunière. **Known for:** Rhône-wines emphasis; artisanal cheese and charcuterie platters; weekly changing three-course prix-fixe option. [$] *Average main: $30* ✉ *Sonoma Hotel, 110 W. Spain St., Sonoma* ✢ *At 1st St. W* ☎ *707/938–3634* 🌐 *www.thegirlandthefig.com.*

★ LaSalette Restaurant

$$$ | PORTUGUESE | Born in the Azores and raised in Sonoma, chef-owner Manuel Azevedo serves cuisine inspired by his native Portugal in this warmly decorated spot with a heated patio out front. The wood-oven whole-roasted fish is always worth trying, and there are usually boldly flavored pork dishes, along with a casserole, pot roast, stew, salted cod, and other hearty fare. **Known for:** authentic Portuguese cuisine; sophisticated spicing; rice pudding with Madeira-braised fig for dessert. [$] *Average main: $31* ✉ *452 1st St. E, Sonoma* ✢ *Near E. Spain St.* ☎ *707/938–1927* 🌐 *www.lasaletterestaurant.com* 🕑 *Closed Wed.*

★ Wit & Wisdom Tavern

$$$ | MODERN AMERICAN | A San Francisco culinary star with establishments worldwide, Michael Mina debuted his first Wine Country restaurant in 2020, its interior of charcoal grays, browns, and soft whites dandy indeed, if by evening vying with outdoor spaces aglow with fire pits and lighted water features. Seasonal regional ingredients—Pacific Coast fish, pasture-raised meats, freshly plucked produce—go into haute-homey dishes, prepared open-fire, that include pizzas, handmade pastas, and the signature lobster potpie with brandied lobster cream and black truffle. **Known for:** 3–5 happy hour's beverage and app selections; many local wines on award-winning list; prix-fixe Night at the Tavern tasting menu. [$] *Average main: $35* ✉ *The Lodge at Sonoma, 1325 Broadway, Sonoma* ✢ *At Leveroni Rd.* ☎ *707/931–3405* 🌐 *www.witandwisdomsonoma.com* 🕑 *Closed Mon. and Tues. No lunch.*

🛏 Hotels

Inn at Sonoma

$$ | B&B/INN | Little luxuries delight at this well-run inn ¼ mile south of Sonoma Plaza whose guest rooms, softly lit and done in pastels, have comfortable beds topped with feather comforters and plenty of pillows. **Pros:** last-minute specials can be a great deal; freshly baked cookies, afternoon wine and cheese; good soundproofing blocks out Broadway street noise. **Cons:** on a busy street rather than right on the plaza; pet-friendly rooms book up quickly; some rooms on the small side. [$] *Rooms from: $275* ✉ *630 Broadway, Sonoma* ☎ *707/939–1340* 🌐 *www.innatsonoma.com* 🛏 *27 rooms* 🍴 *Free Breakfast.*

★ **Ledson Hotel**

$$$ | B&B/INN | With just six rooms the Ledson feels intimate, and the furnishings and amenities—down beds, mood lighting, gas fireplaces, whirlpool tubs, and balconies for enjoying breakfast or a glass of wine—stack up well against Wine Country rooms costing more, especially in high season. **Pros:** convenient Sonoma Plaza location; spacious, individually decorated rooms; whirlpool tub in all rooms. **Cons:** two people maximum occupancy in all rooms; children must be at least 12 years old; front rooms have plaza views but pick up some street noise. [$] *Rooms from: $395* ✉ *480 1st St. E, Sonoma* ☎ *707/996–9779* 🌐 *www.ledsonhotel.com* 🛏 *6 rooms* 🍴 *No Meals.*

★ **MacArthur Place Hotel & Spa**

$$$$ | HOTEL | Guests at this 7-acre boutique property five blocks south of Sonoma Plaza bask in ritzy seclusion in plush accommodations set amid landscaped gardens. **Pros:** verdant garden setting; great for a romantic getaway; appealing common areas. **Cons:** a bit of a walk from the plaza; some traffic noise audible in street-side rooms; pricey in high season. [$] *Rooms from: $705* ✉ *29 E. MacArthur St., Sonoma* ☎ *707/938–2929, 800/722–1866* 🌐 *www.macarthurplace.com* 🛏 *64 rooms* 🍴 *No Meals.*

🍸 Nightlife

Sigh!

WINE BARS | From the oval bar and walls the color of a fine blanc de blancs to retro chandeliers that mimic Champagne bubbles, everything about this sparkling-wine bar's frothy space screams "have a good time." That owner Jayme Powers and her posse are trained in the fine art of *sabrage* (opening a bottle of sparkling wine with a saber) only adds to the festivity. **■ TIP→ Sigh! opens at noon, so it's a good daytime stop, too.** ✉ *120 W. Napa St., Sonoma* ✣ *At 1st St. W* ☎ *707/996–2444* 🌐 *www.sighsonoma.com.*

🏃 Activities

BIKING

Sonoma Adventures

BIKING | Mount a regular bike or one with "pedal assist" on this company's half- and full-day guided tours to area wineries. You can also rent a bike and head off on your own. ✉ *1254 Broadway, Sonoma* ✣ *1/5 mile north of Napa Rd.* ☎ *707/938–2080* 🌐 *www.sonoma-adventures.com* 🎟 *½-day tour from $119, not including tasting fees.*

SPAS

The Spa at the Lodge

SPAS | A restful haven in the rear of the 10-acre Lodge at Sonoma property, the spa contains 11 treatment rooms including two for couples. The signature 80-minute Celestial Body Renewal Ritual begins with an exfoliating shea-butter body scrub, followed by a body wrap and a CBD deep-tissue massage, and there are several other 50- or 80-minute options. Facials, eye and lip treatments, and waxing are also on the menu. Before or after sessions, guests can relax in a landscaped outdoor garden with a pool, a hot tub, and a barrel sauna. ✉ *Lodge at Sonoma, 1325 Broadway, Sonoma* ✣ *At Leveroni Rd.* ☎ *707/931–3434* 🌐 *www.thelodgeatsonoma.com/spa* 🎟 *Treatments from $210.*

Glen Ellen

7 miles north of Sonoma.

Craggy Glen Ellen epitomizes the difference between the Napa and Sonoma valleys. Whereas small Napa towns like St. Helena get their charm from upscale boutiques and restaurants lined up along well-groomed sidewalks, Glen Ellen's crooked streets are shaded with stands of old oak trees and occasionally bisected by the Sonoma and Calabazas creeks. Tucked among the trees of a narrow canyon where Sonoma Mountain and

Benziger tram tours take to the fields to show biodynamic farming techniques in action.

the Mayacamas pinch in the valley floor, Glen Ellen looks more like a town of the Sierra foothills gold country than a Wine Country village.

GETTING HERE AND AROUND

Glen Ellen sits just off Highway 12. From the north or south, take Arnold Drive west and follow it south less than a mile. The walkable downtown straddles a half-mile stretch of Arnold Drive. Sonoma County Transit buses serve Glen Ellen.

◉ Sights

Benziger Family Winery

WINERY | One of the best-known Sonoma County wineries sits on a sprawling estate in a bowl with 360-degree sun exposure. Hosts conducting popular tram tours explain the benefits of the vineyard's natural setting and how biodynamic farming yields healthier, more flavorful fruit. The eco-friendly agricultural practices include extensive plantings to attract beneficial insects and the deployment of sheep to trim vegetation between the vines while simultaneously tilling the soil with their hooves and fertilizing to boot. Known for Chardonnay, Cabernet Sauvignon, Merlot, Pinot Noir, and Sauvignon Blanc, the winery is a beautiful spot for an alfresco tasting, whether you take the tour or not. All visits are by appointment; reserve a tram tour at least a day or two ahead in summer and early fall. ⊠ *1883 London Ranch Rd., Glen Ellen ✛ Off Arnold Dr.* ☎ *888/490–2739* ⊕ *www.benziger.com* 🖃 *Tastings from $40* ⊗ *Closed Tues. and Wed.*

★ Jack London State Historic Park

STATE/PROVINCIAL PARK | The pleasures are pastoral and intellectual at author Jack London's beloved Beauty Ranch, where you could easily spend the afternoon hiking some of the 30-plus miles of trails that loop through meadows and stands of oaks, redwoods, and other trees. Manuscripts and personal artifacts depicting London's travels are on view at the House of Happy Walls Museum, which provides an overview of the writer's life, literary passions, humanitarian and conservation efforts, and promotion of organic farming. His wife Charmian's equally compelling story is also documented. A short hike away lie the ruins of Wolf House, which burned down just before London was to move in. Also open to visitors are a few outbuildings and the restored wood-frame cottage where London penned many of his later works. He's buried on the property. ■ **TIP→ The park hosts hot-ticket musical revues and comedies produced by Transcendence Theatre Company each summer.** ✉ *2400 London Ranch Rd., Glen Ellen* ✣ *Off Arnold Dr.* ☎ *707/938–5216* 🌐 *www.jacklondonpark.com* 🎫 *Parking $10 ($5 walk-in or bike).*

★ Lasseter Family Winery

WINERY | Immaculately groomed grapevines dazzle the eye at John and Nancy Lasseter's secluded winery, and it's no accident: Phil Coturri, Sonoma Valley's premier organic vineyard manager, tends them. Even the landscaping, which includes an insectary to attract beneficial bugs, is meticulously maintained. Come harvest time, the wine-making team oversees gentle processes that transform the fruit into wines of purity and grace, among them a Sémillon–Sauvignon Blanc blend, the Enjoué rosé, and Bordeaux and Rhône reds. Evocative labels illustrate the tale behind each wine. In good weather, guests hear these well-told stories at tastings on the winery's outdoor patio, whose views include the vineyard and the Mayacamas Mountains, where the Lasseters purchased a second vineyard. All visits to the Glen Ellen property are by appointment. ✉ *1 Vintage La., Glen Ellen* ✣ *Off Dunbar Rd.* ☎ *707/933–2800* 🌐 *www.lasseterfamilywinery.com* 🎫 *Tastings from $40.*

🍴 Restaurants

★ Glen Ellen Star

$$$ | **ECLECTIC** | Chef Ari Weiswasser honed his craft at The French Laundry, Daniel, and other bastions of culinary finesse, but his Sonoma Valley outpost revolves around haute-rustic cuisine, much of it emerging from a wood-fired oven. In 2022, Weiswasser turned the day-to-day reins over to a new chef de cuisine, but the mainstay crisp-crusted, richly sauced Margherita and other pizzas continue to thrive in the oven's torrid heat, as do tender whole fish entrées and vegetables roasted in small iron skillets. **Known for:** outdoor dining area; prix-fixe Wednesday "neighborhood night" menu with free corkage; Weiswasser's sauces, emulsions, and spices. [$] *Average main: $33* ✉ *13648 Arnold Dr., Glen Ellen* ✣ *At Warm Springs Rd.* ☎ *707/343–1384* 🌐 *glenellenstar.com* 🕒 *No lunch.*

★ Les Pascals

$ | **CAFÉ** | A bright-yellow slice of France in downtown Glen Ellen, this combination pâtisserie, boulangerie, and café takes its name from its husband-and-wife owners, Pascal and Pascale Merle. Pascal whips up croissants, breads, turnovers, and sweet treats like Napoleons, galettes, and eclairs, along with quiches, potpies, and other savory fare; Pascale creates a cordial environment for customers to enjoy them. **Known for:** memorable French onion soup; shaded back patio; high-test French and Italian coffee drinks. [$] *Average main: $12* ✉ *13758 Arnold Dr., Glen Ellen* ✣ *Near London Ranch Rd.* ☎ *707/934–8378* 🌐 *www.lespascalspatisserie.com* 🕒 *Closed Wed. No dinner.*

🛏 Hotels

★ Gaige House

$$$ | **B&B/INN** | There's no other place in Sonoma or Napa quite like the Gaige House, which blends the best elements of a traditional country inn, a boutique hotel, and a secluded hideaway. **Pros:** short walk to Glen Ellen restaurants, shops, and tasting rooms; idyllic swimming pool and hot tub area; full breakfast with two hot items. **Cons:** sound carries in the main house; least expensive rooms are on the small side; oriented more toward couples than families with children. [$] *Rooms from: $351* ✉ *13540 Arnold Dr., Glen Ellen* ☎ *707/935–0237, 866/207–7146* 🌐 *www.thegaigehouse.com* 🛏 *23 rooms* 🍴 *Free Breakfast.*

★ Olea Hotel

$$$ | **HOTEL** | Husband-and-wife team Ashish and Sia Patel operate this country-casual yet sophisticated boutique lodging. **Pros:** beautiful style; complimentary wine; filling two-course breakfasts. **Cons:** minor road noise in some rooms; fills up quickly on weekends; weekend minimum-stay requirement. [$] *Rooms from: $387* ✉ *5131 Warm Springs Rd., Glen Ellen* ✢ *West off Arnold Dr.* ☎ *707/996–5131* 🌐 *www.oleahotel.com* 🛏 *15 rooms* 🍴 *Free Breakfast.*

Kenwood

4 miles north of Glen Ellen.

Tiny Kenwood consists of little more than a few restaurants, shops, tasting rooms, and a historic train depot, now used for private events. But hidden in this pretty landscape of meadows and woods at the north end of Sonoma Valley are several good wineries, most just off the Sonoma Highway. Varietals grown here at the foot of the Sugarloaf Mountains include Sauvignon Blanc, Chardonnay, Zinfandel, and Cabernet Sauvignon.

GETTING HERE AND AROUND

To get to Kenwood from Glen Ellen, head northeast on Arnold Drive and north on Highway 12. Sonoma Transit buses serve Kenwood from Glen Ellen and Sonoma.

Sights

★ En Garde Winery

WINERY | Sommeliers, critics, and collectors extol the Pinot Noirs and Cabernet Sauvignons of Csaba Szakál, En Garde's Hungarian-born winemaker and owner. To create what he describes as "aromatic, complex, lush, and juicy" wines, Szakál selects top Sonoma County vineyards for the Pinots and the Napa Valley's Diamond Mountain, Mt. Veeder, and other high-elevation sites for the Cabernets. Not afraid to heavy up the oak on the Cabernets, he nevertheless achieves elegance as well. The winemaker is equally precise about hiring staffers for his modest highway's-edge tasting room along Kenwood's brief commercial strip. Well-acquainted with his goals and methods, they provide a wealth of knowledge about wine making and California viticulture. If you're lucky, Szakál will be around to discuss his wines (he loves to), which also include Chardonnay, other whites, and rosé of Pinot Noir. Visits are by reservation, with same-day appointments sometimes possible. ✉ *9077 Sonoma Hwy., Kenwood* ✢ *At Shaw Ave.* ☎ *707/282–9216* 🌐 *www.engardewinery.com* 🎟 *Tastings from $40.*

St. Francis Winery

WINERY | Nestled at the foot of Mt. Hood, St. Francis has earned national acclaim for its pairings of wines and small bites. With its bell tower, red-tile roof, and views of the Mayacamas Mountains to the east, the winery's California Mission–style visitor center occupies one of Sonoma County's most scenic locations. The charm of the surroundings is matched by the wines, among them Cabernet Sauvignon and rich, earthy Zinfandels from the Dry Creek, Russian River, and Sonoma Valleys. The five-course pairings might include Chardonnay with lobster bisque or Cabernet Sauvignon with wine-braised beef ribs. ✉ *100 Pythian Rd., Kenwood* ✢ *Off Hwy. 12* ☎ *707/833–0242* 🌐 *www.stfranciswinery.com* 🎟 *Tastings from $35.*

🍴 Restaurants

Salt & Stone

$$$ | **MODERN AMERICAN** | The menu at this upscale roadhouse with a sloping wood-beamed ceiling focuses on seafood and meat—beef, lamb, chicken, duck, and other options—with many dishes in both categories grilled. Start with the classics, perhaps a martini and oysters Rockefeller, before moving on to well-plated contemporary entrées that might include crispy-skin salmon or duck breast, a fish stew, or grilled rib eye. **Known for:** mountain-view outdoor seating area; weekend brunch; weekday happy hour 2:30–5 except holidays. $ *Average main: $31* ⌂ *9900 Sonoma Hwy., Kenwood* ⊹ *At Kunde Winery Rd.* ☎ *707/833–6326* ⊕ *www.saltstonekenwood.com* ⊗ *No lunch Tues. and Wed.*

🛏 Hotels

⭐ Kenwood Inn and Spa

$$$$ | **B&B/INN** | Fluffy feather beds, custom Italian furnishings, and French doors in most cases opening onto terraces or balconies lend this inn's uncommonly spacious guest rooms a romantic air—more than a few guests are celebrating honeymoons or anniversaries. **Pros:** large rooms; lavish furnishings; romantic setting. **Cons:** far from nightlife; expensive in high season; geared more to couples than families with children. $ *Rooms from: $420* ⌂ *10400 Sonoma Hwy./ Hwy. 12, Kenwood* ☎ *707/833–1293, 800/353–6966* ⊕ *www.kenwoodinn.com* ⇥ *29 rooms* ⌾ *Free Breakfast.*

Petaluma

24 miles southwest of Kenwood, 39 miles north of San Francisco.

The first thing you should know about Petaluma is that this is a farm town—with more than 62,500 residents, a large one—and the residents are proud of it.

Recent years have seen an uptick in the quality of Petaluma cuisine, fueled in part by the proliferation of local organic and artisanal farms and boutique wine production. With the 2018 approval of the Petaluma Gap AVA, the city even has its name on a wine appellation.

GETTING HERE AND AROUND

Petaluma lies west of Sonoma and southwest of Glen Ellen and Kenwood. From Highway 12 or Arnold Drive, take Watmaugh Road west to Highway 116 west. Sonoma Transit buses serve Petaluma. From San Francisco take U.S. 101 (or Golden Gate Transit Bus 101) north.

👁 Sights

Lagunitas Brewing Company

BREWERY | These days owned by Heineken International, Lagunitas began as a craft brewery in Marin County in 1993 before moving to Petaluma in 1994. In addition to its large facility, the company operates a taproom, the Schwag Shop for gifts, and an outdoor beer garden that in good weather bustles even midday. Guides leading the brewery tour, which includes a beer flight, provide an irreverent version of the company's rise to international acclaim. An engaging tale involves the state alcohol board's sting operation commemorated by Undercover Investigation Shut-down Ale, one of several small-batch brews made here. ⌂ *1280 N. McDowell Blvd., Petaluma* ⊹ *½ mile north of Corona Rd.* ☎ *707/778–8776* ⊕ *lagunitas.com/tap-room/petaluma* ⌾ *Tour $10* ⊗ *Taproom closed Mon. and Tues.*

⭐ McEvoy Ranch

FARM/RANCH | The late Nan McEvoy's retirement project after departing as board chair of the *San Francisco Chronicle*, the ranch produces organic extra-virgin olive oil as well as Pinot Noir and other wines, the estate ones from the Petaluma Gap AVA. In good weather, relaxing tastings of oils or wines unfold on a pond's-edge flagstone patio with views of alternating rows of Syrah grapes and mature olive trees. You can preorder lunch to accompany any tasting; for a more private experience, book a pond-side cabana. Walkabout Ranch Tours of four guests or more take in vineyards, gardens, and a Chinese pavilion. All visits require an appointment. ✉ *5935 Red Hill Rd., Petaluma* ✣ *6½ miles south of downtown* ☎ *707/778–2307* 🌐 *www.mcevoyranch.com* 🎫 *Tastings from $25 (olive oil), $35 (wine); tours from $55.*

🍴 Restaurants

★ Central Market

$$$ | MODERN AMERICAN | A participant in the Slow Food movement, Central Market serves creative, upscale Cal-Mediterranean dishes—many of whose ingredients come from the restaurant's organic farm—in a century-old building with an exposed brick wall and an open kitchen. The menu, which changes daily depending on chef Tony Najiola's inspiration and what's ripe and ready, might include spicy duck wings as a starter, a slow-roasted-beets salad, pizzas, stews, two or three pasta dishes, and wood-grilled fish and meat. **Known for:** happy hour (5–6 pm) apps, beer, and wine specials; superior wine list; historic setting. $ *Average main: $27* ✉ *42 Petaluma Blvd. N, Petaluma* ✣ *Near Western Ave.* ☎ *707/778–9900* 🌐 *www.centralmarketpetaluma.com* 🕓 *Closed Mon. and Tues. No lunch.*

★ Pearl Petaluma

$$ | MEDITERRANEAN | Regulars of this southern Petaluma "daytime café" with indoor and outdoor seating rave about its eastern Mediterranean–inflected cuisine—then immediately downplay their enthusiasm lest this unassuming gem become more popular. The menu changes often, but mainstays include *shakshuka* (a tomato-based stew with baked eggs) and a lamb burger dripping with fennel tzatziki. **Known for:** weekend brunch; fun beverage lineup, alcoholic and non; menu prices include gratuity. $ *Average main: $23* ✉ *500 1st St., Petaluma* ✣ *At G St.* ☎ *707/559–5187* 🌐 *pearlpetaluma.com* 🕓 *Closed Tues. and Wed. No dinner.*

Healdsburg

17 miles north of Santa Rosa, 32 miles northwest of Petaluma.

Sonoma County's ritziest town and the star of many a magazine spread or online feature, Healdsburg is located at the intersection of the Dry Creek Valley, Russian River Valley, and Alexander Valley AVAs. Several dozen wineries bear a Healdsburg address, and around downtown's plaza you'll find fashionable boutiques, spas, hip tasting rooms, and art galleries, and some of the Wine Country's best restaurants.

Especially on weekends, you'll have plenty of company as you tour the downtown area. You could spend a day just exploring the tasting rooms and shops surrounding Healdsburg Plaza, but be sure to allow time to venture into the surrounding countryside. With orderly rows of vines alternating with beautifully overgrown hills, this is the setting you dream about when planning a Wine Country vacation.

GETTING HERE AND AROUND

Healdsburg sits just off U.S. 101. Heading north, take the Central Healdsburg exit to reach Healdsburg Plaza; heading south, take the Westside Road exit and pass east under the freeway. Sonoma County Transit buses serve Healdsburg from Santa Rosa.

👁 Sights

★ Aperture Cellars

WINERY | As a youth, Jesse Katz tagged along with his photographer father, Andy Katz, to wineries worldwide, stimulating curiosity about wine that led to stints at august operations like the Napa Valley's Screaming Eagle and Bordeaux's Petrús. In 2009, still in his 20s, Katz started Aperture, a success from the get-go for his single-vineyard Cabernets and Bordeaux blends. Among the whites are Sauvignon Blanc and an old-vine Chenin Blanc that's one of California's best. Katz's wines, which benefit from rigorous farming and cellar techniques, are presented by appointment only in an ultracontemporary hospitality center about 2½ miles south of Healdsburg Plaza. One tasting explores Aperture's various wine-growing sites and their soils, the other the single-vineyard wines. The center's shutterlike windows and other architectural elements evoke Andy Katz's photography career; his images of the Russian River Valley and beyond hang on the walls. ⊠ *12291 Old Redwood Hwy., Healdsburg ⊹ ¼ mile south of Limerick La.* ☎ *707/200–7891* ⊕ *www. aperture-cellars.com* ▨ *Tastings from $60* ⊙ *Closed Tues. and Wed.*

Breathless Wines

WINERY | The mood's downright bubbly (pardon that pun) at the oasis-like garden patio of this sparkling-wine producer tucked away in an industrial park northwest of Healdsburg Plaza. Established by three sisters in memory of their mother, Breathless sources grapes from appellations in Sonoma, Napa, and Mendocino Counties that find their way into sparklers and a few still wines. The small indoor tasting area was fashioned out of shipping containers, though nearly everyone sips in the umbrella-shaded garden in fine weather. You can sample wine by the glass, flight, or bottle; all visits require an appointment, with same-day reservations sometimes possible. ■TIP➡ **Splurge on the Sabrage Experience to learn how to open a bottle with a saber, a tradition supposedly initiated by Napoléon's soldiers.** ⊠ *499 Moore La., Healdsburg ⊹ Off North St.* ☎ *707/395–7300* ⊕ *www. breathlesswines.com* ▨ *Tastings from $28* ⊙ *Closed Tues. and Wed.*

Dry Creek Vineyard

WINERY | Loire-style Sauvignon Blanc marketed as Fumé Blanc brought instant success to the Dry Creek Valley's first new winery since Prohibition, but this stalwart established in 1972 also does well with Zinfandel and Cabernet Sauvignon and other Bordeaux-style reds. Founder David Stare's other contributions include leading the drive to develop the Dry Creek Valley appellation and coining the term "old-vine Zinfandel." The winery's history and wine-making evolution are among the topics addressed at tastings—outdoors under the shade of a magnolia and several redwood trees or in the nautical-theme tasting room. ⊠ *3770 Lambert Bridge Rd., Healdsburg ⊹ Off Dry Creek Rd.* ☎ *707/433–1000* ⊕ *www. drycreekvineyard.com* ▨ *Tastings from $30.*

★ Gary Farrell Vineyards & Winery

WINERY | Pass through an impressive metal gate and wind up a steep hill to reach this winery with knockout Russian River Valley views from the two-tiered tasting room and terrace outside. In 2017 *Wine Enthusiast Magazine* named a Gary Farrell Chardonnay wine of the year, one among many accolades for this winery known for sophisticated single-vineyard Chardonnays and Pinot Noirs. Farrell departed in the early 2000s, but current winemaker Theresa Heredia acknowledges that her philosophy has much in common with his. For the Pinots, this means picking on the early side to preserve acidity and focusing on "expressing the site." The Elevation Tasting of single-vineyard wines provides a good introduction; other tastings involve a winery tour or library wines. Visits are by appointment; same-day reservations are possible on weekdays, but call ahead. ⊠ *10701 Westside Rd., Healdsburg* ☎ *707/473–2909* ⊕ *www.garyfarrellwinery.com* ▨ *Tastings from $55.*

★ Jordan Vineyard and Winery

WINERY | Founders Tom and Sally Jordan erected the French-style château here in part to emphasize their goal of producing Sonoma County Chardonnays and Cabernet Sauvignons—one of each annually—to rival those from the Napa Valley and France itself. Their son John, now at the helm, has instituted numerous improvements, among them the replanting of many vines and a shift to all-French barrels for aging. The signature winery tour and tasting includes a peek at the tank room and its towering oak barrels. The pièce de résistance of the three-hour Estate Tour & Tasting, hosted from spring to early fall, is a stop at a 360-degree vista point overlooking the 1,200-acre property's vines, olive trees, and countryside. As part of these experiences and other seasonal events, the executive chef prepares small bites and dishes whose ingredients come mainly from Jordan's organic garden. Visits are strictly by appointment. ⊠ *1474 Alexander Valley Rd., Healdsburg* ✛ *1½ miles east of Healdsburg Ave.* ☎ *707/431–5250* ⊕ *www.jordanwinery.com* ✉ *Tastings from $90* ⊗ *Closed Tues. and Wed. Dec.–Mar.*

MacRostie Estate House

WINERY | A driveway off Westside Road curls through undulating vineyard hills to this longtime Chardonnay and Pinot Noir producer's steel, wood, and heavy-on-the-glass tasting space. Moments after you've arrived and a host has offered a glass of wine, you'll already feel transported into a genteel realm. Hospitality is clearly a priority, but so, too, is seeking out top-tier grape sources—30 for the Chardonnays, 15 for the Pinots—among them Dutton Ranch, Sangiacomo, and owner Steve MacRostie's Wildcat. With fruit this renowned, current winemaker Heidi Bridenhagen downplays the oak and other tricks of her trade, letting the vineyard settings, grape clones, and vintage do the talking. Tastings, inside or on balcony terraces with views across the Russian River Valley, are all seated and by appointment. ⊠ *4605 Westside Rd., Healdsburg* ✛ *Near Frost Rd.* ☎ *707/473–9303* ⊕ *macrostiewinery.com* ✉ *Tastings from $35.*

★ Ridge Vineyards

WINERY | Ridge stands tall among local wineries, and not merely because its 1971 Monte Bello Cabernet Sauvignon rated second-highest among California reds competing with French ones at the famous Judgment of Paris blind tasting of 1976. The winery built its reputation on Cabernets, Zinfandels, and Chardonnays of unusual depth and complexity, but you'll also find blends of Rhône varietals. Ridge makes wines using grapes from several California locales—Sonoma County, Dry Creek Valley, the Napa Valley, and Paso Robles among them—but the focus is on single-vineyard estate wines such as the Lytton Springs Zinfandel from fruit grown near the tasting room. In good weather, you can sit outside, taking in views of rolling vineyard hills while you sip. ■TIP→ **The educational Century Tour & Library Tasting, a solid value, begins with a spin around the property in an electric cart, followed by a comparative tasting of current and older wines.** ⊠ *650 Lytton Springs Rd., Healdsburg* ✛ *Off U.S. 101* ☎ *408/007 3233* ⊕ *www.ridgewine.com/visit/lytton-springs* ✉ *Tastings from $30.*

★ Silver Oak

WINERY | The views and architecture are as impressive as the wines at the 113-acre Sonoma County outpost of the same-named Napa Valley winery. As in Napa, the Healdsburg facility—an ultramodern, environmentally sensitive winery with a glass-walled tasting pavilion—produces just one wine each year: a well-balanced Alexander Valley Cabernet Sauvignon aged in American rather than French oak barrels. One tasting includes the current Alexander Valley and Napa Valley Cabernets, plus an older vintage. Two or more wines of sister operation Twomey Cellars, which produces Sauvignon Blanc, Pinot Noir, and Merlot, begin a second offering that concludes with the current Cabernets. Hosts at a third pour current and older Cabernets from Napa and Sonoma. Make a reservation for all visits. ✉ *7300 Hwy. 128, Healdsburg ✛ Near Chaffee Rd.* ☎ *707/942–7082* ⊕ *www.silveroak.com* 🍽 *Tastings from $50.*

★ Tongue Dancer Wines
WINERY | Down a country lane less than 2 miles south of Healdsburg Plaza, James MacPhail's modest production facility seems well away from the upscale fray. MacPhail makes wines for The Calling, Sangiacomo, and other labels, but Tongue Dancer's Chardonnays and Pinot Noirs are his handcrafted labors of love. Made from small lots of grapes from choice vineyard sites, the wines impress, sometimes stun, with their grace, complexity, and balance. The flagship Sonoma Coast Pinot Noir, a blend from two or more vineyards, is poured at most tastings, in a mezzanine space above oak-aging barrels or on an outdoor patio. Either the winemaker or his co-owner and wife, Kerry Forbes-MacPhail—she's credited on bottles as the "Knowledge-able One" (and she is)—will host you. As James describes it, they aim to "create an approachable experience for guests we hope will leave as friends." Appointment-only visits are best made a day or more ahead. ✉ *851 Magnolia Dr., Healdsburg ✛ Off Westside Rd.* ☎ *707/433–4780* ⊕ *tonguedancerwines. com* 🍽 *Tastings $30* ☾ *Closed Sun. and Mon.*

 Restaurants

★ Barndiva
$$$$ | AMERICAN | Not one to rest on her laurels, the creative director of this urban-rustic restaurant responded to win-ning a prestigious fine-dining award by welcoming a new chef, mixologist, and wine lead, all with impressive creden-tials themselves. The worth-the-splurge cuisine, hinging on hyperfresh local ingredients from superstar purveyors, comes off even more intricate than before in dishes that might include kanpachi crudo or goat-cheese cro-quette apps or a smoked pork chop with Japanese sweet potato entrée. **Known for:** open-air front and back patios; ornate, well-built cocktails; Friday and weekend brunch. 💲 *Average main: $45* ✉ *231 Center St., Healdsburg ✛ Near Matheson St.* ☎ *707/431–0100* ⊕ *www.barndiva. com* ☾ *Closed Mon. and Tues. No lunch weekdays.*

Bravas Bar de Tapas
$$$ | SPANISH | Spanish-style tapas and an outdoor patio in perpetual party mode make this restaurant, headquartered in a restored 1920s bungalow, a popular downtown perch. Contemporary Spanish mosaics set a perky tone inside, but unless something's amiss with the weather, nearly everyone heads out back for flavorful croquettes, paella, *jamón ibérico, pan tomate* (tomato toast), grilled octopus, skirt steak, and crispy fried chicken. **Known for:** casual small plates; specialty cocktails, sangrias, and beer; Spanish and Sonoma County wines. 💲 *Average main: $33* ✉ *420 Center St., Healdsburg ✛ Near North St.* ☎ *707/433–7700* ⊕ *www.barbravas.com.*

Little Saint
$$$ | VEGETARIAN | Inside a metal-and-glass structure design writers have described as industrial grange-hall chic, the chefs at this "farm-forward gathering place" prepare satisfying plant-based cuisine supporting the founders' goal of creating Healdsburg's first entirely vegan restau-rant. With most ingredients rushed over from Little Saint's nearby 8-acre Russian River farm, the menu items change often. **Known for:** live music and events upstairs some nights; coffee bar, wine shop, and mercantile with made-to-go salads, sandwiches, and dips; sensitive wine pairings, plus beers, ciders, and cocktails alcoholic and non. 💲 *Average*

main: $29 ✉ *25 North St., Healdsburg* ✥ *At Foss St.* ☎ *707/433–8207* 🌐 *www.littlesainthealdsburg.com* 🕒 *Closed Tues. and Wed.*

★ The Matheson

$$$$ | **MODERN AMERICAN** | The location of Dustin Valette's farm-to-table restaurant holds a special place in his heart: the bar and its Wine Wall taps dispensing mostly Sonoma County wines occupy the space where the Geyserville native's great-grandfather ran a bakery a century ago. Valette describes the menu—aged meats creatively adorned, local fish with recently plucked vegetables—as a "love letter" to local agriculture, a point driven home by the large, bright paintings of farm and culinary activity hanging above the dining-room floor. **Known for:** ingredients harvested for peak ripeness; rooftop bar for craft cocktails and bar bites; see-and-be-seen dining. [$] *Average main: $43* ✉ *106 Matheson St., Healdsburg* ✥ *Near Healdsburg Ave.* ☎ *707/723–1106* 🌐 *www.thematheson.com* 🕒 *No lunch.*

★ SingleThread Farm Restaurant

$$$$ | **ECLECTIC** | The seasonally oriented Japanese dinners known as kaiseki inspire the 10-course prix-fixe vegetarian, meat, and seafood menu at the spare, elegant restaurant—redwood walls, walnut tables, mesquite-tile floors, muted-gray yarn-thread panels—of internationally renowned culinary artists Katina and Kyle Connaughton (she farms, he cooks). As Katina describes the endeavor, the micro-seasons of their nearby farm plus SingleThread's rooftop garden of fruit trees and greens dictate Kyle's rarefied fare, prepared in a theatrically lit open kitchen. **Known for:** impeccable wine pairings; dishes customized based on guests' preferences; instinctive service. [$] *Average main: $425* ✉ *131 North St., Healdsburg* ✥ *At Center St.* ☎ *707/723–4646* 🌐 *www.singlethreadfarms.com* 🕒 *Closed Tues. and Wed. No lunch.*

Hotels

★ Harmon Guest House

$$$$ | **HOTEL** | A boutique sibling of the h2hotel two doors away, this downtown delight that debuted in 2018 earned instant LEED Gold status for its eco-friendly construction and operating practices. **Pros:** rooftop bar's cocktails, food menu, and views; connecting rooms and suites; similarly designed sister property h2hotel two doors south. **Cons:** minor room-to-room noise bleed-through; room gadgetry may flummox some guests; minimum-stay requirements some weekends. [$] *Rooms from: $519* ✉ *227 Healdsburg Ave., Healdsburg* ☎ *707/922–5262* 🌐 *harmonguesthouse.com* 🛏 *39 rooms* 🍴 *Free Breakfast.*

★ Hotel Trio Healdsburg

$$ | **HOTEL** | Named for the three major wine appellations—the Russian River, Dry Creek, and Alexander Valleys—whose confluence it's near, this Residence Inn by Marriott 1¼ miles north of Healdsburg Plaza caters to families and extended-stay business travelers with spacious rooms equipped with full kitchens. **Pros:** cute robot room service; full kitchens; rooms sleep up to four or six. **Cons:** 30-minute walk to downtown; corporate feel; pricey in high season. [$] *Rooms from: $282* ✉ *110 Dry Creek Rd., Healdsburg* ☎ *707/433–4000* 🌐 *www.hoteltrio.com* 🛏 *122 rooms* 🍴 *Free Breakfast.*

★ Montage Healdsburg

$$$$ | **RESORT** | Its bungalow-like guest rooms deftly layered into oak- and Cabernet-studded hills a few miles north of Healdsburg Plaza, this architectural sensation that opened fully in 2021 significantly upped Sonoma County's ultraluxury game. **Pros:** vineyard views from spa, restaurant, and swimming pool; outdoor living spaces with daybeds and fire pits; recreational options on-property or nearby. **Cons:** expensive year-round; hefty resort fee; car trip required

for off-property visits. $ *Rooms from: $1,000* ⊠ *100 Montage Way, Healdsburg* ☎ *707/979–9000* ⊕ *www.montagehotels. com/healdsburg* ⌘ *130 bungalows* ⦿ *No Meals.*

★ River Belle Inn

$$$$ | **B&B/INN** | An 1875 Victorian with a storied past and a glorious colonnaded wraparound porch anchors this boutique Russian River property affiliated since 2022 with SingleThread Farms. **Pros:** riverfront location near tasting rooms; cooked-to-order full breakfasts; attention to detail. **Cons:** about a mile from Healdsburg Plaza; minimum-stay requirement on weekends; lacks pool, fitness center, and other amenities. $ *Rooms from: $425* ⊠ *68 Front St., Healdsburg* ☎ *707/955–5724* ⊕ *www.riverbelleinn. com* ⌘ *11 rooms* ⦿ *Free Breakfast.*

▼ Nightlife

★ Lo & Behold Bar and Kitchen

BARS | Two cocktail all-stars and a chef with a fascination for international comfort food opened this bar where patrons wash down fish tacos, kimchi noodles, crispy pork spare ribs, and chicken tenders with craft cocktails that include the Phatty Margarita ("phattened" up with avocado and coconut oil). Good beer and wine list, too. Everything's best enjoyed out back on the patio. ⊠ *214 Healdsburg Ave., Healdsburg* ✛ *Near Mill St.* ☎ *707/756–5021* ⊕ *loandbeholdca.com* ⊙ *Closed Tues. and Wed.*

⬤ Shopping

ART GALLERIES
★ Gallery Lulo

ART GALLERIES | A collaboration between a local artist and jewelry maker and a Danish-born curator, this gallery presents changing exhibits of jewelry, sculpture, and objets d'art. ⊠ *303 Center St., Healdsburg* ✛ *At Plaza St.* ☎ *707/433–7533* ⊕ *www.gallerylulo.com.*

FOOD AND WINE
Dry Creek General Store

FOOD | For breakfasts, sandwiches, bread, cheeses, and picnic supplies, stop by the general store, established in 1881 and still a popular spot for locals to hang out on the porch or in the bar. Beer and wine are also for sale, along with artisanal sodas, ciders, and juices. ⊠ *3495 Dry Creek Rd., Healdsburg* ✛ *At Lambert Bridge Rd.* ☎ *707/433–4171* ⊕ *www. drycreekgeneralstore1881.com.*

🏃 Activities

BICYCLING
Getaway Adventures / Wine Country Bikes

BIKING | This shop several blocks southeast of Healdsburg Plaza is perfectly located for setting up single or multiday treks into the Dry Creek and Russian River valleys by bike, kayak, or both. Private and group tours might include winery stops. If you prefer to explore on your own, you can rent equipment. ⊠ *61 Front St., Healdsburg* ✛ *At Hudson St.* ☎ *800/499–2453* ⊕ *getawayadventures. com* ⊟ *Daily rentals from $39 per day, full-day tours from $144.*

SPAS
★ A Simple Touch Spa

SPAS | Skilled in Swedish, deep-tissue, sports, and other massage modalities, this soothing but unpretentious day spa's therapists routinely receive post-session raves. The most popular treatment involves heated basalt stones applied to the client's body, followed by a massage of choice. Foot reflexology, reiki, and facials are among the other specialties. ■**TIP→ Couples can enjoy any of the massages performed side-by-side by two therapists.** ⊠ *239 Center St., Suite C, Healdsburg* ✛ *Near Matheson St.* ☎ *707/433–6856* ⊕ *asimpletouchspa.com* ⊟ *Treatments from $60.*

Geyserville

8 miles north of Healdsburg.

Several high-profile Alexander Valley AVA wineries, including the splashy Francis Ford Coppola Winery, can be found in the town of Geyserville, a small part of which stretches west of U.S. 101 into northern Dry Creek. Not long ago this was a dusty farm town, and downtown Geyserville retains its rural character, but the restaurants, shops, and tasting rooms along the short main drag hint at Geyserville's growing sophistication.

GETTING HERE AND AROUND

From Healdsburg, the quickest route to downtown Geyserville is north on U.S. 101 to the Highway 128/Geyserville exit. Turn right at the stop sign onto Geyserville Avenue and follow the road north to the small downtown. For a more scenic drive, head north from Healdsburg Plaza along Healdsburg Avenue. About 3 miles north, jog west (left) for a few hundred feet onto Lytton Springs Road, then turn north (right) onto Geyserville Avenue. In town the avenue merges with Highway 128. Sonoma County Transit buses serve Geyserville from downtown Healdsburg.

⊙ Sights

Bannister Wines

WINERY | Brook Bannister's appreciation for his mother's wine-industry achievements inspired him to, as he puts it, forsake his career as a furniture maker "to keep her dream alive." That dream, which Martha "Marty" Bannister initiated in 1989, was to make layered, graceful ageworthy wines. Brook continues this tradition with the core lineup of Chardonnay, Riesling, several Pinot Noirs, and Zinfandel supplemented in recent years by wines from lesser-known grapes. In 2022, Bannister Wines opened a gallery-style tasting room in the 1901 Geyserville Bank structure. Full of stories all its own, it's a fanciful space to sample Brook's well-crafted wines and learn more about this multigenerational labor of love. ⊠ *21035 Geyserville Ave., Geyserville* ✛ *At Hwy. 128* ☏ *707/387–0124* ⊕ *bannisterwines.com* ⊠ *Tastings from $35* ⊙ *Closed Tues. and Wed.*

Francis Ford Coppola Winery

WINERY | The fun at what the film director has called his "wine wonderland," since 2021 owned by Delicato Family Wines, is all in the excess. You may find it hard to resist having your photo snapped standing next to Don Corleone's desk from *The Godfather* or beside other movie memorabilia. A bandstand reminiscent of one in *The Godfather Part II* is the centerpiece of a large pool area where you can rent a changing room, complete with shower, and lounge poolside, perhaps ordering food from the adjacent café. A more elaborate restaurant, Rustic, overlooks the vineyards. As for the wines, the excess continues in the cellar, where the team produces several dozen single-varietal bottlings and blends. You don't need an appointment to taste at the bar but do for seated experiences. All memorabilia may not be on display when you visit—items are sometimes on loan. ⊠ *300 Via Archimedes, Geyserville* ✛ *Off U.S. 101* ☏ *707/857–1400* ⊕ *www.franciscoppolawinery.com* ⊠ *Tastings from $30.*

★ Robert Young Estate Winery

WINERY | Panoramic Alexander Valley views unfold at Scion House, the stylish yet informal knoll-top tasting space of this longtime Geyserville grower. The first Youngs began farming this land in the mid-1800s, raising cattle and growing wheat, prunes, and other crops. In the 1960s the late Robert Young, of the third generation, began cultivating grapes, eventually planting two Chardonnay clones now named for him. Grapes from them go into the Area 27 Chardonnay, among the best whites. The reds—small-lot Cabernet Sauvignons plus individual bottlings of Cabernet Franc, Malbec, Merlot, and Petit Verdot—shine even brighter. Tastings at Scion House, named for the fourth generation, whose members built on Robert Young's legacy and established the winery, are by appointment. Call ahead for same-day reservations. ■ **TIP→ Cab fanatics should consider the Ultimate Cabernet Lovers Experience of top-tier estate wines.** ✉ *5120 Red Winery Rd., Geyserville* ✣ *Off Hwy. 128* ☎ *707/431–4811* 🌐 *www.ryew.com* 🎟 *Tastings from $40* ⏲ *Closed Tues.*

★ Zialena

WINERY | Sister-and-brother team Lisa and Mark Mazzoni (she runs the business, he makes the wines) debuted their small winery's first vintage in 2014, but their Italian American family's wine-making heritage stretches back more than a century. Named for the siblings' great aunt Lena, known for her hospitality, Zialena specializes in estate-grown Zinfandel and Cabernet Sauvignon, some of whose lush mouthfeel derives from techniques Mark absorbed while working for the international consultant Philippe Melka. The Zin and Cab grapes, along with Chardonnay and Sangiovese for the seductive rosé, come from the 120-acre Mazzoni Vineyard, from which larger labels like Jordan also source fruit. Tastings are by appointment only, with same-day visits often possible. ✉ *21112 River Rd., Geyserville* ✣ *Off Hwy. 128* ☎ *707/955–5992* 🌐 *www.zialena.com* 🎟 *Tastings from $30.*

🍴 Restaurants

★ Cyrus

$$$$ | **MODERN AMERICAN** | A decade after his beloved, same-named Healdsburg restaurant closed, celebrity chef Douglas Keane of *Top Chef Masters* and other fame reopened a "2.0" version inside an 8,000-square-foot steel, glass, and concrete structure set in an Alexander Valley vineyard. Keane bills his prix-fixe culinary experience as a "dining journey," with guests (couples'-rate only; single diners charged double) changing rooms a few times for multiple internationally inspired courses based on hyper-seasonal mostly Northern California ingredients. **Known for:** reservations (essential) released in monthly blocks two months in advance; architectural stunner in a rural setting; Bubbles Lounge for cocktails and small bites à la carte (no reservations). [$] *Average main: $295* ✉ *275 Hwy. 128, Geyserville* ✣ *Near Railroad Ave.* ☎ *707/318–0379* 🌐 *www.cyrusrestaurant.com* ⏲ *Closed Mon.–Wed. No lunch.*

Diavola Pizzeria & Salumeria

$$ | **ITALIAN** | A dining area with hardwood floors, a pressed-tin ceiling, and exposed-brick walls provides a fitting setting for the rustic cuisine at this Geyserville mainstay. Chef Dino Bugica studied with artisanal cooks in Italy before opening this restaurant specializing in wood-fired pizzas and house-cured meats, with a few salads and meaty main courses rounding out the menu. **Known for:** talented chef; prime rib sandwich for lunch, chicken under a brick for dinner; outdoor patio. [$] *Average main: $26* ✉ *21021 Geyserville Ave., Geyserville* ✣ *At Hwy. 128* ☎ *707/814–0111* 🌐 *www.diavolapizzeria.com.*

Forestville

13 miles southwest of Healdsburg.

To experience the Russian River Valley AVA's climate and rusticity, follow the river's westward course to the town of Forestville, home to a highly regarded restaurant and inn and a few wineries producing Pinot Noir from the Russian River Valley and well beyond.

GETTING HERE AND AROUND

To reach Forestville from U.S. 101, drive west from the River Road exit north of Santa Rosa. From Healdsburg, follow Westside Road west to River Road and then continue west. Sonoma County Transit buses serve Forestville.

Sights

★ Hartford Family Winery

WINERY | Pinot Noir lovers appreciate the subtle differences in the wines Hartford's team crafts from grapes grown in several Sonoma County AVAs, along with fruit from nearby Marin and Mendocino Counties and Oregon. The winery also produces highly rated Chardonnays and old-vine Zinfandels. If the weather's good, enjoy a flight on the patio outside the main winery building. At private library tastings, guests sip current and older vintages. All visits are by appointment; call ahead on the same day. ⊠ *8075 Martinelli Rd., Forestville ✛ Off Hwy. 116 or River Rd.* ☎ *707/904–6950* ⊕ *www.hartfordwines. com* ⊠ *Tastings from $40.*

★ Joseph Jewell Wines

WINERY | Pinot Noirs from the Russian River Valley and Humboldt County to the north are the strong suit of this winery sourcing from prestigious vineyards like Bucher and Hallberg Ranch. Owner-winemaker Adrian Manspeaker, a Humboldt native, spearheaded the foray into Pinot Noir grown in the coastal redwood country. His storefront tasting room in downtown Forestville (visits by appointment; walk-ins welcomed when possible) provides the opportunity to experience what's unique about the varietal's next Northern California frontier. Manspeaker also makes two Zinfandels; lighter wines include two Chardonnays, Pinot Gris, Vermentino, a sparkling Vermentino, and rosé of Pinot Noir. ■TIP→ **From spring to mid-fall, a private wine educator accompanies small parties on engaging vineyard tastings involving a tour or picnic lunch.** ⊠ *6542 Front St., Forestville ✛ Near 1st St.* ☎ *707/820–1621* ⊕ *www.josephjewell.com* ⊠ *Tastings from $35* ☉ *Closed Mon.–Wed.*

Hotels

★ The Farmhouse Inn

$$$$ | B&B/INN | With a farmhouse-meets-modern-loft aesthetic, this low-key but upscale getaway with a pale-yellow exterior contains spacious rooms filled with king-size four-poster beds, whirlpool tubs, and hillside-view terraces. **Pros:** on-site Farmhouse Inn Restaurant (fine dining) and Farmstand (upscale casual); luxury bath products; full-service spa. **Cons:** mild road noise audible in rooms closest to the street; two-night minimum on weekends; pricey, especially during high season. $ *Rooms from: $1,182* ⊠ *7871 River Rd., Forestville* ☎ *707/887–3300, 800/464–6642* ⊕ *www.farmhouseinn. com* ⇆ *25 rooms* ⦿ *Free Breakfast.*

Activities

Burke's Canoe Trips

CANOEING & ROWING | You'll get a real feel for the Russian River's flora and fauna on a leisurely 10-mile paddle downstream from Burke's to Guerneville. A shuttle bus returns you to your car at the end of the journey, which is best taken on a weekday—summer weekends can be crowded and raucous. ⊠ *8600 River Rd., Forestville ✛ At Mirabel Rd.* ☎ *707/887–1222* ⊕ *www.burkescanoetrips.com* ⊠ *From $55 (kayak), $90 (canoe)* ☉ *Closed mid-Oct.–late May.*

Guerneville

7 miles northwest of Forestville, 15 miles southwest of Healdsburg.

Guerneville's tourist demographic has evolved over the years: Bay Area families in the 1950s, lesbians and gays starting in the 1970s, and these days a mix of both groups, plus techies and outdoorsy types—with coast redwoods and the Russian River always central to the town's appeal. The area's most famous winery is Korbel Champagne

Cellars, established nearly a century and a half ago. Even older are the stands of trees that except on the coldest winter days make Armstrong Redwoods State Natural Reserve such a perfect respite from wine tasting.

GETTING HERE AND AROUND

To get to Guerneville from Healdsburg, follow Westside Road south to River Road and turn west. From Forestville, head west on Highway 116; alternatively, you can head north on Mirabel Road to River Road and then head west. Sonoma County Transit buses serve Guerneville.

Sights

★ Armstrong Redwoods State Natural Reserve

STATE/PROVINCIAL PARK | **FAMILY** | Here's your best opportunity in the western Wine Country to wander amid *Sequoia sempervirens,* also known as coast redwood trees. The oldest example in this 805-acre state park, the Colonel Armstrong Tree, is thought to be more than 1,400 years old. A half mile from the parking lot, the tree is easily accessible, and you can hike a long way into the forest before things get too hilly. ■ **TIP→ During hot summer days, Armstrong Redwoods's tall trees help the park keep its cool.** ✉ *17000 Armstrong Woods Rd., Guerneville* ✥ *Off River Rd.* ☎ *707/869–2015* 🌐 *www.parks.ca.gov* 🎟 *$10 per vehicle, free to pedestrians and bicyclists.*

Restaurants

★ boon eat+drink

$$ | **AMERICAN** | A casual storefront restaurant on Guerneville's main drag, boon eat+drink has a menu built around salads, smallish shareable plates, and entrées that might include a vegan bowl, chili-braised pork shoulder, and local cod with shiitakes. Like many of chef-owner Crista Luedtke's dishes, the signature polenta lasagna—creamy ricotta salata cheese and polenta served on greens sautéed in garlic, all of it floating upon a spicy marinara sauce—deviates significantly from the lasagna norm but succeeds on its own merits. **Known for:** adventurous culinary sensibility; Sonoma County wine selection; sister restaurant Brot for German cuisine in same block. [$] *Average main: $25* ✉ *16248 Main St., Guerneville* ✥ *At Church St.* ☎ *707/869–0780* 🌐 *eatatboon.com* 🕒 *Closed Mon. and Tues.*

Hotels

★ Dawn Ranch

$$$ | **RESORT** | A historic, woodsy 15-acre property that reopened in 2022 as a deluxe, reconnect-with-nature variation on mid-century roadside resorts, Dawn Ranch provides accommodations ranging from one-room, cedar-shingled cabins and larger "chalets" with sitting areas to a cottage and a bungalow. **Pros:** high-quality beds, linens, and bath products; emphasis on unplugging and unwinding; on-site restaurant and full bar with live music some nights. **Cons:** no TVs or phones in rooms (but solid Wi-Fi); some cabins are small; two-night minimum for some stays. [$] *Rooms from: $399* ✉ *16467 Hwy. 116, Guerneville* ☎ *707/869–0656* 🌐 *www.dawnranch.com* 🛏 *53 rooms* 🍴 *No Meals.*

Sebastopol

14 miles southeast of Guerneville.

A stroll through downtown in Sebastopol—formerly known more for Gravenstein apples than for grapes but these days a burgeoning wine hub—reveals glimpses of the past and, perhaps, the future, too. Many hippies settled here in the '60s and '70s and, as the old Crosby, Stills, Nash & Young song goes, they taught their children well: the town remains steadfastly countercultural.

Iron Horse produces sparklers that make history.

GETTING HERE AND AROUND

From Guerneville, take Highway 116 south. From Santa Rosa, head west on Highway 12. Sonoma County Transit buses serve Sebastopol.

⊙ Sights

★ The Barlow

MARKET | A multibuilding complex on a 12½-acre former apple-cannery site, The Barlow celebrates Sonoma County's "maker" culture with tenants who produce or sell wine, beer, spirits, crafts, clothing, art, and artisanal foods. The anchor wine tenant, Kosta Browne, receives only club members and allocation-list guests, but other tasting rooms are open to the public, among them Region wine bar, which promotes small Sonoma County producers. Crooked Goat Brewing makes and sells ales, Golden State Cider pours apple-driven beverages, and you can have a nip of vodka, gin, sloe gin, or wheat and rye whiskey at Spirit Works Distillery. Over at Fern Bar, the zero-proof (as in nonalcoholic)

cocktails entice as much as the traditional ones. The bar serves food, as do Blue Ridge Kitchen (Southern-influenced comfort fare), Acme Pizza, Red Bird Bakery (excellent breakfast and lunch fare), Sushi Koshō, and the affiliated Oyster Bar, and a few other spots. ⊠ 6770 McKinley St., Sebastopol ✛ At Morris St., off Hwy. 12 ☎ 707/824–5600 ⊕ www.thebarlow.net ☎ Complex free; fees for tasting.

★ Dutton-Goldfield Winery

WINERY | An avid cyclist whose previous credits include developing the wine-making program at what's now Hartford Family Winery, Dan Goldfield teamed up with fifth-generation farmer Steve Dutton to establish this small operation devoted to cool-climate wines. Goldfield modestly strives to take Dutton's meticulously farmed fruit and "make the winemaker unnoticeable," but what impresses the most about these wines, which include Chardonnay, Pinot Blanc, Pinot Noir, and Zinfandel, is their sheer artistry. Among the ones to seek out are the Angel Camp Pinot Noir, from Anderson

Valley (Mendocino County) grapes, and the Morelli Lane Zinfandel, from fruit grown on the remaining 1.8 acres of an 1880s vineyard Goldfield helped revive. Lauded as a top Sonoma County winery by *Wine & Spirits* and *Food & Wine* magazines, Dutton-Goldfield is open by appointment but accepts walk-ins when possible. ✉ *3100 Gravenstein Hwy. N/ Hwy. 116, Sebastopol* ✣ *At Graton Rd.* ☎ *707/827–3600* 🌐 *www.duttongoldfield.com* 🎫 *Tastings from $40.*

★ Iron Horse Vineyards

WINERY | A meandering one-lane road leads to this winery known for its sparkling wines and estate Chardonnays and Pinot Noirs. The sparklers have made history: Ronald Reagan served them at his summit meetings with Mikhail Gorbachev; George H. W. Bush took some along to Moscow for treaty talks; and Barack Obama included them at official state dinners. Despite Iron Horse's brushes with fame, a casual rusticity prevails at its outdoor tasting area (large heaters keep things comfortable on chilly days), which gazes out on acres of rolling, vine-covered hills. Tastings are by appointment only. ✉ *9786 Ross Station Rd., Sebastopol* ✣ *Off Hwy. 116* ☎ *707/887–1507* 🌐 *www.ironhorsevineyards.com* 🎫 *Tastings from $35.*

🍴 Restaurants

Handline

$$ | **MODERN AMERICAN** | **FAMILY** | Sebastopol's former Foster's Freeze location, now a 21st-century fast-food palace, won design awards for its rusted-steel frame and translucent panel-like windows. The menu, a paean to coastal California cuisine, includes oysters raw and grilled, fish tacos, ceviche, tostadas, three burgers (beef, vegetarian, and fish), and, honoring the location's previous incarnation, chocolate and vanilla soft-serve ice cream. **Known for:** upscale comfort food; outdoor patio; sustainable seafood and other ingredients. [$] *Average main: $17* ✉ *935 Gravenstein Hwy. S, Sebastopol* ✣ *Near Hutchins Ave.* ☎ *707/827–3744* 🌐 *www.handline.com.*

Ramen Gaijin

$$ | **JAPANESE** | Inside a tall-ceilinged, brick-walled, industrial-looking space with reclaimed wood from a coastal building backing the bar, the chefs at Ramen Gaijin turn out richly flavored ramen bowls brimming with pork belly, wood ear mushrooms, seaweed, and other well-proportioned ingredients. *Izakaya* (Japanese pub grub) dishes like *donburi* (meat and vegetables over rice) are another specialty, like the ramen made from mostly local proteins and produce. **Known for:** artisanal cocktails, beer, wine, and cider; gluten-free, vegetarian options on request; karaage (fried chicken) and other small plates. [$] *Average main: $21* ✉ *6948 Sebastopol Ave., Sebastopol* ✣ *Near Main St.* ☎ *707/827–3609* 🌐 *www.ramengaijin.com* 🕒 *Closed Sun. and Mon.*

Santa Rosa

6 miles east of Sebastopol, 55 miles north of San Francisco.

Urban Santa Rosa isn't as popular with tourists as many Wine Country destinations—not surprising, as there are more office parks than wineries within its limits. Still, this hardworking town has a couple of interesting cultural offerings and a few noteworthy restaurants and vineyards. The city's chain motels and hotels can be handy if everything else is booked, especially since Santa Rosa is roughly equidistant from Sonoma, Healdsburg, and the western Russian River Valley, three of Sonoma County's most popular wine-tasting destinations.

GETTING HERE AND AROUND

From Sebastopol, drive east on Highway 12. From San Francisco, cross the Golden Gate Bridge and continue north on U.S. 101. Santa Rosa's hotels, restaurants, and ieries are spread over a wide area; ⋯ctor in extra time when driving around the city, especially during rush hours. From San Francisco or Marin County, take Golden Gate Transit Bus 101. Sonoma County Transit buses serve Santa Rosa and the surrounding area.

◉ Sights

Balletto Vineyards
WINERY | A few decades ago Balletto was known more for quality produce than grapes, but the new millennium saw vineyards emerge as the core business. About 90% of the fruit from the family's 800-plus acres goes to other wineries, with the remainder destined for Balletto's estate wines. The house style is light on the oak, high in acidity, and low in alcohol content, a combination yielding exceptionally food-friendly wines. Sipping Pinot Gris, rosé of Pinot Noir, or a brut rosé sparkler on the outdoor patio can feel transcendent on a warm day, though the Chardonnays and Pinot Noirs steal the show. The winery also makes Gewürztraminer, Sauvignon Blanc, Syrah, and Zinfandel. ⊠ *5700 Occidental Rd., Santa Rosa* ✛ *2½ miles west of Hwy. 12* ☎ *707/568–2455* ⊕ *www.ballettovineyards.com* ⊡ *Tastings from $25.*

★ Benovia Winery
WINERY | Winemaker-partner Mike Sullivan's Chardonnays and Pinot Noirs would taste marvelous even in a toolshed, but guests to Benovia's unassumingly chic Russian River Valley ranch house will never know. Appointment-only tastings of his acclaimed wines—Benovia also produces Grenache, Zinfandel, and Cabernet Sauvignon—take place in the brown-hued living room or on the open-air patio. From either vantage point, views of the estate Martaella Vineyard all the way to Mt. St. Helena draw the eye. Wine educators leading vineyard tours focus on Benovia's earth-friendly farming practices; a production tour tracks the wine-making process from vineyard to barrel to glass.

Sullivan's handling of two Chardonnays from Martinelli-family grapes typifies his minimalistic approach. He subtly emphasizes minerality in a wine from the Three Sisters Vineyard in the coastal Fort Ross–Seaview AVA. By contrast, a hint of California ripeness emerges in La Pommeraie, from Zio Tony Ranch in the warmer Russian River Valley. ⊠ *3339 Hartman La., Santa Rosa* ✛ *Off Piner Rd.* ☎ *707/921–1040* ⊕ *benoviawinery.com* ⊡ *Tastings from $45.*

★ Charles M. Schulz Museum
ART MUSEUM | FAMILY | Fans of Snoopy and Charlie Brown will love this museum dedicated to the late Charles M. Schulz, who lived his last three decades in Santa Rosa. Permanent installations include a re-creation of the cartoonist's studio, and temporary exhibits often focus on a particular theme in his work. ■TIP➔ **Children and adults can take a stab at creating cartoons in the Education Room.** ⊠ *2301 Hardies La., Santa Rosa* ✛ *At W. Steele La.* ☎ *707/579–4452* ⊕ *www.schulzmuseum.org* ⊡ *$14* ⊗ *Closed Tues. early Sept.–late May.*

Martinelli Winery
WINERY | In a century-old hop barn with the telltale triple towers, Martinelli has the feel of a traditional country store, but sophisticated wines are made here. The winery's reputation rests on its complex Pinot Noirs, Syrahs, and Zinfandels, including the Jackass Hill Vineyard Zin, made with grapes from vines planted mainly in the 1880s by the current owners' ancestors. Noted winemaker Helen Turley set the Martinelli style—fruit-forward, easy on the oak, reined-in tannins—in the 1990s, and the 21st-century team continues this approach. Tastings held (weather permitting) on a vineyard's-edge terrace survey the current releases. All visits are by appointment, best made online. ■TIP➔ **Terrace and Hop Barn tastings survey the portfolio, but serious wine drinkers should consider the Collector's Flight of top-drawer**

Chardonnays, Pinot Noirs, and Zinfandels. ✉ *3360 River Rd.* ✣ *East of Olivet Rd.* ☎ *707/525–0570, 800/346–1627* 🌐 *www.martinelliwinery.com* 🎟 *Tastings from $35.*

★ Safari West

WILDLIFE REFUGE | FAMILY | An unexpected bit of wilderness in the Wine Country, this preserve with African wildlife covers 400 acres. Begin your visit with a stroll around enclosures housing lemurs, cheetahs, giraffes, and rare birds like the brightly colored scarlet ibis. Next, climb with your guide onto open-air vehicles that spend about two hours combing the expansive property, where more than 80 species—including gazelles, cape buffalo, antelope, wildebeests, and zebras—inhabit the hillsides. **■ TIP➔ If you'd like to extend your stay, lodging in semi-glam Botswana-made tent cabins is available.** ✉ *3115 Porter Creek Rd., Santa Rosa* ✣ *Off Mark West Springs Rd.* ☎ *707/579–2551, 800/616–2695* 🌐 *www.safariwest.com* 🎟 *From $105 Sept.–May, from $126 June–Aug.*

🍴 Restaurants

★ Walter Hansel Wine & Bistro

$$$$ | FRENCH | Tabletop linens and lights softly twinkling from this ruby-red roadhouse restaurant's low wooden ceiling raise expectations the Parisian-style bistro cuisine consistently exceeds. A starter of cheeses or French onion soup awakens the palate for entrées like chicken cordon bleu, steak au poivre, or seafood dishes that might include scallops in a rich yet somehow delicate gastrique or subtly sauced wild Alaskan halibut. **Known for:** romantic setting for classic cuisine; prix-fixe option; vegan and vegetarian dishes. [$] *Average main: $38* ✉ *3535 Guerneville Rd., Santa Rosa* ✣ *At Willowside Rd., 6 miles northwest of downtown* ☎ *707/546–6462* 🌐 *walterhanselbistro.com* ⏲ *Closed Mon. and Tues. No lunch.*

The Spinster Sisters

$$$ | MODERN AMERICAN | The versatile chef of this concrete-and-glass grazing spot anchoring the SOFA Santa Rosa Arts District satisfies her diverse devotees with American standards and playful variations on international cuisines. Separated on the menu into three main categories—ocean, garden, and pasture, each with a selection of appetizers, salads, and entrées—the dishes change often but might include trout with French lentils, hanger steak with kale gratin, Tuscan-style St. Louis ribs, and mushroom hand pie with leeks and ricotta. **Known for:** thought-provoking flavors; dessert pastries; local and international wines. [$] *Average main: $31* ✉ *401 S. A St., Santa Rosa* ✣ *At Sebastopol Ave.* ☎ *707/528–7100* 🌐 *thespinstersisters.com* ⏲ *Closed Sun. and Mon. No lunch.*

🛏 Hotels

★ Vintners Resort

$$$ | HOTEL | With a countryside location, a reserved sense of style, and spacious rooms with comfortable beds, the Vintners Resort further seduces with a slew of amenities and a scenic vineyard landscape. **Pros:** café and John Ash & Co. restaurant; vineyard jogging and walking path; facials, massages at Vi La Vita spa. **Cons:** occasional noise from adjacent events center; trips to Healdsburg or downtown Santa Rosa require a car; pricey on summer and fall weekends. [$] *Rooms from: $364* ✉ *4350 Barnes Rd., Santa Rosa* ☎ *800/421–2584* 🌐 *www.vintnersresort.com* 🛏 *78 rooms* 🍽 *No Meals.*

Photo Credits

Front Cover: Art Kowalsky / Alamy Stock Photo [**Description:** Victorian houses in Alamo square, San Francisco]. **Back cover, from left to right:** Jaspe/Dreamstime. Robert Zehetmayer/Dreamstime. Lunamarina/Dreamstime. **Spine:** Holbox / Shutterstock. **Interior, from left to right:** IM_photo/Shutterstock (1). Travelview/Shutterstock (2-3). Pius Lee/ Shutterstock (5). **Chapter 1: Experience San Francisco:** F11photo/Shutterstock (6-7). Scott Wilson/Alamy Stock Photo (8-9). Ekaterina Pokrovsky/Shutterstock (9). Jill Krueger (9). Canyalcin/Shutterstock (10). Photoexhibittimallen/Dreamstime(10). Steve Wood/Shutterstock (10). Pung/Shutterstock (10). Dan Henson/Shutterstock (11). Matt Boylo/Shutterstock (11). Maciej Bledowski/Shutterstock (12). Della Huff/Alamy (12). Gene X Hwang/Orange Photography (12). Snap A Skyline/Shutterstock (12). Zachary Frank/Alamy (13). Courtesy of Tonga Room (14). TJ Muzeni (14). TJ Muzeni (14). Eye35 stock/Alamy (14). Dibrova/Shutterstock (15). Engel Ching/Shutterstock (15). Sundry Photography/Shutterstock (16). Stockimo/Shutterstock (16). Image Professionals GmbH / Alamy Stock Photo (16). Sundry Photography/Shutterstock (16). Zack Frank/Shutterstock (17). Marc Fiorito - Gamma Nine Photography (22). Courtesy of Bluxome Street Winery (22). Courtesy of Boudin Bakery (22). SFCVB/Jack Hollingsworth (23). Courtesy of Blue Bottle Coffee (23). Jill Krueger (24). Jemny/Shutterstock (24). ESB Professional/Shutterstock (24). TJ Muzeni (24). Eug Png/Shutterstock (25). Kropic1/ Shutterstock (25). MNStudio/Shutterstock (25). Morenovel/Shutterstock (25). Courtesy of Kabuki Springs & Spa (26). Peachpappa/ Dreamstime (26). Peachpappa/Dreamstime (26). Frank Farm/ Flickr (26). Alison Taggart-Barone/Parks Conservancy (26). JhvePhoto/ Shutterstock (27). Canadastock/Shutterstock (33). Pius Lee/Shutterstock (35). San Francisco Municipal Railway Historical Archives (36). **Chapter 3: SoMa, Mission Bay, and Dogpatch:** Nounpusher Photography/Shutterstock (63). EQRoy/Shutterstock (69). Sundry Photography/ Shutterstock (77). Hapabapa/iStock (79). **Chapter 4: Union Square, Civic Center, and the Tenderloin:** V_E/Shutterstock (83). Santirf/ Dreamstime (87). Iv-olga/S hutterstock (99). Larry Zhou/Shutterstock (101). Agwilson/Shutterstock (102). **Chapter 5: The Waterfront:** Rramirez125/iStockphoto (105). Checubus/Shutterstock (110). IM_photo/ Shutterstock (113). f11photo/Shutterstock (117). Daniel DeSlover/ Shutterstock (118). PopperFoto/ Alamy (119). Wikipedia (119). Public Domain (119). Eliza Snow/iStockphoto (121). Steve Rosset/Shutterstock (122). **Chapter 6: Chinatown and North Beach:** F11photo/Shutterstock (135). Kongomonkey/ Dreamstime (138). Cura Photography/ Shutterstock (143). Arnold Genthe (Public Domain) (144). Library of Congress Prints and Photographs Division (144). Sandor Balatoni (145). Library of Congress (145). Michael Warwick/Shutterstock (146). Tinamou/Dreamstime (149). Yhelfman/ iStockphoto (151). **Chapter 7: Nob Hill and Russian Hill:** F11photo/Dreamstime (159). Chris LaBasco/Shutterstock (164). **Chapter 8: Pacific Heights and Japantown:** Della Huff/Alamy (173). Andreistanescu/Dreamstime (174). Lunamarina/Dreamstime (175). Checubus/ Dreamstime (175). Rramirez125/ iStockphoto (179). **Chapter 9: The Marina and the Presidio:** Andrew Zarivny/Shutterstock (193). ESB Professional/Shutterstock (194). Phitha Tanpairoj/ Shutterstock (195). Steve Holderfield/ Shutterstock (195). Ivanova Ksenia/Shutterstock (211). **Chapter 10: The Western Shoreline:** Robert Holmes (213). Rteimages/Shutterstock (218). **Chapter 11: Golden Gate Park:** California Travel and Tourism Co. (225) Michael Urmann/ Shutterstock (226). Marina Hose/Shutterstock (227). Zarcar/Shutterstock (228). Andreas Koeberl/Shutterstock (228). CO Leong/Shutterstock (228). STYimages/Shutterstock (229). Robert Holmes (230). Jack Hollingsworth (231). Robert Holmes (231). Mliu92/Flickr (231). Robert Holmes (232). Robert Holmes (232). Janet Fullwood (233). Janet Fullwood (233). Donna & Andrew/Flickr (234). Robert Holmes (234). Andrew Zarivny/Shutterstock (234). **Chapter 12: The Haight, the Castro, Hayes Valley, and Noe Valley:** Luciano Mortula-LGM/ Shutterstock (235). Sepavo/Dreamstime (253). **Chapter 13: Mission District, Bernal Heights, and Potrero Hill:** Kārlis Dambrāns/ Flickr (255). Held Juergen/Alamy (259). Jejim/Shutterstock (263). **Chapter 14: The Bay Area:** Jon Chica/Shutterstock (275). Sundry Photography/iStockkphoto (284). Donovan Jugarap/Shutterstock (291). Topseller/Shutterstock (307). S.Greg Panosian/ iStockphoto (315). Margaret.Wiktor/Shutterstock (343). **Chapter 15: Napa and Sonoma:** Getty Images/iStockphoto (345). Robert Holmes (356). Kevin miller/ iStockphoto (357). Far Niente Dolce Nickel & Nickel (357). Philippe Roy / Alamy (358). Agence Images / Alamy (358). Cephas Picture Library / Alamy (358). Juancat/Shutterstock (359). Roibu/Shutterstock (359). Nickolay Stanev/Shutterstock (359). Yakov Oskanov/ Shutterstock (359). Cavan-Images/Shutterstock (359). Mikeledray/Shutterstock (359). Steve Adamson/Shutterstock (359). Warren H. White (359). Far Niente+Dolce+Nickel & Nickel (368). Smcfeeters/Dreamstime (377). Benziger Family Winery (387). Laurence G. Sterling/Iron Horse Vineyards (401). **About Our Writers.** All photos are courtesy of the writers.

*Every effort has been made to trace the copyright holders, and we apologize in advance for any accidental errors. We would be happy to apply the corrections in the following edition of this publication.

Fodor's SAN FRANCISCO

Publisher: Stephen Horowitz, *General Manager*

Editorial: Douglas Stallings, *Editorial Director*; Jill Fergus, Amanda Sadlowski, *Senior Editors*; Brian Eschrich, Alexis Kelly, *Editors*; Angelique Kennedy-Chavannes, *Assistant Editor*; Yoojin Shin, *Associate Editor*

Design: Tina Malaney, *Director of Design and Production*; Jessica Gonzalez, *Senior Designer*

Production: Jennifer DePrima, *Editorial Production Manager*; Elyse Rozelle, *Senior Production Editor*; Monica White, *Production Editor*

Maps: Rebecca Baer, *Senior Map Editor*; Mark Stroud (Moon Street Cartography), David Lindroth, *Cartographers*

Photography: Viviane Teles, *Senior Photo Editor;* Namrata Aggarwal, Neha Gupta, Payal Gupta, Ashok Kumar, *Photo Editors;* Eddie Aldrete, *Photo Production Intern;* Kadeem McPherson, *Photo Production Associate Intern*

Business and Operations: Chuck Hoover, *Chief Marketing Officer;* Robert Ames, *Group General Manager*

Public Relations and Marketing: Joe Ewaskiw, *Senior Director of Communications and Public Relations*

Fodors.com: Jeremy Tarr, *Editorial Director;* Rachael Levitt, *Managing Editor*

Technology: Jon Atkinson, *Director of Technology;* Rudresh Teotia, *Associate Director of Technology;* Alison Lieu, *Project Manager*

Writers: Trevor Felch, Denise M. Leto, and Daniel Mangin

Editor: Brian Eschrich

Production Editor: Monica White

32nd Edition

ISBN 978-1-64097-624-5

ISSN 1525-1829

All details in this book are based on information supplied to us at press time. Always confirm information when it matters, especially if you're making a detour to visit a specific place. Fodor's expressly disclaims any liability, loss, or risk, personal or otherwise, that is incurred as a consequence of the use of any of the contents of this book.

SPECIAL SALES

This book is available at special discounts for bulk purchases for sales promotions or premiums. For more information, e-mail SpecialMarkets@fodors.com.

PRINTED IN CANADA

10 9 8 7 6 5 4 3 2 1

About Our Writers

Trevor Felch is a lifelong Bay Area resident who has spent countless days catching his breath after climbing San Francisco's hills. He spends most of his time eating and drinking around San Francisco, then writing about those experiences for several local and national publications. When he isn't staring at a laptop or a bakery case full of sourdough loaves and croissants, he's usually swimming or preparing for the next half marathon (remember all those sourdough loaves and croissants?), exploring around town with his girlfriend's dog, or some other activity for soaking up the California sun. He is the author of *San Francisco Cocktails*, a recipe collection and in-depth guide to the Bay Area's cocktail history and leading bars.

Longtime Fodor's writer and editor **Denise M. Leto** roams San Francisco out of sheer love, peeking down overgrown alleyways and exploring tucked-away corners from the Tenderloin to the Richmond, diligently inspecting each bakery along the way. When she's not exploring the city, she can often be found camping in or hiking Northern California's spectacular parks—especially during mushroom season. For this edition, Denise updated the chapters for Union Square, Civic Center, and the Tenderloin; Chinatown and North Beach; Nob Hill and Russian Hill; Pacific Heights and Japantown; the Haight, the Castro, Noe Valley, and Hayes Valley; and the Western Shoreline. She also wrote our special features on cable cars, Chinatown, Golden Gate Park, and Alcatraz.

Daniel Mangin has been a Fodor's Travel writer and editor for over a quarter of a century. The writer of all editions of *Fodor's Napa and Sonoma*, he also contributed to its predecessor *Fodor's InFocus Napa & Sonoma*. As well as the editorial director of the Compass American Guides, Daniel was the series editor of *California Wine Country*. He has also written about wine and wineries for *The California Directory of Fine Wineries*, *Napa Valley Life* magazine, *Marin Magazine*, and other print and online outlets.

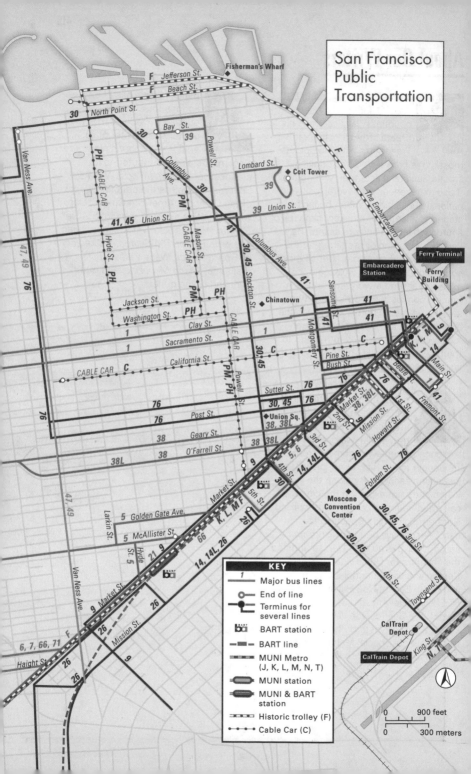